CENTRAL BOHEMIA
Pages 118–133

SOUTH BOHEMIA
Pages 134–157

WEST BOHEMIA
Pages 158–177

NORTH BOHEMIA
Pages 178–193

EAST BOHEMIA
Pages 194–211

ava •

• Ostrava

Frýdek-Místek

• Zlín

• Žilina

• Martin

CENTRAL
SLOVAKIA

Trenčín

Banská
• Bystrica

Zvolen •

• Poprad

• Prešov

EAST
SLOVAKIA

• Košice

Trnava

• Nitra

• Lučenec

WEST SLOVAKIA

WEST SLOVAKIA
Pages 290–305

**CENTRAL
SLOVAKIA**
Pages 306–323

EAST SLOVAKIA
Pages 324–339

EYEWITNESS TRAVEL

CZECH & SLOVAK
REPUBLICS

EYEWITNESS TRAVEL

CZECH & SLOVAK REPUBLICS

LONDON, NEW YORK,
MELBOURNE, MUNICH AND DELHI
www.dk.com

PRODUCED BY Wiedzę i Życie

ART EDITOR Paweł Pasternak
CONSULTANT Jan Bosnovič
GRAPHIC DESIGN Paweł Kamiński
DTP Elżbieta Dudzińska
MAPS Magdalena Polak

CONTRIBUTORS
Marek Pernal, Tomasz Darmochwał, Marek Rumiński,
Jakub Sito, Barbara Sudnik-Wójcikowska

PHOTOGRAPHERS
Dorota i Mariusz Jarymowiczowie, Krzysztof Kur, Oldřich Karasek

ILLUSTRATORS
Michał Burkiewicz, Dorota Jarymowicz, Paweł Marczak

Dorling Kindersley Limited
TRANSLATOR Magda Hannay
EDITORS Jane Simmonds, Emily Hatchwell
SENIOR DTP DESIGNER Jason Little
PRODUCTION CONTROLLER Shane Higgins
Reproduced by Colourscan in Singapore
Printed and bound by South China Printing Co. Ltd, China

First published in Great Britain in 2006
by Dorling Kindersley Limited, 80 Strand, London WC2R 0RL.
Copyright © 2006, 2009 Dorling Kindersley Limited, London
A Penguin Company

Reprinted with revisions 2009

A CIP CATALOGUE RECORD IS AVAILABLE FROM THE BRITISH LIBRARY.

ISBN 978-1-4053-3441-9

FLOORS ARE REFERRED TO THROUGHOUT IN ACCORDANCE WITH BRITISH
USAGE; IE THE "FIRST FLOOR" IS THE FLOOR ABOVE GROUND LEVEL.

Front cover main image: Český Krumlov, South Bohemia

We're trying to be cleaner and greener:

- we recycle waste and switch things off
- we use paper from responsibly managed forests whenever possible
- we ask our printers to actively reduce water and energy consumption
- we check out our suppliers' working conditions – they never use child labour

Find out more about our values and best practices at www.dk.com

---

**The information in every
DK Eyewitness Travel Guide is checked regularly.**

Every effort has been made to ensure that this book is up-to-date at the time of going to press. Some details, however, such as prices, telephone numbers and opening hours are liable to change. The publishers cannot accept responsibility for any consequences arising from the use of this book, and cannot guarantee that any website address in this book will be a suitable source of travel information. We value the views and suggestions of our readers. Please write to: Publisher, DK Eyewitness Travel Guides, Dorling Kindersley, 80 Strand, London WC2 0RL, Great Britain.

Stucco decorations on the façade
of Kinsky Palace, in Prague

CONTENTS

St Wenceslas statue overlooking
the eponymous square, Prague

◁ The imposing buildings of Karlovy Vary, jewel of Bohemia's spas

The Morava river flowing at the foot of Devin Castle, near Bratislava

Colourful roofs, Jindřichův Hradec
Castle, South Bohemia

Jindřichův
Hradec Castle
(pp144–5)

HOW TO USE THIS GUIDE

This guide helps you to get the most out of your visit to the Czech and Slovak Republics. The section at the start of each country entitled *Introducing* provides information about that country's geographic location, history and culture. The sections devoted to each capital and the individual regions describe the major historic sights and tourist attractions, using maps, photographs and illustrations. Information on accommodation and restaurants can be found in *Travellers' Needs*. The *Survival Guide* provides many practical tips.

PRAGUE AND BRATISLAVA AREA BY AREA

The Guide divides Prague into three areas described in individual sections. Sights outside the centre are dealt with in the *Further Afield* chapter. A chapter is devoted to Bratislava; it ends with the historic sights situated away from the town's centre.

Sights at a Glance lists the sights in an area by category, such as: Streets and Historic Buildings, Museums and Galleries, Places of Worship, Parks and Gardens.

2 Street-by-Street Map
This gives a bird's-eye view of the key areas described in each chapter.

A suggested route for sightseeing is indicated by a red dotted line.

Pages referring to Prague have a red thumb tab; Bratislava pages have pink.

1 Area Map
For easy reference, sights are numbered and located on an area map, as well as on the Prague Street Finder on pp108–13.

A locator map shows the area in relation to other parts of the city.

Stars indicate sights that no visitor should miss.

3 Detailed Information
All the major sights are described individually. Practical information includes their addresses, telephone numbers, opening hours and whether they charge for admission. The key to the symbols is on the back flap.

1 Introduction
This section deals with the landscape, history and character of each region, explaining how it has changed over the centuries and describing its visitor attractions.

REGION BY REGION
The guide divides the Czech Republic outside Prague into seven regions, each given a separate chapter. Slovakia is split into three regions outside Bratislava. The most interesting cities, towns, and other places to visit are numbered on a *Regional Map* at the start of each chapter.

2 Regional Map
This map shows the main road network and the overall topography of the region. All the best sights to visit are numbered and there is also information concerning transport.

Story boxes highlight related topics.

Each region of either country can easily be found by its colour coding, shown on the front flap of the book.

3 Detailed Information
All major cities, towns and tourist attractions are described individually. They are listed in order, following the numbering on the Regional Map. *Each entry contains detailed information on important sights.*

For all major sights a Visitors' Checklist gives the practical information you need when planning your visit.

4 Major Sights
At least two pages are devoted to each major sight. Historic buildings are dissected to reveal their interiors. Interesting towns or their centres have maps with the principal sights marked on them.

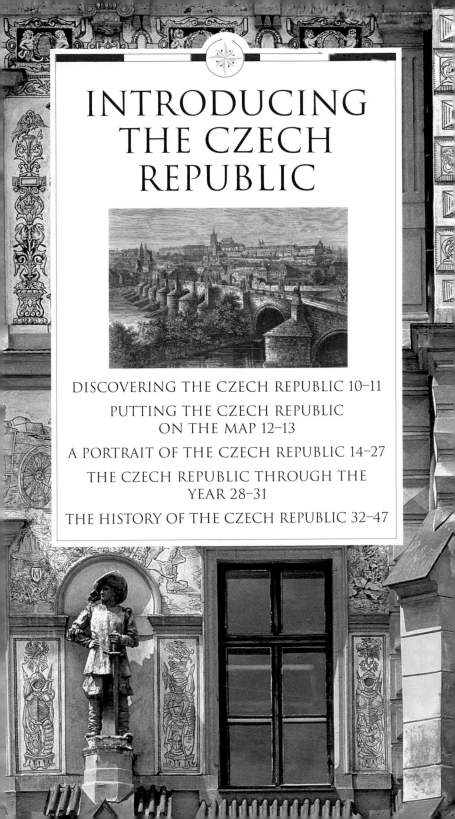

INTRODUCING
THE CZECH
REPUBLIC

DISCOVERING THE CZECH REPUBLIC

With its fortresses and fairy-tale castles, spectacular natural beauty and vibrant nightlife, the Czech Republic has plenty to offer. Located to the east of Germany, the country has been at the crossroads of Europe for centuries and its ancient trading villages

Madonna, Wenceslas Square, Prague

and spa towns testify to the nation's historic wealth. The country's highlands and forested areas are a haven for outdoor enthusiasts and offer a plethora of hiking trails, while the museums, galleries and vibrant nightlife of Prague and other towns will satisfy city-lovers.

![Prague Castle, with the spires of St Vitus's Cathedral at the centre]

Prague Castle, with the spires of St Vitus's Cathedral at the centre

PRAGUE

- **Historic Charles Bridge**
- **Gothic St Vitus's Cathedral**
- **Bustling Old Town Square**
- **Sternberg Palace**

Czech's "Golden City" is at its most evocative in the early hours, when the fog rises off the Vltava River beneath **Charles Bridge** *(see pp68–9)*. Throughout the day, scores flock to **Prague Castle** *(see pp54–5)* to marvel at the Gothic **St Vitus's Cathedral** *(see pp58–9)* and to see the changing of the guard at noon in the first courtyard.

Down below, winding, cobblestone streets and narrow alleys lead to Prague's **Old Town Square** *(see pp72–5)*, where thousands of visitors come to see the unusual Astronomical Clock, Jan Hus Monument and Church of Our Lady before Týn.

Art lovers should not miss the **Sternberg Palace** *(see pp60–61)*, which houses an extensive collection of European art.

CENTRAL BOHEMIA

- **Spectacular castles**
- **Atmospheric Kutná Hora**
- **Mělník vineyards**

With its picture-postcard castles, vineyards and rolling hills, ideal for hiking, Central Bohemia is one of the country's most popular regions.

Among the most visited sights are the 14th-century **Karlštejn Castle** *(see pp132–3)*, the historic town of **Kutná Hora** *(see pp122–3)*, with its wealth of beautiful buildings, such as St Barbara's Cathedral, and **Nelahozeves**

St Barbara's Cathedral in the snow, Kutná Hora

Castle *(see p126)*, housing the country's finest art collection.

To the north of the region, the historic vineyards of **Mělník** *(see p126)* have been producing grapes for wine making since the 14th century.

SOUTH BOHEMIA

- **Medieval Český Krumlov**
- **Renowned Budvar brewery**
- **Hiking in the Šumava mountains**

The region of South Bohemia boasts a wealth of historic sights as well as areas of extraordinary natural beauty.

The UNESCO World Heritage town of **Český Krumlov** *(see p152)*, with its medieval buildings lining the Vltava River, is a popular stop. Nearby, beer fans can tour the **Budvar Brewery** *(see p139)*, where the original Budweiser was fermented more than 100 years ago.

For nature lovers, the dense forest around the **Šumava mountains** *(see pp148–9)* offers hiking, mountain biking and canoeing.

WEST BOHEMIA

- **Karlovy Vary spa resort**
- **Mariánské Lázně walks**
- **Plzeň brewery**

West Bohemia is most noted for its spa resorts but it is also home to several interesting monasteries, large forested areas and a famous brewery.

The spa town of **Karlovy Vary** *(see p174–5)* attracts visitors from around the world who come to bathe in its medicinal waters and to drink at its mineral springs. The town has had its share of famous international visitors, including composer Ludwig van Beethoven and Russian philosopher Karl Marx.

Nearby, the pretty town of **Mariánské Lázně** *(see p169)* is another spa resort. Visitors come here as much for the indoor spa treatments as for the hiking opportunities in the surrounding area.

Beer enthusiasts make the trip to the town of **Plzeň** *(see p162-3)* to visit the Pilsner Urquell brewery where the golden brew is made.

NORTH BOHEMIA

- Beautiful **České Švýcarsko National Park**
- **Terezín's ghetto**
- Architecture of **Liberec**

North Bohemia is home to some well-preserved old towns but it is best known for the **České Švýcarsko National Park** *(see pp188–9)*, also referred to as "Bohemian Switzerland". The park's spectacular gorges, scenic villages and natural rock bridge attract hundreds of hikers every year.

The fortress town of **Terezín** *(see pp190–91)* to the south, became a Jewish ghetto in 1941. Today it is home to a memorial paying homage to 35,000 Jews who passed through the ghetto on their way to concentration camps.

Nearby **Liberec** *(see pp182–5)*, North Bohemia's main city, was a key industrial hub of the Austro-Hungarian Empire; the town is a good example of the region's former glory.

Visiting the sandstone rock formations of Adršpach-Teplice

EAST BOHEMIA

- Skiing in the **Krkonoše**
- Mount **Sněžka** cable car
- **Adršpach-Teplice** rock towns

During the winter months, hikers and skiers flock to the snowy **Krkonoše mountains** *(see pp208–9)* for their cross-country ski routes and good prices. **Mount Sněžka**, the country's highest peak at 1,602 m (5,256 ft), is accessible by cable car and offers stunning views. In warmer weather, the region offers good climbing in the "rock towns" of **Adršpach** and **Teplice** *(see p210)*.

NORTH MORAVIA AND SILESIA

- Historic **Olomouc**
- Gothic castles and fortresses
- Amazing **Javoříčské caves**

Any trip to this region should include a stop at **Olomouc** *(see p216–9)*, a

vibrant, university town and an important seat of the Catholic church. The town's art museum houses excellent collections of Italian works and 20th-century Czech paintings.

The region also boasts several historic buildings including the 13th-century **Sternberg Castle** *(see p221)* in Neo-Gothic style and the 14th-century Gothic fortress of **Bouzov** *(see p220–21)*.

For nature enthusiasts, a trip to the **Javoříčské Caves** will not disappoint *(see p220)*. This extraordinary subterranean complex stretches more than 3 km (2 miles) and features superb stalactite formations.

A street in Olomouc, one of Moravia's oldest towns

SOUTH MORAVIA

- Wine-making in **Znojmo** and **Mikulov**
- **Brno's Špilberk castle**
- Caves of **Moravský kras**

The undulating rows of vines around the pretty towns of **Znojmo** and **Mikulov** trumpet the region's "ice wines" *(see pp238–9)*. During the towns' wine festivals, the grapes are fermented to make burčák, a sweet and fizzy wine.

The gruesome history of the mighty **Špilberk castle** *(see pp230–31)*, in the city of **Brno**, *(see pp 228-9)* makes an intriguing visit, while for a more relaxing experience the underground rivers in the Punkva Caves of the **Moravský kras** region *(see p233)* can be navigated by boat.

Pravčicka brána natural rock bridge, České Švýcarsko National Park

Putting the Czech Republic on the Map

The Czech Republic lies at the heart of Central Europe, sharing borders with Germany, Poland and Austria, as well as Slovakia. Comprising the regions of Bohemia in the west and Moravia in the east, the country covers an area of 78,865 sq km (30,499 sq miles), of which some 80 per cent is made up of mountains and highlands; the highest peak is Sněžka (1,602 m/5,256 ft), in the Krkonoše Mountains of East Bohemia. The Czech Republic has around 10.3 million inhabitants, more than 1 million of whom live in the capital, Prague.

PRAGUE AND ITS ENVIRONS

Neratovice
Kralupy nad Vlt.
Slaný
Kostelec nad Labem
Libčice nad Vlt.
Roztoky
Kladno
Celákovice
Úvaly
Beroun
Černošice
Berounka
Ríčany
Sázava
Vltava

0 kilometres 10

0 miles 5

POLAND

Odra
Legnica
Wrocław
Wałbrzych
Trutnov
Hradec Králové
Sobotin
Opava
Ostrava
Bielsko-Biała
Odra
Olomouc
Frýdek-Místek
Přerov
Morava
Zlín
Žilina
Brno
Martin
Váh
Znojmo
Hodonin
Trenčín
Hollabrun
SLOVAKIA
Váh
Hron
VIENNA
Trnava
Nitra
BRATISLAVA
Eisenstadt
Neusiedler See
Gyor
HUNGARY
Raba

0 kilometres 40

0 miles 20

KEY

✈ Airport

━ Motorway

━ Major road

─ Railway line

─·─ International border

A PORTRAIT OF THE CZECH REPUBLIC

The Czech Republic has blossomed into a vibrant and fascinating place to visit in the post-Communist era. Bohemia and Moravia, neglected under the Communists, now delight visitors with their picturesque towns and cities, well-preserved palaces and castles, and magnificent scenery.

Situated in the centre of Europe, the Bohemian Basin was for centuries a crossroads of trading routes and a place where different religious and national traditions came into close contact. This cultural diversity has produced a rich historical heritage, which survives in remarkable condition: the Czech Republic escaped serious damage during the two World Wars, though the decimation of the Jewish community and the expulsion of German-speakers after 1945 had a devastating effect on Czech society. Wherever you go in the country you will find well-preserved historic buildings and medieval districts, and many attractive towns and villages.

Vase from the Glass Museum in Harrachov

Since the Velvet Revolution of 1989, the Czech Republic has experienced a rapid process of change. While those who lived under Soviet domination have found this economic and social upheaval hard to accept, the younger generations have embraced the change. The speed with which the country is shaking off the aura of its Communist past is astounding. Soviet-style architecture cannot be wiped out overnight, but many cities are now lively cultural and commercial centres. None more so than Prague, which, as well as being a major tourist destination, is carving out a role for itself, both political and cultural, in the newly expanded European Union.

The view from the terrace of the café in Střekov Castle, North Bohemia

◁ East Bohemia's Hrubá Skála Castle, amid colourful autumn scenery

The pace of change in rural areas has been much slower. Here, the people tend to be more inward-looking and are the most sceptical about the country's membership of the EU, ratified in 2004. While 77 per cent of Czechs voted in favour, only just over half of the population voted. There is widespread concern that EU membership will bring rocketing prices and erode the country's vibrant folk culture. This culture is most visible in the country's numerous folk festivals, its music and its art and architecture.

Český Krumlov festival, a typical folk celebration

TRADITION OF DEMOCRACY

The Czechs are very proud of their traditional commitment to democratic values. This means, on the one hand, opposition to any signs of autocracy, and, on the other, a deep-seated belief in the indisputable nature of laws as decreed by the majority. Rules and regulations are respected by Czech society much more than in other European countries. The Czech people's high regard for law and order means that it is rare to encounter any violence while in the country. The widely proclaimed egalitarianism seems rather at odds, however, with the Czech penchant for titles and

*Allegory of Science
by Antonín Břenek*

ranks – a result perhaps of the society's bourgeois roots and the centuries-long rule by Austrian bureaucracy.

SOCIAL HERITAGE

In a country where almost every town and village has an historic castle or chateau, the people's awareness of their history is strong – although this doesn't hold true in areas of the Czech Republic where the chain of local traditions has been broken: by the murder or deportation of entire Jewish communities by the Nazis during World War II, for example, or by the expulsion of German-speakers after the war.

The vagaries of history also help explain the fact that the Czechs are the most secular society in Europe. Closed and empty churches bear witness to the anticlerical feelings of a nation for whom the Catholic Habsburg monarchy was, for centuries, the symbol of national repression. Socially, Czech atheism means that the

Czechs demonstrating during the Velvet Revolution of 1989

often divisive issues of divorce, abortion and childbirth outside marriage raise relatively few eyebrows.

PUBLIC VERSUS PRIVATE

For the Czech people, spending time with family and friends is of paramount importance. Weekends in the country are popular, but the most important venues for socializing are restaurants, pubs and bars. Here, it is easy to strike up a conversation with local people. Visitors shouldn't hesitate to ask if they can join a group of friends at a communal table; indeed, this is common practice. Czechs are well-educated, and are often well-informed about foreign events and politics. It is rare, however, to be invited into a Czech home, which is regarded as a person's oasis of privacy.

The dualism of Czech society is also reflected in its language. The

The historic Sadová Colonnade in the spa town of Karlovy Vary

literary version of Czech (*spisovná čeština*), used in public life, exists side by side with the colloquial version (*hovorová čeština*), which has a different grammar; the latter is used on private occasions by all social groups.

The dramatic changes experienced in the last decade or so have not entirely removed the Czech penchant for retrospection and a nostalgic cult of old things. An attachment to favourite clothes, places and customs occasionally takes on unusual forms. Nowhere else in Europe will you see so many long-haired men who appear to have been transported straight from the 1960s and 70s.

THE CZECH REPUBLIC ABROAD

Most Czechs are deeply patriotic and, by extension, are proud of their country's reputation abroad. The Czech Republic's prestige has undoubtedly been strengthened by the playwright turned politician Václav Havel, admired worldwide for his relentless defence of democracy and civil rights. A major role in the promotion of Czech culture abroad has also been played by a group of prominent authors and artists, including the writers Milan Kundera and Bohumil Hrabal and film director Miloš Forman.

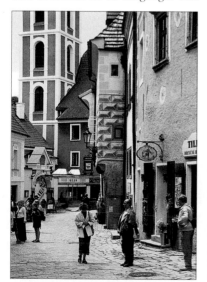

The historic heart of Český Krumlov

Landscape and Wildlife

The Czech Republic's western region of Bohemia is basically a high plateau surrounded by modest mountains, while Moravia is a largely lowland region with just a handful of mountains. A depression called the Moravian Gate (Moravská brána), which separates these regions from the Carpathian mountains to the east, played a major role in shaping the diversity of Central Europe's wildlife. It provided a north-south migration route for many species of plants and animals. The ease of migration, the diversity of climates and soils, plus the varied topography have all contributed to the region's biodiversity. For a visitor, the only problem is the mountainous and wooded terrain, which makes wildlife-spotting tricky.

Stalactite in the Punkva Caves in the Moravian Karst

MOUNTAINS

Most of the mountains in the Czech Republic are lower than 800 m (2,625 ft). The highest are the aptly named Krkonoše (Giant) Mountains in East Bohemia, and it is only here that sub-alpine and alpine flora can be found. The other mountain ranges include the Šumava, an unpopulated wilderness in South Bohemia, and the White Carpathians (Bílé Karpaty) in South Moravia.

HIGHLANDS

Much of the country is made up of the so-called Bohemian-Moravian Highlands plateau (Českomoravská Vysočina), which consists of schist and granite and is furrowed by the valleys of the Vltava and Morava, the Czech Republic's two main rivers, and their tributaries. Its upper sections are covered in forest, while the lower parts are where crops such as rye are cultivated and cattle are bred.

PLANTS

The land in the Czech Republic is less intensively used than in many other European countries. The country's diversity of trees, plants and flowers is shown by the fact that it has the same number of plant species as neighbouring Poland, a country four times the size. These include relatively large numbers of endemic plants. It is of concern, however, that in a listing of rare and endangered plant species in the Czech and Slovak Republics, more than 80 species are singled out as being on the verge of extinction.

Meadows catch the eye in the late spring and summer with their fantastic variety of colourful flower species.

The number of rose species *growing in the Czech Republic is estimated at over 100. Look out for these on the fringes of woodland and in small deciduous thickets.*

FAUNA

The Czech Republic is home to many animals common to Central Europe, though their survival is threatened by industrial development, intensive agriculture and tourism. The most numerous larger mammals are the wild boar, souslik, fox, hare and badger.

The souslik, *or ground squirrel, is related to the marmot and chipmunk. It lives underground in colonies, usually in meadows.*

The mink, *a predatory mammal, inhabits the shores of reservoirs and feeds on fish, frogs and crayfish.*

The gyr falcon, *a bird of prey found primarily in mountain areas, is the world's largest falcon.*

AGRICULTURAL LAND

Some 40 per cent of the Czech Republic is cultivated land. Besides cereals and root crops, a particular feature of the Czech agricultural landscape are the fields of rape, flax, hops and sunflowers. Vineyards are a common sight in some areas, primarily in Moravia, where they grow on south-facing hillsides. Most livestock farming is concentrated around towns.

RIVERS AND LAKES

Bohemia's high plateau is drained by the Labe river (known as the Elbe in Germany), along with its tributary the Vltava, the republic's longest river at 430 km (267 miles). Moravia's principal river is the Morava, which joins the Danube at Bratislava; the scenery along one of its tributaries, the Dyje, is particularly beautiful. The Czech Republic has only a few natural lakes but many artificial reservoirs.

The hop plant *(whose dried flowers are used in the brewing of beer) is endemic in the Czech Republic, often seen in damp woodlands and thickets, or along riverbanks.*

The kingcup, *with its showy golden-yellow flowers, appears in early spring; it favours damp habitats, such as meadows and the banks of streams and ponds.*

The peach-leaved bell-flower *is a beautiful species which grows primarily in oak or hornbeam forests; it flowers in early summer.*

Religious Architecture

The two most momentous periods in the development of Czech religious architecture were the medieval and Baroque eras. The peak of these two architectural heydays were, respectively, the second half of the 14th century and the 18th century (the Late-Baroque era). In between, vicious religious wars in the 15th and 17th centuries seriously affected new architectural development, and also caused brutal damage to many medieval churches.

Basilica of St Procopius in Třebíč, an example of Czech Baroque architecture

ROMANESQUE ARCHITECTURE

The oldest churches in the Czech Republic date from the 9th century. The styles developed during this period culminated in the flowering of Romanesque architecture in the 11th to 13th centuries. Romanesque churches fell into three main categories: rotundas, simple hall churches and triple-aisle basilicas with apses. Sadly, few of these buildings, which were often quite opulent with rich architectural details, have survived intact.

St George's Basilica in Prague (see pp56–7), *begun in the 10th century, was altered often and even partially rebuilt. However, it remains the best-preserved Romanesque basilica in the Czech Republic.*

The Rotunda of St Catherine in Znojmo (see p238) *is one of Moravia's few Romanesque churches to have escaped alteration.*

GOTHIC ARCHITECTURE

From the time Emperor Charles IV chose Prague as his capital in the 14th century, the Czech Lands became one of Europe's most prominent focal areas for the arts. The style in vogue here was known as the "Parler" style, its name derived from that of the prominent German architect Peter Parler and his sons. Its distinctive features include light and airy interiors decorated with intricately carved details.

The Church of St Bartholomew in Kolín (see p124), *which shares many features with St Vitus's Cathedral in Prague, is a prime example of the Parler style.*

St Bartholomew's Cathedral in Plzeň (see .... 14th to 16th centuries, *has massive columns supporting classic Gothic vaulting above the nave.*

The church in Zlatá Koruna (see p156), *attached to the Cistercian monastery, dates from the mid-14th century and was worked on by Peter Parler.*

BAROQUE ARCHITECTURE

The Baroque period was the last great phase in Czech religious architecture. Following the destruction of the Thirty Years' War, a massive rebuilding campaign was launched in Bohemia. In the 17th century the architects of the new style were mainly from Italy, but they were later superseded by more local builders, mainly Germans and Austrians with a few Czechs. Most talented among them were the Bavarian

Christoph Ignaz Dientzenhofer and his son Kilian. They helped to develop the new internal layout of churches, based on interlocking geometrical figures. This spatial sophistication was accompanied by opulent furnishings, stuccowork and frescoes. Often executed by top sculptors and painters, the exuberance of the decoration reached a peak in the Late-Baroque era.

The Church of St Mary Magdalene in Karlovy Vary

(see pp174–5), *designed by Kilian Ignaz Dientzenhofer, was built in the 1730s. Inside are the original fine sculptures and a beautiful main altarpiece.*

The Church of St Nicholas in Malá Strana, in Prague (see pp64–5), *the work of Christoph and Kilian Ignaz Dientzenhofer, is one of the most innovative churches of the time in Europe, with its flowing lines and flamboyant colours. The floorplan of the nave consists of a series of interlocking ellipses.*

The hospital-church complex in Kuks (see p210) *was designed by Italian-born G B Alliprandi in 1707–10. In front of the hospital is a terrace with sculptures by Tyrolean sculptor, Matthias Braun.*

THE 19TH AND 20TH CENTURIES

The 19th century did not see the flowering of any distinct architectural style; the buildings erected during this period drew on earlier styles, often mixing them together. In the 20th century more effort was made to search for new architectural expression. Czech architects adopted the geometric forms of Cubism, and the austere Functionalist style was much in vogue between the World Wars, most visible now in Prague and the Moravian capital of Brno.

The Church of the Most Sacred Heart in Vinohrady, Prague, *built in 1928–32, was so shockingly modern in its day that it was almost Post-Modern. It was the work of the Slovenian architect, Josip Plečnik.*

The Church of St Wenceslas in Prague-Vršovice *was designed in 1929 by the Czech architect Josef Gočár, a leading exponent of the avant-garde. The concrete structure, dominated by a tall bell-tower, is denuded of decoration.*

Czech Music

The Czech Republic has a rich, largely home-grown musical heritage. Psalms written as long ago as the 13th century used the Czech language. It was nationalism which, centuries later, inspired Bedřich Smetana and Antonín Dvořák, the most famous of the unusually large number of composers to emanate from this small country.

Sign on violin-maker's house

Jan Kubelík, famous Czech violinist, in around 1908

RELIGIOUS MUSIC OF THE HUSSITE PERIOD

The earliest surviving pieces of Czech music include choral elements of the Christian liturgy, inter-woven with native folk melodies. The oldest known composition is the 10th–11th-century psalm *Hospodine Pomiluj ny* ("Lord have mercy on us").

During the 15th century the reformist Hussite move-ment began to oppose the Latin singing that was the norm in Czech churches; this in turn inspired the growth of Czech religious songs. Hussite works were published in hymn books both at home and in neigh-bouring countries, including Germany. The subsequent development of music in the Czech Lands occurred during the Renaissance period, when artistic life centred around the imperial court and palaces of the nobility.

AFTER THE DEFEAT AT THE WHITE MOUNTAIN

After the defeat of the Czechs in 1620 at the Battle of the White Mountain, increased repression by the Habsburgs forced many musicians to leave the Czech Lands. Meanwhile, the imperial court, which moved to Vienna, ceased to sponsor Czech composers. Among the few musicians who worked during the 1700s, the most prominent positions went to the church music composers Jan Jakub Ryba and František Brixi.

MOZART IN PRAGUE

Mozart visited Prague for the first time in 1787, and fell in love with the city. He returned here to write *Don Giovanni*, which he ded-icated to "the good people of Prague". The citizens of Prague were entranced by Mozart: opera was already a popular form of entertainment, and was open to everyone rather than just the wealthy classes.

SMETANA AND THE ERA OF NATIONAL REBIRTH

Music played an important role in shaping the Czech national identity.

The first composer whose works espoused the aspira-tions of his countrymen was Bedřich Smetana (1824–84), who was active in the 1848 revolution and, later, the national revival movement. While his music was rooted in German Romanticism, it took its themes primarily from the legends and history of his homeland. Smetana also borrowed elements from Czech folklore. Most popular among his large volume of work is his cycle of six symphonic poems known collectively as *Má Vlast* ("My Country"), written in 1874–79 and whose melodious theme is one of the signatures of Czech music, and his comic opera *The Bartered Bride* (1866), his most famous work internationally.

ANTONIN DVOŘÁK

When Smetana died, he handed the baton to Antonín Dvořák (1841–1904), with whom he had worked at the National

Piano recital given by Bedřich Smetana for his friends

Theatre. Dvořák's first musical experience had been playing the violin in his village band. From these humble beginnings, Dvořák became the source of inspiration for a new generation of Czech musicians and, much later, the most renowned Czech composer in the world.

At heart a peasant, Dvořák was naturally drawn to the folk music tradition of his homeland. He combined this with foreign influences, from Wagner to American folk music. The latter influenced his most famous work, the Ninth Symphony, subtitled *From the New World*. This was written during his stint as director of the New York's conservatory from 1892–5.

Poster advertising a Janáček opera

THE TURN OF THE 20TH CENTURY

Among the large group of composers who worked during the late 19th and early 20th century a prominent place is occupied by Zdeněk Fibich (1850–1900), a pupil of Smetana. Considered, along with his teacher and Dvořák, as one of the fathers of Czech music, Fibich showed little interest in folk music or in patriotic themes; instead, his works were inspired by the music of Berlioz, Schumann and Liszt. His *Poem* is his most famous composition.

Despite being a contemporary of Fibich, Leoš Janáček (1854–1928), born in North Moravia, was a much more modern composer. He resisted the lure of Prague, instead devoting many years of his life to researching the folklore of Bohemia, Moravia

Dvořák's viola, from the Michna Palace

and Slovakia. He wrote down numerous native folk songs, investigated the intonation of the spoken language, and even notated the sounds made by animals and objects: he gave the name "Speech Melodies" to these sounds. While taking his inspiration from the very traditional life and art of country people, Leoš Janáček's music was definitely avant-garde. As a result, his music was not given the recognition that it deserved at the outset. His *Glagolitic Mass* (1926), for which he achieved renown internationally, was composed at the very end of his life.

Two other musicians worth a mention are Josef Suk (1874–1935), the pupil and son-in-law of Dvořák, and violinist Jan Kubelík (1880–1940). While Kubelík achieved fame for his virtuoso technique and interpretation, he was also a composer.

The great German composer and conductor Gustav Mahler (1860–1911) was born in a village near Humpolec in southeast Bohemia. He spent a significant part of his life in Olomouc and Prague.

Another famous name in the Czech Republic is Emma Destinnová, Emy Destinn in

Czech (1878–1930). A soprano singer, she performed with Enrico Caruso at New York's Metropolitan Opera. Her portrait is, to this day, used on 2,000-crown Czech banknotes.

CHOIRS AND DECHOVKY

In the 19th century choirs and amateur wind instrument orchestras known as *dechovky* started to play a significant role in the musical life of Bohemia and Moravia. One such choir, the famous Hlahol ensemble from Prague, founded in 1860, became an important element in the shaping of the Czech national culture. *Dechovky* remain a typical and widely popular form of music-making.

Singer Karel Kryl during a performance

MUSIC AND THE DRIVE FOR DEMOCRACY

Music stagnated during the Communist era: jazz, for example, a hugely popular genre, was proclaimed decadent. Yet music also played a role in the ideological conflict. In 1976, the punk band, the "Plastic People of the Universe", was put on trial for "crimes against the state". This helped ignite the process that led to the creation of the Charter 77 manifesto. Also famous for their resistance to the regime are the singers Karel Kryl and Jaromír Hutka, who, until 1989, were banned from performing.

Art and Decorative Arts

Proof of the wealth of artistic life and traditions in
the Czech Republic is shown by its magnificent
works of painting and sculpture and a wide range of
decorative arts. Artists that made a lasting contribution
to the arts in Europe range from the 14th-century
painter Master Theodoric and the great sculptor of
the Baroque era, Matthias Braun, to Alfons Mucha,
the undisputed master of the Czech Art Nouveau
style. Czech artists and sculptors have always
enjoyed great respect in their country, and their
works of art are, to this day, the pride of numerous
museums, galleries and public places.

**The Krumlov
Madonna**
*(c.1390), the
work of an
anonymous
artist, is one of
the best-known
examples of
the so-called
"Beautiful
Style" in
Czech Gothic
sculpture.*

Master Theodoric, *court painter
to Emperor Charles IV and one of
the greatest Bohemian artists of
the 14th century, painted this* St
Elizabeth, *which can be seen at
Karlštejn Castle.*

**Pose
symbolizing
dancing**

**The
voluptuous
gown** shows
a masterful
portrayal of
movement.

Jan Kupecký (1667–1740), *who spent
most of his life outside his native Bohemia,
was a highly regarded portrait painter
who pioneered a trend for realism in
Late-Baroque painting. This* Self-Portrait
(1711) is his most famous work.

**Ferdinand Brokof and Matthias
Braun,** *who, together with a number
of the Czech Baroque, were responsible
for 12 of the statues on the Charles
Bridge in Prague.*

Přemysl and Libuše, *one of the four group sculptures by Josef Václav Myslbek (1848–1922) now standing in Vyšehrad, once decorated the Palacký Bridge in Prague. The most famous work of the artist is the equestrian statue of St Wenceslas in the capital's Wenceslas Square.*

Intricate floral decoration

Max Švabinský (1873–1962) *was not only a painter but also a hugely talented graphic artist. He designed, among other things, postage stamps and banknotes.*

Soft, flowing lines typical of Art Nouveau

Czech glass, crystal and porcelain *were always highly regarded throughout Europe. The most famous manufacturers included Moser of Karlovy Vary and the Dubí porcelain factory near Teplice.*

ALFONS MUCHA

Among the most outstanding exponents of the European Art Nouveau, Alfons Mucha (1860–1939) developed an instantly recognizable style. Typical subjects of his numerous paintings and posters were female figures: graceful, enigmatic and full of hidden symbols. Those shown here represent *Dance* and *Music*.

This Baroque cupboard *was built of walnut and oak by František Maximilián Kaňka (1674–1766) in c.1740. It is now in the library inside the Clementinum (see p82) in Prague.*

Toyen (1902–80) *was a founding member of the Czech Surrealist movement in the 1930s. Marie Germinova took on the cryptic pseudonym Toyen in order to disguise her gender.*

Czech Literature and Film

The first concerted effort to write in Czech rather than in Latin came in the 14th century, when the work of reformist preachers prepared the way for the writings of Jan Hus. From then on literature flourished in Bohemia, halted only temporarily by the Thirty Years' War. Writers and, more recently, film makers, have played an important role in the nation's history (Václav Havel, a playwright, even became president), and in its search for a cultural identity.

Ninth-century *Book of Gospels*, the oldest in Strahov's library

EARLY CZECH LITERATURE

The dawn of literature in the Czech language is linked with the Slavic writings associated with the 9th-century missionary work of St Cyril and St Methodius. In the 13th century, religious literature, usually chronicles and the lives of the saints, was still in Latin but started to be accompanied by text written in Czech.

The 14th century saw more concerted efforts to write in the Czech language, in lyrical poetry as well as secular and religious prose. Reformist preachers adopted Czech as their preferred language, and it was the trail-blazing reformer, Jan Hus (1369–1415), who made perhaps the most significant contribution to the development of the Czech language of the day. He codified the rules of orthography and extended the readership of the national literature to include the bourgeoisie.

THE HUMANIST PERIOD

The use of the vernacular spread during the 16th and 17th centuries, boosted by the humanist movement and the boom in printing. The crowning glory of this age was the publication of the Kralice Bible (1579–94), a Protestant translation of the Bible in Czech. With the Thirty Years' War, however, came repression. Czech, the language of the reformists, all but died out as a written form, and became little more than a peasant dialect. But Czech was still used by exiles abroad. The most famous exiled writer was Jan Ámos Komenský (1592–1670), also known as Comenius. He won recognition in many fields of science, but became truly famous all over Europe for his ground-breaking ideas on education.

Jan Ámos Komenský

THE LITERATURE OF NATIONAL REVIVAL

The counter-reformation, and the Germanization process that accompanied it, prevented any revival of a national Czech literature in the early 1700s, but by the end of the 18th century the more liberal approach of Joseph II gave Czech scholars the chance to revive their language. A leading role in this campaign was played by Josef Dobrovský (1753–1829), who codified the Czech literary language. Among other leading writers active in the movement of national revival was Karel Hynek Mácha, one of the greatest ever Czech poets.

The second half of the 19th century heralded the arrival of realist literature represented by the great Jan Neruda (1834–91), a poet of world renown and also the author of some fine short stories. His *Tales of the Little Quarter* (1878), set in Prague, is a marvellous portrayal of life in the city.

LITERATURE BETWEEN THE WARS

In the period between the two World Wars, Czech writers did not follow a

The Kralice Bible, the first Czech translation of the Bible

single path. Jaroslav Hašek (1883–1923) wrote *The Good Soldier Švejk*, an hilarious novel that pokes fun at the Habsburg empire. Instantly popular, its hero became a symbol of the Czech nation.

Another prominent figure was Karel Čapek (1890–1938), famous primarily for his plays. These included *R.U.R.* (Rossum's Universal Robots), written in 1921 and the source from which the word "robot" entered the English language. In this and other works, such as his novel *The War of the Newts* (1936), Čapek combines his interest in ordinary life with his love of science fiction.

Franz Kafka (1883–1924), a German-speaking Jew, did not write in Czech, but spent his entire life in Prague and was part of a thriving German-Jewish literary circle. His bleak works were banned during the Communist era.

Scene from Jiří Menzel's film *Closely Observed Trains*

REPRESSION AND LITERARY RESURGENCE

Accompanying the political upheaval of 1948 came curbs on freedom of expression. "Socialist realism" became the only style acceptable to the authorities.

The period of "thaw" in the 1960s, which peaked in 1968 during the Prague Spring, inspired a literary resurgence. Writers such as Josef Škvorecký (b. 1924) and Milan Kundera (b. 1929) penned their first great works during this period. Škvorecký, an ironic chronicler of life during and after World War II, is as famous in his homeland as Kundera. Communist oppression is a common theme in Kundera's often erotic books. A great storyteller, he was influenced by the revered Bohumil Hrabal (1914–97), famously scornful of war in his novella *Closely Observed Trains* (1965).

Russian intervention in 1968 forced many writers to go underground. Some of them decided to emigrate, including Kundera, who shot

to international fame with the publication of his novel *The Unbearable Lightness of Being* (1984). With the Velvet Revolution came a new era, in which literary life could flourish and young writers could work unrestrained.

THEATRE

Czech theatre, which has a long and worthy tradition, hit a peak in the 1950s and '60s with the emergence of many small theatres. One such was the Theatre on the Balustrade, which staged Václav Havel's first play in 1963. Havel tackled the issue of life under totalitarianism and was typical of the Czech theatrical community in his determination to fight repression. Since 1989, the theatre has faced other enemies, such as funding crises, but it is still a potent cultural force.

Milan Kundera, world-famous Czech writer working in Paris

CZECH CINEMA

Czech cinema earned a reputation as far back as the 1930s, mainly thanks to the work of Martin Frič and Karel Zeman. After 1945 film makers struggled to express themselves in the repressive Communist era; it is not by chance that the most avant-garde works of the period were animated films.

The more liberal 1960s saw the golden age of Czech cinema, although the Soviet invasion of 1968 brought this renaissance to a rapid end. This success was associated with the work of a group of young film makers, who created the style known as the "New Wave". In their films they tackled moral and historical judgments of World War II as well as contemporary moral and social issues. One of the young film makers was Miloš Forman, who fled the country after 1968 and later achieved international fame as director of films such as *One Flew Over the Cuckoo's Nest* and *Amadeus*. Other great movies made in this period were *The Party and the Guests* by Jan Němec, and *Closely Observed Trains* by Jiří Menzel.

Czech cinema's greatest success in recent years was *Kolja* (*Kolya*), directed by Jan Svěrák, which won an Oscar for best foreign film in 1997.

THE CZECH REPUBLIC THROUGH THE YEAR

The Czech Republic is a very popular destination in the summer, when Prague and the other main places of interest get unbearably crowded. It is much better to come in late spring or early autumn. While Prague and large towns can still offer plenty of entertainment in winter, castles and palaces in many smaller places tend to be closed from early November to late March. Anyone who loves

A Český Krumlov festival participant

stunning scenery or outdoor activities, on the other hand, can have a great time even then. While large-scale religious festivals don't really exist in the Czech Republic, there are many festivals at which you can see the country's folk traditions in action, admire local crafts and taste traditional cuisine. Throughout the country, throughout the year, there are famous music, film and theatre festivals.

Concert in St Vitus's Cathedral during Prague Spring Festival

SPRING

Many people say that spring arrives earlier in the Bohemian Basin, encircled as it is by mountains, than in neighbouring countries. Whatever the case, the scenery in spring is gorgeous, with fruit trees in blossom along the roadsides.

After the winter break, castles and palaces start to open their gates (some may open only at weekends in March and April); it is still easy to find a hotel room, car parking space or a table at a restaurant.

MARCH

!!! !!!!!! Writers' Festival *(early Jun).* This event brings together writers from all over the world to take part in lectures and workshops.

Prague–Prčice March *(3rd Sat).* Thousands of people walk from the city centre to Prčice (southwest of Prague) to celebrate the arrival of spring.
The Easter Festival of Sacred Music, Brno. It is held in the magnificent setting of the Cathedral of St Peter and St Paul.

Spring flowers in South Bohemia

APRIL

Witch-burning *(30 Apr).* A Czech version of Halloween, celebrated all over the country. Old brooms are burned and bonfires are lit, all to ward off evil spirits.

MAY

Anniversary of the Prague Uprising *(5 May).* The anniversary of the 1945 anti-Nazi uprising is marked by the laying of flowers at the commemorative plaques of those who died.
Prague Spring International Music Festival *(early May–early Jun).* A feast for lovers of classical music, with a busy schedule of concerts, ballet and opera. The festival traditionally begins with a performance of Smetana's *Má vlast* (My Country).
Prague Marathon *(late May).* An annual event since 1995, the marathon route runs through the city's historic centre.
"Without Frontiers" (Bez Hranic) **Theatre Festival** *(late May),* Český Těšín, North Moravia. Performances by some of the top theatre groups from the Czech Republic, Slovakia and Poland.

AVERAGE DAILY HOURS OF SUNSHINE

Sunshine

The greatest number of sunny days occurs between May and August. The fewest occur from November to January, during the winter months, when the hours of daylight are shorter. When the snow falls, of course, everything sparkles in the clear sunlight.

Boy in traditional costume at Strážnice folk festival

SUMMER

In summer the Czech Republic becomes a Mecca for visitors. Prague is truly besieged, but even here there are peaceful parks and quiet museums and churches. While the capital's streets are buzzing well into the night, smaller towns go to sleep much earlier.

The majority of folklore events and cultural festivals are staged in the summer.

JUNE

Concentus Moravia: International Music Festival *(all month)*. Classical concerts featuring international artistes take place in the churches and castles of Moravia's 13 historic towns.
Smetanova Litomyšl: International Opera Festival *(Jun/Jul)*, Litomyšl, East Bohemia. The Czech Republic's biggest outdoor music festival, in Bedřich

Smetana's birthplace. Works by Smetana and other composers are performed.
Five-Petalled Rose Festival *(mid-Jun)*, Český Krumlov, South Bohemia. On the weekend nearest the summer solstice, people dress up in medieval gear and have a great time.
International Folk Festival *(last weekend in Jun)*, Strážnice, South Moravia. One of the biggest and oldest events of its type in Europe.

JULY

International Film festival *(late Jun–early Jul)*, Karlovy Vary, West Bohemia. Launched in 1946, this festival is one of Europe's top film events, along with those held in Cannes, Berlin and Venice.
International Music Festival *(early Jul–mid-Aug)*, Hukvaldy, North Moravia. Devoted to the works of the world-famous

composer, Leoš Janáček, who was born here.
International Music Festival *(mid-Jul–late Aug)*, Český Krumlov, South Bohemia. Staged mostly in the castle. Organ recitals are held in the monastery church here and in churches in neighbouring towns.

AUGUST

Chopin Festival *(mid-Aug)*, Mariánské Lázně, West Bohemia. The great Polish composer visited this famous resort on several occasions and it now has a festival in his honour. In every odd-numbered year there is a piano competition for budding young pianists (held in early July).
International Bagpipe Festival *(mid-Aug)*, Strakonice, South Bohemia. An annual event, staged in the town's castle, this is one of the Czech Republic's biggest international folk festivals.

Crystal Globe award, Karlovy Vary Film Festival

The Five-Petalled Rose Festival, held in June in Český Krumlov

AVERAGE MONTHLY RAINFALL

Rainfall
The heaviest rainfall occurs during the summer months in the Czech Republic's mountainous areas. Other, low-lying regions receive much less precipitation. Winter snowfalls can be reasonably heavy.

AUTUMN

Autumn is generally long and mild, and the weather is normally pleasant until early November. The new cultural season begins, with theatres, concert halls and opera houses reopening after the summer break. Grape harvest festivals are held in wine-making districts, such as Moravia.

Forests all over the country are invaded by armies of mushroom-pickers, since gathering fungi is the favourite autumn activity of many Czechs.

Poster promoting Brno's September tuba competition

SEPTEMBER

Prague Autumn *(Sep–Oct)*, Prague. International festival of classical music, held at the Rudolfinum *(see p82)*.
International Tuba Competition *(3rd week in Sep)*, Brno, South Moravia. Part of Brno's International Music Festival, with year-round events.
International Theatre Festival *(2nd half of Sep)*, Plzeň, West Bohemia. Theatre groups from all over Europe perform.
Organ Festival, Olomouc, North Moravia. Works by Czech and foreign composers

Performers in costume, Prague Autumn music festival

are performed on the organs of Olomouc's Church of St Maurice *(see p216)*.

OCTOBER

The Great Pardubice Steeplechase *(2nd Sun)*, Pardubice, east of Prague. This famous horse race, first held in 1874 and run on Pardubice steeplechase course, is one of the most difficult of its kind in Europe.
Day of the Republic *(28 Oct)*. Despite the splitting up of Czechoslovakia in 1993, the anniversary of the founding of the independent republic in 1918 remains a public holiday.

NOVEMBER

Battle for Freedom and Democracy Day *(17 Nov)*. The anniversary of the Velvet Revolution is celebrated all over the country. In Prague, leading Czech politicians lay wreaths at the monument of St Wenceslas in Wenceslas Square.

Autumn view of St Vitus's Cathedral in Prague

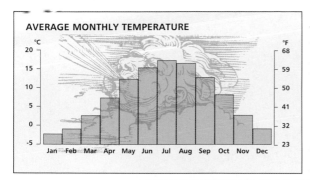

AVERAGE MONTHLY TEMPERATURE

Temperature

Summer is generally warm, with the average temperature approaching 20°C (68°F); the coolest regions are, of course, the mountains. Winters tend to be harsh, with the temperature often dropping below zero in December, January and February.

WINTER

The snowy landscapes of the Czech Republic in winter are stunning, and the Czechs make the most of the snow and ice. Ice hockey is played on frozen ponds throughout the country, and cross-country skiing is another popular activity. Tourist centres in the Krkonoše (Bohemia's highest mountains) stage international sports events, including the prestigious ski-jumping and ski-flying tournaments in Harrachov, and the downhill skiing events in Špindlerův Mlýn. The roads are kept in excellent condition, but driving conditions can be hazardous in the mountains.

Prague fares less well in the winter. On foggy days, which are not uncommon, temperatures can drop as low as -5°C (23°F).

DECEMBER

Christmas and New Year season. Throughout December countless markets sell all kinds of Christmas merchandise, from tree decorations to *svařák* (hot wine); just before Christmas Eve they also sell live carp, the traditional Christmas delicacy. The arrival of the New Year is celebrated with huge and boisterous street parties. Prague experiences a real invasion of visitors at this time, and it is difficult to find a room in a hotel or a pension; restaurants and pubs are busy, too.

Winter scenery in the Krkonoše (Giant Mountains)

Swimming competitions in the Vltava *(26 Dec)*. Hundreds of hearty swimmers congregate on the banks of the Vltava river in Prague to swim in temperatures not much above freezing point 0°C (32°F).

JANUARY

New Year's Day *(1 Jan)*. Public holiday.

A traditional Christmas market stall

FEBRUARY

St Matthew's Fair *(24 Feb–early Apr)*, Prague. Known in Czech as Matějská pouť, this is essentially a giant fun-fair. It is held at Výstaviště fairground in Holešovice.

PUBLIC HOLIDAYS IN THE CZECH REPUBLIC

New Year's Day (1 Jan)
Easter Monday
Labour Day (1 May)
VE Day (8 May)
St Cyril and St Methodius Day (5 Jul)
Anniversary of Jan Hus's death (6 Jul)
Czech State Day (28 Sep)
Foundation of the Republic (28 Oct)
Battle for Freedom and Democracy Day (17 Nov)
Christmas Eve (24 Dec)
Christmas Day (25 Dec)
St Stephen's Day (26 Dec)

THE HISTORY OF THE CZECH REPUBLIC

From the middle ages until the 17th century the Czech Lands played a significant role in European history. Defeat at the start of the Thirty Years' War, however, marked the beginning of three centuries of domination by the Habsburgs. The joint state of Czechoslovakia, founded after World War I, came to an end in 1993.

The Latin name of Bohemia derives from the Boii, one of the two Celtic tribes who, from the 3rd century BC, settled in the territories of the present-day Czech Republic. Towards the end of the 1st century BC, the Celts were dislodged by two Germanic tribes, the Quadi and the Marcomanni. They inflicted several defeats on the Romans who, as a result, decided not to extend their empire beyond the Danube. In the end, it was tribes from the east who displaced the Germanic tribes in the 5th and 6th centuries. In the 7th century Bohemia and Moravia were briefly part of a vast Slav state ruled by the Frankish merchant, Prince Samo.

Bronze head of a Celtic goddess

THE GREAT MORAVIAN EMPIRE

The early 9th century saw the rise of the Moravians. They forged an alliance with the Slavs of Bohemia, and thus the Great Moravian Empire was born. At its peak, in around 885, the empire included Bohemia, Moravia, Silesia and parts of modern Slovakia, Germany and Poland. In response to German ambitions in the region, the second Moravian emperor invited Byzantine missionaries to spread Christianity in the Slavic language. The two monks, the so-called Apostles to the Slavs, were later canonized as St Cyril and St Methodius.

THE PŘEMYSLID DYNASTY

Following the fall of the Moravian empire, brought about by a Magyar invasion in 906, a new political centre emerged in Bohemia under the Přemyslid princes. One of the dynasty's early rulers, Prince (St) Wenceslas, improved his state's relations with Germany but was murdered by his brother Boleslav in 935. Under Boleslav, Bohemia became part of the Holy Roman Empire. In 973 a bishopric (subordinate to the archbishopric of Mainz) was founded in Prague. The murder of Bishop Adalbert, who became the first Czech-born Bishop of Prague in 983, stunned Christian Europe (see p101).

In 1085 Prince Vratislav II received from Holy Roman Emperor Henry IV the (non-hereditary) title of king. He thus became the first crowned ruler of Bohemia.

TIMELINE

Saints Cyril and Methodius

600 BC	1 AD	400 AD	800 AD	1100 AD
	c.167 Invasion of Roman territory by the Quadi and Marcomanni	**450** The Slavs begin moving into the region	**9th century** Foundation of the Great Moravian Empire	**1085** Coronation of Vratislav II, first king of Bohemia
c.500 BC Celtic Boii inhabit territory of present-day Bohemia	**45 AD** Establishment of the Roman province of Noricum, south of the Danube	**863** The Byzantine monks, Cyril and Methodius, arrive in Moravia **983** Adalbert becomes first Czech-born Bishop of Prague		

Bishop Adalbert's bejewelled glove

◁ *St Wenceslas and St Vitus* by Bartholomaeus Spränger, c. 1600

SICILIAN GOLDEN BULL

In exchange for supporting Frederick II of Sicily in his endeavours to secure the Holy Roman Emperor's throne, in 1212 Přemysl king Otakar I received the Golden Bull of Sicily. This edict established the right of succession to the Bohemian crown. Bohemian rulers were also made electors of the emperor.

The Golden Bull, setting out the heredity of the Bohemian crown

The 13th century saw a rapid increase in both the political and economic power of Bohemia. Many towns, including České Budějovice and Hodonín, were founded during this period. The discovery of silver in Kutná Hora and Jihlava helped transform the Bohemian court into one of Europe's richest. Actively encouraged by the Přemyslids, vast numbers of Germans came to settle in Bohemia. They even founded entirely new towns.

Bohemia became the most powerful state within the Empire. During 1254–69 its territory expanded to include parts of what is now Austria. The endeavours of Otakar II to win the throne of Germany and the imperial crown met with opposition from the imperial princes, however. The Bohemian king's death at the Battle of the Moravian Field (Marchfeld), in 1278, put an end to the ambitious monarch's plans.

A period of chaos followed the death of Otakar II. The early death of Václav II was followed by the murder of his heirless son, Václav III, in 1306. This marked the end of the Přemyslid dynasty.

THE LUXEMBURG DYNASTY

By cleverly choosing a member of the Přemyslid family as his wife, John of Luxemburg found himself in a position to secure the Bohemian throne. While John rarely visited Bohemia, his son Charles IV, crowned Holy Roman Emperor in 1355, had much closer links with his kingdom. Charles IV's reign as King of Bohemia (1346–78) is often described as Bohemia's "Golden Age", a period of great economic and cultural growth. Prague, which became the imperial capital, acquired the first university north of the Alps, a new royal palace and a stone bridge across the Vltava river; work started on St Vitus's Cathedral, and the city became the seat of an archbishop. The network of roads and navigable stretches of rivers grew

Miniature of Přemyslid king Václav II

TIMELINE

Přemysl king Otakar II lying dead on the Moravian Field

1200

1212 Otakar I receives the Sicilian Golden Bull.

1250

1278 Otakar II killed in the Battle of the Moravian Field

The seal used by Emperor Charles IV (14th century)

1283 Václav II ascends the throne

1300

1306 Přemyslid dynasty ends with death of Václav III

Charles IV, with a cross from the French Dauphin

EARLY HUSSITE MOVEMENT

In the late 14th century the notion that the source of the social crisis lay in the Church's departure from the teaching of the Gospels began to gain support. One of the advocates of this view was a peasant-born preacher, Jan Hus (1371–1415). He became the main ideologue of the reformation movement, which demanded the curtailing of the Church's influence over state affairs. When, following the Council of Constance in 1415, Hus was burned at the stake as a heretic, unrest spread throughout the country. It reached boiling point in 1419, when several Catholic councillors were thrown out of Prague's New Town Hall's window, in the first "Prague defenestration" *(see p96)*.

rapidly; weaving, as well as the cultivation of cereals, hops and grapes flourished; the mining of silver, gold, iron and tin all increased. There was success abroad, too: through his four marriages Charles IV extend-ed his kingdom north into parts of Poland and Germany. In short, Charles presided over a period of great prosperity and relative peace.

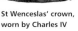

St Wenceslas' crown, worn by Charles IV

Charles IV's son, Václav IV (1378–1419), failed to continue his father's success. Hoping to exploit the weakness of the Church at a time of increasing crisis for the Papacy, he engaged in a dispute with the archbishop of Prague and some sections of the nobility. The consequences of this conflict, including Václav IV's own imprisonment and the weakening of the king's position, coincided with the effects of an outbreak of bubonic plague which, in 1380, ravaged certain parts of Europe.

Jan Hus teaching in Prague's Chapel of Bethlehem

1344 John of Luxemburg killed in the Battle of Crécy

1355 Charles IV crowned Holy Roman Emperor

Crucifix given to Charles IV by Pope Urban V in 1368

1434 Hussites defeated at Battle of Lipany

1350

1400

1344 Establishment of Prague archbishopric

1348 Founding of Prague University

1346 Charles IV crowned King of Bohemia

1415 Jan Hus burned at the stake

1420–31 Emperor Sigismund launches five crusades against the Hussites

The Hussites

In the 15th century, the followers of Jan Hus became a major fighting force. They achieved great successes against the Emperor's crusades, due largely to the skill of their leader, Jan Žižka. The Hussites split into the radical Taborites and the moderate "Utraquists" (from *sub utraque specie*, symbolizing the wish to celebrate Mass with both bread and wine). While the former were finally beaten at Lipany in 1434, the Utraquists recognized papal supremacy in return for consent for the Czech language to be used in church. The Utraquists were active until the Battle of the White Mountain in 1620.

Burning of Jerome of Prague
Jerome of Prague, the Czech theologian and supporter of Jan Hus and John Wycliffe, was burned at the stake in 1416. He was condemned for heresy by the Council of Constance.

The Czech Nobility's Letter of Protest
Several hundred seals of the Bohemian nobility were affixed to a letter protesting the execution of Jan Hus in 1415.

Gilded monstrance, carried by a priest.

Jan Žižka was a brilliant commander and a key strategist of the Hussite army.

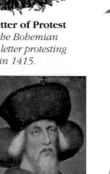

Sigismund of Luxemburg
Boosted by papal support, Emperor Sigismund (1419–37) launched five crusades against the Hussites. They all ended in failure.

Satan Disguised as the Pope
This type of lurid image, satirizing the corrupt Church and the excessively free lifestyle of priests, was painted on placards and carried through the streets.

GOD'S WARRIORS
The early 16th-century *Codex of Jena* illustrated the Hussites' victories. Here, the Hussites, who included artisans, urban merchants and minor nobility, are shown singing their hymn. They are led by their blind leader, Jan Žižka.

Hussite Victory (1420)

In the Battle of Vitkov the Hussites, led by Jan Žižka, won a victory over the Catholic army of Emperor Sigismund.

The chalice was an important symbol for the Hussites, who demanded the right to take wine at Mass.

Farm implements were used as makeshift weapons by the peasants.

The peasant army marched behind Jan Žižka.

REFORMER JAN HUS

Jan Hus was one of the most important religious thinkers of his day. His objections to the Catholic Church's corrupt practices and opulent lifestyle were shared by many Czechs – peasants and nobles alike. His reformist preaching in Prague earned him a huge following and was noticed by the Papacy, which excommunicated him. In 1414 Hus decided to defend his teaching at the Council of Constance. Even though he had received a guarantee of safe conduct from Emperor Sigismund, Hus was imprisoned and burned at the stake in 1415.

Jan Hus at the stake *Wearing the hat of shame given to heretics, Hus became a martyr of the Czech people.*

Hussite Shield

Wooden shields like this one bearing the arms of Prague were used to fill any gaps in the tight formations of military wagons.

Taborite Wagon

Hussite armies struck terror in the whole of Europe. They employed new methods of combat, including the use of reinforced battle wagons.

George of Poděbrady

In 1458 Czech nobles elected a Utraquist – George of Poděbrady – as king. The first and last Hussite king, he reigned until 1471.

Illuminated manuscript of sacred music from Kutná Hora (1471)

GEORGE OF PODĚBRADY

The end of the Hussite wars in 1434 and the dying out of the Luxemburg dynasty were followed by nine years of interregnum, which ended in 1458, when the Czech nobility elected as their king George of Poděbrady (1458–71), a moderate Hussite, who also enjoyed the approval of the Czech Catholics.

The new king of Bohemia, who represented the reforming spirit and preached religious tolerance, was initially accepted by a number of European monarchs. In 1462 George put forward a plan to establish a League of Christian Monarchs to resist the Turkish expansion. This visionary proposal did not, however, meet with approval and the king's position was worsened by the hostile attitude of Rome. In 1466 Pope Paul II excommunicated George and called for a crusade against the "Czech heretics". The ensuing war ended only with the death of King George, in 1471.

THE JAGIELLONIAN DYNASTY

In compliance with the late monarch's wishes, the Czech nobility chose as their new king the Polish Prince Vladislav Jagiello (1471–1516), who, in 1491, also ascended the throne of Hungary and moved his capital to Buda (today's Budapest). The king's absence was exploited by the Bohemian nobility to strengthen their own political and economic power. The fortunes of families such as the Rosenbergs and Pernsteins grew; they founded new towns and supported agriculture and trade.

A treaty concluded at Kutná Hora between Catholics and Utraquists in 1485 laid the foundation for religious peace that lasted more than half a century. Ideas of humanism percolated into the Czech Lands, and local architects created Late-Gothic masterpieces such as Prague Castle's Vladislav Hall (1502).

In 1526 Vladislav's successor, Louis Jagiello, was killed fighting the Turks

Late 15th-century view of Malá Strana in Prague

TIMELINE

1458 George of Poděbrady elected to Bohemian throne

1466 Paul II anounces a crusade against Bohemia

1526–64 Reign of Ferdinand I

1450	1475	1500	1525

1471 Coronation of Vladislav Jagiello, king of Bohemia

1491 Vladislav II becomes king of Hungary

Vladislav Jagiello

1526 Louis Jagiello killed at the Battle of Mohács

Rudolph II and the Danish astronomer Tycho Brahe

at the Battle of Mohács. He left no heir, so based on the political treaty concluded in 1515 between Vladislav and Maximilian I, the throne passed into the hands of the Austrian Habsburgs.

THE HABSBURGS

Ferdinand I (1526–64), the first representative of the Habsburg dynasty, tried to centralize the monarch's power, which met with violent opposition among the Bohemian Estates (essentially the nobility). Tension increased when attempts were made to re-establish the Catholic faith, which eventually eased when an Act of Tolerance, giving the various Christian denominations equal rights, was signed in 1609 by Rudolph II (1576–1611). This emperor, who made Prague his capital and was a great lover of the arts, presided over Bohemia's second Golden Age. Sadly, intensifying

pressure from the clergy, combined with the Emperor's deepening mental illness, forced Rudolph to abdicate in favour of his brother Matthias.

THE THIRTY YEARS' WAR

Rudolph II's Act of Tolerance failed to put an end to the conflict between the Catholic monarch and the non-Catholic Bohemian Estates. In 1618 representatives of the latter threw two of the emperor's envoys out of the windows of Prague Castle. This second "Prague defenestration" signalled an open anti-Habsburg rebellion and marked the beginning of the Thirty Years' War (1618–48), which was to engulf much of Europe.

In 1620 the army of the rebellious Bohemian Estates was crushed by the forces of Emperor Ferdinand II at the Battle of the White Mountain (Bílá Hora), near Prague. The collapse of the insurgence was followed by severe repression in Bohemia: 27 leaders of the anti-Habsburg opposition were executed in Prague's Old Town Square. Around 75 per cent of the land belonging to the Bohemian nobility was confiscated; thousands of families had to leave the country; and dissenters were forced to convert to Catholicism.

Defeat of the Czechs at the Battle of the White Mountain, 1620

Charter for manglers and dyers

1620 Czech defeat at the Battle of the White Mountain

1618 "Prague defenestration". Outbreak of the Thirty Years' War

1621 Execution of 27 leaders of the uprising in Prague

1550	1575	1600	1625
1556 Arrival of Jesuits in the Czech Lands	**1576–1611** Reign of Rudolph II		**1648** Peace of Westphalia ends the Thirty Years' War
1575 Maximilian II confirms religious freedom in Czech Lands	*A ten-ducat coin of Rudolph II*	**1609** Emperor's edict confirming religious freedom and privileges of the Estates **1634** Killing of Albrecht von Wallenstein	

MARIA THERESA AND JOSEPH II

The Thirty Years' War, which ended in 1648 with the Peace of Westphalia, reduced Bohemia's international stature and caused both devastation and depopulation. The war also elevated the position of Catholic noble families, who arrived mostly from abroad and were granted the confiscated estates of Bohemian landowners. Many of the latter went into exile.

Empress Maria Theresa with her children

With the Czech Lands now firmly under Catholic control, a period of intense Counter-Reformation activity followed, spearheaded by the Jesuits. As a result of the campaign, the majority of the population converted to Catholicism. A major role in the shaping of the religious consciousness was played by Baroque art. During this period some outstanding works were created by architects Carlo Lurago, Giovanni Santini, and Christoph and Kilian Ignaz Dientzenhofer; sculptors Ferdinand Brokof and Matthias Braun; and painters Karel Škréta and Petr Brandl. The immigrant Catholic nobility built themselves grand palaces.

Emperor Joseph II, the enlightened despot

Following the war, the legal position of the Czech Crown within the empire changed The Habsburgs were given hereditary rights to the throne and the German language was made legally equal to Czech. The most important national issues were now being decided by the central administration in Vienna.

When Maria Theresa (1740–80) inherited the Habsburg crown, she introduced the principles of the Enlightenment in the empire. Her most notable act was to expel the Jesuits. Her son Joseph II (1780–90) felt an even stronger need for change. He abolished serfdom and even granted certain Christian denominations equal rights. Bohemia's Jews, in

Meeting of Napoleon and Franz II after the Battle of Austerlitz (1805)

TIMELINE

Baroque goblet made of Czech glass (1730)

1648 Peace of Westphalia signed

1711–40 Reign of Charles VI

1781 The Edict of Tolerance allows some freedom of worship

1780–90 Reign of Joseph II

1650	1675	1700	1725	1750	17

1657–1705 Reign of Leopold I

1676–8 Vyšehrad fortifications reinforced with new bastions

1740–80 Reign of Maria Theresa

particular, felt the benefits of this new freedom of worship.

However, Joseph II, often described as an "enlightened despot", was not very popular. In his drive to unify his vast empire, he made German the official language and central-ized power in Austria. The ruthless enforce-ment of his reforms and the Germanization of the Czech Lands bred dissatisfaction.

Joseph's successor, Franz II, was a con-servative who largely swept aside his predecessors' reforms. His most memorable act was to sign a peace treaty with Napoleon following the latter's victory at the Battle of Austerlitz in 1805 *(see p232)*.

Barricades by the Charles Bridge in Prague, June 1848

THE ROAD TO NATIONAL REVIVAL

In response to the unification policies of the Habsburgs, the early 1800s saw the emergence of a new but uncoordinated move-ment to rebuild Czech culture. The fight to restore the position of the Czech language became the key element of the revival programme. New plays and literary works were written in Czech. A vital role in this revival was played by Josef Dobrovský, who wrote a history of the Czech language and literature *(see p26)*.

Franz Joseph I, a staunch supporter of absolute monarchy

THE SPRINGTIME OF NATIONS

In the mid-19th century the Czech Lands, like many other European countries, became a scene of revolutionary struggle against absolute monarchy. The demands included political autonomy and the granting of civic rights, including freedom of speech, assembly, press and religion. In June 1848 an uprising in Prague was quashed by the imperial army. Franz Joseph I, who became emperor that same year, continued the policy of absolute monarchy but could not prevent the decline of the Habsburg Empire. Following the defeat of Austria by Prussia in 1866, the so-called Dual Monarchy of Austria-Hungary was established, creating two independent states under one ruler. This decision was a disappoint-ment to Czech politicians, who failed to win the same rights for the Czech Lands as those enjoyed by Hungary.

The disgruntled Czechs turned their energies to economic activities. New com-panies (such as Škoda) were established, and new theatres and national museums were built. Increasing importance was attached to the standards of education.

1792–1835 Reign of Franz II	1815 Congress of Vienna	1848 The Prague Uprising		1866 Founding of the Austro-Hungarian Empire	1883 Birth of writer Franz Kafka in Prague

1800	1825	1850	1875	1900

| 1792–1814 Wars with France | 1835 First volumes of Josef Jungmann's Czech-German dictionary | 1848 Franz Joseph I succeeds to the throne | 1868–83 Building of the National Theatre in Prague | |

Franz Kafka

The Czech National Revival

Clock on Old Town Hall Tower

The 19th century saw the rapid growth of Czech culture and the shaping of a modern national consciousness. Playing a vital role in this process were musicians, artists and writers, including the composers Bedřich Smetana and Antonín Dvořák, the painter Mikoláš Aleš, sculptor Josef Myslbek and novelist Antonín Jirásek, whose works inspired a huge popular response. The Czech language became the basic tool in the process of shaping the national identity. Theatres and museums sprang up all over the country, emphasizing the importance of Czech culture in the nation's life.

Antonín Dvořák
The conductor and composer Antonín Dvořák (1841–1904) was a major exponent of Czech national music (see pp22–3).

The National Theatre in Prague
When the theatre, one of the symbols of the Czech national revival, burned down in 1881, people from all walks of life contributed money towards its rebuilding. The picture illustrates the ceremonial laying of the cornerstone.

Coat of arms of Prague's Old Town

Smetana's Libuše
Written for the opening of the National Theatre in 1881, this opera drew on legendary Czech history.

OLD TOWN CLOCK TOWER CALENDAR
In 1866 the revolving dial on Prague's famous landmark was replaced by a new one made by Czech painter Josef Mánes. Individual months are symbolized by scenes from peasant life, corresponding with the signs of the zodiac painted on medallions.

Expo 95 Poster
*Vojtěch Hynais
designed this Art
Nouveau poster for
the ethnographic
exhibition of 1895.
It reflects the
new appreciation
of regional
traditions.*

Portrait of a Woman
*A young woman dressed
in traditional costume
poses for a portrait in a
Litomyšl studio, in
c.1860–70.*

**WHERE TO SEE THE
NATIONAL REVIVAL**

Many fine buildings were
built during this period in
Prague and other major cities;
they include the National
Museum in Prague and
Brno's Mahenovo Theatre.
Among the best examples of
Art Nouveau are Prague's
Municipal House *(see pp84–
5)*, with murals by Alfons
Mucha, and the Modern Art
Gallery building in Hradec
Králové, designed by Osvald
Polívka *(see p199)*. Prague's
Rudolfinum *(see p82)* and
the National Theatre *(see
pp94–5)* both have glorious
interiors by great artists
of the day.

National Museum, Prague
*Symbol of the Czech National
Revival, with a glass dome, this
Neo-Renaissance building was
finished in 1890* (see pp90–91).

Mahenovo Theatre, Brno
*Built in 1881, this building
has Corinthian columns and
a lavish gilt interior.*

**Municipal House in
Prague**
*The Art Nouveau
interior is adorned with
allegories of civic virtues
by Alfons Mucha.*

October

Scorpio

Symbols of the months and signs of
the zodiac revolve around the centre.

**The First Automobile in
Prague, 1898**
*Prague businessman, Klubal,
takes a ride around Prague Castle
in the first motor car to be seen
in the capital.*

Assassination of Archduke Ferdinand, 1914

THE FIRST WORLD WAR

Few Czechs (or Slovaks) had the appetite to fight for the empire during World War I, and it was during the war that the idea of a joint Czech and Slovak state independent of Austria arose. Its main champion was Tomáš Masaryk, a professor at Prague University. In 1916, together with Edvard Beneš, he created the Czechoslovak National Council, based in Paris, which was later recognized by the Allies as the representative of the future Czechoslovakia. In May 1918, in Pittsburgh, USA, representatives of Czech and Slovak émigré organizations signed an agreement that provided for the creation of a joint Czechoslovak state after the war.

The political endeavours were supported by the military efforts of Czechs and Slovaks fighting on the side of the Allies. Czechoslovak legions fought in Italy, France and Russia. Back at home, where there had been growing anti-Habsburg dissent, the Czechoslovak National Council became the supreme political authority. On 28 October 1918, as the Austro-Hungarian Empire collapsed, the independent Czechoslovak Republic was declared in Prague. Tomáš Masaryk was its first president.

CZECHOSLOVAKIA

Thanks to the industry established under the Habsburgs, Czechoslovakia flourished economically. However, the ethnic situation was much more problematic. The new state had a diverse population made up of some 6 million Czechs, 2 million Slovaks, and 3 million Germans, as well as communities of ethnic minorities including Ukrainians and Hungarians. While the Czechs were generally content with their new situation, the other ethnic groups were much less satisfied with their lot.

It was thanks to the skills of Tomáš Masaryk that Czechoslovakia became such a progressive and staunchly democratic nation. The new Czechoslovak constitution ensured that there was, at least for the moment, peaceful coexistence among the ethnic minorities by ensuring that any area

Signing of the Pittsburgh Agreement, in 1918

TIMELINE

Woman wearing Czech national costume

1918 Pittsburgh Agreement

1920–21 Formation of the Small Entente, an alliance between Czechoslovakia, Romania and Yugoslavia

1910   1915   1920   1925

1914 Assassination of Archduke Franz Ferdinand in Sarajevo. Outbreak of World War I

1916 Czechoslovak National Council created in Paris

1918 Founding of the Czechoslovak Republic. Tomáš Masaryk becomes president

Poster for 10th Sokol Rally, aimed at promoting sport

with an ethnic community exceeding 20 per cent of the population would be officially bilingual. This relative calm disappeared in the 1930s. On top of the economically devastating Wall Street Crash of 1929 came political instability; this coincided with the growing threat posed by the Third Reich. Hitler's rise to power in 1933 helped to activate the disgruntled German minority living in northern Bohemia and Moravia (the Sudetenland). They found a voice in the Sudeten German Party (SdP), a far-right group with direct links with the Nazis. The retirement in 1935 of President Masaryk, to be replaced by Edvard Beneš, couldn't have come at a worse time.

WIR DANKEN UNSERM FÜHRER

Poster showing the area of the Protectorate

THE MUNICH TREATY

Following the Nazi annexation of Austria in March 1938, Czechoslovakia became Hitler's next target. Later that year he demanded the Sudetenland. In a bid to avoid war, President Beneš agreed that the heads of France (Daladier) and Great Britain (Chamberlain) should negotiate with Hitler and Mussolini to settle the dispute. In September 1938 the four powers signed the notorious Munich Agreement, which handed Sudetenland to the Nazis. Czechoslovakia lost 5 million inhabitants and a vast chunk of its land. President Beneš resigned and left the country.

The nation carved out by the Munich Agreement survived

only for another six months. In March 1939 Hitler forced the ineffectual Emil Hacha (Beneš's successor) to agree to make Bohemia and Moravia a German Protectorate. Nazi troops marched into Bohemia.

Repression against the population, while not as brutal as that seen in Poland, intensified after 1941, when Reinhard Heydrich was appointed Reich protector. A concentration camp was established in Terezín for the Jews brought from Germany, Austria, Holland and Denmark, as well as from the Protectorate. In 1942 Heydrich was assassinated by Czech paratroopers trained in England.

German troops entering Prague in March 1939

1934 Election success of the Sudeten German Party	1935 Edvard Beneš succeeds Masaryk as the country's president	1938 Munich Agreement	1942 Assassination of Reinhard Heydrich
1930	**1935**	**1940**	

Edvard Beneš, president of Czecho-slovakia 1935–38

1939 Creation of the Bohemia and Moravia Protectorate. Start of the German occupation

Celebrating Gottwald's new government, 1948

"VICTORIOUS FEBRUARY"

On 5 May 1945, in the closing days of World War II, there was an armed uprising in Prague against the Nazis. Four days later the city was liberated by the Red Army. Beneš returned to the country as its president. The reprisals against Czech German-speakers were inevitable. Thousands died and more than 2 million were forcibly expelled (or fled).

The years immediately after the war were marked by the rapid rise of the Communist Party (KSČ). It was the party with the most votes at the 1946 election, its leader, Klement Gottwald, became prime minister and several Party members joined the cabinet. While the Communists had great popular support, there was growing dismay among the non-Communist members of the cabinet. In February 1948, 12 of them resigned, hoping thereby to bring an end to Gottwald's premiership; in the event, he managed to orchestrate a Communist coup, without the military assistance that Stalin had offered. Failing in health, Beneš resigned. This so-called "Victorious February" opened an era of Stalinization, bringing with it

blanket nationalization and massive industrialization. There was also repression and persecution. Farmers opposed to the collectivization of the land were sent to work in the mines or to prison; clergymen were sent to concentration camps. Many people opted to emigrate.

THE "PRAGUE SPRING"

In the 1960s a reform movement within the Communist Party took shape. It demanded a liberalization of the Stalinist approach to economics, politics and individual free-doms. After failed attempts to win over and then repress the reformers, in January 1968 President Novotný was forced from office. The new First Secretary, Alexander Dubček, declared his wish to build "a socialism with a human face". The subsequent democratic reforms, which met with an enthusiastic reception, embraced all aspects of social and political life.

Funeral of Czech student Jan Palach, in 1969

Citizens of Prague queuing for food in 1965

TIMELINE

Alexander Dubček

1945 The Prague uprising. End of World War II	1949–55 Period of the most notorious political trials	1966 Oscar for Jiří Menzel's film *Closely Observed Trains*	
1948 "Victorious February" – Communists assume full power in the country	**1957** Antonín Novotný becomes President	**1968** "Prague Spring". Armed intervention by Warsaw Pact countries	**1977** "Charter 77" manifesto

It all came to an abrupt end on 21 August 1968, when, on Soviet orders, troops from the Warsaw Pact nations invaded Czechoslovakia. Dubček and other reformers were sent to Moscow, and people protested in the streets. Among the few who died was a student Jan Palach, who set fire to himself in Wenceslas Square.

An invading Russian tank after the "Prague Spring" of 1968

The suppression of the "Prague Spring" returned orthodox Communists to power. Dubček was replaced by Gustáv Husák, a man totally subservient to the Soviet Union. During the next 21 years of "normalization", totalitarian rule was re-established and all dissent quashed. Many intellectuals fled abroad.

In 1977, a group of politicians and intellectuals, including the playwright Václav Havel, signed a document demanding basic human rights. This so-called Charter 77 became a rallying-point for all dissidents.

THE VELVET REVOLUTION

In the autumn of 1989 the wave of democratic changes that was sweeping across Europe reached Czechoslovakia. In response to a mass demonstration in the capital, Václav Havel and Alexander Dubček appeared on a balcony in Wenceslas Square on 22 November. Their call for a general strike was enough to cause the

Crowds in Wenceslas Square in Prague: the Velvet Revolution

downfall of the Communist regime. A hastily formed new political party, the Civic Forum, embarked upon negotiations with the outgoing government. On 29 December 1989 Václav Havel became president.

THE VELVET DIVORCE

Without the strong, centralizing authority of the Communists, the historical tensions between Prague and Slovakia reappeared. The Civic Forum split into two (the centre-left Civic Movement and the right-wing Civic Democratic Party), and the 1992 general elections brought to power parties intent on breaking up the joint state. On 1 January 1993 the Czech Republic was established. Václav Havel remained its president for two terms of office, until 2003. He was replaced by Václav Klaus. In 1999 the Czech Republic became a member of NATO and in 2004 joined the European Union.

1984 Jaroslav Seifert awarded Nobel Prize for Literature for his poetry
Václav Havel

1997 Oscar for Jan Svěrák's film *Kolya*

2004 The Czech Republic becomes member of the EU

2007 Czech Republic joins the Schengen Agreement, abolishing border controls with all of its members

1985	1995	2005	2015

1989 "Velvet Revolution". Václav Havel becomes president

1993 Czechoslovakia splits. Founding of the Czech Republic

1999 Czech Republic joins NATO

Serious floods in the Czech Republic, August 2002

PRAGUE
AREA BY AREA

Prague at a Glance

Most major historic sites in Prague are found in the city centre within the three districts marked on the map. From Staré Město (Old Town) and Josefov (Jewish Quarter) it is only a short distance to Charles Bridge and, beyond, Malá Strana (Little Quarter), from where a steep uphill climb ends at Prague Castle and Hradčany.

HRADČANY AND MALÁ STRANA
(pp52–69)

St Vitus's Cathedral
houses the Bohemian crown jewels. These fine relics, shown rarely in public, include the St Wenceslas crown and the royal orb, pictured (see pp58–9).

Wallenstein Palace,
a Baroque palace built in the 1620s for Count Albrecht von Wallenstein, was intended to outshine Prague Castle (see p66).

The Church of St Nicholas in the centre of Malá Strana, is perhaps the most magnificent of the many fine examples of Baroque architecture in Prague (see pp64–5).

Maisel Synagogue *was founded in 1591 by Mordechai Maisel, then mayor of the Jewish Quarter. Now it houses one of the world's most magnificent collections of Judaica (see p79).*

STARÉ MĚSTO AND JOSEFOV *(pp70–85)*

NOVÉ MĚSTO *(pp86–99)*

| 0 metres | 200 |
| 0 yards | 200 |

Prague's Main Station *features some exquisite Art Nouveau decoration, as do many other buildings in Nové Město (see p91).*

HRADČANY AND MALÁ STRANA

The history of Prague began with the Castle, founded in the 9th century high above the Vltava river. Among the buildings enclosed within the castle walls were three churches and a monastery. In around 1320 a settlement called Hradčany was founded in part of the outer bailey. The

Stained-glass window in St Vitus's Cathedral

castle complex has undergone numerous reconstructions.

Malá Strana ("little quarter") occupies the slopes beneath Prague Castle and has changed little since the 1700s. Its maze of streets abounds in lavishly decorated Baroque palaces and churches. Once the realm of nobles, Malá Strana is now home to artists and musicians.

SIGHTS AT A GLANCE

Churches, Monasteries and Monuments
Belvedere ⑥
Černín Palace ⑪
Charles Bridge pp68–9 ㉒
Church of Our Lady beneath the Chain ⑲
Church of Our Lady Victorious ⑳
Church of St Nicholas pp64–5 ⑭
Church of St Thomas ⑯
Loreto ⑩
Old Royal Palace ③
St George's Basilica ④

St Vitus's Cathedral pp58–9 ②
Strahov Monastery ⑫
Wallenstein Palace ⑮

Museums and Galleries
Prague Castle Picture Gallery ①
Sternberg Palace pp60–61 ⑧

Historic Streets, Squares and Parks
Castle Square ⑨
Golden Lane ⑤
Little Quarter Square ⑰
Nerudova Street ⑬

Palace Gardens ⑱
Petřín Hill ㉑
Royal Garden ⑦

KEY

▢ Street-by-Street map
See pp54–5

Ⓜ Metro station

🚊 Tram stop

✝ Church

🚠 Cable car

ℹ Tourist information

0 metres 200
0 yards 200

GETTING THERE

An easy way to get there is by tram 22 or 23 to Pražský hrad (Prague Castle) or to Pohořelec, or by tram 12, 18, 22 or 23 to Malostranské náměstí. You can also take the metro to Malostranská or Hradčanská stations; both are within walking distance of most historic sites.

◁ **The closely packed rooftops above the narrow streets of Malá Strana**

Street-by-Street: Prague Castle

Despite periodic fires and invasions, Prague Castle has retained churches, chapels, halls and towers from every period of its history, from the Gothic splendour of St Vitus's Cathedral to the Renaissance additions of Rudolph II, the last Habsburg to use the castle as his principal residence. The courtyards date from 1753–75, when the whole area was rebuilt in Late Baroque and Neo-Classical styles. The castle became the seat of the Czechoslovak president in 1918, and the current president of the Czech Republic has an office here.

★ St Vitus's Cathedral
This relief decorates St Vitus's Golden Portal ❷

The Powder Tower, used in the past for storing gunpowder and as a bell foundry, is now a museum.

Gothic reliquary of St George's arm in St Vitus's Cathedral

To Royal Garden

President's office

Prague Castle Picture Gallery
Renaissance and Baroque paintings hang in the restored stables of the castle ❶

Second courtyard

Matthias Gate (1614)

First courtyard

To Castle Square

Steps down to Malá Strana

Church of the Holy Rood

The castle gates are crowned by copies of 18th-century statues of Fighting Giants by Ignác Platzer.

The South Gardens, laid out in the old ramparts, contain 18th-century statues.

★ Golden Lane
The picturesque artisans' cottages along the inside of the castle wall were built in the late 16th century for the castle's guards and gunners ❺

LOCATOR MAP
See Street Finder, map 2.

Dalibor Tower takes its name from the first man to be imprisoned in it.

White Tower

Old Castle steps down to Malostranská metro

URSKÁ

Lobkowicz Palace houses works of art from the Lobkowicz family's private collection. It is also a venue for concerts.

★ St George's Basilica
The vaulted chapel of the royal Bohemian martyr St Ludmilla is decorated with 16th-century paintings ❹

0 metres	60
0 yards	60

KEY

– – – Suggested route

★ St George's Convent
The convent houses 19th-century Czech art such as this piece titled Summer Countryside with Chapel *by Adolf Kosárek* ❹

★ Old Royal Palace
The uniform exterior of the palace conceals many fine Gothic and Renaissance halls. Coats of arms cover the walls and ceiling of the Room of the New Land Rolls ❸

STAR SIGHTS

★ Golden Lane

★ Old Royal Palace

★ St George's Basilica and Convent

★ St Vitus's Cathedral

Titian's *The Toilet of a Young Lady* in
Prague Castle Picture Gallery

Prague Castle Picture Gallery ❶

OBRAZÁRNA PRAŽSKÉHO HRADU

Prague Castle, second courtyard. **Map**
2 D2. *Tel 224 373 531.* ᵂᵂᵂ *Malostranská, Hradčanská.* 🚋 *22, 23.* ⏰
10am–6pm daily (to 4pm in winter).
📷 ♿ **www**.obrazarna-hradu.cz

The gallery was created in
1965 to display, among other
works, what remains
of the great art collection of
Rudolph II, Bohemia's own
Renaissance king *(see p39).*
Though many works were
looted in 1648 by the occupying Swedish army, some fine
paintings remain, including
works by Hans von Aachen
and Bartolomeus Spranger.
 Paintings from the 16th–
18th centuries make up the
bulk of the gallery's collection;
highlights include Titian's
The Toilet of a Young Lady
and Rubens' *The Assembly of
the Olympic Gods.* Master
Theodoric, Paolo Veronese,
Tintoretto and the Czech
Baroque artists Jan Kupecký
and Petr Brandl are among
other painters represented.
The sculptures include a copy
of a bust of Rudolph II by
Adriaen de Vries.
 You can see the remains of
the castle's first church, the
9th-century Church of Our
Lady, believed to have been
built by Prince Bořivoj, the
first Přemyslid prince to be
baptized a Christian.

St Vitus's Cathedral ❷

See pp58–9.

Old Royal Palace ❸

STARÝ KRÁLOVSKÝ PALÁC

Prague Castle, third courtyard.
Map 2 D2. *Tel 224 373 102.*
ᵂᵂᵂ *Malostranská, Hradčanská.*
🚋 *22, 23.* ⏰ *Apr–Oct: 9am–
6pm daily; Nov–Mar: 9am–4pm
daily.* 📷 ♿ ♿
www.hrad.cz

The vast complex of
the Old Royal Palace
consists of several layers.
The first palace on the
site, remains of which are
still visible in the basement,
was built by Soběslav I in
around 1135. Two further
palaces were built above
the original, in the 13th and
14th centuries, followed by
the Gothic Vladislav Hall,
designed by Benedikt Ried
for King Vladislav Jagiellon
in the 1490s. This vast and
opulent hall is the highlight
of the palace. It has superb
rib vaulting and is lit by large
windows that heralded the
advent of the Renaissance
in Bohemia. The room was
used not only for state
functions, but also for
jousting. The architect's
unusual staircase design,
with gently sloping steps,
allowed knights to enter
the hall without having to
dismount from their horses.
 The adjacent Ludvík Wing
was, in 1618, the scene of
the famous defenestration
which led to the outbreak
of the Thirty Years' War. All
Saints' Church, behind the
Vladislav Hall, was built by

**The Riders' Staircase, Vladislav Hall
in the Royal Palace**

Peter Parler but was badly
damaged in the great fire
of 1541. The same fire
destroyed Ried's Diet Hall,
but this was rebuilt so its
intricate Late Gothic vault
can still be enjoyed.

St George's Basilica and Convent ❹

BAZILIKA A KLÁŠTER SV. JIŘÍ

Jiřské náměstí. **Map** 2 E2. *Tel 257
531 644.* ᵂᵂᵂ *Malostranská,
Hradčanská.* 🚋 *22, 23 to Pražský
hrad (Prague Castle).* ⏰ *Apr–Oct:
9am–6pm daily; Nov–Mar 9am–
4pm daily.* 📷 ♿ ♿
www.ngprague.cz

The building of St George's
Church began before 920,
during the reign of Prince
Vratislav, making it the oldest
remaining part of Prague
Castle. The church's two
distinct light-coloured stone
towers date from after the
1142 fire. The wonderful,
austere interior contains
the 10th-century tomb of
Vratislav I, found opposite
the presbytery. Also buried
in the church are Prince
Boleslav II, who died in
992, and Princess Ludmilla
(grandmother of St Wenceslas),
who was murdered in 921
and is revered as the first
Bohemian saint; her 14th-
century tombstone is located
in the Gothic side chapel.
The south portal of the
church features a 16th-
century relief depicting St
George and the dragon.
 The adjacent former
Benedictine nunnery is the
oldest convent building in
Bohemia. It was founded
in 973 by Princess Mlada,
sister of Boleslav II.
Throughout the Middle
Ages the convent, together
with St George's basilica,
formed the heart of the castle
complex. Many times rebuilt,
the convent and its religious
functions finally ceased to
operate in 1782.
 Today the convent building
houses a magnificent collection of Bohemian Mannerist
and Baroque art, including
some fine examples of

work by artists such as Jan Kupecký, Petr Brandl, Bartolomeus Spranger, Matthias Braun and Ferdinand Brokof.

Golden Lane ❺

ZLATÁ ULIČKA

Map 2 E2. ⚈ Malostranská, Hradčanská. ⚈ 22, 23. ⚈

Named after the goldsmiths who lived here in the 17th century, this short, narrow street is one of the prettiest in Prague. One side of the lane is lined with tiny, brightly painted houses which were built right into the arches of the castle walls. They were constructed in the late 16th century for Rudolph II's 24 castle guards. A century later the goldsmiths moved in and modified the buildings. But by the 19th century the area had degenerated into a slum and was populated by Prague's poor and the criminal community. In the 1950s all the remaining tenants were moved and the area restored to something like its original state. Most of the houses were converted into shops selling books, Bohemian glass and other souvenirs for visitors, who now flock to this narrow lane.

Golden Lane has been home to some well-known writers, including Franz Kafka *(see pp26–7)*, who stayed at No. 22 with his sister for a few months in 1916–17.

Despite the street's name, Rudolph II's alchemists never produced gold here. Their labs were in Vikářská, the lane between St Vitus's and the Powder Tower (Mihulźa).

One of the tiny houses in Golden Lane

Belvedere ❻

BELVEDÉR

Prague Castle, Royal Garden. **Map** 2 E1. ⚈ Malostranská, Hradčanská. ⚈ 22, 23. ⚈ 10am–6pm Tue–Sun during exhibitions only. ⚈ ⚈

Built in the 16th century by Ferdinand I for his beloved wife Anne, the Belvedere is the popular name for Queen Anne's Palace (Letohrádek královny Anny), one of the finest Italian Renaissance buildings north of the Alps. An arcaded summerhouse with Ionic columns, it is topped by a roof shaped like an inverted ship's hull clad in blue-green copper. The main architect, Paolo della Stella, also designed the reliefs inside the arcade. In the garden stands the Singing Fountain, so-called for its musical sound.

Bronze Singing Fountain in the Belvedere gardens

PARADISE GARDEN

The South Gardens below Prague Castle were developed in stages, the oldest part being the Paradise Garden, first laid out in 1559. In the 1920s, as part of President Masaryk's plan to revamp the castle, Josip Plečnik, a Slovenian architect, redesigned the gardens. He was responsible for the spiralling Bull Staircase, which leads from the Paradise Garden up to Prague Castle.

Plečnik's ingenious Bull Staircase

Spring flowers in Prague Castle's Royal Garden

Royal Garden ❼

KRÁLOVSKÁ ZAHRADA

Prague Castle, U Prašného mostu. **Map** 2 D2. ⚈ Malostranská, Hradčanská. ⚈ 22, 23. ⚈ May–Oct: 10am–6pm daily (to 7pm May & Sep, to 9pm Jun–Aug). ⚈ ⚈ ⚈ www.hrad.cz

Of the gardens around Prague Castle, the Royal Garden, on the north side, is the most important historically. It was laid out for Ferdinand I in 1534, and became famous for its rare and exotic plants. Some fine examples of 16th-century garden architecture have survived, notably the Belvedere and the Ball Game Hall (Míčovna). The latter is covered in much-restored but still beautiful Renaissance *sgraffito*.

The garden is a beautiful place for a stroll, especially in spring when thousands of tulips bloom in its immaculate beds. This is where tulips (originally from Turkey) were first acclimatized to the North European climate.

St Vitus's Cathedral ❷

CHRÁM SV. VÍTA

Work began on the city's most distinctive landmark in 1344. Peter Parler was largely responsible for the grandiose Gothic design, though the building was not finally completed for another 600 years. The cathedral contains the tomb of "Good King" Wenceslas, some fine works of art, among them an exquisite Alfons Mucha window.

Chancel
The chancel, first built by Parler and repaired in Neo-Gothic style, is remarkable for its vault, counterpointed by the intricacy of the webbed tracery.

Twin west spires

Triforium

Rose Window
Designed by František Kysela in the 1920s, the window above the portals depicts scenes from the biblical story of the Creation.

West front

Gargoyles
On the ornate west front gutter spouts are given their traditional disguise.

Nave

Main entrance

TIMELINE

c.925 Rotunda of St Vitus built by St Wenceslas

1359 Masterbuilder Peter Parler summoned to continue work on the cathedral

Bust of Peter Parler on triforium

1619 Calvinists take over cathedral as house of prayer

1929 Consecration of completed cathedral, nearly 1,000 years after death of St Wenceslas

1000	1200	1400	1600	1800

1060 Building of triple-aisled basilica begins on orders of Prince Spytihněv

Tomb of Přemysl Otakar II

1421 Hussites occupy St Vitus's

1589 Royal tomb completed

1872 Joseph Mocker begins work on west nave

1344 King John of Luxemburg founds Gothic cathedral. French architect Matthew of Arras begins work

1770 New steeple added to tower after fire

For hotels and restaurants in this region see pp344–5 and pp372–3

★ Flying Buttresses
The slender buttresses that surround the exterior of the nave and chancel, supporting the vaulted interior, are richly decorated like the rest of the cathedral.

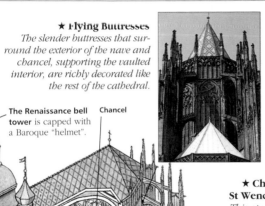

The Renaissance bell tower is capped with a Baroque "helmet".

Chancel

VISITORS' CHECKLIST

Prague Castle, third courtyard.
Map 2 D2. ᴹ Hradčanská,
Malostranská. 22, 23 to
Pražský hrad (Prague Castle) or to
U Prašného mostu. **Cathedral**
◻ Nov–Mar: 9am–4pm daily;
Apr–Oct: 9am–5pm daily (except
during services). 🛈 📷 ♿
Steeple ◻ Apr–Oct: 9am–
4pm daily. 🖼 📷

★ Chapel of St Wenceslas
This opulent, jewel-studded chapel, home to the saint's tomb, is the highlight of a visit to St Vitus's. This bronze ring hangs on the chapel's north portal.

To Old Royal Palace
(see p56)

The tomb of St Wenceslas is connected to an altar, decorated with semi-precious stones.

★ Golden Portal
Until the 19th century this was the main cathedral entrance, and it is still used on special occasions. Above it is a mosaic of The Last Judgment *by 14th-century Venetian craftsmen.*

Gothic Vaulting
The skills of architect Peter Parler are never more clearly seen than in the delicate fans of ribbing that support the three Gothic arches of the Golden Portal.

STAR FEATURES

★ Chapel of
St Wenceslas

★ Flying Buttresses

★ Golden Portal

Sternberg Palace ⑧

ŠTERNBERSKÝ PALÁC

Franz Josef Sternberg founded the Society of Patriotic
Friends of the Arts in Bohemia in 1796. Fellow
noblemen would lend their finest sculptures and
pictures to the society, which had its headquarters in
the early 18th-century Sternberg Palace. Since 1949,
the fine Baroque building has housed the National
Gallery's collection of European art, with its superb
range of Old Masters.

The Lamentation of Christ
*The frozen, sculptural
figures make this one of the
finest paintings by Lorenzo
Monaco (1408).*

Cardinal Cesi's Garden in Rome
*Henrick van Cleve's painting (1548) provides a
valuable image of a Renaissance collection of
antiquities. The garden was later destroyed.*

First
floor

Garden
Room

Stairs to
second
floor

Ground
floor

Stairs to
first floor

STAR FEATURES

★ Scholar in his Study
by Rembrandt

★ Head of Christ by
El Greco

★ The Martyrdom
of St Thomas by
Rubens

Ticket
office

Passageway
to Castle
Square

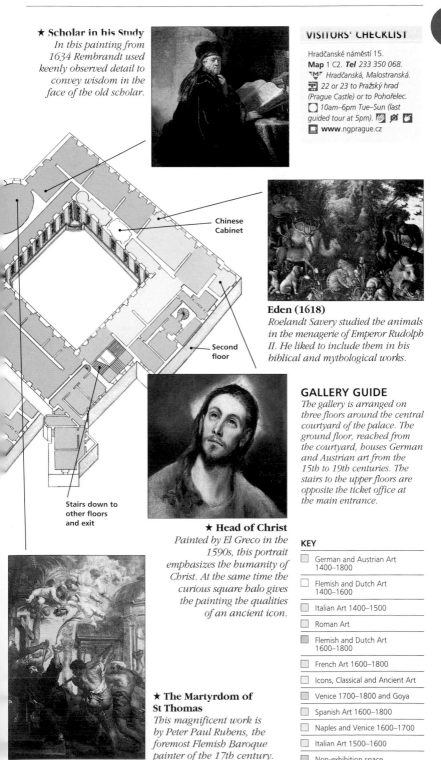

★ Scholar in his Study
In this painting from 1634 Rembrandt used keenly observed detail to convey wisdom in the face of the old scholar.

Chinese Cabinet

Eden (1618)
Roelandt Savery studied the animals in the menagerie of Emperor Rudolph II. He liked to include them in his biblical and mythological works.

Second floor

GALLERY GUIDE
The gallery is arranged on three floors around the central courtyard of the palace. The ground floor, reached from the courtyard, houses German and Austrian art from the 15th to 19th centuries. The stairs to the upper floors are opposite the ticket office at the main entrance.

Stairs down to other floors and exit

★ Head of Christ
Painted by El Greco in the 1590s, this portrait emphasizes the humanity of Christ. At the same time the curious square halo gives the painting the qualities of an ancient icon.

KEY

☐	German and Austrian Art 1400–1800
☐	Flemish and Dutch Art 1400–1600
☐	Italian Art 1400–1500
☐	Roman Art
☐	Flemish and Dutch Art 1600–1800
☐	French Art 1600–1800
☐	Icons, Classical and Ancient Art
☐	Venice 1700–1800 and Goya
☐	Spanish Art 1600–1800
☐	Naples and Venice 1600–1700
☐	Italian Art 1500–1600
☐	Non-exhibition space

★ The Martyrdom of St Thomas
This magnificent work is by Peter Paul Rubens, the foremost Flemish Baroque painter of the 17th century.

Castle Square ⑨

HRADČANSKÉ NÁMĚSTÍ

Map 2 D3. Ⓜ *Malostranská, Hradčanská.* 🚃 *22, 23.*
Schwarzenberg Palace
🅞 *call for times.*

The vast, grand square in front of Prague Castle was once the home of workshops and artisans' houses, but after the devastating fire of 1541 they were replaced by a series of imposing palaces. These were built by Czech and foreign nobles, eager to live close to the court of the Habsburgs. On the south side, the huge 16th-century Schwarzenberg Palace (Schwarzenberský palác) is one of the most beautiful Renaissance buildings in Prague, with graceful attics and magnificent *sgraffito* that gives the impression that the façade is clad in Italian-style diamond-point stonework.

The broad, western end of the square is taken up by the Thun-Hohenstein Palace (Thun-Hohenšteinský palác), a much more austere affair built in 1689–91. Its roof is crowned with statues by F M Brokoff.

On the north side of the square, between the castle and Sternberg Palace, is the Archbishop's Palace (Arcibiskupský palác), a 16th-century building with a fancy Rococo façade in pink and white, added in the 1760s.

The Renaissance Martinic Palace (Martinický palác), at the corner of Castle Square and Kanovnická Street, has *sgraffito* depicting scenes from the Bible and mythology.

The square's high terrace affords a famous view that embraces virtually the entire city.

The Loreto's entrance, with statues of St Joseph and St John the Baptist

Loreto ⑩

Loretánské náměstí, Hradčany. **Map** 1 C3. **Tel** *220 516 740.* 🚃 *22, 23 to Pohořelec.* 🅞 *9am–12:15pm, 1– 4:30pm Tue–Sun.* 📷 🅥 🔔 *7:30am Sat, 5pm Sun.* **www**.loreta.cz

The religious complex of Prague's Loreto, occupying virtually the entire west side of Loretánské náměstí, was built in 1629, shortly after the victory of the Catholic forces in the Battle of the White Mountain. Its founder was Kateřina of Lobkowicz, a Czech aristocrat who was eager to promote the legend of the Santa Casa – the "holy house" in which Archangel Gabriel told Mary about the future birth of Jesus, and which, in 1295, was miraculously transported to the Italian town of Loreto. Replicas of the house were erected all over Bohemia and Moravia, the grandest of which lies at the heart of

Capital on Černín Palace

Prague's Loreto complex. In it, stuccoes and statues show characters from the Old Testament and scenes from the life of the Virgin Mary. The Santa Casa is enclosed by lavishly decorated 17th-century cloisters, which meet on one side at the Baroque Church of the Nativity.

The Loreto's treasury has many valuable liturgical vessels, among which the collection of monstrances (for displaying the host) is particularly precious: one dazzling monstrance is encrusted with no fewer than 6,222 diamonds.

Every hour an unusual concert is played by 27 bells in the Loreto's Baroque tower.

Černín Palace ⑪

ČERNÍNSKÝ PALÁC

Loretánské náměstí 5. **Map** 1 B3. **Tel** *224 181 111.* 🚃 *22, 23.* 🅞 *public hols only.* **www**.mzv.cz

Begun in 1669 for Count Černín of Chudenice, the Imperial Ambassador to Venice, the Černín Palace was Prague's first truly Baroque building, though later changes do not make this obvious. Its 150-m (490-ft) long façade, with a row of vast Corinthian half-columns, towers over the small, grassy square that lies between it and the Loreto.

The huge building suffered as a result of its prominent position on one of Prague's highest hills. It was looted by the French in 1742 and badly damaged in the Prussian bombardment of the city in 1757. In 1851 the now-impoverished Černín family sold the palace to the state and it became a barracks. Following the creation of Czechoslovakia in 1918, the palace was restored to its original design and became the Ministry of Foreign Affairs. Thirty years later, a few days after the Communist coup, the Foreign Minister Jan Masaryk, the popular son of Czechoslovakia's first

Schwarzenberg Palace, with its *sgraffito* decoration, in Castle Square

President, Tomáš Masaryk, died as the result of a fall from a top-floor window of the palace. He was the only non-Communist in the new government. No one really knows whether he was pushed or jumped, but he is still widely mourned.

Strahov Monastery ⑫

STRAHOVSKÝ KLÁŠTER

Královská Kanonie Premonstrátů na Strahově, Strahovské nádvoří 1/132, Strahovská. **Map** 1 B4. **Tel** 220 516 671. 🚋 22, 23 to Pohořelec. ⬜ 9am–noon, 12:30–5pm daily. **Theological Hall, Philosophical Hall, Church of Our Lady, Picture Gallery** ⬜ 9am–noon, 1–5pm daily. ⬛ Easter Sun, 25 Dec. 🎫 📷 🔟 www.strahovskyklaster.cz

When it was founded by Vladislav II in 1140, to serve an austere religious order, the Premonstratensians, Strahov rivalled Prague Castle in size. Burnt down in the 13th century, then rebuilt, Strahov acquired its present magnificent, Baroque form in the 18th century. In 1783, during the reign of Joseph II, the monastery managed to escape dissolution by cleverly declaring itself an educational establishment, citing its vast library. The monks were finally driven out of Strahov in 1950 by the Communists. Now, following the Velvet Revolution, the monastery has resumed its original function, and monks can sometimes be seen going about their daily business.

The abbey courtyard is entered via a Baroque gateway sporting a statue of St Norbert, the founder of the Premonstratensian Order. The nearby 17th-century Church of St Roch now houses one of Prague's finest art galleries. The main monastery church is the vast Church of Our Lady, whose façade features expressive statues by Johan Anton Quitainer. The lovingly restored Baroque interior dazzles with its opulence. Besides the magnificent altars and furnishings, including the

Philosophical Hall, Strahov Monastery

pulpits, particularly striking are the impressive frescoes covering the ceiling and the walls above the arcades.

Inside the monastery itself, the two Baroque libraries are among the most beautiful in Europe. The first of these, the Philosophical Hall (Filosofický sál), was built expressly to house the books (and splendid bookcases) from Louca monastery, in Moravia, dissolved by Joseph II. The breathtaking vault is decorated with a 1782 fresco depicting mankind's *Quest for Truth*. The second, the Theological Hall (Teologický sál), dates from the 16th century and is equally impressive with its beautiful frescoes filling the stucco frames, and superb furnishings, including a number of 17th-century astronomical globes.

Nerudova Street ⑬

NERUDOVA ULICE

Map 2 D3. 🚇 Malostranská. 🚋 12, 20, 22, 23.

A picturesque narrow street leading up to Prague Castle, Nerudova is named after the poet and journalist Jan Neruda, who wrote many

short stories set in this part of Prague. From 1845 to 1857 he lived in the house called At the Two Suns (No. 47). Bustling, noisy and crowded during the day, Nerudova Street becomes deserted at night – the souvenir shops and offices have gradually ousted the ordinary residents.

Until the introduction of house numbers in 1770, the city's dwellings were distinguished by signs. Nerudova Street's houses have a splendid selection of these, featuring symbols, emblems and heraldic beasts made of stone, stucco or metal, painted or carved; they often indicate a profession or particular interest of the former occupants.

Proceeding up Nerudova's steep slope, look out in particular for the Red Eagle (No. 6), the Three Fiddles (No. 12), the Golden Horse-shoe (No. 34), the Green Lobster (No. 43) and the White Swan (No. 49), as well as the Old Pharmacy museum at No. 32.

There are also a number of grand Baroque buildings, most of which have now become embassies. Among them are the Thun-Hohenstein Palace (No. 20, now the Italian embassy), whose entrance is framed by an imposing portal featuring two spread-wing eagles, by Matthias Braun, and Morzin Palace (No. 5, the Romanian embassy). The latter has a façade with two vast statues of Moors (a pun on the name Morzin) sculpted by Ferdinand Brokof and supporting the semicircular balcony on the first floor. Another impressive façade is that of the Church of Our Lady of Unceasing Succour, the church of the Theatines, an order founded during the Counter-Reformation.

Sign of Jan Neruda's house, 47 Nerudova Street

Church of St Nicholas ⑭

KOSTEL SV. MIKULÁŠE

The Church of St Nicholas divides and dominates the two sections of Malostranské náměstí (Little Quarter Square). Building began in 1703, and the last touches were put to the glorious frescoed nave in 1761. It is recognized as the masterpiece of father-and-son architects Christoph and Kilian Ignaz Dientzenhofer, Prague's greatest exponents of High Baroque, though neither lived to see the church's completion. The statues, frescoes and paintings inside are by leading Baroque artists, and include a fine Passion Cycle (1673) by Karel Škréta. Renovation in the 1950s dealt with the damage caused by 200 years of leaky cladding.

Altar Paintings
The side chapels hold many works of art. This painting of St Michael is by Francesco Solimena.

★ Pulpit
Dating from 1765, the ornate pulpit is by Richard and Peter Prachner. It is lavishly adorned with golden cherubs.

Baroque Organ
A fresco of St Cecilia watches over the superb organ, built in 1746 by Tomás Schwarz. There were originally three Schwarz organs here.

Entrance
from west side
of Little Quarter
Square

Chapel of St Anne

Chapel of St Catherine

STAR FEATURES

★ Dome Fresco

★ Pulpit

★ Statues of the Church Fathers

Façade
St Paul, by John Frederick Kohl, is one of the statues that grace the curving façade. It was completed in 1710 by Christoph Dientzenhofer, who was influenced by Italian architects Borromini and Guarini.

The dome was completed by Kilian Ignaz Dientzenhofer in 1751, shortly before his death.

The belfry, added in 1751–56, was the last part to be built. Visitors can climb up it to admire the view.

★ **Dome Fresco**
Franz Palko's fresco, The Celebration of the Holy Trinity *(1752–3), fills the 70-m (230-ft) high dome.*

High Altar
A copper statue of St Nicholas by Ignaz Platzer surmounts the high altar. Below it, the painting of St Joseph is by Johann Lukas Kracker, who also painted the nave fresco.

★ **Statues of the Eastern Church Fathers**
The statues of the four great teachers by Ignaz Platzer stand at the base of the four columns supporting the dome. Pictured here is St Cyril.

THE DIENTZENHOFER FAMILY

Christoph Dientzenhofer (1655–1722) came from a family of Bavarian master builders. His son Kilian Ignaz (1689–1751) was born in Prague and educated at the Jesuit Clementinum *(see pp82–3).* They were responsible for the greatest treasures of Jesuit-influenced Prague Baroque architecture. The Church of St Nicholas, their last work, was completed by Kilian's son-in-law, Anselmo Lurago.

Kilian Ignaz Dientzenhofer

The main hall of Wallenstein Palace

Wallenstein Palace and Garden ⑮

VALDŠTEJNSKÝ PALÁC

Valdštejnské náměstí 4. **Map** 2 E3. Ⓜ *Malostranská.* **Tel** *257 071 111.* 🚋 *12, 18, 20, 22, 23.* **Palace** ⬤ *10am–5pm Sat & Sun (subject to change).* 🚫 ♿ *from Valdštejnská.* **Garden** ⬤ *Apr–Oct: 10am–6pm daily (to 8pm in Aug).* 📷 ♿ *from Valdštejnské náměstí.* 🖥 www.senat.cz

The first large secular building of the Baroque era in Prague, the palace stands as a monument to the fatal ambition of imperial military commander Albrecht von Wallenstein (1583–1634). His string of victories over the Protestants in the Thirty Years' War *(see p39)* made him vital to Emperor Ferdinand II. Already showered with titles, Wallenstein soon started to covet the crown of Bohemia. When he dared to negotiate independently with the enemy, he was assassinated on the emperor's orders.

Wallenstein spent only 12 months in the palace that he had had built in 1620–30. Intended to overshadow even Prague Castle, the palace was designed by Andrea Spezza who, like most of the artists who helped decorate the building, was Italian. The superb main hall has a ceiling fresco of Wallenstein himself portrayed as Mars, the god of war, riding in a triumphal chariot. Today, the palace is the home of the Czech Senate.

The restored gardens are laid out as they were when Wallenstein dined in the huge garden pavilion that looks out over a fountain and rows of bronze statues.

Church of St Thomas ⑯

KOSTEL SV. TOMÁŠ

Josefská 8. **Map** 2 E3. **Tel** *257 532 675.* Ⓜ *Malostranská.* 🚋 *12, 20, 22, 23.* ⬤ *for services.* ✝ *12:15pm Mon–Sat, 9:30am, 11am (in English), 12:30pm Sun.* 🚫 ♿

Founded by Wenceslas II in 1285 as the monastery church of the Augustinians, the original Gothic church was completed in 1379. During

Glass coffin with relics of St Justus, in St Thomas's Church

the Hussite period this was one of the few churches to remain Catholic, and, as a result, it suffered serious damage. Further misfortune arrived in 1723, when the church was struck by lightning. Kilian Ignaz Dientzenhofer was called in to rebuild it. The shape of the original church was preserved, but, apart from the spire, the church today retains little of its Gothic origins.

Frescoes adorn the dome and the curving ceiling in the nave, while above the altar are copies of paintings of St Thomas and St Augustine by Rubens. The English-speaking community of Prague meets in this church.

The Baroque Church of St Nicholas in Little Quarter Square

Little Quarter Square ⑰

MALOSTRANSKÉ NÁMĚSTÍ

Map 2 E3. Ⓜ *Malostranská.* 🚋 *12, 20, 22, 23.*

This sloping square, busy with trams and people stopping for a drink or bite to eat, has been the centre of activity in Malá Strana since its foundation in 1257. It began as a marketplace in the outer bailey of Prague Castle. Most of the houses here have a medieval core, but all were rebuilt during the Renaissance and Baroque periods.

The square is dominated by the Church of St Nicholas *(see pp64–5)*, opposite which is the vast Neo-Classical façade of Lichtenstein Palace. Other important buildings include Malá Strana's Town

Hall, with its fine Renaissance façade and Sternberg Palace, built on the site of the outbreak of the 1541 fire, which destroyed most of the district.

Palace Gardens below Prague Castle ⑱

PALACOVE ZAHRADY POD PRAZSKYM HRADEM

Valdštejnské náměstí. **Map** 2 F2. ᴹ Malostranská. **Tel** 257 010 401. 🚋 12, 18, 20, 22, 23. ⚪ Apr–Oct: 10am– 6pm daily (to 9pm Jun, Jul, to 8pm Aug). 📷

When, in the 1500s, nobles started building palaces on the slopes below Prague Castle, they also laid out formal gardens based on Italian Renaissance models. Redone in the 18th century, when Baroque statuary and fountains were added, some of the gardens now form a public park. As well as offering superb views of the city, the gardens are full of interest. The Kolowrat-Černín Garden is undoubtedly the finest, with its highly decorated pavilion and assortment of staircases, balustrades and loggias, as well as fountains, pools and Classical statuary.

Church of Our Lady beneath the Chain ⑲

KOSTEL PANNY MARIE POD ŘETĚZEM

Lázeňská. **Map** 2 E4. ᴹ Malostranská. **Tel** 257 530 876. 🚋 12, 20, 22, 23. ⚪ for concerts & services. ✝ 9:30am Sat & Sun.

This church, the oldest in Malá Strana, was founded in the 12th century. King Vladislav II presented it to the Knights of St John, the order later known as the Knights of Malta. It stood in the centre of the Knights' heavily fortified monastery guarding the approach to the old Judith Bridge. The church's name refers to the chain used in the Middle Ages to close the monastery gatehouse.

Detail from the Church of Our Lady beneath the Chain

In the 14th century, the original Romanesque church was demolished. What can be seen today dates largely from a Baroque facelift performed in 1640 by Karel Škrěta.

The painting on the high altar shows the Virgin Mary and John the Baptist coming to the aid of the Knights of Malta in the famous naval victory over the Turks at Lepanto in 1571.

Church of Our Lady Victorious ⑳

KOSTEL PANNY MARIE VÍTĚZNÉ

Karmelitská. **Map** 2 E4. **Tel** 257 533 646. 🚋 12, 20, 22, 23. ⚪ 9am–7pm Mon–Sat (to 8pm Sun). ✝ 9am, 6pm Mon–Sat, 10am, noon (English), 5pm (French), 6pm (Italian), 7pm Sun.

Originally built in the early 17th century by German Lutherans, the church was given to the Carmelites by the

Catholic authorities after the Battle of the White Mountain . They rebuilt the church and renamed it in honour of the famous victory.

Although the building itself is of little interest, the church attracts many visitors who come to see the Pražské Jezulátko, better known by its Italian name, *il Bambino di Praga* – a wax effigy of the infant Jesus in a glass case in the south aisle. This figure has a record of miracle cures and is one of the most revered images in the Catholic world. It was presented to the Carmelites by one of the Lobkowicz family's Spanish brides in 1628. The figure has a vast number of clothes, some of which are in the museum.

Petřín Hill ㉑

PETŘÍNSKÉ SADY

Map 2 D5. 🚋 6, 9, 12, 20, 22, 23, then take funicular railway from Újezd.

Petřín Hill, to the west of Malá Strana, is the highest of Prague's nine hills, and an area of greenery much loved by local citizens.

A path winds up the slopes of Petřín, offering fine views of Prague, but it is also fun to take the funicular from Újezd. Once at the top, there are many paths to explore and several attractions, including a mini version of the Eiffel Tower (Rozhledna), built in 1891, which can be climbed, and a mini Gothic castle (Bludiště), containing a hall of distorting mirrors which is hugely popular with children.

ALBRECHT VON WALLENSTEIN

Albrecht von Wallenstein (Valdštein) was born in Bohemia in 1583. He studied in Italy and later converted to Catholicism and joined the army of Rudolph II. He rose to lead the Imperial armies in Europe, and during the Thirty Years' War he scored numerous victories over the Protestants. In 1630 he negotiated secretly with the Protestants and then joined them. For this, he was killed in 1634 by mercenaries acting on the orders of the Emperor Ferdinand.

Wallenstein, politician and commander

Charles Bridge 22
KARLŮV MOST

Prague's most familiar monument was built by Peter
Parler for Charles IV in 1357, and replaced the ruined
Judith Bridge; it was the only bridge across the Vltava
until 1741. Due to wear and tear, many of the statues
that witness the constant parade
of people across the bridge
are copies.

MALÁ STRANA

Malá Strana
Bridge Tower

Judith Bridge
Tower, 1158

St Adalbert, 1709
*Adalbert, Bishop of Prague,
founded St Lawrence Church on
Petřín Hill in 991. The Czechs
know him as Vojtěch (see p101).*

St Vitus,
1714

Tower
entrance

St Wenceslas, 1858

Christ between
St Cosmas and
St Damian, 1709

St John de Matha,
St Felix de Valois and
the Blessed Ivan, 1714

St Philip
Benizi, 1714

STARE MĚSTO

**Thirty Years'
War**
*In the last hours of
this war, Staré Město
was saved from the
Swedish army. The
truce was signed in
the middle of the
bridge in 1648.*

St Francis Xavier
*The Jesuit
missionary is
supported by
Moorish and
Oriental
converts.
The sculptor
Brokof is
seated on the
saint's left.*

St Norbert, St Wenceslas
and St Sigismund,
1853

St Christopher,
1857

St Anne, 1707

St Francis Borgia, 1710

St John the Baptist, 1857

St Cyril and
St Methodius, 1938

St Joseph, 1854

★ St Luitgard, 1710
The most artistically remarkable statue on the bridge, sculpted by Matthias Braun at the age of 26, shows the crucified Christ appearing to the blind Cistercian nun.

VISITORS' CHECKLIST

Map 2 F4, 3 A4. 🚋 12, 22, 23 to Malostranské náměstí or 17, 18 to Karlovy lázně . **Staré Město Bridge Tower** ⬜ 10am–5pm daily (Mar: to 6pm, Apr–May, Oct: 7pm, Jun–Sep: 10pm). **Malá Strana Bridge Tower** ⬜ Apr–Oct: 10am–6pm daily.

★ St John Nepomuk, 1683
Reliefs on the bridge depict the martyrdom of St John Nepomuk. Here the saint has been polished bright from people touching his image for good luck.

St Cajetan, 1709

St Augustine, 1708

St Vincent Ferrer and St Procopius, 1712

St Jude Thaddaeus, 1708

St Anthony of Padua, 1707

St Nicholas Tolentino, 1708

St Ludmilla, 1710

Steps to Kampa Island

St Francis of Assisi, with two angels, 1855

Crucifix
For 200 years this crucifix stood alone on the bridge. The gilded Christ dates from 1629 and the Hebrew words "Holy, Holy, Holy Lord" were paid for by a Jew as punishment for blasphemy.

Staré Město Bridge Tower

Tower entrance

Madonna and St Bernard, 1709

Pietà, 1859

The Madonna, St Dominic and St Thomas, 1708

St Barbara, St Margaret and St Elizabeth, 1707

★ Staré Město Bridge Tower
This fine Gothic tower was an integral part of the old town's fortifications. The sculptures, like the tower, are by Peter Parler.

STARÉ MĚSTO AND JOSEFOV

In the 11th century the settlements built around Prague Castle spilled over onto the right bank of the Vltava. Thus Staré Město, the Old Town, was created. With time, houses and churches built around the market square developed into an irregular network of streets, many of them surviving to this day. In the Middle Ages this area was home to two

Art Nouveau detail on house in Kaprova

distinct Jewish communities, Ashkenazi and Sephardi Jews. These groups gradually merged and became confined to a ghetto. The discrimination they suffered was partially relaxed in 1784, by Joseph II, and the Jewish Quarter was named Josefov in his honour. The ghetto area was razed in the 1890s, but the Town Hall and some synagogues were saved.

SIGHTS AT A GLANCE

Churches and Synagogues
Church of Our Lady before Týn ❸
Church of St Giles ❿
Church of St James ❹
Maisel Synagogue ❾
Old-New Synagogue pp78–9 ❼
Pinkas Synagogue ⓫
Spanish Synagogue ❻

Historic Buildings
Clementinum ⓮
Jewish Town Hall ❽
Municipal House ⓳
Old Town Hall pp74–5 ❶

Museums and Galleries
Convent of St Agnes ❺
Museum of Decorative Arts ⓬
Smetana Museum ⓰

Historic Streets
Celetná Street ❷
Charles Street ⓯

Theatres and Concert Halls
Estates Theatre ⓲
Rudolfinum ⓭

Cemeteries
Old Jewish Cemetery pp80–81 ❿

KEY

▦	Street-by-Street map *See pp72–3*
Ⓜ	Metro station
🚋	Tram stop
✚	Church
✚	Synagogue
ℹ	Tourist information

0 metres   250
0 yards   250

GETTING THERE

Můstek on metro lines A and B and Staroměstská on line A both serve the Old Town and Josefov. While trams do not cross the Old Town, it is only a short walk from the tram stop near Charles Bridge. For Josefov, take tram 17 or 18 to náměstí Jana Palacha. For the Convent of St Agnes, buses 126, 135 and 207 are convenient.

◁ **View over the rooftops of Staré Město**

Street by Street: Staré Město

Free of traffic and ringed with historic buildings, Prague's Old Town Square (Staroměstské náměstí) ranks among the finest public spaces in any city. Nearby streets, including Celetná, are also pedestrianized. In summer, café tables spill out onto the cobbles, and although the area draws visitors in droves, the unique atmosphere has not yet been destroyed. Prague's colourful history comes to life in the buildings around the square.

Kinský Palace (palác Kinských), by Kilian Ignaz Dientzenhofer, has a stucco façade crowned with statues of the four elements.

The Church of St Nicholas has an imposing façade which dominates one corner of Old Town Square.

Old Town Square is depicted in this late 19th-century water-colour by Václav Jansa, which shows how little Staroměstské náměstí has changed in more than 100 years.

S T A R O M Ě S T S K É
N Á M Ě S T Í

M A L É
N Á M Ě S T Í

Ž E L E Z N Á

The Jan Hus Monument was erected in 1915, on the 500th anniversary of the religious reformer's burning at the stake as a heretic. To the Czechs, he is a hero.

The House at the Two Golden Bears has a carved Renaissance portal which is the finest of its kind in Prague.

U Rotta, now Hotel Rott, is a former ironmonger's shop, decorated with colourful paintings by the 19th century artist Mikoláš Aleš.

★ **Old Town Hall**
The town hall's famous astronomical clock draws a crowd of visitors every hour ❶

The Štorch House has painted decoration based on designs by Mikoláš Aleš showing St Wenceslas on horseback.

0 metres   100

0 yards   100

KEY

- - - - Suggested route

Church of Our Lady before Týn
The church's Gothic steeples are the Old Town's most distinctive landmark ③

Týn courtyard

LOCATOR MAP
See Street Finder, maps 3–4

Church of St James
This wooden Pietà, on the main altar, was made in the 15th century ④

★ **Municipal House**
This Art Nouveau building is a popular concert venue ⑲

JAKUBSKÁ

STUPARTSKÁ

UPRAŠNÉ

CELETNÁ

House of the Black Madonna

Powder Gate, a much-restored Gothic gate, is a relic of when there was a royal palace located here, at the entrance to the Old Town.

OVOCNÝ TRH

Estates Theatre
The theatre featured in director Miloš Forman's film Amadeus ⑱

Ovocný trh, once Prague's fruit market, is now a pedestrian street.

Celetná Street
This ornamental Baroque plaque is the sign of the House at the Black Sun, on famous Celetná Street ②

The Carolinum
formed the heart of the university founded by Charles IV in 1348. A beautifully carved Oriel window projects from the oldest surviving part.

STAR SIGHTS

★ Municipal House
_____
★ Old Town Hall

Old Town Hall ❶

STAROMĚSTSKÁ RADNICE

One of the most striking buildings in Prague, the Old Town Hall was established in 1338 by King John of Luxemburg. Over the centuries several nearby houses were knocked together as the Town Hall expanded, and it now consists of a row of colourful Gothic and Renaissance buildings; most of these have been restored after damage inflicted by the Nazis in 1945. The 69-m (228-ft) tower offers a great view.

Old Council Hall
This 19th-century engraving features the well-preserved 15th-century ceiling.

Old Town Coat of Arms
Above the inscription, "Prague, Head of the Kingdom", is the coat of arms of the Old Town, which was adopted in 1784 for the whole city.

Tourist information and entrance to Tower

Temporary art exhibitions

EXECUTIONS IN THE OLD TOWN SQUARE

A bronze tablet below the Old Town Hall chapel records the names of the 27 Protestant leaders executed here by order of Emperor Ferdinand II on 21 June 1621. This was the result of the humiliating defeat at the Battle of the White Mountain, which also led to the emigration of Protestants unwilling to give up their faith, a Counter-Reformation drive by the Catholic Church and a campaign of Germanization.

★ Old Town Hall Tower

In 1364 the tower was added to the private house of Wolflin of Kámen. Its gallery provides a fine city view.

Viewing gallery

VISITORS' CHECKLIST

Staroměstské náměstí 1.
Map 3 C3. **Tel** 724 508 584.
Ⓜ Staroměstská, Můstek.
🚋 17, 18. ◯ Apr–Oct: 9am–6pm daily (from 11am Mon); Nov–Mar: 9am–5pm daily (from 11am Mon).

Oriel Chapel

The original stained-glass windows on the five-sided chapel were destroyed in the last days of World War II, but were replaced in 1987.

Oriel Chapel Ceiling

The chapel, built on the first floor of the tower in 1381, has an ornate ceiling, which has recently been restored.

The house of Wolflin of Kámen was purchased by the authorities in 1338.

Steps to gallery

★ Astronomical Clock

Mechanical figures perform above the zodiac signs in the upper section; the lower section is a calendar.

Calendar

Entrance hall decorated with mosaics

Gothic Door

This late Gothic main entrance to the Town Hall and Tower was carved by Matthias Rejsek. The entrance hall is filled with wall mosaics after designs by the Czech painter Mikoláš Aleš.

STAR FEATURES

★ Astronomical Clock

★ Old Town Hall Tower

Celetná Street ❷

CELETNÁ ULICE

Map 3 C3. Ⓜ️ *Náměstí Republiky,
Můstek.* **House of the Black
Madonna** *Tel 224 211 746.*
⭕ *10am–6pm Tue–Fri.* 🖼️ ♿ 📷

One of the oldest streets
in Prague, Celetná follows
an old trading route from
eastern Bohemia. Its name
comes from the plaited bread
rolls that were first baked
here in the Middle Ages. It
gained prestige in the 14th
century as a section of the
so-called Royal Route, which
linked the Royal Court (on
the site of the Municipal
House) and Prague Castle via
Old Town Square; it was used
during coronation processions.

Most of the houses along
Celetná Street date from the
Middle Ages. The foundations
of Romanesque and
Gothic buildings can
be seen in some of
the cellars, but most of
the houses with their
picturesque signs are
the result of Baroque
remodellings.

At No. 34, the House
of the Black Madonna
(Dům U Černé Matky
Boží) is an
exception, being a
splendid example of
Cubist architecture
designed by Josef
Gočár dating from
1912. (Note that the
distinctive polychrome figure
of the Madonna with Child
comes from an earlier house
that stood on this site.) The
building is home to a small
but interesting collection of
Czech Cubism, including
paintings, sculpture, furniture
and architectural plans.

The 1759 Pachts' Palace,
across the street, has a balcony
that rests on the shoulders of
four miners and soldiers
sculpted by Ignaz Platzer.
The most impressive example
of Baroque architecture is
Hrzánský Palace (No. 558)
whose façade features busts,
gargoyles and stuccoes, as
well as a portal with caryatids.
Used for state dinners, the
palace has been visited by
numerous heads of state.

The towering nave of the Church
of Our Lady before Týn

Church of Our Lady before Týn ❸

KOSTEL MATKY BOŽÍ PŘED
TÝNEM

Staroměstské náměstí 604. **Map**
3 C3. *Tel 602 204 213.*
Ⓜ️ *Staroměstská, Můstek.*
⭕ *10am–1pm, 3–5pm
Tue–Sun.* ⭕ *in winter.* ✝️
*6pm Wed–Thu, 8am Sat,
9:30am & 9pm Sun.* 🖼️ 📷

**House of the Black
Madonna**

Dominating the Old
Town Square are
the magnificent
multiple steeples of
this historic church.
The present Gothic
building was started
in 1365 and soon
became associated
with the reform movement in
Bohemia. From the early 15th
century until 1620 Týn was
the main Hussite church in
Prague. It was taken over by
the Jesuits in the 17th century,
and it was they who were
responsible for the Baroque

renovation inside, which jars
with the Gothic style of the
original church.

On the northern side is a
beautiful entrance portal (1390)
decorated with scenes of
Christ's passion. The dark
interior has notable features,
including Gothic sculptures
of *Calvary*, a pewter font
(1414) and a 15th-century
Gothic pulpit. The Danish
astronomer Tycho Brahe
(1546–1601) is buried here.

Church of St James ❹

KOSTEL SV. JAKUBA

Malá Štupartská. **Map** 3 C3.
Tel 224 828 816. Ⓜ️ *Můstek,
Náměstí Republiky.* ⭕ *10am–noon,
2–3:45pm Mon & Sat,
10:30am Sun.* 📷

This attractive Baroque
church was originally the
Gothic presbytery of a
Minorite monastery. The
order (a branch of the
Franciscans) was invited to
Prague by King Wenceslas I
in 1232. The Baroque
reconstruction occurred after
a fire in 1689, allegedly
started by agents of Louis
XIV. More than 20 side altars
were added, decorated with
works by painters such as Jan
Jiří Heinsch and Petr Brandl.

The tomb of Count Vratislav
of Mitrovice (1714–16),
designed by Johann Bernhard
Fischer von Erlach and with
sculptures by Brokof, is the
most beautiful Baroque tomb
in Bohemia. The count is said
to have been accidentally
buried alive: his corpse was
later found sitting up in the

Baroque organ loft in the Church of St James

tomb. There is an equally macabre tale surrounding a 400-year old mummified forearm to be found hanging on the right of the entrance. The story goes that when a thief tried to steal the jewels from the Madonna on the high altar, the Virgin grabbed his arm and held on so tightly that it had to be cut off.

The acoustics in the nave are excellent and concerts are often held here. The splendid organ dates from 1702.

Panel (c.1370) showing a kneeling Charles IV, in St Agnes's Convent

Convent of St Agnes ❺

KLÁŠTER SV. ANEŽKY ČESKÉ

U Milosrdných 17. **Map** 3 C2. **Tel** 224 810 628. ꝑ Náměstí Republiky, Staroměstská. ꝑ 17 to Law Faculty (Právnická fakulta), 5, 8, 14 to Dlouhá třída. ꝑ 133 to Řásnovka. ◯ 10am–6pm Tue–Sun. ◐ ∅ ◉ ◔ www.ngprague.cz

The convent of the Poor Clares was founded by Princess Agnes, sister of King Wenceslas I, in 1234, and was one of the first Gothic buildings in Bohemia. It functioned as a convent until 1782, when the Order was dissolved by Joseph II.

Following painstaking restoration, the premises now house a magnificent collection of medieval art belonging to the National Gallery in Prague. Among its most precious exhibits are works by two outstanding Czech artists of the 14th century: the so-called Master of the Vyšší Brod Altar, who adorned a monastic altarpiece with exquisite scenes from the life of Christ, and Master Theodoric. The latter's splendid series of panels for the chapel of Karlštejn Castle are the unmissable works in the gallery. Other works worth seeing include the moving *Crucifixion* from Prague's Na Slovanech Monastery, 14th-century panels by the Master of Třeboň, and an anonymous sculpture of the Madonna and Child, much influenced by the famous Krumlov *Madonna*.

The early 16th century is represented by works by the Master of Litoměřice; these include the Holy Trinity triptych and the *Visitation of the Virgin Mary*.

Spanish Synagogue ❻

ŠPANĚLSKÁ SYNAGÓGA

Vězeňská 1. **Map** 3 B2. ꝑ Staroměstská. ꝑ 17, 18. ꝑ 133 to Řásnovka. ◯ Apr–Oct: 9am–6pm Sun–Fri; Nov–Mar: 9am–4.30pm Sun–Fri. ◔ www.jewishmuseum.cz

Prague's first synagogue, known as the Old School (Stará škola), once stood on this site. In the 11th century the Old School was the centre of the Sephardic Jewish community, who lived strictly apart from the Ashkenazi Jews, who were concentrated around the Old-New Synagogue.

The present Moorish building dates from the second half of the 19th century. The ornate exterior gives way to an even more fantastically decorative and gilded

Ten Commandments motif on the Spanish Synagogue façade

interior. The rich stucco decorations are reminiscent of the Alhambra in Spain, hence the name. Once closed to the public, the Spanish Synagogue is now home to a permanent exhibition dedicated to the history of the Jews of Bohemia.

Old-New Synagogue ❼

See pp78–9.

Jewish Town Hall ❽

ŽIDOVSKÁ RADNICE

Maiselova 18. **Map** 3 B3. **Tel** 222 319 002. ꝑ Staroměstská. ꝑ 17, 18. ꝑ 133. ◉ to the public.

The core of this attractive pink and white building is the original Jewish Town Hall, built in 1570–77 by the hugely rich mayor, Mordechai Maisel. In 1763 it acquired its flowery Late Baroque image; further alterations were made in the early 20th century.

On the roof stands a small wooden clock tower with a distinctive green steeple. Another clock, on one of the gables, has Hebrew figures and, since Hebrew reads from right to left, hands that turn in an anti-clockwise direction.

Jewish Town Hall, with its two clocks

Old-New Synagogue ❼

STARONOVÁ SYNAGÓGA

Built around 1270, this is the oldest synagogue in Europe and one of the earliest Gothic buildings in Prague. The synagogue has survived fires, the slum clearances of the 19th century and many Jewish pogroms. Residents of the Jewish Quarter have often had to seek refuge within its walls and today it is still the religious centre for Prague's Jews. It was originally called the New Synagogue until another synagogue (later destroyed) was built nearby.

Right-hand Nave
The glow from the chandeliers provides light for worshippers who sit in the seats lining the walls.

Stepped brick gable (14th century)

★ Jewish Standard
The historic banner of Prague's Jews is decorated with a star of David and, within it, the hat that had to be worn by Jews in the 14th century.

These windows formed part of the 18th-century extensions built to allow women a view of the service.

Candlestick holder

The cantor's platform (or *bima*) is surrounded by a wrought-iron Gothic grille.

Entrance in Červen St.

★ Five-Rib Vaulting
Two massive octagonal pillars inside the hall support the five-rib vaults: one rib was added to the traditional four ribs.

Entrance Portal
The tympanum above the door in the south vestibule is decorated with bunches of grapes and vine leaves.

East Façade
The east and the west façades possess an austerity that is in strong contrast with the Gothic interior.

The tympanum above the Ark is decorated with 13th-century leaf carvings.

★ **Rabbi Löw's Chair**
A star of David marks the chair of the Chief Rabbi, placed where Rabbi Löw once sat. A 16th-century scholar, he was Prague's most revered Jewish sage (see p80).

The interior is dim since the small windows do not allow much light in.

STAR FEATURES

- ★ Five-Rib Vaulting
- ★ Jewish Standard
- ★ Rabbi Löw's Chair

The Ark
This is the holiest place in the synagogue as it holds the sacred scrolls of the Torah *(the first five books of the Bible) and of the books of the Prophets.*

Maisel Synagogue ❾

MAISELOVA SYNAGÓGA

Maiselova 10. **Map** 3 B3. Staroměstská. 133. Apr–Oct: 9am–6pm Sun–Fri; Nov–Mar: 9am–4.30pm Sun–Fri. Jewish hols. **www**.jewishmuseum.cz

When it was first built, in the late 16th century, this was a private house of prayer for use by mayor Mordechai Maisel and his family. It was also the most richly decorated synagogue in the city. Maisel, who made a fortune lending money to Rudolph II, funded the extensive Renaissance reconstruction of the ghetto.

The original building was a victim of the fire that also devastated the Jewish Town in 1689, and a new synagogue was built in its place. Its present Gothic aspect dates from the early 20th century.

The synagogue now houses a superb collection of Jewish silver and other metalwork dating from Renaissance times. It includes early examples of items used in the Jewish service, such as Torah crowns and finials, used to decorate the rollers which hold the text of the Torah (the five books of Moses), shields (hung on the mantle draped over the Torah) and pointers (used by readers to follow the text).

By a tragic irony, most of these treasures were brought to Prague by the Nazis from synagogues all over Bohemia and Moravia.

18th-century silver Torah crown in the Maisel Synagogue

Old Jewish Cemetery ⓾
STARÝ ŽIDOVSKÝ HŘBITOV

This remarkable site was, for over 300 years, the only burial ground permitted to Jews. Founded in 1478, it was slightly enlarged over the years but still basically corresponds to its medieval size. Due to the lack of space people had to be buried on top of each other, up to 12 layers deep. Today, you can see over 12,000 gravestones crammed into the tiny area, but an estimated 100,000 people are thought to have been buried here. The last burial was in 1787.

View across the cemetery towards the western wall of the Klausen Synagogue

Jewish printers, Mordechai Zemach (d. 1592) and his son Bezalel (d. 1589), are buried under this square gravestone.

The Pinkas Synagogue is the second-oldest in Prague *(see p82).*

David Gans' Tombstone
The tomb of the writer and astronomer (1541–1613) is adorned with the symbols of his name – a star of David and a goose (Gans in German).

Rabbi Kara Tomb (1439), the oldest in the cemetery

Rabbi David Oppenheim (1664–1736)
The chief rabbi of Prague owned the largest collection of Hebrew manuscripts and prints in the city.

The gravestone of Moses Beck

Klausen Synagogue

Main entrance

The Nephele Mound was where infants who died under a year old were buried.

★ 14th-century Tombstones
Embedded in the wall are fragments of Gothic tomb-stones brought here from an older Jewish cemetery in Staré Město.

RABBI LÖW AND THE GOLEM

The 16th-century scholar and philosopher Rabbi Löw was thought to possess magical powers. It is claimed that he created a figure, the Golem, from clay and then brought it to life. When his creature went berserk, the rabbi is said to have hidden it in the Old-New Synagogue *(see pp78–9).*

VISITORS' CHECKLIST

Široká 3 (main entrance). **Map** 3
B3. *Tel* 222 317 191 (bookings).
M Staroměstská. 17, 18.
Apr–Oct: 9am–6pm Sun–Fri,
Nov–Mar: 9am–4:30pm Sun–Fri
(last adm 30 mins before closing).
www.jewishmuseum.cz

Prague Burial Society
*Founded in 1564, the group carried out ritual burials
and performed charitable work. In this 18th-century
painting, members of the society wash their hands after
leaving the cemetery.*

**The Museum of
Decorative Arts**
(see p82)

★ **Tombstone of Rabbi Löw**
*The most visited tomb in the
cemetery is that of Rabbi Löw
(1520–1609). Visitors place a
pebble on the grave as a
mark of respect.*

**The Neo-
Romanesque
Ceremonial Hall**

Mordechai Maisel
(1528–1601) was Mayor of
Prague's Jewish Town and a
philanthropist *(see p79)*.

**Tombstone of
Hendela Bassevi**
*The highly decorated
tomb (1628) was built in
honour of the beautiful wife of
Prague's first Jewish nobleman.*

UNDERSTANDING THE GRAVESTONES

From the late 16th century onwards, tombstones in the
Jewish cemetery were decorated with symbols denoting the
background, family name or profession of the deceased.

**Blessing
hands:
Cohen family**

**A pair of
scissors:
tailor**

**A stag:
Hirsch or
Zvi family**

**Grapes:
blessing or
abundance**

STAR FEATURES

★ 14th-century
Tombstones

★ Tombstone of
Rabbi Löw

Stage of the Dvořák Hall in the Rudolfinum

a fraction of it is ever on display. Pride of place goes to the Bohemian glass, of which there are many fine Baroque and 19th- and 20th-century pieces. Other exhibits include Meissen porcelain, Gobelin tapestries, costume, textiles, photographs and some exquisite furniture.

Rudolfinum ⑬

Alšovo nábřeží 12. **Map** 3 A3.
Staroměstská. 17, 18.
133. **Philharmonic**
Tel 227 059 352.
www.czechphilharmonic.cz

Now the home of the Czech Philharmonic Orchestra, the Rudolfinum is one of the most impressive landmarks on the Old Town bank of the Vltava. Many of the major concerts of the Prague Spring music festival are held here. The most impressive of the various concert halls is the sumptuous Dvořák Hall, one of the finest creations of 19th-century Czech architecture.

The Rudolfinum itself is a superb example of Czech Neo-Renaissance style. The curving balustrade is adorned with statues of distinguished Czech, Austrian and German composers and artists.

Between 1918 and 1939 the Rudolfinum was the seat of the Czechoslovak parliament.

Pinkas Synagogue ⑪

PINKASOVA SYNAGÓGA

Široká 3. **Map** 3 B3.
Staroměstská. 17, 18.
133. Apr–Oct: 9am–6pm
Sun–Fri; Nov–Mar: 9am–4:30pm.
www.jewishmuseum.cz

The synagogue was founded in 1479 by Rabbi Pinkas and enlarged in 1535 by his great-nephew Aaron Meshulam Horowitz. It has been rebuilt many times since. Excavations have turned up fascinating relics of life in the medieval ghetto, including a *mikva*, or ritual bath. The core of the present building is a hall with Gothic vaulting. The gallery for women was added in the early 17th century.

The synagogue now serves as a memorial to all the Jewish Czechoslovak citizens who were imprisoned in Terezín concentration camp *(see pp190–91)* and later deported to various Nazi extermination camps. The names of the 77,297 who did not return are inscribed on the synagogue walls. There is also a display of haunting children's drawings from Terezín camp.

Museum of Decorative Arts ⑫

UMĚLECKOPRŮMYSLOVÉ MUZEUM

17. listopadu 2. **Map** 3 B3. **Tel** 251 093 111. Staroměstská. 17, 18. 133. 10am–6pm Wed–Sun (to 7pm Tue). www.upm.cz

The museum's collection of glass is one of the largest in the world, but space constraints mean that only

Stained-glass window from inside the Museum of Decorative Arts

Clementinum ⑭

KLEMENTINUM

Křižovnické náměstí 4 or Mariánské náměstí 5. **Map** 3 A4. **Tel** 221 663 111. Staroměstská. 17, 18. **Baroque Library, Astronomical Tower and Chapel of Mirrors** 10am–4pm (to 8pm Apr–Oct, to 6pm Nov–Dec) Mon–Fri, 11am–6pm Sat, Sun. www.dreyer.cz

In 1556 emperor Ferdinand I invited the Jesuits to Prague to undo the work of the Hussites and help bring the Czechs back into the Catholic fold. They took over the former Dominican monastery which, over two centuries, the Jesuits turned into the largest complex of buildings in the city after Prague Castle. They built the Church of St Saviour (1593–1714), adorned with large statues of the Apostles by Jan Bendl (1659).

The most brutal expansion, which involved the demolition of 30 houses, occurred after the Jesuits were given control of the university. The sumptuous Baroque library (Barokní sál), with a splendid trompe-l'oeil ceiling, dates from 1727. The lovely Chapel of Mirrors (Zrcadlová kaple), and the Astronomical Tower (Astronomická věž), offering great views, are also 18th-century. In 1773, when the pope dissolved their Order, the Jesuits left Prague. The Clementinum eventually became the National Library.

Former Jesuit Church of St Saviour in the Clementinum

Charles Street ⓯

KARLOVA ULICE

Map 3 A4. ⓜ Staroměstská.

Dating back to the 12th century, this narrow, winding street was part of the Royal Route, along which coronation processions passed on the way to Prague Castle. Many original Gothic and Renaissance houses remain, most converted into shops to attract tourists.

A café in the House at the Golden Snake (No. 18) was established in 1714 by an Armenian, Deodatus Damajan, who handed out slanderous pamphlets from here. It is now a restaurant.

At No. 3, At the Golden Well has a magnificent Baroque façade and stucco reliefs of saints including St Roch and St Sebastian, who are believed to offer protection against plagues.

A 19th-century sign on the House at the Golden Snake, Charles Street

Smetana Museum ⓰

MUZEUM BEDŘICHA SMETANY

Novotného lávka 1. **Map** 3 A4. **Tel** 222 220 082. ⓜ Staroměstská. 🚋 17, 18. 🕐 10am–5pm Wed–Mon. 🎥 📷 fee. **www**.nm.cz

On a spit of land beside the Vltava, a former Neo-Renaissance waterworks has been turned into a memorial to Bedřich Smetana (1824–84), the father of Czech music. The one-room museum contains documents, letters, scores and musical instruments from the composer's life and work.

Smetana was an ardent patriot and his music helped inspire the Czech national revival. Deaf towards the end

of his life, he never heard his cycle of symphonic poems *Má Vlast* (My Country), being performed. The opera, *The Bartered Bride*, brought him the greatest renown abroad.

The riverside museum was particularly badly damaged when the Vltava flooded the Old Town in 2002.

Church of St Giles ⓱

KOSTEL SV. JILJÍ

Husova. **Map** 3 B4. **Tel** 224 220 235. ⓜ Národní třída. 🚋 6, 9, 17, 18, 22. 🕐 by appointment. 🕐 7am & 6:30pm Mon–Fri, 6:30pm Sat, 9:30am, 6:30pm Sun. 📷

Despite a beautiful Gothic portal on the south side, the inside of this church is essentially Baroque. Founded in 1371, it became a Hussite church in 1420. Following the Protestant defeat in 1620, Ferdinand II gave the church to the Dominicans, who built on a huge friary. The monks were booted out under the Communists, but they have since been able to return.

The vaults of the church are decorated with frescoes by the painter Václav Vavřinec Reiner, who is buried in the nave. The main fresco, a glorification of the Dominicans, shows St Dominic and his friars helping the pope defend the Catholic Church from non-believers.

Façade of the Smetana Museum, decorated with *sgraffito*

The Estates Theatre, once the most important theatre in Prague

Estates Theatre ⑱

STAVOVSKÉ DIVADLO

Ovocný trh 1. **Map** 3 C4. *Tel 224 902 322.* Ⓜ Můstek. ☐ *by appt only – call 224 902 231.* ♿ **www.**estatestheatre.cz

Built in 1783 by the German-speaking Count Nostitz Rieneck, the theatre is one of the finest examples of Classical elegance in Prague. Its white, gold and blue auditorium resembles a luxury chocolate box. While performances were given in Czech or Italian occasionally, until 1920 the main language used on stage was German.

The theatre is renowned for its premieres of operas by Mozart. On 29 October 1787 the public was treated to the world premiere of *Don Giovanni*, with Mozart himself conducting from the piano. Acknowledging the connection between Mozart and the theatre, the interior was used by Miloš Forman in his famous Oscar-winning film *Amadeus* (1984).

In 1834 *Fidlovačka*, a comic opera by Josef Kajetán Tyl, was performed here for the first time. One of its songs, *Kde domov můj?* (Where is My Home?), later became the Czech national anthem. More than a century later, in the spirit of the national revival, the theatre was renamed after Tyl, though it has since reverted to its original name.

The Carolinum (Karolinum) is the core of Prague University founded by Charles IV. In the 15th and 16th centuries, the university led the movement to reform the church. It was later taken over by the Jesuits.

Municipal House ⑲
OBECNÍ DŮM

Prague's most prominent Art Nouveau building was built in 1905–11 on the site of a former royal palace. It includes Prague's top concert venue, as well as other smaller halls, a restaurant and café. The flamboyant and exciting interior, decorated with works by leading Czech artists, including Alfons Mucha, is well worth savouring. The guided tour is excellent and also good value.

★ Mosaic by Karel Špillar
The façade includes a vast semicircular mosaic depicting Homage to Prague, *by Karel Špillar.*

Glass Dome
The imposing glass dome, a local landmark, towers above Hollar's Hall, a circular room next to the exhibition rooms.

★ Mayor's Salon
This splendid room has furniture by J Krečuk and murals depicting Czech heroes by Mucha.

Main Hall
Lifts in the main hall have beautiful Art Nouveau details and ornaments.

VISITORS' CHECKLIST

Náměstí Republiky 5. **Map** 4 D3.
Tel 222 002 101. Náměstí Republiky. 5, 8, 14. **Gallery** only during exhibitions: 10am–6pm daily. by arrangement. **www**.obecnidum.cz

★ **Smetana Hall**
The auditorium seating 1,500 is occasionally used as a ballroom. The box to the left of the stage is reserved for the President of the Republic, the one to the right for the Mayor.

Decorative Detail
This delightful detail by Alfons Mucha is found in the Mayor's Salon.

Side Portal
Here, the carved decoration is in perfect harmony with the architecture.

Magnificent glass dome

Figures
seen on all sides of the building are by Czech artists who combined Classical and historic symbols with modern motifs.

The wing facing U Obecniho Domu Street includes four dining rooms with original panelling, mirrors and clocks.

Shops

STAR FEATURES

★ Mayor's Salon

★ Mosaic by Karel Špillar

★ Smetana Hall

Decorative Elements
Lavish stucco decoration covers all sides of the Municipal House; seen here are floral motifs, typical of the Art Nouveau style (see p97).

NOVÉ MĚSTO

Art Nouveau decoration in Wenceslas Square

The new town, or Nové Město, founded in 1348 by Charles IV, was planned around three central market squares: the Horse Market (Wenceslas Square), the Cattle Market (Charles Square) and the Hay Market (Senovážné Square). Twice as large as the Old Town, the district was inhabited mainly by merchants and craftsmen. In the late 1800s a large section of the New Town was demolished and completely redeveloped, giving it the appearance it has today.

There are many historic sites and attractions in Nové Město. Wenceslas Square, a wide boulevard housing restaurants, hotels and shops, is surrounded by fine buildings and is busy day and night. For some peace and quiet, head for the park in Charles Square.

SIGHTS AT A GLANCE

Churches
Church of Our Lady of the Snows **2**
Church of St Cyril and St Methodius **18**
Church of St Stephen **8**
Church of St Ursula **15**
Slavonic Monastery **10**

Theatres
National Theatre pp94–5 **14**
State Opera **5**

Historic Squares, Buildings and Gardens
Charles Square **12**
Dancing House **13**
Faust House **11**

Franciscan Garden **3**
Main Station **7**
New Town Hall **17**
U Fleků **16**
Wenceslas Square **1**

Museums and Galleries
Dvořák Museum **9**

Mucha Museum **6**
National Museum **4**

GETTING THERE
The area is well served by the metro, with two main stations, Můstek and Muzeum, in Wenceslas Square, and others at Karlovo náměstí and Národní třída. Tram routes from most parts of the city pass through Charles Square.

KEY
▨	Street-by-Street Map *See pp88–9*
✠	Church
Ⓜ	Metro station
⯐	Tram stop
🚉	Train station
ℹ	Tourist information

0 metres 250
0 yards 250

◁ **Art Nouveau sculptures on the Hlalol Choir Building (1905) on Masarykovo nábřeží**

Street-by-Street: Around Wenceslas Square

Hotels and restaurants occupy many of the buildings around Wenceslas Square, though it remains an important commercial centre. As you walk along look up at the buildings, most of which date from the beginning of the 20th century, when the square was redeveloped. There are some fine examples of the Czech decorative styles used during that period. Many blocks have dark, covered arcades leading to shops, theatres and cinemas.

Koruna Palace
(1914) is an ornate block of shops and offices. Its corner turret is topped with a crown (*koruna*).

Statue of St Lawrence at U Pinkasů

U Pinkasů, housed in a building with Gothic, Renaissance and Baroque features, started serving Pilsner Urquell in 1843.

Church of Our Lady of the Snows
The towering Gothic building is only part of a vast church planned during the 14th century ❷

M Můstek

M Můstek

M Můstek

M Můstek

Jungmann Square is named after Josef Jungmann (1773–1847), an influential linguist and lexicographer, and there is a statue of him in the middle. The Adria Palace (1925) used to be the Laterna Magika Theatre (*see p94*), which was where Václav Havel's Civic Forum worked in the early days of the 1989 Velvet Revolution.

Lucerna Palace

Franciscan Garden
A small park, which features this striking fountain, is laid out in an old monastery garden ❸

Wiehl House was completed in 1896. The five-storey building is in striking Neo-Renaissance style, with a loggia and colourful *sgraffito*. Mikoláš Aleš designed some of the Art Nouveau figures.

STAR SIGHTS

★ National Museum

★ State Opera

★ Wenceslas Square

For hotels and restaurants in this region see pp346–7 and pp376–7

★ **Wenceslas Square**
The dominant features of the square are the bronze equestrian statue of St Wenceslas (1912) and the National Museum behind it. St Wenceslas, a Přemyslid prince who was murdered by his brother Boleslav, is the patron saint of Bohemia ❶

LOCATOR MAP
See Street Finder, maps 3, 4 & 6

The Assicurazioni Generali Building was where Franz Kafka worked as an insurance clerk for ten months in 1906–7.

The Monument to the Victims of Communism is on the spot where Jan Palach killed himself in protest against the regime. Since the Velvet Revolution an unofficial shrine has been maintained here.

Hotel Evropa's façade and the interior of the hotel (1906) have retained most of their original Art Nouveau features.

Café Tramvaj 11

★ **State Opera**
Meticulously refurbished in the 1980s, the interior still has the luxurious red plush, crystal chandeliers and gilded stucco of the original late-19th-century theatre ❺

Fénix Palace

Muzeum M

Muzeum M

Muzeum M

St Wenceslas Monument

★ **National Museum**
The grand building with its monumental staircase was completed in 1890 as a symbol of national prestige ❹

| 0 metres | 100 |
| 0 yards | 100 |

KEY

- - - - Suggested route

Wenceslas Monument in Wenceslas Square

Wenceslas Square ❶

VÁCLAVSKÉ NÁMĚSTÍ

Map 3 C5. 🚇 *Můstek, Muzeum.*
🚋 *3, 9, 14, 24.*

The square has witnessed many key events in recent Czech history. It was here that the student Jan Palach burnt himself to death in 1969, and in November 1989 a protest rally in the square against police brutality led to the Velvet Revolution and the overthrow of Communism.

Wenceslas "Square" is something of a misnomer, for it is some 750 m (2,460 ft) long and only 60 m (196 ft) wide. Originally a horse market, today it is lined with hotels, restaurants, clubs and shops, reflecting the seamier side of global consumerism.

The huge equestrian statue of St Wenceslas in front of the National Museum was erected in 1912. Cast in bronze, it is the work of Josef Myslbek, the leading Czech sculptor of the late 19th century. At the foot of the pedestal there are several other statues of Czech patron saints. A memorial near the statue commemorates the victims of the former regime. Walking down the square

from the monument, there are several buildings of interest. To the left, down a passage, is Lucerna Palace, built in the early 20th century by Václav Havel, father of the former Czech president. It is now a shopping and entertainment complex. The cinema is worth a visit to see its Art Nouveau furnishings.

On the opposite side of the square, at No. 29, stands the lavishly decorated Art Nouveau Grand Hotel Evropa, built in 1903–6. This is a wonderfully preserved reminder of the golden age of hotels. Its magnificent façade is crowned with gilded nymphs, while inside the original bars, the mirrors, panelling and light fittings have survived virtually intact.

Church of Our Lady of the Snows ❷

KOSTEL PANNY MARIE SNĚŽNÉ

Jungmannovo náměstí 18. **Map** 3 C5. **Tel** 224 490 350. 🚇 *Můstek.* 🕐 *9am–7pm daily.* ⛪ *7am, 8am, 6pm Mon–Fri; 8am, 6pm Sat; 9am, 10:15am, 11:30am, 6pm Sun.* 📷 ♿

Charles IV founded this church in 1347 to mark his coronation. The name refers to a 4th-century miracle in Rome, when the Virgin Mary appeared to the pope in a dream telling him to build a

The soaring Church of Our Lady of the Snows

church on the spot where snow fell in August. Charles's church was to have been over 100 m (330 ft) long, but was never completed. The towering building we see today was just the presbytery of the projected church.

The church had a checkered history until, in 1603, the Franciscans restored it. The intricate net vaulting of the ceiling dates from this period. Most of the interior decoration is Baroque. Note the splendid three-tiered altar, crowded with statues of saints.

Franciscan Garden ❸

FRANTIŠKÁNSKÁ ZAHRADA

Jungmannovo náměstí 18. **Map** 3 C5. 🚇 *Můstek.* 🕐 *Apr–Sep: 7am–10pm daily; Sep–Oct: 7am–8pm daily; Nov– Mar: 8am–7pm daily.* ♿

Originally the physic garden of a Franciscan monastery, the area was opened to the public in 1950 as a quiet oasis close to Wenceslas Square. By the entrance is a Gothic portal leading to the U františkánů cellar restaurant. In the 1980s some beds were replanted with herbs of the kinds cultivated by the Franciscans in the 17th century.

National Museum ❹

NÁRODNÍ MUZEUM

Václavské náměstí. **Map** 6 E1. **Tel** 224 497 111. 🚇 *Muzeum.* 🕐 *Oct– Apr: 9am–5pm daily; May– Sep: 10am–6pm (but closed first Tue of month).* 🎦 📷 *for a fee.* **www**.nm.cz

The vast and magnificent Neo-Renaissance building at one end of Wenceslas Square houses the National Museum. Designed by Josef Schulz as a triumphal affirmation of the Czech national revival, the museum was completed in 1890. The entrance is reached by a ramp flanked by allegorical

statue seated by the door are History and Nature; in front is a fountain with an allegorical figure symbolizing the Czech nation and the Czech rivers. If you look closely at the façade you can pick out pockmarks left by shells from Warsaw Pact tanks during the invasion of Prague in 1968. Unmissable overhead is a gilt-framed glass cupola.

Inside, the monumental staircase lit by grand brass candelabras leads to the Pantheon, a dome-topped hall. This contains statues and busts of the most prominent figures in Czech political, intellectual and artistic life. The vast room with windows overlooking Wenceslas Square has four huge paintings by Václav Brožík and František Ženíšek and Vojtěch Hynais.

While the rich marbled decoration is impressive, it overwhelms the museum's displays devoted mainly to mineralogy (including one of Europe's largest collections of rocks), archaeology, anthropology, numismatics and natural history. The museum is due to close in 2011 for renovation.

Grand staircase in the National Museum

State Opera ❺

STÁTNÍ OPERA PRAHA

Wilsonova 4. **Map** 4 E5.
Tel 224 227 266 (box office).
Ⓜ Muzeum. ☐ for performances only. **www**.opera.cz

The first theatre built here, the New Town Theatre, was pulled down in 1885 to

Façade of the State Opera, formerly the New German Theatre

make way for the present building. This was originally known as the New German Theatre, built to rival the Czech National Theatre (see pp94–5). By attracting top-quality conductors and musical directors, including Mahler, the theatre gained a reputation for staging some of the best German operas outside Germany; this is due partly to the excellent acoustics. Nowadays, the opera house stages both traditional and modern works.

A Neo-Classical frieze decorates the pediment above the loggia at the front of the theatre. Inside, original paintings in the auditorium and on the curtain have been preserved. In 1945 the theatre became the city's principal opera house.

Mucha Museum ❻

MUCHOVO MUZEUM

Panská 7. **Map** 4 D4. **Tel** 221 451 333. Ⓜ Mstek, Nám´stí Republiky. 🚊 3, 5, 9, 14, 24, 26. ☐ 10am–6pm daily. ◻ ◻ ◻ **www**.mucha.cz

The 18th-century Kaunicky Palace is home to the first museum dedicated to Alfons Mucha, the Czech master of Art Nouveau (see p25). The exhibits include paintings, drawings, sketchbooks and photographs (some taken by Mucha) as well as personal memorabilia. Special attention is paid to the artist's time in Paris. The documentary film is

also well worth seeing. The central courtyard is given over to a café in the summer.

Main Station ❼

HLAVNÍ NÁDRAŽÍ

Wilsonova 8. **Map** 4 E5.
Ⓜ Hlavní nádraží.

Prague's main railway station, designed by Josef Fanta and constructed in 1901–9, is one of the finest examples of Czech Art Nouveau architecture. The vast structure is magnificently decorated, with the walls and ceilings covered with allegorical figures, animals and floral motifs. The turrets of the two towers that flank the building's central section rest on the shoulders of giant Atlantes. Even before the building was completed the nudity of these youths caused heated controversy between the local moralists and the sculptor – Stanislav Sucharda.

The main station façade, hiding an equally impressive interior

Church of St Stephen **⑧**

KOSTEL SV. ŠTĚPÁNA

Štěpánská. **Map** 5 C2.
🚋 4, 6, 10, 16, 22, 23. ◐ only for services. ⛪ 11am Sun. 📷

Founded by Charles IV in 1351 as the parish church of the upper Nové Město, St Stephen's was finished in 1401 with the completion of the multi-spired steeple. In the late 17th century the Branberg Chapel was added; it is now home to the tomb of the prolific Baroque sculptor Matthias Braun. Most of the subsequent Baroque additions were removed when the church was scrupulously re-Gothicized in the 1870s. There are some fine Baroque paintings, however, including a picture of St John Nepomuk by Jan Jiří Heinsch to the left of the pulpit. But the church's greatest treasure is a stunning Gothic panel painting of the Madonna, known as *Our Lady of St Stephen's*, which dates from 1472.

The Michna Summer Palace, home of the Dvořák Museum

Gothic pulpit in St Stephen's

Dvořák Museum **⑨**

MUZEUM ANTONÍNA DVOŘÁKA

Ke Karlovu 20. **Map** 6 D2. **Tel** 224 923 363. ᴹ IP Pavlova. 🚌 148. ◐ 10am–5pm Tue–Sun and for concerts 📷 📷 📷 www.nm.cz

One of the most enchanting secular buildings of the Prague Baroque, this red and ochre villa now houses the Dvořák Museum. On display

are Dvořák scores, as well as photographs and memorabilia of the 19th-century Czech composer, including his piano, viola and desk.

The building, designed by the great Baroque architect Kilian Ignaz Dientzenhofer, has an elegant tiered mansard roof. It was built in 1720 for the Michnas of Vacínov and was originally known as the Michna Summer Palace.

In the 19th century the villa and garden fell into decay, but both have been heavily restored. The garden statues and vases, from the workshop of Matthias Braun, date from about 1735. Inside, the ceiling and walls of the large room on the first floor, often used for recitals, are decorated with 18th-century frescoes.

Slavonic Monastery **⑩**

KLÁŠTER NA SLOVANECH

Vyšehradská. **Map** 5 B2. **Tel** 221 979 296. ᴹ Karlovo náměstí. 🚋 3, 4, 14, 18, 24. **Monastery church** ◐ 9am–4pm Mon–Fri. **Cloisters** ◐ by appointment. 📷 📷 www.emauzy.cz

Both the monastery and its church were almost destroyed in an American air raid in 1945; it was one of the

few historic buildings in the city to be damaged during World War II. When the church was reconstructed, it was given two concrete spires, which form an incongruous part of the city's skyline.

The monastery was founded in 1347 by Croatian Benedictines, whose services were held in the Old Slavonic language, hence its name "Na Slovanech". In the course of Prague's tumultuous religious history, the monastery has since changed hands many times. In 1446 a Hussite order was formed here, then in 1635 the building was acquired by Spanish Benedictines. In the

The vaulted cloisters in the Slavonic Monastery

For hotels and restaurants in this region see pp346–7 and pp376–7

18th century the complex was given a thorough Baroque treatment, but then in 1880 it was taken over by German Benedictines, who decided to rebuild virtually everything in Neo-Gothic style.

The complex, also known as the Emmaus Monastery, is now functioning again since the return of monks exiled under Communism. Some historically important 14th-century wall paintings are preserved in the cloisters, though many were damaged in World War II.

Baroque façade of Faust House

Faust House ⓫

FAUSTŮV DŮM

Karlovo náměstí 40, 41. **Map** 5 B3. Karlovo náměstí. 3, 4, 14, 16, 18. to the public.

This Ornate Baroque mansion is the object of one of Prague's most enduring legends: namely, that this house, whose origins can be traced to the 12th century, was once the home of the notorious Dr Faustus.

In the 16th century an English alchemist-cum-con man Edward Kelley lived here. However, it was the experiments of alchemist Count Ferdinand Mladota of Solopysky, who owned the house in the 1700s, which gave rise to its association with the legend of Faust.

Charles Square ⓬

KARLOVO NÁMĚSTÍ

Map 5 B2. Karlovo náměstí. 3, 4, 6, 10, 14, 16, 18, 22, 23, 24.

The southern part of Nové Město resounds to the rattle of trams, as many routes converge in this part of the city. The public garden in Charles Square, laid out in the mid-19th century, offers a peaceful and welcome retreat, though its trees do make it hard to enjoy broad vistas within the square. The statues in the park are of various figures from Czech history.

Prague's largest square – it is almost twice the size of Wenceslas Square – was laid out when Charles IV was establishing Nové Město in 1348. Built at its centre was a wooden tower, where the coronation jewels were put on display once a year. Some time later the tower was replaced by a chapel. It was from here, in 1437, that the famous document informing the Czechs about the concessions granted to the Hussites by the pope and the council in Basle was read out for the first time.

Until the 19th century Charles Square was used mainly as a cattle market, and for selling firewood, coal and other goods. On its north side is the New Town Hall *(see p96)*, while on the south side is the magnificent church of St Ignatius. Built by Carlo Lurago in the 1660s, this is a prime example of Baroque Jesuit architecture, intended to symbolize the strength and the power of the faith. The façade is topped by a statue of the church's patron saint, St Ignatius of Loyola, framed by a radiant sunburst. The Church's rules allowed only Christ and the Virgin Mary to be represented in this fashion, but the Jesuits succeeded in obtaining an exemption from the pope for their Prague church.

Detail from a house in Charles Square

Inside, the profusion of gilts is truly dazzling.

To the right of St Ignatius stands the rather featureless former Jesuit college, also designed by Carlo Lurago. It is now a teaching hospital that is attached to Charles University, which makes use of several buildings in and around this square.

Dancing House, nicknamed "Fred and Ginger"

Dancing House ⓭

TANČÍCÍ DŮM

Resslova 9. **Map** 5 B2. **Tel** 224 920 686. Karlovo náměstí. 3, 4, 6, 10, 14, 16, 18, 22, 23, 24. **Restaurant** noon–2pm Tue–Sat; 7–10:30pm Mon–Sat.

On the banks of the Vltava, west of Charles Square, is an extraordinary building affectionately named the "Dancing House". Its other popular name – "Fred and Ginger" – alludes to the fact that its silhouette brings to mind the famous American dancing pair, Fred Astaire and Ginger Rogers. The glass and concrete structure which, in fact, is two buildings with different façades and of different heights, is the 1996 work of Californian architect Frank Gehry and his associate Vlado Milunič. It was awarded a special prize by *Time*, the American magazine, for blending modern architecture with an older, historical environment. The French restaurant on the top floor, Las Perle de Prague *(see p377)*, has great views.

National Theatre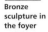

NÁRODNÍ DIVADLO

This gold-crested theatre is a cherished symbol of the Czech cultural revival. Work on the original Neo-Renaissance building, designed by Josef Zítek and funded largely by voluntary contributions, began in 1868. After the devastating fire of 1881 *(see opposite)*, however, Josef Schulz was given the job of rebuilding it; all the best Czech artists of the day contributed to the new theatre's superb decoration. In the 1970s and 80s the theatre was restored and the New Stage (Nová Scena) was built by Karel Prager.

The theatre from Slovanský ostrov (island)

Bronze sculpture in the foyer

A bronze three-horse chariot, designed by Bohuslav Schnirch, carries the Goddess of Victory.

The Laterna Magika, where shows combine film, theatre, dance and light.

The New Stage auditorium

★ Auditorium
The elaborate ceiling, painted by František Ženíšek, is adorned with allegorical figures representing the arts.

STAR FEATURES

★ Auditorium

★ Lobby Ceiling

★ Stage Curtain

The five arcades of the loggia are decorated with lunette paintings by Josef Tulka, entitled *Five Songs*.

★ Lobby Ceiling
This ceiling fresco is the final part of a triptych painted by František Ženíšek in 1878, depicting the Golden Age of Czech Art.

★ Stage Curtain
This sumptuous red and gold stage curtain, showing the origin of the theatre, is the work of Vojtěch Hynais.

VISITORS' CHECKLIST

Národní 2, Nové Město. **Map** 3 A5. **Tel** 224 912 673. Ⓜ Národní třída. 17, 18, 22, 23 to Národní divadlo. **Auditorium Tel** 221 714 152. ◯ Sat & Sun for tours. 8:30–11am. www.nationaltheatre.cz

Façade Decoration
This standing figure on the attic of the western façade is one of the many figures representing the Arts sculpted by Antonín Wagner in 1883.

The roof, sky-blue and covered with stars, is said to represent the sky – the summit that all artists should aim for.

The President's Box
The former royal box, lined in red velvet, is decorated with paintings of famous historical figures from Czech history by Václav Brožík.

FIRE IN THE NATIONAL THEATRE

On 12 August 1881, just days before the official opening, the National Theatre was completely gutted by fire. It was thought to have been started by metal-workers on the roof. Just six weeks later enough money had been collected to rebuild the theatre. It was finally opened two years late in 1883 with a performance of Smetana's opera *Libuše* (see p42).

Renaissance painted ceiling in the New Town Hall

Chujkrch of
St Ursula ⑮

KOSTEL SV. VORŠILY

Ostrovni 18. **Map** 3 A5. **Tel** 224
930 502. Ⓜ Národni třída.
🚋 6, 9, 18, 22, 23. ⬆ 5pm Sat;
11am, 5pm Sun. ◯ daily – call 221
714 130. ⊘ 🔲

The delightful Baroque
church of St Ursula was
built as part of an Ursuline
convent founded in 1672.
The original sculptures still
decorate the façade, and in
front of the church stands a
group of statues featuring
St John Nepomuk with angels
(1740), the work of Ignaz
Platzer the Elder.

The light airy interior has a
frescoed, stuccoed ceiling,
beautiful Baroque furnishings,
and on the various altars
there are lively Baroque
paintings. The main altar
has one of St Ursula.

The adjoining convent was
returned to the Ursuline
order in 1989 and is now a Catholic
school. Part of the ground
floor is used for secular
purposes: it houses the
Klášterní Vinárna (Convent
Restaurant).

U Fleků ⑯

Křemencova 11. **Map** 5 B1.
Ⓜ Národni třída, Karlovo náměstí.
🚋 6, 18, 22. **Tel** 224 934 019. See
Restaurants p376. **www**.ufleku.cz

A short walk south from the
Church of St Ursula is one of
the city's most famous (and
also most touristy) beer halls,
U Fleků. Records have it
that beer has been brewed
here since 1459. The owners
of the large beer hall have

kept up the tradition of
brewing: the current brewery,
the smallest in the capital,
produces and serves special
strong, dark beer, sold
exclusively on the premises.

New Town Hall ⑰

NOVOMĚSTSKÁ RADNICE

Karlovo náměstí 23. **Map** 5 B1.
Ⓜ Karlovo náměstí. 🚋 3, 4, 6,
10, 14, 16, 18, 22, 24. **Tel** 224 948
229. **Tower** ◯ May–Sep:
10am–6pm Tue–Sun. 🖼

In 1960 a statue of Hussite
preacher Jan Želivský was
unveiled at the New Town
Hall. It commemorates the
first and bloodiest of Prague's
defenestrations. On 30 July
1419 Želivský led a crowd of
demonstrators to the Town
Hall to demand the release of
some prisoners. When they
were refused, they stormed
the building and threw the
Catholic councillors they found
inside out of the windows.
Those who survived the fall
were finished off with pikes
in the street.

Façade of the Baroque Church of St Ursula

The Town Hall already
existed in the 14th century;
the Gothic tower was added
in the mid-15th century and
contains an 18th-century
chapel. In the 16th century an
arcaded courtyard was added.

After the four towns of
Prague were coalesced in
1784 the Town Hall ceased to
be the seat of the municipal
administration and became a
courthouse and prison. It is
now used for cultural and
social events.

Church of St Cyril
and St Methodius ⑱

KOSTEL SV. CYRILA A METODĚJE

Resslova 9. **Map** 5 B2.
Tel 224 916 100. Ⓜ Karlovo
náměstí. 🚋 3, 4, 6, 10, 14, 16, 18,
22, 23, 24. ◯ Oct–Mar: 10am–4pm
Tue–Sun; Apr–Sep: 10am–5pm
Tue–Sun. 🖼 ⊘ ♿

This Baroque church, with
a pilastered façade and a
small central tower, was built
in the 1730s. It was dedicated
to St Charles Borromeo and
served as the church of a
community of retired priests,
but was closed in 1783.
In the 1930s the church was
restored and given to the
Czechoslovak Orthodox
Church. It was rededicated
to St Cyril and St Methodius,
the 9th-century Greek monks
who brought Christianity to
the Czechs and who are often
referred to as the "Apostles to
the Slavs" (see p33).

In 1942 the parachutists who
had assassinated Reinhard
Heydrich, the
Nazi governor of
Czechoslovakia, hid
in the crypt along
with members of the
Czech Resistance.
Surrounded by
German troops, they
took their own lives
rather than surrender.
Bullet holes made by
the German machine
guns during the siege
can still be seen
below the memorial
plaque on the outer
wall of the crypt,
which now houses
a museum.

Art Nouveau in Prague

The decorative style known as Art Nouveau originated in Paris in the 1890s. Its influence quickly spread internationally as most of the major European cities quickly responded to its graceful, flowing forms. In Prague, as in the rest of central Europe, the movement was known as the Secession. It reached its height in the first decade of the 20th century but died out during World War I, when the style seemed frivolous and even decadent. There is a wealth of Art Nouveau in Prague, mainly in Josefov and Nové Město, with the style perhaps at its most expressive in the decorative and applied arts: artists adorned every type of object – from doorknobs to lamps and vases – with plant-like forms in imitation of the natural world from which they drew their inspiration.

Façade detail, 10 Masaryk Embankment

ARCHITECTURE

Architecturally, the new style was a deliberate attempt to break with the 19th-century tradition of monumental buildings. In Art Nouveau the important feature was ornament, either painted or sculpted, often in the form of a female figure, applied to a fairly plain surface. This technique was ideally suited to wrought iron and glass, which were both light and strong and became popular materials. The style created buildings of lasting beauty in Prague.

Hotel Meran, 1904
This grand Art Nouveau building is notable for its fine detailing both inside and out.

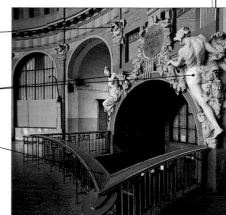

Ornate pilasters

Decorative statues

Brass and wrought-iron balustrade

One of the many examples of Art Nouveau decoration in Prague's Main Station *(see p91)*

ALFONS MUCHA

Many painters, sculptors and graphic artists were influenced by Art Nouveau. One of the style's most successful exponents was Alfons Mucha (1860–1939). He is celebrated chiefly for his posters, yet he also designed stained glass, furniture, jewellery, even postage stamps *(see p91)*.

Poster for Sokol Movement
This beautiful colour lithograph by Mucha, for the Sokol gymnastic movement, dates from 1912.

Iridescent green vase made of Bohemian glass

FURTHER AFIELD

Visitors to Prague, finding the historic centre so full of sights, often ignore the suburbs. It is true that once visitors venture away from the centre, language can become a problem. However, it is well worth the effort, both to escape the crowds and also to realize that Prague is a living city as well as a picturesque time capsule. The majority of the museums and other attractions are easily reached by Metro, tram, bus or even on foot. The sights of particular interest include the Mozart Museum;

Statuette of Mozart, on show at the Mozart Museum

the Trade Fair Palace, with its superb modern art collection; the former monastery at Zbraslav, now a repository for some impressive Asian art and artifacts; the Břevnov Monastery, co-founded by St Adalbert; Vyšehrad, the rocky seat of the Přemyslid princes; Žižkov, site of a famous Hussite victory and of a giant monument that towers over Prague; Bílá Hora (White Mountain), which remains the symbol of national calamity; and the Troja Palace, a splendid 17th-century villa with a French garden.

SIGHTS AT A GLANCE

Museums and Galleries
Mozart Museum ❶
Trade Fair Palace
  pp102–3 ❹
Zbraslav Chateau ❽

Monastery
Břevnov Monastery ❻

Historic Districts
Vyšehrad ❷
Žižkov ❸

Historic Sites
White Mountain and Star
  Hunting Lodge ❼

Historic Building
Troja Palace pp104–5 ❺

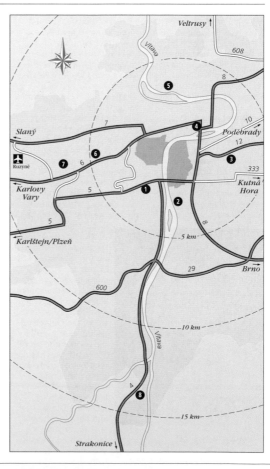

0 km 2

0 miles 2

KEY

- Central Prague
- Greater Prague
- ✈ Airport
- ▬ Major road
- ═ Local road

◁ **Part of the garden staircase of the 17th-century Troja Palace**

Mozart Museum ❶

BERTRAMKA

Mozartova 169. *Tel 257 317 465.*
Anděl. 🚊 *4, 7, 9, 10.*
⬜ *Apr–Oct: 9:30am–6pm daily;*
Nov–Mar: 9:30am–4pm daily. 📷
Ⓧ 🖥 🎵 www.bertramka.com

Though slightly off the
beaten track, in a busy,
traffic-ridden district, the
museum is well signposted.
The Czech people's reverence
for Mozart means that the
composer is treated more
like a Czech than an
Austrian citizen.

Bertramka is a 17th-century
farmhouse, enlarged in the
following century into a
comfortable suburban villa in
walled grounds. Mozart and
his wife Constanze stayed
here as the guests of the
composer František Dušek
and his wife Josefina in 1787,
when Mozart was working on
Don Giovanni. He composed
the overture to the opera in
the garden pavilion just a few
hours before its premiere at
the Nostitz Theatre, now the
Estates Theatre *(see p84).*

The house, which has a
small exhibition devoted to
Mozart, is at its best in the
late afternoon when the
crowds have gone home.
There is a café in the
courtyard in which to enjoy
the peace and quiet. In
summer, recitals take place
on the terrace.

Bertramka, the villa now housing the Mozart Museum

Vyšehrad ❷

Map 5 B5. *Vyšehrad.*
🚊 *3, 7, 16, 18, 24, 97.*
www.praha-vysehrad.cz

According to legend
Vyšehrad was the original
seat of the Přemyslid family,
and it was from here that
Princess Libuše, the mythical
mother of Prague, saw the
future glory of her city.
Research has proved that as
early as the 10th century the
wooded outcrop above the
Vltava river, south of Nové
Město, was the site of a
fortified settlement. Vyšehrad
("The Castle on the Heights")
later rose to the rank of a
royal residence, though its
privileged status was soon
overshadowed by Prague
Castle, on the opposite side
of the river.

The fortress is entered from
the south via two gates: the
Tábor Gate (17th century)
and the slightly later Leopold
Gate. The oldest
remaining structure on
the hill is the 11th-
century Rotunda of St
Martin, the oldest
complete Romanesque
building in the capital,
albeit greatly restored.

The mighty walls on
top of the crag give a
magnificent view of
the river and town of .
Vyšehrad. The hillside
park below contains
some interesting
sculptures of Czech
legendary figures,
including Libuše
and her ploughman
spouse, Přemysl
(after whom the early
Bohemian kings were
named).

Portal of St Peter and Paul Church, Vyšehrad

The most imposing building in
Vyšehrad is the vast, Neo-
Gothic church of St Peter and
St Paul (sv. Petra a Pavla).
Nearby is Vyšehrad Cemetery,
conceived by the National
Revival movement and found-
ed in 1869 as the burial ground
for the greatest contributors to
Czech cultural life. Buried here
are composers Antonín Dvořák
and Bedřich Smetana, poet Jan
Neruda, and artists Alfons
Mucha and Mikoláš Aleš.

Equestrian statue of Jan Žižka

Žižkov ❸

*Jiřího z Poděbrad, Želivského,
Flóra.* 🚊 *9, 11.* 🚌 *133, 168, 207.* **TV
Tower Tel** *242 418 778.* ⬜ *10am–
11pm daily.* 📷 🍴 www.tower.cz

This area was the scene of
an historic battle in 1420, in
which a tiny force of Hussites
defeated an army of several
thousand Crusaders. In 1877
the area around Vítkov was
renamed Žižkov in honour of
the leader of the Hussites, Jan
Žižka; in 1950 a 9-m (30-ft)
high bronze statue of Žižka
on horseback was erected on
the hill. It stands in front of
the vast National Monument
(1927–32), built as a symbol
of the Czech struggle for
independence and later used

as a mausoleum for early Communist leaders.

The ugly, futuristic Žižkov TV Tower, reaching over 100 m (328 ft) high, was built in the 1970s. There are fine views over the city from its eighth-floor viewing platform.

Trade Fair Palace ❹

See pp102–103.

Troja Palace ❺

See pp104–105.

Břevnov monastery, designed largely by the Dientzenhofers

Břevnov Monastery ❻

BŘEVNOVSKÝ KLÁŠTER

Markétská 28. **Tel** 220 406 111. 🚇 8, 15, 22, 25. 🚌 only, Sat & Sun; tour times vary. 📷 🚫 www.brevnov.cz

From the surrounding suburban housing you would never guess that Břevnov is one of the oldest inhabited parts of Prague. A flourishing community grew up here around the Benedictine abbey founded in 993 by Prince Boleslav II and Bishop Adalbert (Vojtěch) – Bohemia's first monastery. An ancient well called Vojtěška marks the spot where the prince and bishop are said to have met and decided to found the monastery.

The gateway, courtyard and most of the present monastery buildings are by the great Baroque architects

SAINT ADALBERT

Adalbert, born in Bohemia as Vojtěch, became Bishop of Prague in 982. Dismayed by the heathen behaviour of its people, however, he resigned. He ended up at the court of Prince Boleslav in Poland, from where, in 997, he set out on a mission to convert the Prussians. They welcomed Adalbert by murdering him. Boleslav brought the martyr's body back and buried it in Gniezno cathedral in Poland. Canonized in 999, St Adalbert became the patron saint of Poland.

The Martyrdom of St Adalbert

Christoph and Kilian Ignaz Dientzenhofer *(see p65)*: the monastery church of St Margaret (sv. Markéty) is Christoph's work. Essentially a substantial reworking of the original 10th-century church, it is based on a floorplan of overlapping ovals, as ingenious as any of Bernini's churches in Rome. For four decades the Ministry of the Interior used St Margaret's as storage space. Also of interest is the abbey's meeting hall, or Theresian Hall, with a painted ceiling dating from 1727.

White Mountain and Star Hunting Lodge ❼

BÍLÁ HORA/LETOHRÁDEK HVĚZDA

🚇 1, 22 (White Mountain), 18 (Star Hunting Lodge). **White Mountain** 🚪 24 hrs daily. **Star Hunting Lodge Tel** 235 357 938. 🚪 Apr–Oct: 10am–5pm Tue–Sun (to 6pm May–Sep). 📷 🚫

The Battle of the White Mountain, the decisive first battle of the Thirty Years' War fought on 8 November

1620, affected the two main communities of Prague in different ways. For the Protestants it was a disaster that led to 300 years of Habsburg domination; for the Catholic supporters of the Habsburgs it was a triumph, so they erected a memorial chapel on the hill. In the early 1700s this was converted into the grander Church of Our Lady Victorious and decorated by leading Baroque artists.

In the 16th century the woodland around the White Mountain battle site had been a royal game park. The Star Hunting Lodge (Letohrádek Hvězda), completed in 1556, survives today. This fascinating building has a six-pointed star design – *hvězda* means star. In 1950 it became a museum dedicated to the writer of historical novels Alois Jirásek (1851–1930), and the painter Mikoláš Aleš (1852–1913). This is now closed for reconstruction.

The museum has exhibits relating to the Battle of the White Mountain and Czech culture.

The 16th-century Star Hunting Lodge, close to Bílá Hora

Trade Fair Palace ❹

VELETRŽNÍ PALÁC

The national gallery in Prague opened its Centre for Modern and Contemporary Art in 1995, housed in a reconstruction of a former Trade Fair building of 1929. Its vast, skylit spaces make an ideal backdrop for the collection, which ranges from French 19th-century art through superb examples of Impressionist and Post-Impressionist painting, to works by Munch, Klimt and Picasso, and a fine collection of Czech modern art.

The Virgins (1913)
This colourful work is typical of Gustav Klimt's distinctive erotic style.

Screening Room

The Blind (1926)
Among the sculptures on display is this intriguing work by František Bílek.

Fourth Floor

Third Floor

★ George of Poděbrady and Matthias Corvinus
Mikoláš Aleš (1852–1913) painted many patriotic historical scenes. Here, the King of Hungary signs a treaty with King George in 1469.

Cleopatra (1942–57)
This striking painting by Jan Zrzavý made him a major representative of Czech modern art.

Pomona (1910)
This figure is by Aristide Maillol, a pupil of Rodin, several of whose works are included in the museum's superb display of bronzes.

STAR FEATURES

- ★ Evening in Hradčany by J. Schikaneder
- ★ George of Poděbrady and Matthias Corvinus by M. Aleš
- ★ Torso by Z. Pešánek

★ Evening in Hradčany (1909–13)
This fascinating painting by Jakub Schikaneder captures the magic and nostalgia of Prague at dusk.

Grand Meal (1951–55)
The works of the Czech artist Mikuláš Medek range from post-war Surrealism to 1960s Abstraction.

★ Torso (1936)
Zdeněk Pešánek was a pioneer of kinetic art, here combining an organic form with neon lighting.

Egg Object (1976)
Crafted by sculptor Jiří Kolář, this egg is one of the late 20th-century works on display in the museum.

Second floor

Stairs to all floors

Stairs to all floors

Main entrance

First Floor

Mezzanine Floor

Ground Floor

KEY

- ▢ 19th & 20th-century European Art
- ▢ Czech Art 1900–1930
- ▢ 19th & 20th-century French Art
- ▢ Czech Art 1930–present day
- ▢ Non-Czech Modern Art
- ▢ Temporary Exhibition space
- ▢ Non-exhibition space

The façade's concrete and glass bands are typical of 1920s Functionalist architecture.

Troja Palace ⑤

TROJSKÝ ZÁMEK

One of Prague's most striking summer palaces, Troja was built in the late 1600s by Jean-Baptiste Mathey for Count Sternberg, member of a leading Bohemian aristocratic family. Lying at the foot of the Vltava Heights, the palace was modelled on a Classical Italian villa, while its garden was laid out in formal French style. The superb interior is full of extravagant frescoes expressing the Sternbergs' loyalty to the Habsburg dynasty. Troja houses a good collection of 19th-century art.

Terracotta urn on the garden balustrade

Defeat of the Turks
This turbaned figure, tumbling from the Grand Hall ceiling, symbolizes Leopold I's triumph over the Turks.

Belvedere turret

Statue of Olympian God

Statues of sons of Mother Earth

Personification of Justice
Abraham Godyn's image of Justice gazes from the lower east wall of the Grand Hall.

The two sons of Mother Earth which adorn the oval-shaped staircase (1685–1703) are part of a group of sculptures by Johann Georg Heermann and his nephew Paul, showing the struggle of the Olympian Gods with the Titans.

For hotels and restaurants in this region see pp347–9 and p377

★ Grand Hall Fresco
*The frescoes in the Grand Hall
depict the story of the first
Habsburg Emperor, Rudolph I,
and the victories of Leopold I
over Christianity's arch-
enemy, the Ottoman Empire.*

Stucco
decoration

STAR FEATURES

★ Chinese Rooms

★ Garden
  Staircase

★ Grand Hall Fresco

★ Chinese Rooms
*Several rooms feature 18th-century murals of
Chinese scenes. This room makes a perfect
backdrop for a ceramics display.*

Zbraslav
Chateau ❽

ZÁMEK ZBRASLAV

Ten km (6 miles) south of
Prague, Zbraslav Chateau is a
little out of the way but well
worth a visit. The bus ride
from Smíchovské nádraží
station takes only 15 minutes.

The building was founded
as a Cistercian monastery by
King Wenceslas II in 1292,
to serve as the royal burial
ground. The king was a
frequent visitor to Zbraslav
and was duly buried here in
1305. He and Wenceslas IV
were, in the end, the only
kings to be buried here.
In 1499 King Vladislav II
granted the monastery licence
to produce paper; the result
was Bohemia's first paper mill.

Destroyed during the Hussite
Wars, the monastery was
rebuilt in 1709–39, only to be
abolished in 1785 and turned
into a sugar factory. Reconstruction in the early 1900s
turned Zbraslav into a chateau,
which was handed over to
the National Gallery in 1939.

It now houses an impressive
collection of Asian art, including art and artefacts from
China, Japan, India, Southeast
Asia and Tibet. The collection
of Japanese sculpture features
some exhibits which blind or
partially sighted people are
encouraged to touch. There is
also some Islamic art.

**Zbraslav Chateau, home to a fine
exhibition of Asian art**

PRAGUE STREET FINDER

The map references given for all the sights described in the Prague chapter, and also for the hotels and restaurants listed in Travellers' Needs *(see pp344–9 and 372–7)* refer to the street maps in this section. The key map (right) shows the area of Prague covered by the Street Finder. This map includes sight-seeing areas, as well as districts for hotels and restaurants.

In keeping with Czech maps, none of the street names on the Street Finder has the Czech word for street, *ulice*, included (though you may see it on the city's street signs). Churches, buildings, museums and monuments are marked on the Street Finder with their English and Czech names.

KEY TO STREET FINDER

▮	Major sight
▮	Place of interest
▯	Other building
Ⓜ	Metro station
🚆	Train station
🚌	Bus station
🚋	Tram stop
🚋	Funicular railway
⛴	Riverboat boarding point
🚕	Taxi rank
P	Parking garage
i	Tourist information office
✚	Hospital with emergency unit
🛡	Police station
✝	Church
✡	Synagogue
⊠	Post office
═	Railway line
—	City wall
═	Pedestrian street

SCALE OF MAP PAGES

0 yards	200
	1:8,400

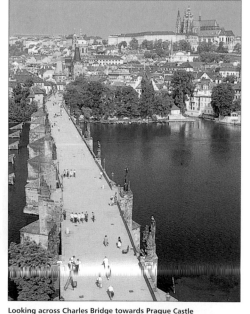

Looking across Charles Bridge towards Prague Castle

Aerial view of the Baroque Church of St Nicholas in Old Town Square

2 **3** **4**

MILADY HORÁKOVÉ

NÁBŘEŽÍ EDVARDA BENEŠE

NA FRANTIŠKU

REVOLUČNÍ

Hradčany and Malá Strana

Staré Město and Josefov

NERUDOVA

Karlův most

WILSONOVA

ÚJEZD

SMETANOVO NÁBŘEŽÍ

NÁRODNÍ

5 **6**

Nové Město

ANGLICKÁ

SLEZSKÁ

ŽITNÁ

KORUNNÍ

JEČNÁ

RAŠÍNOVO NÁBŘEŽÍ

SOKOLSKÁ

LEGEROVA

SVORNOSTI

RADLICKÁ

SVOBODOVA

VNISLAVOVA

SEKANINOVA

JAROMÍROVA

KŘESOMYSLOVA

The imposing twin towers of the Church of St Peter and St Paul atop the rocky outcrop at Vyšehrad

CZECH REPUBLIC
REGION
BY REGION

The Czech Republic at a Glance

The Czech Republic is a country with over 70 per cent of its land occupied by uplands full of rolling hills and sweeping valleys. It comprises three historic regions. Bohemia, the largest, has a central basin surrounded by ranges of mountains and hills. To the east it borders Moravia, a paradise for lovers of good wine, which stretches eastwards to the border with Slovakia. The third and smallest region, Silesia, is a highland area to the north, bordering Poland.

České Švýcarsko, *an area of extraordinary sandstone formations, is best symbolized by Pravčická brána – the largest natural rock bridge in Central Europe* (see pp188–9).

Plzeň's Great Synagogue *features a magnificent vaulted ceiling. Built in the 19th century, the synagogue only recently regained its former splendour following many years of reconstruction* (see p162).

NORTH BOHEMIA
(pp178–193)

CENTRAL BOHEMIA
(pp118–133)

PRAGUE
(pp48–113)

WEST BOHEMIA
(pp158–177)

SOUTH BOHEMIA
(pp134–157)

Český Krumlov's *Old Town has lovingly restored houses with ornamented portals and pediments, as well as richly decorated façades* (see pp152–3).

St James's Church, Kutná Hora *is the oldest church in a town that is famous for its silver mining and its vast St Barbara's Cathedral. St James's has* ⁓⁓⁓⁓⁓⁓ ⁓⁓⁓⁓ ⁓⁓⁓⁓⁓ ⁓ *⁓⁓⁓ ⁓⁓⁓⁓⁓ ⁓⁓⁓⁓ ⁓⁓⁓⁓⁓ built as there were fears that it might collapse due to the instability of the ground, which had been disturbed by mining operations* (see pp122–3).

◁ The castle and the houses of the Old Town beside the Vltava river, Český Krumlov

Častolovice Palace, *returned in 1989 to Franziska Diana Sternberg-Phipps, is among the best-preserved castles in East Bohemia. Now its historic interiors serve as an exclusive hotel and a museum* (see p211).

Bouzov Castle, *formerly the property of the Order of Teutonic Knights, was given its Neo-Gothic form in the late 19th and early 20th centuries. Now it is a favourite setting for films whose action takes place in the Middle Ages* (see pp220–21).

EAST BOHEMIA
(pp194–211)

NORTH MORAVIA AND SILESIA
(pp212–223)

SOUTH MORAVIA
(pp224–241)

0 kilometres — 50

0 miles — 25

The village of Křtiny
is home to an important Baroque church. Also in the village is a Baroque residence that was converted in the first half of the 19th century by František Xavier of Dietrichstein into a small castle, where this coat of arms can be seen (see p232).

CENTRAL BOHEMIA

*T*he region surrounding Prague offers the combined attractions
of an extraordinary landscape with its magnificent rock
formations furrowed by river canyons, as well as a wealth of
historic towns and spectacular castles. Situated relatively close to the
city, these sights provide visitors and locals alike with superb
opportunities for exploration.

From the 6th century AD, Central Bohemia (Střední Čechy) saw the arrival of numerous Slav tribes, who built settlements and fortresses here. In the 9th century the Czechs emerged as the dominant people in the region. The first duke in the Přemyslid dynasty, which held sway in Bohemia from the 9th century, was a Christian, and many ecclesiastical remains in Central Bohemia testify to the importance of this new influence. Nowhere else in the country are there so many examples of Romanesque and Early Gothic stone architecture. At Sázava Monastery, founded in the 11th century, the Old Slavonic liturgy continues to be celebrated in the tradition of the missionaries St Cyril and St Methodius *(see p33)*.

Nearly every town in Central Bohemia has an historic town centre. The old silver-mining town of Kutná Hora has over 300 excellently preserved buildings from the Middle Ages and the Baroque eras.

In a region of many castles, the most famous is undoubtedly Karlštejn – an imposing Gothic fortress built by Emperor Charles IV to house the crown jewels and religious relics. More recent history is reflected at Konopiště Castle, owned by the Archduke Franz Ferdinand. Many of the castles are set on craggy hilltops, and some of the more beautiful rock formations of the area can be seen at Český Kras, not far from Karlštejn. This fertile region also has a wine-growing area around the historic town of Mělník.

The formal Baroque façade of Dobříš Palace

◁ Křivoklát Castle, overlooked by a monument to Joseph Fürstenberk, one of the castle's former owners

Exploring Central Bohemia

For those on a short visit to the Czech Republic, the central part of the Bohemian Basin provides an excellent cross-section of all the attractions that this beautiful country has to offer. Within an hour's journey, or certainly a day trip, from Prague are a variety of spectacular castles. Karlštejn, with its turrets and towers and immaculate interiors, is one of the most-visited places in the country; it has some interesting walking trails nearby. Other, less-visited, castles, such as Křivoklát and Kokořín, offer quieter opportunities for exploration. The town of Kutná Hora, with its atmospheric old centre and Gothic Cathedral of St Barbara, is also hugely popular. Superb Renaissance buildings can be seen in Nelahozeves, and Dobříš Palace is a Baroque treasure.

Schwarzenberg coat of arms made of bones, Sedlec ossuary, Kutná Hora

SEE ALSO

• **Where to Stay** pp349–50

• **Where to Eat** pp378–9

KEY

═══ Motorway

──── Main road

····· Minor road

──•── Main railway

──── Minor railway

──── Regional border

KOKOŘÍN CASTLE
Teplice
MĚLNÍK **8**
VELTRUSY CHATEAU **9**
NELAHOZEVES **10**
Neratovice
Kralupy nad Vltavou
Slaný
Řevničov
Nové Strašecí
Kladno
Rakovník
LÁNY **11**
← Karlovy Vary
PRAGUE
HLAVNÍ MĚSTO PRAHA
KŘIVOKLÁT CASTLE **12**
Loděnice
Beroun
Velká Amerika
Zbraslav
Zdice
ČESKÝ KRAS **14**
KARLŠTEJN CASTLE **15**
TOČNÍK CASTLE **13**
Koněpruské Caves
STŘEDOČESK
Hořovice
Mníšek p. Brdy
Sázava
Plzeň
DOBŘÍŠ PALACE **16**
Týn nad S
Jince
Dubno
PŘÍBRAM **17**
Obory
18
Sedlčany

Svatá Horá Church above the mining town of Příbram

GETTING AROUND

The capital provides a convenient starting point
for exploring the sights of Central Bohemia. The
local transport network is well developed and
reliable. Railway lines offer regular services north
through Mělník and Mladá Boleslav, east through
Kolín and Kutná Hora, south via Konopiště and
west to Karlštejn and Křivoklát. Buses from
Prague and between towns also serve the
region well.

**Entrance to the grounds of
Sázava Monastery**

SIGHTS AT A GLANCE

Benátky nad Jizerou ④
Český Kras ⑭
Dobříš Palace ⑯
Karlštejn Castle pp132–3 ⑮
Kokořín Castle ⑦
Kolín ②
Konopiště Castle ⑱
Křivoklát Castle ⑫
Kutná Hora pp122–3 ①
Lány ⑪
Mělník ⑧
Mladá Boleslav ⑤
Mnichovo Hradiště Palace ⑥
Nelahozeves ⑩
Poděbrady ③
Příbram ⑰
Sázava Monastery ⑲
Sternberg Castle ⑳
Točník Castle ⑬
Veltrusy Chateau ⑨

| 0 km | 20 |
| 0 miles | 20 |

The imposing Hall of Mirrors in Dobříš Palace

Kutná Hora ●

A rich source of silver from the 13th to the 18th centuries, Kutná Hora (Kuttenberg) was the second most important town in Bohemia, after Prague. Its wealth funded many beautiful buildings, including St Barbara's Cathedral; the Italian Court (Vlašský Dvůr), which housed the royal mint and later the town hall; the 14th-century Gothic Church of St James (sv. Jakub); and the 15th-century Stone House (Kamenný Dům). Since 1995 the historic centre of Kutná Hora has been on the UNESCO Cultural Heritage List. Three km (2 miles) northeast of the centre is the suburb of Sedlec, home to an extraordinary ossuary where bones accumulated over centuries were put together by carver František Rint in 1870 to form crosses, a coat of arms and even a chandelier.

Cathedral's Front Façade
In 1388 Peter Parler planned this five-aisled building, with three tented spires. The last architectural additions were in the late 19th century.

★ Vault
The central nave with its magnificent geometric vaulted ceiling was designed in the early 16th century by Benedikt Ried. It incorporates coats of arms from local craft guilds.

Organ
The Baroque organ case dating from 1740–60 hides a much newer mechanism installed in the early 20th century by the local organmaker Jan Tuček.

ST BARBARA'S CATHEDRAL

Dedicated to the patron saint of miners, St Barbara's Cathedral (sv. Barbora) is one of Europe's most spectacular Gothic churches. Both the interior and exterior are richly ornamented, and the huge windows ensure it is filled with light. Many of the side chapels are decorated with interesting frescoes, some of which depict miners at work and men striking coins in the mint, reflecting the sources of the town's wealth.

STAR FEATURES

★ High Altar

★ Vault

Pulpit
The pulpit dating from 1655 is decorated with four stone reliefs produced in 1566 by Master Leopold, depicting the four Evangelists.

Oak Stalls
The late 15th-century stalls, originally designed for St Vitus's Cathedral in Prague, feature Gothic spired canopies and carved balustrades.

Stained-glass Window
The Art Nouveau stained-glass windows designed by František Urban were added in the early 20th century.

★ High Altar
The central scene of the Neo-Gothic high altar (1901–5), a replica of the original, depicts the Last Supper.

Balustrade
The stone balustrade of the presbytery includes the initials of King Vladislav Jagiello ("W") and his son Ludwig ("L").

Sgraffito in the courtyard of the castle in Benátky nad Jizerou

Kolín ❷

Road map B2. 🏛 *30,000.* 🚃 *from Prague.* 🚉 *from Prague.* 🚌 *Na Hradbách 157.* **Tel/Fax** *321 712 021.*

Founded in the 13th century by German colonists, the town of Kolín centres around the **Charles Square** (Karlovo náměstí). On the western side of the square is the **town hall** (radnice), originally Gothic, and rebuilt in the 19th century in the Neo-Renaissance style.

Kolín's dominant feature is its Early Gothic **Church of St Bartholomew** (sv. Bartoloměj), begun in 1261. The choir of this triple-aisled basilica is by Peter Parler – builder of St Vitus's Cathedral in Prague. In the **Regional Museum**, an exhibition details the battle fought nearby on 18 June 1757 during the Seven Years' War between Britain and France.

Arms of Kolín on its town hall

🏛 **Regional Museum**
Brandlova 27. **Tel** *321 723 841.*
○ *Tue–Sun.*

Poděbrady ❸

Road map B2. 🏛 *14,000.* 🚃 🚉 *from Prague.* 🚌 *from Prague.* 🚌 *Jiřího náměstí 1/1.* **Tel** *325 612 505.*

Strategically located on the Labe (Elbe) river on the trade route linking Prague with East Bohemia, Silesia and Poland, Poděbrady was built in the mid-12th century. George of Poděbrady (Jiří z Poděbrad) was elected the King of Bohemia in 1458.

The town's oldest historic sight is **Poděbrady Castle**. Begun in the second half of the 13th century and altered many times since, it is not particularly attractive architecturally, but its magnificent location on the riverbank and its Gothic tower topped by a Baroque cupola – the town's symbol – make it worth visiting. The castle chapel with its traces of medieval frescoes houses an exhibition on King George.

In 1905 the town's life changed when a German dowser, von Bülow, discovered a local source of mineral water and Poděbrady became famous as a spa. Its waters still draw many visitors.

⛪ **Poděbrady Castle**
Tel *325 612 640.* ○ *May–Oct: Tue–Sun.* 🌐 www.polabskemuzeum.cz

Benátky nad Jizerou ❹

Road map B2. 🏛 *6,800.* 🚃 *from Prague.*

With a name that translates as Venice (Benátky) on the Jizera, this town was founded in the mid-13th century, on the flood-prone River Jizera. Its main historic sight is the **Castle**, built in 1526–7. A particularly striking element of its decor is the 16th-century Renaissance *sgraffito* on the courtyard façade. In 1599 Emperor Rudolph II bought the estate and allowed the castle to be used by his court astronomer and alchemist Tycho Brahe, who built a small observatory and laboratory here, where he produced an elixir against plague. It was also here that Brahe met with another famous star-gazer, Johannes Kepler, in 1600. The castle acquired its Baroque form in the 18th century.

⛪ **Benátky nad Jizerou Castle**
Tel *326 316 595.* ○ *Jun–Oct: Tue–Sun.* 🌐

Poděbrady Castle, on the Labe

Mladá Boleslav ➎

Road map B2. 43,500. 2 km (1 mile). *from Prague.* Železná 107. **Tel** 326 322 173.

Famed as the home of Škoda cars, Mladá Boleslav (Jungblunzau) is dominated by a vast four-storey **Castle**. It stands on the site of a former Přemyslid stronghold, which was established here in the late 10th century. The present heavy silhouette is the result of its mid-18th-century conversion into army barracks. Traces of the Renaissance style can still be glimpsed in the arcaded courtyard. The castle is now the home of the local museum.

More interesting is the permanent archaeological exhibition in the Gothic Temple Palace in the town square, with its display of local finds. The Protestant **Church of Bohemian Unitas Fratrum** (Unity of Bohemian Brethren) at 123 Českobratrské Náměstí, dating from 1544–54, now an art gallery, is a reminder of the town's former prominence as a centre of Reformation in the 16th century.

In the northern district of town is the interesting **Škoda Museum** with its exhibition of motorcycles and cars that have been produced here since the early 20th century.

⛪ **Mladá Boleslav Castle**
Tel 326 322 542. Tue–Sun.

🏛 **Škoda Museum**
V Klementa 294. **Tel** 326 831 134. daily. www.skoda-auto.com

Mnichovo Hradiště Palace ➏

Road map B2. *from Prague.* *from Prague.* **Tel** 326 773 098. Jan–Mar: by appt; Apr, Oct: 8:45am–3pm Sat, Sun, public hols; May–Sep: 8:45am–4pm Tue–Sun. www.mnichovo-hradiste.cz

This Renaissance palace, built in about 1606 by Václav Budovec of Budov, is in the industrial town of Mnichovo Hradiště (Münchengrätz). Following the Battle of the White Mountain in 1620 (*see p39*), its owner – one of the leaders of the anti-Habsburg

The castle in Mladá Boleslav, now a museum

insurrection – was beheaded and his confiscated estate passed to Count Albrecht von Wallenstein. Mnichovo Hradiště remained in the Wallenstein family until the mid-20th century.

The present Baroque form of the palace is due to extensive rebuilding at the turn of the 17th and 18th centuries. The opulent interiors are furnished with Baroque and Rococo furniture. The ceiling in the main hall of the palace has a particularly striking fresco.

The court theatre, which opened in 1833, is unusual in that it still has many of its original costumes and stage settings. The palace Chapel of St Anne is Albrecht von Wallenstein's final resting place. After his murder in 1634, his body was taken to the monastery at Valdice, near his centre of power in Jičín (*see p207*). It was moved here in 1785 near to the body of his first wife.

Kokořín Castle ➐

Road map B2. *from Mělník.* **Tel** 315 695 064. May–Sep: 9am–4pm Tue–Sun; Apr, Oct: 9am–noon, 1–3pm Sat, Sun, public hols. Nov–Mar: by appt. www.hrad-kokorin.cz

In a region of forests and sandstone rocks lies Kokořín Castle, notable for its spectacular 38-m (125-ft) tall tower, which offers a sweeping panorama. Built in the 14th century, the castle suffered severe damage in the 15th century during the Hussite Wars and was later abandoned. The Špaček family restored it in the early 20th century. Its ruins inspired many 19th-century painters and poets, including the Czech Romantic poet Karel Hynek Mácha (1810–36). The understated castle rooms house exhibits relating to its history.

A sculpture from Kokořín Castle

ŠKODA

The bicycle and motorcycle manufacturers Laurin and Klement made their first motor car in Mladá Boleslav in 1905. Named Voiturette, it had a 1-litre, 7-HP engine and cruising speed of 45 km/h (28 mph). They continued to develop and improve on their models, and, in a quest for the means to expand, they merged with the existing Škoda company in the 1920s. This highly successful company became synonymous with the Czech motor industry. Since 1991 Škoda Auto has belonged to the Volkswagen Group of Companies.

A 1937 Škoda Rapid II

The fountain in Mělník's market square

Mělník ⓧ

Road map B2. 🏛 *19,500.* 🚗 🚌
from Prague. 🅷 *Náměstí Míru 11.*
Tel *315 627 503.* **www**.melnik.cz

Perched high on an escarpment, surrounded by vine-
yards, Mělník lies at the confluence of the two biggest
Czech rivers, the Labe (Elbe)
and the Vltava. The town
centres on its market square
(Náměstí Míru), dominated by
the Renaissance town hall
(radnice) with its clock tower.
The Baroque arcaded houses
around the square have vast
cellars that were used for
storing wine. The town has
been a wine-producing centre
since the 14th century, and
the square's fountain
commemorates that heritage.
    The Gothic **Church of St
Peter and St Paul** (sv. Petr a
Pavel) is a conspicuous
structure, with its tall onion-
domed tower. Inside, a beautiful vault and an interesting
ossuary can be viewed.
    The Lobkowicz family **Castle**
is a vast edifice adjacent to
the church, its walls covered
with some of the oldest
sgraffito in Bohemia, dating
from 1533. Inside is an impressive array of Czech Baroque
art including works by Jan
Kupecký *(see p24)*, Karel
Škréta and Petr Brandl. The
paintings are hung in well-
restored castle rooms, including the grand bedchamber and
the study of the Chancellor
George Christian. The castle's
vast 14th-century three-level
wine cellars occupy over
1,500 sq m (16,000 sq ft).
Here you can see lavishly
decorated old wine casks,

and also sample some of the
wines produced in Mělník.

♠ **Mělník Castle**
Svatováclavská 19. **Tel** *315 622
121.* ◯ *daily.* 📷 🎟
www.lobkowicz-melnik.cz

Veltrusy Chateau ⓧ

Road map B2. 4 km (2 miles) N of
Kralupy nad Vltavou. 🚗 🚌 *from
Prague.* **Tel** *315 781 146.* ◯ *May–
Sep: 9–11am, 1–4pm Tue–Sun.* 📷 🚫

Built during the first half of
the 18th century by the
aristocratic Chotek family, the
château was designed by
František Kaňka. Its floor plan
is in the shape of a cross,
with a domed rotunda at the
centre. Inside are interesting
Baroque and Empire-style
decorations and furnishings,
including inlaid Dutch
furniture, Chinese, Japanese
and Viennese porcelain and
Dutch decorated earthenware.
    The main attraction of the
château is, however, its vast
English-style park, one of the
best-preserved in Europe. It
occupies nearly 300 ha (750
acres) and was established in

Pavilion of the Friends of Villages
and Gardens in Veltrusy Park

1764–85. Its creator, Rihard
van der Schott, who created
the imperial gardens in Vienna,
took advantage of the watery
conditions that existed on the
banks of this stretch of the
Vltava river. Numerous
pavilions in Classical and
Romantic styles were built
from 1792 to 1830 amid
meadows, ponds and canals.
Attractions include the Doric
Pavilion; the Pavilion of the
Friends of Villages and
Gardens; the Egyptian Cabinet;
a bridge with the sphinx
inspired by Napoleon's Egypt
expedition; the Empire-style
Pavilion of Maria Theresa and
the Neo-Gothic Red Mill.
    In 2002 Veltrusy suffered cat-
astrophic flooding and is now
being restored. Only the park
is partially open to visitors.

Nelahozeves ⓧ

Road map B2. 🏛 *1,200.*
🚗 🚌 *from Prague.*

The village of Nelahozeves
is the birthplace of the
composer Antonín Dvořák *(see
pp22–3)*. Today the modest
building where he was born,
opposite the church, houses
a small **museum**.
    Nelahozeves has a
huge Renaissance
Castle, which since
1623 has belonged to
the Lobkowicz family.
In 1950 the estate was
nationalized by the
Communists, but in
1992 it was returned
to the family. The
courtyard façades are
decorated with beauti-
ful *sgraffito*. Inside are

Sgraffito on the castle in Nelahozeves

original wooden coffered ceilings with stucco decorations. The **Roudnice Lobkowicz Collection**, the largest private art collection in the country, includes paintings by Rubens, Breughel and Veronese, as well as porcelain and furniture. There are also impressive music archives and a library. A new exhibition, entitled *Private Spaces*, explores the life of the Lobkowicz family.

Dvořák's Birthplace
Tel 315 785 099. Apr–Sep: Sat, Sun (closed 1st weekend in month).

Castle and Roudnice Lobkowicz Collection
Tel 315 709 121. Tue–Sun.

Lány ⓫

Road map B2. 1,600.
from Prague to Stochov (2 km/1 mile). *Tel 313 502 078.*

In 1929 Slovenian architect Josip Plečnik remodelled the Renaissance **Palace** in the village of Lány into the summer residence of the president of the Czech Republic. Its first occupant was Tomáš Garrigue Masaryk *(see p44)*, the first democratically elected President, and a highly popular figure, who was buried in the village cemetery in 1937. The palace is not open, but it is worth exploring its beautiful **park**. The former Baroque granary now houses the **Tomáš G Masaryk Museum** of the former president's life.

Lány Park
Apr–Oct: Wed, Thu, Sat, Sun.

Masaryk Museum
Tel 313 502 450. May–Oct: daily.

The vast Royal Hall in Křivoklát Castle

Křivoklát Castle ⓬

Road map B2. 13 km (8 miles) SE of Rakovník. from Prague. *Tel 313 558 120.* Mar: 9am–noon, 1–3pm Sat, Sun; Apr–Oct: 9am–noon, 1–3pm Tue–Sun (May, Sep: to 4pm; Jun–Aug: to 5pm); Nov, Dec: 9am–3pm Sat, Sun.
www.krivoklat.cz

Built in the mid-13th century by Přemysl Otakar II, Křivoklát (Pürglitz) was the childhood home of Emperor Charles IV. From 1493 to 1522 it was remodelled by King Vladislav Jagiello and his son Ludwig. Lying in a beautiful area of woodland, the castle is dominated by its 42-m (130-ft) cylindrical Great Tower. This adjoins the red roofs and spires of the three-wing palace and chapel. The most beautiful interior is that of the Royal Hall with its star-spangled vault, the second-largest room of its type in Bohemia, after the Vladislav Hall in Prague Castle.

Relief from Křivoklát Castle

Točník Castle ⓭

Road map B2. 15 km (9 miles) SW of Beroun. from Prague via Beroun or Zdice. *Tel 311 533 202.* Mar, Apr, Oct: 10am–noon, 1–4pm Sat, Sun; May, Jun, Sep: 10am–noon, 1–5pm Tue–Sun; Jul, Aug: 9am–noon, 1–6pm Tue–Sun.
www.tocnik.com

Točník was one of the last castles to be built in Bohemia during the Middle Ages, commissioned in about 1394 by Wenceslas IV as a new royal residence following the fire which destroyed the nearby Žebrak Castle. In the 16th century Točník was remodelled in Renaissance style. After the Thirty Years' War it was abandoned. Now, although partly ruined, it still provides a rare example in Bohemia of the monumental architecture of the turn of the 14th and 15th centuries. The mighty, five-storey edifice of the royal palace can be seen from afar.

The red roofs of the village of Lány at sunset

The Velká Amerika gorge, Český Kras

Český Kras ⓐ

Road map B2. 🚌 to Beroun.

The land around Karlštejn
and along the banks of the
Berounka river, southwest of
Prague, known as the Český
Kras, or Bohemian Karst, is
the largest karst region in
Bohemia, made up of
picturesque limestone
formations. At over 800 m
(2,600 ft) long, the
Koněpruské Caves, 5 km
(3 miles) south of Beroun, are
the largest cave system in the
republic open to visitors.

Between the towns of
Mořina and Kozulupy, about
5 km (3 miles) north of
Karlštejn, is one of the most
extraordinary sights of the
Český Kras. The disused and
now flooded quarry known
as **Velká Amerika** (Great
America) has provided
dramatic settings for
numerous Western films.

Along the road that links
Loděnice with Srbsko is the
village of **Sv. Jan pod Skalou**
(St John by the Rock). Set in a
ravine, at the foot of a mighty
crag, is the Baroque Church
of the Nativity of St John the
Baptist (Narození Jana Křtitele),
built by Carlo Lurago in 1657.
From inside the church there
is access to three travertine
caves – the site of a cult of St
Ivan, a 9th-century hermit.

📌 **Koněpruské Caves**
Tel 311 622 405. ◻ Apr–Oct: daily.
◻ 🖾 http://jeskyne.cesky-kras.cz

Karlštejn Castle ⓑ

See pp132–3.

Dobříš Palace ⓒ

Road map B3. 23km (14 miles) SW
of Prague. 🚌 from Prague. **Tel** 318
521 240. ◻ Apr, May: 8:30am–5pm
daily; Jun–Oct: 8am–5:30pm daily;
Nov–Mar: 8:30am–4pm daily. 🖾 🖾
www.zamekdobris.cz

This Rococo palace was
built in 1745–65. The owner
of the estate, Jindřich Pavel
Mansfeld, commissioned
French architect Jules de
Cotte and Italian interior
designer G N Servadoni to
prepare the design. The
palace remained in the hands
of the Colloredo-Mansfeld
family until 1942 when it was
confiscated by the Nazi
authorities and turned into a
residence for the German
Reich Protector. Nationalized
by the Communists, it was

returned to its former owners
after 1989. Now it charms
visitors with its restored
interiors, which are furnished
in a combination of late
Baroque, Rococo and Neo-
Classical styles.

The French garden, one
of the most beautiful in the
Czech Republic, is set out on
five levels and featuring a
huge cascading fountain.

Příbram ⓓ

Road map B3. 👥 35,300.
🚊 🚌 from Prague.

Founded in the 13th
century, the town of Příbram
(Pribrans) was famous for its
mines, which over the
centuries yielded some 3.6
million tons of silver, as well
as lead and antimony. In the
country's biggest **Mining
Museum** (Hornické muzeum),
in the district of Březové
Hory, in the disused mine of
Ševčínský důl, visitors can
take a ride on an under-
ground train along a 300-m
(1,000-ft) section of the mine,
at a depth of 1,600 m (5,250
ft). The mine's ornate early
19th-century pithead has been
listed as a UNESCO World
Industrial Heritage site.

On top of a hill above the
town is **Svatá Hora** (Holy
Mountain), the Marian
Sanctuary, once the biggest
and most famous pilgrimage
site in the entire Austro-
Hungarian Empire. Built by
Carlo Lurago in 1658–75 on
the site of an earlier Gothic
church, the Early Baroque
complex has a church with
vivid frescoes depicting the
Sanctuary's history.

The palace in Dobříš from the gardens

◁ Winter scene at Sternberg Castle

🏛 **Mining Museum**
Tel *318 626 307.* ⬤ *Nov–Mar:*
Tue–Fri; Apr–Oct: Tue–Sun.

Underground exhibition
⬤ *Apr–Oct: as museum;*
Nov–Mar: by appt Tue–Sun. 📷 📹

⛪ **Church of Svatá Hora**
Tel *318 626 351.* ⬤ *daily.*

**Hunting trophies in the corridors
of Konopiště Castle**

Konopiště Castle ⑱

Road map B3. 2 km (1 mile) W of
Benešov. 🚆 🚌 to Benešov. *Tel* *317
721 366.* ⬤ *Apr, Oct: 9am–12:30pm,
1–3pm Tue–Sun (to 4pm Sat & Sun);
May–Sep: 9am–12:30pm, 1–5pm
Tue–Sun; Nov: 9am–3pm Sat, Sun, by
appt Tue–Fri.* 📷 📹 *3 routes.* 🖥

One of the most popular
tourist sites in the Czech
Republic, Konopiště Castle
belonged to the heir to the
Austrian throne, Franz
Ferdinand. The Gothic
castle has richly furnished
apartments, a collection of
Late Gothic paintings in the
chapel, and a gallery of the
Archduke's artefacts relating
to the cult of St George. It
also houses a famous
collection of the weapons of
Franz Ferdinand, including
items produced by the best
armourer and gunsmith
workshops in Europe. But
many visitors are particularly
amazed by the Crown Prince's
collection of about 300,000
hunting trophies: countless
antlers and stuffed animals
line the corridors and
numerous rooms of the castle.
Three tour routes explore the
different collections
    The huge park of 225 ha
(555 acres) contains a

The Austrian Archduke Franz
Ferdinand bought Konopiště in
1887. For the Archduke,
criticized by the Habsburg Court
for marrying a Bohemian
noblewoman Sophie Chotek, the
castle was a refuge from the
hostilities of Viennese society.
Franz Ferdinand lived in his
Bohemian home until his death
alongside his wife at the hands
of an assassin in Sarajevo – the
event that led to the outbreak of
World War I in 1914.

terraced garden, many
statues, a deer park, a lake
and a superb rose garden.

Sázava Monastery ⑲

Road map B2. 18 km (11 miles) SE of
Benešov. 🚆 🚌 from Prague. *Tel* *327
321 177.* ⬤ *May–Aug: 9am–5pm
Tue–Sun; Sep: 9am–4pm Tue–Sun;
Apr, Oct: 9am–3pm Sat, Sun, public
hols; by appt Tue–Fri.* 📷 📹
www.klaster-sazava.cz

Founded in 1032, this
Benedictine monastery has
remained a centre of the
Slavonic liturgy, and to this
day every Sunday an Old
Slavonic liturgy mass is celebrated here. A new church
was started in 1315, but only
the tower and a wall of one
of the naves, with high Gothic
windows, were completed;
these remain today. The
original frescoes in the church
date from the time of Charles
IV and include unusual images
of the life of the Virgin Mary.

Sternberg Castle ⑳

Road map B2. Český Šternberk. 🚆
🚌 from Prague to Český Šternberk
zastávka. *Tel* *317 855 101.* ⬤ *Apr
& Oct: 9am–5pm Sat, Sun, public
hols; May–Sep: 9am–5pm Tue–Sun
(Jun–Aug: to 6pm); last adm 45 mins
before closing. All year: groups of
10 and over by appt daily.* 📷 📹

The sprawling edifice on
top of a high cliff above the
Sázava river valley is a truly
impressive sight. The early
Gothic castle erected on this
site in the mid-13th century
by the Sternberg (Šternberk)
family was captured and
destroyed by the army of King
George of Poděbrady in 1467.
At the turn of the 15th and 16th
centuries the owners restored
the demolished walls and
extended the fortifications. The
17th-century Baroque interiors
contain some striking Italian
stucco work, especially in the
Knights' Hall. Some of the
rooms house displays of engravings and historic weapons.

View of Sternberg Castle above the Sázava river

For hotels and restaurants in this region see pp349–50 and pp378–9

Karlštejn Castle ⑮

This imposing Gothic castle is one of the most frequently visited historic sites in the Czech Republic. It was built for the Holy Roman Emperor Charles IV in 1348 as a royal residence and a treasury where imperial insignia and crown jewels as well as documents, works of art and holy relics were stored. In the 16th century Karlštejn (Karlstein) was remodelled in Renaissance style. The castle owes its present form to the restoration work carried out in the 19th century, mainly by Josef Mocker, who returned the building to its original appearance. At that time the castle was given its ridge roofs as a typical feature of medieval architecture.

Grand Tower

★ **Holy Cross Chapel**
The walls of the Holy Cross chapel are hung with a unique collection of 129 portraits of saints and monarchs – works of Master Theodoric, court painter to Charles IV.

Voršilka Tower Gate
The Voršilka Tower was once the castle's main entrance. Now the entrance is via the gate below the Tower, and along the former moat.

The first floor of the Grand Tower features two rooms, which in the 19th century were turned into a museum with a collection of pictures depicting Karlštejn and other castles.

The Well Tower
The Well Tower is situated at the lowest point of the castle complex. Inside is an old wooden treadwheel for hauling water, operated by two people.

STAR FEATURES

★ Holy Cross Chapel

★ St Mary's Tower

For hotels and restaurants in this region see pp349–50 and pp378–9

★ St Mary's Tower
One of the paintings in the church of St Mary depicts Charles IV receiving two thorns from the crown of Jesus from the French Dauphin, Charles.

VISITORS' CHECKLIST

Road map B2. 🚆 *from Prague (30-min walk from stn to Karlštejn).* **Tel** 274 008 154. ⏱ *9am–noon, 1–3pm Tue–Sun (May, Jun, Sep: to 5pm; Jul, Aug to 6pm).* **Chapel** ⬤ *Nov–May.* 📷 🎫 *2 routes (reservation compulsory for route II).* **www**.hradkarlstejn.cz

St Catherine's Chapel
Used as a place of meditation by Charles IV, this tiny chapel has walls that are richly decorated with paintings and semi-precious stones.

Madonna Statue
The 14th-century marble statue of the Madonna, in the royal bedchamber, belonged to King Charles IV.

The Imperial Palace's first floor was used by courtiers; the second by the Emperor himself for private and official functions.

Vassals' Hall of the Imperial Palace
A striking feature of the Vassals' Hall is the late Gothic altarpiece from St Palmatius's Church in the village of Budňany at the foot of Karlštejn Castle.

SOUTH BOHEMIA

Wooded hills and spreading meadows characterize much of South Bohemia, while in the flatter, central area around Třeboň hundreds of glittering medieval fish ponds, still used for raising carp, can be seen. The backbone of the region is the Vltava river. This rises in the Šumava Mountains to the southwest, a remarkably unspoilt area of dense forests and tiny villages.

In the 13th century several fortified towns were established in South Bohemia (Jižní Čechy), with the aim of defending the king's rule. The foremost of them, České Budějovice, is now the region's capital and source of Budvar, the famous local beer.

The deciding influence on the life of South Bohemia in the Middle Ages was often exerted by two powerful aristocratic families – the Rožmberks (Rosenbergs) and the lords of Hradec. Both built numerous castles and fortified towns, known as "Rose Towns" after the red rose of the Rožmberks and the black rose of the Hradecs. Český Krumlov, owned by the Rožmberk family is the region's top tourist destination for the picture-postcard perfection of its old town and its fascinating castle, but many other historic towns, such as Jindřichův Hradec and Třeboň are equally rich in well-preserved buildings.

South Bohemia played a prominent role in the history of the Hussite movement. Tábor became the main centre of the more radical faction of the religious reformers who strongly opposed the 15th-century social conditions.

In the 17th century the Bavarian Schwarzenberg family achieved great power in the region. It is to them that the fortress in Hluboká nad Vltavou, the most frequently visited castle in this part of the country, owes its fairy-tale Neo-Gothic form. One of the most magnificent collections of Late Gothic art is found here in the Aleš South Bohemian Gallery.

Boubín forests, the last remaining virgin backwoods of Šumava, southwest Bohemia

◁ Decorated towers of the Castle and the Church of St Justus in Český Krumlov

Exploring South Bohemia

The historic sights of South Bohemia, its magnificent scenery and its opportunities for hiking and canoeing satisfy a wide range of interests. The architectural variety is astonishing as well-preserved grand squares and churches jostle for attention with the traditional architecture of Holašovice. Individual buildings stand out: the fairy-tale castle in Hluboká, for example, with its bristling turrets, and the vast, soaring cooling towers of the Temelín power station. In the southern part of the region, along the border with Austria, runs the Šumava mountain range. It is worth making time to explore the Vltava river and its villages, not forgetting to sample the local beers in any of the many Bohemian beer halls.

Coat of arms above the entrance to Hluboká Castle

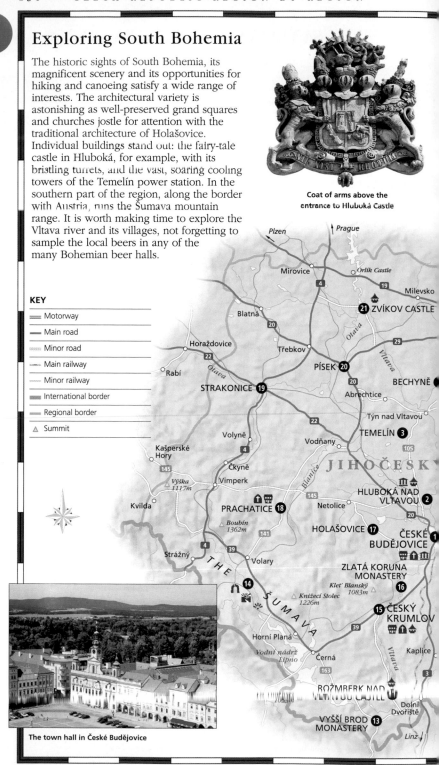

KEY

▬▬	Motorway
▬▬	Main road
▪▪▪	Minor road
▬▬	Main railway
----	Minor railway
▬▬	International border
▬▬	Regional border
△	Summit

Plzeň

Prague

Mirovice

Orlík Castle

Milevsko

21 ZVÍKOV CASTLE

Blatná

Horažďovice

Třebkov

PÍSEK 20

BECHYNĚ

Rabí

Otava

STRAKONICE 19

Abrechtice

Týn nad Vltavou

TEMELÍN 3

Volyně

Vodňany

Kašperské Hory

Čkyně

JIHOČESK

Výška 1117m

Vimperk

HLUBOKÁ NAD VLTAVOU 2

Netolice

Kvilda

PRACHATICE 18

Boubín 1362m

HOLAŠOVICE 17

ČESKÉ BUDĚJOVICE 1

Strážný

Volary

ZLATÁ KORUNA MONASTERY 16

Klet' Blanský 1083m

THE

14

Knížecí Stolec 1226m

ČESKÝ KRUMLOV 15

Š U M A V A

Horní Planá

Kaplice

Vodní nádrž Lipno

Černá

ROŽMBERK NAD VLTAVOU CASTLE

Dolní Dvořiště

VYŠŠÍ BROD MONASTERY 13

Linz

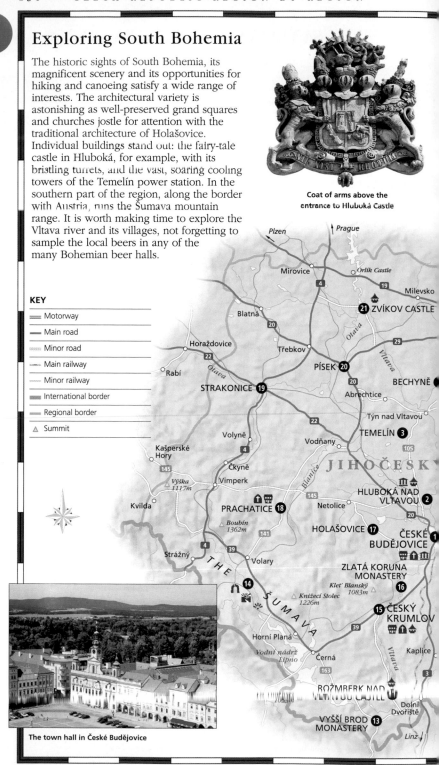

The town hall in České Budějovice

SIGHTS AT A GLANCE

SEE ALSO

GETTING AROUND

The main transport artery of the region is the north-south highway 3 linking Prague with Linz in Austria. The capital of South Bohemia – České Budějovice – is linked by a network of local buses with all the neighbouring towns. Buses provide fast and relatively frequent access to most parts of the region. Trains serve much of the region, even mountainous areas, although routes may take a little planning. Check the frequency of buses and trains during weekends and public holidays.

The frescoed Grand Hall at Bechyně Castle

České Budějovice ❶

Founded by Přemysl Otakar II in 1265, the town of České Budějovice (Budweis) fast became the stronghold of the king's power in South Bohemia. As early as the 13th and 14th centuries it had two magnificent churches and mighty town walls. Spared by the Thirty Years' War, it was subsequently destroyed by the great fire of 1641. Today, the capital of South Bohemia is an important industrial centre, not least for its internationally renowned Budvar Brewery.

Náměstí Přemysla Otakara II – one of Europe's largest squares

Exploring the Town

The town's well-preserved historic centre lies on a peninsula created at the confluence of the rivers Vltava, Malše and Mlýnská stoka. It has maintained its original layout with a central square and surrounding streets in a grid pattern. Most sights are within this compact central area.

🏛 Náměstí Přemysla Otakara II

The town square bears the name of the town's founder. Measuring 133 x 133 m (436 x 436 ft), the huge square is surrounded by arcaded houses built mostly during the Middle Ages, and now – after numerous alterations by their German owners – with Renaissance and Baroque façades. At the square's centre stands the Baroque Samson's Fountain, built in 1727, with a sculpture of Samson and the lion. It was produced by Josef Dietrich, and for a while it was the only source of water for the town's population. Look out for cobblestones laid in 1934 in a distinctive pattern of large squares.

Coat of arms on the town hall

🏛 Town Hall

Náměstí Přemysla Otakara II. **Tel** 386 801 413. 🕐 **Tours:** Jul & Aug: 10am, 2pm, 4pm Mon–Fri; 10am, 2pm Sat, Sun; May, Jun, Sep: 2pm daily. 🏷🎫

The southwest corner of the town square is occupied by a Baroque, white and blue town hall (radnice) with three towers, built by Antonio Martinelli in 1727–30 to replace a Renaissance building. Allegorical statues of Providence, Justice, Wisdom and Honesty stand on the roof. On top of the tallest tower is a statue of the Czech lion, and on the left side is the medieval standard ell measure (the "forearm") used when measuring cloth. The Debating Hall features *The Judgement of Solomon* (1730) by Jan Adam Schöpf.

🔒 Dominican Monastery and Church of the Sacrifice of the Virgin

Piaristické náměstí. 🕐 10am–5pm daily.

Built at the same time as the founding of České Budějovice, and altered by Peter Parler in the 14th century, is this interesting former monastery.

Inside the church (Kostel Obětování Panny Marie), cross-rib vaulting can be seen. The furnishing is mostly Neo-Gothic, but there is also a spectacular Rococo pulpit dating from 1759, and 17th-century organs. The large stone amphibian seen on the side wall by the church entrance, is a reminder of the local legend about the creature, who was guarding the treasure supposedly hidden on the site, and tried to prevent the start of the church building. The Gothic cloister also has two original tracery windows that are lovely examples of medieval stonemasonry work.

🏛 Butchers' Market

Krajinská 13.

The Renaissance butchers' market (Masné krámy) now houses a restaurant. On its top are three stone masks, and the year of building: 1531.

🏛 Black Tower

U Černé věže. **Tel** 386 801 413. 🕐 Apr–Jun, Sep, Oct: noon–6pm Tue–Sun; Jul, Aug: 10am–6pm daily. 🏷

Standing next to St Nicholas's Cathedral is the Gothic-Renaissance Black Tower (Černa věž) dating from 1577, formerly serving as a belfry and the town's observation tower. In 1723 two bells were placed in the belfry; in 1995 a third bell was added – Budvar – presented to the town by the nearby brewery. The

The three-towered façade of the town hall

View of the Black Tower and town square with Samson's fountain

reward for climbing the 225 winding stairs to the top at a height of 72 m (236 ft), is the magnificent panorama.

St Nicholas's Cathedral

U Černé věže.

On a small plot at the north-eastern corner of the town square is St Nicholas's Cathedral (Chrám sv. Mikuláše). This triple-aisled edifice started as a church in the 13th century. The original Gothic building burned down in 1641 and was rebuilt a few years later in the Baroque style. Inside, take a look at the pulpit and an interesting

1740 painting *Death of the Virgin Mary* in the south chapel; also at the main altarpiece by Leopold Huber (1791).

South Bohemia Museum

Dukelská 1. *Tel* 387 929 311.
◯ 9am–12:30pm & 1–5pm Tue–Sun. **www**.muzeumcb.cz
Established in 1887, this museum (Jihočeské muzeum) is the oldest of its kind in South Bohemia. It houses a natural science collection, regional exhibits and 16th–18th-century art.

Železná Panna

Zátkovo nábřeží.
This tower, erected in the 14th century, was used as a prison

Painting from a house (No. 140) close to Železná Panna

VISITORS' CHECKLIST

Road map B3. 👥 99,700.
🚋 Novohradská 393.
🚌 Žižkova 32.
🛈 Náměstí Přemysla Otakara II 2.
Tel 386 801 413.
www.c-budejovice.cz
🎭 City Hall Summer (Festival of Music and Theatre): Jul–Aug.

and torture chamber. Its name translates as "Iron Maiden" after the instrument of torture (and death) used here whose shape resembled a woman.

Motorcycle Museum

Piaristické náměstí. *Tel* 387 200 849
◯ Mar–Oct: 9am–5pm Wed–Sun.
The small motorcycle museum (Motocyclové muzeum) housed in the former Salt House has numerous well-preserved old Czech machines and some Harley-Davidsons.

Environs

North of the centre is the famous, state-owned **Budvar Brewery**, where beer has been made since the 19th century; visits can be arranged direct or via the tourist information office.

Budvar Brewery

Karolíny Světlé 4. *Tel* 387 705 347.
◯ 9am–4pm daily by appt.

ČESKE BUDĚJOVICE TOWN CENTRE

Black Tower ⑤
Butchers' Market ④
Dominican Monastery and Church of the Sacrifice of the Virgin ③
Motorcycle Museum ⑨
Náměstí Přemysla Otakara II ①
St Nicholas's Cathedral ⑥
South Bohemia Museum ⑦
Town Hall ②
Železná Panna ⑧

| 0 metres | 200 |
| 0 yards | 200 |

Key to Symbols *see back flap*

Sumptuously furnished Tapestry Room in Hluboká Castle

Hluboká nad Vltavou ❷

Road map B3. 🏰 *4,500.* 🚌 *from České Budějovice or Prague.* ℹ *Zborovská 80.* **Tel** *387 966 164.*

Hluboká village is known for its **Castle**, regarded by many as Bohemia's most beautiful aristocratic residence. Built in the 13th century by Wenceslas I, the Gothic castle was re-modelled several times: in the 16th century in Renaissance style; then under the owner-ship of the Schwarzenbergs in the 18th century in Baroque style; and from 1839 to 1871 in the style of the English Neo-Gothic. It has 11 towers and over 120 rooms filled with furniture and paintings.

In the castle's former riding school is the **Aleš South Bohemian Gallery** (Alšova jihočeská galerie), a superb collection of 57 Flemish tapes-tries and excellent Bohemian medieval art. The *Adoration of Infant Jesus* by the Master of Třeboň (1380) is a highlight.

♣ **Hluboká Castle**
Tel *387 843 911.* ◯ *Apr–Jun, Sep, Oct: Tue–Sun; Jul, Aug: daily.* 📷 🎫

Aleš South Bohemian Gallery
◯ *daily.* **www**.ajg.cz

Environs
In the Baroque **Ohrada Hunting Lodge**, just south of Hluboká, is a hunting, fishing and forestry museum, filled with hunting trophies.

🏛 **Ohrada Hunting Lodge**
Tel *387 985 340.* ◯ *Apr, May, Sep, Oct: Tue–Sun; Jun–Aug: daily.*

Temelín ❸

Road map B3. 🚆 *from České Budějovice.* 🚌 *from České Budějovice or Prague.* **Tel** *381 102 639.* ◯ *Jul, Aug: 9am–5:30pm daily; Sep–Jun: 9am–4pm daily (appt recommended).*

The atomic power station in Temelín was started under the Communists in 1983, using Soviet technology, and com-pleted in the 1990s using US and European technology. Designed to provide up to 20 per cent of the Czech Republic's electricity, it finally opened in 2000. Prior to that it became famous for the protests it provoked in the Czech Republic and other European countries, particularly Austria, whose border is a mere 50 km (30 miles) away. Critics of the project point out that from the time of its commissioning in 2000 there have been frequent failures. A stop at the station's visitor centre provides information on the functioning of Temelín, but much more impressive is

Coat of arms, Bechyně Castle

the close-up view of its 150-m (500-ft) high cooling towers.

Environs
In **Albrechtice**, 5 km (3 miles) north of Temelín, by the Baroque Church of St Peter and St Paul, is an unusual cemetery. In 1841–54 108 small shrines were built here, each painted in a naïve style to record events in the life of the deceased.

Bechyně ❹

Road map B3. 🏰 *5,700.* 🚆 *from Tábor.* 🚌 *from České Budějovice or Prague.* ℹ *Soukenicka 57.* **Tel** *381 213 822.*

The most beautiful view of this picturesque spa resort is from the Rainbow (Duha) bridge, 50 m (160 ft) above the Lužnice river. The train ride from Tábor takes you over this bridge, and is a pleasant way to arrive. Bechyně's spring waters attract those seeking treatment for rheumatism and metabolic disorders.

The **Castle** is the town's oldest sight. A 12th-century Gothic fortress given a Renaissance make-over four centuries later, it now houses an exhibition of its history. In the former synagogue near the main square is the **Firefighters' Museum** (Hasičské muzeum), with sev-eral old fire engines on display.

♣ **Bechyně Castle**
Tel *381 213 143.* ◯ *Jun–Aug: Tue–Sun; Sep–May: by appt.* 📷

🏛 **Firefighters' Museum**
Tel *602 840 275.* ◯ *May: Thu–Sun; Jun–Sep: Tue–Sun.*

Environs
Týn nad Vltavou, 11 km (7 miles) south of Bechyně, has a market square with many Renaissance houses, the most prominent of them being the town hall with its arcades and richly ornamented Rococo façade. In the 1699 Baroque

Towers of Temelín nuclear power station

palace is an interesting regional museum.

🏛 Týn nad Vltavou Museum
Náměstí Miru. *Tel* 385 772 302.
◯ Mar–May, Sep–Dec: Mon–Fri;
Jun–Aug: Tue–Sun.

Tábor ❺

See pp142–3.

Pelhřimov ❻

Road map B3. 🏯 *16,000.* 🚊 🚌
from Prague. 🚹 *Masarykovo náměstí
10. Tel 565 326 924.* 🎪 *Festival of
Records and Curious Performances:
mid-Jun.* www.pelhrimovsko.cz

The charming town of
Pelhřimov has a medieval
pedigree. It retains its defence
walls with two tower gates,
and the Gothic **Church of St
Bartholomew** (sv. Bartoloměj).
The town square has houses
with Renaissance and Baroque
façades and pediments. No. 13,
originally Baroque, is particularly
striking: Pavel Janák gave it a
Cubist façade in 1913–15.

A singular attraction of
Pelhřimov is its Festival of
Records and Curious
Performances, held in mid-
June for those who want to
earn a place in the *Guinness
Book of World Records.* Some
of these extraordinary feats
are documented in the
Museum of Records
(Muzeum rekordů a kuriozit)
in one of the town's Gothic
gates. Those taller than 205
cm (80 in), and adults shorter
than 145 cm (57 in) or
measuring more than 135 cm
(53 in) around the waist, are
admitted free of charge.

🏛 Museum of Records
Tel 565 321 327. ◯ Apr–Sep:
daily; Oct–Mar: Sat, Sun. 🏷

Environs
Λ **Motorcycle Museum** is
housed in a 14th-century
castle in the tiny village of
Kámen (meaning "rock"),
which lies 15 km (9 miles)
west of Pelhřimov. There are
numerous exhibits from the
National Technical Museum in
Prague, including an 1898
Laurin and Klement motorcycle.

Baroque gable on a house in Pelhřimov

In **Žirovnice**, 20 km (12 miles)
south of Pelhřimov, is a
sprawling Renaissance **Castle**
featuring historic interiors and
a museum of wickerwork and
button-making – products for
which the town became
famous in the 19th century.
Počátky, situated nearby, is a
charming small town with a
beautiful Baroque church and
a picturesque market square.

🏛 Motorcycle Museum
Tel 565 426 619. ◯ May–Sep:
Tue–Sun; Apr, Oct: Sat, Sun.

⚜ Žirovnice Castle
Tel 565 494 095. ◯ May–Sep:
Tue–Sun.

The Gothic Červená Lhota Castle

Červená Lhota Castle ❼

Road map B3. 🚊 *8 km (5 miles)
Kardašova Řečice. Tel 384 384 228.*
◯ Apr, Oct: 9:30am–4:30pm Sat, Sun,
public hols; May–Sep: 9:30am–4:30pm
Tue–Sun (Jun–Aug: to 5:15pm). 🏷 🎥

Enjoying an exceptionally
scenic location amid forests,
the Červená Lhota Castle is on

an island at the centre
of a small lake. The
original Gothic castle
was remodelled in the
16th century into a
Renaissance residence
named Nova Lhota. In
the early 17th century
the island was linked
with the mainland by
a stone bridge and the
castle roof was
covered with red tiles,
which subsequently
gave it its name
(*červená* means "red").
The German composer Karl
Ditters von Dittersdorf lived
here until his death in 1799.

In 1945 the castle was taken
out of private hands by the
state and turned first into a
children's hospital and later
into a cultural establishment
open to visitors. Displayed
inside are furnishings
representing periods from the
Renaissance to Biedermeier in
the mid-19th century, as well
as porcelain and tapestries.
The castle is surrounded by a
scenic park, where there is
also a castle chapel. In
summer it is possible to hire a
boat to go on the lake, and to
take a ride in a horse and
carriage around the grounds.

Environs
Pluhův Žďár, 2 km (1 mile)
south of Červená Lhota, is a
14th-century fortress
transformed in the 18th
century into a Baroque
residence. The last owners of
the palace before World War
II were the president Edvard
Beneš and his brother Vojta.
The family descendants, who
regained possession of the
castle in 1992, are happy to
admit visitors.

Soběslav, 11 km (7 miles)
to the west, is famous with
Czech visitors for its 16th-
century love story involving
one of the most powerful
Bohemian lords, Peter Vok of
Rožmberk, and a miller's
daughter Zuzana Vojířova. It
now delights visitors with its
picturesque town square
flanked by historic houses,
and two fine Gothic churches:
St Vitus (sv. Víta) and Our
Lady (Panny Marie). Both are
worth visiting for their
magnificent arched ceilings.

Tábor ❺

A military camp established in 1420 by
Hussite refugees from Prague grew into
the town of Tábor, named after the
mountain where Christ's Transfiguration
took place. Radical Hussite reformers
(see pp36–7) became known as
Taborites, and fought battles throughout
Bohemia, but were finally defeated in
1434. Today, the lively Old Town retains
its maze-like narrow streets and
alleyways. It lies between the town walls,
the Lužnice river and Jordán lake, a short walk
west of the new town.

**Church of the
Transfiguration**
*This image of Christ
is from the beauti-
ful Baroque pulpit
of this Neo-Gothic
church. There is
also an unusual vault
over the presbytery. Its
tall bell tower offers a
panorama of the town.*

★ Town Hall
*On the main square, Žižkovo náměstí,
is the Town Hall (1440–51). Inside, the
Grand Hall features superb net vaulting.
The Hussite Museum (Husitské
muzeum) now occupies the building.*

ZIZKOVO
NAMESTI

ARBEITEROVA

RADNICKÁ

MARTÍNKA Z HÚSKY

KLOKOTSKÁ

A stroll along
Klokotská takes you to
Bechyňska brána
(gate) and tower –
the only one left.

KEY

– – – Suggested route

STAR SIGHTS

★ Škoch House

★ Town Hall

★ Ulice Pražská

★ Škoch House
*This gable of Škochův dům
is one of the finest
examples of Gothic-
Renaissance
architecture in
Bohemia. The
gables of houses
facing the
main square
are astonish-
ingly varied.*

Ctibor House
One of the town's most interesting houses (Ctiborův dům), this is a magnificent example of the Late Gothic, built in 1532. Its gable with tracery decorations crowns the cream-white façade.

VISITORS' CHECKLIST

Road map B3. 👥 37,000. 🚌
🚏 ℹ️ Žižkovo náměstí 2. **Tel**
381 486 230. www.tabor.cz
🎭 Hussite Festival: Sep. **Hussite Museum Tel** 381 254 286.
⭕ Nov–Apr: Mon–Fri; May–Sep: daily. 🖥️ www.husmuzeum.cz

Statue of Jan Žižka
The monument to the Hussite military leader was officially unveiled in 1877 but was badly cast and had to be recast in 1884.

HRNČÍRSKÁ

ŠPITÁLSKÁ

TRŽNÍ

LUČINOVA

KOŽEŠNÍCKÁ

STŘELNICKÁ

PRAŽSKÁ

ŠIROKÁ

The 1603 house at No. 210 – a very fine Flemish Renaissance building – has an intricate gable decorated with figurative and floral *sgraffito*.

★ Ulice Pražská
The extraordinary Renaissance houses flanking the street that runs from the southeast corner of the main square were built after the Great Fire of 1532.

0 metres   20
0 yards   20

Stark House
The façade of Starkův dům (No. 157), dating from 1526, is decorated with lavish 1570 sgraffito inspired by nature and history.

Jindřichův Hradec ⑧

One of the most beautiful towns in South Bohemia, situated among medieval fish ponds, Jindřichův Hradec (Neuhaus) lies slightly off the main tourist track. It was founded in the 13th century by the lords of Hradec. The Old Town, a peaceful, interesting area, centres on the main square (náměstí Míru), lined with vividly coloured houses, many of which were rebuilt after a fire in 1801. Northwest of the square are cobbled alleys leading to the Church of the Assumption of the Virgin Mary (Nanebevzetí Panny Marie), with a tower offering excellent views. To the west of the Old Town is the huge castle.

★ Rondel
The interior of this 1592 music pavilion is decorated with the family tree tracing the descent of Adam II of Hradec from the biblical Adam.

Adam II's Bedchamber
The spread on the Baroque bed is decorated with symbols of the marriage of Adam II and Katherine de Montfort.

Prince Adam's palace was designed by Baldassare Maggi in 1561.

Černín's Dining room
The dining room houses a valuable dining service made of "habanska majolica", collected during the 17th century.

JINDŘICHŮV HRADEC CASTLE
Beside the Vajgar fish pond lies this 13th-century castle, once the main residence of the lords of Hradec. Originally a Gothic building, it was made into a Renaissance palace by Italian architects in the late 16th century. Antonio Cometa added the three-tiered courtyard arcades at this time.

The Spanish Wing
The vast state room of the Renaissance Spanish Wing was built to a design by Baldassare Maggi. Its grand furnishings include this 16th-century wardrobe.

VISITORS' CHECKLIST

Road map B3. 23,000.
from Prague or České Budějovice. Panská 136.
Tel 384 363 546.
Castle **Tel** 384 321 279.
Apr–Oct: Tue–Sun.
3 tour routes. **www**.jh.cz

The Black Tower, the 32-m (104-ft) high tower, dating from the early 13th century, was used as a prison.

The Red Tower Kitchen
The kitchen with its open hearth and four corner chimneys projecting above the roof of the tower was built around 1500 and is still in use. This is the best-preserved kitchen of its type in the Czech Republic, and includes the original equipment.

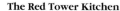

★ Holy Spirit Chapel
The chapel frescoes uncovered during reconstruction works in about 1727 depict scenes from the life of Christ and other biblical motifs.

The Royal Hall
The paintings hung in the vaulted hall are portraits of the former rulers of Bohemia.

STAR FEATURES

★ Holy Spirit Chapel

★ Rondel

Slavonice **❾**

Road map B3. 🏠 *4,500.* 🚉 *from Telč.* 🚌 *from Prague.* 🛈 *Náměstí Míru 480.* **Tel** *384 493 320.* www.slavonice-mesto.cz

Slavonice (Zlabings), situated next to the Austrian border, is a pleasant, sleepy little town with a street layout preserved unchanged since the 13th century.

An exceptional number of its Gothic and Renaissance houses feature decorative *sgraffito* and opulent gables. The houses at Nos. 25 and 46 Dolní náměstí are particularly stunning with their beautiful ground-floor vaulted ceilings; also worth a visit is the house at No. 517 Horní náměstí, whose first-floor rooms are decorated with 16th-century wall paintings depicting scenes from the Apocalypse.

There are also two Gothic-Renaissance town gates and two Gothic churches. The **Church of the Assumption of the Virgin Mary** (Nanebevzetí Panny Marie) has some valuable frescoes; the **Church of St John the Baptist** (sv. Jana Křtitele) features an interesting vault above the presbytery.

Environs
The imposing ruins of **Landštejn Castle** lie 9 km (6 miles) east of Slavonice. It was built in the early 13th century, modelled on German or Austrian fortresses. The ground floor of one of its

Sgraffito-decorated house in Slavonice

mighty square towers is occupied by a chapel.

⛰ Landštejn Castle
Tel *384 498 580.* ☐ *Apr & Oct: Sat & Sun; May–Aug: Tue–Sun.* 📷

Renaissance arcades in the inner courtyard of the Castle in Třeboň

Třeboň **❿**

Road map B3. 🏠 *9,000.* 🚉 🚌 *1 km (0.5 miles).* 🛈 *Masarykovo náměstí 103.* **Tel** *384 721 169.* www.mesto-trebon.cz

Situated among hills and fish ponds, Třeboň (Wittingau) has a tiny medieval centre dominated by a huge castle; it is also a spa town. It was founded in the 12th century, and the Rožmberk family took over during the 14th century. During their rule it reached the peak of its glory, with exceptionally fast economic development. The Rožmberks funded the development of local fish ponds into more formal fish farming, a system of 6,000 ponds that remain productive today.

Coat of arms from Nové Hrady

The main square, Masarykovo náměstí, is lined with Renaissance and Baroque houses; in the square stand a Renaissance ten-sided fountain and a 1781 Marian column. The Renaissance town hall has a façade with three semi-circular arcades and a 31-m (100-ft) high tower added in the 17th century. To the east, the square ends with a 1527

gate (Hradecká brána). The **Church of St Giles** (sv. Jiljí) on Husova has an unusual twin-aisled interior.

The town's huge Renaissance **Castle** was built in the first half of the 16th century on the site of a Gothic fortress. Inside, visitors can view the Renaissance Rožmberk apartments and the 19th-century living quarters of the last owners – the Schwarzenbergs, who owned many estates throughout South Bohemia.

⛰ Třeboň Castle
Tel *384 721 193.* ☐ *Apr–Oct: Tue–Sun.* 📷

Environs
On the opposite side of the Svět pond from Třeboň stands the vast **Schwarzenberg Mausoleum** (Schwarzenberská hrobka). This three-storey edifice with its monumental stairs and lofty tower was built in Neo-Gothic style in 1877. It is the resting place of 27 members of the Schwarzenberg family.

⚰ Schwarzenberg Mausoleum
☐ *Apr–Oct: Tue–Sun.*

Nové Hrady **⓫**

Road map B3. 🏠 *2,600.* 🚉 *5 km (3 miles).* 🛈 *Náměstí Republiky 46.* **Tel** *386 362 195.* www.novehrady.cz

To the east of the town square stands the **Church of St Peter and St Paul** (sv. Petr a Pavel), which has a magnificent presbytery vault and monumental Baroque furnishings dating from the late 17th century. Nearby is the Empire-style palace built in 1801–10 for the Buquoy family.

The 13th-century **Castle** was built to guard the trading route between Bohemia and Austria. Damaged, first during Hussite wars and again by a gunpowder explosion in 1557 and then the earthquake of 1605, it was given its present Baroque form in the 18th century. The entrance to the castle leads over a bridge that

Entrance to the 13th-century Nové Hrady Castle

spans the deep brick-lined moat, the largest moat in the Czech Republic.

⚓ **Nové Hrady Castle**
Tel 386 362 135. ☐ *Apr & Oct: Sat, Sun; May, Jun, Sep: Tue–Sun; Jul, Aug: daily.* 🌐 📷

Environs
Žumberk, 6 km (4 miles) west of Nové Hrady, is worth a short detour for its late 15th-century Gothic fortress and the unusual four-aisle church built in 1455 and featuring a lovely vault resting on six slender columns.

Rožmberk nad Vltavou Castle ⑫

Road map B3. 🚉 *4 km (2 miles). Tel 380 749 838.* ☐ *Apr & Oct: 9am–4pm Sat & Sun; May & Sep: 9am–4pm Tue–Sun; Jun–Aug: 9am–5.15pm Tue–Sun.* 🌐 📷

The 13th-century fortified estate of the powerful Rožmberk family towers on a hilltop above the tiny village at its base. The Rožmberks used it as a base for running their estates in the region from the 13th to the 17th century. It consists of the Upper Castle, the only remains of which are now the Jacobean Tower, closed to visitors; and the Lower Castle, originally Gothic and in the 16th century re-modelled in the Renaissance style. In 1840–57 the then owners, the Buquoy family, renovated the castle, giving it its English Neo-Gothic features.

Inside are displayed collections of precious glass, paintings, weapons, porcelain and furniture, and there is a marvellous frescoed Banquet Hall.

Environs
On the border with Austria 8 km (5 miles) to the east is the small town of **Dolní Dvořiště**. The church of St Giles (sv. Jiljí) here is the prime example of the South Bohemian Gothic style, featuring magnificent net-vaulting over the presbytery and all the aisles.

To the north, west and south of Dolní Dvořiště there are remains of the horse-drawn train lines that once linked České Budějovice with Linz. Built in 1825–31, it was the first railway of its kind in Continental Europe. The total route was 131 km (81 miles) long, and the journey took 14 hours. The most numerous fragments of the railway (embankments, pillars, bridges) can be seen near the village of Suchodol, 2 km (1 mile) to the north of Dolní Dvořiště.

Vyšší Brod Monastery ⑬

Road map B3. 🚉 *from České Budějovice.* 🚌 *from Český Krumlov. Tel 380 746 627.* ☐ *May–Sep: 9am–4:15pm Tue–Sat, 1:15–4:15pm Sun; Oct–Apr: by appt.* 🌐 📷 **Postal Museum** ☐ *Apr–Oct: 9am–noon, 1–5pm Tue–Sun (last adm 4pm).* 🌐

In the mid-13th century the Rožmberk family founded a Cistercian monastery here. The completion of the entire complex took the whole of the next century, when Peter Parler was invited to help with its construction. The damage inflicted by the Hussite army in 1422 was soon repaired due to the monastery's effective fortifications.

During the 17th and 18th centuries new Baroque buildings were added to the older parts of the church. The Communists closed the monastery in 1950, imprisoning the monks. Since the 1990s it has been undergoing major renovation work.

The most beautiful room is the Chapter House dating from 1285–1300, its vaulted ceiling supported by a single column. Also very impressive is the Rococo library, entered by a hidden door, decorated with frescoes and topped with a ceiling adorned with gold leaf. It houses 70,000 volumes. Inside the Church of the Assumption of the Virgin Mary (Nanebevzetí Panny Marie), the aisles and the church sacristy have beautiful Gothic vaults. The main altarpiece dates from 1644–46. The works of art found in the monastery are of the highest quality; they include the *Crucifixion* by the Master of Vyšší Brod, which was only recently returned to the Cistercians by the National Museum in Prague.

The outer buildings of the monastery now house a Postal Museum (Poštovní muzeum) devoted to the history of mail delivery in the Czech Republic since 1526, including uniforms and post coaches.

Entrance to the Cistercian Monastery in Vyšší Brod

A Tour of the Šumava

The Šumava mountains *(see also pp150–51)* form a natural border between the Czech Republic, Germany and Austria. This is the largest forested area in Central Europe at 120 km (75 miles) long and up to 45 km (28 miles) wide. The unspoilt Boubín Virgin Forest has been a reserve since 1858. Nearby, some of the densest woodland makes up the Šumava National Park *(see also p166)*. The whole area, preserved in part due to a period during the Cold War when it was closed off, was made a UNESCO biosphere reserve in 1990. The Šumava offers superb trekking, canoeing and cycling.

Velhartice ⑨
The castle at Velhartice, now a ruin, was built in the late 13th and early 14th century. The four-span stone bridge was erected in about 1430 *(see also p166)*.

Rabí ⑧
The Czech Republic's largest medieval fortress, Rabí is made up of Gothic ruins dominated by a square tower that offers a great viewpoint *(see also p157)*.

ŠUMAVA NATIONAL PARK

Srní ⑦
The pretty village of Srní has a couple of pleasant places to stay. The village, surrounded by forests and meadows, makes a good base for trekking, mountain biking and, in winter, skiing.

Map labels:
Klatovy · Strakonice · Sušice · Otava · Kašperské Hory · Strakor · Vimperk · BOUBÍN VIRGIN FOREST · Passau · Vltava

22 · 187 · 149 · 670 m (2198 ft) · 171 · 971 m (3186 ft) · 149 · 902 m (2959 ft) · 171 · 170 · 171 · 4 · 76 (25) · 1317 m (4321 ft) · 169 · 145 · 168 · 1317 m (3665 ft) · 145 · 1302 m (4272 ft) · 1314 m (4311 ft) · 6 · 167 · 1362 m (4469 ft) · 1265 (414) · 167 · 39 · 4

Kvilda ⑥
The highest altitude parish in the Czech Republic (1,065 m/ 3,495 ft above sea level). Kvilda is a quiet winter sports centre in an area of peat bogs.

KEY

- ▬ Tour route
- ▬ Other scenic routes
- ▬ Other roads
- �554 Viewpoint
- —·· International border

For additional map symbols *see back flap*

Volary ⑤

The town of Volary has some 20
original wooden houses, built by
Tyrol farmers who settled here in
the 16th century. It is also a
gateway to Boubín. A single-track
train service links Volary with
České Budějovice.

Schwarzenberg Canal ④

Close to the hamlet of Jeleni
vrchy is a 429-m (1,407-ft)
long underground tunnel, a
fragment of the 1789
Schwarzenberg Canal linking
the Vltava with the Danube.

Lake Lipno ③

The man-made water reservoir, Lipno, built
in 1950–59, is often referred to as the "South
Bohemian Sea". Ferries cross regularly, and
it offers excellent facilities for sport and
recreation, attracting many local visitors.

Rožmberk nad Vltavou ②

The castle, perched high above the
Vltava river valley, was the home
of the Rožmberks – one of
the most powerful
Bohemian families (*see
also p147*).

Klet' Mountain ①

This mountain is the
highest peak (1,083 m/
3,553 ft) in the Blanský
forest area. On top is a
stone observation tower,
the oldest in the Czech
Republic, built in 1825.
There is a chairlift to the
top, and in fine weather it
offers views of the Alps.

0 km 10
0 miles 10

Písek
Prachatice
141
1008 m (3307 ft)
143
143
165
953 m (3127 ft)
České Budějovice
① Klet'
Blanský les
39
E55 3
166
656 m (2152 ft)
Český Krumlov
1226 m (4022 ft)
39
744 m (2441 ft)
918 m (3012 ft)
Kaplice
1049 m (3442 ft)
Horní Planá
39
162
160
④
Lake Lipno
163
③
②
984 m (3228 ft)
791 m (2595 ft)
813 m (2667 ft)
1053 m (3455 ft)
935 m (3067 ft) Vyšší Brod
163
Linz

Linz **A stream flowing through part of the Šumava mountains** ▷

Český Krumlov ⑮

An astonishingly beautiful and well-preserved small medieval town, Český Krumlov (Krumau) is one of the most visited in the Czech Republic. Founded in the 13th century, it belonged to the Rožmberk dynasty from 1302 to 1611. The family crest of a five-petalled red rose is one of the most often seen motifs in Český Krumlov. The Eggenbergs held sway for 100 years, then the Schwarzenbergs took over from 1717 to 1947. In 1992 it was added to the UNESCO World Cultural Heritage List.

Exploring the town

The historic town centre is situated on the rocky banks of the sharply meandering Vltava. The Inner Town (Vnitřní Město), with its market square, town hall and St Vitus's Church, is located on the right bank, in an area enclosed on three sides by water. The left side meander features the castle and the village called Latrán. The town centre is closed to cars.

Coat of arms on the town hall

🏛 Egon Schiele Centrum

Široká 71. **Tel** 337 704 011.
◯ 10am–6pm daily. 🖼 🅿 ◻ ♿
www.schieleartcentrum.cz
A former brewery building not far from the market square now houses a gallery devoted to Austrian artist Egon Schiele (1890–1918), who lived in Český Krumlov in 1911. On display are watercolours and drawings, including several famous male and female nudes, which in Schiele's day caused a scandal. He was driven out of the town for employing young local girls to pose for him. There are other temporary exhibitions of contemporary works.

🏛 Náměstí Svornosti

The most imposing building in the market square, náměstí Svornosti, is the town hall. Occupying a corner site on the north side, it was created in the mid-15th century by combining two Gothic houses. The Marian plague column at the centre of the square was erected in 1716 as a thanksgiving for sparing the town from the Black Death in 1682.
Matthäus Jäckel, a Prague sculptor, placed a statue of the Madonna at the top, and at the foot of the column, in one of the niches, a figure of St Roch, the saint invoked for protection against plague.

🏛 Church of St Vitus

St Vitus's Church (sv. Víta) provides a visual counterbalance to the lofty tower of the castle. Dating from the early 15th century, and built on the site of an earlier church, this triple-aisled Gothic edifice features one of the oldest examples of net vaulting in Europe. The sanctuary by the north wall of the presbytery is a splendid example of stonemasonry dating from about 1500. The Early Baroque high altar, made in 1673–83, has paintings depicting St Vitus and the coronation of the Virgin Mary. The Late Gothic porch has an unusual vault in the shape of octagonal stars.

Gothic wall paintings dating from 1430 can be seen on the north wall of the side aisle (*The Crucifixion, St Veronica, St Elizabeth with a beggar, Mary Magdalene, St Katherine* and *St Bartholomew*). The church once housed the famous *Krumlov Madonna* of 1390, regarded by many as the finest example of the International Gothic style, now kept in the Art History Museum, Vienna. Its 15th-century replica can be seen in the National Gallery, Prague.

The imposing nave of the Church of St Vitus

🏛 Ulice Horní

Regional Museum ◯ May–Sep: 10am–5pm daily; Oct–Apr: 9am–4pm Tue–Fri; 1–4pm Sat, Sun.
Horní street, off the market square, was once terminated by a town gate, demolished in 1839. At No. 159 is the Chaplaincy (Kaplanka) dating from 1514–20, with a beautiful Gothic gable and Renaissance window jambs. At No. 155 is the former Prelature built in the 14th century and remodelled several times since. Adjoining it is the former Jesuit College (No. 154), designed by Baldassare Maggi and now a hotel. At No. 152, the **Regional Museum** includes a fascinating scale model of the town in 1800.

Part of the façade of the former Jesuit College in Ulice Horní

The arcaded bridge linking Krumlov Castle with its Theatre

⛪ Latrán

The old quarter of Latrán was once a village inhabited by craftsmen and merchants, who provided services for the castle. It is linked to the Inner Town by a bridge over the Vltava. Still remaining is a complex of late-Gothic and Baroque buildings including the Minorite monastery, the **Convent of the Poor Clares** and a church. The entire complex was linked with the castle by a covered walkway running over Latrán. Close by is the Renaissance **Budějovice gate**, the only one left of the original eight town gates.

♣ Krumlov Castle

Zámek 59. **Tel** 380 704 711. ⬛ Apr–Sep: 9am–5pm Tue–Sun (Jun–Aug: to 6pm). 🎟️ 🎟️ 2 routes. ⬛

Perched high up on a rock, the castle is the second only to Prague Castle in terms of its size. The oldest part of this sprawling complex is Dolní Hrad, also known as Hrádek, with a tall, cylindrical tower painted in colourful designs, built in 1580.

The castle has a total of 300 rooms. The most beautiful are the stately Rožmberk Rooms with wooden vaults and Renaissance wall frescoes, completed in 1576 under the patronage of Vilém Rožmberk. Particularly unusual is the Hall of Masks, which is vividly

VISITORS' CHECKLIST

Road map B3. 🏘️ 14,800. 🚉 1 km (0.5 mile) N of Krumlov Castle. 🚌 ℹ️ Náměstí Svornosti 2. **Tel** 380 704 622. **www**.ckrumlov.cz/infocentrum 🎭 Five-Petalled Rose Festival: mid-Jun; International Music Festival: mid-Jul–Aug.

decorated with some extra-ordinary trompe-l'oeil paintings depicting carnival scenes.

A spectacular 17th-century tiered bridge (Plášťovy most), complete with statues, links the Upper Castle with its Theatre.

🎭 Castle Theatre
See pp154–5.

Entrance to the Minorite Monastery in Latrán

ČESKÝ KRUMLOV TOWN CENTRE

Key to Symbols see back flap

Český Krumlov: Castle Theatre

The Baroque theatre (Zámecké divadlo) in Krumlov Castle is virtually unique in that its interior, furnishings, stage settings, costumes and stage machinery are so numerous and so well preserved. It was rebuilt on the site of a previous theatre in 1767 to a commission by Prince Josef Adam Schwarzenberg. The scene-shifting machinery was constructed by Lorenz Makh from Vienna. Following a 30-year refurbishment in the 20th century, the theatre offers a fascinating glimpse of 18th-century theatrical life.

★ **Painted Ceiling**
The ceiling mural above the auditorium and wall paintings were by Viennese artists Leo Märkl and Hans Wetschel.

Costumes
The theatre wardrobes house 540 original costumes for men, women and children.

A theatre building was built in 1682 by Prince Johann Christian Eggenberg, under the supervision of the Italian builders G A de Maggi and G M Spinetti.

Sundial
A sundial adorns the Renaissance House, which, since the building of the new theatre, now houses wardrobes, laundries and stables.

Wind Machine
The sound of wind was simulated by turning a revolving drum, loosely covered with a linen cloth.

Stage Scenery
Among the surviving scenery are 13 complete typical stage sets including 11 backcloths, 40 ceilings, 100 props, 50 machines for creating special effects and 250 wings.

★ Stage
This setting represents a military camp; other preserved sets include a forest, a town, a prison, a garden, a harbour, a cathedral and a colonnaded hall.

Plášťový most (bridge), linking the theatre with the castle, was built in 1691.

Auditorium
Rising wooden benches are provided for the audience, and the centre of the circle has a comfortable royal box. The auditorium would have been lit by chandeliers with oil lamps.

Scene-shifting Machinery
A sophisticated system of ropes and pulleys, which still works well, allowed for fast shifting of the wings. The same device or a similar one controlled the lifting and lowering of the backcloth, the ceiling and the curtain.

STAR FEATURES

★ Painted Ceiling

★ Stage

Remains of the Late Gothic fortified walls of the castle.

Zlatá Koruna Monastery ⑯

Road map B3. 🚌 *from Prague or České Budějovice.* **Tel** *380 743 126.* 🚪 *Apr–Oct: 9am–3:15pm Tue–Sun (Jun–Aug: to 5:30pm).* 🎫 🚗 *2 routes.*

Founded in 1263 by Přemysl Otakar II, this Cistercian monastery has at its centre a courtyard surrounded by cloisters. Adjoining is the Church of the Assumption with a pentagonal presbytery dating from about 1500. The main altarpiece is a magnificent example of monumental Rococo architecture.

The Chapterhouse, built in 1280–1300, features vaulting supported by two Gothic columns. The Chapel of the Guardian Angels, at the southern end of the monastery grounds, is a beautiful two-storey church from the late 13th century, featuring the original rib vaulting on both levels. Another building houses a **Museum of South Bohemian Literature** (Památník písemnictví jižních Čech).

Intricate vaulting in the Chapterhouse at Zlatá Koruna Monastery

Holašovice ⑰

Road map B3. 15 km (9 miles) W of České Budějovice. 👥 *335.* 🚌 *from České Budějovice.* 📞 *387 982 145.*

This picturesque village contains a splendidly preserved set of early 19th-century historic buildings grouped around a central fish pond, which is used jointly by all the inhabitants. Nowhere else is such a collection of buildings found in its original setting. The stone buildings – including both homes and farmsteads as well as a pub – represent the architectural style known as Folk Baroque, found only in this part of Bohemia, and are characterized by colourful façades with white stucco ornamentation. The gables differ from house to house. Most of them face the central square and pond, and have an entrance gate leading to a yard. Larger homesteads have brick granaries resembling small fortresses.

Providing an enchanting glimpse of traditional rural life, this tiny village was declared a UNESCO World Cultural and Natural Heritage Site in 1998. Holašovice was the setting for the 1932 film version of *The Bartered Bride* by Bedřich Smetana.

Prachatice ⑱

Road map B3. 👥 *11,800.* 🚉 *from České Budějovice.* 🚌 *from Prague.* 🛈 *Velké náměstí 1.* **Tel** *388 312 563.* 🎫 *Gold Trail Festival: mid-Jun.*

The town's tiny centre is surrounded by a ring of defensive walls, with a mighty entrance gate. It was a key point along the salt trade route into Bohemia. The lovingly restored town square (Velké náměstí) has a 17th-century **Old Town Hall** (Stará radnice), its façade decorated with *sgraffito*. Many buildings are covered with *sgraffito;* No. 31 has the finest, of the Last Supper (1563). The **Church of St James** (sv. Jakuba) has magnificent net vaulting.

Folk Baroque buildings overlooking the fish pond in the village of Holašovice

Strakonice ⓳

Road map B3. ⚲ 23,500.
🚆 from Plzeň. 🚌 from
Prague. 🛈 Velké náměstí
2. Tel 383 700 700.
🎵 International Bagpipe
Festival: mid-Aug.
www.strakonice.net

In the 19th
century, Strakonice
was a textile
manufacturing town
and centre of the
woollen industry. It
became most famous
for making fezzes.
At one point nearly
5 million a year
were being ex-
ported to Turkey,
India, Arabia and Egypt. Also
made here are Czech bagpipes
(*dudy*); the International
Bagpipe Festival every August
attracts large numbers of
bagpipe enthusiasts.

Situated at the confluence
of the Otava and Volyňka
rivers, Strakonice has a 13th-
century **Castle**, one of the
oldest stone buildings in the
Czech Republic. Until 1694
this was the headquarters of
the Knights of St John in
Bohemia. The castle still
features original Gothic
details, which can also be
seen in the cloisters and
porch of the adjacent **Church
of St Procopius** (sv. Prokop).
The **Regional Museum** in the
castle has displays of fezzes,
bagpipes and motorcycles
(also made in the town).

In the town itself, the main
square (Velké náměstí) has a
couple of beautifully decorated buildings: the town hall
(radnice) and a savings bank.

⚑ **Strakonice Castle and
Regional Museum**
Tel 383 321 537. 🕐 May–Oct:
Tue–Sun. 🎫 📷 www.muzeum.
strakonice.cz

Environs

About 20 km (12 miles) west
of Strakonice, **Rabi** fortress
(*see also p148*), built in the
early 14th century, became a
target of Hussite army attacks
in 1420. After a long siege it
was captured by the troops of
Jan Žižka (*see pp36–7*), who
is thought to have been
blinded in one eye here.

**Statue of St Barbara in
the Regional Museum
in Strakonice Castle**

Písek ⓴

Road map B3. ⚲ 30,000.
🚆 from Tábor. 🚌 from
Prague. 🛈 Heydukova 97.
Tel 382 213 592.
www.icpisek.cz

On the Otava river,
Písek was at the
centre of a gold-
panning region and is
named after the sand
from which gold is
separated. Přemysl
Otakar II founded the
town in the 13th
century. Its main
draw today, the
medieval bridge,
survives from that
time, making it
older than Prague's Charles
Bridge (*see pp68–9*). It has
several statues of saints,
including St John Nepomuk.

The fascinating **Prácheňské
Museum**, in the former royal

**Gothic entrance gate to the castle
in Zvíkov**

castle, has an exhibition on the
town's history, including 20th-
century upheavals, and the
region's natural environment.

🏛 **Prácheňské Museum**
Velké nám´stí 114. Tel 382 201
111. 🕐 Mar–Dec: Tue–Sun. 🎫

Zvíkov Castle ㉑

Road map B3. 🚌 from Písek to
Zvíkovské Podhradí, 1.5 km (1 mile).
Tel 382 285 676. 🕐 Apr, Oct:
9:30am–noon, 1–4pm Sat, Sun,
public hols; May–Sep: 9:30am–noon,
1–4:30pm Tue–Sun (Jun–Aug: to
5:30pm). 🎫

Originally built on the Vltava
river, Zvíkov now overlooks
the artificial lake that has
resulted from the Orlík dam
downstream. Zvíkov was built
in the reign of Přemysl Otakar
II in the mid-13th century, and
during the Thirty Years' War it
became the final stronghold of
the Protestant army in South
Bohemia. The oldest part of
the castle is its mighty keep.
The royal palace has an interesting chapel of St Wenceslas
with lovely medieval frescoes
on the first floor.

Environs

The Neo-Gothic **Orlík Castle**,
14 km (9 miles) north of
Zvíkov, belongs to the
Schwarzenberg family, and its
historic interiors illustrate this
prominent family's history.

⚑ **Orlík Castle**
Tel 382 275 101. 🕐 Apr–Oct:
Tue–Sun.

ST JOHN NEPOMUK

Jan of Pomuk, known as John Nepomuk,
was from 1389 the vicar-general of the
Prague Archbishopric. In 1393, on the
orders of Wenceslas IV, he was imprisoned, tortured and then drowned
in the Vltava. Later sources claim that
he was murdered for refusing to reveal
the secret of the queen's confession.
Canonized in 1729, John Nepomuk
became a phenomenon of the Baroque
period. Because he is regarded as the
patron saint of good reputation and
bridges, and guardian against floods,
countless statues of the saint were placed
by bridges. His was the first statue on
Prague's Charles Bridge (*see p69*).

WEST BOHEMIA

This border region, strongly affected by its proximity to German neighbours, attracts visitors for its natural beauty, its spa resorts, and, not least, its excellent beer. Fortresses on the frontiers of the former Přemyslid state are reminders of its distant past; its more recent past can be seen in the areas from which, after World War II, many Germans were expelled, leaving traces of their long presence.

Some of the most interesting historic sites of West Bohemia (Západní Čechy) include the structures that were built to defend the Kingdom of Bohemia; they include the castles of Přimda, Velhartice and Švihov, as well as a number of smaller fortresses scattered along the foothills of the Šumava mountains.

Several magnificent monasteries, including Kladruby, Plasy and Teplá, are truly outstanding sights. Founded in the Middle Ages these Gothic centres of monastic life were remodelled during the Baroque era and now provide excellent examples of the art that was intended to serve the ideas of Counter-Reformation.

The famous spa resorts of Karlovy Vary (Karlsbad), Mariánské Lázně (Marienbad) and Františkovy Lázně (Franzensbad) played a significant role in European history. Their habitués were the rich and influential from the worlds of politics and culture, including Goethe, Gogol, Chopin, Wagner, Russian Emperor Peter the Great, British King Edward VII and Austrian Emperor Franz Josef I.

Yet the attractions of West Bohemia are not limited to historic relics. Its capital, Plzeň, is a flourishing industrial centre, the home of Pilsner beer. The town of Domažlice near the German border retains aspects of Slav folk culture. The region also offers intriguing natural phenomena at Soos – a strange landscape of small mud geysers – and the beautiful Černé and Čertovo lakes near the Šumava mountains.

Façade of the sanatorium (Bath V) overlooking Smetana Park in Karlovy Vary

◁ Statue of the Plzeň Madonna on the high altar of the Church of St Bartholomew, Plzeň

Exploring West Bohemia

The region's capital and its biggest town, Plzeň, is an interesting place to visit and gives a flavour of the region. It is also the home of the world-renowned beer *(see p167)*. The main tourist attractions of West Bohemia are its spa resorts of Karlovy Vary and Mariánské Lázně. Monasteries are another highlight *(see pp176–7)*, and there are numerous small picturesque towns. The large forested areas of Český and Slavkovský Les form a backdrop to a number of the towns and offer many kilometres of hiking and cycling trails, and, in winter, excellent skiing facilities.

The monumental columns of the Mill Spring Colonnade in Karlovy Vary

SIGHTS AT A GLANCE

SEE ALSO

Coat of arms from the palace in Lázně Kynžvart

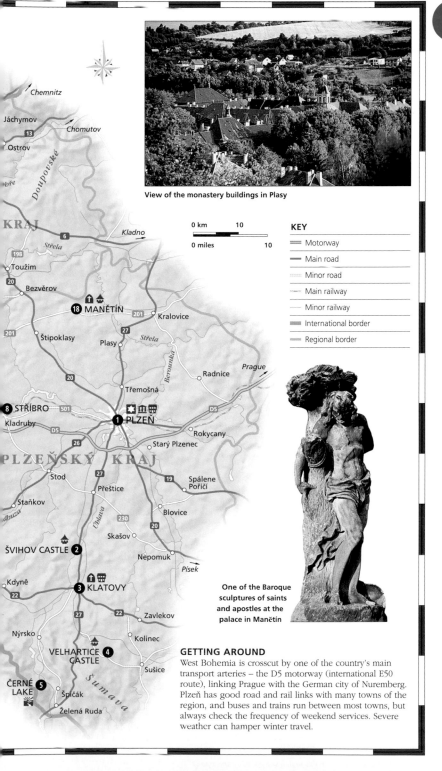

View of the monastery buildings in Plasy

KEY

━━ Motorway

━━ Main road

┅┅ Minor road

╍╍ Main railway

─── Minor railway

▬▬ International border

▬▬ Regional border

One of the Baroque
sculptures of saints
and apostles at the
palace in Manětín

GETTING AROUND

West Bohemia is crosscut by one of the country's main transport arteries – the D5 motorway (international E50 route), linking Prague with the German city of Nuremberg. Plzeň has good road and rail links with many towns of the region, and buses and trains run between most towns, but always check the frequency of weekend services. Severe weather can hamper winter travel.

Plzeň ❶

The large and bustling capital of West Bohemia, Plzeň (Pilsen) has two main industries that contribute to its vibrant atmosphere. It is mainly associated with beer, producing Pilsner Urquell (Plzeňský Prazdroj) in the brewery founded here in 1842 *(see p167)*. Since the late 19th century a large Škoda factory in the city has made armaments as well as cars. The city was established in 1295 by Wenceslas II, at the crossroads of the main trading routes between Bohemia, Bavaria and Saxony.

Plague Column on Náměstí Republiky

Exploring the City

The majority of Plzeň's historic sites are found on the left bank of the Radbuza river. The historic centre, laid out in a grid pattern, is surrounded by Plzeňske sady – a green belt created on the site of the old town walls in the 19th century. On the opposite eastern side of the Radbuza is Plzeň's brewery, the Prazdroj.

🏛 Náměstí Republiky

The market square, Náměstí Republiky, is one of the largest in the country, measuring 139 x 193 m (456 x 633 ft). Standing at its centre is the Church of St Bartholomew. The square is fringed by a number of beautifully decorated houses, with the best-preserved along the south side.

Particularly striking are the Red Heart House (U červeneho srdce), built in 1894 and sporting magnificent *sgraffito* by Czech painter Mikuláš Aleš, of two mounted knights in full tournament gear; and the Baroque Archdeanery building (Arciděkanství) on the west side. A market is held in the square every Friday.

🏛 Church of St Bartholomew

See pp164–5.

🏛 Town Hall

Náměstí Republiky. ⬜ *8am–6pm daily.*
The Renaissance town hall (stará radnice), one of the loveliest buildings of its kind in Bohemia, was designed by Italian architect Giovanni de Statio. This four-storey edifice with its magnificent gables was built in 1554–59. The interesting *sgraffito* decorations on the façade are the work of J Koul, produced during 1907–12. Standing in front of the town hall is a Plague Column, erected in 1681 in thanksgiving for the fact that the plague epidemic suffered at that time was only mild.

🏛 Císařský dům

Náměstí Republiky 41.
An imposing Renaissance edifice to the left of the town hall, dating from 1606, twice played host to Emperor Rudolph II. Now it houses the tourist information office. The next door Pechlátovský dům was created by combining two smaller, Renaissance buildings and adding a Neo-Classical façade.

A statue on Císařský dům

🏛 Great Synagogue

Sady Pětatřicátníků 11. *Tel 377 223 558.* ⬜ *Apr–Oct: 11am–5pm Sun–Fri.* ⬤ *Jewish religious festivals.*
The Great Synagogue (Velká synagóga) is the world's third-largest Jewish sacred building, after the Jerusalem and Budapest synagogues. It was built in the 1890s, funded by voluntary donations from the Plzeň Jewish community. Its architect, Rudolf Štech, designed it in a romantic "Moorish-Romanesque" style. It could accommodate 2,000 worshippers, and in addition, the high balcony, intended for women, could take up to 800. Following World War II the building and its furnishings, including the unique organ located above the Torah, suffered gradual deterioration. In 1998 the synagogue was reopened after careful restoration.

Twin towers with onion domes of the Great Synagogue

🏛 Tyl Theatre

Smetanovy sady 16. *Tel 378 038 070.*
Plzeň's theatre (Divadlo J K Tyla) is named after Josef Kajetan Tyl, Czech playwright and novelist, and a champion of national culture in the 19th century. This striking Neo-Classical-style building was erected in 1902 and, just like the National Theatre (turn to Prague, its design was intended to symbolize and reinforce Czech patriotism. The figures on the theatre's façade are allegories of Opera and Drama. The beautiful stage curtain was painted by Augustin Nějmece.

For hotels and restaurants in this region see pp352–3 and pp382–3

Frescoes in the Franciscan Monastery Chapel

🏛 West Bohemian Museum

Kopeckého sady 2. *Tel 377 329 380.* 🕙 9am–5pm Tue–Sun. 🖬 www.zcm.cz

This large museum (Západočeské muzeum) is a Neo-Baroque building with a magnificent Art Nouveau interior dating from 1898. Take time to look at the reliefs on the staircase and the Art Nouveau library furnishings. Exhibits include Charles IV's armoury, and a beautiful glass and porcelain collection in the vast, stately Jubilee Hall.

⛪ Franciscan Monastery and Church of the Assumption

Františkánská.

The early Gothic monastery is one of the town's oldest buildings. Off the lovely cloisters is the 13th-century Chapel of St Barbara, with a stellar vault supported by a single column; the chapel is decorated with frescoes from about 1460. The monastery's Church of the Assumption has a main altarpiece painting of the Annunciation, a copy of Rubens' work. The Gothic Madonna, below the painting, is from the late 14th century.

🏛 Brewing Museum

Veleslavínova 6. *Tel 377 235 574.* 🕙 Jan–Mar: 10am–5pm daily; Apr–Dec: 10am–6pm daily.

Appropriately housed in an old malt house, this museum (Pivovarské muzeum) traces the history of brewing in Plzeň, with a fascinating range of beer-related exhibits.

🍺 Prazdroj Brewery

U Prazdroje 7. *Tel 377 062 888.* 🕙 Jan–Mar: 10am–5pm daily; Apr–Dec: 10am–6pm daily. 🖬 🖬

The opulent brewery (pívovar) building, with its imposing Empire-style gate, is a 1917

work of architect H Zapala. The attractions here – besides tasting Plzeňský Prazdroj (Pilsner Urquell) beer – include the chance to explore its 10-km (6-mile) long cellars, used from 1838 until 1930 to store the fermenting brew *(see p167).*

Façade of the West Bohemian Museum

PLZEŇ CITY CENTRE

Brewing Museum ⑨
Church of St Bartholomew ②
Cisařský dům ④
Franciscan Monastery and Church of the Assumption ⑦
Great Synagogue ⑤
Náměstí Republiky ①
Prazdroj Brewery ⑩
Town Hall ③
Tyl Theatre ⑥
West Bohemian Museum ⑧

0 metres 200
0 yards 200

Key to Symbols see back flap

Cathedral of St Bartholomew

The Gothic Cathedral of St Bartholomew (Chrám sv. Bartoloměje) dominates Plzeň market square from its position in the centre. Its 102-m (335-ft) spire – the tallest in Bohemia – can be seen from all over the city, and was used in the 19th century by the imperial land surveyors in laying out transport routes around Plzeň. Construction of the church continued from the late 13th century until 1480. The Sternberg Chapel, adjoining the south wall of the presbytery, is an early 16th-century addition, featuring an unusual keystone at the centre of the vault, and Renaissance paintings.

★ Cathedral Tower
Originally the cathedral had two towers. One collapsed when struck by lightning in 1525.

Sculptures in the Cathedral
The church houses a large number of sculptures, including the figures of St Barbara, St Katherine and St Wenceslas seen on the pillars of the main nave.

This small tower is over the main nave.

The tower has a balcony at the top, which is open to the public.

Stained-Glass Windows
The magnificent windows in the aisles and the presbytery, which provide the entire church interior with beautiful light, were fitted in the early 20th century.

STAR FEATURES
★ Cathedral Tower
★ Plzeň Madonna
★ Sternberg Chapel

Main door

Pulpit
The Gothic pulpit of sandstone, as well as the magnificent traceried canopy above it, date from the same period as the rood arch figures, and were made in about 1360.

VISITORS' CHECKLIST

Náměstí Republiky 35. **Tel** *377 223 112.* ☐ *Apr–Oct: 9am–4pm Sat–Sun (May–Sep: Tue–Sun).* 🖼
Tower ☐ *10am–6pm daily; Jan & Feb: phone to check.* 🖼
http://info.plzen-city.cz

★ Plzeň Madonna
The statue of the Virgin Mary dating from about 1390, set at the centre of the main altarpiece, is an outstanding example of the International Gothic style.

The presbytery
was given its present form in around 1360.

Pendant Boss, Sternberg Chapel
In the vault of the chapel, this unusual hanging keystone is a unique Late Gothic detail.

★ Sternberg Chapel
The Sternberg family founded this chapel in the early 16th century. It has a beautiful altar (right) and marvellous Renaisssance paintings.

Entrance

Rood Arch
Standing on the beam of the rood arch are figures in a Calvary scene. The crucifix was made in the 1470s by the Bohemian Master of Plzeň.

Side tower of Švihov Castle rising above the moat

Švihov Castle ❷

Road map A3. 🚋 🚌 *from Prague or Plzeň.* **Tel** *376 393 378.* ⭕ *Apr, Oct: 9am–noon, 1–3pm Sat, Sun & public hols; May–Sep: 9.30am–noon, 1–4pm Tue–Sun (Jun–Aug: to 5pm).* 📷 🎥 *2 routes.* **www**.hradsvihov.cz

This beautifully preserved Gothic castle, surrounded by water and meadows, has provided a fairytale backdrop for numerous films. Built in 1480, it is a relatively recent castle for Bohemia. Following the Thirty Years' War it was condemned to demolition by Ferdinand III, but its then owners – the Czernín family – successfully avoided carrying out the Emperor's orders. The entire estate now includes two palaces, a tower, and the defence walls with four bastions. The grand hall of the south castle has a lovely coffered ceiling. The 1515 wall painting in the castle chapel, *Saint George Slaying the Dragon*, includes Švihov in the background.

Klatovy ❸

Road map A3. 🏛 *23,000.* 🚋 🚌 *from Prague or Plzeň.* ℹ️ *Náměstí Míru 63.* **Tel** *376 347 240.* **www**.klatovy.cz

One of the richest towns in Bohemia in the 15th century, Klatovy was founded by Přemysl Otakar II. In the 16th century, Klatovy achieved international fame for its carnations, grown from seeds brought from Nancy in 1813.
The town's dominant feature is the Renaissance **Black**

Tower (Černá věž) – a lofty stone structure in the south-west corner of the town square (náměstí Míru).
Close by is the Baroque **Jesuit Church** (Jezuitský kostel), the work of Giovanni Orsi and Carlo Lurago, built in 1655–75. It was renovated in 1717 by Karl Dientzenhofer, who is credited with designing its magnificent doorway. The interior includes valuable Baroque furnishings, furniture pieces and vivid trompe-l'oeil paintings. The fascinating **catacombs** beneath the church

Black Tower, town hall and Jesuit church in Klatovy

contain scores of mummified bodies of monks. The **White Unicorn Apothecary** (U bílého jednorožce) on the west of the square has its original 17th-century interior lined with bottles and jars of intriguing ingredients. It was a working pharmacy until the 1960s.

🏛 **Catacombs**
⭕ *Apr: Sat, Sun; May–Sep: Tue–Sun.*

🏛 **White Unicorn Apothecary**
Tel *376 326 362.* ⭕ *by appt.*

Velhartice Castle ❹

Road map A3. 🚋 *from Plzeň.* **Tel** *376 583 330.* ⭕ *Apr, Oct: 9am–4pm Sat, Sun; May, Sep: 9am–5pm Tue–Sun; Jun–Aug: 9am–6pm Tue–Sun.*

Between the towns of Klatovy and Sušice, the castle was built at the turn of the 13th and 14th centuries, on a rocky outcrop. It consisted of two palace buildings connected by a huge four-span stone bridge – the only one of its kind in Bohemia *(see also p148)*. In the 18th century a new Renaissance palace was built next to the old one. The castle's most famous owner was Bušek of Velhartice, a secretary to Charles IV. Today, Velhartice is in ruins.

Černé Lake ❺

Road map A3. 🚋 *from Plzeň to Železná Ruda.*

By the German border, at the northwest tip of the Šumava *(see pp148–9)*, lies a beautiful glacial lake known as Black (Černé) Lake. Čertovo (Devil's) Lake is nearby. They are within the National Park area, near the towns of Špičák and Železná Ruda, and can be reached by walking from Špičák station. Black Lake is the largest, the deepest (over 40 m/130 ft) and the lowest-lying lake on the Bohemian side of the Šumava. Its name is believed by some to derive from the reflection in its water of the dark forest wall; others attribute it to the dark silt on the bottom; others put it down to the water's high acidity, which prevents most organisms from populating it.

The serene glacial waters of Černé Lake

Pilsner Urquell

Pilsner beer, produced in Plzeň since 1842, is prized for its outstanding clarity, golden colour and transparency. The beer-making tradition in Plzeň goes back to the times of Wenceslas II, who granted 260 of the town's citizens a licence to produce this golden liquid. Its quality was poor, however, until the Plzeň brewery was established on the banks of the

Bottle of Pilsner Urquell

Radbuza in 1842 after a dozen or so independent breweries were amalgamated. Purpose-built, the brewery *(see p163)* was erected on sandy soil, which made it easy to build tunnels and cellars. Word of the new beer, Pilsner Urquell, quickly spread around Europe, and it was widely imitated. "Pilsner" soon became the generic name for beer produced by similar methods.

The information centre, *the starting point for a visit, is in a modernized section of the old brewery.*

Cellars and tunnels *of the brewery, some 10 km (6 miles) long, are open to the public. Here, visitors can see how the beer is produced and stored using traditional methods.*

In the vast *information centre visitors can view the unique equipment and procedures of beer-making which are not used elsewhere in Europe.*

The label *on the bottles containing the original beer includes at its centre a picture of the entrance gate.*

The wooden casks *containing beer are stored for three months in the maze of long tunnels that were manually dug under the brewery.*

In the past *the beer was matured at low temperatures, in oak or beech barrels sealed inside with resin.*

The brewery entrance gate, *in the shape of a triumphal arch, was erected in 1892, the 50th anniversary of the first golden Pilsner being produced.*

Domažlice ❻

Road map A3. 🏘 *11,000.* 🚊
🚌 *from Plzeň.* ℹ️ *Náměstí Míru 51.*
Tel 379 725 852. 🎭 *Chod Folk
Festival: Aug.* **www**.idomazlice.cz

This quiet, interesting town,
situated on an old trading
route, has at its centre a long,
narrow town square (náměstí
Míru), lined by pretty gabled
houses. Dominating the square
is the leaning **tower** of the
Gothic Church of the Nativity
of the Virgin Mary (Děkanský
kostel Narození Panny Marie).
At 56 m (184 ft) tall, it offers a
magnificent panorama from its
top. Inside the church are
some lovely Baroque frescoes.

The **Castle**, southwest of the
square, was once a fortified
Gothic building. All that
remains is the cylindrical tower
and some 18th-century buildings, now housing the **Chod
Museum** (Muzeum Chodska),
which traces the town's history.
Domažlice was the base of
the Chods, a Slav group who
guarded the border region
from the 11th century on.

More on the Chods can be
discovered in the **Jindàich
Jindàich Museum** outside the
old town to the east. Jindřich
Jindřich was a composer and
collector of Chod folk items.
The display recreates a Chod
cottage interior.

⚓ **Chod Castle and Museum**
Tel 379 776 009. ⏲ *Tue–Sun.* 📷

🏛 **Jindřich Jindřich Museum**
Náměstí svobody 61. *Tel 379 722
974.* ⏲ *Jan–Apr, Oct–Dec:
Mon–Fri; May–Sep: Mon–Sat.*

**Holy Trinity Chapel at Horšovský
Týn Castle**

**Gabled house in Domažlice
town square**

Horšovský Týn ❼

Road map A3. 🏘 *5,000.* 🚌 *from
Prague or Domažlice.* ℹ️ *S Května 50.*
Tel 379 415 151.

The bishops of Prague used
to own this town, which
has a square (náměstí
Republiky) of
Baroque houses
with lovely Gothic
doorways. In 1258
Bishop Jan III of
Dražice built a
fortified Gothic
Castle here. All that
remains is the west
wing and the chapel
in the south tower.
This features beautiful
cross-vaulting supported by
slender columns, an early
Gothic doorway and Renaissance wall paintings. In the
16th century the castle was
transformed into a Renaissance
palace surrounded by a park.
Inside is an interesting
exhibition on the life of the
nobility over the last 400 years.

⚓ **Horšovský Týn Castle**
Tel 379 423 111. ⏲ *Apr, Oct:
Sat, Sun, public hols; May–Sep:
Tue–Sun; 26 Dec–1 Jan: daily.*
📷 *4 routes.* 📷

Stříbro ❽

Road map A2. 🏘 *7,600.* 🚌 *from
Prague.* 🏛 ⏲

The name Stříbro means
"silver" after the silver mines
that existed here from as early
as the 12th century. The town
centre is partly flanked by

14th-century walls. Within a
tower that forms part of the
walls on Plzenská is a winery.

The late Gothic **Church of
All Saints** (Všech svatých) has
interesting Baroque frescoes.
The 1543 **town hall** (radnice)
sports a façade with lavish
sgraffito gables. The former
Minorite Monastery, dissolved
during the reforms introduced
by Joseph II, now houses an
exhibition that includes a history
of silver- and lead-mining.

🏰 **Minorite Monastery**
Tel 379 622 214. ⏲ *9am–noon,
1–4pm Tue–Fri, 9am–2pm Sat.* 📷

**A figure from
Stříbro winery**

Environs
About 6 km (4 miles)
southeast of Stříbro, near
the village of Kladruby, is
**Kladruby Monastery and
Church** (*see also pp176–7*).
The 12th-century Benedictine
monastery was founded by
Vladislav I, remodelled by
Kilian Ignaz Dientzen-
hofer, and includes
Baroque sculptures
by Matthias Braun.
The monastery
church of the
Assumption of the
Virgin Mary (kostel
Nanebevzetí
Panny Marie) was
the lifetime achieve-
ment of Giovanni
Santini, beautifully
combining Gothic and
Baroque outside and in.

🏰 **Kladruby Monastery**
Tel 374 631 773. ⏲ *Jan–Mar & Nov,
Dec: by appt; Apr, Oct: Sat, Sun;
May–Sep: Tue–Sun.* 📷 📷 *2 routes.*

Přimda Castle ❾

Road map A3. 🚌 *from Bor.*

Standing by the motorway to
the Czech-German border
crossing in Rozvadov are the
ruins of Přimda – the oldest
stone castle in Bohemia. Built
in the Romanesque style in the
12th century, it was for four
centuries one of the strongholds guarding the road into
the kingdom. Now its most
imposing part is its massive
keep, whose lower section,
with its 4-m (13-ft) thick wall,
was once used as a prison.

Mariánské Lázně ⑩

Road map A2. 🏘 *14,000.*
🚇 🚌 *from Prague.* 🛈 *Hlavní 47.*
***Tel** 354 622 474.*
www.marienbad.com
🎭 *Chopin Festival: Aug.*

Although the therapeutic powers of the local springs were recognized from the 16th century, it was only in the second half of the 19th century that Mariánské Lázně (formerly Marienbad) became a European spa resort. Its guests at that time included Chopin, Mark Twain, Freud, Kafka and British King Edward VII.

Fresco on the colonnade in Mariánské Lázně

Today Mariánské Lázně has a much quieter ambience, very different from the cosmopolitan bustle of Karlovy Vary *(see pp174–5)*, and is open to all. Visitors have at their disposal about 40 cold mineral water springs that are strongly saturated with natural carbon dioxide. The mountain air remains refreshing, and there are plenty of walks here.

The town has some fine historic buildings spectacularly set on the wooded slopes. The most prominent is the Neo-Baroque spa **colonnade** (kolonáda) built in 1889 of cast iron. At one end of this is the **Cross spring** (Křížový pramen) in an 1818 Empire-style pavilion. Behind the colonnade is the octagonal Neo-Byzantine **Church of the Assumption of the Virgin Mary** (Nanebevzetí Panny Marie). The **Town Museum** (Městské muzeum), in the house once inhabited by Goethe, traces the spa's history. There is a small **Chopin Museum** in the building in which the composer stayed.

🏛 **Town Museum**
Goethovo Náměstí 11. ***Tel** 354 622 740.* ⬤ *Tue–Sun.*

🏛 **Chopin Museum**
Hlavní 47. ***Tel** 354 622 617.*
⬤ *Apr–Oct: Tue, Thu, Sun.*

Lázně Kynžvart ⑪

Road map A2. 🏘 *1,600.* 🚇 *from Prague, Plzeň, Cheb, Mariánské Lázně.*

Nestling in dense woodland, the small town of Lázně Kynžvart (Königswart) competed with Mariánské Lázně in the 19th century in terms of fame. It is now a children's spa.

The town's best-known historic site is the **Palace** of Klemens von Metternich – the creator of the Holy Alliance and from 1821 the all-powerful Chancellor of Austria. This Neo-Classical residence, built in 1820–33 by Viennese architect Pietro Nobile, houses a large assortment of furniture, paintings, sculpture, porcelain and other objects from Metternich's own collection. The park, established at the same time as the palace, is one of the most beautiful English-style gardens in Bohemia.

Perched on top of a wooded hill are the Gothic ruins of Kynžvart **Castle**, which up to the Thirty Years' War still served as a strategic defence structure. The **New Baths**, in the promenade of the spa centre, occupy a Neo-Gothic building built in 1863.

♠ **Kynžvart Palace**
***Tel** 354 691 424.* ⬤ *Feb, Mar, Nov, Dec: by appt; Apr, Oct: Sat, Sun, public hols; May–Sep: Tue–Sun.* 🎫 🎫
www.kynzvart.cz

Cheb ⑫

Road map A2. 🏘 *32,000.* 🚇 *from Prague, Karlovy Vary, Mariánské Lázně.* 🛈 *Náměstí Krále Jiřího z Poděbrad 33.* ***Tel** 354 440 302.*
www.mestocheb.cz

Only 10 km (6 miles) from the border with Germany, Cheb (Eger) is one of Bohemia's oldest towns. From the late 19th century on there was resistance here to Czech nationalism, as well as anti-Semitic feeling. The town was incorporated into the Third Reich in 1938; after the war, most of its German population was forcibly removed.

At the centre is the funnel-shaped market square (náměstí krále Jiřího z Poděbrad), with colourful 17th-century houses. The Špalíček, at its lower, narrow end, consists of 11 medieval half-timbered German-Jewish merchant houses. Also on the square is the **Cheb Museum** (Chebské Muzeum) in the house where Albrecht von Wallenstein was murdered *(see p67)*.

The 13th-century **Church of St Nicholas** (sv. Mikuláše) was given its Baroque features by Balthazar Neumann, a Cheb native. The **Castle** is Cheb's oldest site, built after 1167. Its ruins include the Black Tower (Černá věž), and a beautiful Romanesque chapel.

🏛 **Cheb Museum**
***Tel** 354 400 620.* ⬤ *Nov–Mar: Wed–Sun; Apr–Oct: Tue–Sun.*
www.muzeumcheb.cz

♠ **Cheb Castle**
***Tel** 354 422 942.* ⬤ *Apr–Jun, Sep, Oct: Tue–Sun; Jul, Aug: daily.* 🎫

View of the Church of St Nicholas and the roofs of the old town in Cheb

Františkovy Lázně ⑬

Road map A2. 🏘 5,200. 🔲 🚌
from Prague, Cheb. 🛈 *Americká 2.*
Tel 354 543 162.

The spa town of Františkovy
Lázně (Franzensbad) was
established in 1793, by the
decree of Emperor Franz I.
The local spa waters and mud
baths became famous for their
effectiveness in the treatment
of heart, urinary tract, gynae-
cological and rheumatic conditions. The streets are in a
compact grid layout around
the main street, Národní, and
the buildings are Neo-Classical.
The town has successfully
resisted any industrial
development and remains an
oasis of greenery and calm.

The symbol of Františkovy
Lázně is the statue of František,
a naked boy with a fish. One
small highly polished part of
the statue attests to the popular
belief that stroking it assists
conception. Amid the gardens,
cafés and Neo-Classical buildings is a rotunda over the
Františkův pramen, a pavilion
over the **Grauber spring**
(Glauberovy pramen), an
1882 **music pavilion**, and
the 1820 **Church of the Holy
Cross** (Povýšeni sv. Kříže).

Environs
Seeberg Castle, 5 km (3 miles)
northwest of the town, is a
former Romanesque fortress
with lavishly furnished 19th-
century interiors.

⛪ Seeberg Castle
Tel 354 595 360. ⚪ *Mar, Nov:*
Sat, Sun; Apr–Oct: daily. 📷

The rotunda of Františkův pramen

**Mofettes in the Soos
Nature Reserve**

Soos Nature Reserve ⑭

Road map A2. 6 km (4 miles) NE of
Cheb. **Tel** 354 542 344. ⚪ *Mar,*
Apr, Oct, Nov: 10am–4pm daily;
May, Sep: 10am–5pm daily; Jun:
9am–6pm daily; Jul, Aug:
8am–6pm daily. 📷

The Soos nature
reserve is a
marshy area of
extraordinary hot
springs, quite
exceptional in this
part of Europe,
and testifying to
relatively recent
volcanic activity.
Established in
1964, the reserve
covers an area of
2 sq km (three-quarters of a
square mile). A special 1,200-m
(4,000-ft) wooden trail gives
visitors a chance to gaze at
the lunar landscape full of
bubbling gaseous springs
called mofettes (or bog
volcanoes), as well as
some rare salt-loving
plants (halophytes).
The footpath leads
along the bottom of a
dried lake with a
yellow and white crust
of crystallized salt. The
local **museum** has an
interesting exhibition
devoted to the region's
natural history, the
plants and animals and
the Earth's geological
history; also on display
are numerous stuffed
animals. Tickets to the
reserve include ad-
mission to the museum.

Chlum sv. Máří ⑮

Road map A2. 10 km (6 miles) E of
Cheb (near Kynšperk nad Ohří)
🚌 *from Prague, Karlovy Vary.*
Tel 352 682 091.

Chlum SV. Máří is one of
the most famous sites of the
Marian cult in Bohemia. The
church that formerly stood on
this site was plundered in the
15th century by the Hussite
army, and demolished in
1620 by the local Protestant
nobility. Built on its ruins in
the late 17th century by
Christoph Dientzenhofer is
the present imposing triple-
aisled church. The Chapel of
Mercy, which also serves as
the church vestibule, features
a late 13th-century Gothic
statue of the Virgin Mary,
famous for its miracles.

The church has exception-
ally lavish furnishings. All
of the vaulted ceilings,
including that of
the dome, are
covered with 17th-
century paintings
by Johann Jakob
Steinfels. The aisle
around the church
(the ambulatory),
with its colonnade
opening onto the
courtyard, and
the corner chapels,
are by Giovanni
Santini.

**Statue of the Virgin
Mary, Chlum sv. Máří**

Loket ⑯

Road map A2. 🏘 3,200. 🚌 *from*
Prague, Karlovy Vary. 🛈 *T G*
Masaryka 12. **Tel** 352 684 123.
🎭 *Loket Summer Cultural Festival:*
late Jul. **www**.loket.cz

The tiny town of Loket
(Elbogen) lies in a rocky
crook of the Ohře River; its
Czech and German names
both mean "elbow". The
town, which just like Český
Krumlov is washed around on
three sides by running waters,
is an exceptionally scenic
place. Thanks to china clay in
last two centuries it has been
renowned for its fine
porcelain. The picturesque
market square (náměstí T G
Masaryka) sports a plague
column and numerous

◁ **Towers of the Gothic castle in Loket**

Houses and town hall in Loket market square

interesting Gothic houses. It also features a graceful Early Baroque **town hall** (radnice) built in 1682–96. It was thoroughly restored in 1989.

The Gothic **castle** has well-preserved towers, gates, walls and keeps. In 1319 John of Luxemburg used it to imprison his wife Eliška of the Přemysl family, and their three-year-old son, Wenceslas, later Emperor Charles IV.

The town was frequently visited by Goethe who in 1823, in the house called **Bílý kůň** on the main square, now a hotel *(see p353)*, met for the last time with the great love of his declining years, Ulrika von Levetzow. At that time he was 74 years old; she was 19. She refused his marriage proposal and died unmarried at the age of 93.

♣ **Loket Castle**
***Tel** 352 684 104.* ◻ *daily.* ▨

Environs
In Bečov nad Teplou, 10 km (6 miles) southeast of Loket, is a **Castle** and **Palace** complex, a unique example of combining a medieval fortress with a Baroque residence. This majestic structure stands perched on a high rock above the Tepla river valley. Its oldest, Gothic section, dating from the first half of the 14th century, has never been modified and remains in its original state.

At the foot of the medieval castle its successive owners have made their own mark on the castle, building a Renaissance residence in the 16th century, and an octagonal, domed Baroque

palace with a tower two centuries later. The state rooms and the large library have survived particularly well.

Displayed in the palace chapel is one of the most precious ecclesiastical objects in Europe – the Romanesque reliquary of St Maurus, made in the Benedictine monastery in Florennes, in present-day Belgium. It was brought to Bohemia in the 19th century, by the then owner of Bečov – Alfred de Beaufort. Before the end of World War II, the Beauforts, who collaborated with the Germans, left their home in a hurry, burying the reliquary, which is encrusted with gold, silver and precious stones, under the chapel floor. Following long years of searching it was found in 1985.

♣ **Bečov Castle and Palace**
***Tel** 353 999 394.* ◻ *Jan, Feb, Dec: by appt; Apr, Oct: Sat, Sun; May–Sep: Tue–Sun.* ▨ ▨ *2 routes.*

Karlovy Vary ⑰

See pp174–5.

Manětín ⑱

Road map A2. ▨ *1,300.* ▨ *from Prague, Plzeň.*

The earliest records of the town of Manětín date from 1169, when King Vladislav II donated it to the Knights of St John of Prague. It now has a large collection of Baroque sculpture, resembling a vast open-air gallery.

Manětín Palace occupies one entire side of the long market square. Built after 1712 to a design by Giovanni Santini, it features an interesting staircase decorated with allegories of the four elements. The interiors and surroundings have been decorated with 18th-century sculptures produced by local artists Josef Herscher and Štěpán Boroviec. Their figures of the saints and apostles stand on the terrace before the palace's north façade, by the main routes towards Plzeň, Nečtin and Rabštejn and on many further sites around the town. Among the sculptures are an image of the Holy Trinity, and figures of St John Nepomuk, St Florentius, St Anne, St Joseph, St Sebastian, St Donatus, and the Archangel Michael.

Works by Herscher and Boroviec can also be found in the **Church of St John the Baptist**, linked with the palace by a covered corridor, and in the Baroque **Church of St Barbara**. There are also fine paintings by Petr Brandl – the *Baptism of Christ* in the first, and the *Death of St Isidore* and the *Killing of St Wenceslas* in the second church.

♣ **Manětín Palace**
***Tel** 373 392 283.* ◻ *Apr, Oct: Sat, Sun, public hols; May–Sep: Tue–Sun.* ▨ ▨

The castle in Bečov nad Teplou

Karlovy Vary 🔟

World-famous for its mineral springs, the town of Karlovy Vary (Karlsbad) was founded by Charles IV in the mid-14th century. Legend has it that he discovered it when one of his dogs fell into a hot spring (*vary* means "hot spring") when out hunting. Since the 18th century the rich and famous have flocked here to take the waters. The town is also known for its china – the first porcelain factory opened in the early 19th century – and for Moser glassware.

Wooden Market Colonnade and castle tower

Exploring the town

The spa district of Karlovy Vary starts in T G Masaryka Street, which runs into Zahradní; the spas continue south along the banks of the Teplá river, in the valley flanked on both sides by wooded slopes. The two streets that follow the river, lined with pleasant 19th- and 20th-century houses, are linked by numerous road- and foot-bridges. All the mineral springs are also found along the river, as well as the historic colonnades and the majority of interesting architectural sights.

🏛 Imperial Baths

Mariánskolázeňska 2.
The imposing Imperial Baths or Kaiserbad (Lázně I), looking more like a theatre than a medical establishment, was once the most opulent building in Karlovy Vary. Built in 1892–5, they feature a magnificent Neo-Renaissance façade and Art Nouveau decorations, inside and out.

🏛 Karlovarské Museum

Nová Louka 23. *Tel 353 226 252.*
⏰ 9am–noon, 1–5pm Wed–Sun.
The museum, established in 1853, has collections relating to the region's history and its natural environment; also on display are glass and porcelain items and handicrafts. Besides permanent displays there are also topical exhibitions organized throughout the year.

🔲 Karlovy Vary Theatre

Divadelní náměstí 21. *Tel 353 225 801.*
The Karlovy Vary theatre (Městské divadlo), built in 1884–86, is the work of Viennese architects Ferdinand Fellner and Hermann Helmer, who designed many theatre buildings all over Europe. It is worth stepping inside to see the magnificent interior decor, which includes paintings by Gustav Klimt, his brother Ernst, and Franz Matsche. A collective work of all three artists is the curtain, on which they painted their joint self-portrait. Following many years of reconstruction the theatre was opened again in 1999.

🔲 Church of St Mary Magdalene

Kostelní náměstí.
Dating from 1732, and among the best work of Kilian Ignaz Dientzenhofer, this church (sv. Máří Magdalény) is one of the finest examples of Baroque architecture in Bohemia. The single-aisled church with an oval floor plan has an impressively spacious interior with fine decor. The high altar features an image of Mary Magdalene from 1752. It is flanked by Jakob Eberle's 1759 sculptures of St Augustine, St Jerome, St Peter and St Paul. It is also worth taking a closer look at the lavishly decorated side altars, the dome and the magnificent galleries high up. The wavy façade with two towers features a splendid semi-circular stairway.

Detail above Karlovy Vary Theatre entrance

🏛 Market Colonnade

Lázeňská. *Tel 353 362 100.*
This lovely white wooden colonnade, Tržní kolonáda, designed in Swiss style by Ferdinand Fellner and Hermann Helmer, was built on the site of a former town hall, which was demolished in 1879. It contains two springs. In 1991–2 it underwent a thorough reconstruction, although it has kept its original appearance.

BOHEMIA'S SPA RESORTS

Clustered in the western part of the country, spa resorts (lázně) began to emerge and flourish in the 18th century. Crowds of patients and prominent figures of the day visited spas, initially to take medicinal baths, and later to drink spring waters in truly exclusive company and opulent surroundings. During the Communist era, spa cures were open to all who needed them, and spa treatments remain popular in the Czech Republic today. The spas also attract numerous German, Austrian and Russian visitors, and during the past 20 years many have been restored to their former glory.

Karlovy Vary in 1891

For hotels and restaurants in this region see pp352–3 and pp382–3

Columns of the Mill Spring Colonnade

VISITORS' CHECKLIST

Road map A2. 🎪 51,500.
🚉 Main and local stations. 🚌
Varšavská. 🛈 Lázeňská 1. **Tel** 355
321 176. **Fax** 353 224 667.
🛈 Západní 2A. **Tel** 353 232 838.
Fax 353 232 839. 🎬 International Film Festival: late Jun–Jul.
www. karlovyvary.cz

🏛 Mill Spring Colonnade
Mlýnské nábřeží.
Built in 1871–81 by Josef Zítek, creator of the National Theatre in Prague *(see pp94–5)*, the Mill Spring Colonnade (Mlýnská kolonáda) is the largest of the resort's colonnades, and one of its most opulent. The Neo-Renaissance gallery, 132 m (430 ft) long and 13 m (43 ft) wide, has a coffered ceiling resting on 124 columns with Corinthian capitals. Inside are five springs, with a water temperature exceeding 50°C (120°F). Statues at each end represent the twelve months of the year.

🏛 Park Spring Colonnade
Dvořákovy sady.
On the west bank of the Teplá, right at the centre of town, stands Sadová Kolonáda – a beautiful painted wrought-iron structure made of columns decorated with sculptures, terminating in two pavilions. The colonnade was designed by Ferdinand Fellner and Hermann Helmer in 1880–81. It stands in the Dvořákovy sady gardens.

Gilded domes of the Church of St Peter and St Paul

⛪ Church of St Peter and St Paul
Krále Jiřího. ◻ 10am–5pm daily.
This church (sv. Petr a Pavel) with its five gilded domes, built in 1893–7 by G Wiedermann, is among the world's largest Russian Orthodox churches. It was built for the Russian aristocracy, who in the 19th century flocked to Karlovy Vary in great numbers.

⛰ Diana Viewpoint
Funicular. ◻ 9:15am–4:45pm (to 6:45pm Jun–Sep) daily.
Behind the town's top hotel, the Grand Hotel Pupp *(see p352)*, at the southern end of Stará Louka, is the lower station of the funicular, which runs to the top of the Hill of Friendship. Built in 1912, the funicular rises 167 m (550 ft), covering a distance of 435 m (1,425 ft). At the top is the Diana viewpoint, providing a great view over the resort.

KARLOVY VARY TOWN CENTRE

Church of St Mary Magdalene ④
Church of St Peter and St Paul ⑧
Diana Viewpoint ⑨
Imperial Baths ①
Karlovarské Museum ②
Karlovy Vary Theatre ③
Market Colonnade ⑤
Mill Spring Colonnade ⑥
Park Spring Colonnade ⑦

0 metres 200
0 yards 200

Key to Symbols *see back flap*

West Bohemian Monasteries

In the Middle Ages West Bohemia experienced the emergence of numerous centres of monastic life. The most prominent were the abbeys: the Benedictine in Kladruby *(see p168)*, the Cistercian in Plasy and the Premonstratensian in Teplá. In the Baroque era the medieval buildings were converted by the leading architects of the day into vast church and monastery complexes, with opulent interior decor and furnishings.

The Cistercian Monastery in Plasy, *about 20 km (12 miles) north of Plzeň, was founded in 1144–45, by Vladislav II. Giovanni Santini and the French-born architect Jean-Baptiste Mathey gave it its present Baroque appearance.*

The lantern *above the cupola of Kladruby Church, which gives it its distinctive silhouette, was designed by Giovanni Santini in 1716–18. Topped with a golden crown, it filters a beautiful light into the building.*

Inside Kladruby Church, *the nave is 85 m (280 ft) long, the longest in Bohemia. The interior was designed by Santini, including the highly decorative vaulting. The tomb of the monastery's founder, Vladislav I, is at the front of the church, to the left.*

The lavishly decorated façade *of the church dates from 1726, which is confirmed by the date in the porch of the main entrance. The statue of the Madonna stands on top of the façade in a niche above the tall window, dates from 1716.*

The Premonstratensian Monastery, Teplá, 15 km (9 miles) east of Mariánské Lázně, was founded in 1193. The spectacular Neo-Baroque Monastery library was added in the 1900s and houses about 100,000 volumes.

The Teplá Monastery Church of the Annunciation of the Virgin Mary is a beautiful Romanesque building, part of the original 12th-century monastery complex. Much of the rest of the complex was built in Baroque style in 1689–1721 by K I Dientzenhofer.

The mosaic seen above the beautiful portal of the Romanesque-Gothic Church of the Annunciation, in Teplá, depicts the Virgin Mary and Child.

AVE MARIA · GRATIA PLENA

KLADRUBY MONASTERY

This Benedictine monastery, founded in 1114 by Vladislav I, became a major centre of Přemyslid power. Early in the 18th century, St Mary's, the original church, was remodelled by Giovanni Santini in Baroque style with some obvious Gothic elements. It is considered to be the greatest achievement of this brilliant Czech-born architect. In 1785 the monastery was closed and rebuilt as a chateau to designs by K I Dientzenhofer (see p65).

The new building was designed by K I Dientzenhofer as a chateau.

Mariánsky Týnec has belonged to the Cistercians from nearby Plasy Monastery since 1230. Giovanni Santini was responsible for numerous Baroque additions in the first half of the 18th century.

NORTH BOHEMIA

O ne of the most prosperous and industrial parts of the country for many centuries, divided in two by the Labe (Elbe), North Bohemia is a diverse and rewarding region to explore. The attractive main city of Liberec offers a good taste of Czech culture, while slightly off the beaten track are a surprising number of castles and atmospheric old towns.

The wealth of North Bohemia (Severní Čechy) was based principally on the region's natural resources. Iron ore and coal were mined here from the Middle Ages. During the past few centuries the production of fine porcelain has played a significant role in its economy. Unfortunately the intensive exploitation of raw materials, especially strip-mining for lignite (brown coal), and industrial overdevelopment have ravaged the region's landscape. Since 1989, much has been done to reduce pollution and limit the ecological damage, but even now the dominant features of much of North Bohemia are factory chimneys and areas of lunar landscape left by mining works.

While the region has shared much of its history and culture with Bohemia, a considerable section of its population has been German. Many surviving relics of Gothic architecture bear witness to the mingling of Czech and Saxon cultures. In 1938 a large part of North Bohemia, dominated by Germans, was incorporated into the Third Reich, who set up Terezín as a concentration camp. The forcible expulsion of all local Germans after World War II left many towns and villages deserted. These have since been resettled, but some border areas remain underpopulated. Roma (Gypsies) live in many areas, and tension exists between them and the local Czechs.

Tucked away in the region are some remarkably well-preserved or lovingly restored castles, towns and monasteries. The weird geological formations of České Švýcarsko ("Czech Switzerland") attract many visitors interested in outdoor activities.

Part of a gable on a slate-tiled house in Úštěk

◁ The castle of Děčín overlooking the Labe

Exploring North Bohemia

The jewels of North Bohemian architecture – Litoměřice, Louny, Žatec, Kadaň and Úštěk – must be included in the itinerary of any visitor exploring this part of the country. Their amazingly well-preserved old towns are truly impressive, although to restore individual buildings to their former glory still requires a great deal of work and money. The region's main city, Liberec, is a thriving centre, with some excellent art collections. The extraordinary rock formations are the main feature of České Švýcarsko, where the Labe (Elbe) has cut a narrow gorge on its way through the Czech Republic to Germany.

Palace in Teplice

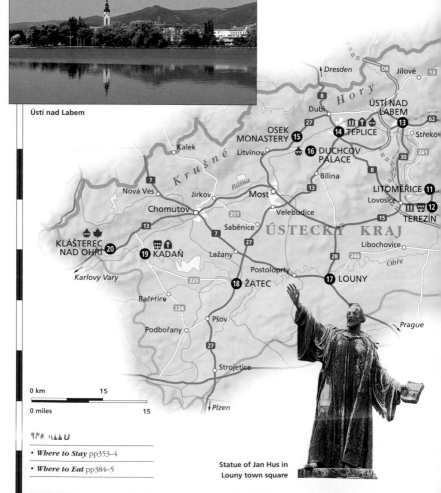

Ústí nad Labem

Dresden — D8 — Jílové 13

Hory

8

Dubi — ÚSTÍ NAD LABEM — 13 — 62

27 — 🏛 ⛪ — Střeko

OSEK MONASTERY 15 — 14 TEPLICE

Kalek — Litvínov — 🏛 16 DUCHCOV PALACE — 30 — 261

Krušné — Bílina — Bílina — 8

Nová Ves — Jirkov — Most — 13 — LITOMĚŘICE 11

Chomutov — Velebudice — Lovosice — 🏛 🏛 12

251 — TEREZÍN

13 — Saběnice — ÚSTECKÝ KRAJ — 15

KLÁŠTEREC NAD OHŘÍ 20 — 19 KADAŇ — Lažany — 27 — Libochovice — 28 — 246

Karlovy Vary — 225 — Postoloprty — Ohře

Račetice — 18 ŽATEC — 17 LOUNY

224 — Pšov

Podbořany — Prague

27

Strojetice

0 km — 15

0 miles — 15

♦ Plzen

Statue of Jan Hus in Louny town square

GETTING AROUND

The easiest way of getting to North Bohemia from Prague is along D8 motorway (the international E55 route), which in future will link the Czech capital with Dresden. The wide road 10 goes to Liberec, and towards the Polish border. The main transport route cutting across the entire region, from Liberec all the way to Chomutov, is the popular and often congested road 13. Buses and trains provide reasonable coverage of North Bohemia but are less frequent during weekends and holiday periods.

Interior staircase, Liberec Town Hall

Arable land beside the road linking Kadaň with Žatec

KEY

═══	Motorway
═ ═	Motorway under construction
───	Main road
⋯⋯	Minor road
⌁⌁	Main railway
───	Minor railway
▬▬	International border
▬▬	Regional border
△	Summit

SIGHTS AT A GLANCE

Liberec ❶

As early as the 16th century Liberec (Reichenberg) was a major weaving centre. With the 19th-century industrial revolution, large textile factories and metalwork plants brought true prosperity to the city. Between the two World Wars Liberec was the main political centre of the Czech Germans; under German occupation it was made the capital of Sudetenland. After the war it regained its position as North Bohemia's main city, while also becoming a tourist centre.

Lavishly decorated façade of F X Šaldy Theatre

Exploring the city

Liberec is rich in historic buildings, similar to many Czech towns, but also has equally interesting, modern buildings, which can be seen between the main square and Sokolovské náměstí. Sights outside this area include the Oblastní Gallery, and a little further east from the centre, the Severočeské Museum.

⊞ Náměstí Dr E Beneše

Liberec's main square, and the entire town, are dominated by the Neo-Renaissance town hall (see pp184–5). In front of the town hall is a fountain by Franz Metzner dating from 1927. By the steps of the town hall is a modest monument to those who died fighting in 1968 after the Warsaw Pact invasion.

The houses around the square are not as uniformly well preserved as in many other old towns, and mostly [illegible] centuries, but a few fine ones survive, among them the Posta Café opposite the theatre, with beautiful Neo-Renaissance stuccoes, chandeliers and furnishings.

⊞ Town Hall (Radnice)

See pp184–5

🖼 F X Šaldy Theatre

Náměstí Dr E Beneše 22. **Tel** 485 104 188. ⏰ 10am–6pm (until 7pm on performance days) Mon–Fri.

At the rear of the town hall is the F X Šaldy Theatre (Divadlo F X Šaldy), designed in 1883 by the Viennese architects Ferdinand Fellner and Hermann Helmer. Its ornate façade has an allegory of Art holding a torch, and a figure of Apollo surrounded by dolphins. Inside, take a look at the curtain painted by Gustav Klimt.

Façade of an early 19th-century building in Sokolovské náměstí

⊞ Sokolovské Náměstí

This square includes some houses with highly ornate façades, but its main sight is the Church of St Anthony (sv. Antonína). This triple-aisled edifice has a 70-m (230-ft) tall tower. Built in 1579–87 and remodelled in the 19th century in Neo-Gothic style, it is the town's oldest brick building. Its interior is dominated by a 10-m (33-ft) high altarpiece with figures of the patron saints of Bohemia.

⊞ Wallenstein Houses

Větrná.

Just off Sokolovské náměstí in narrow Větrná street are some of the oldest and most interesting buildings in Liberec: the Wallenstein Houses (Valdštejnské domky). The three buildings of timber-frame construction and with street-facing gables date from 1678–81. They were once inhabited by cloth-makers, and one was an inn.

The half-timbered Wallenstein Houses

♿ Church of the Holy Cross

Malé Náměstí. **Tel** 485 108 506.

This Baroque church (sv. Kříže) with a cross-shape floorplan was built by Johann Josef Kunz in 1753–61 on the site of an older church that stood on a former plague cemetery. Its richly fitted interior includes a statue of the Virgin Mary holding the dead body of Christ, which dates from 1506. The beautiful Plague Column (1719) standing behind the church came from the workshop of Matthias Braun.

Liberec Castle – one of the town's early brick buildings

🛕 Liberec Castle
U tiskárny. ⬤ *to visitors.*
The original Renaissance palace dating from 1583–7 was remodelled several times. It has a Renaissance chapel with a lovely coffered ceiling, and beautifully carved wooden oratory supported by five columns. There are plans to turn the castle into a showcase for local crystalware.

🏛 Oblastní Gallery
U tiskárny. **Tel** *485 106 325.*
◯ 10am–6pm Tue–Sun. 🎦
www.ogl.cz
One of the finest galleries in the Czech Republic, this has been housed in the 1872 Neo-Renaissance villa of a textile industrialist, Baron Johann Liebig. Much of the art collection was donated to the town in 1904 by the Liebig family; it now includes works by 16th–18th century Dutch and Flemish artists; 19th-century French landscapists and many superb modern paintings and sculptures by Czech artists. There is also a recently opened exhibition of 19th-century German and Austrian painting.

Dvorek v Benátkách by August Pettenkofen, Oblastní Gallery

🏛 Severočeské Museum
Masarykova 11. **Tel** *485 246 111.*
◯ 9am–5pm Tue–Sun. 🎦
This eclectic museum is housed in a Neo-Renaissance building erected in 1897–8. The large, varied collection includes glass, ceramics, porcelain, textiles, furniture, clocks and jewellery, much of it locally produced. There are also photography, archaeology and history exhibitions. Particularly valuable is its extraordinary collection of mechanical music instruments.

Environs
A further walk eastwards along the tree-lined Masarykova leads to the **Botanical Gardens** and the **Zoo**, the oldest (1904) in Bohemia. To the southwest of the centre is one of Liberec's landmarks, **Ještěd** peak. On the 1012-m (3,320-ft) summit, reached by cable car, is a 1960s tower, part of a hotel, which offers superb views.

LIBEREC TOWN CENTRE

Church of the Holy Cross ⑥
F X Šaldy Theatre ③
Liberec Castle ⑦
Náměstí Dr E Beneše ①
Oblastní Gallery ⑧
Sokolovské Náměstí ④
Town Hall ②
Wallenstein Houses ⑤

0 metres 200
0 yards 200

Key to Symbols *see back flap*

Liberec Town Hall

A majestic edifice, the town hall (radnice) was built in the German Neo-Renaissance style in 1888–93 to a design by Viennese architect Franz Neumann. The size and ornamentation were intended to highlight the status and wealth of the town, which in the late 19th century was one of the main industrial centres of the Austro-Hungarian Empire. The councillors and townsfolk were undoubtedly flattered by the fact that the silhouette of the new building was strongly reminiscent of Vienna's town hall.

★ Main Façade
The symmetrical façade sports a 65-m (210-ft) tower; in 2005 a knight with a banner was placed at the top.

Staircase Ceiling
The painting by A Groll on the ceiling of the main staircase depicts a female figure symbolizing Liberec and the god of trade, Mercury.

★ Staircase
The main staircase to the first-floor state rooms emphasized the town's wealth with its use of marble and its sheer size.

Entrance Hall
Marble stairs, illuminated by stained-glass windows donated by the guild of bakers, lead from the hall to the first-floor rooms.

Above the main entrance is the date of completion, and a relief by Theodore Friedel.

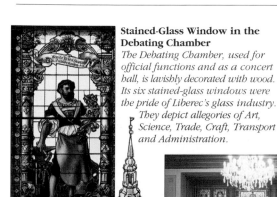

Stained-Glass Window in the Debating Chamber

The Debating Chamber, used for official functions and as a concert hall, is lavishly decorated with wood. Its six stained-glass windows were the pride of Liberec's glass industry. They depict allegories of Art, Science, Trade, Craft, Transport and Administration.

VISITORS' CHECKLIST

Náměstí Dr E Beneše 1. **Tel** 485 101 709. **Fax** 485 243 589. ▢
Oct–Apr: 9am–4pm Mon–Fri;
May–Sep: 9am–4pm Mon–Fri;
9am–noon Sat, Sun (visits booked
via Liberec info centre - see p183)
▨ ▰ by appt. www.liberec.cz

Drawing Room

A large stained-glass window in the Drawing Room shows Liberec's old town hall, demolished in 1893.

Mayoral Offices

The first-floor drawing room is a part of the office of the town's mayor; it is used to hold official meetings.

Side Entrance

Flanked by two ornate columns (right), this door leads to the town's information centre.

STAR FEATURES

★ Main Façade

★ Staircase

Tomb of Frederick I, his wife and son, Church of the Holy Cross, Frýdlant

Frýdlant ❷

Road map B2. 🏛 *7,500.*
🚉 🚌 *from Liberec.* 🛈 *Náměstí T
G Masaryka 99.* **Tel** *482 312 552.*

The small town of Frýdlant
(Friedland) is dominated by
its vast, sprawling castle.
Frýdlant Castle reputedly
inspired Franz Kafka as the
setting for his famous novel
The Castle. An earlier Gothic
fortress was extended in the
16th century by an Italian
architect, Marco Spazzio di
Lancio, commissioned by the
von Redern family who
owned the castle from 1558.
Following the Battle of the
White Mountain in 1620, this
opulent residence became the
property of the powerful
Albrecht von Wallenstein, who
assumed the title of Duke of
Frýdlant. The Swedes, who
occupied the castle at the end
of the Thirty Years' War,
strengthened its defence walls
and built fortified barbicans.
    The castle was opened to
the public as early as 1801.
Now it is possible to view its
magnificently restored interiors,
including the Knights' Hall,
Portraits Hall and Trophies
Room. Inside are many valuable pieces of furniture,
tapestries, porcelain,
ceramics, chandeliers, suits of
armour and uniforms. The
collection of paintings is
outstanding, with works by
Karel Škréta, Václav Vavřinec
Reiner and others. The castle
museum has an exhibition on
the Thirty Years' War.
    The beautiful **Church of the
Holy Cross** (sv. Kříž), built by

Italian architects in the mid-
16th century, has a lavishly
decorated interior and a monumental mausoleum (1610) to
the von Redern family.

🏰 **Frýdlant Castle**
Tel *482 312 130.* ⬜ *Apr, Oct:
Wed–Sun; May–Sep: Tue–Sun.* 🖼
📷 *3 routes.* **www**.npu.cz

Hejnice ❸

Road map B2. 7 km (4 miles) SE of
Frýdlant. 🏛 *2,700.* 🚌 *from Liberec.*

Hejnice is a small, pleasant
village with a spa. Visitors
come mainly for its **Church of
the Visitation of the Blessed
Virgin Mary** (Navštívení Panny
Marie), one of the Czech
Republic's major pilgrimage
centres. On this site, according
to tradition, the Virgin Mary
has bestowed miraculous
graces and favours since the
13th century. The earlier stone
Gothic church was replaced
by a magnificent Baroque one

in 1729, able to accommodate
7,000 worshippers.
    The main altarpiece has a
14th-century Gothic Madonna.
During the Reformation, when
the district was ruled by the
Protestant Redern family, the
church was closed, and the
statue transferred to Frýdlant
Castle. When the statue
survived a fire in the castle in
1615 this was taken as a sign
that it should be returned,
and it was soon afterwards.

🏛 **Church of the Visitation
of the Blessed Virgin Mary**
Tel *482 360 211.* ⬜ *daily.* 🕓 *4pm
Tue–Sun, 9am Sun.* **www**.mcdo.cz

Environs
Hejnice is the best starting
point for forays into **Jizerské
mountains**, a natural extension
of the Krkonoše massif. The
most scenic hiking route (well
signposted, about 30 km/18
miles long) leads from Hejnice
to the top of Smrk (1,122 m/
3,680 ft) with a superb view
over the peat moor Na Čihadle.

Jablonné
v Podještědí ❹

Road map B2. 🏛 *3,800.*
🚉 🚌 *from Liberec.* 🛈 *Náměstí
Míru 23.* **Tel** *487 829 970.*

One of the oldest villages in
Bohemia, Jablonné (Gabel)
was founded in 1240. Activity
centres around the main square
(náměstí Míru), where cafés
overlook the **Basilica of St
Lawrence and St Zdislava** (sv.
Vavřince a Zdislavy). This
Baroque edifice with its lofty
dome was built in 1699. In

View of the pilgrimage church in Hejnice

the Baroque crypt below the high altar is the tomb of St Zdislava, who lived in the 13th century, the wife of the local lord of Lemberk *(see below)*. In 1995 she was canonized. The façade includes Baroque statues of saints, including St Zdislava and St Lawrence.

🔒 Basilica of St Lawrence and St Zdislava
Tel 487 762 105. ☐ May–Sep: Tue–Sun. **www**.zdislava.cz

Environs
About 2 km (1 mile) northeast of the village is **Lemberk Castle**, St Zdislava's home, which has interesting displays on her life.

⛪ Lemberk Castle
Tel 487 762 305. ☐ Apr, Oct: Sat & Sun; May–Sep: Tue–Sun. 🏷️ 🖥️ http://szlemberk.xf.cz

The Basilica of St Lawrence and St Zdislava in Jablonné v Podještědí

Sychrov Palace ❺

Road map B2. 🚊 from Liberec. **Tel** 482 416 011. ☐ Jan–Mar: 10am–2pm daily; Apr, Sep, Oct: 9am–3:30pm daily; May–Aug: 9am–4:30pm daily; Nov, Dec: 10am–2pm daily. 🏷️ 🖥️ **www**.zamek-sychrov.cz

The palace stands in the romantic valley of the Mohelka river. An earlier Baroque building was remodelled in the 19th century in Neo-Classical, and later in Neo-Gothic style. From 1820 to 1945 the palace belonged to the aristocratic French Rohan family, who assembled a large collection of art here. Now the Rohan Gallery has a superb collec-

tion of French portrait paintings, unrivalled outside France. Antonín Dvořák came several times to Sychrov to rest between 1877 and 1880. The palace is surrounded by a large English-style garden with many exotic trees. Here, concerts are held over the summer months.

Česká Lípa ❻

Road map A2. 🏛️ 40,000. 🚊 from Děčín, Liberec. 🚌 from Prague. ℹ️ Náměstí T G Masaryka 2. **Tel** 487 881 105. **www**.mucl.cz

In the 15th century, Česká Lípa (Böhmisch Leipa) was one of the major centres of the Hussite movement. Later, in the 19th century it gained a reputation as a dynamic centre of the textile industry, producing popular printed fabrics. Today Česká Lípa is an industrial town with some interesting architectural sights.
The main square is lined with attractive houses. All that remains of the former Renaissance castle is the lovely decorated 1583 **Red House** (Červený dům), with a magnificent loggia running along its first floor. The **Church of the Holy Cross** (sv. Kříž) was founded in 1381 and bears evidence of later remodelling. The **Regional Museum** has a small collection of local historic materials. It is housed in the former Augustinian monastery, founded in 1627 by Albrecht von Wallenstein.

🏛️ Regional Museum
Tel 487 824 145. ☐ Mar, Apr, Oct–Dec: Wed–Sun; May–Sep: Tue–Sun. 🏷️ **www**.muzeumcl.cz

České Švýcarsko ❼

See pp188–9.

Baroque castle in Děčín

Děčín ❽

Road map A2. 🏛️ 134,000. 🚊 🚌 from Prague. ℹ️ Prokopa Holého 8. **Tel** 412 531 333.

Lying on both sides of the Labe (Elbe), Děčín (Tetschen) is made up of the more industrial Podmokly on the left bank, and the older Děčín on the right. In Děčín the **Church of the Holy Cross** (sv. Kříž) is an ornate Baroque building from the late 17th century. The town square has a lovely 1906 Art Nouveau fountain. Dominating the town is the **castle**, a royal fortress built in the 13th century and adapted in the 17th and 18th centuries. Entrance is via Dlouhá jízda, a steep, narrow alley built in the 1670s. The castle has a superb rose garden.

⛪ Děčín Castle
Tel 412 518 905. ☐ Mar–Dec: daily; Jan–Feb: Thu–Sun. 🏷️ 🖥️

Houses in the main square in Česká Lípa

České Švýcarsko ❼

Information sign on a hiking trail

An extraordinary area of natural beauty, České Švýcarsko is a landscape of forests and fantastically shaped sandstone rocks, crisscrossed by gorges and ravines. This region was attracting tourists as early as the 19th century, when the Romantic poets first dubbed it the "Czech Switzerland" (It is also referred to as "Bohemian Switzerland"). The National Park established over this area, in 2000, continues to attract many visitors, mainly from Germany.

Pravčicka brána
This is the largest natural rock bridge in Central Europe, at 26 m (85 ft) long, 7–8 m (25 ft) wide, and rising to a height of 16 m (52 ft).

From Mezní Louka a red hiking trail leads to the stone bridge of Pravčická brána, 6.5 km (4 miles) away. From here you can continue on the same trail to Hřensko, a further 2.5 km (2 miles).

Falcon's Nest
This small castle (1881), by the Pravčicka brána, belonged to the Clary-Aldringen family. It now houses a restaurant and the National Park Museum.

0 km   1
0 miles   1

Hřensko

Děčín

Labe (Elbe)

62

Mezní Louka

Mežná

Kamenice

Kamenická Stráň

Kamenice Gorge
This narrow gorge runs between vertical walls of rock 50–150 m (165–500 ft) high. Boat trips go up- or downstream. The footpath along its banks was built in the 19th century by Italian workers.

Tichá Soutěska
Known as the "quiet gorge", this section of Kamenice Gorge stretches for 960 m (3,150 ft).

For hotels and restaurants in this region see pp353–4 and pp383–5

Wildlife in the National Park
České Švýcarsko used to be rich in animal species. Although the animal diversity is not as great as it once was, the Park remains a haven for wildlife, including European beaver, river otter, lynx, which settled here in the 1930s, and the Alpine chamois, introduced in 1907.

VISITORS' CHECKLIST

Road map B2. 🚌 *from Děčín.*
🛈 *Hřensko 82.* **Tel** *412 554 286.* **www**.pbrana.cz
National Park Museum
Falcon's Nest. **Tel** *604 238 209.*
⏰ *Apr–Oct: 10am–6pm daily; Nov–Mar: 10am–4pm Sat, Sun.*

Tourist Trails
The entire area of the Park has a network of clearly signposted hiking and cycling trails.

Sokolí vrch
▲
486 m
(1594 ft)

Doubice

Ostroh
▲
484 m
(1588 ft)

unštejn

soká Lípa   Jetřichovice

Rynartice

Šaunštejn
The high rock platform, which once was the site of the small Šaunštejn Castle, known also as Robbers' castle (Loupežnický hradek), can now be reached only by a series of vertical stepladders.

Jetřichovice
This scenic village, whose timber houses now provide beds for the many walkers, makes a good base for forays into the rocky Jetřichovické range.

KEY

═ Road

--- Hiking trail

≈ River

� Viewpoint

Benešov nad Ploučnicí ❾

Road map B2. 🚶 *4,200.* 🚍 💬
from Děčín. 🛈 *Náměstí Míru 1.*
Tel *412 589 811.*

Two 16th-century castles are
the pride of Benešov, an
attractive town centred
on its main square.
The 15th-century
**Church of the
Nativity of the
Virgin Mary**
(Narozeni Panny
Marie) has a 16th-
century sandstone
pulpit. There is
also a fine Renais-
sance town hall.

**Gable of the town hall
in Benešov**

The castles are in the Saxon
Renaissance style, rare in
Bohemia. Both adjoin the
15th-century city walls. The
Upper Castle is partially open
to the public due to renovations following a 1969 fire.
The **Lower Castle** has some
interesting interiors.

🏛 **Benešov Castles**
Tel *412 586 575.* ☐ *Apr, Oct:
Wed–Sun; May–Sep: Tue–Sun.* 📷

Úštěk ❿

Road map B2. 🚶 *1,600.*
🚍 💬 *from Litoměřice.* 🛈 *Mírové
náměstí 47.* **Tel** *416 795 368.*
www.mesto-ustek.cz
The picturesque buildings of
Úštěk have provided locations
for numerous films. This
sleepy town lies on a narrow

Picturesque houses in Úštěk town square

rocky ridge, its former Gothic
castle in ruins, but retaining a
pleasant inner courtyard. The
mightiest part of the town's
fortifications is Pikartská věž,
with 2-m (6-ft) thick walls, now
housing the local **art gallery**.
The narrow town square
features several Gothic
houses with street-facing
gables. The **Church
of St Peter and St Paul**
(sv. Petr a Pavel)
has an altarpiece
by Karel Škréta.
Unique to the
town are the birds'
houses (ptačí
domky), wooden
homes perched
on a rocky ledge.
They were inhabited by Jewish families and then in the
19th century by Italians who
worked on the construction
of the railway.

🏛 **Art Gallery**
☐ *Jul, Aug: Tue–Sun.* 📷

Litoměřice ⓫

Road map B2. 🚶 *26,000.*
🚍 💬 *from Prague.* 🛈 *Mírové
náměstí 15/7.* **Tel** *416 732 440.*

The beautiful town of
Litoměřice was founded in
the 13th century. The zenith of
its glory was in the mid-15th
century, when it was among
the largest towns in Bohemia.
Following the Thirty Years'
War, in 1655, it became the
seat of a new diocese, the
main centre for re-
introducing Catholicism
to North Bohemia.
The Renaissance
town hall (radnice) in
the main square
(Mírové náměstí) has
Gothic arcades; it now
houses the **Regional
Museum**. Nearby is
the 1537 **House at the
Chalice** (Dům u
Kalicha), with a goblet-
shaped roof finial –
symbol of the Hussites.
In several other old
buildings on the square
is the superb collection
of religious paintings
in the **Diocesan
Museum** (Muzeum
litoměřické diecéze).

Near the square, in the **North
Bohemian Art Gallery**
(Severočeská galerie výtvar-
ného uměni) are Bohemia
Gothic altar paintings by the
Master of Litoměřice.
During the late 17th and
early 18th centuries the archi-
tect Ottavio Broggio changed
many of the town's buildings.
His father Giulio remodelled
St Stephen's Cathedral (sv.
Štěpána), a vast basilica just
west of the town centre.

🏛 **Regional Museum**
Mírové Náměstí 40. **Tel** *416 731
339.* ☐ *Tue–Sun.* 📷

🏛 **Diocesan Museum**
Mírové Náměstí 24. **Tel** *416 732
382.* ☐ *Tue–Sun.*

🏛 **North Bohemian Art
Gallery**
Michalská 7. **Tel** *416 732 382.* ☐
Tue–Sun. 📷 **www**.galerie-ltm.cz

**Detail of a wall-painting in the
House at the Chalice, Litoměřice**

Terezín ⓬

Road map B2. 🚶 *1,900.* 💬 *from
Prague, Litoměřice.* 🛈 *Náměstí ČSA
179.* **Tel** *416 782 616.*
www.terezin.cz

In 1780 Joseph II began the
construction of a fortified
garrison to stop the potential
advance of an enemy from the
direction of Dresden. The fortress, called Terezín (Theresien-
stadt) in honour of the
Emperor's mother, Maria
Theresa, took 11 years to build.
The resulting structure consists of the octagonal **Main
Fortress** (Hlavní pevnost) and
the rectangular **Small Fortress**
(Malá pevnost). A system of
corridors, 29 km (18 miles)
long, runs under the town.
Within the Main Fortress is
Terezín town centre.

Fountain in Lázeňský Sad, the spa park in Teplice

In the Krásne Březno district, near the castle, stands the Gothic-Renaissance **Church of St Florian**, built in 1597–1603 and featuring a magnificent Renaissance main altarpiece, the work of Master T Lindner of Freiberg, dating from 1605; there is also a lovely vault.

Teplice ⓮

Road map B2. 🏛 53,000. 🚉 🚌 from Prague. 🛈 Náměstí Svobody 2. Tel 417 510 666. www.teplice.cz

Teplice is the oldest health resort in Bohemia. The curative effects of local spring waters were recognized as far back as the 15th century, but it was only in the 19th century that the development of hydrotherapy in Teplice began in earnest. In 1879 the fate of the resort hung in the balance when after a nearby mining disaster the spa waters stopped flowing for a while.

Much of the old town centre was destroyed by the Communists, but the **palace**, built in 1585–1634, survives, and was later rebuilt in Baroque and Neo-Classical styles. In the palace chapel it is worth taking a closer look at the Renaissance altarpiece now used as a tombstone – a fine 1420 work by an Italian master. The palace also houses **Teplice Museum. St John's church** (sv. Jan) in the town square has rich Baroque paintings inside.

🏛 **Teplice Museum**
Zámecké Náměstí 14. Tel 417 537 869. ◻ Tue–Sun. ▨

From the second half of the 19th century the Small Fortress was used as a jail for political prisoners; Serb student Gavrilo Princip, the assassin of Archduke Franz Ferdinand, was kept here until his death. In 1940 the Small Fortress became a prison and, later, a concentration camp within the Protectorate of Bohemia and Moravia. In the autumn of 1941 the Germans transformed the Main Fortress into a ghetto for the Jews, who were brought here from all over Europe, and subsequently dispatched to death camps.

The **Ghetto Museum** inside the main fortress uses artefacts, photographs and videos to give a detailed and shocking picture of ghetto life. This continues in the **Magdeburg Barracks** where the cramped conditions are reconstructed. Exhibits also cover the ghetto's rich cultural life.

🏛 **Small Fortress**
Principova Alej 304. Tel 416 782 225. ◻ daily. ▨

🏛 **Ghetto Museum and Magdeburg Barracks**
Komenského. Tel 416 782 577. ◻ daily. ▨

Ústí nad Labem ⓭

Road map B2. 🏛 97,000. 🚉 🚌 from Prague. 🛈 Hradiště 9. Tel 475 220 233. www.usti-nl.cz

A major river port on the Labe (Elbe), Ústí nad Labem (Aussig) is an industrial and trade centre. The 14th-century **Cathedral Church of the Assumption of the Virgin Mary** (Nanebevzetí Panny Marie) has a lovely late Gothic altarpiece dating from 1498. Its tower, following the Allies'

bombing of Ústí in the final stages of World War II, was pushed out of plumb by nearly 2 m (6 ft). A fine example of modern engineering and architecture is the **Mariánsky Bridge** over the Labe (Elbe), opened in 1998 – an unusual suspended structure that is supported by a single pylon.

Environs
A couple of kilometres from the town centre are the ruins of **Střekov Castle**, perched on a steep rock above the Labe. In 1842 they inspired Wagner to compose his *Tannhäuser*.

Interior of the church of the Assumption in Ústí nad Labem

THE TEREZIN GHETTO

Terezín ghetto was intended to keep in isolation Jews brought here from all parts of occupied Europe. The conditions were, ostensibly, shown as adequate for survival, and an International Red Cross delegation was persuaded twice that the ghetto was a self-governing Jewish "town". In fact, at least 35,000 perished in the ghetto, and over 100,000 prisoners passed through on their way to near-certain death in concentration camps.

Part of the Jewish cemetery in Terezín

Duchcov Palace across the water

Osek Monastery ⑮

Road map B2. 🚪 🚌 *from Teplice.*
Tel *417 822 138.* ◻ *Apr–Oct:*
10am–4pm Tue–Sun (Jun–Aug: to
5pm); Sun & public hols: from 1pm.
🖥 *www.osek.cz*

The main attraction of Osek
(Ossegg) is its Cistercian
monastery founded in
1196. The interior of
the monastery
church overflows
with lavish Baroque
furnishings and
ornaments, added as
part of the 17th-
century revival of
Catholicism in
Bohemia. Ottavio
Broggio made the
exterior alterations.
The spectacular
wall and ceiling
stucco is by
Giacomo Corbellini.
　The adjacent monastery has
an early Gothic chapterhouse;
its ceiling is supported by two
columns with magnificent
capitals. At its centre stands an
exceptionally lovely, UNESCO-
listed Romanesque lectern,
made of stone, supported on
two intertwined posts. The
inner courtyard is surrounded
by cloisters, which are linked
with the church by a pre-1240
Romanesque portal.

**Sculpture of St Matthew,
Osek monastery church**

Duchcov Palace ⑯

Road map B2. 🚪 🚌 *from Prague.*
Most. **Tel** *417 835 301.* ◻ *Apr,*
Oct: 9am–4pm Wed–Sun; May–Sep:
9am–6pm Tue–Sun. 🖼 🖼

The imposing Baroque palace
of the Wallenstein family was
where Giacomo Casanova

spent the final years of his
life *(see box, opposite)*.
The north wing, a former
bedroom and study, houses
a few of his mementoes.
　The guests entertained by the
Wallensteins here included
Haydn, Mozart, Goethe
and Schiller. The family
had the palace re-
modelled in the
early 19th century
in Neo-Classical
style. Be sure not to
miss the large ball-
room with its ceiling
painted by Václav
Vavřinec Reiner. Out-
side, the main court-
yard and the stairway to
the English-style garden
is decorated with
sculptures by
Matthias Braun.

Louny ⑰

Road map B2. 🚶 *20,000.* 🚌 *from*
Prague. 🚏 *Mírové náměstí 35.*
Tel *415 621 102.* **www.**mulouny.cz

The town of Louny (Laun)
was founded in the 13th
century by Přemysl Otakar II,
on the old trading route that

led to Saxony. Much was
destroyed by a fire in 1517.
Standing to this day are fragments of its original defensive
walls and one imposing 16th-
century gate – Žatecká brána
– sporting the town's emblem.
　A treasured survivor is its
Late Gothic **Church of St
Nicholas** (sv. Mikuláš), built
in 1520–38 by Benedikt Ried,
on the ruins of a church. The
building's conspicuous roof,
in the shape of three tents,
resembles that of St Barbara's
Cathedral in Kutná Hora
(see pp122–3). The walls are
supported on all sides by tall
buttresses. The south vestibule
with its "donkey back" portal
features exceptionally intricate
net vaulting. Inside, take a
look at the Baroque high
altarpiece dating from the
early 18th century, the twin
side altars and the Late Gothic
pulpit from 1540.
　The **town hall** was built at
the end of the 19th century to
replace an earlier 14th-century
building. Also built in the
19th century, and recently
restored, is the **synagogue**.

🔒 **Church of St Nicholas**
◻ *Tue–Sun.* 🖼

The lavishly decorated façade of the town hall in Louny

For hotels and restaurants in this region see pp353–4 and pp383–5

Žatec ⑱

Road map A2. 🚊 20,000. 🚌 from Prague, Louny. 🛈 Náměstí Svobody 1. **Tel** 415 736 156. **www.**mesto-zatec.cz

Žatec's pride is not limited to its excellent locally grown hops, used for Pilsner Urquell and other beers worldwide. Žatec (Saaz) also has a well-preserved old town, with many interesting buildings. Particularly striking are the numerous Gothic, Renaissance and Baroque houses with their original doorways, gates and arcades. One of the loveliest is the **Hošt'alkov House**, from around 1500. The town's oldest church is the **Church of the Assumption of the Virgin Mary**, originally Romanesque, remodelled in the Baroque period, and in the 19th century reconstructed in the Gothic style.

Oriel of a house in the main square (No. 184) in Kadaň

Kadaň ⑲

Road map A2. 🚊 18,000. 🚊 🚌 from Prague, Klášterec. 🛈 Mírové náměstí 1. **Tel** 474 319 550.

Despite the fact that most of the town burned down in 1811, Kadaň (Kaaden) is still one of the best-preserved historic cities in Bohemia, and the beautiful surroundings make the town a lively and interesting place to visit.

The medieval town is almost fully encircled by defensive walls, accessed by a number of gates. A small Gothic gate is reached via the narrow Hangman's Lane (Katová ulička) leading from the south side of the main square; until the 17th century the only person entitled to use the gate was the town's hangman. Kadaň's **town hall** (radnice) dates from the early 14th century; its tower is 54 m (177 ft) high. The **Church of the Fourteen Holy Martyrs** (Čtrnáct svatých Pomocníků), an ornate Late Gothic building, contains the marble sarcophagus of John of Lobkowicz, which dates from 1517, by the north wall of the presbytery.

Perched on top of a rock above the Ohře river is a former royal **castle**, dating from the 13th century, and currently undergoing extensive reconstruction.

Klášterec nad Ohří ⑳

Road map A2. 🚊 16,200. 🚊 🚌 from Prague. 🛈 Náměstí E Beneše 86. **Tel** 474 376 431.

Following the Battle of the White Mountain in 1620, Klášterec nad Ohří (Klösterle-an-der-Eger) fell into the hands of the Thun family. They built their Renaissance **palace** a short distance from the village. Over the centuries the original palace has undergone many changes, some made by the Italian architects Rossi de Luca and Carlo Lurago, who designed the adjacent church of the Holy Trinity. In 1856 the palace was remodelled into a fashionable Romantic edifice by changing the shape of the façades, raising the roofs and towers, and adding decorative elements in the spirit of Neo-Gothic. The palace has retained this form. The interiors have lost their original furnishings, but now house an impressive collection of Czech porcelain.

The adjacent English park is beautifully laid out, with rare species of trees, sculptures by Jan Brokof and the tomb of the Thun-Hohenstein family displaying their family tree in the form of a porcelain relief.

🏛 Palace and Park
Tel 474 375 436. ◯ Apr, Oct: Sat, Sun, public hols; May–Sep: Tue–Sun. 🏛 🎫

GIACOMO CASANOVA

The notorious Venetian adventurer and seducer arrived in Duchcov in 1785 and took on the position of palace librarian. He was also hired to entertain the castle's owners – members of the Wallenstein family. In Duchcov Casanova wrote most of his *Memoirs*. He died in 1798 and was buried in the cemetery of the nearby Church of St Barbara, although the exact location of his grave is not known.

Portrait of Giacomo Casanova

The palace in Klášterec nad Ohří

EAST BOHEMIA

S *cenery is the star attraction in much of East Bohemia, an area of exceptional diversity. The flat, somewhat monotonous landscape around Hradec Králové and Pardubice forms a marked contrast with the dramatic scenery to the north in the Krkonoše mountain range, which draws visitors in summer and winter alike to Sněžka, the highest peak in the Czech Republic.*

The capital of East Bohemia (Východní Čechy), Hradec Králové, is a town that has passed through many stages of development – from Slav settlement, through medieval stronghold and Baroque fortress, to showcase for spectacular Modernist architecture in the 1920s. The region's other large towns – Pardubice, with its famous steeplechase course, and Litomyšl, with its imposing Renaissance palace and its links with the Czech national composer, Bedřich Smetana – are also beautiful and interesting places to explore.

The Krkonoše and Orlické mountain ranges form the northern border of the region and the country. They attract many visitors keen on skiing and hiking. Within the Krkonoše range, the Krkonoše National Park and its flora are strictly protected. The region near Turnov and Jičín includes Český ráj (the "Bohemian Paradise"), a land full of castle ruins and extraordinary geological formations, exceptionally rich in precious minerals.

Central and eastern parts of East Bohemia are characterized by the extensive, flat plain around the River Labe (Elbe). The towns in this region suffered badly in the Thirty Years' War *(see p39)*, and their prosperity declined. This resulted in recolonization and Germanization, but also in the development of Baroque art and architecture. East Bohemia has many fine works by Kilian Ignaz Dientzenhofer, Giovanni Santini and Matthias Braun. A special place among the historic buildings of the region must be given to the castle and church complex in Kuks – a unique structure born on a whim of Count Špork.

Hydroelectric power station on the Labe (Elbe), in Hradec Králové

◁ **Prachovské skály, nicknamed the "Gate to the Bohemian Paradise" in Český ráj**

Exploring East Bohemia

The geological formations of East Bohemia, such as Český ráj and the Adršpach and Teplice Rocks, are among the most beautiful in Central Europe. Aside from these, the most interesting sight in the northern part is Jičín, formerly the centre of the vast estate of Albrecht von Wallenstein. Nearby, the Krkonoše mountains attract walkers and skiers. In the centre of the region are the two major towns of Hradec Králové and Pardubice. Further south, the Renaissance town of Litomyšl is a must for any visitor.

Cathedral of the Holy Ghost, Hradec Králové

SIGHTS AT A GLANCE

Terrace and steps linking Nové Město nad Metují Palace and gardens

Wałbrzych

16

ADRŠPACH-TEPLICE ROCKS
Trutnov   17

Úpice   14

NÁCHOD 18   Kłodzko

KUKS
Jaroměř   NOVÉ MĚSTO 19 NAD METUJÍ
JOSEFOV   KRAJ

Velká Deštná 1115m

OPOČNO 21   Dobruška

11   298
Orlice
ČASTOLOVICE   Solnice
PALACE 22
Borohrádek   Rychnov nad Kněžnou
6   Holice   Čestice Kostelecká

35   11   Žamberk
Loučná
Letohrad   Jablonné n. Orl.
17   Vysoké Mýto   Choceň   Ústí nad Orlicí   43   11
   Opava
PARDUBICKÝ   KRAJ   14
   Lanškroun
NOVÉ HRADY 3   Česká Třebová
PALACE   2 LITOMYŠL
Hlinsko   Proseč   35
34   43   Olomouc
   Moravská Třebová
   Svitavy
Polička
Svratka   Brno

GETTING AROUND

The main transport artery of the region is the D11 motorway leading from Prague to Hradec Králové, the region's capital. Hradec Králové also lies on the main railway linking Prague with Moravia and Slovakia. From Hradec Králové roads and railway lines radiate out to all parts of the region. Buses are reasonably efficient throughout East Bohemia. Trips to more remote places are possible on public transport, but need more advance planning.

KEY

▬▬	Motorway
──	Main road
┈┈	Minor road
──	Scenic route
──	Main railway
──	Minor railway
▬▬	International border
▬▬	Regional border
△	Summit

0 kilometres   20
0 miles   10

SEE ALSO

Part of the **17th-century arcaded market square in Jičín**

Hradec Králové ●

The capital of East Bohemia, at the confluence of the Labe (Elbe) and Orlice rivers, Hradec Králové (Königgrätz) is one of the most beautiful towns in Bohemia. It first appears in historic records as early as 1225 and later became an important Hussite and then Counter-Reformation centre. In the 20th century the town acquired a new face when architects Jan Kotěra and Josef Gočár built many Modernist structures outside the medieval centre on the east and west banks of the Labe.

Town Hall and White Tower in Velké náměstí

Exploring the Town

The oldest part of the town, with historic buildings clustered around the two medieval squares, occupies high ground between the two river *(see also pp200–1)*. The New Town, built in 1920–30, starts on the east, and continues on the west bank of the Labe.

🏛 Velké náměstí

One of the most opulent buildings in the former market square is the old town hall (radnice). This Gothic edifice, erected before 1418, was remodelled in the late 16th century in the Renaissance style. At that time it was used as the town prison. In 1786 it acquired two clock towers.

On the south side of the square stands the Bishop's Palace, one of the town's finest Baroque buildings. Its designer was G Santini Aichl, who also designed its magnificent entrance portal. Adjacent is the charming, small-scale Baroque Špulak House (Dům U Špuláků). It was remodelled in 1750 by F Kermer. The 20-m (66-ft) column was erected in

Relief from the house opposite the cathedral

1717 in thanksgiving for sparing the town from the plague of the previous year. The monument is probably by sculptor and architect G B Bullo. Adjoining the square to the northeast is the smaller medieval square Malé náměstí.

🔒 Cathedral of the Holy Ghost

The magnificent brick Gothic Cathedral of the Holy Ghost (Katedrála sv. Ducha), founded in 1307, is evidence of the town's wealth in the early 14th century. In 1424 the

church was the temporary burial site of Jan Žižka, leader of the Hussite movement. Striking features of its plain interior are the Late Gothic, 15th-century high altar, and in the south aisle, the Baroque altarpiece with a painting of St Anthony, by Petr Brandl. The pewter baptismal font, dating from 1406, is one of the oldest in Bohemia.

🏛 White Tower

Franušova 1. **Tel** *495 511 455.*
⭘ *Apr–Sep: 9am–noon, 1–5pm daily.*
The 72-m (235-ft) tall Renaissance belfry next to the cathedral was erected in 1589. The white stone used as the building material gave the structure its name White Tower (Bílá věž), though the stone is now grey. The bell inside, nicknamed "Augustin", is Bohemia's second-largest. Do not be misled by the replacement clock that was fitted in the White Tower in 1829: the small hand points to the minutes, and the large one to the hours!

🔒 Church of the Assumption of the Virgin Mary

The church (Nanebevzetí Panny Marie) was built for the Jesuit Order by Carlo Lurago in the mid-17th century. One hundred years later the church burned down and only the chapel of St Ignatius Loyola, with its wall paintings and a picture by Petr Brandl of the glorification of the saint, was spared. The present façade, graced with two towers, dates from 1857. The former Jesuit College, the long building to the right of the church, dates from 1671–1710.

Interior of the Church of the Assumption of the Virgin Mary

Entrance hall of the Modern Art Gallery

🏛 **Modern Art Gallery**

Velké náměstí 139/140. *Tel 495 514 893.* ⬤ *9am–noon, 1–6pm Tue–Sun.* 📷 www.galeriehk.cz

The striking five-storey Art Nouveau building of the Modern Art Gallery (Galerie moderního umění) was designed in 1912 by Osvald Polívka. Inside is a superb and extensive collection of works by the finest Czech artists of the 19th and 20th centuries, including Jan Zrzavý, Jan Preisler, Josef Váchal, Václav Špála, Josef Čapek and Jiří Kolář.

✚ **Former Synagogue**

Československé armády.

This distinctive building has a magnificent dome recently overlaid with sheet copper. It was built in 1904–5 to a design by Václav Weinzettel, in the Art Nouveau style, with some Oriental elements. Apart from the prayer hall it also included the domestic quarters of the rabbi, the shammash and the caretaker; there was also a meeting room and space for the archives. The building served the Jewish community until World War II. After 1960 it was acquired and renovated by the Hradec Králové Research Library, and it remains a library today.

🏛 **East Bohemia Regional Museum**

Eliščino nábřeží 465. *Tel 495 514 624.* ⬤ *9am–5pm Tue–Sun.* 📷 ♿

The monumental building of East Bohemia's Regional Museum (Krajské Museum Východních Čech) is one of

View of the Labe from the Pražský Bridge

the prime examples of Bohemian Modernism. It was built in 1909–12 to a design by Jan Kotěra. Inside, through the doorway flanked by gigantic statues, are some interesting exhibits, in particular a scale model of the town from 1865, complete with all of its fortifications.

🏛 **Pražský Bridge**

The Pražský Bridge was designed in 1910 by Jan Kotěra. The 60-m (200-ft) long structure replaced the oldest bridge in Hradec Králové, dating from 1796. In 1910–12 Kotěra added four pavilions to house shops; he also gave it distinctive lighting and masts with the town's emblem. The bridge leads into the section of the new town over the river built by Modernist Josef Gočár.

HRADEC KRALOVE TOWN CENTRE

Cathedral of the Holy Ghost ②
Church of the Assumption of the Virgin Mary ④
East Bohemia Regional Museum ⑦
Former Synagogue ⑥
Modern Art Gallery ⑤
Pražský Bridge ⑧
Velké Náměstí ①
White Tower ③

0 metres   200

0 yards   200

KEY

🟦 Street-by-Street *see pp200–1*

Key to Symbols *see back flap*

Street-by-Street: Hradec Králové Old Town

The historic sights of the Old Town are
clustered around its former market square,
Velké náměstí, and the adjoining, smaller
Malé náměstí. Charming streets lined with
beautiful houses are juxtaposed with the
opulent edifices of museums, churches,
theatres and palaces. Make a point of going
down the narrow street that runs behind the
White Tower to see the recently restored
historic houses, and then ascend the tower
to gain a bird's-eye view of the Old Town
stretching beneath.

★ **Town Hall**
*The façade of
this three-storey
building is
decorated with
the national
emblem of the
former
Czechoslovakia.*

St Clement Chapel
*Squeezed between the Town Hall and the
White Tower is the Baroque St Clement
Chapel (1716). It would be easy to miss it,
were it not for its golden crown glittering
in the sunlight, visible from any point
in the main square.*

The White Tower is the
work of Burian Vlach, in
1574–89. It offers a
superb view of the town
from the top.

Plague Column

ROKYTARSKÉHO

K. TOMANA

| 0 metres | 100 |
| 0 yards | 100 |

★ **Cathedral of the
Holy Ghost**
*This Gothic brick church
founded in 1307 has slender
stained-glass windows and a
magnificent high altar.*

"Bono publico"
*This Empire-style
rotunda with three
three cupolas was built
in 1810 on the site of
the Fisherman's Gate,
which once formed
part of the town's
fortifications.*

KEY

– – – Suggested route

Malé Náměstí
In this smaller square is a 1718 statue of St John Nepomuk with two angels. Its fine buildings include the houses at No. 129 with Renaissance sgraffito on the façade, and No. 127 with a beautiful hall ceiling.

Former Synagogue
The synagogue was built in 1904–5 for the 300-strong Jewish community in the town.

DLOUHÁ

DLOUHÁ

KLICPEROVA

ÚZKÁ

TOMKOVA

MALÉ NÁMĚSTÍ

MÝTSKÁ

VELKÉ NÁMĚSTÍ

NA KROPÁČI

Municipal Library
The library building with its beautifully decorated portal stands next to Klicperovo divadlo, one of the best regional theatres in the Czech Republic.

Modern Art Gallery

Church of the Assumption of the Virgin Mary

Former Canons' Houses
Seen along the south side of the square are former canons' houses – lovely Renaissance buildings with eye-catching gables.

STAR SIGHTS

★ Cathedral of the Holy Ghost

★ Town Hall

Architectural decorations on the façade of the Knights' House, Litomyšl

Litomyšl ❷

Road map C2. 🏔 10,150. 🚉 *from Prague.* 🚌 *from Prague, Hradec Králové.* 🛈 *Smetanovo náměstí 72.* **Tel** *461 612 161.* 🎭 *International Opera Festival (late Jun).* **www**.litomysl.cz

One of Bohemia's oldest historic towns, Litomyšl (Leitomischl) is small but dynamic, dominated by its fine Renaissance palace, and its associations with composer Bedřich Smetana *(see p22).* The town was established over 1,000 years ago on the trading route that linked Bohemia with Moravia. In the 11th century Prince Břetislav II founded a Benedictine monastery here. The settlement that sprang up nearby was accorded municipal status in 1259 by Přemysl Otakar II; in 1344 the town became the seat of the second bishopric in Bohemia, after Prague. Captured by Hussites in the 15th century, it became a centre of the Bohemian Brethren community.

In 1567 the town fell into the hands of Vratislav of Pernštejn, Chancellor of the Bohemian Kingdom, who built a magnificent Renaissance palace, the main seat of his family.

Pernštejn Palace is to the northeast of the main square (Smetanovo náměstí). Built in 1568–81, it was included in 1999 on the UNESCO World Cultural Heritage List. The finial-topped building features two courtyards. The main one, square-shaped, is flanked on three sides by three-storey arcades. The fourth wall is lavishly decorated with *sgraffito.* The external *sgraffito* is regarded as the most beautiful of its kind in the former Austro-Hungarian Empire.

Inside the palace, highlights among the many rooms include historic furnishings include the Battle Hall and the Great Dining Hall. Particularly striking is the late 18th-century theatre, one of the oldest and best-preserved in Europe. Smetana made his debut as a pianist in this theatre.

Opposite the palace is the birthplace of Bedřich Smetana, now the **Smetana Museum**. The building used to belong to the brewery as Smetana's father was a brewer. One of the town's attractions is the annual International Opera Festival in June, which brings together many outstanding opera performers.

Amid the lavishly decorated arcaded Baroque houses in the long, thin **main square** is the **Knights' House** (Dům U Rytířů), with magnificent Renaissance façade decorations including vivid knights, merchants and creatures. It now houses an art gallery. Close to the palace stands the Early Baroque **Church of the Finding of the Holy Cross** (Nalezení sv. Kříže) built in 1730 by Giovanni Alliprandi. Its façade is winged by two obliquely positioned towers, while the richly decorated interior is dominated by larger-than-life figures of the four Evangelists. The originally Gothic **Church of the Exaltation of the Holy Cross** (Šénové Náměstí) has an interesting semicircular entrance portal dating from 1605, flanked by Tuscan columns.

⛪ **Pernštejn Palace**
Tel *464 615 067.* ⬜ *Apr, Oct: Sat, Sun, public hols; May–Sep: Tue–Sun.* 🖼 **www**.chateau-litomysl.cz

🏛 **Smetana Museum**
Zámecký Pivovar. **Tel** *461 615 287.* ⬜ *Apr, Oct: Sat, Sun, public hols; May–Sep: Tue–Sun.* 🖼

Nové Hrady Palace ❸

Road map C2. 🚌 *from Litomyšl, Chrudim.* **Tel** *469 325 353.* ⬜ *May–Sep: 10am–4pm daily; Oct: 10am–4pm Sat, Sun.* 🖼 📷

Bohemia's most beautiful Rococo palace is in the small town of Nové Hrady. Commissioned by Count Jean Antonín Harbuval de Chamaré, it was built in 1774–7 by a Tyrolean architect Josef Jäger, in the

Nové Hrady Palace viewed from its English-style gardens

For hotels and restaurants in this region see pp354–5 and pp385–6

Façades of houses in Havlíčkův Brod

style of a French summer residence. The sloping site was used to set off the stately character of the building: it has often been called the "Bohemian Versailles".

The salmon-pink palace consists of the central building with two wings embracing a raised courtyard, which forms a terrace above the lower floor of the entrance section. All of it is completed by an imposing three-part gate dating from 1782. Palace interiors feature original Rococo furnishings. The main hall on the first floor has some interesting Rococo stuccoes. The adjoining English-style park features Baroque Stations of the Cross, dating from 1767.

Havlíčkův Brod ❹

Road map C3. 🏠 *24,500.* 🚉 🚌 from Prague. 🛈 *569 497 111.*

Scenically located on the banks of River Sázava, Havlíčkův Brod was until 1945 known as Německý Brod ("German Ford"). The town's current name comes from the name of Karel Havlíček-Borovský – a poet and a prominent member of the Czech patriotic movement, who studied and worked here in the 19th century.

The historic centre is focused on the quadrangular **market square** (Havlíčkovo náměstí) surrounded by Baroque houses with lavishly decorated façades. Rising above their roofs is the massive tower of the 13th-century **Church of the Assumption of the Virgin Mary** (Nanebevzetí Panny Marie) with a lovely high altar, with

four levels of angels and saints; the church also has some interesting side altars. The church tower houses one of Bohemia's biggest bells, "Vilém", dating from 1300.

At the square's centre is a Marian column decorated with figures of saints Andrew, Florian, John Nepomuk and Wenceslas. Nearby is a stone fountain in the shape of the Greek sea god Triton.

Lipnice nad Sázavou ❺

Road map B3. 🏠 *620.* 🚌 from Havlíčkův Brod.

This village is where the novelist Jaroslav Hašek lived from 1921 until his death in 1923. He is now buried in the local cemetery. It was in Lipnice that he wrote the second, third and fourth (unfinished) volumes of his comic masterpiece, *The Good Soldier Švejk*.

Statue of Jaroslav Hašek in Lipnice nad Sázavou

The twin-towered silhouette of **Lipnice Castle** dominates the landscape. This mighty Gothic edifice was built in the early 14th century as a fortress guarding the trade route from Havlíčkův Brod to Humpolec. The main body of the castle and the tower date from this period. After a fire in 1869 it fell into ruin. It is currently undergoing extensive

reconstruction. The 14th-century chapel is decorated with fine frescoes.

🏰 **Lipnice Castle**
Tel 569 486 189. ⭕ *Apr, Sep, Oct: Sat, Sun, public hols; May–Aug: Tue–Sun.* 📷 📹

Ledeč nad Sázavou ❻

Road map B3. 🏠 *6,000.* 🚉 🚌 from Prague. 🛈 Husovo náměstí 60. *Tel 569 721 471.* www.ledecns.cz

Perched on a high escarpment on the right bank of the Sázava is the 12th-century **Ledeč Castle**. Currently it is being restored, but the ground floor houses a **Regional Museum**, with ethnographic exhibits and old weaponry.

The town itself, on the left bank of the river, is dominated by the **Church of St Peter and St Paul** (sv. Petr a Pavel) in the square. Originally Gothic, the church was remodelled in Baroque style. The town has some interesting reminders of the Jewish community, who were forcibly removed from here in 1942; they include an early 18th-century **synagogue** and a **Jewish cemetery** established in 1601, one of the oldest in Bohemia, with many Baroque tombstones.

🏰 **Ledeč Castle (museum)**
Tel 569 721 128. ⭕ *Apr, Oct: Sat, Sun; May–Sep: Tue–Sun.* 📷

Hall housing an exhibition of sculpture in Lipnice Castle

Žleby Castle 7

Road map B2. 🚉 🚌 *from Čáslav.*
Tel *327 398 121.* ⏰ *Apr, Oct: 9am–*
4pm Sat, Sun, public hols; May–Sep:
9am–4:30pm Tue–Sun. 🏛 🎫 *2*
routes. **www**.zamek-zleby.cz

This fairytale castle has
undergone dramatic changes
over the centuries. In the 13th
century, Žleby Castle was a
Gothic defensive fortress. In
the 16th century it was
remodelled in Renaissance
style, and in the 19th century
its owners, the Auersperg
family, gave it a romantic Neo-
Gothic look. The castle sports a
massive tower with a pointed
roof, and an entrance portal
decorated with an unusual
relief of a bison. The Auersperg
family fled at the end of
World War II, leaving behind
the contents of their home.

On the courtyard's ground
and first floors are Renaissance
and Baroque arcades, partially
glazed with lovely stained-
glass windows produced in
Germany and Switzerland.
Palace rooms were decorated
extravagantly in the 1840s. The
palace chapel, built in 1853–8,
has unusually lavish furnishings
including Renaissance figures
of St John the Evangelist and
St John the Baptist, made of
terracotta in the Florence
workshop of Giovanni della
Robbia. In the adjacent game
park are herds of white stags.

Environs
About 6 km (4 miles) to the
northwest is the town of
Čáslav, which has a

**Bison relief above the entrance to
Žleby Castle**

Flower-filled courtyard of Slatiňany Palace

rectangular square with a
Baroque town hall, and
houses in a variety of styles,
from Gothic to Empire. The
Late Gothic Church of St Peter
and St Paul (sv. Petr a Pavel)
has a 13th-century presbytery
supported by two vast
buttresses, and fine portals in
the west and south walls.

Slatiňany Palace 8

Road map C2. 🚉 🚌 *from Pardubice.*
Tel *469 681 112.* ⏰ *Apr, Oct:*
9:30am–3pm Sat, Sun, public hols;
May–Sep: 9am–4pm Tue–Sun. 🏛 🎫

A place of interest for all
horse lovers, Slatiňany Palace
was built in the 16th century
in Renaissance style. At the
turn of the 18th and 19th
centuries it was remodelled
in Neo-Gothic style. In 1947
it became home to an
equestrian museum, unique in
Europe. It has nearly 2,100
exhibits associated with horse
breeding. There are also
paintings, prints, sculptures,
porcelain and tapestries
devoted to the subject of
horses; and a collection of
saddles and harnesses. In the
large English-style palace park
are paddocks used for horses
bred at the local stud farm.

Environs
The main reason to visit
Chrudim, 6 km (4 miles)
northwest of Slatiňany, is its
fascinating Puppet Museum
(Muzeum loutkářských
kultur). It started with the
collection of Jan Malik, a
Czech pedagogue and
historian, of puppets
worldwide. The town hosts a
Puppet Festival in July. The

museum is in the town's
most beautiful Renaissance
structure – the Mydlářovský
dům – with a two-storey
arcaded façade and a slender
tower resembling a minaret.
Nearby, on the main square,
is the Gothic Church of the
Assumption of the Virgin Mary
(Nanebevzetí Panny Marie).
Also in the square is an
imposing Plague Column.

🏛 **Puppet Museum**
Břetislavova 74. **Tel** *469 620 310.*
⏰ *daily.* 🏛 **www**.puppets.cz

**Highly ornate ceiling in
Pardubice Castle**

Pardubice 9

Road map C2. 🏘 *90,000.* 🚉 *from*
Prague. 🈺 *Třída Míru 60.*
Tel *466 613 223*

A large centre of industry,
commerce and administration,
Pardubice (Pardubitz) has a
pedigree going back to the
14th century. Following great
fires in 1507 and 1538, the
town was rebuilt in the form
that has survived to the

present day. As well as its architecture, Pardubice is known for the production of the explosive Semtex in a factory in its suburb of Semtim.

To fans of horse-racing, Pardubice is known for the Velká Pardubická – a steeplechase race held annually since 1874. The course of 6,900 m (over 4 miles) includes 31 jumps. The most difficult of them – the notorious Taxis – was the cause of so many injuries to horses and riders that it has been redesigned in recent years. The Velká Pardubická is regarded as more gruelling than the Grand National, run at Aintree, even though it is not quite as long.

As in so many Bohemian towns, **Pardubice Castle** dominates, and was once the favourite residence of Emperor Ferdinand I and his court. Now it houses the **Museum of East Bohemia** with some eye-catching frescoes in the Renaissance Knights' Halls.

The town has about 100 Gothic and Renaissance houses. They surround the **market square** (Pernštýnské náměstí). Particularly striking is Jonah's House (Dům U Jonáše) at No. 50, with a relief depicting the Prophet being spat out by the whale. The Neo-Renaissance town hall, dating from 1894, sports at the top, between two towers, a copper figure of a knight – the town's guardian.

In the town's modern square (náměstí Republiky) is the **Church of St Bartholomew** (sv. Bartoloměj), a Gothic edifice with a slender spire at the centre of the roof. It contains a fine Renaissance tombstone of Vojtěch of Pernštejn, and a monumental sculpture depicting Calvary, dating from 1736. Also in the square is the boldly Art

Pardubice market square with the Plague Column and town hall

Nouveau **Municipal Theatre** (Městské divadlo).

🏛 **Pardubice Castle and Museum of East Bohemia**
Tel 466 513 263. ◷ 10am–6pm Tue–Sun. 🖼 www.vcm.cz

Environs

On a large spreading plain 5 km (3 miles) south of Pardubice is an 8-m (26-ft) high solitary hill, **Kunětická Hora**. The castle on its top is the dominant feature of the district. Built in the 15th century by the Hussites, it was captured by the Swedes in the Thirty Years' War. In the early 20th century reconstruction works started, which are still going on. In good weather the 35-m (115-ft) tower affords a view of the distant Krkonoše. A castle houses a small museum of its history.

🏛 **Kunětická Hora Castle**
Tel 466 415 428. ◷ Apr, Sep, Oct: Sat, Sun, public hols; May–Aug: Tue–Sun. 🖼

Hrádek u Nechanic Palace ⑩

Road map C2. 🚌 *from Hradec Králové. Tel* 495 441 244. ◷ Apr, Oct: 9am–4pm Sat, Sun, public hols; May–Sep: 9am–5pm Tue–Sun (Sep: to 4pm). 🖼 🖼 www.hradeku nechanic.cz

The palace in Hrádek u Nechanic is one of the finest Romantic buildings in Bohemia. Commissioned by Count František Arnošt Harrach, this grand Neo-Gothic residence, complete with crenellations, was built in 1839–57. The lengthy building works were supervised by the Viennese architect Karl Fischer.

Particularly attractive rooms are the Golden Hall, with lovely panelled ceilings and an impressive fireplace; also the Knights' Hall, which is decorated with laboriously worked, ostentatious wood-carvings along the lower sections of the walls and around the doors. Much of the furniture was imported from Germany and Austria in the 19th century.

Around the palace are sweeping, landscaped gardens and a golf course.

The romantic, Neo-Gothic Hrádek u Nechanic Palace

Karlova Koruna Palace at Chlumec nad Cidlinou

Chlumec nad Cidlinou ⓫

Road map B2. 🏯 5,300. 🚌 🚆 from Hradec Králové. ⓘ Kozelkova 26. **Tel** 495 484 121.

The pleasant riverside town of Chlumec nad Cidlinou is known for the **Karlova Koruna Palace**. Designed by Giovanni Santini, it was built in 1721–3. The owner, Count František Kinský, named it "Charles's Crown" in honour of Emperor Charles VI, who stayed here in 1723, following his coronation as King of Bohemia. The palace has an unusual central cylindrical section and three radially spreading wings. Inside are paintings and memorabilia of the Kinský family, who after 1989 regained ownership of the palace from the Czech government. The Chapel of the Annunciation (1740) is also by Santini.

⛪ **Karlova Koruna Palace**
Tel 495 484 519. ◻ May–Sep: Tue–Sun; Apr, Oct: Sat, Sun, public hols. 🎟

Jičín ⓬

Road map B2. 🏯 17,000. 🚌 🚆 from Prague. ⓘ Valdštejnovo náměstí 1. **Tel** 493 534 390. 🎭 Fairytale Festival (Sep). **www**.jicin.org

Jičín (gitschin) borders the Český ráj nature reserve and makes an ideal place to stay while exploring the surrounding countryside. Jičín reached the peak of its glory during the Thirty Years' War, when the supreme commander of the Imperial Army, Albrecht von Wallenstein, made it the centre of his vast Duchy of Friedland. Here, this most powerful Bohemian warlord built his residence, minted his own money and dreamt of founding a university. All these plans collapsed after the assassination of Wallenstein in Cheb, in 1634 (see p169); yet the town has retained many mementoes of the ambitious duke.

A silent witness to his unfulfilled plans is the town's

Tour of Český ráj ⓭

Česky ráj, or "Bohemian Paradise", is the oldest protected nature reserve in the Czech Republic. The scenic landscape is full of extraordinary geological formations: "rock towns", "gates" and high-rise "towers" popular with climbers. There are also a number of medieval castles and an extensive network of walking trails. Jičín and Turnov make good bases for exploring.

Valdštejn Castle ④
The seat of the famous Wallenstein family, it was partially remodelled in the Romantic Neo-Gothic style in the 19th century.

Kost Castle ③
This 14th-century fortress is dominated by a 32-m (105-ft) high White Tower, with nearly 4-m (13-ft) thick walls. Used originally as the final refuge of the castle's defenders, it now houses a museum of torture.

KEY

■ Tour route

= Other road

❋ Viewpoint

square, built by Wallenstein and now named after him – Valdštejnovo náměstí. It is surrounded on all sides by superb and well-preserved 17th-century arcaded houses. Standing at the southeast corner of the square is the former ducal castle, now housing a **Regional Museum**. The most interesting of its historic interiors is the Conference Hall where Tsar Alexander I of Russia, King Frederick William III of Prussia and Emperor Francis I of Austria formed the Holy Alliance against Napoleon in 1813. The **Jesuit Church of St James the Great** (sv. Jakuba Většího) beside the castle is of Baroque design, and dates from 1627. Just to the west of the main square is the 14th-century **Church of St Ignatius** (sv. Ignáce).

The town's tallest building is the 16th-century quadrangular

Coat of arms at
Jičín Castle

Valdice Gate (Valdická brána). At 52 m (170 ft) high its tower affords a lovely view of the town from the top. The Valdice Gate now houses the **Radek Pilař Museum** devoted to a Czech animator and illustrator of fairytales (1931–93). He is one of several local artists and writers celebrated in the annual Fairytale Festival.

Environs
Wallenstein ordered the planting of an avenue of over 1,200 lime trees in two straight lines over 2 km (1 mile) long, leading from Jičín to his 1630 park pavilion, known as **Libosad**. This is now a quiet, somewhat overgrown spot.

Near Libosad is the town of **Valdice** (Walditz), with its

17th-century Baroque Carthusian monastery. The monastery was turned into a prison by the Habsburgs, used later by the Communists to house political prisoners, and it still serves as a top-security prison, one of the harshest in Bohemia.

🏛 **Regional Museum**
Tel *493 532 204.* ◻ daily. 🖼
🏛 **Radek Pilař Museum**
◻ daily.

Interior of the Church of St James, Jičín

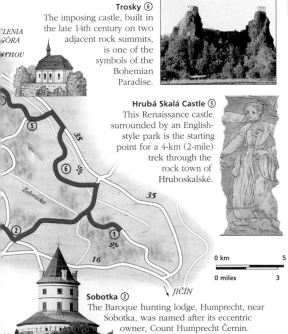

Trosky ⑥
The imposing castle, built in the late 14th century on two adjacent rock summits, is one of the symbols of the Bohemian Paradise.

Hrubá Skalá Castle ⑤
This Renaissance castle surrounded by an English-style park is the starting point for a 4-km (2-mile) trek through the rock town of Hruboskalské.

ŻELENIA
GÓRA
urnov

0 km 5
0 miles 3

Sobotka ②
The Baroque hunting lodge, Humprecht, near Sobotka, was named after its eccentric owner, Count Humprecht Černín.

TIPS FOR DRIVERS

Tour length: 50 km (31 miles).
Stopping-off points: The best accommodation and choice of eating places can be found in nearby Jičín. On the tour route, the Hrubá Skalá Castle is now a hotel with bars and restaurants.

Prachovské skály ①
Prachovské skály reserve is a huge rock town featuring sandstone rocks scattered amid trees, and several breathtaking viewpoints.

Krkonoše ⑭

The Krkonoše range (Riesengebirge) stretches along the Polish-Czech border for about 35 km (22 miles). Krkonoše means "Giant Mountains". On the Polish side, the mountains slope more steeply, while on the south side they open out into numerous valleys. The Krkonoše National Park (KRNAP) opened in 1963, an area of 385 sq km (150 sq miles) within the range, and provides a habitat for many indigenous species of plants. Particular care is taken of the local spruce forests, which in the past have suffered greatly due to environmental pollution. A network of clearly marked hiking trails, plus hundreds of chairlifts and ski runs, as well as snowboarding facilities, make this an excellent holiday region, winter or summer.

Spirit of Krkonoše
Legend tells of a wicked and – later – a benign spirit of Krkonoše, called Rýbrcoul.

Ceramic Altar, Harrachov
The glassworks established here in the 18th century made the local products famous worldwide. In the Church of St Wenceslas, glass and ceramics are used to decorate its interior.

Jelenia Góra

Harrachov

Prague   1022 m (3353 ft)

910 m (2985 ft)

1294 m (4245 ft)

1210 m (3970 ft)

1509 m (4951 ft)

Labe (Elbe)

1435 m (4708 ft)

1235 m (4052 ft)

Rokytnice nad Jizerou

1218 m (3996 ft)

Horní Mísečky

Jablonec nad Jizerou

1038 m (3405 ft)

Vítkovice

Benecko

Strážné

Jizera

Poniklá

Křižlice

Mrklov

Víchová nad Jizerou

Valteřice

Vrchla

Labe (Elbe)

Semily

Jičín

14

Mumlov Waterfall
This 8-m (26-ft) high waterfall on the Mumlava river is an attractive destination for a walk along the trail from the nearby ski resort of Harrachov.

Vrchlabí
This small town in the foothills of the mountains has a Renaissance castle, many times remodelled; its owners included Albrecht von Wallenstein.

VISITORS' CHECKLIST

Road map C2. ![i] *Svatopetrská
173, Špindlerův Mlýn.* **Tel** *499
523 656.* ![i] *Náměstí Míru 233,
Vrchlabi (National Park
Information).* **Tel** *499 422 136.*
Emergency (Mountain rescue)
Horské služby. **Tel** *112 or 155.*
www.spindleruvmlyninfo.cz

Studnični hora

*This is the third-highest peak in Bohemia; its eastern
and southern slopes are notorious for their frequent
avalanches. Snow here may reach 14 m (46 ft) deep.*

Rich Plantlife

*The varied environment, including mountain
forests, meadows, glacial basins, sub-Arctic peat
moors and ridge fells, supports many rare plants.*

Sněžka

*At 1,602 m (5,256 ft), this is
the highest peak in the
Krkonoše range and in the
Czech Republic. The summit
can be reached by cablecar
from Pec pod Sněžkou, the
region's main ski resort.*

Špindlerův Mlýn

*The main tourist centre in
Krkonoše makes an
excellent base for mountain
forays; its earliest historic
records date back to the
16th century.*

KEY

═	Secondary road
═	Other road
≋	River
✲	Viewpoint

Tiger, an inmate at Dvůr Králové Zoo

Dvůr Králové

Road map C2. 🏛 *16,400.* 🚃 *from Hradec Králové.*

The local zoo is what makes this town such a popular destination. It is one of the largest in Europe, and special care is lavished on African animals, including zebras, giraffes, white rhinos and a huge herd of antelopes. The star attraction is the evening safari – a ride on a special bus over the site where the animals roam free.

Founded in the 13th century, the town itself has several fine historic buildings and an arcaded main square. The **Church of St John the Baptist** (sv. Jana Křtitele) has a 64-m (210-ft) tower. The Renaissance town hall is decorated with *sgraffito*.

> 🦌 **Dvůr Králové Zoo**
> *Tel* 499 329 515. ⬭ *daily (evening safaris Jul, Aug: 7:30–9:30pm daily).* 🖼 www.zoodk.cz

Kuks 🔟

Road map C2. 🚃 🚌 *from Hradec Králové, Prague.* **Historic hospital complex** *Tel* 499 692 161. ⬭ *Apr, Oct: 9am–4pm Sat, Sun, public hols; May–Sep: 9am–5pm Tue–Sun (Sep: to 4pm).* 🖼 🎫 *2 routes.*

The history of the founding, the growth and the sudden decline of Kuks is quite extraordinary. The spa resort, of European fame, was built in 1694–1724 by Count František Antonín Špork and visited by Europe's elite, including J S Bach. In 1740, just two years after Špork's death, it was partially swept away by the rising waters of the Labe (Elbe) in the course

of one night. Now the remaining evidence of the town's former glory is its magnificent hospital and the Holy Trinity Church, both the work of Giovanni Alliprandi. On the hospital terrace are figures depicting the *Virtues* and *Vices*; apart from the figure of *Fraud* they were all produced by Matthias Braun in 1715–18.

Environs
In a forest about 5 km (3 miles) away it is worth taking a look at Betlém (Bethlehem) – a gallery of scenes and figures representing the Nativity. These were carved by Matthias Braun directly into the rocks, again at the behest of Špork.

Statues symbolizing the *Virtues*, on Kuks hospital terrace

Adršpach-Teplice Rocks 🔟

Road map C2. 15 km (9 miles) E of Trutnov. 🚃 *from Trutnov.* 🏛 *Horní Adršpach 128.* **Tel** 491 586 012. www.skalyadrspach.cz

The two rock towns at Adršpach and Teplice (Teplicko-Adršpašské skály) are fascinating sandstone formations, the region's finest. The Adršpach rock town can be explored on a marked trail that takes in some of the most spectacular rock formations. The path leads to Adršpach lake, and on to the Teplice rock town. The area attracts hikers and rock climbers and can be busy in high season.

Náchod 🔟

Road map C2. 🏛 *21,300.* 🚃 🚌 *from Prague.* 🏛 *Kamenice 144.* **Tel** 491 420 420.

On the major trade route from Bohemia to Poland, Náchod was founded in the 13th century. Above the town is a Gothic **Castle**, subject to Renaissance and later Baroque remodelling. Some of the interiors date from when the castle was owned by Ottavio Piccolomini, an officer serving with Albrecht von Wallenstein. Piccolomini was given the castle as a reward by Emperor Ferdinand II for his part in the murder of his commander.

The Gothic **Church of St Lawrence** (sv. Vavřinec) in the town square (náměstí T G Masaryka) has a rare 15th-century pewter baptismal font. The two onion-domed towers, nicknamed Adam and Eve, are 40 m (130 ft) tall. The Neo-Renaissance **town hall** (radnice) is decorated with *sgraffito* designed in 1909 by Mikoláš Aleš. **U Beránka Hotel** has an Art Nouveau interior and theatre auditorium.

Embedded in the pavement of Karlovo náměstí is a horse-shoe, reputedly lost by King Frederick's horse in 1618 as he escaped through Náchod to Silesia after his defeat at the Battle of the White Mountain.

> 🏰 **Náchod Castle**
> *Tel* 491 426 201. ⬭ *Apr, Oct: Sat, Sun, public hols; May–Sep: Tue–Sun.* 🖼 *2 routes.*

Art Nouveau panels on a house façade in Náchod market square

Nové Město nad Metují ⓳

Road map C2. 🏛 10,000. 🚊 🚌 from Prague, Náchod. 🛈 Na Zádomí 1226. **Tel** 491 470 331.

Set in a beautiful location in the crook of a river, Nové Město (Neustadt) is surrounded on three sides by water. Its charming Renaissance **market square** (Husovo náměstí) has arcaded houses with joint gables decorated with finials. This uniform design of an entire frontage of a square is unique in Europe. The unusual **Castle**, in a corner of the square, was originally Gothic, and owes its present form to restoration carried out during 1909–15. The castle interiors provide a unique aesthetic experience: its Renaissance furnishings stand side by side with Art Nouveau and Cubist furniture. There are 1654 Baroque stuccoes by Giovanni Bianco, and 20th-century works by Czech artists Josef Myslbek and Max Švabinský among others. The corner tower, called Máselnice, or the "butter churn" after its domed shape, affords a magnificent view. Matthias Braun created the Baroque sculptures by the bridge over the castle moat.

♣ **Nové Město Castle**
Tel 491 470 523. ⬜ Apr, Oct: Sat, Sun, public hols; May, Jun, Sep: Tue–Sun; Jul, Aug: daily. 🎟 🗗

Josefov ⓴

Road map C2. 🏛 12,000. 🚊 to Jaroměř, 1 km (0.5 mile) N of Josefov.

One of the prime historic sites of 18th-century military architecture, Josefov (Josefstadt) is a vast fortress town, erected in the reign of Joseph II. Ironically it never played any military role. Its extensive system of underground corridors, 45 km (28 miles) long, runs on two and in some places on three levels.

The 5-km (3-mile) long section of prisons is open to the public, who have to carry candles to light the darkness.

♣ **Fortifications**
Tel 442 812 343. ⬜ Apr, Oct: Sat, Sun; May–Sep: Tue–Sun. 🎟 🗗

Opočno ⓴⓵

Road map C2. 🏛 3,200. 🚊 🚌 from Hradec Králové, Prague.

The beautiful and well-preserved **Opočno Castle** is perched dramatically above its small town. It was built for the Colloredo family, on the site of an earlier Gothic fortress, in 1562–7. The only remaining part of the original structure is the cylindrical tower.

Statue of Emperor Joseph II, in Josefov

The unusual courtyard, with three-storey arcades on three sides, opens out into a park on the once-enclosed fourth side. Inside is an impressive collection of arms and armour. There is also a gallery with works of Italian, Bohemian and Dutch masters, and a library of over 12,000 volumes.

In Kupka square (Kupkovo náměstí) is the **Church of the Nativity** (Narození Páně), which has a splendid Baroque *Way of the Cross* in the ambulatory. There are a number of beautiful houses, including the Baroque house at No. 14. In Trčka square (Trčkovo náměstí) there are Renaissance houses at Nos. 9 and 13.

♣ **Opočno Castle**
Tel 494 668 216. ⬜ May–Sep: Tue–Sun; Apr, Oct: Sat, Sun & public hols. 🎟 🗗 2 routes.

Častolovice Palace ⓴⓶

Road map C2. 8 km (5 miles) SW of Rychnov nad Kněžnou. 🚊 🚌 from Prague. **Tel** 494 323 646. ⬜ May–Sep: 9am–6pm daily. 🎟 🗗 www.zamek-castolovice.cz

Originally a Renaissance building, Častolovice Palace was remodelled in the late 19th and early 20th centuries in Neo-Gothic and Neo-Renaissance styles. Its opulent interiors have been arranged with a great deal of expertise by the current owner of the palace – Franziska Diana Sternberg-Phipps, who regained the estate after 1989.

The most impressive room is the Knights' Hall (Rytířský sál), hung with portraits of the Sternbergs, and featuring a ceiling with images from the Old Testament. The dining room ceiling is painted with the biblical story of Tobias; and in two other rooms the coffers include illustrations from Ovid's *Metamorphoses*.

The palace courtyard features magnificent colourful paintings from about 1600, depicting figures of emperors and battle scenes, and a Baroque fountain. There is a pleasant, landscaped English-style park around the palace.

The arcaded courtyard of Opočno Castle

NORTH MORAVIA AND SILESIA

This region of the Czech Republic is associated mainly with the historic town of Olomouc and the industrial landscape of the Silesian mines and steelworks. Yet it has other facets: the beautiful mountain ranges of Jeseníky and Beskydy; Bouzov and Hradec castles; a large number of traditional Wallachian wooden houses; and the fascinating Javoříčské Caves.

From the earliest days of the Czech state until the 17th century the capital of Moravia was Olomouc. This lovely town, full of historic sights, is now a major educational and cultural centre and an excellent base for exploring its picturesque environs. The eastern border of North Moravia (Severní Morava) is defined by the Beskydy range, a region furrowed by deep valleys with fast-running rivers. Beskydy is the site of an open-air museum (skansen), the largest and most interesting in the Czech Republic, located in Rožnov pod Radhoštěm.

The central and northern parts of the region are occupied by the Jeseníky mountains covered with dense evergreen forests and still maintaining, to a large degree, an atmosphere of the days before vast industrialization took place.

Silesia has been disputed territory historically. It was part of the Bohemian lands until 1745 when Empress Maria Theresa lost almost the whole of Silesia to Prussia. Today, Czech Silesia has its capital in Opava, a town that suffered severe devastation in the course of the Thirty Years' War and again in World War II. The much larger town of Ostrava is a centre of mining and steel industries and one of the main economic hubs of the Czech Republic. An unusual aspect of today's Silesia is the presence of a 40,000-strong Polish minority – a homogenous native community which retains its language and culture.

Plumlov Palace overlooking Plumlov Reservoir

◁ **Astronomical clock at the town hall in Olomouc**

Exploring North Moravia and Silesia

The best point from which to start exploring this region is the historic town of Olomouc, to which it is worth allocating at least a few days. From here on, heading north for the Jeseníky mountains, it is possible to see the impressive Bouzov and Sternberg castles and visit the subterranean world of the Javoříčské Caves.

Further east are the Beskydy mountains, with their wooden churches and traditional wooden buildings, offering walking opportunities and a break from the industrial landscapes elsewhere in the region.

Priessnitz Park in Jeseník, named after the founder of the nearby spa

SIGHTS AT A GLANCE

Coach from Náměšť na Hané Palace

*Map labels:*
Javorník
Žulová
Mikulovice
6 JESFNÍK
44
Filipovice
Jeseníky Hora
Vrbno
Hanušovice
Mravenečník 1341m
Praděd 1491m
451
Morava
Velké Losiny
Sobotín
Bruntál
Hradec Králové
11
Šumperk
11
Rýmařov
Valšov
44
Zábřeh
45
Úsov
Moravský Beroun
Mohelnice
444
Uničov
Hradec Králové
35
BOUZOV CASTLE **5**
Litovel
7 ŠTERNBERK CASTLE
JAVOŘÍČSKÉ CAVES **4**
OLOMOUCKÝ KRAJ
NÁMĚŠŤ NA HANÉ PALACE **3**
46
1 OLOMOUC
55
150
PLUMLOV PALACE **2**
Prostějov
Morava
Přerov
46
Brno
Vrchoslavice
55

KEY

═══ Motorway

= = Motorway under construction

━━ Main road

┄┄ Minor road

── Scenic route

┄┄┄ Main railway

── Minor railway

▬▬ International border

▬▬ Regional border

△ Summit

Sculptures on the façade of St Wenceslas
Cathedral in Olomouc

Třemešná

Krnov

45

57

Malé
Heratice

OPAVA **8**

Kravaře

Bohumín

Slavkov

Hlučín

11

56

67

RADEC NAD MORAVICÍ
CASTLE **9**

Poruba

Orlova

Karviná

vorce

Moravice

Kajlovec

10 OSTRAVA

Bílovec

47

58

56

Havířov

11

Český
Těšín

MORAVSKOSLEZSKÝ KRAJ

48

Fulnek

Odra

Postat

47

Hladké
Životice

Frýdek-Místek

Třinec

Odry

48

11 PŘÍBOR

Frýdlant n. Ostr.

11

NOVÝ
JIČÍN **12**

Kopřivnice

13 HRANICE

48

Ostravice

Lysá Hora
△ 1323m

Jablunkov

LIPNÍK
NAD BEČVOU

57

Frenštát pod
Radhoštěm

58

Smrk
1275m △

Bečva

35

Radhošť
1129m △

Beskydy

56

Valašské Meziříčí

15 🏛 ⚜

Bystřice p. Hostýnem

150

150

ROŽNOV POD
RADHOŠTĚM

Bílá

57

Velké Karlovice

Žilina

Vsetín

Karolinka

GETTING AROUND

Ostrava airport has flights to
and from Prague and several European
cities. After World War I the railway line linking
Prague with Ostrava was Czechoslovakia's main transport
artery and connection with Slovakia. Today it remains one
of the main trunk-lines in this part of Europe. Around the
region, train transport is good to major towns, but
relatively sparse off the beaten track due to the mountains.
Buses are often the easiest means of public transport.

| 0 km | 10 |
| 0 miles | 10 |

SEE ALSO

- **Where to Stay** pp355–6

- **Where to Eat** pp387–8

Olomouc ❶

According to legend, Olomouc (Olmütz), one of Moravia's oldest towns, was founded by Julius Caesar. In fact it did not come into existence until the 7th century, when it was a major centre. In 1063 it was made a bishopric and in 1187 the capital of Moravia. Its university was founded in 1573. From 1655 the town became a military stronghold. Today it is a prosperous and vibrant industrial city off the main tourist trail, retaining its beautiful religious buildings.

Stained-glass window in St Maurice Church

Exploring the town

The fine historic town centre is second only to Prague's old town in terms of size. Its oldest part centres on the main square of Horní náměstí *(see also pp218–19)*, and is surrounded by a ring of parks and the remains of the medieval town walls. This part of the city is fascinating to explore for its lively atmosphere as well as its architecture.

🔒 Church of St Maurice

Úzká.
This huge 15th-century edifice with two asymmetrical towers resembles a medieval fortress. The church (sv. Mořice) has a highly unusual architectural detail in the form of an external staircase enclosed within a round cage. The interior is impressive with beautiful stained-glass windows and a vast 1505 wall painting. The church organ made by Silesian organ maker Michael Engler in 1745 is the largest in Central Europe.

🏛 Horní náměstí

The main square has at its centre the 13th-century town hall (radnice), which was greatly extended in the 15th century, when it acquired its astronomical clock *(see pp212 and 219)*, beautifully vaulted Gothic Debating Hall and the chapel dedicated to St Jerome.

The huge Holy Trinity Column (sousoší Nejsvětější Trojice) in front of the town hall is on the UNESCO World Cultural Heritage List. This unique example of European Baroque sculpture was erected in 1716–17. Its three tiers are peopled with historic figures and saints. Standing in the market square are three out of the total number of seven of Olomouc's fountains. The largest of them, made in 1725 by Jan J Schauberger, is the Caesar Fountain, sporting an [equestrian statue] of the legendary founder of the town. The other two are the Arion Fountain and the Hercules Fountain on which the hero is depicted holding a white eagle – the town symbol.

Top of the Holy Trinity Column

🔒 Church of St Michael

Žerotínovo náměstí. ⬜ 10am–noon, 2:30–3:30pm Wed, 2:30–3:30pm Fri.
The Dominicans, who arrived in Olomouc in about 1240, soon began to build their monastery and Church of St Michael (sv. Michala) on the town's most elevated site. In the 14th and 15th centuries it was destroyed by fire, and in the 17th it suffered damage from the Thirty Years' War. It was rebuilt in 1673–99 in Baroque style. The architect, Giovanni Pietro Tencalla, designed the first three-domed edifice in Moravia. Most of the furnishings date from the Baroque period, including its magnificent organs – the work of Josef Sturmer and Augustine Thomasberger. In 1829 the main façade of the building was decorated with statues of the Virgin Mary and the Saviour, produced in the 18th century by Ondřej Zahner; they are among the finest examples of Baroque in Olomouc.

Sculptures in the cloisters of the Church of St Michael

🔒 St Jan Sarkander Chapel

Na Hradě. *Tel 603 282 975.*
This chapel (sv. Jana Sarkandera) is a Neo-Baroque building designed by E Sochor in 1909–12. It was erected on the site of the town prison, and an old torture chamber still runs beneath it.

🔒 Church of Our Lady of the Snows

Denisova. ⬤ to sightseers.
Built in 1712–22 by Olomouc Jesuits, this church (Panny Marie Sněžné) served until 1778 as the university church. In recent years it has under-

Sculptures on the dome of St Jan Sarkander Chapel

gone a thorough restoration. Features of its wavy façade are the monumental portal including four columns, a balustraded balcony and a cartouche with the letters JHS, designed by Václav Bender. The lavishly decorated interior includes some interesting Baroque paintings.

🏛 Olomouc Art Museum

Denisova 47. *Tel 585 514 111.*
⏺ 10am–6pm Tue–Sun. 🖼
The town art gallery (Muzeum umění) is in an historic building superbly modernized. It

has a range of paintings by Italian artists from the 14th century onwards, plus an excellent collection of 20th-century Czech works.

⛪ St Wenceslas Cathedral

Václavské náměstí.
Not many traces remain of the Romanesque church that was built on this site in 1107. The present church (sv. Václav) owes its shape to the initiative of Archbishop Bedřich Fürstenberg, who ordered its reconstruction to be carried out in 1883–92, in Neo-Gothic style.

Decorative motifs on the pillars inside St Wenceslas Cathedral

VISITORS' CHECKLIST

Road map C3. 🏠 106,000.
🚆 2 km (1 mile) E of centre (Jeremenkova). *Tel 584 722 175.*
🚌 Sladkovského 41. *Tel 585 313 848 (ext. 292).* 🛈 Horní náměstí. *Tel 585 513 385.*
⏺ 8am–7pm daily.
www.olomouc-tourism.cz

⛪ Přemyslid Palace

Václavské náměstí. *Tel 585 514 111.*
⏺ Apr–Sep: 10am–6pm Tue–Sun.
Museum: Tue–Sun. 🖼 🎵
One of Olomouc's most picturesque buildings is the Romanesque palace beside St Wenceslas Cathedral. It was built after 1126 by Bishop Jindřich Zdík. In its day this was one of the most magnificent works of residential architecture in Europe. The bishop's rooms with their beautifully carved Romanesque windows and columns have no equal in the Czech Republic. The Olomouc Archdiocesan Museum opened here in 2006 and includes some fine paintings collected by bishops of Olomouc. There is also the Mozarteum concert hall.

TOWN CENTRE

Church of Our Lady of the Snows ⑤
Church of St Maurice ①
Church of St Michael ③
Horní náměstí ②
Olomouc Art Museum ⑥
Přemyslid Palace ⑧
St Jan Sarkander Chapel ④
St Wenceslas Cathedral ⑦

Key to Symbols see back flap

KEY
Street-by-Street see pp218–19

Street-by-Street: Horní náměstí

Olomouc's cobbled main square is famous, above all, for its grand Town Hall, and the remarkable highly decorated Holy Trinity Column. Equally impressive are its three fountains: the Caesar Fountain of 1725, the 1687 Hercules Fountain, and the newest – the 2002 Arion Fountain. The square is a popular meeting place, especially around the Holy Trinity Column, and its many sidestreets offer pleasant and interesting places to explore.

Edelmann Palace
One of the most opulent buildings in the square is the Renaissance palace dating from 1572–86, built for the wealthy local merchant Václav Edelmann.

Hercules fountain

28. ŘÍJNA

RIEGROVA

HORNÍ NÁMĚSTÍ

PAVELČÁKOVA

★ Holy Trinity Column
The massive Baroque column is crowned by figures representing the Holy Trinity. Below is the Archangel Michael with his fiery sword.

★ Town Hall
The magnificent external staircase built in 1591 is decorated with heraldic emblems. The slender tower, which dominates the entire building, affords a lovely view over the market and the surrounding streets.

Arion Fountain
The work of Ivan Theimer and a Tuscan artist, Angela Chiantelli, this fountain depicting the ancient poet Arion was produced in 2002 to a design created by the Olomouc councillors 350 years ago.

| 0 metres | 100 |
| 0 yards | 100 |

Coat of Arms, Town Hall
The shield of Olomouc was placed next to the town hall's stairs in 1591. It features the Moravian chequered eagle.

Chapel Oriel
In 1488 the remodelled chapel of the town hall was given a lavishly decorated oriel, unique in the Czech Republic.

Caesar Fountain
The equestrian statue of Caesar on this 1725 fountain is modelled on one of Constantine the Great in the Vatican Museum in Rome.

KEY
- - - Suggested route

TOWN HALL CLOCK

The first clock was placed in the Gothic niche on the north wall of the town hall in the early 15th century. The mechanism displaying astronomical data was added in 1573. After damage in World War II it was remodelled so that wooden figures of proletarians replaced those of saints. A mosaic added at the same time also shows workers *(see also p212)*.

The clock by Master Hanuš with its new figures and mosaic

STAR SIGHTS

★ Holy Trinity Column

★ Town Hall

OPLETALOVA
OSTRUŽNICKÁ
ZTRACENA
MAHLEROVA
MICHALSKÁ
DOLNÍ NÁMĚSTÍ

Plumlov Palace beside Plumlov Reservoir

Plumlov Palace ❷

Road map C3. 7 km (4 miles) W of
Prostějov. 🚌 from Prostějov, Olomouc.
Tel 582 393 217. ☐ Apr–Jun, Sep:
10am–noon, 2–6pm Sat, Sun, public
hols; Jul, Aug: 10am–6pm Tue–Sun. 📷

An astonishing sight, Plumlov
Palace is a tall, three-storey
structure (there are two
further, intermediate storeys
inside), which is also
unusually flat. The entire
façade is lavishly decorated
with columns, cornices,
stuccoes and balustrades.

The palace's unusual shape
is due to its history. The 17th-
century prince-bishop Karl
Eusebius of Liechtenstein,
Lord of Valtice, designed a
huge four-wing palace that
was to be the most beautiful
residence in Moravia.
Unfortunately his son, Jan
Adam, saddled by his father
with the responsibility of
accomplishing the task, was
unable to meet the financial
demands associated with the
project. The family became
embroiled in arguments about
financial affairs and
consequently, by the end of
the century, only one wing
was completed and roofed.
This now serves as a small
museum and a venue for a
variety of cultural events.

Náměšť' na Hané Palace ❸

Road map C3. 13 km
(8 miles) W of Olomouc.
🚌 🚌 from Prostějov,
Olomouc. **Tel** 585 952 184.
☐ Apr, Oct: 9am–4pm Sat,
Sun; May–Sep: 9am–5pm
Tue–Sun. 📷

The palace, with its
mansard roof typical
of late 18th-century
French architecture,
was built in 1760–63
by Ferdinand
Bonaventura Harrach.
Its two ground-floor
wings surround a
courtyard that ends
with a gate leading to
the palace garden. Laid
out in the shape of a
perfect circle, the
garden is crisscrossed
by four avenues of lime trees
leading to the four points of
the compass.

Riches of the interior
include the Red and the
Gold Parlours with Rococo,
Classical and Empire furnishings; there is also an extensive
library. Large collections of
Meissen porcelain and the
stately coaches are housed in
the ground-floor wings, from
the collection of the Olomouc
Archbishopric.

The palace Chapel of
the Holy Trinity took an
extraordinarily long time to
be completed; the building
works started in 1672 and
ended 50 years later. In 1834
it was remodelled in the
Empire style.

Javoříčské Caves ❹

Road map C3. 4 km (2 miles) S of
Bouzov. 🚌 bus from Bouzov. **Tel** 585
345 451. ☐ Apr, Oct: 9am–3pm Tue–
Sun; May–Sep: 8am–4pm Tue–Sun. 📷

The maze of limestone caves
(jeskyně) discovered here in
1938 stretches for over 3 km
(2 miles). One part of the
subterranean complex, nearly
700 m (2,300 ft) long, is open
to the public. Its chambers,
some of which are more than
10 m (33 ft) high, feature extraordinary stalactite formations
in the shapes of waterfalls,
bulging columns and curtains.

Inside the "Giants' cathedral",
Javoříčské Caves

Bouzov Castle ❺

Road map C3. 🚌 12 km (7 miles)
Mohelnice. **Tel** 585 346 201. ☐ Apr:
9am–3pm Sat, Sun; May–Oct: 9am–
4pm Tue–Sun (Aug: to 6pm). 📷 📷

Founded in the 14th century,
Bouzov Castle (Busau) was
probably the birthplace of

Interior of the palace in Náměšť' na Hané

George of Poděbrady, the future king of Bohemia. In 1696 Bouzov became the property of the Teutonic Knights. It gradually fell into disrepair until the end of the 19th century, when the Order's Grand Master, Archduke Eugene Habsburg, commissioned Georg von Hauberisser to remodel the structure in the Romantic spirit. As a result, Bouzov acquired the form of a huge Gothic fortress complete with towers and turrets.

In 1939 the castle became the headquarters of a Nazi SS unit. After the war it was taken over by the Czech state authorities, and now, impeccably maintained, it is among the Czech Republic's most popular historic sites.

Its interiors, lavishly decorated with paintings and sculptures, include the luxurious apartments of the Grand Master; the Column Hall; Royal Quarters and Guest Rooms; Chapel and Armoury; castle kitchens and fortress defence system.

Jeseník **6**

Road map C2. 🏔 13,000.
🚌 🚊 from Olomouc.
ℹ Masarykovo náměstí 1.
Tel 584 498 155.

One of the towns in the Jeseníky peaks, away from the industry of the lower-lying parts of Moravia, Jeseník (Freiwaldau) has a castle known as the Water Fortress

Arcaded cloister in the courtyard of Šternberk Castle

Relief image of Priessnitz, in Jeseník

for its now-dry moat. Built at the turn of the 13th and 14th centuries, it withstood a siege by the Swedes in 1641. The fortress was given its present shape in the mid-18th century. It now houses the **Regional Museum**. Perched above the town, on a hillside, is the small spa resort of **Lázně Jeseník**, founded by Vinzenz Priessnitz, who advocated cold-water therapy. It was at the height of its fame in the 19th century.

🏛 **Regional Museum**
Tel 584 401 070. ☐ Sep–Jun: Tue–Sat; Jul, Aug: Tue–Sun. 📷

Šternberk Castle **7**

Road map C3. 🚉 🚌 from Olomouc.
Tel 585 012 935. ☐ Apr, Oct: 9am–4pm Sat, Sun, public hols; May–Sep: 9am–5pm Tue–Sun.
📷 📹 2 routes.

The oldest surviving part of the castle, the cylindrical tower, dates from the second half of the 13th century. The remaining buildings of this medieval structure took a lot of battering during the 15th-century Hussite wars, and in the course of the Thirty Years' War, in 1618–48. In the 19th century Jan II of Liechtenstein rebuilt the decaying castle in Neo-Gothic style. Now it is home to the Liechtenstein collection, which includes furniture, paintings, sculptures and fireplaces. The second floor has an interesting exhibition of furnishings brought from Northern Moravian castles, which after 1945 were closed to the public.

Opava **8**

Road map D2. 🏔 61,500. 🚉 from Prague. ℹ Horní náměstí 67. Tel 553 756 143. www.infocentrum.opava.cz

The capital of Austrian Silesia following the Austro-Prussian war of 1742, Opava (Troppau) started life as an important trading centre. Its most interesting historic sites include the vast 14th-century

brick **Church of the Assumption of the Virgin Mary** (Nanebevzetí Panny Marie), a splendid example of Silesian Gothic. Masaryk Street (Masarykova třída) is a handsome street that includes the 18th-century palaces of the Sobek and Blücher families.

The oldest museum in the Czech Republic, founded in 1814, is the **Silesian Municipal Museum** (Slezské zemské Museum). Its opulent building was erected in 1893–5 to a design by Viennese architects Scheinringer and Kachler. It has history, ethnography and natural history displays. Its other division, in Hlučín-Darkovicki, includes Czech fortifications erected in the late 1930s – a rare example of well-preserved military technology of that time.

🏛 **Silesian Municipal Museum**
U Muzea 1. Tel 553 756 143.
☐ Tue–Sun. 📷

Altar in the Church of the Assumption in Opava

Courtyard view of the red castle in Hradec nad Moravicí

Hradec nad Moravicí Castle ⑨

Road map D2. 🚌 *from Jeseník, Opava, Přerov.* **Tel** *553 783 444.* ⭕ *Apr, Oct, Dec: 10am–4pm Sat, Sun, public hols; May–Sep: 9am–5pm Tue–Sun.* 🎫 🎫 *2 routes.*

As early as the 9th century a Slav settlement stood here. The fortress, built in the 11th century, kept watch over the Polish-Czech borderland. Following consecutive reconstructions, including late 16th-century Renaissance works and late 18th- to early 19th-century Neo-Classical remodelling, the castle acquired its present Romantic Neo-Gothic form in 1860–67. Its owners, the ducal family of Lichnovský of Voštice, turned it into a centre of culture and music. Now the lovingly restored interiors exhibit paintings, porcelain and mementoes associated with visits from Beethoven, Liszt and Paganini.

Ostrava ⑩

Road map D2. 🏚 *320,000.* 🚉 *Ostrava střed, Frydlantská.* 🚌 *Vítkovická 2.* ℹ️ *Nádražní 7/686.* **Tel** *596 123 913* **www**.ostravainfo.cz

The third-largest city in the Czech Republic, Ostrava (Ostrau) expanded rapidly from 1763 onwards, when rich coal deposits were discovered nearby. The development of mines, steelworks, and construction and chemical plants turned Ostrava and its environs into an industrial district. Pollution was a huge problem, but since many mines and

steelworks closed in the 1990s, the city has been cleaned up and regeneration is underway.

The centre has been declared a historic zone. Masarykovo náměstí, the main square, has one of the city's oldest buildings: the 17th-century **Old Town Hall** (Stará radnice). Some of Ostrava's finest buildings date from the 1920s. They include the former **Anglo-Czech Bank** designed by Josef Gočar; the Constructivist Arts Centre (Dům umění), now the **Gallery of Arts and Crafts** (Galerie Výtvarného Umění), and the **New Town Hall**, north of the old centre. In Petřkovice suburb is a vast open-air **Mining Museum** (Hornické muzeum), where visitors can see an old mine.

🏛 **Gallery of Arts and Crafts**
Jurečkova 9. **Tel** *596 112 566.* ⭕ *Tue–Sun.* **www**.gvuostrava.cz

🏛 **Mining Museum**
Pod Landekem 64. **Tel** *596 131 803.* ⭕ *Tue–Sun.* **www**.muzeumokd.cz

Příbor ⑪

Road map D3. 🏚 *9,000.* 🚉 🚌 *from Přerov.* ℹ️ *Náměstí Sigmunda Freuda 19.* **Tel** *556 455 444.* **www**.pribor-mesto.cz

The birthplace of Sigmund Freud, Příbor (Freiberg) is in the foothills of the Beskydy. Its quiet market square (náměstí Sigmunda Freuda) is surrounded by Renaissance houses with Baroque façades. At its centre is a 1713 statue of the Virgin Mary. The town is dominated by the tower of the **Church of St Mary** (sv. Marie), which has a Gothic statue of the Madonna dating from 1400. The former 1694 Piarist college houses the **Příbor Museum** with some Freud mementos.

Fountain in Příbor market square

Houses in Poštovna, near Masarykovo náměstí in Ostrava

For hotels and restaurants in this region see pp355–6 and pp387–8

🏛 Příbor Museum
Lidická 50. *Tel 556 725 191.*
◯ *Tue, Thu, Sun.* 🖾

Nový Jičín ⑫

Road map D3. 👥 *27,000.* 🚆 *from Olomouc.* ℹ *Úzká 27. Tel 556 711 888.* **www**.novyjicin.mic.cz

The old part of Nový Jičín (Neutitschein) has maintained its original square layout dating from the Middle Ages. The striking house of Mayor Ondřej Řepa, dating from 1563 and known as the **Old Post Office** (stará pošta), features a two-storey arcaded loggia. The "White Angel", continuously used as a pharmacy since 1716, has a 1790 Neo-Rococo façade.

In a Gothic former castle is the fascinating **Hat Museum** (Kloboučnické muzeum) – the town was known in the 19th century for producing hats.

🏛 Hat Museum
Tel 556 701 156. ◯ *Tue–Sun.* 🖾

Hranice ⑬

Road map D3. 👥 *8,000.* 🚆 *from Ostrava, Přerov.* ℹ *Masarykovo náměstí 71. Tel 581 607 479.*

In Hranice is a recently reconstructed Late-Renaissance **castle**, a four-wing structure with an arcaded courtyard. The most opulent building in the market square is the Baroque **Church of St John the Baptist** (sv. Jana Křtitele) dating from 1763. At one corner of the square stands the Neo-Gothic town hall, built in the first half of the 16th century. Several nearby houses have interesting Renaissance façades. The **Municipal Museum** also lies on the main square; it contains local history exhibits.

Emblem of Hranice at the Municipal Museum

🏛 Municipal Museum
Masarykovo náměstí 71. *Tel 581 601 160.* ◯ *Tue–Sun.* 🖾

The castle housing the Hat Museum in Nový Jičín

Lipník nad Bečvou ⑭

Road map D3. 👥 *8,500.* 🚉 🚆 *from Přerov.* ℹ *Náměstí T G Masaryka 41. Tel 581 773 763.*

The town's historic core centres on its L-shaped market square, lined with Renaissance and Baroque houses. Its most eye-catching buildings are the **Town Hall** (radnice), and the 1609 bell tower. The **Church of St Jacob** (sv. Jakub) has a unique Renaissance tower. Another place of interest is the Late-Gothic former **synagogue**.

Environs
Helfštýn, 4 km (2 miles) southeast of Lipník, is the largest of the Moravian castles. This 14th-century Gothic edifice was several times extended. The drive to the castle complex leads through five gates and across four courtyards. The last features ruins of a Late-Renaissance palace, whose basement houses an interesting historical exhibition.

Rožnov pod Radhoštěm ⑮

Road map D3. 👥 *17,200.* 🚉 🚆 *from Valašské, Meziříčí.* ℹ *Palackého 484. Tel 571 655 196.*

To the south of Radhošť mountain lies a small town (its name means Rožnov under Radhošť) that is immensely popular for its **Wallachian**

Open-Air Museum (Valašské muzeum v přírodě). This consists of three open-air exhibitions (or skansen) of beautiful traditional wooden buildings of the Wallachs of the Beskydy region. The Wallachs were sheep farmers who lived in Moravia and parts of Slovakia. The skansen, established in 1925, aim to preserve and illuminate their culture and way of life with examples from the 17th to the 20th centuries.

From the museum it is possible to walk up **Radhošť** mountain, which at 1,129 m (3,700 ft) above sea level provides extraordinary views of the surrounding peaks and villages. On its top stands a Byzantine-style wooden chapel of St Cyril and St Methodius, dating from 1898.

🏛 Wallachian Open-Air Museum
Palackého 147. *Tel 571 757 111.* ◯ *daily (some areas May–Sep only).* 🖾 🎥 **www**.vmp.cz

Portal of the Church of St Jacob in Lipník nad Bečvou

SOUTH MORAVIA

T*he wealth of historic remains in this region would enthral most visitors. Around virtually every corner you are likely to come across lovely towns and villages or imposing monasteries, castles and palaces. The stunning Renaissance town of Telč, the archbishop's residence in Kroměříž, and the Lednicko-Valtický park and palace complex are all UNESCO World Heritage sites.*

South Moravia (Jižní Morava), once a frontier region of the Roman Empire, was the cradle of the first state set up by the Slavs, who arrived in the region from Eastern Europe. The so-called Great Moravian Empire *(see p33)* lasted from 830 until the early 10th century, when Magyars made incursions into Moravian territory. In the subsequent centuries South Moravia was the scene of some of the most momentous events in the history of the Czech Lands.

The capital of the region (and of the whole of Moravia) is Brno. This university town, the second largest in the Czech Republic, is often neglected by visitors, but it has a pleasant and compact historic centre as well as a modernist landmark, Mies van der Rohe's Villa Tugendhat.

Elsewhere in the region there are architectural treasures from most periods: Znojmo's magnificent Romanesque rotunda; the splendid Gothic castle of Pernštejn; the Renaissance gem of Telč; and the Baroque castle in Valtice. Besides the buildings that testify to Moravia's strong links with Catholicism, there are also many sights associated with the history of the region's Jewish population, including those in Boskovice, Mikulov and Třebíč.

While South Moravia's hills and forests are similar to Bohemia's, the southern part of the region is flatter and more open. Home to fertile vineyards, it has a long tradition of winemaking. Around Mikulov and other southern towns it is worth visiting the historic cellars, and tasting the highly respected wines.

Fountain in front of the elegant arcades in Kroměříž gardens

◁ **Detail of the Romanesque gateway at the Porta Coeli convent in Tišnov**

Exploring South Moravia

Brno is the most convenient place to begin a visit. As well as having some attractions of its own, the city is also within easy reach of other places of interest, such as Pernštejn Castle and the breathtaking caves of the Moravský kras. South of Brno much of the land was once owned by the Liechtenstein family, who built many of the churches and castles here, including Lednice and Vranov. The neglected hilly region in the west is home to the idyllic town of Telč, while in the eastern reaches beats the heart of Moravia's folk culture.

Svitavy

Hradec Králové

Brněnec

Nové Město na Moravě

ŽĎ'ÁR NAD SÁZAVOU 8

Brnĕnec

43

Letovice

Bystřice nad Pernštejnem 150

BOSKOVICE 4

Prague

Nedvedice

Meziříčko 37

PERNŠTEJN CASTLE 6

Rájec-Jestřebi

JIHLAVA 9

Kamenice

Křižanov 387

MORAVSKÝ KRAS 5

Kostelec

Velké Meziříčí

Velká Bíteš

TIŠNOV 7

Blansko 379

Stonařov

VYSOČINA

KŘTINY 3

Třešt

406

Trnava

38

Ostravačice

TŘEBÍČ 11   23

Oslava

385

Svratka

43

TELČ 10   23

Hory

Jihlava

Rosice

D1

BRNO 1

360

JAROMĚŘICE NAD ROKYTNOU CHATEAU 12

Hrotovice

152

Ivančice

Rajhrad

52

Moravské Budějovice

Moravský Krumlov

D2

Jemnice

361

JIHOMORAVSKÝ

152

Bojanovice

Pohořelice

BÍTOV 13

Uherčice

38

Vranovice

VRANOV NAD DYJÍ CHATEAU 14

53

Litobratřice 52

ZNOJMO 15

Dyje

415

MIKULOV 16

38

LEDNICKO-VALTICKÝ AREÁL 17

Hevín

Valtice

Vienna

Oriel of a house in Telč's main square

GETTING AROUND

Brno lies at the junction of major transport routes. The D1 motorway cuts through the centre of the region linking Prague to Brno, and ending near Kroměříž, in the east. The D2 heads south from Brno to . . . . through the eastern part of the region, through Otrokovice and Břeclav, is the main railway line linking Warsaw with Vienna, via Bratislava, but generally the train network in South Moravia is not as good as in Bohemia.

SIGHTS AT A GLANCE

Bítov **13**

Boskovice **4**

Brno pp228–31 **1**

Buchlovice Chateau **18**

Jaroměřice nad Rokytnou
   Chateau **12**

Jihlava **9**

Kroměříž pp240–41 **20**

Křtiny **3**

Lednicko-Valtický areál **17**

Luhačovice **22**

Mikulov **16**

Moravský kras **5**

Pernštejn Castle **6**

Slavkov u Brna **2**

Telč **10**

Tišnov **7**

Třebíč **11**

Velehrad Monastery **19**

Vranov nad Dyjí Chateau **14**

Žďár nad Sázavou **8**

Zlín **21**

Znojmo **15**

SEE ALSO

• **Where to Stay** pp356–7

• **Where to Eat** pp388–9

**Statue of the Three Graces in
the palace gardens at Valtice**

KEY

═══ Motorway

═ ═ Motorway under construction

──── Main road

········ Minor road

╍╍╍ Main railway

──── Minor railway

▬▬▬ International border

▬▬▬ Regional border

Lednice castle gardens, in the Lednicko-Valticky areál

Brno ❶

Now the second-largest city in the Czech Republic, Brno (Brünn) occupies the site of what, in the 9th century, was the main settlement in the Great Moravian Empire. The city that you see today first developed at the foot of Petrov Hill, where the Přemyslids built a castle in the 11th century. In 1641, the walled town became the new capital of Moravia but didn't develop significantly until the 19th century. World War II devastated the city and, despite being totally rebuilt, Brno has never quite regained its former lustre. Even so, thanks to its buoyant theatre life and numerous museums, Brno has become a major cultural centre.

View of the St Peter and St Paul Cathedral

Exploring the town

Brno's Old Town, with the city's main historic sites and museums, is focused around two squares: Zelný trh and náměstí Svobody. Two major landmarks outside the Old Town are the twin-towered cathedral atop Petrov Hill, and **Špilberk fortress**, to the west (see pp230–31). The other sites of interest are Villa Tugendhat and the Augustinian Monastery.

🔒 Cathedral of St Peter and St Paul

Petrov Hill. ⬜ 8:15am–6:15pm daily. ✝ 7:30am, 9am, 10:30am Sun; 7:30am Sat (in Latin).

The cathedral (katedrála sv. Petra a Pavla), with its soaring towers visible from afar, stands on the site which, in the 11th and 12th centuries, was the probable site of Brno's first castle. Originally Romanesque, the church acquired a Gothic appearance in the 1200s, but countless subsequent alterations eventually obliterated its

original shape. It was restored to its Gothic form in the late 1800s. Of most interest inside is the crypt of the original church. There are also great views from the tower.

🔒 Church of the Holy Cross

Kapucínské náměstí. 5.
Crypt ⬜ 9am–noon, 2–4pm Tue–Sat (also May–Sep: Mon), 11–11:45am, 2–4:30pm Sun.

The austere façade of the Church of the Holy Cross (kostel sv. Kříže), near the foot of Petrov Hill, is typical of other Capuchin churches elsewhere in Europe. The rather macabre attraction here are the mummified monks (dressed) in the crypt.

🏛 Zelný trh

This square (literally "cabbage market") has served as a vegetable market since the Middle Ages, and has even kept its original, sloping shape. Its main adornment, the Parnassus Fountain, is Brno's finest piece of sculpture. Made to a design by Fischer von Erlach in the 1690s, it combines the best traits of Baroque naturalism, trompe-l'oeil and theatrics. Among the rather motley group of buildings around Zlený trh is the home of

the Reduta theatre. Currently under renovation, this is the oldest theatre building in Brno. The Dietrichstein Palace (Ditrichšteinský palác), at the square's southern end, has a fine entrance portal (1700) and is home to the **Moravian National Museum**, devoted to Brno's early history.

Sculptures by Anton Pilgram on the Old Town Hall's doorway

🏛 Old Town Hall

Radnická 8. ⬜ Apr–Sep: 10am–6pm daily; Oct–Mar: 8am–6pm Mon–Fri, 9am–5pm Sat & Sun.

Just off Zelný trh, the Old Town Hall (Stará radnice) is the oldest secular building in Brno, dating from 1240. In 1510 a doorway was cut into the tower on Radnická and framed by a superb Gothic portal. This work by Anton Pilgram is decorated at the lower level with figures of knights and, above, with figures of the town's aldermen. At the centre is the allegorical figure of Blind Justice. A pinnacle above the statue is deliberately twisted, said to be Pilgram's revenge for being underpaid for his work. The main tourist office is here, and there are views from the tower.

🏛 New Town Hall

Panenská.

The "New" Town Hall (Nová radnice), the seat of the city council, dates mainly from the 1700s. It was built inside a former Dominican monastery; the Dominican **St Michael's Church** stands

Eighteenth-century sculpture outside St Michael's Church

nearby. Gothic cloisters survive inside the town hall. The first courtyard is skirted by Renaissance buildings and has a lovely sundial (1728).

🏛 Náměstí Svobody
Brno's main square buzzes with life, its many restaurants and cafés being popular meeting places. The chief landmark is the Baroque **plague column**, while the architecture around the square spans 400 years. Its finest buildings include the Schwartz House (Schwarzův palác), with an ornate 16th-century façade decorated with *sgraffito*, and the House of the Four Mamlases (Dům u čtyř mamlasů) (1928), whose four comical Atlas figures strain to support the building.

🏛 Moravian Gallery
Husova 18, Husova 14 and Moravské náměstí. *Tel 532 169 131.* ⬚ *10am–5pm Wed–Sun (to 6pm May–Oct).* 📷
The Moravská galerie is spread over three premises. The most unusual collection is at the Uměleckoprůmyslové muzeum or UPM (at Husova 14), dedicated to the applied arts. It has some fantastic exhibits, including superb late 19th-century furniture and Art Nouveau glassware.

🏛 Villa Tugendhat
Černopolni 45. 🚋 *3,5, 11.* *Tel 545 212 118.* ⬚ *10am–6pm Wed–Sun.* 📷 📷 *compulsory.*
One of the most famous buildings designed in the spirit of Functionalism, Villa Tugendhat was built by

German architect, Ludwig Mies van der Rohe in 1929–30. By covering a steel frame with glass, van der Rohe achieved a superb effect of linked space both inside and outside the building. Fortunately, alterations made by the Communists did not manage to ruin the building.

🔒 Augustinian Monastery
Mendlovo náměstí. *Tel 543 424 010.* **Museum** ⬚ *10am–6pm Tue–Sun (to 5pm Nov–Mar).* 📷 ♿
This monastery (Augustiniánský klášter) has a fine Gothic church, but it is famous above all as the place where Gregor Mendel (1822–84) discovered and formulated his theory of genetics. The monk's contribution to modern biology was acknowledged only after his death. A **museum** dedicated to his work, known as the Mendelianum, is in the monastery's west wing.

Brno's náměstí Svobody, with its Baroque plague column (1680)

BRNO CITY CENTRE

Cathedral of St Peter and St Paul ①
Church of the Holy Cross ②
Moravian Gallery ⑦
Náměstí Svobody ⑥
New Town Hall ⑤
Old Town Hall ④
Zelný trh ③

Villa Tugendhat
MAREŠOVA
MORAVSKÉ NÁMĚSTÍ
KOLIŠTĚ
Sady Osvobození
ŽEROTÍNOVO NÁMĚSTÍ
BRANOLOVA
Moravian Gallery ⑦ (Místodržitelský palác)
JOŠTOVA
KOMENSKÉHO NÁMĚSTÍ
JEZUITSKÁ
ROOSEVELTOVA
ÚDOLNÍ
SOLNIČNÍ
ČESKÁ
RAVNOVA
JAKUBSKÉ NÁMĚSTÍ
BĚHOUNSKÁ
KOLIŠTĚ
SKRYTÁ
DVOŘÁKOVA
MALINOVSKÉHO NÁMĚSTÍ
Moravian Gallery ⑦ (Pražákův palác)
Špilberk
Plague Column ⑥
KOBLIŽNÁ
NÁMĚSTÍ SVOBODY
JÁNSKÁ
Moravian Gallery ⑦ (UPM)
⑤ New Town Hall
PÁNSKÁ
KOŽÍ
ORLI
NOVOBRANSKÁ
BENEŠOVA
Augustinian Monastery
PELLICHOVA
HUSOVA
St Michael's Church
MĚČOVA
④ Old Town Hall
0 metres 250
0 yards 250
PEKAŘSKÁ
STAROBRNĚNSKÁ
③ ZELNÝ TRH
Morvian National Museum
② Church of the Holy Cross
LEITNEROVA
KOPEČNÁ
Cathedral of St Peter and St Paul ①
NÁDRAŽNÍ
🖂 Brno train station
Bus station 200 m (220 yards)

Key to Symbols *see back flap*

Brno: Špilberk

A hilltop castle was built on this site by a Moravian margrave, the future Přemysl Otakar II, in the 13th century, but Špilberk gained the status of a true royal residence only 400 years later, when it was transformed into a mighty Baroque fortress. After the Napoleonic wars, the castle became a prison and gained a reputation as one of the harshest symbols of Habsburg repression. Špilberk was also used as a prison by the Nazis. Displays inside relate to Brno and the castle. Concerts and plays are staged here in summer.

Coat of Arms
The coat of arms with a twin-headed eagle and an imperial crown is a reminder that Špilberk was one of the main fortresses defending the mighty Habsburg Empire.

"From Renaissance to Modernism"
This permanent exhibition displays works by painters and sculptors associated with Brno, from the mid-16th century to 1945.

"From Castle to Fortress"
The rooms devoted to the history of Špilberk also have an excavated area showing some of the citadel's earliest foundations.

"The City of Špilberk"
This extensive exhibition seeks to bring to life the history of Brno, from its earliest records in 1091 to the end of World War II.

STAR FEATURES

★ Chapel

★ Dungeons

Baroque Pharmacy
From the mid-18th until the early 20th century the pharmacy belonged to a convent in Brno. Its historic furnishings include hundreds of jars, instruments and the original cupboards.

VISITORS' CHECKLIST

Špilberk. *Tel* 542 123 616. **Dungeons** 🔲 9am–5pm Tue–Sun (Jul, Aug; daily). **Pharmacy** May–Sep: 9am–6pm Tue–Sun. **Exhibitions** Apr–Oct: 9am–5pm Tue–Sun; Nov–Mar: 10am–5pm Wed–Sun. 🎵 📷 www.spilberk.cz

Tower
The tower at the northeast corner of the castle provides an excellent viewpoint overlooking the entire Špilberk area. It is also used for staging exhibitions.

★ Dungeons
This maze of dark, dank subterranean corridors was transformed, in the reign of Emperor Joseph II, into a series of unbelievably gruesome prison cells, particularly those in the north wing.

★ Chapel
Little remains of the original Gothic castle. The Gothic look of the eastern wing, and of the chapel, dates from controversial reconstruction work carried out in the 1990s.

The façade and ornamental lake of the Baroque chateau in Slavkov u Brna

Slavkov u Brna ❷

Road map C3. 🚶 *6,000.* 🚊 🚌 **ℹ**
Palackého 1/126. **Tel** *544 220 988.*

The plains between Brno and Slavkov (Austerlitz) were, in 1805, the site of the great battle in which Napoleon defeated the Austrians and Russians *(see box)*. Before the battle, Emperor Francis II and Tsar Alexander I stayed at the Baroque **Slavkov Chateau** (zámek Slavkov), which Napoleon chose as his base following his victory.

The vast, imposing building, with its squat central dome, has some beautifully preserved rooms. The finest of these is the Ancestors' Hall (Sál předků) with its lovely painting and stucco decoration. It was here that Napoleon and the defeated Emperor and Tsar signed their peace treaty. In the museum is a model of the battlefield.

♣ Slavkov Chateau
Palackého náměstí 1. **Tel** *544 221 204.* ◻ *Apr–May, Sep–Nov: Tue–Sun; Jun–Aug: daily.* 🖼 🌐
www.zamek-slavkov.cz

Křtiny ❸

16 km (10 miles) west of Brno.
Road map C3. 🚶 *770.* 🚌

Hidden amid forests and rocks northeast of Brno is Křtiny. Home to a castle, the village is more famous for its **Church of Our Lady**, one of the crowning achievements of Moravian Baroque architecture. Designed by the superb Baroque architect, Giovanni Santini, this large pilgrimage

Vaulted ceiling in the Church of Our Lady, Křtiny

church was built between 1712 and 1750. Inside, the nave has a definite Byzantine feel, with its frescoed domes in garish colours illuminated by light from numerous windows. The high altar itself, crowned with a baldachin, is a riot of colour. Here can be found the venerated 15th-century statue of Our Lady.

The interior is decorated with works by leading artists of the Czech Baroque. The wall paintings (1747) are by Johann J Etgens, and the Way of the Cross stations by the Jesuit painter, Ignaz Raab.

🔒 Church of Our Lady
Křtiny. **Tel** *516 439 189.*

Boskovice ❹

Road map C3. 🚶 *11,400.* 🚊 🚌
ℹ *Masarykovo náměstí 1.* **Tel** *516 488 677.* **www**.boskovice.cz

The town of Boskovice, 48 km (30 miles) north of Brno, is one of the most beautiful in the region with two impressive historic sights.

The first is the ruined 13th-century **Boskovice Castle** (hrad Boskovice), which was obtained by the Dietrichstein family in the 17th century but abandoned by them in the 18th. The vast structure, one of the biggest of its kind in Moravia, still has its original defensive walls, complete with a gate and a tower.

Nearby is the magnificent **Boskovice Chateau** (palác Boskovice), built from 1819–26 by the Dietrichsteins. With its clean architectural lines, it is the finest example of the Empire style in Moravia. Of particular interest inside are the main hall,

Gate and walls of the impressive castle ruins in Boskovice

THE BATTLE OF AUSTERLITZ

On 2 December 1805, Napoleon's 75,000-strong forces crushed the 90,000-strong combined Russian and Austrian armies near the town of Slavkov. The battle claimed the lives of some 33,000 Russian and Austrian troops, and about 7,000 French. The Monument of Peace (Mohyla míru), a soaring Art Nouveau pyramid, was erected on the battlefield, 8 km (5 miles) south-west of Slavkov, in 1912. The fields around are scattered with crosses.

The Monument of Peace

library and Neo-Classical furnishings. There is also an exhibition illustrating the everyday life of the Czech nobility in the 19th century.

Boskovice, once home to a large Jewish community, has one of the best preserved former Jewish ghettoes in the country, encompassing some 80 buildings. These include the richly decorated Grand Synagogue *(see p237)* on Taplova Street. The large Jewish cemetery, established in the 17th century, is now overgrown with trees.

♠ **Boskovice Castle**
Tel 516 452 043. ☐ *Apr, Oct: Sat, Sun, public hols; May, Sep: Tue–Sun; Jun–Aug: daily.* ▨
♠ **Boskovice Chateau**
Tel 516 452 241. ☐ *May–Sep: Tue–Sun.* **www**.zamekboskovice.cz

Macocha Abyss, created by the collapse of a cave roof

Moravský kras ❺

Road map C3. ▨ to Blansko from Brno; from Blansko to Skalní Mlýn. ℹ Skalní Mlýn. **Tel** 516 413 575 ♿ Some caves accessible: phone for information. **www**.caves.cz

The limestone karst region of the Moravský kras covers an area of some 85 sq km (33 sq miles) north of Brno, and is hollowed out by a vast system of caves. Four caves are open to the public, three of which can be reached on foot from Skalní Mlýn (5 km/3 miles from Blansko), home to the main Moravský kras information centre.

The first, the **Punkva Caves** (Punkevní jeskyně) are the largest in the whole region.

MORAVIA'S KARST

In the Moravský kras, as in similar regions elsewhere, the karst formations are the result of the action of rain-water on limestone rock: over millions of years the water dissolves the rock, creating cracks which are then eroded by the constant flow. Great cave systems and deep gorges often result. Limestone-rich water dripping through the porous roofs of the caves often creates stalactites and stalagmites. Moravia's karst is famous for its rivers that repeatedly vanish and re-emerge. The word "karst" comes from the German name of the limestone plateau near Trieste.

Stalactites and stalagmites in the Punkva cave

On the one-hour tour, which includes a boat ride along the Punkva underground river, visitors can expect to see some fantastic stalactites and stalagmites, and to gaze in wonder up the 1,387-m (4,550-ft) Macocha Abyss (propast Macocha). To be sure of a place on this very popular cave tour, book ahead in the high season. It is also possible to visit the rim of the abyss separately.

The second, **Kateřinská Cave**, is the region's largest single cavern, measuring 100 m (328 ft) in length. The third, the **Balcarka Cave**, is small but has breathtakingly colourful stalactites and stalagmites. Evidence of prehistoric human dwellings has also been discovered here.

The caves are the big attraction but the scenery of the Moravský kras is worth seeing in its own right, with its densely wooded ravines.

Visitors in need of a break from the geological tour should stop off 5 km (3 miles) north of Blansko at Rájec-Jestřebi for a look at **Rájec nad Svitavou Chateau**, an unusual Moravian example of French Baroque built in the 1760s. Part of the attraction is the collection of 16th-century Dutch and Flemish paintings assembled by the Salm family, the original residents.

▨ **Punkva Cave**
Tel 516 418 602. ☐ *Jan–Oct: Tue–Sun.* ▨ ▨ ♿
▨ **Katerinska Cave**
Tel 516 413 161. ☐ *Mar, Apr, Oct, Nov: Tue–Sun; May–Sep: daily.* ▨ ▨ ♿
▨ **Balcarka Cave**
Tel 516 444 330. ☐ *Mar, Apr, Oct, Nov: Tue–Sun; May–Sep: daily.* ▨ ▨ ♿
♠ **Rájec nad Svitavou Chateau**
Tel 516 432 013. ☐ *Apr, Oct: Sat & Sun; May–Sep: daily.*

The French-style Rájec nad Svitavou Chateau, in the Moravský kras

Pernštejn Castle ❻

Road map C3. 🚉 🚌 *Nedvědice,*
2 km (1 mile) from Pernštejn.
Tel *566 566 101.* ☐ *Apr, Oct: 9am–*
noon, 1–3pm Sat, Sun, public hols;
May–Sep: 9am–noon, 1–4pm Tue–
Sun (Jul & Aug: to 5pm). 📷 ☑

The road that leads from the
village of Nedvědice, at the
foot of Pernštejn, gives an
unforgettable view of the
sheer walls, towers and turrets
of the Gothic castle. This,
one of the biggest and best-
preserved Gothic strongholds
in the Czech Republic, was
damaged by fire in 2005 and
is now only partially open to
the public. But the dizzying
spectacle can still be enjoyed.

Barbican of the impressive Gothic fortress of Pernštejn

Rebuilding work in the 15th
and 16th centuries turned the
medieval *hrad* into a fortress
so powerful that it withstood
all attempts by the Swedish
army to capture it during
the Thirty Years' War. The
various sections of the castle
are linked by a labyrinth of
secret passages, corridors and
winding staircases. The most
interesting rooms include the
Knights' Hall and the library.
There are superb views of the
surrounding hills.

**Tišnov's Porta Coeli, showing its
Romanesque gateway**

Tišnov ❼

Road map C3. 🚶 *8,500.* 🚉 🚌

If you drive from Brno to
Pernštejn, or take the train (a
lovely route), it is well worth
stopping off at Tišnov in
order to visit the Cistercian
convent, **Porta Coeli** ("Gate of
Heaven"), in the suburb

of Předklášteří. The nunnery,
founded in the 13th century,
is named after the church's
Romanesque gateway on the
west front. Reminiscent of
French cathedral portals, it is
surprisingly ornate given the
traditional austerity of the
Cistercian Order.

🏛 Porta Coeli
Tel *549 412 293.* ☐ *Tue–Sun.* 📷

Žd'ár nad Sázavou ❽

Road map C3. 🚶 *27,000.* 🚉 🚌
🛈 *náměstí Republiky 24.* **Tel** *566*
625 808. **www**.zdarns.cz

Located in the uplands of
the so-called Vysočina,
this industrial town is of little
interest in itself. The draw
here is the former Cistercian
monastery, 3 km
(2 miles) north. This
is largely the work of
the visionary Giovanni
Santini, who oversaw
the Baroque redesign
of the Gothic monas-
tery in the early 1700s.
The complex is now
known as **Žd'ar Castle**
(zámek Žd'ar) and
encompasses various
museums. The Book
Museum (Muzeum
Knihy) is particularly
good.

The most beautiful
and extraordinary
sight, however, is
found on a hilltop

above the castle, namely the
St John Nepomuk Church
(sv. Jan Nepomucký). Built in
1720, this is one of Santini's
most eccentric works. Both
its design and decoration
repeatedly allude to the
number five: the story goes
that when John Nepomuk had
his tongue cut out and was
thrown off the Charles Bridge
in Prague five stars appeared
above his head. The church is
in the shape of a five-pointed
star, which is matched by the
extraordinary, zigzagging
cloisters. The interior is full
of images of the saint, with
repetitive use made of the
five stars.

🏛 Žd'ar Castle and St John
Nepomuk Church
Tel *566 629 152.* ☐ *Apr–Oct: Sat,*
Sun & public hols; May–Sep: Tue–
Sun; Nov–Mar: groups only, by
appt. 📷 ☑ **www**.zamekzdar.cz

Cloisters at St John Nepomuk Church

Jihlava �ⓐ

Road map C3. 🏘 52,000. 🚉 🚌
ℹ️ *Masarykovo náměstí 19.* **Tel** *567 167 158.* www.jihlava.cz

In the Middle Ages Jihlava (Iglau) grew from a small village into one of the richest towns in the Czech Lands: its fortunes were transformed by the discovery in the 13th century of nearby silver deposits. While the modern era has certainly left its mark, Jihlava retains a fine historic centre, still encircled by medieval defensive walls.

The cobbled main square, Masarykovo náměstí, is vast. While blighted by a hideous shopping complex, the square has scores of Renaissance and Baroque houses with fine façades, portals and finials. Running beneath the square is a maze of **catacombs** (katacomby), originally storage cellars, which extend for some 25 km (15 miles). The entrance is in the square, next door to the Baroque Church of St Ignatius (sv. Ignác).

It is worth having a stroll around the rest of the old town. Look out for the one remaining gateway in the old walls, brána Matky Boži.

⛪ Catacombs
Tel *567 167 887.* ◐ *Apr–Oct: daily for tours.* 📷 📷

Telč 🟓

Road map B3. 🏘 6,000. 🚉 🚌
ℹ️ *náměstí Zachariáše z Hradce 10.* **Tel** *567 112 407.* www.telc-etc.cz

This UNESCO-listed town is outstandingly beautiful. The turning point for Telč came in 1530, when a fire devastated the town. Lord Zachariáš, the governor of Moravia, brought in Italian master builders and architects to rebuild the castle. These craftsmen ended up rebuilding virtually all the houses in the Renaissance style, endowing the town with an architectural uniformity that has survived to this day. The main square, náměstí Zachariáše z Hradce, is arcaded and has a fine array of pastel-coloured houses. At

Telč Castle, overlooking one of the old fishponds

one end is **Telč Chateau** (zámek Telč), a magnificent Renaissance building. Inside, highlights are the rooms with superb coffered ceilings, such as the Knight's Chambers. It also has fine collections of arms and porcelain.

Modern Telč is separated from the old town by two fishponds which virtually surround the tiny historic centre.

⛫ Telč Chateau
Tel *567 243 943.* ◐ *Apr–Oct: Tue–Sun.* 📷 📷 www.telc.eu

Třebíč 🟕

Road map C3. 🏘 41,000. 🚉 🚌
ℹ️ *Karlovo náměstí. 53.* **Tel** *568 847 070.* www.kviztrebic.cz

Two reasons to visit this industrial town are the **Basilica of St Procopius** (Bazilika sv. Prokopa) and its historic Jewish quarter. The church once belonged to a monastery, founded by the

Přemyslids in 1101 and, in the 1600s, transformed into a castle. The 13th-century church was heavily restored in the Baroque period but retains its lovely Romanesque portal, adorned with floral and geometric patterns. Take a look at the beautiful rosette window in the apse and the unusual "dwarfs' gallery" running outside. The enormous crypt features 50 columns, each with a different capital.

The restored Jewish quarter in Třebíč, between the Jihlava river and Hrádek hill, is on UNESCO's World Heritage list. With many original buildings intact, it is still possible to feel something of the atmosphere of the old ghetto. Stroll along colourful Leopold Pokorný Street and look inside the richly frescoed Rear (New) Synagogue, or Zadní/Nová synagóga (*see p237*).

⛪ Basilica of St Procopius
Zámek 1. **Tel** *568 610 022.* ◐ *daily.* 📷 📷
reservations preferred.

Stained-glass window in the Church of St Ignatius, Jihlava

Jaroměřice nad Rokytnou Chateau ⑫

Road map C3. 🚇 🚌 *2 km (1 mile) away in Popovice.* **Tel** *568 440 237.* ⬜ *Apr, Oct: 8am–4pm Sat, Sun, public hols; May, Jun, Sep: 9am–5pm Tue–Sun; Jul–Aug: 9am–6pm Tue–Sun.* 🅿🚻 **www**.zamek-jaromerice.cz

This small town, 14 km (9 miles) south of Třebíč, is dwarfed by the Baroque chateau (zámek Jaroměřice nad Rokytnou), one of the biggest palace complexes in Europe with a sprawling park. Essentially a reconstruction incorporating elements of older buildings, the work began in 1700 and was led by the famous Austrian Baroque architect, Jakob Prandtauer. It took 37 years to complete. The man who ordered the chateau's construction, Johann Adam von Questenburg, turned it into an influential centre for the arts.

Among the highlights of a tour are the two lavishly decorated halls, Taneční sál and Hlavní sál. Visitors can also see the library and theatre, as well as a large porcelain collection, or enjoy a stroll around the formal gardens. In the grounds is the monumental Church of St Margaret (sv. Markéty), with a magnificent dome decorated with elaborate frescoes.

The colossal Baroque castle complex of Jaroměřice nad Rokytnou

despite much rebuilding work. The interior, mainly Neo-Gothic, has a fascinating armoury, featuring more than 1,000 firearms dating from the 14th–19th centuries. More bizarrely, the castle has a collection of stuffed animals, including 50 stuffed dogs, all collected by the castle's last owner. Part of the enjoyment of visiting the fortress is the climb up from the village, as well as the great views.

Bítov itself has an unusual history. The medieval village was rebuilt in the 1930s, following the flooding of the original village during the creation of the Vranov reservoir. Visitors can see how the planners tried to recreate the layout of the old village, with a market square and a series of narrow streets.

Coat of arms above Bítov Castle gate

♠ **Bítov Castle**
Tel *515 294 622.* ⬜ *Apr, Oct: Sat, Sun, public hols; May–Sep: Tue–Sun.* 🅿🚻🚫 *in some parts.*

Bítov ⑬

Road map C3. 🏘 *500.* 🚌

The village of Bítov is set amid the densely wooded hills of the Podyjí National Park. Perched dramatically on a hill high above the Dyje river, 3 km (2 miles) from the village, is **Bítov Castle** (hrad Bítov), built in the 11th century to defend the Přemyslid kingdom's southern borders. The castle has managed to keep its medieval character,

Environs
In Uherčice, 6 km (4 miles) west of Bítov, is the Baroque **Uherčice Chateau** (zámek Uherčice). Parts of the building are closed during renovation work, but the vast English style park remains open in the summer. The chateau boasts some fine stucco decoration.

🏰 **Uherčice Chateau**
Tel *515 298 396.* ⬜ *Jun: Sat, Sun & public hols; Jul–Aug: Tue–Sun.*🅿

Vranov nad Dyjí Chateau ⑭

Road map C3. 🚌 **Tel** *515 296 215.* ⬜ *Apr, Oct: 9am–noon,1–4pm Sat, Sun, public hols; May, Jun, Sep: 9am–noon, 1–5pm Tue–Sun; Jul–Aug: 9am–noon, 1–6pm Tue–Sun.* **Garden** *by appt.* 🅿🚻 *4 routes.*

The village of Vranov is overshadowed by its fairytale chateau (zámek Vranov nad Dyjí), which is dramatically sited on a cliff high above the Dyje river. First erected in the 13th century, the castle was rebuilt to a Baroque design by the illustrious Austrian architect, J B Fischer von Erlach, in the late 17th century.

The highlight inside is the Ancestors' Hall (Sál předků), with its great dome lavishly decorated with frescoes by Johann Michal Rottmayr. The extravagantly furnished and decorated interiors give an insight into aristocratic life at the start of the 19th century. The chapel is a delightful work by Fischer von Erlach.

Intricate ceramic artifact in Vranov nad Dyjí Chateau

Jewish Historic Sites

There were more than 136,000 Jews living in Bohemia, Moravia and Silesia in 1939. By the end of World War II, however, as a result of the Nazi extermination programme, there were just 15,000 left. The community, which for centuries was an essential part of Czech cultural life, left behind countless historic relics. Jewish communities built synagogues and other religious buildings; they founded schools and maintained large cemeteries. The best known historic sites associated with Czech Jews are found in Prague and Plzeň, but there are also many sites in South Moravia. The Jewish quarters in Boskovice, Mikulov and Třebíč, as well as others in Brno, Lipník nad Bečvou, Hranice and Holešov, now provide a valuable testimony to the part played by Jewish religion and culture in the history of the region.

The Renaissance New Synagogue in Třebíč *dates from the early 17th century. Its recently restored interior includes some remarkable, strikingly colourful wall paintings.*

The restored Jewish ghetto in Třebíč *features two synagogues and a vast cemetery that contains 3,000 graves, dating from 1641 to the 1930s.*

Boskovice's Grand Synagogue, *built in 1698, features lavish Baroque decoration. Used as a storehouse under Communist rule, this fine building has now been restored (see p233).*

Mikulov, *which, from the 16th century, was the seat of Moravia's chief rabbi, has a vast overgrown cemetery, with beautifully carved headstones dating back to 1618.*

Brno's hall of prayers, *built in Neo-Renaissance style in 1900, stands at the entrance to Moravia's largest Jewish cemetery. It is the site of some 9,000 tombstones, many of them brought here from 17th- and 18th-century cemeteries.*

Castle towering above the red rooftops of Mikulov

Znojmo ⑮

Road map C3. 36,000.
Obroková 10. **Tel** 515 222 552.

In a splendid spot above the Dyje river, Znojmo is one of Moravia's oldest towns, with a warren of small streets at its heart. The best of its historic sights is the Romanesque Rotunda of St Catherine (sv. Kateřiny), with some beautifully preserved frescoes and portraits of Přemyslid princes. The rotunda is inside **Znojmo Castle** (Znojemský hrad), a large part of which is now a brewery.

Znojmo's Gothic Cathedral of St Nicholas (sv. Mikuláš) has a charming Baroque pulpit in the shape of a vast globe.

♣ **Znojmo Castle**
Tel 515 222 311.
Apr: Sat & Sun; May–Sep: Tue–Sun. limited access.
www.znojmuz.cz

Mikulov ⑯

Road map C3. 8,000.
Náměstí 1. **Tel** 519 510 855.
www.mikulov.cz

Built on a hillside close to the Austrian border east of Znojmo, Mikulov is picture postcard pretty. The town is full of delightful streets, with some fine Renaissance and Baroque houses. **Mikulov Castle** (zámek Mikulov), 13th-century but much altered, was burned down by the retreat-

ing Germans in the final days of World War II and then painstakingly rebuilt. It is worth visiting to see the fine vaults, for centuries used to store locally made wine.

West of the castle is the once thriving Jewish quarter, with an atmospheric, over-

♣ **Mikulov Castle**
Tel 519 510 255. Apr–Oct: Tue–Sun.

Lednicko-Valtický areál ⑰

Road map C3. Valtice & Lednice. to Valtice from Mikulov. **Valtice** Náměstí Svobody 4. **Tel** 519 352 978. **Lednice** Zámecké náměstí 68. **Tel** 519 340 986. **www**.radnice-valtice.cz

Near the Austrian border are Valtice and Lednice, two towns linked by the Lednicko-Valtický areál – a beautiful UNESCO-listed park scattered with follies such as temples, artificial ruins, arches and colonnades. Each town

has a chateau built by the Liechtensteins, once one of the Czech Lands' most powerful families. The two chateaus are linked by a 7-km (5-mile) avenue of lime trees.

Valtice Chateau (Valtický zámek) is a Baroque reworking of a Renaissance palace, designed by the leading architects of the early 18th century, among them J B Fischer von Erlach. Its state rooms are furnished with Baroque and Rococo flamboyance.

Lednice Chateau (zámek Lednice) is a Neo-Gothic, fairlytale creation dating from the mid-1800s. The heavily panelled and richly furnished interiors are well worth seeing, but the other big attraction of Lednice is the landscaped grounds, complete with lakes and a 60-m (196-ft) minaret, the tallest of its kind outside the Islamic world.

♣ **Valtice Chateau**
Tel 519 352 423. Apr–Oct: daily. **www**.valtice.cz

♣ **Lednice Chateau**
Tel 519 340 128. Apr, Oct: Sat & Sun; May–Sep: Tue–Sun.

Colonnade, one of the follies in the grounds of Valtice Chateau

Buchlovice Chateau ⑱

Road map D3. 🚌 **Tel** 572 434 240.
🕐 Apr, Oct: 9am–noon, 1–4pm
Tue–Sun; May, Jun, Sep: 9am–noon,
1–5pm Tue–Sun; Jul, Aug: 9am–
noon, 1–6pm daily. 📷
www.zamek-buchlovice.cz

East of Brno on the fringes
of the Chřiby hills is the
delightful Buchlovice
Chateau. Built in the 18th
century in the style of a
country house, it consists of
two symmetrical semicircular
buildings set around a central
octagon. Inside are some
opulently furnished rooms,
while outside is a magnificent
Baroque garden, with an
impressive array of trees,
rhododendrons and fuchsias.

Velehrad's monastery church

Velehrad Monastery ⑲

Road map D3. 🚌 **Tel** 572 420
149. 🕐 7am–6pm daily.

Velehrad has one of the
Czech Republic's most
popular pilgrimage centres,
in the form of its Cistercian
Monastery (klášter Cisterciáků).
Founded in the 1200s, it commemorates the work of saints
Cyril and Methodius (see
p33). The present monastery
buildings are 18th-century
Baroque, though the church
follows the shape of the first
Romanesque building. There
are some exquisitely carved
stalls and a lapidarium, with
remains of the original church.

View of Buchlovice Chateau from the garden

Kroměříž ⑳

See pp240–41.

Zlín ㉑

Road map D3. 👥 90,000. 🚊 🚌
ℹ️ Náměstí Míru 12. **Tel** 577 630 270.

The history of this town is
inextricably linked with
Tomáš Baťa, who founded a
shoe factory here in 1894. He
invited a group of architects
to build a town to house his
workers, and as a result
several Functionalist buildings
sprang up here in the 1920s
and 30s. While Zlín has lost the
utopian feel of a planned city,
it has a unique atmosphere.

Zlín is the birthplace of the
playwright Tom Stoppard,
who fled the Nazis with his
family and settled in England.

Luhačovice ㉒

Road map D3. 👥 5,500. 🚊 🚌
ℹ️ Masarykova 950. **Tel** 577 133 980.

Less grand than the spa
towns of west Bohemia,
Luhačovice is nonetheless

Moravia's largest spa town.
The springs of **Luhačovice Spa**
are used to treat digestive,
metabolic and respiratory
disorders. For most visitors,
however, the main reason to
come here is to admire the
work of Dušan Jurkoviče, the
Slovak architect who brought
his folk-inspired Art Nouveau
style to Luhačovice in the
early 20th century. Most
notable is the Jurkovičuv dům.

🔥 **Luhačovice Spa**
Lázeňské náměstí 436. **Tel** 577 682
111. **www**.spaluhacovice.cz

Luhačovice, an unpretentious spa town with Art Nouveau villas

---

MORAVIA'S WINE

The wine-making tradition in Moravia dates back
to the 13th century. The local climate favours the
late ripening of grapes, producing wines with a
full, spicy flavour. Most of the vineyards are
given over to white grape varieties. The best
known are Veltínské zelené, with an aromatic
honey flavour and Müller-Thurgau, with a
smooth, medium-sweet flavour and low acidity.
When travelling around, especially near Mikulov,
look out for the sklepy, or wine cellars, where
you can taste and buy wine. The region is a
hive of activity during the grape harvest.

White wine from a Moravian wine producer

Kroměříž 20

This is an appealing yet quite sleepy town, with some lovely and extensive gardens as well as fine architecture – many of the buildings in the heart of Kroměříž, still partially enclosed within the original walls, have survived the Communist period relatively unscathed. The main square, Velké náměstí, has been carefully restored in the last ten years and is one of the prettiest in Moravia. The main attraction, just north of the square, is the magnificent, UNESCO-listed palace of the bishops of Olomouc, who had their seat here between the 12th and 19th centuries.

North Façade
The north front has a portico that doubles as a balcony. The formal garden below links up with the landscaped grounds.

Bedroom
The bedroom and the adjacent study form the Winter Quarters. The pseudo-Renaissance 19th-century furniture came from Venice.

The Vassals' Hall
The magnificent ceiling fresco (1759) in the hall (Mansky sál) is the work of Viennese artist F A Mauelbertsch. He was paid 12,300 ducats, an incredible sum at the time.

Main entrance

Throne Room
The throne and the baldachin were used by the Olomouc archbishops. Other furnishings here date from the late 18th century.

ARCHBISHOP'S PALACE

The vast Baroque palace (Arcibiskupský zámek) has some splendidly furnished rooms whose Rococo flourishes featured in Miloš Forman's film *Amadeus*. It also houses the impressive art collection of the Liechtenstein family, a major influence in the town. This collection (the second largest in the republic) features some superb works of art, including *The Flaying of Marsyas*, a famous painting by Titian, and *King Charles I and his wife Henrietta Maria* by Van Dyck. Veronese and Cranach are among the other painters represented.

★ **Assembly Hall**
The name of this superb Rococo room alludes to talks held here by the exiled Austrian Imperial Parliament in 1848–9, during which they drafted a new constitution. This became famous for its stated principle: "All the power within the state stems from the people."

VISITORS' CHECKLIST

Road map D3. 🚶 30,000. 🚉 Palace **Tel** 573 502 011. 🕐 Apr, Oct: 9am–4pm Sat & Sun; May, Jun, Sep: 9am–5pm Tue–Sun; Jul, Aug: 9am–6pm Tue–Sun. Or by appt. 🏷 📷 2 routes. **Garden** 🕐 Jun–Oct: 7am–7pm daily; Nov–Mar: 7am–4pm daily. 🌧 when raining. **www**.azz.cz

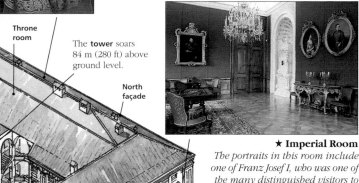

Throne room

The **tower** soars 84 m (280 ft) above ground level.

North façade

★ **Imperial Room**
The portraits in this room include one of Franz Josef I, who was one of the many distinguished visitors to the palace. The emperor and Tsar Alexander III went hunting together here and their trophies can be seen in the Hunting Hall.

Staircase
Accessed via a fine staircase is the palace's art gallery (Zámecká obrazárna), which has an impressive collection of European paintings from the 16th and 17th centuries.

Library
The library rooms were laid out in 1694. Still in beautiful condition, they house 90,000 volumes dating from the 16th and 17th centuries.

STAR FEATURES

★ Assembly Hall

★ Imperial Room

INTRODUCING SLOVAKIA

DISCOVERING SLOVAKIA

Slovakia, tagged on to the southeast end of the Czech Republic in the heart of Central Europe, combines a dynamic economy with a wealth of natural assets: mountains, lakes, unspoilt valleys and meadows, spectacular ice caves and national parks. The capital, Bratislava, sits at the western tip of the country and borders both

Fountain in Bratislava

Austria and Hungary. The Small Carpathian mountain range runs through West Slovakia and boasts a blossoming viticulture while Central Slovakia's lush valleys are home to medieval mining towns and villages nestling in the shelter of the mighty Tatras mountains. In the east, the region is dotted with dozens of caves and quaint wooden churches.

BRATISLAVA

- **Historic Old Town**
- **Architectural treasures**
- **Romantic ruins of Devín**
- **Winemaking region**

Spectacularly located on the Danube River between Vienna and Budapest, Bratislava effortlessly combines the history, culture, architecture and cuisine of three very different nations: Slovakia, Austria and Hungary.

History and hedonism intertwine in the Slovak capital's **Old Town** *(see pp276–7)* where, in the warmer months, cafés set their tables outside, in front of ancient Baroque palaces. The Old Town's pedestrian cobbled streets are ideal for strolling around and the centre boasts an impressive variety of architectural styles from the turreted **Castle** *(see p278)* on the north embankment of the Danube to the pocket-sized **St Martin's**

The cobbled streets of Bratislava's Old Town

Cathedral *(see pp280–1)*, a Gothic treasure. The pretty pink **Primate's Palace** *(see pp278–9)* is a fine example of Neo-Classical architecture, while the **Little Blue Church** *(see p284)* is an unusual Art Nouveau building.

To the northwest of Bratislava's urban sprawl and upstream on the Danube is **Devín** *(see p285)*, a ruined castle teetering on a high crag above the river. The castle and surrounding region are popular among nature lovers and sports enthusiasts, and the riverside paths offer an idyllic retreat from the summer heat.

The local winemaking tradition of the Small Carpathian mountains has its roots in the town of **Rača** *(see p285)* on Bratislava's outskirts. Grape harvest festivals are held here and in **Modra** *(see p286)*. The crisp white wines from this region are of good quality and excellent value; vineyards are dotted around the area.

Dining out on one of Bratislava's pedestrianized streets, Old Town

WEST SLOVAKIA

- **Castles and romantic palaces**
- **Trnava's religious treasures**
- **Piešt'any's spa**

The sun-drenched plains of West Slovakia were once the scene of conflict in Slovakia's busy history. Eighteenth-century Hungarian nobles built many palaces and castles only to ruin them in the heat of battle. Some, like **Mojmírovce Palace** *(see pp304–5)*, have been restored as luxury hotels, located in magnificent park surroundings. Others, such as **Beckov Castle** and **Čachtice Castle** *(see pp300–1)*, are testimony-in-rubble to the region's turbulent past. The latter is where "Blood Countess" Elizabeth Báthory was walled up as punishment for her bloodthirsty behaviour.

The town of **Trnava** *(see pp296–9)* has a magnificent

◁ The idyllic scenery of Pribylina at the foothills of the Western Tatras

Beautiful scenery of the popular Tatras Mountains

collection of religious buildings as well as a vibrant student population, while the historic towns of **Trenčín** *(see p301)* and **Nitra** *(see p304)* are guarded by impressive castles perched on hills above the towns. Like Trnava, Trenčín and Nitra have lively pubs, cafés and clubs, dedicated to the youthful population.

The famous spa resort of **Piešťany** *(see p300)* provides refuge at the restored Art Nouveau **Thermia Palace** *(see p360)*, Slovakia's first five-star spa hotel, set on an island in the Váh River.

Imposing ruins of Beckov Castle, West Slovakia

CENTRAL SLOVAKIA

- **Intriguing folk museums**
- **Historic mining towns**
- **Spectacular Tatras Mountains**

The fertile central region is dotted with isolated and unusual villages, existing as living folk museums, and many are classed as UNESCO World Cultural Heritage Sites. **Vlkolínec** *(see p322)*, nestled on the side of a hill,

is a village of timber houses where traditional crafts and rural pursuits can still be seen. Nearby **Čičmany's** *(see p322)* remarkable cottage wall decorations are the most famous surviving examples of Slovak folk architecture.

The historic mining towns of **Banská Štiavnica** *(see p314)*, **Banská Bystrica** *(see pp310–13)* and **Kremnica** *(see p315)* all have vibrant, youthful centres as well as some of the country's best historic monuments to gold, silver and copper mining from the Middle Ages.

Nature lovers and sports enthusiasts flock to the **Tatras Mountains** *(see pp316–17)* where skiing, hiking, caving and rafting can be enjoyed in glorious surroundings.

The region also has its fair share of château-like palaces, such as the turreted **Bojnice Castle** *(see pp320–21)*, which was built by nobles in the 18th and 19th centuries. These buildings provide a good insight into Slovakia's complicated history.

EAST SLOVAKIA

- **Košice's cultural gems**
- **Amazing limestone caves**
- **Ruins of Spiš Castle**

Slovakia's second-largest city, **Košice** *(see pp328–31)* is graced with a fine collection of historic buildings along its main street, **Hlavná**. The jewel in the crown is the Gothic masterpiece, **St Elizabeth's Cathedral** *(see p328)*.

East of Košice is the town of **Svidník** *(see p333)* which is home to some of the renowned wooden buildings of the Greek-Catholic Ruthenian community. The towns of **Bardejov** *(see p333)* and **Levoča** *(see pp334–5)* offer beautiful squares flanked by Renaissance buildings while the **Slovak Karst** *(see pp336–7)* region includes an extensive and unusual cave system.

Popular among visitors are the imposing ruins of **Spiš Castle** *(see pp338–9)* which are visible for miles and offer spectacular views.

Gothic St Elizabeth's Cathedral, Košice

Putting Slovakia on the Map

Located in the central part of Europe, Slovakia – more formally known as the Slovak Republic – is a landlocked country bordering Poland, Ukraine, Hungary, Austria and the Czech Republic. It covers an area of 49,036 sq km (18,930 sq miles) and its population is 5.43 million. The capital, Bratislava, with a population of 430,000, lies near the border with Austria, on the Danube. Other large centres include Košice and Prešov in the east, Žilina in the north, and Nitra near the capital. The Carpathian mountain range stretches across most of Slovakia's territory.

KEY

✈ Airport

▬ Motorway

▬ Major road

— Railway line

–·– International border

BRATISLAVA AND ENVIRONS

Smolenice
Malacky
509
51
Časta
502
Suchá
n. Parnou
Zohor
Lozorno
503
Modra
504
Pezinok
Šenkvice
Stupava
Svätý Jur
502
Záhorská
Bystrica
D1
Senec
62
BRATISLAVA
Jelka
Hainburg
a.d. Donau
9
Zlaté Klasy
510
572
Lehnice
503

503
D2
2
2
49
Morava
63
Danube (Dunaj)
2
D4

0 km 10
0 miles 5

Svidník
77
77
73
Laborec
Poprad
68
Torysa
Poprad
18
D1
Prešov
72
66
61
18
74
262
Košice
50
Užhorod
AKIA
50
I A
UKRAINE
Ondava

Lučenec
50
67
3
50
71
26
Tisza
4

0 km 40
0 miles 20

Miskolc

Eger

3
M3

HUNGARY

Szolnok
4

EUROPE

FINLAND
NORWAY
SWEDEN
ESTONIA
REPUBLIC
OF
IRELAND
UNITED
KINGDOM
DENMARK
LATVIA
LITHUANIA
RUSSIA
BELARUS
NETHERLANDS
GERMANY
POLAND
ATLANTIC
OCEAN
BELGIUM
LUXEMBOURG
CZECH
REPUBLIC
SLOVAKIA
Bratislava
UKRAINE
FRANCE
AUSTRIA
HUNGARY
SWITZERLAND
ROMANIA
SLOVENIA
CROATIA
PORTUGAL
ANDORRA
BOSNIA AND
HERZEGOVINA
SERBIA
BULGARIA
SPAIN
CORSICA
MONTENEGRO
MACEDONIA
ALBANIA
SARDINIA
ITALY
GREECE
MOROCCO
ALGERIA
TUNISIA

POLAND
Nida
73
7
Wisła
Tarnów
Kraków
28
47
Nowy Sącz
67
D1

Jánožik šluduje za kňaza.

Jánošikov útek s lenayy.

Jánošik ide do hôr.

Smeť Jánošikovho

nošik bohatim berie chudobným ďáva

Jánošikova družina sa veseli

A PORTRAIT OF SLOVAKIA

For nine centuries Slovakia was a province of the Kingdom of Hungary; later, in the 20th century, it was for 70 years part of Czechoslovakia. Gaining its independence in 1993, it is one of Europe's youngest countries. Its attractions include its natural environment, beautifully preserved architecture and rich folk culture.

Although it has plenty of attractions, Slovakia remains a relatively little-known country, with few visitors. The most popular destination is the capital city of Bratislava, with its historic architecture, shops and visitor facilities. Lovers of good wine will most likely be familiar with the region of the Small Carpathians, which traditionally produces very drinkable Slovak wine; winter sports enthusiasts crowd into ski resorts in the Tatras mountains, and in the Malá (Small) and Velká (Great) Fatra ranges. Slovaks, particularly the young, are generally welcoming and hospitable to visitors, and proud of their country and its history.

Decorative clay hive

Due to Slovakia's mountainous character, there are considerable areas of wilderness, with the environment unscathed by development. There are not many other countries in Central Europe with such large areas of unspoilt mountains, meadows and ancient forests. There are also deep gorges, spectacular caves and meandering rivers. Almost one half of the land is devoted to agriculture, while mineral resources include iron, brown coal, copper, magnesium and salt.

FOLK CULTURE

In Slovakia, traditional folk culture forms a part of everyday life and customs. Costumes in a variety of

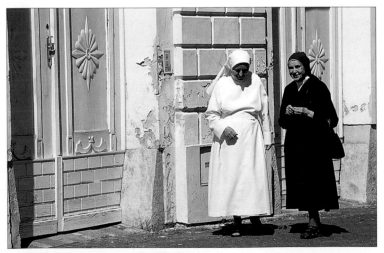

Nuns in St Nicholas's Square, Trnava, West Slovakia

◁ Illustration from the life of Jánošík, the popular Slovak Robin Hood figure, by L'udovit Kamenik (1959)

View from Bratislava Castle of the Danube with the New Bridge on the right

styles, ornaments and colours are not confined to museums; they are also worn (particularly in Central and Eastern Slovakia) during local festivities and celebrations, especially by the women. Pottery, basket work and other handmade products are still used in many homes for everyday purposes. Wooden folk buildings exist in situ and are also preserved in open-air museums to form traditional villages or skansen.

ETHNIC MINORITIES

Of Slovakia's population of 5.4 million, over 85 per cent are Slovaks, according to official statistics. The most significant minorities are the Hungarians, found mainly in the south, Roma (Gypsies), Ukrainians, Czechs, Poles, and Ruthenians (Rusyns) in the east. Slovak-Hungarian relations are now friendly, but until recently there were scars of

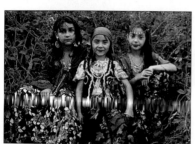

Roma children in Svina

the dramatic national conflict that arose in the second half of the 19th century. The situation of the Roma minority, the second-largest at about 350,000, is hard. In many regions, mainly in the east, large Roma communities live in great poverty, without any prospect of improving their lot.

RELIGIOUS LIFE

Slovakia, as opposed to the secularized Czech Republic, is a country where religious life and traditions remain very strong. The majority of the population, nearly 70 per cent, declare themselves to be Roman Catholics, but there are sizeable groups attached to Protestant (7 per cent), Greek Orthodox and United Reformed (both 4 per cent) churches. Only 13 per cent of Slovaks regard themselves as atheists. Devotion to religious life is evident not only at times of religious feasts and colourful celebrations. Churches throughout the country, particularly in smaller towns and villages, fill up with the faithful during Sunday mass and other services.

Statue of St Cyril, by Jozef Bart

INDEPENDENCE

The 19th-century process of national rebirth strengthened the feeling of national identity among Slovaks and consolidated their aspirations to become an independent nation. The desire for autonomy within the Austro-Hungarian Empire and later Czechoslovakia, voiced by consecutive generations of politicians,

Chairlift station in Skalnaté pleso, the High Tatras

had never been realized. Ironically, the first opportunity to achieve a semblance of independence arose within the puppet state created according to Hitler's wishes in 1939; the Slovak National Uprising against the Germans of 1944 is a key event in the national consciousness. The dream of independence came true only through the "Velvet Divorce", following the break-up of Czechoslovakia in January 1993. Slovakia became a member of the EU and NATO in 2004.

Slovak Republic in the European Union

SLOVAKIA'S DIVERSE ATTRACTIONS

An undeniable trump card of modern Slovakia is the wide range of attractions it offers to those interested in outdoor activities. Winter sports enthusiasts will appreciate the local skiing conditions – the best in Central Europe. Marked cycle routes of 3,500 km (2,175 miles) allow cyclists to undertake long-distance expeditions, while several thousand hiking trails lead through the most beautiful mountainous areas. Liptovská mara and other artificial reservoirs offer good sailing and windsurfing; the waters of the Váh, Hron and Nitra rivers enable white-water rafters to indulge their popular passion.

Beautiful churches in styles ranging from the Romanesque to Art Nouveau are a feature of many towns and cities. In the Slovak landscape numerous castles and ruined fortresses stand out. Those in lowland areas – such as Spiš Castle – have huge fortifications. Those in the mountains, such as Oravský, mostly cling, like eagles' nests, to the rocks. The abundance of castles testifies to the region's turbulent history, a history that makes an essential and vivid contribution to Slovakia's appeal.

St Martin's Cathedral in Spišská Kapitula, East Slovakia

Landscape and Wildlife of Slovakia

Alpine orchid

Slovakia surprises visitors with its diversity of scenery and wealth of wildlife. Mountains and highlands constitute over 60 per cent of the country's area. Many of these mountainous areas have been given National Park status to protect the landscape and wildlife, but also to allow visitors access to these rewarding areas. Slovakia's mountain ranges form part of the huge Carpathian range. The Central Carpathians include Slovakia's highest mountain massif – the Tatras.

Dunajec river valley in the Pieniny National Park, Central and East Slovakia

LOWLANDS

The lowland areas are concentrated in the south of the country. In the southwest, dunes and forests growing on sandy soil dominate. The areas further to the east, including the Danube Lowland, where the Váh joins the Danube, and the East Slovakian Lowland, are intensely farmed. The most popular crops, besides cereals, include sugar beet, tobacco, hops, rape and sunflowers.

Water chestnuts *were eaten in times of famine. They grow in ponds and old river beds, including the valleys of the Danube, Cisa and Latorica rivers, but are becoming increasingly rare.*

Sunflowers *are widely cultivated throughout Slovakia. In the summer, when the crops flower, vast areas of the Danube Lowland and East Slovakian Lowland are covered with a yellow carpet.*

THE KARST REGION

Slovenský kras, the Slovak Karst region, is a limestone plateau that occupies the southern part of the Slovenské Rudohorie mountains, close to the Hungarian border. The area has been shaped by surface and underground waters, as they cut their way through the limestone rock. The scenery here is extremely diverse in terms of karst formations, with ravines, funnels, and numerous caves containing stalactites and stalagmites.

Jasovská jaskyňa, *a cave with particularly lovely stalactites, is home to several species of bats.*

Slovenský kras *is the largest legally protected karst area in Central Europe. Brown bears and wolves roam here.*

Dwarf irises, *small perennial rhizomatous plants with purple, yellow, white or pinkish flowers, growing wild in the Slovak Karst and other areas, are now in serious danger of extinction.*

FORESTS

It is estimated that forests cover over 30 per cent of Slovakia's territory. In the mountainous regions the forests are predominantly natural, with spruce, sycamore and beech; lower sections are covered with oak forests. Pine and mixed forests have colonized the poorer soils. Acid rain has affected Slovakia's forests, but not as severely as in the Czech Republic.

Turk's cap lilies *grow wild in most areas, but are slightly more common in the Carpathians. The species is legally protected.*

Virgin forests *survive in some of the more inaccessible mountain regions of Slovakia, with trees up to 130 m (425 ft) tall.*

MOUNTAINS

The most spectacular and highest of all the Slovak mountain ranges are the Tatras. Formed of granite and limestone, they support a wide variety of plant and animal life, including deer, foxes, boar and golden eagles. Particularly interesting are the alpine grasses, and the meadow vegetation found at lower levels.

Blue sow thistle *grows in the forest belt and at sub-alpine levels; it has lovely purple-blue flowers, although white and pink varieties do occur. It often grows with the Austrian leopard's-bane in dense thickets.*

The High Tatras *are the only alpine group within the Carpathians and the smallest alpine range in Europe. They occupy 260 sq km (100 sq miles) and rise to over 2,500 m (8,200 ft); the highest peak – Gerlachovský štít is 2,654 m (8,707 ft) high. The range includes about 1,000 peaks.*

FAUNA

Slovak fauna is not as diverse as its flora but it does feature many interesting species. Along with the animals that inhabit lowlands, such as deer, fox and bear, there are also species typical of high mountain zones – chamois and marmot. Forested riverbanks are home to waterfowl such as cormorant, heron and crane. In the areas around the Danube, marshy meadows are home to the great bustard, now an endangered species.

The brown bear *is the largest land predator in Slovakia. It is a good swimmer, and can climb steep slopes.*

The lynx, *a predator of the cat family, inhabits upper and lower forest zones; it is becoming in-creasingly rare.*

The great bustard *inhabits Central and Eastern Europe. It is the world's heaviest flying bird.*

Slovak Architecture

From medieval times until the fall of the Habsburgs Slovak architecture was linked with Hungarian culture. The south of the country also looked to Vienna for its inspiration, while the north tended to follow local traditions. Bratislava, which for a long time was the capital of the Hungarian kingdom, acquired many splendid residential buildings. For centuries the finest buildings in Slovakia were churches, particularly those of the Late Gothic, and the opulent Baroque monasteries. The 19th and 20th centuries saw a rapid development of urban architecture.

The town hall in Bardejov, combining Gothic and Renaissance features

MIDDLE AGES

The predominant architectural features of the early Middle Ages were fortified towns and castles. Small churches were built until the mid-14th century. Rapid growth of religious architecture – particularly in Bratislava and the Spiš region – took place during the 15th century. The spectacular Gothic churches in Levoča, Bardejov and Kremnica date from this period.

St Martin's Cathedral *in Bratislava, built at the turn of the 14th and 15th centuries, is among the city's finest religious buildings* (see pp280–81).

St Elizabeth's Cathedral *in Košice* (see pp328–31) *is a splendid example of Peter Parler's style, which emanated from Prague* (see p20).

RENAISSANCE

Renaissance architecture concentrated mainly on secular buildings: castles, courts and palaces. It reached its apogee in the second half of the 16th and the early 17th century. The Italian styles, modified in Austria, south Germany, and Poland, acquired their specific local flavour in Slovakia. For instance, high roofs, ornate attics and plain undivided façades, with rustication at the corners, became its typical features.

Thurzo House *in Levoča, although many times rebuilt, has kept some strong Renaissance elements, including the loggia, cloisters and buttresses* (see p334).

The town hall *(ratúš) in Levoča, originally Gothic, was turned into one of Slovakia's finest Renaissance builings in the early 17th century with arcades and a clock tower* (see pp334–5).

BAROQUE

Slovakia is particularly rich in Baroque architectural works, some of which are of international standing. Many were built in Bratislava, the coronation city of the Hungarian kings, in the 18th century. The royal status of the city attracted wealthy investors and prominent artists from Vienna, including G B Martinelli, A G Bibiena and G R Donner. At that time many monasteries were built in southern and central Slovakia, particularly for the Franciscan and Jesuit orders.

The monastery church in Jasov *(1750–66), with the opulence of its Late-Baroque architecture, was designed by Austrian architect Anton Pilgram. It draws on Italian-Austrian stylistic forms* (see p337).

The Summer Palace *built for the Primate of Hungary, Franco Barkóczy, in Bratislava in 1761–5, was heavily influenced by Vienna's Baroque architectural forms.*

19TH AND 20TH CENTURIES

During the past two centuries the development of Slovak architecture has gone hand-in-hand with Central European trends. The first half of the 19th century was dominated by Neo-Classical and Romantic styles, particularly in the flourishing sphere of residential architecture. The second half of that century was marked particularly by the development of urban architecture: apartment blocks and municipal buildings, designed in eclectic and historical styles. The early 20th century saw the arrival of splendid Art Nouveau and Modernist projects. Communist architecture blighted many towns, but since 1989 there has been extensive restoration of old town centres.

The English-style park *that surrounds the Andrássys' residence in Betliar (see p336) is adorned with fountains, artificial ponds with cascades, grottoes and a variety of pavilions.*

The Manor House *in Dolná Krupá (1818–28), designed by Anton P Riegl, is a superb example of a Neo-Classical residence with a distinctive central columned portico and side breaks* (see p295).

The Slovak National Theatre *in Bratislava* (see p282) *was built in Neo-Renaissance style during 1885–8 by Viennese architects Ferdinand Fellner and Hermann Helmer, who specialized in designing theatres and opera houses.*

This detail *from a house in Košice is typical of decorations used at the turn of the 19th and 20th centuries.*

SLOVAKIA THROUGH THE YEAR

Although interesting at any time of the year, Slovakia is never swamped by waves of tourists. In winter the snow-covered slopes attract skiers; spring is a time of magnificent flowers, particularly in the meadows; summer is the best time for exploring the country. Autumn attracts those who wish to taste Slovak wines – the pride of local producers. There is a full calendar of cultural events the whole year round, although they tend to be of a local character. Folk festivals, one of the country's main attractions, are especially popular among visitors. Slovakia is rich in religious traditions. Catholic feasts are celebrated throughout the country; Orthodox festivals are mainly observed in the eastern regions. Traditional pilgrimages to places of worship continue to attract large numbers of participants.

Man in a regional costume, Nitra district

Braided willow twigs for an Easter folk ritual

SPRING

Main festivals of the spring calendar are associated with Easter, when religious celebrations are accompanied by a variety of bucolic customs, such as egg painting, preparing decorated food baskets for blessing, or *šibačka* – an old fertility ritual involving mock-whipping girls with braided willow twigs.

Easter Easter festivities begin on "Green Thursday". Church bells are tied up to silence them, and their ringing is replaced by sounds of wooden rattles until "White Saturday". On Easter Sunday churches fill with the faithful. On Easter Monday water, which is believed to bring health and prosperity, is poured over women.

MARCH

Swimming Competitions *(19–20 Mar)*, Trnava, West Slovakia. The main international swimming event in Slovakia.

APRIL

Devin-Bratislava Run *(10 Apr)*. The capital's inhabitants welcome the arrival of spring by running the 12-km (7-mile) route from Devin. The run is regarded as one of the most important events of its kind in Europe.
Komárno Lehára *(late Apr)*, Komárno, West Slovakia. Singing competition held every two years in memory of the composer Franz Lehár, who was born here.
Flora Bratislava *(28 Apr–1 May)*. International flower fair on the banks of the Danube.
Festival duchov a strašidiel *(late Apr–early May)*, Bojnice, Central Slovakia. Festival of ghosts and spirits held in the castle: banquets, firework displays and theatrical performances.

MAY

Lumen *(early May)*, Trnava, West Slovakia. International Festival of Gospel Music.
Bratislava's Days of Europe *(1–10 May)*. International open-air music festival first held in 1996.
Košice Music Spring International Festival *(whole of May)*, East Slovakia. Held since 1955.
International Dolls' Festival *(late May)*, Poprad, East Slovakia. Exhibitions of dolls in national costumes.
Sám na javisku *(May)*, Trenčin, West Slovakia. Festival of theatre.

Flowering spring meadows in the High Tatras

AVERAGE DAILY HOURS OF SUNSHINE

Hours
10
8
6
4
2
0

Jan Feb Mar Apr May Jun Jul Aug Sep Oct Nov Dec

Sunshine

The largest number of sunny days in Slovakia occurs, naturally enough, in the summer, between June and August, although there is also fine weather in May and September. The cloudiest months are usually November, December and January.

SUMMER

Most folk festivals take place in the summer, when many regions, towns and villages present their local customs and cuisine. The largest events offer a chance to meet artists from many parts of the world.

Golden fields in the Small Carpathians in midsummer

JUNE

Folk Festival *(3–4 Jun)*, Humenné, East Slovakia.
Eurofolklor International Folklore Festival *(late Jun)*, Banská Bystrica, Central Slovakia.
ArtFilm Festival *(second half of Jun)*, Trenčianske Teplice, West Slovakia. Week-long event with competitions for the best avant-garde and experimental productions.

JULY

Folk Festival *(early Jul)*, Detva near Zvolen, Central Slovakia.

Pilgrimage to Marian Sanctuary *(1st Sat in Jul)*, Levoča, East Slovakia. The best-attended pilgrimage in Slovakia, with hundreds of thousands of Catholics, marking the start of many such pilgrimages in Slovakia.
International Handicraft Exhibition *(mid-Jul)*, Kežmarok, East Slovakia.
International Folk Festival in Novohrad *(27–31 Jul)*, Lučenec, Central Slovakia. A unique European-scale event, held at the same time on both sides of the Slovak-Hungarian border.

AUGUST

Jánošík Days *(3–6 Aug)*, Terchová, Central Slovakia. The country's biggest folk festival celebrating the highland robber, Juraj Jánošík (1688–1713).
Kysucer Pilgrimage *(15 Aug)*, Oščadnica near Žilina, Central Slovakia. Colourful,

Folk festival in Detva, Central Slovakia

lively and often crowded religious festivities.
Folklore Festival *(mid-Aug)*, Poprad, East Slovakia, on the edge of the High Tatras.
International Historic Fencing Festival *(mid-Aug)*. This is one of the attractions that brings to life the vast ruins of Spiš Castle, East Slovakia.
Dobrofest *(late Aug)*, Trnava, West Slovakia. The only festival in the country organized in memory of Jan Dopjera, who founded the guitar-making firm, Dobro, in the United States.

Summer concert in the courtyard of the Old Town Hall, Bratislava

AVERAGE MONTHLY RAINFALL

Rainfall
June is one of the warmest but also one of the wettest months in Slovakia. The best time to visit the country is late spring or early autumn – when it's warm with less rain.

AUTUMN

One of the most important events in the Slovak calendar is the September grape harvest festival – boisterous, jolly celebrations organized in all of the country's vine-growing areas. This is a unique opportunity to sample *burčiak* – a freshly fermented sweet grape juice, which is supposed both to purify the system and to rejuvenate the body, although overindulgence can give you a headache!

SEPTEMBER

Coronation Celebrations *(early Sep)*, Bratislava. Actors dressed in historic costumes re-enact a royal coronation, and with great pomp and ceremony march through the streets of the Old Town.

Full house at Bratislava Jazz Days festival

St Hubert's Day *(17 Sep)*, Přibylina, near Ružomberok, Central Slovakia. Celebrations associated with hunting customs and traditions, combined with shooting competitions.
Radvanský jarmok *(Sep)*, Banská Bystrica, Central Slovakia. Colourful handicrafts market.
Biennale of Illustration *(first half Sep–end of Oct)*, Bratislava. Regular international exhibition of illustrations for books for children and young readers; takes place in odd-numbered years.
Bratislava Jazz Days *(3rd week in Sep–mid-Oct)*, Bratislava. International jazz festival, and one of the most important events of its kind in Central Europe. Participants include top jazz musicians and singers from all over the world.

OCTOBER

Bratislava Music Festival *(first half of Oct)*, Bratislava. The main Slovak festival of classical music.
International Jazz Festival *(early Oct)*, Košice, East Slovakia.
Malokarpatský Marathon *(Oct)*, Trnava, West Slovakia. A popular marathon attracting thousands of competitors.

NOVEMBER

Košice Days of Traditional Folk Music *(16–25 Nov)*, Košice, East Slovakia. Folk event, in a variety of forms: concerts, dance shows, discussion meetings. It takes place at various venues throughout the town.
Festival of Greek-Catholic Choirs *(Nov)*, Košice, East Slovakia.
Christmas Fair *(25 Nov–23 Dec)*, Bratislava. One of Bratislava's most popular events. The town fills up with stalls selling handicrafts that make excellent Christmas presents.

Autumn at Gerlachovský štít, the Tatras

AVERAGE MONTHLY TEMPERATURE

Temperature
Large variations in altitude cause the weather to vary between individual regions of Slovakia. The average summer temperature is about 20°C (68°F); at high altitudes it does not exceed 15°C (59°F). Winters tend to be cold, with temperatures often dropping below freezing.

WINTER

The early part of winter is dominated by Christmas and New Year celebrations. Epiphany marks the beginning of the carnival season, which continues until Ash Wednesday.

DECEMBER

International Film Festival *(2–10 Dec)*, Bratislava. Festival for cinema lovers. Besides European films it also includes works by independent producers.

Christmas *(24–26 Dec)*. On Christmas morning people put up the Christmas tree (usually a spruce) in their home. During traditional Christmas Eve supper people break wafer bread spread with honey and nuts, or garlic. Honey symbolizes love; garlic health. The main dish is usually carp. In the evening they also unwrap their presents.

New Year's Eve Ball *(31 Dec)*, Bratislava. Some 50,000 citizens of Bratislava and several thousand visitors meet in the town centre to participate in live concerts and an open-air disco. Fireworks and light displays on the banks of the Danube create an unforgettable atmosphere.

JANUARY

Epiphany *(6 Jan)*. In many villages and small towns this is an opportunity to see boys sporting royal crowns, singing carols and collecting small donations.

FEBRUARY

Shrovetide is the traditional end of carnival season. Boisterous parties often last from Sunday until midnight on Tuesday before Ash

Cable car to Lomnický štít, the Tatras

Wednesday. The final carnival procession is the traditional "burial of the double bass", after which the music ceases for the entire period of Lent.

Gajdošské fašiangy *(last Sun before Ash Wed)*, Mala Lehota near Ždiar, Central Slovakia. International bagpipe-players' rally.

PUBLIC HOLIDAYS IN SLOVAKIA

Anniversary of the Independent Slovak Republic (1 Jan)
Epiphany (6 Jan)
Good Friday
Easter Monday
Labour Day (1 May)
VE Day (9 May)
St Cyril and St Methodius Day (5 Jul)
Anniversary of Slovak National Uprising (29 Aug)
Constitution Day (1 Sep)
Feast of St Mary, the Patron Saint of Slovakia (15 Sep)
All Saints' Day (1 Nov)
Christmas Eve (24 Dec)
Christmas Day (25 Dec)
Boxing Day (26 Dec)

Cinema foyer at the International Film Festival, Bratislava

THE HISTORY OF SLOVAKIA

From the Middle Ages until the 20th century the fate of the Slovak nation was bound up with the fortunes of the Kingdom of Hungary. The national aspirations of the Slovak people were realized only following the creation of the independent Slovak Republic in 1993.

PREHISTORY

Archaeological discoveries point to the presence of man in the area of present-day Slovakia during the Middle Paleolithic era (200,000–35,000 BC). The Moravian Venus, a famous Paleolithic statuette discovered near Piešt'any (West Slovakia) in 1940, was made around 23,000 years ago. From the 5th century BC the area was colonized by the Celts who, as in the Czech Lands, were displaced in around 10 BC by the Marcomanni, a German tribe. They, in turn, were attacked by the Romans, but the Marcomanni were a troublesome enemy, and the Romans eventually pulled back south of the River Danube.

The Moravian Venus

THE GREAT MORAVIAN EMPIRE

During the 5th and 6th centuries the Slavs arrived in the Danube Lowlands, but they were later conquered by the nomadic Avars. A Frankish merchant called Samo led a Slavic rebellion in 623 and managed to create a kingdom encompassing west Slovakia and parts of Bohemia and Moravia. But it wasn't until 795 that the Avars were decisively beaten by Charlemagne, at the head of an alliance of Franks and Moravians. This cleared the way for the establishment of two Slavic principalities, out of which grew the Great Moravian Empire. By 885, this included parts of present-day Slovakia, Germany and Poland, as well as the whole of Bohemia and Moravia. From 863 two Greek monks, Cyril and Methodius took on the task of Christianizing the people of the empire.

UNDER HUNGARIAN RULE

The Moravian empire came to an end in the 9th century, destroyed by the invading Magyars. They took control of the Danube Lowlands, including what is now Slovakia, which remained part of Hungary until 1918. From this moment the Czechs (under Frankish rule) and Slovaks were exposed to differing social, cultural and political influences, a direct result of which was the "Velvet Divorce" of 1993. Also, the Slavic unity under the Great Moravian Empire has, periodically, fuelled dreams of Panslavism.

TIMELINE

1900–700 BC Bronze items from this period have been found in present-day Slovakia

A bronze vessel dating from the 8th–7th centuries BC

863 The Greek monks, Cyril and Methodius, arrive in Moravia

833 The foundation of the Great Moravian Empire

800 BC	500 BC	100 BC	AD 600	950

5th century BC First Slovak coins minted by the Celts

700–500 BC The earliest examples of stone architecture in Slovakia

1st–4th centuries AD Roman military camp Gerulata exists near Bratislava

5th–6th centuries Slav tribes colonize Danube Lowlands

Jewellery from the Great Moravian Empire

◁ *Jan Francisci: Captain of Slovak Insurgents* by Peter Michal Bohúň, 1848–50

St Stephen, founder of the Kingdom of Hungary

MONGOL INVADERS AND GERMAN SETTLERS

Having been a highly disruptive force in central Europe, the Magyars settled down under St Stephen I (997–1038), the first King of Hungary. Initially, the Hungarians were reasonably just rulers, allowing the Slovaks to keep their own language and culture. The economy prospered, thanks largely to mining and trade. This progress was interrupted by a Mongol invasion in 1241–42, but the subsequent rebuilding of the devastated country initiated another period of prosperity. The country's rulers granted privileges to many towns, built many castles, and invited in large numbers of German settlers (a similar process was underway in the Czech Lands). The new arrivals brought with them new skills, particularly useful in

the field of mining. In the 14th century the region of Banska Štiavnica and Kremnica yielded a quarter of Europe's silver and gold.

TURKISH EXPANSION AND THE ARRIVAL OF THE HABSBURGS

Although Bohemia's Hussite armies disrupted the generally peaceful existence of its neighbour, the turning point in Slovakia's history was the Battle of Mohács (1526), in which the invading Turkish army crushed the forces of King Louis Jagiello, ruler of both Hungary and the Czech Lands. Louis died in battle leaving no heir, paving the way for Ferdinand I, a Habsburg, to become king *(see p38)*. With the Turks occupying most of the Hungarian plain, the only significant part of the Hungarian kingdom left in Ferdinand's hands was the territory of Slovakia, essentially Upper Hungary. In 1536 Bratislava (Pressburg) became capital of this much-reduced kingdom.

Lying between Christian Europe and the Muslim Turkish Empire, Slovakia was ravaged by raids and military campaigns. In 1663 the Turks invaded again, captured Nové Zámky, the

The invasion of the Mongols in 1241

TIMELINE

1000 St Stephen crowned king of Hungary

1025 Slovak lands become part of the Kingdom of Hungary

1173–96 Bela III rules Hungary

1342–82 Reign of Louis the Great in Hungary

| 1000 | 1100 | 1200 | 1300 | 1400 |

Document granting town privileges to Trnava (1238)

1241–42 Mongol invasion

1335 Meeting of the kings of Bohemia, Poland and Hungary in Vyšehrad

Two men working in a smithy, a 16th-century altarpiece in Rožnava

mightiest castle in Hungary, and won more land. There was also home-grown trouble. In addition to the Reformation, to which the Habsburgs responded by bringing in the Jesuits, there was resistance by Hungarian nobles to the monarchy's centralist policies. This led to numerous acts of defiance, most famously in 1678 and 1703, led by Imre Thököly and Ferenz Rákoczi II respectively.

THE ENLIGHTENMENT AND SLOVAK NATIONAL REVIVAL

The enlightenment reforms of Maria Theresa and her son Joseph II in the 18th century had a big impact in the empire *(see p41)*. While German was made the official language, the role of national languages was also acknowledged. The codification of a Slovak vernacular became crucial to the forging of a national identity. The first codification of Slovakian was by a Catholic priest called Anton Bernolák, in 1787, but it received little suppport. In the 1830s a new generation of Slovaks, mostly anti-Magyar and pro-Czech, began to make themselves heard. The leading figure in this nationalist movement was L'udovít Štúr, who helped codify a new literary language; this became the basis of modern Slovakian.

By 1848, revolutions had broken out all over Europe, including in Hungary. Štur and his fellow activists demanded self-determination for Slovakia, but this was rejected by the leaders of the Hungarian revolution. The Slovak nationalists took a gamble by offering to support the Habsburgs in their fight against Hungarian insurgents. Their hope that the emperor would appreciate the loyalty and would look favourably on the request for Slovak independence proved futile.

After suppressing the 1848 revolution, Emperor Franz Joseph II restored absolute monarchy. All was not well in the empire, however, and in 1867 Hungary was granted autonomy by Austria under the so-called "Dual Monarchy".

1848 Revolution: detail of a painting by P M Bohúň

		1740–80 Reign of Maria Theresa	**1780–1790** Reign of Joseph II	
1526 Louis Jagiello killed at Mohács	**1683** Turks defeated at the Battle of Vienna		**1787** First codification of Slovak language by Father Bernolák	
1500	**1600**	**1700**	**1800**	
1458–90 Reign of Matthias Corvinus	**1536** Bratislava (Pressburg) becomes capital of the Kingdom of Hungary		**1840s** L'udovit Stur becomes leader of the Slovak nationalist movement	
	1663 Turks capture Nové Zámky		*L'udovit Štur (1815–56)*	

Bratislava – City of Coronations

The modern capital of Slovakia, originally known as Pressburg, was first granted royal privileges in the 13th century. But it was the victory of the Turks at Mohács in 1526 that marked the start of great things for Bratislava. The town became capital of the much-reduced Kingdom of Hungary, and was made the coronation city of the Hungarian kings. For three centuries the town hosted coronation ceremonies for 19 Hungarian monarchs, including Maria Theresa and Joseph I. Bratislava's heyday was in the 18th century during the reigns of Maria Theresa and Joseph II.

Crown of the Hungarian Kings
This crown is commonly believed to be that worn by King Stephen I, but its authenticity has long been questioned.

Maria Theresa, 1740–80
Empress Maria Theresa often took up residence at Bratislava Castle, and as a result numerous aristocrats from neighbouring Vienna chose to build palaces here.

The Primate's Palace
Built in 1778–81, this white Neo-Classical palace became a favourite place to stay for many members of the Habsburg family. Leopold II was said to have stayed here in 1790 following his coronation as emperor.

The ceremony was attended by prominent state and Church dignitaries, including Jan Pálffy, governor of Hungary.

After the passing of the procession, the crowd scrambled to touch the cloth that lined the pavement.

The Wedderin Bell
The bell housed in St Martin's Cathedral rang to signal that a new monarch had ascended the throne of Hungary.

Bratislava – Centre of Culture
Bratislava's musical life flourished under Empress Maria Theresa. The imperial orchestra (with Joseph Haydn its leading composer) gave many concerts here, as did the six-year-old Mozart in 1762.

Bratislava Castle

Coronation of Leopold II
After his coronation ceremony on 15 November 1790, Leopold II knighted 33 noblemen in the Franciscan church.

The city walls, which the queen entered via Michael's Gate.

BRATISLAVA, 1741
This painting shows the coronation procession of Empress Maria Theresa on 25 June 1741. Modern visitors to Bratislava can walk the coronation route through the city (see p280).

Maria Theresa is carried in the state coach to St Martin's Cathedral for the coronation ceremony.

Pressburg Peace
The Primate's Palace was the venue for the signing, on 26 December 1805, of the peace treaty between Napoleon and Franz II following the Battle of Austerlitz.

A village in East Slovakia before World War I

THE AUSTRO-HUNGARIAN ERA
The situation for Slovakia worsened drastically after the creation of the Austro-Hungarian monarchy in 1866. The Hungarian government, having a free hand in the shaping of internal policy, embarked on a process of ruthless Magyarization of non-Hungarian communities. The Slovak language was banned from schools, and the national cultural organization, Matica Slovenska, was abolished. Economically devastating was the handing over of vast swathes of land to Hungarian settlers. By the early 20th century almost one-third of the Slovak population, driven by poverty and persecution, had fled abroad, mainly to the USA.

WORLD WAR I
The lack of success in their attempts to win autonomy within the Hungarian state drove Slovak politicians to forge closer links with Czech activists, led by Tomáš

Masaryk *(see p44)*. This cooperation intensified after the outbreak of World War I. In 1918, in Pittsburgh USA, representatives of Czech and Slovak emigré organizations signed an agreement providing for the creation of a joint state, in which Slovakia's autonomy would be guaranteed.

THE FIRST CZECHOSLOVAK REPUBLIC
With the Austro-Hungarian empire in tatters, the independent Czechoslovak Republic was declared in Prague on 28 October 1918. While the new state was composed of two countries with different histories, cultural traditions and ethnic compositions, President Masaryk and other leading politicians in Prague steadfastly promulgated the concept of a single country. The rejection of Slovakia's bid for autonomy caused disappointment among Slovakians. Ironically, autonomy came with the arrival of the Nazis.

THE SLOVAK STATE, 1939–45
When Hitler took the Sudetenland, and with Czechoslovakia in crisis, the Slovaks seized their chance to declare independence. However, the new

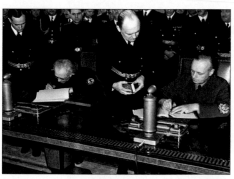

Ribbentrop and the Slovak prime minister signing a pact in 1940

TIMELINE

Stollwerck chocolate label

1867 Creation of the Austro-Hungarian monarchy

1896 German confectionery company, Stollwerck, opens a factory in Bratislava

1938 Parliament proclaims the Slovak Republic

1850   1875   1900   1925

1874–75 Slovak language banned in schools, and abolition of Matica Slovenska

1900 Tomáš Masaryk starts advocating closer cooperation between the Czechs and Slovaks

1918 Czechs and Slovaks sign, in Pittsburgh, a document proclaiming the creation of Czechoslovakia government, headed by Jozef Tiso, became little more than a Nazi puppet state. Tiso banned opposition parties and deported thousands of Jews. Slovakia became the base of the Nazis' military industry and also actively supported the German army. Tiso's regime was popular since Slovakia was, for the first time, able to set up its own national institutions. But the support was not universal, and in August 1944 elements of the Slovak army, assisted by Communist partisans, launched the Slovak National Uprising. German troops quashed the revolt.

Soviet tanks on the streets of Bratislava in 1968

Reborn in 1945, the state of Czechoslovakia initially continued the pre-war democratic traditions of the First Republic. In 1948, however, it fell under the total control of the Communist Party *(see p46)*. The era of Stalinist repression that followed affected both the democratic activists and the staunch Communists, who were often accused – like Gustáv Husák – of "Slovak nationalism".

THE "PRAGUE SPRING"

In January 1968 reformists in the Communist Party reacted to the authorities' reluctance to adopt a more liberal course by taking control of the government. The democratic reforms of the so-called Prague Spring came to an abrupt end, however, on 21 August with an invasion by Warsaw Pact troops. The orthodox Communists returned to power and during the "normalization" process that followed, totalitarian rule was re-established and all dissent suppressed.

THE SLOVAK REPUBLIC

After the "Velvet Revolution" of 1989, when the Communist government was overthrown *(see p47)*, Czechoslovakia was finally in the hands of democrats. The country was not destined to remain a joint state, however, and on 1 January 1993 the sovereign Slovak Republic was proclaimed, headed by Michal Kováč. While democracy in the Slovak Republic has seemed extremely fragile at times, the position of the new state within the international community was confirmed when, in 2004, Slovakia joined NATO and the European Union.

President of Slovakia, Ivan Gasparovič

1944 Slovak National Uprising

1969 Alexander Dubček removed from office as First Secretary of the Communist Party

Slovak Constitution

ÚSTAVA SLOVENSKEJ REPUBLIKY

2005 Slovakia elected to a two-year term on the UN Security Council

1950	1975	2000	2025

1948 Communists take control of Czechoslovakia

1968 "Prague Spring"

1989 Velvet Revolution

2004 Slovakia joins NATO and becomes EU member

2007 Slovakia joins the Schengen agreement, abolishing border controls with all of its members

1945 Liberation of Slovakia by the Red Army

1993 Creation of the Slovak Republic

SLOVAKIA REGION BY REGION

Slovakia at a Glance

This small Central European country displays a diverse topography. Although there are lowlands in the west of Slovakia, most of the territory is taken up by forest-clad mountains. The Small Carpathian mountains start just north of Bratislava. Central Slovakia is dominated by the Tatras range, which includes Slovakia's highest peak. In the east of the country is the Slovak Karst, which has huge limestone caves.

The Slovak Agricultural Museum, Nitra, *is one of Slovakia's most interesting, full of historic implements for agriculture and wine-making, as well as displays illustrating folk and social history* (see p304).

The Church of St Jacob *in Trnava, built in 1640 on the site of a previous Early Gothic church, acquired some Baroque elements in 1712. The interior furnishings date from the 17th and 18th centuries* (see pp296–7).

CENTRAL SLOVAKIA
(pp306–323)

BRATISLAVA
(pp272–289)

WEST SLOVAKIA
(pp290–305)

The Chapel of St John the Alms-giver *was added to St Martin's Cathedral in Bratislava during the Baroque period, it holds the remains of the Saint* (see pp280–81).

The altar of Our Lady of the Rosary, *made by an Austrian Master in 1500–20, is one of many outstanding artefacts displayed inside Zvolen Castle* (see p314).

◁ **The majestic ruins of the medieval Spiš Castle**

Rohače, the start of the Western Tatras, is a uniquely picturesque region, less crowded than the High Tatras to the east. It is worth taking a walk along one of the trails to admire the mountain scenery, glistening lakes and cascading waterfalls (see p316).

The Church of St James in Levoča *contains 18 altars, masterpieces of medieval and Renaissance religious art (see p334).*

EAST SLOVAKIA
(pp324–339)

0 km 30

0 miles 30

The Slovenský kras *(Slovak Karst) is the largest karst area in Europe, with exceptionally diverse wildlife, and glorious scenery. The beauty of the landscape and the many caves make this region highly attractive (see pp336–7).*

Hlavná in Košice, *the town's main promenade, is lined with magnificent Gothic, Baroque and Neo-Classical buildings. This detail is from No. 37 (see p328).*

BRATISLAVA

The capital of Slovakia lies very near the country's south-western border. It straddles the River Danube (Dunaj) at the southern end of the Small Carpathian mountains. From here it is a mere 2 km (1 mile) to the border with Austria, and only 10 km (6 miles) to the border with Hungary. In clear weather both neighbouring countries can be seen from Bratislava Castle.

Bratislava has been the capital of Slovakia since 1993, when the country was proclaimed an independent state. Through its long history it has always been a major centre of the country's social and cultural life, as well as its administrative capital. It was known as Pressburg to German-speakers and as Pozsóny to Hungarian speakers.

A settlement founded by Celts in the 2nd century BC later became the base of a Roman garrison, and by the 10th century one of the main centres of the Great Moravian Empire. In 1291 it was granted town privileges by the Hungarian King Andrew III and gradually it strengthened its position within the Crown Lands of St Stephen. It assumed a particularly important role after the capture of Buda by the Turks, in 1541, when it was the capital of Hungary for nearly 200 years.

Pressburg reached the zenith of its glory during the reign of Maria Theresa. In the 19th century, it became the centre of the Slovak independence movement. After World War I and the creation of Czechoslovakia, the capital of the Slovak part of the country assumed the name of Bratislava. In 1939–45, when Slovakia was an ally of the Third Reich, Bratislava was spared destruction. Many people believe that, paradoxically, postwar development, involving the demolition of the historic centre, caused much more damage to the city. Today, the old town of Bratislava, lovingly restored, provides a charming setting for countless cafés, pubs and clubs.

Bratislava Castle with its lofty corner towers

◁ A Gothic entrance into the Old Town Hall

Exploring Bratislava

The majority of historic sights in Bratislava can be found in the compact old town centre, on the left bank of the Danube. The area is split in two by a busy main road, which was built in the late 1960s, cutting right through the old town. The landmark castle is to the west of the main road. The best point from which to view the city's layout is the restaurant at the top of the New Bridge (Nový most). Outside of the centre there are interesting villages and wine-growing areas, which are ideal for day trips.

SIGHTS AT A GLANCE

Churches
Franciscan Church **4**
Poor Clares Church **15**
St Martin's Cathedral pp280–81 **8**

Buildings and Squares
Academia Istropolitana **7**
Bratislava Castle **1**
Grassalkovich Palace **17**
House at the Good Shepherd **13**
Michael's Gate **5**
Mirbach Palace **6**
Námestie SNP **16**
New Bridge **14**
Old Town Hall **2**
Pálffy Palace **12**
Primate's Palace **3**
Reduta **10**
Slavín Monument **18**
Slovak National Gallery **11**
Slovak National Theatre **9**

Environs
Bernolákovo **32**
Červený Kameň **27**
Devín Castle **21**
Little Blue Church **20**
Malacky **30**
Marianka Shrine **29**
Modra **26**
Pezinok **25**
Rača **22**
Rusovce **23**
St Andrew's Cemetery **19**
Stupava **28**
Svätý Jur **24**
Veľké Leváre **31**

0 metres   200
0 yards   200

For additional map symbols *see back flap*

VISITORS' CHECKLIST

Road map C4. 🏛 *430,000.*
✈ *Štefanika, 9 km (6 miles)
NE.* 🚆 *Hlavna stanica, Pražska,
1 km (0.5 mile) N.* **Tel** *(02) 524
959 06.* 🚌 *Mlynske nivy.* 🛈
Klobučnícka 2. **Tel** *(02) 544 337
15.* **www**.bratislava.sk

GETTING AROUND

Central Bratislava is best seen
on foot. The Old Town is very
compact, and many of the
major places to visit are
grouped in and around it. For
longer distances within the city
and into its environs, there is a
fast and efficient network of
buses, trams and trolleybuses.
These also run at intervals
throughout the night, starting
from Námestie SNP. From April
to October ferry and sightseeing
boats run from a jetty on the
Danube at Fajnorovo nábrežie.

SEE ALSO

• **Where to Stay** pp358–9

• **Where to Eat** pp390–91

The main square and castle in Bratislava

KEY

▪	Street-by-Street map *See pp276–7*
✈	Airport
🚋	Tram stop
🚌	Bus stop
🅿	Parking
🛈	Tourist information
⊠	Post office
✝	Church
▬	Pedestrianized street

Street-by-Street: Old Town

The centre of Bratislava's historic Staré mesto district consists of two interlinked squares: Hlavné námestie and Františkánské námestie. The first has the distinctive Old Town Hall. This square was also part of the coronation route of the Hungarian kings (*see p280*), now marked by golden crowns embedded in the pavement. The pride of Františkánské námestie, apart from its lovely trees, is the Marian Column erected in 1657. Both squares are popular meeting places, with some attractive cafés.

Michael's Gate
This is the only gate that remains from the medieval fortifications. In the 18th century it was topped with a statue of the Archangel Michael ❺

Mirbach Palace
This Rococo palace, one of Bratislava's finest architectural relics, now houses the City Gallery ❻

This statue of Napoleon's soldier is one of several life-sized figures in the Old Town, including a worker poking his head out of a round manhole and a newspaper photographer aiming his lens from around a corner.

Marian column

ZAMOČNÍCKA

BIELA

FRANTIŠ-KÁNSKE NÁMESTIE

SEDLÁRSKA

HLAVNÉ NÁMESTIE

ZELENÁ

RYBÁRS

In Hlavné námestie, the main square of Bratislava and its former marketplace, is the 1572 Maximilian Fountain designed by Andreas Luttringer. On a tall plinth at the centre of the fountain is the figure of Roland, a knight who defended the townspeople's rights. The square has been beautifully renovated, and seasonal stalls add to its bustle and atmosphere.

0 metres 50

0 yards 50

★ Franciscan Church

Bratislava's oldest religious building, this Gothic-style church was erected in the 13th century. Several times remodelled, it acquired its Baroque form in the 18th century ❹

LOCATOR MAP
See city map, pp274–5

The Jesuit Church *(see p278)* was built in 1636–8 by Protestants. Its greatest treasure is the Rococo pulpit by Ľudovít Gode.

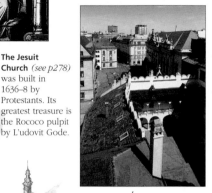

★ Primate's Palace

One of the city's finest Neo-Classical structures, this palace was built in 1778–81 by Melchior Hefele for the Archbishop Jozef Batthyány ❸

The Museum of Music is in the birthplace of Johann Nepomuk Hummel (1778–1837), a celebrated composer and pianist. The Renaissance house in Klobučnicka has displays about his life and works, and the history of music in Bratislava.

STAR SIGHTS

★ Franciscan Church

★ Primate's Palace

The Museum of Wine Production, part of the City Museum, displays wooden grape presses over 200 years old.

KEY
− − − Suggested route

Old Town Hall
The Stará radnica, many times remodelled and rebuilt since the 13th century, is now home to the City Museum ❷

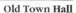

Bratislava Castle ❶

BRATISLAVSKÝ HRAD

Slovak National Museum *Tel* *(02) 54 41 14 44.* ○ *9am–5pm Tue–Fri, 10am–6pm Sat, Sun (last adm: 45 mins before closing).* www.snm.sk

Bratislava Castle on the north embankment of the Danube

Perched forbiddingly on a large, rocky hill above the Danube, Bratislava's stronghold is first mentioned in 907. It was at a strategic location on the Danube, at the crossing of trade routes, including the ancient Amber Route. Fortified in the 11th and 12th centuries, the castle was rebuilt in Gothic style in the 15th century, and in 1552–60 remodelled into a Renaissance residence. In 1750–60, it was given beautiful Rococo furnishings. In 1811 the castle burnt down; it was rebuilt in the 1950s.

Inside are several sections of the **Slovak National Museum**. The largest collections are from the Slovak History Museum (Slovenské historické múzeum), including furniture, clocks and folk artifacts. In the Treasury of Slovakia (Klenoty davnej minulsloti Slovenska) is the tiny *Venus of Moravany*, a fertility figure carved from a mammoth tusk about 25,000 years ago. A Music Museum (Hudobné Múzeum) has some fascinating folk instruments.

Bratislava's eclectic Old Town Hall in the main square

Old Town Hall ❷

STARÁ RADNICA

City Museum *Tel* *(02) 59 20 51 30.* ○ *10am–5pm Tue–Fri, 11am–6pm Sat, Sun.*

The charming Old Town Hall in Primaciálne námestie was created in the 15th century by combining a number of residential houses. At the turn of the 16th and 17th centuries it was rebuilt in Renaissance style. In the 18th century its much older corner tower was remodelled in Baroque style; this tower can be climbed for excellent views. Mounted on its lower section is a plaque marking the level of flood waters recorded in February 1850. Higher up, to the left of the Gothic window, is another historic relic – a cannon-ball embedded in the wall since the 1809 siege of Bratislava by Napoleon's army. It is worth taking a look at the unusual colourful roof covering of the building on the side of Primaciálne námestie.

The town hall houses the **City Museum** (Mestské múzeum). Displayed within its splendid vaulted interiors are exhibits associated with the history of Bratislava, including an unusual collection of 17th–19th-century painted shooting targets.

Opposite the town hall stands the **Jesuit Church of the Holy Saviour**. It was built in 1636–8 for Bratislava's Protestant community, which explains its wide, plain façade with no tower. Its interesting Baroque furnishings include a fine Rococo pulpit.

Primate's Palace ❸

PRIMACIÁLNY PALÁC

Primaciálne námestie 1. *Tel (02)* *35 63 94.* ○ *10am–5pm Tue–Sun.*

The most beautiful palace in Bratislava was built during 1778–81 to a design by Melchior Hefele, for Jozef Batthyány, the primate of Hungary and archbishop of Esztergom. Its Neo-Classical pink-and-gold façade features a magnificent pediment that is crowned with the archbishop's coat of arms, topped with a giant-size cardinal's hat. The figures of angels on the façade hold the letters I and C, a reference to the motto in the cardinal's coat of arms – Iusticia (Justice) and Clementia (Mercy).

The palace, which is now the seat of the town's mayor, is partly open to the public. Its most opulent room is the Hall of Mirrors, where in 1805 the Peace Treaty of Pressburg was signed between Napoleon and Francis I, after the French victory at the Battle of Austerlitz. Other first-floor rooms are given to a branch of the Municipal Gallery with a modest collection of paintings and six unique English tapestries dating from 1632,

The courtyard fountain at the Primate's Palace

For hotels and restaurants in this region see pp358–9 and pp390–91

depicting the love story of Hero and Leander. The strikingly bright tapestries were discovered in a hidden compartment during building works in the early 20th century.

Franciscan Church ❹

FRANTIŠKÁNSKÝ KOSTOL

Františkánske námestie.
🗋 *10:30am–5pm Mon–Fri.*

The Franciscan Church behind an inconspicuous Baroque façade is the oldest religious building in Bratislava. Built in the 13th century, it was consecrated in 1297 in the presence of King Andrew II. Subsequent remodelling works obliterated its original Gothic form, but it is still possible to see the medieval rib vaulting above the presbytery. Particularly impressive is the two-tier 14th-century chapel of St John the Evangelist. During coronation pageants in Bratislava the church was used for knighting ceremonies, in which the new monarch appointed Knights of the Golden Spur.

The church's furnishings, mainly Baroque, date from the 17th and 18th centuries; an older, 15th-century Pietà in a side altar is a highlight.

Statue from the Franciscan Church

Michael's Gate ❺

MICHALSKÁ BRÁNA

Michalská ulica 24. **Museum of Weapons and Town Fortifications Tel** *(02) 54 43 30 44.* 🗋 *Oct–Apr: 9:30am–4:30pm Tue–Sun; May–Sep: 10am–5pm Mon–Fri, 11am–6pm Sat, Sun.* 📷

Built in the first half of the 14th century, Michael's Gate is the only surviving original gateway to the medieval city. In 1753–8 its Gothic tower was raised to the present 51 m (167 ft), by the addition of

Buildings of the Academia Istropolitana, site of a 15th-century university

a Baroque cupola, and the statue of Archangel Michael was placed at the top. The tower now houses the **Museum of Weapons and Town Fortifications** (Múzeum zbraní a mestského opevnienia).

The viewing terrace affords a stunning panorama of the city and beyond. The small building next to the gate is Bratislava's oldest pharmacy – At the Red Lobster.

Mirbach Palace ❻

MIRBACHOV PALÁC

Františkánske námestie 11. **City Gallery Tel** *(02) 54 43 15 56.* 🗋 *11am–6pm Tue–Sun.* www.gmb.sk

The Rococo Mirbach Palace opposite the Franciscan Church has a beautiful façade

Michael's Gate with its striking Baroque cupola

with stuccoes and a triangular pediment. The building was erected in 1768–70 by a rich brewer, Martin Spech. Its subsequent owner, Count Karol Nyary, ordered his family crest to be placed in the tympanum. The last owner of the palace, Emil Mirbach, bequeathed the building to the town.

Now it is an art gallery, currently holding the main collection of Bratislava's **City Gallery** (Galéria mesta Bratislavy). Exhibits include examples of 17th- and 18th-century Baroque painting. Two of the first-floor halls have walls almost entirely covered with colourful 18th-century engravings set in wood panelling.

Academia Istropolitana ❼

Ventúrska 3. 🎵

The oldest university in present-day Slovakia, the Academia Istropolitana was founded by King Matthias Corvinus in 1465. It occupied two residential town houses belonging to Štefan Gmaitel. The university trained its students in three faculties. Following the death of King Matthias in 1490, the university closed down.

This building, with its stone entrance portal and oriel windows, is now a national cultural monument. Modernized in the 1960s, it houses the Bratislava Academy of Music; check with tourist information offices for times of occasional performances.

St Martin's Cathedral 🔞

DÓM SV. MARTINA

This Gothic edifice, with a wide nave flanked by two aisles, was built on the site of an earlier, 14th-century Romanesque church. Between 1563 and 1830 eleven Hungarian kings and eight queens were crowned here. It is possible to walk the former coronation route through the Old Town, starting from here, by following a series of golden crowns embedded in the pavement. In the late 19th century the church was rebuilt in Neo-Gothic style by Jozef Lippert, and its interior was refurbished along more purist lines.

Structure of the Cathedral
Due to vibrations from heavy traffic on the nearby major road to the New Bridge (see p283), the cathedral is being damaged. It frequently undergoes repair work.

Presbytery
After completing the hall the builders realized that the section by the altar was too small. They added a presbytery with a splendid net vault; the coat of arms on it is that of Matthias Corvinus.

★ Sculpture of St Martin
This dramatic sculpture, by Georg Raphael Donner (1734), was originally made for the main altar. St Martin is shown in Hungarian dress cutting his cloak to share with a beggar.

Chapel of St John the Almsgiver
In 1732, commissioned by Archbishop Esterházy, Georg Raphael Donner built the side chapel of St John the Almsgiver (sv. Ján Almužník), in which the saint's remains were laid to rest.

St Anne's Chapel

The tower, 85 m (280 ft) tall, is topped with a slender cupola, and includes a tiny copy of the Hungarian crown, a reminder that this was once the venue of royal coronations.

VISITORS' CHECKLIST

Rudnayovo náměstí 1. **Tel** (02) 544 313 59. ⬜ Apr–Oct: 9–11:30am, 1–5pm Mon–Sat, 1:30–11pm Sun (Nov–Mar: times vary). 🕆 8am & noon Mon–Sat, 7:45am, 9am, 10:30am, noon, 5pm Sun. 🈁

Interior

In the late 19th century the Baroque furnishings were replaced with new, Neo-Gothic ones. The main altar was removed and its angels paying homage to St Martin were transported to Budapest.

Stained-Glass Windows

The windows in the presbytery and the aisles date from the second half of the 19th century; they were mostly produced by the Viennese company of K Geyling.

The Canons' Chapel and the Chapel of the Czech queen Sophia are adjacent to the sacristy under the tower.

Main portal with Neo-Gothic vestibule

STAR FEATURES

★ Altar of St Anne's Chapel

★ Sculpture of St Martin

★ Altar of St Anne's Chapel
The central field of the ornate altarpiece in this chapel depicts the scene of the Crucifixion.

Façade of the Neo-Renaissance Slovak National Theatre

Slovak National Theatre **9**

SLOVENSKÉ NÁRODNÉ DIVADLO

Hviezdoslavovo námestie 1. *Tel* (02) 54 43 30 83. **Advance ticket sales:** Komenského námestie. ☐ 8am–5:30pm Mon–Fri, 9am–1pm Sat.

This imposing Neo-Renaissance theatre on the east side of Hviezdoslavovo námestie was built in 1884–6. Its creators were two Viennese architects who specialized in theatres, Ferdinand Fellner and Hermann Helmer. The façade is decorated with busts including Goethe, Liszt and Shakespeare. At the centre of the tympanum is a sculptural group including the Muse of Comedy, Thalia. Opera and ballet performances are regularly staged here; the sumptuous interiors can only be seen by attending a performance.

The beautiful fountain in front of the theatre depicts the Trojan youth Ganymede flying on the back of Zeus, who has become an eagle. Made in 1880 of bronze and marble, the fountain is the work of V Tilger.

Reduta **10**

Palackého 2. *Tel* (02) 54 43 33 51. ☐ ┌ ┐ ┌ ┐ ┌ ┐ ┌ ┐ 8am–2pm Wed. **www.**filharm.sk

Close to the Slovak National Theatre is the imposing building of the Reduta, built in 1913–18, with a grand lobby and staircase. It used to stage social and artistic events, symphony concerts and theatre performances. Today the Reduta is the home of the Slovak Philharmonic, and every autumn it is the principal venue for the Bratislava Music Festival. The part of the building on the side of Mostova houses a casino and a stylish restaurant.

Slovak National Gallery **11**

SLOVENSKÁ NÁRODNÁ GALÉRIA

Riečna 1. *Tel* (02) 54 43 45 87. ☐ 10am–6pm Tue–Sun. ● 21 & 24 Apr, 1 & 8 May. 📷 ☐ **www.**sng.sk

Established in 1948, the National Gallery occupies a building that was created by combining the four-wing 18th-century Baroque naval barracks, designed by G Martinelli and F Hildebrandt, and, in the 1970s, V Dědeček's house. In 1990 the gallery's collections were also placed in the neighbouring Neo-Renaissance Esterházy Palace. A long structure designed by I Feigler Jr and built in 1870–76, Esterházy Palace is reminiscent of an Italian Renaissance town palace. On the ground floor is the legendary Berlinka café, one of the most popular in town.

The gallery boasts a number of magnificent works of art. The finest are the collections of 13th- and 14th-century Slovak art including altarpieces and statues from churches of the Spiš region in eastern Slovakia.

Modern Slovak art is also well represented, with models of buildings, photographs, ceramics, jewellery and posters, making an eclectic overview of the country's creative output over the last hundred years.

As well as Slovak artists, the collection also holds works by a number of foreign masters, including Caravaggio, Rubens, Manet and Picasso.

Pálffy Palace **12**

PÁLFFYHO PALÁC

Panska 19/21. **City Gallery** *Tel* (02) 54 43 36 27. ☐ 11am–6pm Tue–Sun. 📷 **www.**gmb.sk

The 1747 Baroque Pálffy Palace serves as another extension to Bratislava's **City Gallery** (Galéria mesta Bratislavy); the main collection is in the Mirbach Palace *(see p279)*. Its distinctive portal is decorated

The Reduta, home of the Slovak Philharmonic

with images of war trophies, reminders of the fact that one of its first owners was Marshal Leopold Pálffy.

The Palace displays collections of Gothic panel painting, Central European painting, 19th-century sculpture and 20th-century Slovak painting and sculpture. It is this 20th-century section that holds the most interest, with its varied portrayals and interpretations of Slovak life.

House at the Good Shepherd ⓭

DOM U DOBRÉHO PASTIERA

Židovska 1. *Tel (02) 54 41 19 40.*
Museum of Clocks ☐ *10am–5pm Mon–Fri, 11am–5pm Sat, Sun.*

One of the town's finest examples of Rococo architecture is the House at the Good Shepherd, named after the statue of the Good Shepherd on its corner. Built in 1760–65, it is now one of the few remaining original houses in the area at the foot of the castle. It is colloquially referred to as the "house like an iron", because of its tall flat wedge shape, dictated by the plot on which it was erected. It is believed to be the narrowest building in Europe, and there is only one room on each floor. It houses a **Museum of Clocks** (Múzeum hodín), a branch of the City Museum. The exhibits date from the 17th to the 20th centuries and are mostly the works of Bratislava's clockmakers.

New Bridge ⓮

NOVÝ MOST

Staromestská.

Also known as the bridge of the Slovak National Uprising (most SNP), this steel construction, which is suspended from one pylon on the south bank of the Danube (Dunaj), opened in 1972. At the top of the pylon is a restaurant, reached by a lift, which provides views of the city on the north bank, and of the vast housing estates of Petržalka on the south. Built by the Communists, this estate houses around 150,000 of the city's inhabitants.

To build the New Bridge, and the major Staromestská highway that cuts through the city and over the bridge, a section of the old city was destroyed, including the former Jewish quarter at the foot of Bratislava Castle, just outside the old city walls.

Poor Clares Church ⓯

KLARISKÝ KOSTOL

Klariská ulica.

The former church and convent of St Clare stand near the 14th-century walls, which surrounded the city until the 18th century, when they were dismantled on the orders of Empress Maria Theresa. The remaining fragments are a meticulous reconstruction.

The 14th-century Gothic, single-nave church should, in line with the strict rules binding the mendicant and contemplative orders, be plain and have no ostentatious tower, only a small bell rung at times of prayer. This rule has been broken twice in Bratislava: the nearby Franciscan Church *(see p279)* and the Poor Clares Church were both given towers. The convent's fine church tower, dating from 1400 and richly decorated with sculptures, is built on a rarely seen pentagonal ground-plan.

The convent itself was built after the great fire of 1590, in

Richly decorated tower and spire of the Poor Clares Church

Renaissance style. From the second half of the 18th century until 1908 it housed the Law Academy and the Catholic Theological Seminary; one of its students was the Hungarian composer Béla Bartók. It has been restored, and now it serves as a venue for exhibitions and, due to the church's excellent acoustics, concerts.

Námestie SNP ⓰

Námestie SNP.

The square of the Slovak National Uprising has been used for public gatherings for centuries. Celebrations that accompanied royal coronations were held here, and more recently it saw gatherings of activists in 1989 just before the fall of Communism.

Just off the square is the **Church and Monastery of the Brothers of Mercy** (kostol a kláštor milosrdných bratov). Here, the monks, who devoted themselves to caring for the sick, built a large complex of buildings outside the city walls. The Early Baroque façade with its angular tower (1728) is clearly visible on many old drawings. The most interesting artifacts are the 18th-century altars and the tombstone of Ján Onell (1745). The still-functioning hospital played an important role during the plague that ravaged Europe in 1710–13.

Figure from the House at the Good Shepherd

National flags flying in front of Grassalkovich Palace

Grassalkovich Palace ⑰

GRASSALKOVIČOV PALÁC

Hodžovo námestie 1. **Gardens** *Štefánikova ulica.* ☐ *daily.*

This Baroque palace, built in 1760 to a design by A Mayerhoffer, was originally the residence of Anton Grassalkovich, chairman of the Royal Hungarian Chamber, the Royal Crown's Guardian and one of the closest advisors to Empress Maria Theresa. The palace was considerably extended towards the end of the 18th century. In 1939 it became the seat of Monsignor Josef Tiso, president of the Slovak Republic during World War II. It is still the residence of the President. Standing guard in front of the palace are soldiers in colourful historic uniforms. In the late 18th century the palace was surrounded by a French garden, which was returned to its former glory in 1999 and is now open to the public.

Figure of an angel, St Andrew's Cemetery

Slavín Monument ⑱

Slavín.

The vast Soviet monument to the Red Army soldiers killed in battles with the Nazis around Bratislava in the closing stages of World War II stands on Slavín hill in the north-western part of the city. The 40-m (130-ft) obelisk by Ján Svetlik is topped by a bronze

figure by Alexander Trizulijak of a Red Army soldier holding a banner flapping in the wind. The adjacent mausoleum is used as a venue for official celebrations. The monument is surrounded by a cemetery containing 6,845 war graves. The front terrace affords a fine prospect of Bratislava to the south and views of the distant Small Carpathian mountains to the north.

St Andrew's Cemetery ⑲

ONDREJSKÝ CINTORÍN

Entrance on Pol'na.
☐ *7am–dusk daily.*

The oldest and most interesting graveyard in Bratislava, St Andrew's Cemetery is a well-kept green oasis resembling a town park and is popular with the locals for a stroll. Founded in 1784, it covers an area of 6 ha (15 acres) and entry to it is through St Andrew's Chapel, which was built by the architect I Feigler in 1861.

The cemetery is the resting place of many prominent citizens of Bratislava and Slovakia. Its avenues are lined with many tombs belonging to famous families. Among those buried here are sculptor Alois Rigele; historian Ján ... Ferko Urbánek.

The cemetery has an exhibition of tomb monuments and details from memorials of the 19th and 20th centuries.

Little Blue Church ⑳

MODRÝ KOSTOLIK

Bezručova ulica.

The unusual Art Nouveau Little Blue Church owes its name to its blue roof tiles and walls. Its designer, Ödön Lechner, was a Hungarian architect, one of the most famous creators of Art Nouveau in Budapest. The church was built in 1907–13 and dedicated to St Elizabeth (sv. Alžbeta) of Hungary, daughter of King Andrew II of the Arpad family, who was born in Bratislava Castle in 1207. Her portrait can be seen above the church's portal.

Monument to the Red Army soldiers on Slavín Hill

For hotels and restaurants in this region see pp358–9 and pp390–91

Devín Castle ㉑

8 km (5 miles) W of the centre of Bratislava. 🚌 *28, 29.* 🚊 *from Central Bratislava.* **Tel** *(02) 65 73 01 05.* ⭕ *10am–5pm Tue–Fri, 11am–6pm Sat, Sun.* 🖼

At the point where the Morava river flows into the Danube stand the looming ruins of Devín Castle perched on a high rock. The rock was once the site of a Celtic settlement; later on the Romans built their fortress here; and in the 9th century Prince Rastislav, King of Great Moravia, chose it for his stronghold. It changed hands many times until in 1809 it was blown up by the French during the Napoleonic Wars.

In the 19th century, during the period of national rebirth, it became a prominent symbol in the shaping of Slovak national identity, promoted by the nationalist L'udovít Štúr *(see p286).*

During the 1980s the castle area, separated from Austria only by the Danube, was closed to the public. Now it is a favourite spot for a stroll for Bratislavans. It also features the remains of the Roman fortress and a museum of archaeological finds in a reconstructed fragment of the castle.

The ruins of Devín Castle, high above the Danube

Rača ㉒

8 km (5 miles) NE of the centre of Bratislava. 🚶 *21,000.* 🚌 *52, 55, 56, 59, 65, 515.* 🚊 *3, 5. 11.* 🏠 *Kubačova 21.* **Tel** *(02) 44 88 32 76.* 🍇 *Grape Harvest (mid-Sep).*

The small winemaking town of Rača has a history going back to Roman times. Its earliest written records, from 1245, mention a settlement on the southeastern slopes of the Small Carpathians. During the Middle Ages the locally produced wine was regarded as the region's best, and exported to Silesia and Austria. In 1767 Empress Maria Theresa granted Rača's producers a licence to produce *terezianska frankovka,* so declaring the local red wine worthy of the imperial table.

In order to protect their products against interference

and fakes, Rača's winemakers marked their barrels by scorching special marks on them. Winemaking traditions are still a significant part of the local culture, and the annual grape harvest festivals, here and in Modra *(see p286),* attract many visitors.

Rusovce ㉓

9 km (6 miles) S of the centre of Bratislava. 🚶 *1,700.* 🚌 *91, 191.*

The remains of a Roman military camp called Gerulata were discovered in the suburban district of Rusovce in 1961. It had stood here from the 1st to the 4th centuries AD, and was one of

the command posts that guarded the northern border of the Roman Empire along the Danube. Archaeological excavations unearthed fragments of fortifications, cult sites, tombstones and small everyday objects, many of which are displayed in the **Gerulata Museum**.

Another popular attraction is the 19th-century Neo-Gothic **Zichy Castle**. This houses part of the collection of the Slovak National Gallery, and is surrounded by a vast English-style park.

🏛 **Gerulata Museum**
Gerulatská 69. **Tel** *(02) 62 85 93 32.* ⭕ *May–Oct: 10am–5pm Tue–Sun.* 🖼

⛪ **Zichy Castle**
🚫 *for renovation.*

The fairytale Zichy Castle in Rusovce

Altar in the Church of St George, Svätý Jur

Svätý Jur ㉔

Road map C4. 14 km (9 miles) NE of the centre of Bratislava. 🚌 *4,500.* 🚌 🚎 www.svatyjur.sk

A wine-producing centre, Svätý Jur lies in an extremely picturesque setting surrounded by vineyards with the remains of its ancient walls visible here and there. Its first records date from 1209 but this small town reached the peak of its prosperity in the 17th and 18th centuries, and most of its historic buildings date from that time. In the early 17th century Emperor Rudolph II granted it town privileges, and in 1615 Matthias II conferred on it numerous further rights.

The town's highlight is the modest 13th-century **Church of St George** (sv. Juraj). Its Gothic interior contains many beautiful wall-paintings, stone epitaphs and a carved altarpiece depicting the church's patron saint fighting the dragon. The altarpiece was carved from white sandstone, in 1527, by Anton Pilgram.

Standing below the church is an early 17th-century Renaissance mansion that belonged to the Pálffy family and is now the home of the new Academia Istropolitana *(see p279)*. The nearby Baroque **Church of the Piarist Order** (Piaristický klástor), with its steep roof, has the tallest clock tower in town.

Pezinok ㉕

Road map C4. 20 km (12 miles) NE of the centre of Bratislava. 🚌 *20,500.* 🚌 🚎 ℹ *Radničné námestie 9.* **Tel** *(033) 641 25 50.* www.pezinok.sk

Pezinok's winemaking tradition dates back to the late Middle Ages. The first vine growers were German settlers, who arrived in the 13th century. In 1615 Matthias II granted Pezinok the status of a free royal town and the town's walls were constructed. The **Old Town Hall** was built in the 17th century and rebuilt after a fire in Neo-Classical style. Kaviakov, the Renaissance house at No. 4 Štefanika, with its attractive oriel window and inner courtyard, houses the **Small Carpathian Museum** (Malokarpatské múzeum), devoted to local winemaking traditions and Pezinok's history. Hiking and skiing are popular in the nearby mountains.

🏛 **Small Carpathian Museum**
Tel *(033) 641 20 57.* 🕐 *Apr–Oct: Tue–Sun.*

Modra ㉖

Road map C4. 30 km (19 miles) NE of the centre of Bratislava. 🚌 *8,600.* 🚎 ℹ *Dukelská 38.* **Tel** *(033) 647 22 12.* 🎎 *Grape Harvest (mid-Sep).* www.modra.sk

An annual highlight in Modra (Modern), sometimes called the "jewel" of the Small Carpathians, is the September grape harvest festival. The oldest of its five churches is the Catholic **Church of St John the Baptist** (sv. Ján Krstitel), from the beginning of the 14th century. Buried in its cemetery is one of the heroes of the Slovak national movement, L'udovít Štúr (1815–56), whose life is illustrated by an exhibition in the local **Štúr Museum**, in the former town hall. His statue also dominates the main square. Modra is renowned for its majolica pottery *(see p399)*.

🏛 **Štúr Museum**
Štúrova 54. **Tel** *(033) 647 27 65.* 🕐 *Mon–Fri.* 🌐 www.snm.sk

Old Town gate, Modra

Červený Kameň ㉗

Road map C4. 8 km (5 miles) N of Modra. 🚌 **Tel** *(033) 690 58 03.* 🕐 *Nov–Feb: 9:30am–3:30pm daily; Apr–Aug: 9am–5pm daily; Sep, Oct: 9am–4pm daily (to 5pm Sat, Sun).* 🌐 📷

One of the best-preserved Slovak castles, Červený Kameň (Red Stone) owes its magnificent appearance to the

The Old Town Hall in Pezinok

Coats of arms from the well in the courtyard of Červený Kameň Castle

fact that from 1580 until the end of World War II it remained in the hands of the the wealthy Pálffy family. A mighty edifice with four corner towers, it was acquired in the 16th century by the German banking family, the Fuggers, on the site of a 13th-century fort. Anton Fugger, one of the richest men in 16th-century Europe, converted the fort into a Renaissance castle with huge cellars, 70 m (230 ft) long and 9 m (30 ft) high, which were used as a warehouse. After the Pálffy family took over, they converted it into a splendid Baroque residence. At the end of World War II they fled the country.

The castle's magnificent interiors include many excellently preserved pieces of furniture, porcelain and historic furnishings. The eye-catching features of the octagonal castle chapel are its lavishly decorated walls and ceilings, and marble altars, while the castle pharmacy still has the original cabinets dating from 1752. An unusual feature of the castle is the 1656 *sala terrena*, a startling artificial grotto with trompe-l'oeil paintings and stuccoes.

The castle also houses some interesting collections from the Slovak National Museum. There are historic weapons dating from the 15th to the 19th centuries. There is also a gallery of paintings with some fine family portraits of the Habsburgs, Pálffys and their courtiers. Many other exhibits illuminate the lives and living conditions of the aristocracy here and in other Slovak castles from Renaissance times until the 19th century.

Environs
Částá, about 1 km (half a mile) east of Červený Kameň, has been a centre of winemaking for several centuries. Its 15th-century Gothic **Church of St Imre** (sv. Emeryk) has some interesting medieval paintings, and in several private wine cellars in the town you can taste the local wines.

Stupava ㉘

Road map C4. 🏛 8,100. 🚌 �'
(02) 65 93 41 10.

An important trading centre for several centuries, Stupava – known at the time as Ztumpa – is mentioned in the donation letter of the Hungarian King Bela IV as early as 1269. The local fairs were famous, and the town charged a three per cent tax on all goods sold, which contributed to its growing wealth.

The seat of the changing owners of Stupava was a modest-sized **Castle**, which in the second half of the 19th century was rebuilt in Romantic style, with some Rococo elements. Placed above the entrance is the

Figure from the Church of St Stephen, Stupava

Károlyi family crest. Unfortunately, the building burned down in 1947 and its subsequent reconstruction completely changed its appearance. The castle is surrounded by a lovely English-style garden with some rare species of trees.

The town's most notable religious building is the **Church of St Stephen** (sv. Štefana), the patron saint of Hungary. This Baroque edifice, erected on the site of a castle mentioned in 1271, was most recently remodelled in 1867. Close by is a Baroque chapel surrounded by a high wall with the Stations of the Cross.

Also of interest in Stupava are some well-preserved Baroque and Neo-Classical burghers' houses along Hlavná. The pillory, erected in 1766 for the punishment of minor offences, is still standing. The town's **Synagogue**, dating from 1803, is a square-shaped building with massive walls that give it a rather forbidding appearance. Although it is listed as a UNESCO World Architectural Heritage Site, the synagogue is sadly much neglected; attempts are being made to restore it. Inside, four huge pillars divide the vault into twelve segments. The ceiling and the walls still feature beautiful paintings in cobalt blue and dark red.

Stupava has also been a well-known centre for ceramics, which is commemo-rated in the **Museum of Ferdiš Kostka**, a famous Slovak potter (1878–1951). It displays the original stone tiles, sculptures and vessels by Kostka with his decorations depicting the lives of the local inhabitants.

🏛 **Museum of Ferdiš Kostka**
F Kostku 26. **Tel** (02) 65 93 48 82.
⏰ Tue–Sat (Sat to 1:30pm). 🗷

Miraculous statue of the Madonna, the Mariánka Shrine

Mariánka Shrine ㉙

Road map C4. 12 km (7 miles) NW of Bratislava. 🚌 **Tel** (03) 65 93 60 07. ◯ daily.

The charming sanctuary in Mariánka, a small town northwest of Bratislava, is the oldest site of the Marian cult in the territory of the former Hungarian Kingdom. The Gothic **Church of Our Lady** (Panny Márie), built in 1377, was founded by King Louis I of Hungary. Inside are five Baroque altars dating from 1717–35. The jewel of the church is the wooden statue of Our Lady, dating probably from the 13th century, made famous by numerous miracles. In the 17th century, during the wars with Turkey, the revered statue was hidden five times in the nearby Pajštún Castle *(see below)*. The adjacent monastery is as old as the church. The building was given its present shape in 1711–14, when Cardinal Kristián August, Archbishop of Esztergom and Primate of Hungary, chose Mariánka – known at the time as Mariatál – for his summer residence.

Starting behind the church is a scenic footpath with thirteen Baroque Stations of the Cross. The path leads up to the site of a miraculous spring, which has a Baroque rotunda chapel built above it. Its founder, Count Jan Macholanyi, is depicted, with his family, in one of the ceiling paintings. Standing in front of the chapel are two Baroque statues by Georg Raphael Donner.

Environs

A popular but steep 90-minute walk from Mariánka via the town of Borinka leads to the remains of **Pajštún Castle**, once a magnificent Renaissance seat of the Pálffy family. The castle was unfortunately destroyed by a passing detachment of troops from Napoleon's army and today is just a pile of ruins. According to legend, the place is haunted by a knight on a charger, who each night jumps from the castle walls. The surrounding district offers several interesting and fairly difficult climbing trails.

Malacky Synagogue

Malacky ㉚

Road map C4. 🏠 17,770. 🚉 🚌
🛈 Radlinskeho 1. **Tel** (034) 796 61 00. **www**.malacky.sk

Belonging to the Balassy family, Malacky was granted town privileges in 1573. Its main attraction and a place of pilgrimage is the Baroque **Church of the Assumption of the Virgin Mary** (Nanebovzatia Panny Márie), built for the Franciscan order in 1653. Its "sacred stairs" are, according to tradition, a copy of those ascended by Christ as he entered the courtroom in Jerusalem, where he was sentenced to death. Pilgrims climb the ascending left-hand side of the staircase on their knees. Placed under every step are relics of saints. The right-hand side may be descended on foot. The entrance at the back of the church leads to the crypt, a resting place of members of the Pálffy family and several hundred Franciscan monks.

The **Synagogue**, built in 1886, sports a twin-towered façade, clearly inspired by Middle Eastern architecture.

🛈 **Church of the Assumption of the Virgin Mary**
◯ Mon, Wed, Fri.

Vel'ké Leváre ㉛

Road map C4. 🏠 3,220. 🚌

Once a military base guarding the borders of the Hungarian Kingdom, this small town was first mentioned in historic records in 1378. It has houses, quite unique in Europe, built by the Anabaptists (locally known as Habans), members of a religious community who arrived here in 1588 from Swiss and South German territories. They exerted an enormous influence on the life of the local population and left behind a number of fine historic buildings. The **Haban Houses** (Hábanske domy) display distinctive design and are often painted blue. A display of Haban pottery can also be seen. In 1981 Hábanský dvor (mansion) was declared a legally protected monument of folk architecture.

In the 16th century the Kollonič family, who originated from Croatia, built a three-wing Baroque **Palace** here, surrounded by a sprawling English-style garden. Both palace and garden are closed to visitors.

In 1729–33 Cardinal Žigmund Kollonič, Archbishop of Vienna, erected an imposing twin-towered parish church. Its consecration date coincided with the 50th anniversary of the victory over the Turks at Vienna, in 1683.

The Baroque Bernolákovo Palace, now a luxury hotel

The twin-towered parish church in Veľké Leváre

Bernolákovo ❷

Road map C4. 🏚 4,500. 🚉 🚌
🛈 Hlavná 111. **Tel** (02) 45 99 39 11.

From the 13th century until 1948 Bernolákovo was known as Čeklí. It was renamed in honour of Anton Bernolák, author of the first book on Slovak grammar, who was the local priest here between 1787 and 1791.

The vast **Bernolákovo Palace** is regarded as the finest piece of secular Baroque architecture in Slovakia. It was built during 1714–22 for the Esterházy family, to a design by Johann Bernard Fischer von Erlach. The three wings surround its exquisite courtyard. Each of them sports a tower and is covered with a differently shaped roof. The entrance

gate is adorned with the Esterházy family crest and rich ornaments. The buildings stand surrounded by a sprawling French-style park with allegorical statues by Ľudovít Gode. It also features the Baroque Chapel of St Anna, dating from 1716.

Now the palace has been turned into a luxury hotel, part of the Bratislava Golf and Country Club. It has both a nine and an 18-hole golf course, the latter being well-known throughout Europe.

Senec ❸

Road map C4. 🏚 14,700. 🚉 🚌
🛈 Mierové námestie 8. **Tel** (02) 45 92 32 06. **www**.senec.sk

The small town of Senec has been a major trading centre for many centuries and is now a gateway to the nearby Sunny Lakes resort. In Senec is one of the oldest relics of Renaissance architecture in Slovakia – the **Turkish House** (Turecký dom), which dates from 1560. The building, with its round

corner turret and scalloped roof parapet, was built by Kristóf Bat'an as the seat of the local administration. The building withstood attack by Turkish forces in 1663. It is now an upmarket restaurant.

While here it is worth taking a look at the Gothic **Church of St Nicolas** (sv. Mikuláš) surrounded by walls, built in 1326 and subsequently remodelled in Baroque style. Inside are four fine Rococo altars. The market square features a 16th-century pillory, used until 1848, and a Plague Column dating from 1747. The most interesting of the surrounding buildings is the crumbling **Synagogue**, built in 1904 in Art Nouveau style with the use of floral motifs. In 1930 Jews constituted about 25 per cent of the town's population, but since World War II they are a small community.

Two kilometres (1 mile) southeast of the town is the popular **Sunny Lakes** (Slnečné jazerá) resort built on the shores of two warm-water lakes, with hotels, camp sites, jetties, water slides and children's playgrounds.

The 1560 Turkish House in Senec

WEST SLOVAKIA

For visitors arriving first in the Slovak capital, Bratislava, West Slovakia becomes the gateway to the rest of the country. The main topographic features of the region are the great plain of the Danube river, the wide valley of the middle and lower Váh river and the gentle slopes of the Small Carpathian mountains stretching from the Váh valley to the outskirts of Bratislava.

The western section of Slovakia differs significantly from the rest of the country in that it is the most highly developed and most industrialized region. West Slovakia has few forests; the landscape consists mainly of flat, open plains, with rich, fertile soils. Its only mountain range, the Small Carpathians, is a low, undramatic chain.

The most interesting historic sights in West Slovakia are its old towns, Trnava and Nitra. The former, once referred to as the "Slovak Rome", owes this nickname to the impressive number of churches built within a small area of the historic town centre. Nitra was, in the early 9th century, the seat of the Slav ruler, Prince Pribina, the founder of the first Christian church in Slovak territory.

Visitors are drawn in their thousands to Piešt'any, famous for its spa centres, located on an island on the Váh river. Trenčianske Teplice is another historic spa. Nearby Trenčín boasts a history going back to the days of the Roman Empire. To this day there are the traces of a fortified camp of the Roman legions, Laugaricio.

In the 16th and 17th centuries, the southern part of the region was the scene of conflict due to the Ottoman Empire's expansion into the Kingdom of Hungary. During that time, a key role was played by the splendid Renaissance fortress, Nové Zámky; its loss in 1663 and subsequent recovery from Turkish hands after 22 years was an important chapter in the history of Christian-Ottoman conflict in Europe.

Trinity Column in Trojičné námestie, Trnava

◁ The imposing ruins of the clifftop Beckov Castle

Exploring West Slovakia

Slovakia's western region offers a wide variety of visitor attractions. Those interested in history will find here remnants of every era, ranging from the region's earliest civilizations, in Dunajská Streda, to the numerous magnificent Gothic, Renaissance, Baroque and Neo-Classical buildings in Trnava, Nitra and Levice. Nature lovers can enjoy the endless hiking trails that crisscross the Small Carpathians, while visitors seeking to improve their health can take advantage of the famous thermal waters of the Piešt'any spa.

SEE ALSO

- *Where to Stay* pp359–61
- *Where to Eat* pp391–2

St Nicholas's Church in Trnava

KEY

═══	Motorway
▬	Main road
═══	Minor road
─	Scenic route
┼─	Main railway
─	Minor railway
▬	International border
▬	Regional border
△	Summit

Map labels: 54, HOLÍČ 4, Kopčany, Radošovce, Nové Mesto nad Váhom, Brno, 51, Myjava, 581, ČACHTICE CASTLE 12, Čachtice, SENICA 3, 500, Dojč, BREZOVÁ POD BRADLOM 5, Košariská, Kúty, 499, 6, DOBROVODSKÝ CASTLE 6, PIEŠŤANY 10, D2, Morava, 501, PLAVECKÝ CASTLE 1, Plavecký Mikuláš, Záruby 767m △, 502, Smolenice Castle 2, SMOLENICE CASTLE, DOLNÁ KRUPÁ 7, D1, 2, Vápenná 752m △, Hlohovec, Malacky, 501, BRATISLAVSKÝ KRAJ, TRNAVA 8, Váh, 61, Lozorno, 502, Pezinok, 61, Sered, D2, Svätý Jur, TRNAVSKÝ KRAJ, 62, Rača, Senec, Sládkovičovo, 2, D1, GALANTA 18, BRATISLAVA, Zlaté Klasy, Vienna, Danube (Dunaj), 63, Malý Dunaj, 503, D4, 2, Horná Potôň, Šamorín, DUNAJSKÁ STREDA 9, Baka, Dolný Štál, 63, Vel'ký Meder, Medvedov, Gjôr

SIGHTS AT A GLANCE

Beckov Castle 13	Nitra 17
Brezová pod Bradlom 5	Nové Zámky 20
Čachtice Castle 12	Piešt'any 10
Dobrovodský Castle 6	Plavecký Castle 1
Dolná Krupá 7	Senica 3
Dunajská Streda 9	Smolenice Castle 2
Hlohovec 11	Topol'čiansky Castle 11
Holíč 4	Tovarniky Castle 16
Komárno 21	Trenčianske Teplice 15
Levice Castle 22	Trenčín 14
Mojmírovce Palace 19	*Trnava pp296–9* 8

0 kilometres 20

0 miles 10

Zlín

Žilina

57

Váh

61

Dubnica nad Váhom

50

D1

15 TRENČIANSKE
TEPLICE

14 🏛 ♟

TRENČÍN

**TRENČIANSKY
KRAJ**

13 ♟
BECKOV
CASTLE

50

Prievidza

Bánovce nad
Bebravou

11 TOPOĽČIANSKY
CASTLE

**TOVARNIKÝ
CASTLE** **16**

499

Radošina

Topoľčany

514

64

Preselány

Dolné
Trhovište

Výčapy
Opatovce

Zvolen

65

Lužianky

Koliňary

513

17 NITRA

🏛 ✝

511

Cabaj-
Čápor

Ivanka

51

19 MOJMÍROVCE
PALACE

22 LEVICE CASTLE 🏛

Kalnica

51

Saľa

Komjatíce

76

Hron

75

75

64

Tekovské
Lužany

Šarovce

Demandice

**NITRIANSKY
KRAJ**

Šurany

Želiezovce

573

75

Kolta

Pastovce

NOVÉ ZÁMKY **20** 🏛

Dvory
nad Žitavou

Pohronský
Ruskov

Kolárovo

Pribeta

76

Hurbanovo

Kamenny
Most

Salka

561

Váh

64

Svätý Peter

Gbelce

Zemianska
Olča

63

Mužla

Štúrovo

21 KOMÁRNO

63

Danube (Dunaj)

Budapest ↑

Beckov Castle on its rocky outcrop

GETTING AROUND

The predominantly lowland character of West
Slovakia means that its transport network is fairly
well developed. Good bases for exploring the
region are Bratislava and Trnava, which have
numerous transport links radiating outwards. The
main highway is the D1 motorway, which runs
southwest to northeast. Trains are also fast and
efficient along this northeast route via Trnava and
Trenčín. Buses are a better choice towards Nitra
and Levice, and a good bus network connects the
region's smaller towns and villages.

Portrait of Juraj Illésházy,
Trenčín Museum

Plavecký Castle ruins, in the Small Carpathian mountains

Plavecký Castle ❶

Road map C4. 35 km (22 miles) N of Senec. 🚌 to Plavecké Podhradie.

The lofty ruins of Plavecký Castle form a distinctive feature of the Small Carpathian mountains when viewed from the western side. The castle was built as a royal fortress guarding the border region in 1256–73. Many times remodelled since, it now bears traces of Gothic and Renaissance styles. From the 17th until the 20th century it was the property of the Pálffy family. In the early 18th century, following Rákóczi's anti-Habsburg insurrection in 1703 (see p263), the castle was captured by the emperor's army. Since then it has fallen into disrepair. In good weather the ruins can be reached by a half-hour uphill walk from the village of Plavecké Podhradie.

Smolenice Castle ❷

Road map D4. 20 km (12 miles) NW of Trnava. 🚌 **Tel** (033) 558 61 94 (hotel reception). www.kcsmolenice.sav.sk

In the foothills of the Small Carpathian mountains, Smolenice Castle towers above Smolenice village below. The castle was built in the 14th century as the final fortress defending the passes of this ╥╥╥╥╥╥╥╥╥╥╥╥╥╥╥ range. The site, which initially belonged to the king and subsequently to a series of Hungarian families, fell into ruin in the 18th century and in the following century was destroyed by fire. In the early

20th century its last owners – the Pálffy family – rebuilt the structure in the Gothic style.

Now the castle is used by the Slovak Academy of Science, mainly as a hotel and conference venue, and some of its rooms have been opened to the public. Surrounded by an English-style garden and located in an exceptionally beautiful area, the castle has a romantic, fairy-tale silhouette.

Senica ❸

Road map D3. 44 km (27 miles) NW of Trnava. 🏠 20,000. 🚆 Železničná. 🚌 Hurbanova. ℹ Bus terminal. **Tel** (034) 651 64 59. ◷ 9am–5pm Mon–Fri.

As recently as the early 20th century, Senica was a sleepy little town populated mostly by craftspeople and farm workers. Historic records mention the fact that shoemakers formed the most numerous group of local

tradespeople. Social and political changes turned it into a flourishing centre of trade and industry, with a 20,000-strong population. The Gothic **Chapel of St Anna** (sv. Anna) is the oldest historic relic in Senica. The Castle now houses the **Záhorská Gallery** (Záhorská galéria), whose collection documents the art of the Slovak-Czech-German-Hungarian border region. The building, designed by Viennese architect Franz A Hillebrandt, features an opulent columned hall on the ground floor, which is now used for exhibitions.

There is a **Catholic Church** dating from the first half of the 17th century and featuring an Early Baroque altarpiece.

The eastern part of the town has a fascinating **Jewish cemetery**, with original 18th- and 19th-century tombstones (masebhas).

Sculpture, Chapel of St Anna in Senica

🏛 **Záhorská Gallery**
Sadová 619/3. **Tel** (034) 651 29 37. ◷ Tue–Sun. 📷

Holíč ❹

Road map C3. 80 km (50 miles) N of Bratislava. 🏠 11,400. 🚌 ℹ Zámocká 2. **Tel** (034) 668 51 55.

Once an important border town, Holíč lies along the trading route that linked the two capital cities of Buda in Hungary and Prague in Bohemia. Duties levied on the transported goods

Entrance hall of Smolenice Castle

provided a major source of revenue for the local authorities. The main historic sight in Holíč is its Baroque **Castle**. This four-storey edifice built on a "U"-shaped floorplan, and enclosed within massive defensive walls and a moat, was once a Renaissance fortress built in the face of the Turkish threat. In the 18th century, Maria Theresa's husband, Francis Stephen of Lorraine, converted it into a Habsburg summer residence. Now it is a venue for cultural and folklore events, and houses the **Jaroslava Prílučíka Ethnographic Museum** (Mestské múzeum Jaroslava Prílučíka), the eclectic collection of one of the oldest inhabitants of Holíč.

↟ Jaroslava Prílučíka Ethnographic Museum
◯ *Mon–Sat.* 🖾

A house in Brezová pod Bradlom

Brezová pod Bradlom ❺

Road map D3. 48 km (30 miles) N of Trnava. 🚌

On top of Bradlom Hill, at 543 m (1,780 ft), stands the monumental tomb of General Milan Rastislav Štefánik (1880–1919), one of the founders of Czechoslovakia. The general, a close associate of Tomaš G Masaryk and Edvard Beneš, was killed in 1919 in an air crash near Bratislava, while returning to the country where he was due to assume the office of war minister in the newly formed government. The monument was built in 1927–8 to a design by Slovak architect Dušan Jurkovič. It is a vast structure of light grey stone. Steps lead up to the tomb, which has an obelisk at each corner.

Brezová pod Bradlom also has Slovakia's only monument to Jan Hus (*see pp36–7*).

Environs
The family home of General Štefánik, in the village of Košariská (4 km/2 miles from Brezová pod Bradlom), is an interesting **museum** devoted to his life.

↟ Štefánik Museum
***Tel** (034) 624 26 26.*
◯ *daily.*

View from Dobrovodský Castle

Dobrovodský Castle ❻

Road map D3. 30 km (19 miles) N of Trnava. 🚌

Standing on a wooded hill above the village of Dobrá Voda, Dobrovodský Castle belonged in the 14th century to the system of fortresses that guarded the road (no longer in existence) running along the ridge of the Small Carpathians. In the 16th century it was so vast that access to the upper castle was via three separate entrances, each protected by its own defensive wall.

In the ensuing centuries the importance of Dobrovodský Castle gradually diminished, and, following the 1762 fire that consumed the buildings, it was never rebuilt. Now the picturesque ruins are crumbling, although the remains of the two towers, the round turret, the entrance gate and the defensive walls are still very impressive.

Dolná Krupá ❼

Road map D3. 7 km (4 miles) NW of Trnava. 🏘 *2,250.* 🚌 *from Trnava.*

The Neo-Classical palace in Dolná Krupá was a stately home of the Brunswick family. This two-storey building with a columned portico was erected on earlier foundations in 1793–4.

The large English-style garden that stretches in front of the palace includes a small music pavilion, whose history is connected with the visits to Dolná Krupá by Ludwig van Beethoven who was friends with the Brunswick family. Tradition has it that it was here in 1801 that the composer wrote his famous *Moonlight Sonata*. The pavilion houses a small **Beethoven Museum** containing displays about his life and work.

↟ Beethoven Museum
***Tel** (033) 557 72 71.* ◯ *May–Sep: Tue–Sun; Oct–Apr: Mon–Fri.* 🖾

Neo-Classical Brunswick Palace in Dolná Krupá

Trnava 🔞

Trnava (Nagyszombat) was granted town privileges in 1238, making it one of Slovakia's oldest towns. In the 16th and 17th centuries, at the height of the Turkish threat, it was the seat of the Hungarian primate and the headquarters of the Church of Hungary. The town acquired numerous churches, convents and monasteries, becoming known as the "Slovak Rome". The first university in Hungary was founded here in 1635. Highlights for visitors are its religious buildings and relaxed ambience.

St Joseph's column in St Nicholas's Square

Exploring Trnava

The historic town centre is enclosed within the old walls, which form an almost complete square. The main Holy Trinity Square is at its heart. Among the restored historic buildings in the Old Town are some modern structures erected in the postwar years. The main shopping street is the pedestrianized Hlavná.

🏛 St Nicholas's Square

This spindle-shaped square (námestie sv. Mikuláša) by the old city walls was in the Middle Ages the focus of the town. At its centre is the 1731 Baroque column of St Joseph, surrounded by chapter buildings including the **Archbishop's Palace**. The Palace was built by Pietro and Antonio Spazzi in 1562. During the 16th and 17th centuries, this imposing Renaissance edifice was the seat of the Hungarian primates whose residence in Esztergom had been appropriated by the Turks. The archbishops went back to Esztergom in 1820, but a Slovak archbishopric was re-established here in 1990.

🔒 Cathedral of St Nicholas

The twin towers of the Cathedral of St Nicholas (sv. Mikuláša), with their distinctive bell-shape cupolas, are one of Trnava's chief landmarks. The church was built in 1380–1421. Its outside walls are supported by mighty buttresses, particularly imposing in the presbytery. The towers – initially of unequal size – were given their present shape after a fire in 1676. They are still not identical; a close look will reveal that the southern one is slightly narrower. Inside, the main attraction is the octagonal chapel of the Virgin Mary added in 1741 to the left aisle of the church. It contains the miraculous picture of the Trnava Madonna, which is particularly revered in Slovakia. The richly gilded Renaissance-Baroque main altarpiece dates from 1639. Built into the side walls of the chapels are a number of interesting Renaissance and Baroque tombstones.

The twin towers of St Nicolas's Cathedral

Interior of the Church of the Assumption of the Virgin Mary

🔒 Church of the Assumption of the Virgin Mary

The Order of the Poor Clares settled in Trnava during the Middle Ages. This church (Nanebovzatia Panny Márie) was built for the nuns in the 13th century as an aisleless Romanesque structure. Following a 17th-century fire it was extended and remodelled in the Baroque style, which can be seen to this day. The original features of the interior include the early 18th-century high altar and three side altars.

🏛 Museum of West Slovakia

Muzejné námestie 3. **Tel** (033) 551 29 14. ◯ 8am–5pm Tue–Fri, 11am–5pm Sat, Sun. 📷

One of the largest in West Slovakia, this interesting and varied museum (Západoslovenské múzeum) is housed in the 13th-century convent adjacent to the Church of the Assumption of the Virgin Mary. Following administrative restructuring of the empire's institutions carried out during the reign of Joseph II, the building became a military hospital, and then a warehouse. In 1954 it became a new museum with the aim of continuing Trnava's museum traditions.

The collections, on two floors of the building, are highly diverse and include archaeological finds, an exhibition of religious art, ethnography and natural history displays and a unique collection of bells.

⚙ Synagogue
Halenárska 2. **Tel** (033) 551 46 57. ◷ 10am–noon, 1–5pm Tue–Fri, 1–6pm Sat, Sun. **www**.snm.sk

The imposing edifice of Byzantine-Moorish style was built in the 19th century to a design by Viennese architect Jakub Gartner. Now it houses a centre of modern art and the Museum of Jewish Culture; it is also used as an exhibition and concert hall. Standing in front of the synagogue is a black marble monument designed by Artur

19th-century synagogue in Byzantine-Moorish style

Szalatnai-Slatinský dedicated to the memory of Trnava's Jews murdered in the Holocaust.

🏛 Music Museum
M S Trnavského 5. **Tel** (033) 551 25 56. ◷ 9am–5pm Tue–Fri, 11am–5pm Sat, Sun.

The Music Museum occupies Dom hudby, which used to be the home of one of Trnava's most famous citizens – the composer Mikulas Schneider Trnavský (1881–1958). It displays objects and mementos associated with the Slovak musician; it also serves as a concert venue.

🚩 University Church of St John the Baptist
See pp298–9.

⛪ Holy Trinity Square
The town's main square, Trojičné námestie, sports a lofty Municipal Tower dating from 1574, with a viewing gallery. Its cupola is crowned with a golden statue of Our Lady. There is also an 18th-century Plague Column. Close by is the 1831 **Municipal Theatre** (Trnavské divadlo), the oldest

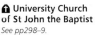
Holy Trinity statue, Holy Trinity Square

theatre building in Slovakia. Just north of the square, the Holy Trinity Church (now known in Slovak as Jesuitský kostol) was built in the early 18th century by the Trinitarian monks. It has been used by the Jesuits since 1853. To the west of the square is the single-towered Church of St Jacob (sv. Jakub), built in 1640 and given a Baroque remodelling in 1712.

🚩 Church of St Helen
Trnava's oldest church (sv. Helena), at the southern end of Hlavná, dates from the 14th century. Adjoining its north façade is the original tower with Gothic windows; seen above the portal are statues of the saints.

VISITORS' CHECKLIST
Road map D4. 46 km (28 miles) NE of Bratislava. 🚗 68,300.
🚍 Kollárova. 🚆 Staničná.
🛈 Trojičné námestie 1. **Tel** (033) 323 64 40. **Fax** (033) 551 10 22. ◷ 9am–5pm Mon–Fri; May–Sep: also 8am–noon Sat, 2–6pm Sun. **www**.trnava.sk

TRNAVA CITY CENTRE
Cathedral of St Nicholas ②
Church of the Assumption of the Virgin Mary ③
Church of St Helen ⑨
Holy Trinity Square ⑧
Museum of West Slovakia ④
Music Museum ⑥
St Nicholas's Square ①
Synagogue ⑤
University Church of St John the Baptist ⑦

0 metres   400
0 yards   400

Key to Symbols see back flap

RYBNÍKOVA
HORNÉ BASTY
University Church of St John the Baptist ⑦
INVALIDSKÁ
HLBOKÁ
ŠTEFÁNIKOVA
PEKÁRSKA
HORNOPOTOČNA
Cathedral of St Nicholas
ST NICHOLAS'S SQUARE ②
Music Museum ⑥ ①
Archbishop's Palace
HVIEZDOSLAVOVA
Holy Trinity Church
HOLY TRINITY SQUARE ⑧
Synagogue ⑤
HALENÁRSKA
Church of St Jacob
DIVADELNÁ
Municipal Theatre
ZAMOČNÍCKA
VAJANSKÉHO
TROJIČNÁ
HLAVNÁ
PAULÍNSKA
OROLSKÁ
KAPITULSKÁ
Church of the Assumption of the Virgin Mary ③
Museum of West Slovakia ④
HOSPODÁRSKA
Trnávka
STRELECKÁ
Church of St Helen ⑨

Train and bus stations
300 m (330 yards)

Trnava: University Church of St John the Baptist

The first monumental Baroque structure in Slovakia and one of the country's largest religious buildings, the University Church (Univerzitný kostol sv. Jána Krstitela) was constructed in 1629–37. The building, intended as the church for the Jesuit-run university, was founded by Count Miklós Esterházy. The first mass was celebrated here by the Archbishop of Esztergom, Imrich Lósi. From 1777, when the university was moved to Buda, the church was used by war veterans; later on it became the local parish church. It has a richly ornamented Italianate interior.

Main Façade
The twin-towered façade, divided by protruding cornices, is decorated with statues of St Joachim, St Anna, St Elizabeth and St Zachary.

Main Portal
The Latin inscription above the entrance mentions Count Miklós Esterházy, the church's founder.

Pilasters decorate the façade

Figures of the apostles were placed in niches on the south side

Interior
Walls, vault, arcades and windows are decorated with rich stucco ornamentation – figurative, floral and geometric — by Rossi, Tornini and Conti.

For hotels and restaurants in this region see pp359–61 and pp391–2

St John's Pulpit
The Baroque pulpit is decorated with figures depicting the Fathers of the Church. It was built in 1640 by B Kniling and V Stadler.

VISITORS' CHECKLIST

Univerzitne námestie.
Tel & **Fax** *(033) 551 45 86.*
◯ *May–Sep: 8am–noon, 2–5pm and 30 min before each mass.*
✝ *7:30am daily; 9:30 and 11:30am Sun.*
📷 📷

★ The High Altar
This magnificent Baroque gilded wooden altar-piece (1640) depicts the scene of Christ's baptism.

Ornate Door
Above the richly carved wooden door leading to the sacristy is an ornate metal grille with gilded elements.

★ Vaulted Ceiling
The paintings on the arched vaulting of the presbytery ceiling depict scenes from the life of St John the Baptist.

STAR FEATURES

★ The High Altar

★ Vaulted Ceiling

Distinctive modern buildings in Dunajská Streda town centre

Dunajská Streda ⑨

Road map D4. 45 km (28 miles) SE of Bratislava. 🏛 *10,000.* 🚉 🚌
ℹ️ *Hlavná 50.* **Tel** *(031) 555 65 21.*
🕐 *9am–5pm Mon–Fri.*

The town lies on Žitný ostrov, an island cut off from the main flow of the Danube by the Little Danube (Malý Dunaj). Archaeological discoveries here provide evidence of settlements in this area since the early Bronze Age and confirm the importance of the island under the Great Moravian Empire *(see p261).* The earliest written records of the town date from the 12th century. Materials relating to the island's colonization can be seen in the **Regional Museum** (Žitnoostrovné múzeum) in Žltý kaštel, a pleasant Neo-Classical building erected in the 18th century.
   The greatest attraction, however, is now the **town centre**, which in 1995–9 Imre Makovec returned to its former ambience by building a series of unusual white buildings with tiled roofs, decorated with arches, towers and wooden ornaments.

🏛 **Regional Museum**
Múzejná 2. **Tel** *(031) 552 24 02.*
🕐 *Tue–Sat.* 🎫

Piešt'any ⑩

Road map D3. 40 km (25 miles) S of Trenčín. 🏛 *30,000.* 🚉 🚌 *W of*
⬚⬚⬚⬚⬚⬚⬚ 🚌 ⬚⬚⬚⬚⬚⬚⬚ *P*
Tel *(033) 774 33 55.* 🕐 *9am–5pm Mon–Fri.* **www**.spapiestany.com

A health resort that is amous all over Europe, Piešt'any offers treatment for rheumatic and arthritic conditions. For

many years the town spa was owned by the Erdödy family, who in 1822 built the first spa house here. The town became a popular resort visited by Beethoven and Mucha, among others. The spa facilities are located on the edge of the beautiful park, on the right bank of the Váh river, and on the spa island. Near the park is a pavilion, built in 1894 and now housing a concert hall and the **Spa Museum** (Balneologické múzeum). The **Columned Bridge** to the island is a fine example of 1930s Functionalist architecture.

🏛 **Spa Museum**
Beethovenova 5. **Tel** *(033) 772 28 75.* 🕐 *Tue–Sun.*

Topol'čiansky Castle ⑪

Road map D3. 56 km (35 miles) NE of Trnava. 🚌 *to Podhradie.*

On a high rocky ledge above the village of Podhradie are the scenic ruins of

Topol'čiansky Castle, with a remarkable tower topped by a ridge roof. Originally a royal castle built in the mid-13th century, it became a stronghold of the Hussite army in 1431–4. In subsequent wars for control of Hungary it was captured and burned down, and later on changed hands many times. Its last owners, the Stummer family, abandoned what was left of the castle in the mid-18th century and moved to a large castle in Tovarníký *(see p304).*

Čachtice Castle ⑫

Road map D3. 15 km (9 miles) S of Beckov. 🚉 🚌 *to Čachtice.*

The conspicuous remnants of Čachtice Castle stand on a rocky hill (375 m/ 1,230 ft) between the towns of Čachtice and Višňové, offering a magnificent view of the surrounding area – the Small

Tower of Topol'čiansky Castle

Carpathians and the Myjava Plateau. This fortified stronghold, whose construction was started in the first half of the 13th century, was part of the defence system that guarded the western border of the Hungarian Kingdom. Over the following centuries the most famous person associated with Čachtice was the "Blood Countess" Elizabeth Báthory, wife of the district chief and Hungarian army captain, Ferenc Nádasdy. In 1585–1610 she ordered over 600 young girls to be

Čachtice Castle, dominating a rocky peak

blood, which she used to maintain her youth. The investigations confirmed the charges and Elizabeth was imprisoned for the rest of her life within the walls of her residence. In 1708 the castle was captured and from then on it began to fall into ruin.

Beckov Castle ⓭

Road map D3. 20 km (12 miles) SW of Trenčín. 🚌 🕐 *May–Oct: 9am–6pm Tue-Sun.*

The castle ruins, looming on top of the 70-m (230-ft) rock above the small town of Beckov, provide a truly unforgettable sight. The structure was built at the turn of the 12th and 13th centuries as a link in the chain of Hungarian fortifications stretching along the Váh river valley. In the 14th century the owner of Beckov was a powerful warlord, Matúš Čák. Later the castle – converted into a Gothic and Renaissance residence – was owned by the Stibor and Bánffy families. In 1729 the fortress burned down and was never rebuilt. Now the most impressive part is the upper castle with its grand rectangular tower. There are also ruins of two palaces and a chapel.

Beckov Castle, perched above a breathtaking drop

Trenčín ⓮

Road map D3. 80 km (50 miles) NE of Trnava. 🏠 *60,000.* 🚉 🚌 *Železničná.* ℹ️ *Sládkovičova.* **Tel** *(032) 743 35 05.* **www.**trencin.sk

Straddling the Váh river, the town of Trenčín has a well-preserved historic centre. In ancient times the site was occupied by a Roman military camp, Laugaricio. It is still possible to see an inscription carved into the rock face below the castle concerning the victorious battle fought here in AD 179 with the German tribe the Quadi.

Trenčín's huge Gothic **Castle** *(see pp302–3)* has recently undergone a thorough restoration. Built in the 11th century, it became, two centuries later, the property of Matúš Čák, one of Hungary's most powerful

magnates, the "Lord of the Váh and the Tatras". The dominant feature of the castle's silhouette is its tower, Matúšova veža, erected during the times of Čák. Adjoining it are the stately Gothic palaces built by Sigismund of Luxemburg and Louis of Hungary. Now they are occupied by the **Trenčín Museum** (Trenčinaske múzeum) as an exhibition venue, with reconstructed interiors of 11th-century feudal houses; a gallery of paintings from the Illésházy family estate; and an exhibition of historic arms. In the courtyard is Omar's well, 80 m (260 ft) deep, which was dug between 1557 and 1570.

The town itself centres on the main square, Mierové

Bathhouse in the Sina sanatorium, in Trenčianske Teplice

námestie. The Baroque **Piarist Church** (Piaristický kostol) here, from the mid-17th century, has attractive trompel'oeil paintings. The yellow Parish Church (Farský kostol), at the base of the lane to the castle, was rebuilt after a fire in 1528.

⚓ **Trenčín Castle**
Tel *(032) 743 56 57.* 🕐 *daily.* 📷
🏛 **Trenčín Museum**
Mierové námestie 46. **Tel** *(032) 743 44 31.* 🕐 *Tue–Sun.*

Trenčianske Teplice ⓯

Road map D3. 14 km (9 miles) E of Trenčín. 🏠 *5,000.* 🚉 🚌 🎬 *ArtFilm Festival (late Jun).* **www.**teplice.sk

The spa town of Trenčianske Teplice has a beautiful location on a site rich in mineral waters, which from the 14th century were known throughout the Hungarian kingdom for their therapeutic properties. From 1582 the town belonged to the aristocratic Hungarian Illésházy family. The most famous building is the Turkish bathhouse (1888), in which Moorish arches surround the central courtyard with spa waters spouting from stone fountains; women are not allowed in. There is also an exotic bathhouse in the 19th-century Sina sanitorium.

Trenčín Castle above the historic town of Trenčín ▷

Tovarniky Castle ⑯

Road map D3. 6 km (4 miles) NW of
Topol'čany. 🚌 to Topol'čany ⬤ to
the public.

The small town of Tovarnicky
boasts a large castle. This
fortified structure, surrounded
by a moat, was built during
the time of the Turkish threat.
In the late 18th century it was
remodelled to form a
comfortable Baroque
residence. The extensive
rebuilding turned the former
closed quadrangle of the
walls into a three-wing palace
with attractive two-colour
façade decorations and
mouldings, and a courtyard
open on one side.

Inhabited until 1945, the
castle later fell into disrepair.
In recent years both castle
and grounds have been
undergoing a complete
reconstruction. The works,
carried out by private owners,
are still not finished, but it is
already possible to see from
the outside the restored
buildings, which are set in a
beautiful English-style garden.

Tovarniky Castle and gardens

Romanesque rotunda at
St Emeram's Cathedral in Nitra

Nitra ⑰

Road map D4. 90 km (56 miles) E
of Bratislava. 🚗 90,000. 🚉 🚌
Stanična. 🚊 Štefánikova 1.
Tel (037) 741 09 06. **www**.nitra.sk

In early medieval times
Nitra was already a political
and commercial centre of the
Slav tribes north of the
Danube. At the turn of the 8th
century this area was an independent principality, ruled by

Prince Pribina, the first known
ruler of the Slavs. The Turks
caused great destruction here
in the 16th and 17th centuries.
Since the 19th century Nitra
has grown into a sprawling
modern city.

The old town's dominant
feature is the **Castle**, on a
rocky ledge in the crook of the
Nitra river. It is surrounded by
17th-century walls whose one
gate is accessed via a stone
bridge. The main building of
the castle complex is **St
Emeram's Cathedral**
(Katedrálny Biskupský Chrám
sv. Emerama), consisting of
three churches that were joined
in the 18th century. They
comprise the 11th-century
Romanesque rotunda of St
Emeram, the Gothic upper
church, and the lower church
built in the 17th century.

At the foot of the castle is
the Upper Town. Its centre,
Pribinovo námestie, is flanked
by Baroque and Neo-
Classical buildings. On the
south side is the **Grand
Seminary**, now housing the
Diocesan Library (Diecézna
knižnica) with its valuable
collection of books and
incunabula. Situated
outside the walls is the
Lower Town with a
twin-towered **Piarist
Church** (kostol
Piaristov), containing
magnificent frescoes.

The striking 1991
Andrej Bagar Theatre
(Divadlo Andrej Bagara)
overshadows the Neo-
Renaissance town hall,
which houses the **Nitra
Museum** (Nitranske
múzeum). In the
museum are displays
on archaeology,
history and the
natural world.

Just east of the Nitra river is
the **Slovak Agricultural
Museum** (Slovenské
pol'nohospodarské múzeum),
a fascinating collection of
reconstructed traditional farm
buildings, shops and houses,
with original machinery.

🏛 **Nitra Museum**
Štefánikova trieda 1. **Tel** (037) 651
00 00. ⬤ Tue–Sun. 🖼

🏛 **Slovak Agricultural
Museum**
Dlhá 92. **Tel** (037) 657 25 53.
⬤ Mar–Oct: Tue–Sun.

Galanta ⑱

Road map D4. 35 km (22 miles) E of
Bratislava. 🚗 16,000. 🚉 🚌

Founded in the 13th century,
Galanta is in the Danube
Lowland. It has two Esterházy
palaces. The **Renaissance
Palace** (Renesaníný kástiel)
houses exhibits on the
town's history, the
Esterházy family, and
the Hungarian com-
poser Zoltán Kodály.
The other palace, not
open to the public, was
built in 1860 in English
Neo-Gothic style.

♣ **Renaissance Palace**
Esterházyovcov.
⬤ Tue–Sun. 🖼

Mojmírovce
Palace ⑲

Road map D4. 15 km (9
miles) S of Nitra. 🚌
Tel (037) 779 82 01.

The history of
Mojmírovce
Palace (Kaštiel
Mojmírovce) is

Statue of St Urban in
Mojmírovice Park

linked with the members of the Huňady family, who settled here in about 1657 and soon became the richest local landowners. In 1721 Huňady built an opulent Baroque residence, and close to it established a park with many exotic trees and shrubs, regarded as one of the most magnificent in the Hungarian Kingdom. They also founded a famous horse stud. The family members lived in the palace until the end of World War II.

After 1945 the building was used as an army hotel, a surgery and a school, until 1960, when it was left to deteriorate. Now, following its reconstruction and modernization, it has been made into a luxury hotel, which still attracts visitors with its magnificent park surroundings.

Nové Zámky ⓴

Road map D4. 39 km (24 miles) S of Nitra. 🏙 42,000. 🚉

In the 16th century, Nové Zamký had a powerful **fortress**, intended to resist the attacks by the Turks. Built in 1576–80 and based on the finest models of Renaissance military architecture, the fortress was hexagonal in shape, with solid bastions at each corner. After the Turkish expansionist threat, the fortress ceased to have any military significance, and it was demolished on the orders of Emperor Charles VI in 1724. One of its remaining mementos is the historic Calvary – a set of Late-Baroque Stations of the Cross, dating from 1779, in the southeast section of the fortifications.

Also in the town are the 17th-century Franciscan Church and Monastery, now the home of the **Regional Museum** (Múzeum Jána Thaina), which has displays on local history and weaponry. The Trinity Column in Hlavné Námesti dates from 1749.

🏛 **Regional Museum**
Pribinova 6. **Tel** (035) 640 00 32.
⭕ Tue–Sat.

Part of Europe Place in Komárno

Komárno ㉑

Road map D4. 72 km (45 miles) S of Nitra. 🏙 40,000. 🚉 🚌 1.5 km (1 mile) from town centre.
🛈 Župná 5. **Tel** (035) 773 00 63.
🎪 Komárno Days (late Apr–early May); Komárno Lehara (late Apr).

Situated on the Slovak-Hungarian border, at the point where the Váh flows into the Danube, Komárno was mentioned in historic records under the name of Camarum as early as 1205. The original trading settlement, along a key transport route that crossed the Danube, was devastated by the Mongol raid of 1243. In 1745 Komárno was granted the status of a royal free town by Empress Maria Theresa.

The town is worth visiting, not for its historic buildings, as few remain, but as a major centre of Slovak national minorities. Its street signs are in both Slovak and Hungarian, and the Hungarian influence is strong. Komárno Days festival is a lively event celebrating Slovak and Hungarian cultures. Every other year another festival, the Komárno Lehara, includes a singing competition in honour of Franz Lehár (1870–1948), the composer of famous operettas and a native of Komárno.

The modern complex known as Europe Place

A female deity figure, Levice Regional Museum

(Nádvorí Európy) comprises pavilions in a variety of architectural styles from different parts of Europe. There are also fountains, statues and a viewing tower. The whole thing constitutes an unusual shopping and leisure centre, the largest in this part of Slovakia.

Levice Castle ㉒

Road map D4. 60 km (37 miles) E of Nitra. 🚉 🚌

The castle in Levice was built in the second half of the 13th century to defend the monastery in Hronsky Baňadik and the mining centres to the north. Its central structures were the Gothic palace and the round tower. In the 16th century Levice became one of the 15 fortresses defending the country against attacks by the Turks. Castle fortifications were so powerful that they withstood the 1578 siege by the Sultan's army. The Turks captured Levice only in 1663, but the next year they were defeated in the great battle at the gates of the fortress, by the Emperor's army led by Louis de Souches.

The castle was destroyed during Rákóczi's insurrection against the Habsburgs, in 1703 (see p263). The Esterházy family, which became the owners of Levice in the 18th century, decided not to rebuild it. Even so, the ruins of the castle are well preserved. The Renaissance building (1571) in the lower courtyard houses an interesting **Regional Museum** with exhibits on the history of the castle and local archaeology.

🏛 **Regional Museum**
Sv. Michala 40. **Tel** (036) 631 21 12. ⭕ daily (Nov–Mar: closed Sat).

CENTRAL SLOVAKIA

*M*any people regard the central region of Slovakia as the true heart of the country, not only geographically, but also in a spiritual sense. There is no doubt that the region played a crucial part in building Slovak national identity, and – particularly in the eyes of foreigners – presents the most stereotypical image of Slovakia as the land of mountains, castles and caves.

There are many reasons why Central Slovakia is regarded as the region that made the greatest contributions to the country's history. It was here, in 1861, that the plan for national rebirth was unveiled; here the Slovak language was codified for the first time; and here the Slovak National Uprising against the Nazis broke out in 1944. In the local mountains the most famous Slovak outlaw, the brave Jánošík, robbed the rich and helped the poor. This is also the only land mentioned in the Slovak national anthem, *Thunder above the Tatras*.

Situated in the northern part of the region, the Tatras are the highest and most formidable mountains in Slovakia. Shrouded in legends, photographed, painted and described by countless artists, throughout the year they attract visitors for rock-climbing, hiking and skiing. It is worth combining a visit to the Tatras with a trip to the neighbouring Pieniny – beautiful "small-scale" mountains on the border with Poland, which are famous for the scenic Dunajec canyon.

The urban heart of Central Slovakia is Banská Bystrica, a town filled with magnificent historic sights, many of them bearing witness to the past history of the region, which grew rich on the mining of gold, silver and other precious metals. Other man-made attractions in Central Slovakia include numerous architectural sights, such as the fairy-tale castle in Bojnice; Oravský Castle, perched on a craggy cliff; and the timber houses in Čičmany and other villages.

View of snowy peaks in the Tatras, from Starý Smokovec

◁ White, geometric decoration on the façade of a house in Čičmany

Exploring Central Slovakia

Central Slovakia offers numerous attractions, not only for those interested in history and folklore, but also for sports enthusiasts. This is primarily a mountainous region, encompassing the bleak High Tatras, and the gentler, forested Low Tatras. In these areas, winter travel, even by car, can prove very difficult, particularly in bad weather. At any time of the year, be prepared for sudden changes in weather and temperature. The cities and villages provide good bases for exploring the countryside and are interesting destinations in themselves.

SEE ALSO

• *Where to Stay* pp362–4

• *Where to Eat* pp392–4

Part of the castle complex,
Banská Bystrica

SIGHTS AT A GLANCE

A 15th-century work by
an unknown artist in
Zvolen Fortress

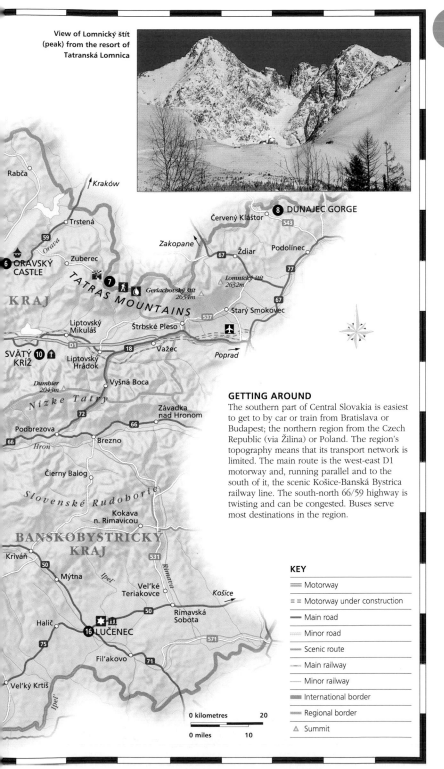

View of Lomnický štít (peak) from the resort of Tatranská Lomnica

Rabča

Kraków

Trstená

8 DUNAJEC GORGE

Červený Kláštor

543

Zakopane

67 Ždiar

Podolínec

77

59

Orava

6 ORAVSKÝ CASTLE

Zuberec

Lomnický štít 2632m

7

Gerlachovský štít 2654m

T A T R A S   M O U N T A I N S

67

537 Starý Smokovec

K R A J

Liptovský Mikuláš

Štrbské Pleso

D1

18 Važec

Poprad

SVÄTÝ KRÍŽ 10

Liptovský Hrádok

Dumbier 2043m

Vyšná Boca

N i z k e   T a t r y

Závadka nad Hronom

72

66

Podbrezová

66 *Hron*

Brezno

Čierny Balog

S l o v e n s k é   R u d o h o r i e

Kokava n. Rimavicou

BANSKOBYSTRICKÝ KRAJ

Kriváň

50

Mýtna

Ipeľ

531

Rimava

Veľké Teriakovce

Košice

50

Rimavská Sobota

Halič

16 LUČENEC

571

75

Fiľakovo

71

Veľký Krtíš

Ipeľ

GETTING AROUND

The southern part of Central Slovakia is easiest to get to by car or train from Bratislava or Budapest; the northern region from the Czech Republic (via Žilina) or Poland. The region's topography means that its transport network is limited. The main route is the west-east D1 motorway and, running parallel and to the south of it, the scenic Košice-Banská Bystrica railway line. The south-north 66/59 highway is twisting and can be congested. Buses serve most destinations in the region.

KEY

▬▬	Motorway
= =	Motorway under construction
▬	Main road
⋯	Minor road
—	Scenic route
⋯	Main railway
—	Minor railway
▬	International border
▬	Regional border
△	Summit

0 kilometres   20

0 miles   10

For additional map symbols *see back flap*

Banská Bystrica ❶

Bańska Bystrica (Neusohl) is one of Slovakia's oldest towns. In 1255 it was granted royal privileges associated with the mining of gold, silver and copper, which brought wealth to the town and its inhabitants from medieval times. The town's prosperity is evident in many fine examples of religious and secular architecture. Banská Bystrica's main contribution to modern history is that in 1944 it became the centre of the Slovak National Uprising (Slovenské národné povstanie, or SNP).

The house at the end of Národna, with a passage to the market square

Exploring the town

The historic sights are concentrated on the route that runs along the pedestrianized Dolná, the large market square Námestie SNP, and Horná. The middle section of this area is occupied by Námestie Štefana Moyzesa – the central square, flanked by buildings of the old castle complex. Built in the 12th and 13th centuries, it consists of both religious and secular buildings. All that remains of the original town walls and the castle's 18 bastions are three bastions and one long section of the wall within the castle area. The castle complex also includes the parish Church of Our Lady (see pp312–13); the Church of the Holy Cross; the Matthias House; the barbican with a tower; and the town hall.

🔒 Church of the Holy Cross

🚫 for reconstruction works.
✝ 9am Sun.
This aisleless, Late-Gothic church (Hrend Pelho ha Kríža), dating from 1492, was once known as the "Slovak church", since the majority of its congregation consisted of Slovaks. In 1782 a new entrance was added on the

south side, with a carved date 1452, instead of 1492, on the portal. The interesting features of the interior include the 1652 stone font and the main altarpiece with statues of the Virgin Mary and Mary Magdalene, the work of Vavrinec Dunajský in 1834.

🏛 Matthias House

The astonishingly tall, six-storey Matthias House (Matejov dom) was built in 1479 for Beatrice, wife of the Hungarian King Matthias Corvinus. The south façade sports a Gothic portal, a stone balcony and the coats of arms

The Old Town Hall (1500)

of Matthias Corvinus and of the town, the latter dated 1479. Behind the Matthias House is the old cemetery.

🏛 Barbican and Town Walls

In the 16th century the town was surrounded by mighty walls intended to protect it against Turkish invasion. Only some of the old fortifications have survived. Still standing are the Pisárska, Banicka and Fraska bastions. The former defence tower with a draw-bridge and barbican is in Námestie Štefana Moyzesa. Hanging inside the tower are three bells; the heaviest weighs nearly 10 tonnes.

🔒 Church of Our Lady

See pp312–13.

🏛 Old Town Hall

Municipal Gallery Námestie Štefana Moyzesa 25. **Tel** (048) 412 48 64. ◯ 9am–5pm Tue–Fri, 10am–4pm Sat, Sun.
Adjacent to the Church of Our Lady is the Old Town Hall (Stará radnica), a plain white building with a small tower and an arcaded loggia. Built in about 1500, it was remodelled in Renaissance style, in the second half of the 16th century. Now it is the home of Banská Bystrica's Municipal Gallery (Štátna galéria).

🏛 Námestie SNP

Central Slovak Museum Tel (048) 412 58 97. ◯ 9am–5pm Mon–Fri, 1– 4pm Sun (also Jul–Aug: 9am–1pm Sat).
Thurzo House (Thurzov dom) is the most beautiful building in the market square. Its core consists of two Gothic houses, which at the turn of the 15th and 16th centuries became the property of the Thurzo family. The building was given its present appearance in the second half of the 16th century, when its façade was decorated with Renaissance sgraffito. Since 1958 the palace has been the home of the **Central Slovak Museum** (Stredoslovenské múzeum). Its

collections illustrate the region's history, from prehistoric times to the early 20th century.

The Renaissance **clock tower** was built in 1552. In the past it served as an observation post, a prison and torture chamber. During reconstruction works carried out in 1762 and 1784 it was found that the tower was not vertical. Now its top is out of line by 68 cm (27 in). In the 19th century brass bands used to give concerts from the top-floor gallery. The place offers a magnificent view of the entire town and environs.

The 18th-century Jesuit church standing at the corner of the square, designed in Early-Baroque style, was modelled on the Il Gesú church in Rome. The resemblance is, however, far from obvious, particularly since in 1844 the church was given two square towers without cupolas.

The Baroque Marian column at one corner of the square dates from 1719. In the late 1960s it was decided to remove this from Námestie SNP and replace it with a granite obelisk honouring the Red

Detail of the house at No. 9 Dolná

Army. The column was moved to a position in front of the Church of Our Lady. It was returned to its original site in 1993.

🏠 Dolná

At the extension of Námestie SNP are two streets with historic houses: Horná (Upper) and Dolná (Lower). **Bethlenov dom** at No. 8 Dolná is where in 1620 the Hungarian parliament elected Gábor Bethlen, prince of Transylvania, as the king of Hungary. The Latin inscription on the façade reads: "The Lord's blessing enriches the common people". The tower at the side of the courtyard is an original medieval structure.

The striking silhouette of the SNP Museum

VISITORS' CHECKLIST

Road map E3. 🏘 82,100.
🚉 🚌 1 km (0.5 mile) E of town centre; local train station just over Hron river S of town centre.
ℹ️ Námestie SNP 14. **Tel** (048) 415 50 85. ⏰ Oct–Apr: 9am–5pm Mon–Fri; May–Sep: 8am–7pm Mon–Fri, 9am–1pm Sat.

🏛 SNP Museum

Kapitulská 23. **Tel** (048) 412 32 58.
⏰ 9am–6pm Tue–Sun (to 4pm Oct–Apr). **www**.muzeumsnp.sk
The Museum of the Slovak National Uprising is housed in a concrete building in two sections linked by a bridge. The building was erected in 1965, to a design by Dušan Kuzma. The extensive exhibits focus on the history of Slovakia in 1938–1945, with particular emphasis on the 1944 uprising against the Nazis, and on the fate of Slovak Jews. The surrounding park contains an exhibition of the weapons used by the insurgents, including tanks. Among its most interesting exhibits is an original Li-2 aircraft with full interior equipment, with visitor access.

BANSKÁ BYSTRICA TOWN CENTRE

Barbican and Town Walls ③
Church of the Holy Cross ①
Church of Our Lady ④
Dolná ⑦
Matthias House ②
Námestie SNP ⑥
Old Town Hall ⑤
SNP Museum ⑧

0 metres 200
0 yards 200

Key to Symbols see back flap

Banská Bystrica: Church of Our Lady

Construction of the church (Nanebovzatia Panny Márie) began in 1255. In the early 14th century the church was widened and given a Gothic sacristy. Two centuries later it acquired the presbytery, the oratory and the side chapels, and its famous altar of St Barbara. Following a great fire in 1761 the church was rebuilt in Baroque style; in 1770 its interior was given new, magnificent furnishings.

View of the Church
The church's tower – grey with red decorations – is a town landmark. The simple arches of the tower windows indicate their Romanesque origin.

Interior
The most striking features of the beautiful interior are the pulpit and the organ loft. The bronze font, by Master Jodok, is a masterpiece of medieval metalwork.

★ Altar of St Barbara
The ornate Gothic altar-piece of St Barbara (patron saint of miners), in the north side chapel, is the church's greatest treasure. Made by Master Pavol of Levoča, it depicts the Madonna and Child, St Barbara and St Jerome.

Christ on the Mount of Olives
The vivid Baroque sculpture outside the church depicting Christ and saints was renovated in 1995.

Vault Paintings

The imposing Baroque paintings covering the barrel-vault are by Anton Schmidt. They were made during the renovation of the church, which followed the 1761 town fire.

VISITORS' CHECKLIST

Námestie Š Moyzesa.
Tel (048) 412 45 31.
6:30am, 4:40pm daily:
7am, 8:30am, 9:45am, 11am
(children), 4:30pm Sun.
only during mass and
celebrations.

Main Altarpiece

Paintings in the main altarpiece (1774) are by Jan Lukas Kracker. They portray the Assumption of the Virgin Mary and the Holy Trinity.

★ Side Altar

The south chapel, to the right of the nave, contains a 15th-century Gothic triptych of St Mary Magdalene, one of the most treasured items of the church's original furnishings.

Porch

The "new" main entrance in the porch, with a stellar vault and an attractive portal, was added in 1473–1516.

STAR FEATURES

★ Altar of St Barbara

★ Side Altar

Zvolen Castle, a superbly preserved example of Gothic-Renaissance architecture

Zvolen ❷

Road map D3. 20 km (12 miles) S of Banská Bystrica. 42,000.
Námestie Svobody 22. **Tel** *(045) 530 32 19.* 9am–5pm Mon–Fri. **www**.zvolen.net

A settlement was established here by Bela IV in the mid-13th century. In 1326 Zvolen, known at the time in German as Altsohl, and in Hungarian as Zólyom, was granted town privileges. It soon became a trading centre and in the 19th century also a centre of the timber industry.

Zvolen Castle is in the town centre. Construction began in the reign of King Louis of Hungary, before 1382. At the start of the 15th century it became the property of the Thurzos, one of Hungary's richest families. The new owners rebuilt the castle in Renaissance style and reinforced its system of fortifications. Now, carefully restored, it is one of Slovakia's best-preserved examples of 16th-century architecture. The castle chapel has a Gothic portal. In the 18th-century Baroque hall is a magnificent coffered ceiling divided into 78 fields filled with portraits of Habsburg kings and emperors. The castle houses permanent exhibitions of Gothic stonework and 16th–18th-century Tuscan art from the Slovak National Museum.

In the market square is the late 14th-century Catholic **Church of St Elizabeth** (sv. Alžbety). Inside is the chapel of Our Lady of Sorrows, dating from 1650. Amid the Gothic and Renaissance houses on the square is the Protestant **Church of the Holy Trinity** (sv. Trojice), built in 1921–3. It includes a Neo-Gothic altarpiece with a huge figure of Christ.

On the southwestern outskirts of the town are the ruins of **Pusty Fortress**. Scattered over a vast area in the middle of a forest are fragments of walls, bastions and gates of one of the biggest fortresses in medieval Europe.

♠ Zvolen Castle
Tue–Sun. Tue (Oct–Apr).

The Hall of Mirrors in the Palace of St Anton near Banská Štiavnica

Banská Štiavnica ❸

Road map D4. 40 km (25 miles) S of Banská Bystrica. 10,000.
Námestie sv. Trojice 6. **Tel** *(045) 692 05 25.* www.banskastiavnica.sk

Between the 13th and 18th centuries Banská Štiavnica was one of Europe's main mining centres, and grew into the third-largest town in the Hungarian Kingdom. At the centre is Holy Trinity square (Námestie sv. Trojice), lined with Gothic and Renaissance houses. It has a sandstone Baroque Holy Trinity monument. On the south side is the 15th-century **Church of St Catherine** (sv. Katerína), with lovely net vaulting.

The **Old Castle** (Starý zámok) was turned from a church into a fortress when the town was threatened by the Turks. Currently being restored, it has some interesting artifacts. The whitewashed **New Castle** (Nový zámok), on a hillock to the south of the centre, was also built against the Turks. The town has a magnificent **Mining Museum** (Banské múzeum), with several sites, including an open-air area outside the centre.

♠ Old Castle
Starozámocká 11. **Tel** (045) 691 31 13. May–Sep: daily; Jan, Mar, Apr, Dec: Tue–Sun; Feb, Oct, Nov: Tue–Fri.

♠ New Castle
Novozámocká 22. **Tel** (045) 691 15 43. May–Sep: daily; Feb, Mar: Tue–Sun; Jan, Apr: Tue–Fri.

🏛 Mining Museum
Kammerhofská 2. **Tel** (045) 694 94 22. May–Sep: daily; Jan, Feb: Tue–Fri; Mar, Apr, Oct–Dec: Mon–Fri. www.muzeumbs.sk

Environs
In the village of Antol, 5 km (3 miles) southeast of Banská Štiavnica, is the Baroque **Palace of St Anton**, with beautiful interiors. It houses a museum.

♠ Palace of St Anton
Tel (045) 691 39 32. May–Sep: Tue–Sun; Oct–Apr: Tue–Sat. 2 routes.

Kremnica ❹

Road map D3. 20 km (12 miles) W of Banská Bystrica. 🏠 6,000. 🚆 ⛟ 🛈 *Štefánikovo námestie 35/44*. **Tel** *(045) 674 28 56*.

This little mountain town was one of the richest in the Hungarian Kingdom from the 14th to the 19th centuries. Its source of wealth was the nearby gold mines. The history of gold mining and of the mint, which minted the highly valued "Kremnica ducats", and which still operates, are traced in the interesting **Museum of Coins and Medals** (Múzeum mincí a medailí) in the main square, Štefánikovo námestie. Also in the square is a gold-covered Baroque Marian column. In the 15th-century **Castle** is the Gothic **Church of St Catherine** (sv. Katerína).

🏛 **Museum of Coins and Medals**
Štefánikovo námestie 10/19. **Tel** *045) 674 26 96*. ◯ *Tue–Sat*. 📷

Statue of St Stephen, Church of St Catherine, Kremnica

Martin ❺

Road map D3. 68 km (42 miles) NW of Banská Bystrica. 🏠 61,000. 🚆 *Bitánkova*. ⛟ 🛈 *M.R. Štefánika 9/A*. **Tel** *(043) 423 87 76*. ◯ *9am–5pm Mon–Fri, 9am–1pm Sat*.

A symbol of the Slovaks' struggle for a place among the nation states of Europe,

Gothic Church of St Martin in historic Martin

Martin was where the famous Martin Memorandum was announced in 1861 proclaiming the Slovak national rebirth programme. In 1918 the Slovak National Council approved the Martin Declaration expressing the wish to form, with the Czechs, the state of Czechoslovakia.

The town is rich in historic sites, such as the 13th-century **Church of St Martin** (sv. Martin). The **Slovak National Museum in Martin** (Slovenské národné múzeum) has many collections, both in the main building and in branches, mainly focusing on Slovak folk exhibits. One of the most spectacular is the **Slovak Village Museum** (Múzeum slovenskej dediny). This open-air museum 2 km (1 mile) south of the town is a huge collection of traditional wooden buildings principally from the Orava region in the north of Slovakia.

🏛 **Slovak National Museum in Martin**
Malá Hora 2. **Tel** *(043) 413 10 11*. ◯ *Tue–Sun*. 📷 www.snm.sk

🏛 **Slovak Village Museum**
Jahodnícke Háje. **Tel** *(043) 413 26 86*. ◯ *Tue–Sun (Jul, Aug: daily)*. 📷

Oravský Castle ❻

Road map E3. 80 km (50 miles) N of Banská Bystrica. 🚆 ⛟ *to Oravský Podzámok*. **Tel** *(043) 581 61 11*. ◯ *May–Mar: daily*. 📷

Resembling an eagle's nest clinging to a mighty 120-m (400-ft) cliff, Oravský Castle is first mentioned in historical records of 1267. New parts of the castle were added gradually to the original citadel up until the 17th century. In 1800 the castle burned down, and restoration began only in 1953. Some of the castle's quarters are now used by the Orava Museum to display its archaeological, historical and ethnographic collections.

Viewing terrace on the walls of the Oravský Castle

SLOVAK TRADITIONAL ARCHITECTURE

Historic wooden buildings are among Slovakia's greatest attractions. In almost every village it is still possible to see buildings erected centuries ago, using traditional methods, often without the use of nails. Many regions feature conservation sites of traditional architecture. The best known are Vlkolínec and Čičmany *(see p322)*, both in Central Slovakia. Many treasures of traditional architecture have been gathered in open-air museums (skansen). The largest of them, the Slovak Village Museum in Martin, features 100 houses from northern Slovakia. In East Slovakia, in Bardejov *(see p333)*, is one of the oldest open-air museums. In the same region are the Unitarian churches in the area around Svidník *(see p333)*.

A timber house (1792) in the Slovak Village Museum

Tatras Mountains 7

Logo of the Tatra National Park

Slovakia's Northern Tatras mountains consist of three ranges: the Western Tatras (Západné Tatry), the High Tatras (Vysoké Tatry) and the small area of Belianské Tatry, a strictly protected reserve that is closed to the public. All are within the Tatra National Park. The most spectacular range, the High Tatras, is a magnet for walkers.

View from Around Zuberec
Zuberec, a village at the mouth of the Rohácska Dolina (valley), affords magnificent views of Rohače, the start of the Western Tatras.

Roháčsky Waterfall
This is one of the most scenic attractions of the 5-km (3-mile) long post-glacial valley, Roháčska Dolina.

Habovka

Osobitá *1687 m (5535 ft)*

Zuberec

1663 m (5456 ft)

Grzes *1653 m (5423 ft)*

Krzesanica *2122 m (6962 ft)*

Salatin *2050 m (6726 ft)*

1806 m (5925 ft)

Volovec *2064 m (6772 ft)*

2176 m (7139 ft)

2158 m (7080 ft)

Baranec *2184 m (7165 ft)*

2194 m (7198 ft)

Bystrá *2248 m (7375 ft)*

Kamienista *2121 m (6959 ft)*

WESTERN TATRAS

LIPTOVSKÉ TATRY

Jaloveckýp.

584

Liptovský Mikuláš
The town, in a valley surrounded by peaks, is an interesting and convenient base for the Liptov region.

Brobrovec

Smertianka

Liptovský Mikuláš

537

Belá

Pribylina

Hybica

973

D1 E5

Vážh

18

Východná

D1 E50

Prouba

Hybe

Liptovský Hrádok

BANSKÁ BYSTRICA

72

Liptovský Hrádok
Liptovský Hrádok is [.............] of its 14th-century castle, later extended into a Renaissance palace and now housing an Ethnography Museum.

KEY

▤	Motorway
▭	Minor road
▬	Other road
≈	River
---	National border
✲	Viewpoint

For hotels and restaurants in this region see pp362–4 and pp392–4

Ždiar

Founded in the 17th century, the village of Ždiar features many recently restored wooden highland houses with a variety of decorations.

VISITORS' CHECKLIST

Road map E3. ✈ *Poprad-Tatry.* 🚂 *from Poprad to Tatranská Lomnica, Starý Smokovec, Štrbské Pleso.* 🅸 *Starý Smokovec.* **Tel** *(052) 442 34 40.* ⏰ *8:30am–4pm Mon–Fri, 8am–1pm Sat (May–Sep: daily).*

Lomnický štít

Lomnický štít, the second-highest peak in the Tatras, is accessible by cable car.

BUKOWINA TATRZAŃSKA

Javorina

Ždiar

Havran
2152 m
(7060 ft)

2019 m
(6624 ft)

SPIŠSKÁ BELÁ

67

Kasprov Vrch
1985 m
(6512 ft)

BELIANSKE TATRY

Šviníca
2301 m
(7549 ft)

Ka pa

Široká
2210 m
(7250 ft)

Lomnický štít
2632 m
(8635 ft)

TATRAS

2438 m
(7999 ft)

Rysy
2499 m
(8199 ft)

Tatranská Lomnica

2428 m
(7966 ft)

Gerlachovský štít

Slavkovský štít
2452 m
(8045 ft)

Kriváň
2494 m
(8182 ft)

2654 m
(8707 ft)

HIGH

Starý Smokovec

Štrbské Pleso

537

534

0 km   5

0 miles   3

Biely Váh

poprad

18

Važec

Štrba

Starý Smokovec

This attractive spa complex has several hotels, pensions and restaurants that blend well with their woodland surroundings.

Gerlachovský štít

The Tatras' highest peak, Gerlachovský štít (2,654 m/8,707 ft), can be climbed only with a professional guide.

Dunajec Gorge ⑧

Road map E3. **Rafting** *Apr–Oct: 8am–7pm daily, various operators.*
🖥 *www.pieniny.sk*

The Dunajec river flows from west to east, dividing Slovakia and Poland, through Pieniny National Park. This was combined with a park in Poland to form the first international nature reserve in Europe, in 1932. Through this extraordinarily picturesque mountain scenery the river has cut a magnificent 9-km (6-mile) long canyon, whose white limestone walls rise vertically, in some places to the height of 500 m (1,640 ft) above the water level. From April to October it is possible to experience an unusual thrill: floating through the Dunajec Gorge on a wooden raft steered by the local highlanders.

The route, which runs along the most beautiful section of this mountain river, starts in Červený Kláštor and ends in Lesnica. Červený Kláštor, a former Carthusian monastery, is now the **Červený Kláštor Museum** with displays on the monks and the region's history. The **Monastery Church** has an interesting Gothic vault with Baroque polychrome paintings; its refectory is decorated with medieval frescoes depicting scenes from the Passion.

🏛 **Červený Kláštor Museum**
Tel *(052) 82 29 55.* ⏰ *Apr–Oct: daily.* 🖥

Wooden rafts navigating the Dunajec Gorge

Valley of the Five Spiš Tarns in the Slovak High Tatras ▷

Bojnice Castle ❾

The romantic, turreted Bojnice Castle is one of
Slovakia's greatest tourist attractions. Rising high
above the town, it was originally built in the 12th
century. In the 13th century it passed into the hands
of the most powerful Hungarian warlord of the time,
Matúš Čák. In 1527 the Thurzo family converted the
castle into a comfortable Renaissance residence, and
in the 19th century its last owner, Count Ján František
Pálffy, remodelled it into a stately residence resembling
the Gothic castles of France's Loire valley.

Pálffy's Tomb
*From the castle crypt,
containing the
magnificent marble
tomb of Ján Pálffy, a
passage leads to a
cave inside
the hill.*

Chapel
*The chapel with its magnifi-
cent stuccoed and painted
vault was built in the
17th century, in a
former bastion.*

★ Golden Hall
*The magnificent vault, made
of pine and covered with gold
leaf, was modelled on the
interior of the Venetian
Academy of Fine Arts.*

Music Room
*The present Music Room was
once Ján Pálffy's bedroom. The
piano pictured was made in
Vienna in 1884.*

The castle courtyards
are used in the
summer as venues for
tournaments and
falconry shows.

Castle Grounds

Bojnice is in a large park with many rare species of trees, including what is claimed to be the oldest lime tree in Slovakia. In summer, events are staged in the grounds.

VISITORS' CHECKLIST

Road map D3. 5 km (3 miles) from Prievidza. 🚌 🚆 *from Bratislava.* **Tel** *(046) 543 05 35.* ⬛ *May, Jun, Sep: 9am–5pm Tue–Sun; Jul, Aug: 9am–5pm daily; Oct–Apr: 10am–3pm Tue–Sun.* 🎟 🎫 *2 routes.* 🎵 **www**.bojnicecastle.sk

Central Castle

The rooms of the central castle are furnished in Gothic style. The top floor features the Knights' Hall.

Neo-Gothic gallery

Entrance tower and gate

Well in the Fourth Courtyard

The well standing in the smallest of the castle's courtyards was once linked to an old thermal spring. Its decorative grille was made in 1895.

★ Bojnice Altarpiece

The altarpiece painted by Nardo di Cione – the only complete surviving work by the artist – is the most important piece from Ján Pálffy's collection. It was painted in the mid-14th century, using tempera paint on a wooden panel.

STAR FEATURES

★ Bojnice Altarpiece

★ Golden Hall

Traditional timber church, Svätý Kríž

Svätý Kríž ⑩

Road map E3. 20 km (12 miles) E of Ružomberok. 🏘 *680.* 🚌 *from Ružomberok.*

The Protestant Evangelic Lutheran Church in the village of Svätý Kríž is one of the largest timber churches in Europe. This vast building has an area of 659 sq m (7,090 sq ft). It was transported to its present site from the village of Palúdza, which in 1982 was flooded to form the artificial lake of Liptovská Mara.

The church was built in 1774, when Emperor Leopold let Protestants put up churches, on condition that they were built of timber and outside town boundaries. It was constructed by a local carpenter, Jozef Lang, with 40 helpers, without the use of a single nail and without help from any architect. It took them eight months and 22 days. The church can accommodate 6,000 people.

🏛 **Evangelic Lutheran Church**
Tel *(044) 559 26 22.* ◯ *daily.* 🖼
🕇 *Sun 9am.*

Environs
Vlkolínec, near the large, industrial town of Ružomberok, was in 1993 named a UNESCO World Cultural Heritage Site as a unique example of a well-preserved complex of 45 timber houses in a typical village of the Liptov region. Interesting features include the old well, which still supplies the village with water, and the 1770 belfry of the Baroque Church of the Virgin Mary.

Žilina ⑪

Road map D3. 29 km (18 miles) NW of Martin. 🏘 *90,000.* 🚊 🚌 🛈 *Burianova medzierka 4.* **Tel** *(041) 662 14 78.*

A good base for the nearby Malá Fatra mountains, the town of Žilina has a particularly striking main square, Marianské námestie. Arcades run along all four sides of the square market place at the centre of the old town. The most conspicuous of its colourful restored buildings are the Old Town Hall, the Baroque Church of St Paul (sv. Pavel) and the Jesuit monastery in the south-western corner of the square. Standing at the centre is the 1738 Marian Column.

Interesting sites along Farska include the **Holy Trinity Church** (Najsvätejšie Trojice) dating from around 1400, and the nearby **Burian Tower**, a 46-m (150-ft) tall Renaissance structure topped with a cupola identical to that of the adjacent church tower. In Námestie A Hlinku is the **Museum of Art** (Považská galéria) with a collection by modern Slovak artists. On a hillside at the west end of the town, in Závodská sesta, stands the **Church of St Stephen** (sv. Štefana), one of the oldest in Slovakia, contain-ing 14th-century wall paintings.

🏛 **Museum of Art**
Štefánikova 2. **Tel** *(041) 562 24 15.* ◯ *Tue– Sun.* 🖼

Čičmany ⑫

Road map D3. 40 km (25 miles) S of Žilina. 🏘 *200.* 🚌 *from Žilina.*

This village in the Rajčanka valley resembles a set of gingerbread houses. For the last 200 years, the wooden walls of its buildings have been decorated with white geometric patterns painted with lime. In 1921 a fire consumed a large portion of Čičmany, but the village was rebuilt by its inhabitants in its original form. In the two-storey Raden's house (No. 42) is the **Považské Museum** with photographs, embroidered costumes, and furniture illustrating village life. There is an interesting section on tinkers.

🏛 **Považské Museum**
Tel *(041) 500 15 11.* ◯ *Sep–Jun: Tue–Sun; Jul, Aug: daily.* 🖼

Traditional white painted decoration on a house in Čičmany

Vel'ké Uherce Palace ⑬

Road map D3. 48 km (30 miles) N of Levice. 🚊 🚌 ⬤ *to the public.*

Enjoying a lovely location on mountain slopes, the village of Vel'ké Uherce is known for its huge palace surrounded by an English-style park. The original Renaissance castle was built in 1622 by Michal Bossanyi. Remodelled in the 18th century in Gothic style, it was given the appearance of a Neo-Gothic residence in the spirit of English Romanticism in the second half of the 19th century. Until 1945 the palace was owned by the Thonet family, one of the world's

Coat of arms, Vel'ké Uherce Palace

biggest furniture manufacturers. After World War II the nationalized property was badly damaged. Reconstruction works, which started in the 1990s, have ceased and now the interiors provide only a vague indication of the palace's former glory. The park, although neglected, remains impressive.

The south wing of Topol'čianky Palace, now a museum

Topol'čianky Palace **⓮**

Road map D4. 30 km (19 miles) N of Levice. **Museum Tel** (037) 630 11 11. ☐ May–Aug: 9am–3pm Tue–Fri, noon–4pm Sat, Sun; Sep–Apr: 10am–3pm Tue–Fri, noon–4pm Sat, Sun.

One of Slovakia's most beautiful historic buildings, the Topol'čianky Palace was built in the 15th century on the site of an older building. Over the following centuries the original Gothic palace changed hands several times, becoming the property of the Hungarian families of Rakoczy, Erdödy and Zichy, who during the Renaissance period turned it into a four-wing residence surrounding an arcaded courtyard. The Neo-Classical south wing with its splendid portico was added in the 18th century. In 1890 the palace became one of the Habsburgs' residences, and during 1923–51 was used as the summer residence of the presidents of Czechoslovakia.

Now the Renaissance part is being used as a hotel, while the Neo-Classical wing houses a museum with a collection of the palace's historic furniture

and paintings. The magnificent English-style park with an attractive hunting lodge and world-famous stud deserves a separate visit.

Environs

About 10 km (6 miles) to the south is the **Mlyňany Arboretum**, established in 1892 by Štefan Ambrózy-Migazzi, a Hungarian fascinated by botany and dendrology. Today this is Slovakia's richest collection of coniferous trees. The site, an area of 67 ha (165 acres), features nearly 2,400 different species, representing all regions of the world.

Particularly interesting are the specimens brought back by scientific expeditions to China and Korea, planted on a 20-ha (50-acre) site devoted to Far Eastern flora; also worth exploring is the equally exotic collection of North American plants.

🌿 Mlyňany Arboretum
Veska nad Žitavou 178. **Tel** (037) 633 45 71. ☐ daily.

Hronský Beňadik Abbey **⓯**

Road map D4. 20 km (12 miles) N of Levice. ☐ ☐ **Tel** (045) 689 31 93. ☐ Jul, Aug: 9:30am–5:30pm Mon–Fri; Sep–Jun: by appt.

The Benedictine abbey in Hronský Beňadik was mentioned by historic sources as early as 1075. In the late 14th century its Romanesque buildings were rebuilt in the Gothic style. The magnificent triple-naved church with an impressive portal and a beautiful vault is from that period. The most interesting features of the interior include the Gothic wall painting depicting the legend of St George; also St Scholastica's altar with 15th-century carved figures of the Virgin Mary and St Benedict. In the 16th century, during the period of growing Turkish threat, the monastery assumed military significance, guarding

Sculpture at Hronský Beňadik Abbey

access to the rich mining towns of Central Slovakia. It was at that time converted into a fortified stronghold, by strengthening its outside walls, blocking up the vast Gothic windows and erecting bastions.

Lučenec **⓰**

Road map E4. 80 km (50 miles) SE of Banská Bystrica. 🏠 30,000. ☐ ☐ ☐ Masarykova 14. **Tel** (047) 433 15 13.

One of the centres of Slovakia's Hungarian national minority, Lučenec has been known since the 13th century under a variety of names, including Lucheneh, Lušeniča and Losonc. In 1919 it found itself within the borders of Czechoslovakia, and during 1938–45 belonged briefly to Hungary. In its fairly small market square, Kubínyiho námestie, is the former Neo-Gothic Calvinist church of 1853, with an unusual ceramic-tiled roof and a tower crowned with a gilded cockerel. Inside is the **Novohradské Museum**, its collection illustrating the region's culture, including glass, furniture and musical instruments.

In Filakovska, south of the market square, stands an enormous Art Nouveau **synagogue** dating from 1926, one of the largest in Europe, which has now deteriorated.

🏛 Novohradské Museum
Kubínyho Námestie 3. **Tel** (047) 433 25 02. ☐ Tue–Fri, Sun.

The former Art Nouveau synagogue in Lučenec

EAST SLOVAKIA

Many regard East Slovakia as the most fascinating part of the country. The region's cultural riches, particularly evident in the large number of towns that have maintained or restored their medieval character, go hand in hand with the beauty of its natural environment: the astonishing karst scenery and the mountainous areas barely touched by civilization.

Situated in the western part of East Slovakia, southeast of the Tatras Mountains, is the Spiš region (known as Zips in German, and Szepes in Hungarian), a historic land rich in examples of Late-Gothic art that bear witness to the centuries-long intermingling of the Slovak, Hungarian, German, Polish, Ruthenian (Rusyn) and Jewish cultures. The places listed on the UNESCO World Cultural Heritage roster – Levoča, Spiš Castle and the charming village of Žehra – attract the greatest numbers of visitors, but interesting historic sites can be found in almost every village.

The area to the south of Spiš offers not only hilly, wooded scenery but also a fascinating subterranean world. The vast cave systems are a world-class attraction of the Slovenský kras (Slovak Karst) and of the nearby Slovenský ráj (Slovak Paradise). Some of the dripstone formations (stalagmites and stalactites) that occur here are unequalled anywhere else in Europe. Both areas attract hikers.

Košice, in the central part of the region, is Slovakia's second-largest city, boasting the magnificent Cathedral of St Elizabeth and the carefully restored old town. The historic town centre of nearby Prešov is also well preserved.

The eastern part of the region, along the border with Poland, is sparsely populated and offers remote and tranquil wilderness and pretty wooden churches. Bardejov has a fine medieval centre, while Svidník has an open-air exhibition of traditional wooden folk architecture. The remote, unspoilt Vihorlat mountains to the south provide superb hiking opportunities.

Spiš Castle, above the small town of Spišské Podhradie

◁ Richly decorated walls of the Orthodox Church of the Holy Spirit, Medzilaborce

Exploring East Slovakia

East Slovakia offers a great variety of attractions. The historic towns and villages of Spiš, with the former capital of the region – Levoča – are real treasure-houses of Slovakia's history. Košice, now the vibrant regional capital, enjoys a well-deserved reputation as the cultural heart of the region. What's more, there is magnificent, unspoiled scenery, and, scattered all over the region, small wooden village churches. Slovenský kras delights its visitors with the natural riches of the four great limestone caves that are open to visitors.

A tablet in the Church of St James, Levoča

Reservoir at Košicka Bela, northwest of Košice

KEY

═══	Motorway
≡ ≡	Motorway under construction
───	Main road
⋯⋯	Minor road
───	Scenic route
╍╍╍	Main railway
───	Minor railway
───	International border
───	Regional border
△	Summit

SIGHTS AT A GLANCE

Bardejov **6**
Kežmarok **7**
Košice pp328–31 **1**
Levoča pp334–5 **9**
Medzilaborce **4**
Podolínec **8**
Prešov **2**
Spišská Kapitula **12**
Spiš Castle pp338–9 **11**
Svidník **5**
Vihorlat **3**

Tour
Slovenský kras pp336–7 **10**

0 kilometres   20
0 miles   10

GETTING AROUND

Košice – the main town of the region – has an airport with domestic flights to Bratislava, and several international flights. Košice is also the major hub of bus transport. The main road running through East Slovakia is the 18 (international E50) leading from Žilina in Central Slovakia through Prešov, to Košice. East Slovakia is also crossed by the main Slovak railway line, which runs from Bratislava via Žilina to Košice, with an extension to Humenné.

The restored Košice Gate in the eastern district of Levoča

Krásna Hôrka Castle in the Slovenský kras

SEE ALSO

• **Where to Stay** pp364–5

• **Where to Eat** pp394–5

Košice ●

Košice's coat of arms

Slovakia's second-largest city has roots reaching back to the 12th century. At the crossroads of major trade routes, it was granted in 1347 the same town privileges as the then capital of Hungary, Buda. In 1369 King Louis the Great gave the town its coat of arms, making it the first town in Europe to receive this by royal decree. Due to its proximity to the Hungarian border, the city has always had a large Hungarian population. Its historic old town now superbly restored, Košice is a lively, interesting city.

The Plague Column and beautiful houses in Hlavná

Exploring the town

The most interesting sights in Košice are clustered within its large historic centre. The main street, Hlavná, whose spindle shape is typical of the eastern region's towns, runs north–south, with the main squares, Hlavné námestie and Námestie slobody, and the cathedral in the centre (see also pp330–31).

🏛 Hlavná

This lovely avenue, full of shops and cafés, makes for an enjoyable evening stroll. The most striking of its buildings are the Gothic Levoča House (Levočský dom) and the old town hall, its façade decorated with sculptures of ancient heroes by Anton Kraus. The Plague Column (1722–3) is Košice's most beautiful piece of Baroque sculpture.

⛪ St Michael's Chapel

Hlavná 26.

The church (sv. Michal) was built in the 14th century, on the site of a cemetery south of St Elizabeth's Cathedral. The lower section of the building served as an ossuary. The upper section was used for celebrating masses for the souls of the dead. In the early 20th century 17 old tombstones from the cemetery were built into the chapel walls. Highlights include the altarpiece depicting St Michael the Archangel; the lovely stone tabernacle; and, above the sacristy door, the oldest coat of arms of Košice.

⛪ St Elizabeth's Cathedral

Hlavná 28. **Tel** (055) 622 15 55.

Dominating the main square, and of great interest inside

Detail from St Elizabeth's Cathedral

and out, St Elizabeth's Cathedral (Dóm sv. Alžbety) is the largest church in Slovakia, and a supreme achievement of the European Gothic. Its construction began in 1378. The main, western façade of this five-aisled church was originally meant to have two towers, but by 1477 only one was built. In 1508 works were completed on the beautifully vaulted presbytery. In 1775 the second tower of the cathedral was built, topped with a Rococo copper cupola. The present form of the church is the result of reconstruction that began in the late 19th century and restored the cathedral to its former appearance, close to the original design. Inside, the spectacular main altarpiece has 48 panels. Take time also to see the relief work over the north and west doors.

🏛 Urban Tower

Hlavná.

The Urban Tower (Urbanova veža) stands to the north of St Elizabeth's Cathedral. Built in the 14th century, it was remodelled in Renaissance style in 1628. St Urban's bell was cast in 1557 and installed inside the tower. Dedicating it to St Urban was intended to honour the patron saint of viniculture: wine production has always been a source of Košice's wealth.

🏛 Singing Fountain

Hlavné námestie.

In the square between the cathedral and the theatre is the Singing Fountain (Spievajúca fontána), which spouts water to recorded music. At night, the pearly jets are lit up by coloured lights that correspond to the rhythm of the music. The fountain is at the centre of a narrow water channel that runs the length of the square.

Singing Fountain in Hlavné namestie

State Theatre

Hlavná 58. **Tel** (055) 622 12 31.
☐ performances only. **ww**.sdke.sk
The imposing building of the
State Theatre (Štátne divadlo)
was built in 1897–99, to a
design by Adolf Lang. Its lofty
dome is topped with the
torch-bearing figure of Dawn.
The interior, with its beautiful
auditorium and lyre-shape
floor plan, features a
magnificent ceiling
with paintings of
scenes from
Shakespeare. The
foyer and the rest
of the theatre are
richly decorated
with stuccoes.

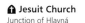

**Bas-relief from the
Jesuit Church's façade**

Jesuit Church

Junction of Hlavná
and Univerzitna.
The church (Univerzitný
kostol sv. Trojice), one of the
finest remaining Baroque
structures in Košice, was built
in 1681 by the Jesuit order. Its
austere, Early-Baroque façade
bearing traces of the
Renaissance style hides a
lavishly furnished interior,
which includes a 17th-century
pulpit and stalls and a 19th-
century main altar. The
central nave and all the side
chapels are beautifully
decorated with magnificent
trompe-l'oeil paintings.

Executioner's Bastion

Hrnčiarska 7. ☐ 9am–5pm Tue–Sat.
The bastion (Katova bašta)
takes its name from the
nearby house, which was
once the home of the town's
hangman. This semicircular
structure was built in about
1500 and served defensive
purposes, housing eight guns.
The lower section of the
bastion is reinforced with
slanting buttresses.

East Slovak Museum

Námestie Maratónu
mieru 2. **Tel** (055) 622 13
61. ☐ 9am–5pm Tue–
Sat, 9am–1pm Sun.
One of Slovakia's
oldest museums,
the East Slovak
Museum (Východoslovenské
múzeum) was established in
1872 as the Upper Hungary
Museum. Its vast collections,
numbering half a million
exhibits, are displayed in an
early 20th-century Neo-
Renaissance building. The
impressive façade is decorated with the town's coat of
arms and the carved figures
of Perseus and Vulcan. The
museum's greatest attraction is
the "golden treasure of Košice"
– a huge find of nearly 3,000
gold coins dating from the
15th to the 17th centuries.

Former Synagogue

Puškinova.
The former synagogue was
built in 1926–7. In 1992 a
bronze memorial plaque was
added to the front of the
building to commemorate
over 12,000 Jews who were
taken from Košice to
concentration camps in 1944.

**The Neo-Renaissance building
housing the East Slovak Museum**

KOŠICE CENTRE

East Slovak Museum ⑨
Executioner's Bastion ⑧
Former Synagogue ⑩
Hlavná ①
Jesuit Church ⑦
St Elizabeth's Cathedral ③
St Michael's Chapel ②
Singing Fountain ⑤
State Theatre ⑥
Urban Tower ④

0 metres   300
0 yards   300

KEY

▨ Street-by-Street see pp330–31

Key to Symbols see back flap

Street-by-Street: Around St Elizabeth's Cathedral

The long main street, Hlavná, the loveliest
avenue in Slovakia, follows the old trade
route through the town. It widens in its
middle section where it is crosscut by
Alžbetina and Mlynská streets. This is the
town's central point, marked by the lofty
spire of St Elizabeth's Cathedral and the
pointed, angular cap of the Urban Tower.
The area is awash with stately Baroque and
Neo-Classical buildings set amid greenery.

Singing Fountain
*Built in 1986 by Russian experts, this
huge fountain was the first attraction
of its kind in Czechoslovakia.*

Urban Tower
*Following the
Great Fire of Košice
in 1556 the once
Gothic tower was
rebuilt in
Renaissance style.
It was then that
it acquired the
Urban Bell.*

HLAVNÉ
NÁMESTIE

Urban Bell
*The 5-tonne (some
say 7-tonne) bell was
removed from the
tower and
placed in the
square in the
1960s.*

ALŽBETINA

Archbishop's Palace
*The palace is one of the newest buildings in
Hlavná. It was constructed in 1804, on the
site of two older houses.*

0 metres		20
0 yards		20

KEY

- - - Suggested route

★ St Elizabeth's Cathedral

The resplendent Gothic main altarpiece (1474–7), with 48 panel pictures in its side-wings, depicts various scenes. Some parts include sculpture and illustrate the life of St Elizabeth, a Hungarian princess and patron saint of the town and the church.

Hlavná 39
Built for the Smidegh family in 1593, this house is one of many magnificent buildings on Hlavná.

★ St Michael's Chapel

The Archangel Michael is the patron saint of the 14th-century chapel in the cemetery by St Elizabeth's Cathedral. He is depicted in a doorway relief weighing the souls of the dead.

MLYNSKÁ

NÁMESTIE SLOBODY

Hlavná 26
This 1901–2 Art Nouveau house is one of several notable Art Nouveau façades in the street.

STAR SIGHTS

★ St Elizabeth's Cathedral

★ St Michael's Chapel

Rakoczy Palace (Regional Museum) in Prešov

Prešov ❷

Road map F3. 38 km (24 miles) N of Košice. 🏛 *91,000*. 🚗 🚌
🛈 *Hlavná 67.* **Tel** *(051) 773 11 13.*
www.pis.sk

Slovakia's third-largest town is first heard of in 1247. It was a thriving centre of salt mining from the 13th century, and mining ceased only in the 19th century. During the 16th and 17th centuries it became a Reformation stronghold. One of the major events in the town's history was the 1687 Prešov massacre, when 24 Protestants were publicly executed on the town square for allegedly supporting an anti-Habsburg insurrection.

Dominating the town's historic district is the 1347 Gothic **Church of St Nicholas** (sv. Mikuláš), on the main street, Hlavná. It has magnificent Gothic paintings and Baroque furnishings, particularly its 17th-century high altar with figures of saints carved

by Josef Hartmann. In front of the church is a Baroque Plague Column and the 19th-century Neptune's Fountain. Opposite is the late 16th-century Renaissance **Rakoczy Palace**, now a **Regional Museum** (Šarišské múzeum). The suburb of **Solivar** features an interesting complex of historic buildings associated with salt mining.

🏛 **Regional Museum**
Hlavná 85. **Tel** *(051) 773 47 08.*
◯ *Tue–Fri, Sun.* 📷

Vihorlat ❸

Road map F3. E of Košice. 🚌

A small range of volcanic mountains, Vihorlat runs near the border with Ukraine. This is one of the quietest, least populated corners of Slovakia. The local attractions include the lovely reservoir, Zamplinská Širava (Slovak Sea), surrounded by camp sites. In the Vihorlat Nature

Reserve is **Sninský Crag** (Sninský Kameň), a steep climb to 1,005 m (3,300 ft), the final section ascended by steel ladders. From the top it is possible to see the emerald lake of **Morské oko** (Sea Eye) sparkling in the crater of an extinct volcano.

Medzilaborce ❹

Road map F3. 43 km (27 miles) E of Svidník. 🏛 *6,000*. 🚗 🚌

This small town, close to the border with Poland, owes its fame to the American painter Andy Warhol, leading creator of pop art. His parents, Ruthenian immigrants, came from the neighbouring village of Miková. The **Warhol Family Museum of Modern Art** (Múzeum moderného umenia) in Medzilaborce is in a chunky concrete building. On display are 18 of Warhol's original screen prints, including his iconic paintings of Campbell's soup cans, the blue cat and Ingrid Bergman as a nun. There are also mementos associated with his family.

The town was severely damaged during the two World Wars, but its attractive 18th-century Greek Orthodox **Church of the Holy Spirit** (sv. Ducha) has survived.

🏛 **Warhol Family Museum of Modern Art**
A Warhola 749/26. **Tel** *(057) 748 00 72.* ◯ *Tue–Sun.* 📷

ANDY WARHOL (1928–1987)

The real name of the king of pop art was Andrej Varchola. Born in the USA to Ruthenian parents, he studied painting and design. In 1942 he began to sign his works "Andy Warhol". Six years later he had his first one-man show in New York. In about 1960 he started to paint pictures of everyday objects, banknotes, metro tickets and cigarettes. He executed his works with the precision of an illustrator, often choosing advertising motifs for his topics. His most famous works include the widely copied series of portraits of Marilyn Monroe.

Statue of Andy Warhol in Medzilaborce

Screen of icons in the Church of the Holy Spirit in Medzilaborce

Czechoslovak Army Monument at the Dukla Pass near Svidník

Svidník ❺

Road map F3. 53 km (33 miles) NE of Prešov. 🏛 *13,000.* ▦

In the autumn of 1944, the Battle of Dukla Pass was fought against the Nazis near Svidník. Many thousands of Red Army soldiers were killed here. The **Battle of Dukla Museum** (Vojenské múzeum) is dedicated to this event. The modern building in the shape of an anti-tank mine houses thousands of exhibits associated with the battle. Some tanks and vehicles used in the battle are on display outside and en route to the Dukla Pass.

The **Museum of Ukraine-Ruthenian Culture** (Múzeum ukrajinsko-rusínskej kultúry) has artifacts of the Greek-Catholic Ruthenian minority. Part of the museum, on a separate site, is an open-air skansen of traditional Ruthenian wooden buildings.

🏛 **Battle of Dukla Museum**
Bardejovska 25. **Tel** (054) 752 13 98. ⏱ *Tue–Sun.*

🏛 **Museum of Ukraine-Ruthenian Culture**
Centrálna 258. **Tel** (054) 788 21 00. ⏱ *Tue–Sun.* ✉ www.muk.sk

🏛 **Skansen**
Nad Svídníckym Amfiteátrom. **Tel** (054) 752 29 52. ⏱ *May–Oct: daily.* 🎫

Environs
At the Dukla Pass (20 km/12 miles north of Svidník) is the **Czechoslovak Army Monument.**

Bardejov ❻

Road map F3. 42 km (26 miles) N of Prešov. 🏛 *32,000.* ▣ ▦ *from Prešov.* ℹ *Radničné námestie 21.* **Tel** (054) 541 61 86. www.e-bardejov.sk

Mentioned by chroniclers as early as 1241, this large town has retained its medieval character. The superbly preserved old town's long market square, Radničné námestie, is flanked on three sides by over 40 houses built on typically narrow plots, with street-facing gables. The finest is No. 13, originally a Gothic structure remodelled in Renaissance style, now part of the **Šariš Museum**. The early 16th-century **town hall** at the centre of the square has Renaissance windows, an oriel and stone portals. The top façade bears a statue of the Knight Roland. Another branch of the Šariš Museum is here.

The fourth side of the square is occupied by the **Basilica of St Giles** (sv. Egídius), a magnificent church with 11 medieval side altars. The town, on the UNESCO World Cultural Heritage list, also has very well-preserved medieval defensive walls.

🏛 **Šariš Muzeum**
Radničné námestie 48. **Tel** (054) 472 49 66. ⏱ *May–Sep: daily; Oct–Apr: Tue–Sun.* 🎫

Madonna in the Bardejov town hall

Kežmarok ❼

Road map E3. 74 km (46 miles) W of Prešov. 🏛 *17,000.* ▣ ▦ ℹ *Hlavné námestie 46.* **Tel** (052) 452 40 47. www.kezmarok.net

Kežmarok's most imposing historic sight is the vast, Neo-Byzantine **Lutheran Church** (Nový evanjelický kostol), work of the Viennese architect Theophil von Hansen. It contains the mausoleum of Count Imre Thököly, hero of Hungarian anti-Habsburg insurrections *(see p263).* In contrast, the old **Protestant Church** (Drevený kostol)

nearby, built in 1717 of red spruce and yew, has a richly decorated main altar, a carved pulpit and a stone font dating from 1690 that is older than the church itself. To the north of the town square with its Neo-Classical town hall stands a 15th-century **castle** built by Imre Zápolya, and remodelled by the Thököly family into a Renaissance residence; today it is the **Kežmarok Museum**.

🏛 **Kežmarok Museum**
Hradné námestie 42. **Tel** (052) 452 26 18. ⏱ *May–Sep: Tue–Sun; Oct–Apr: Mon–Fri.* 🎫

Main altar in the Protestant Church in Kežmarok

Podolínec ❽

Road map E3. 16 km (10 miles) N of Kežmarok. 🏛 *3,000.* ▦ ℹ *Námestie Mariánske 3.* **Tel** (052) 439 12 05.

This small town in the Poprad river valley has a history going back to 1292. At the centre of its main square, flanked by Renaissance houses, is the late 13th-century **Church of the Ascension of the Virgin Mary** (Nanebovzatia Panny Marie), its presbytery decorated with Gothic wall paintings. The beautiful Renaissance belfry in front of the church, with a lavishly decorated attic, is from 1659.

The nearby mid-17th-century **Piarist Church and Monastery** have an interesting history. For three centuries the monastery was home to the Piarist college founded by the bailiff of Spiš. In 1950–51 the Communists turned it briefly into a concentration camp for Slovak monks.

The Renaissance Thurzo House in the old centre of Levoča

Levoča ⑨

Road map E3. 56 km (35 miles) W of Prešov. 👥 *14,000.* 🚌 🚎 ℹ️ *Námestie Majstra Pavla 58.* **Tel** *(053) 451 37 63.* **www**.levoca.sk

The former capital of the affluent region of Spiš, Levoča is situated between the High Tatras and Slovenské Rudohorie mountains. The town has an immaculately preserved historic centre, full of magnificent Gothic, Renaissance, Baroque and Neo-Classical buildings. Its main square, Námestie Majstra Pavla, features the Gothic **Church of St James** (sv. Jakub). This houses a unique set of 18 altarpieces, a magnificent collection of medieval and Renaissance sacred art. The most splendid of them – the 18.6-m (61-ft) high main altarpiece – is the world's tallest Gothic altar. The over 2-m (6-ft) high statues of the Madonna, St James and St John the Evangelist are all by Master Pavol of Levoča, an outstanding sculptor of the Late Gothic, who also carved several other altarpieces in the church. Just south of the church is the former **Town Hall** *(see right).*

Among nearly 60 historic houses around the main square are the striking **Thurzo House** (Thurzov dom) crowned with a Renaissance attic, and the **House of Master Pavol of Levoča**, now a museum of his life and work. At the edge of the historic district is the 14th-century **Old Minorites' Church** (Starý kláštor minoritov) that has a dazzling Baroque interior.

🏛 **House of Master Pavol**
Námestie Majstra Pavla 20. **Tel** *(053) 451 34 96.* ⭕ *daily (by appt Mon).* 📷

Levoča: Town Hall

One of the town's most distinguished buildings, the town hall (radnica) was erected in 1550 in Gothic style, replacing an earlier building that had been destroyed by fire. In the early 17th century it was remodelled along Renaissance lines. The bell tower dates from 1656–61, which, in the 18th century, was decorated with Baroque elements. The Neo-Classical pediments were added in the 19th century. The town hall is still used for civic functions, and it also houses the main branch of the Spiš Museum on the first floor, with exhibits on regional history.

★ **Arcades**
The original town hall did not have any galleries. The two-tier arcades were added to the central part of the building in 1615.

CAGE OF DISGRACE

The wrought-iron contraption by the south wall of the town hall is the 16th-century "Cage of Disgrace", in which women who had committed minor crimes were locked up and put on public display. It used to stand in the park belonging to the Probstner family, who gave it to the town in 1933.

Town's Coat of Arms
This consists of a red shield with a double cross supported by two lions.

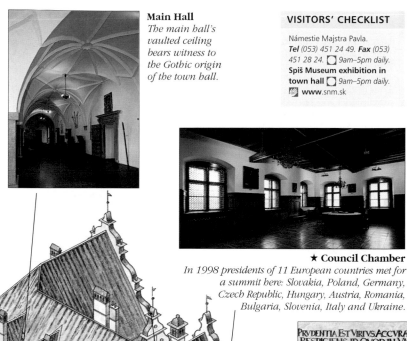

Main Hall
The main hall's vaulted ceiling bears witness to the Gothic origin of the town hall.

VISITORS' CHECKLIST

Námestie Majstra Pavla.
Tel *(053) 451 24 49.* **Fax** *(053) 451 28 24.* ◯ *9am–5pm daily.*
Spiš Museum exhibition in town hall ◯ *9am–5pm daily.*
📷 **www**.snm.sk

★ Council Chamber
In 1998 presidents of 11 European countries met for a summit here: Slovakia, Poland, Germany, Czech Republic, Hungary, Austria, Romania, Bulgaria, Slovenia, Italy and Ukraine.

PRVDENTIA EST VIRTVS ACCVRATE RESPICIENS ID QVOD IN VNA QVAQVE ACTIONE DECET.

★ Wall Paintings
The authentic Renaissance paintings on the south elevation of the building depict the civic virtues of restraint, courage, justice and patience.

The Neo-Classical pediments date from the 19th century.

Coat of Arms
The town's coat of arms can be found above the central arch of the ground-floor arcades, on the west side of the building.

STAR SIGHTS

★ Arcades

★ Council Chamber

★ Wall Paintings

A Tour of the Slovensk Kras ❿

Limestone caves characterize the Slovak Karst, which runs in a wide arc along the Slovak-Hungarian border. Most of the country's karst phenomena occur here, including the vast majority of its 4,450 caves. Four of them – Domica, Gombasecká, Ochtinská aragonitová and Jasovská – are partly open to the public. A fifth cave, Dobšiná ice cave, is in the Slovenský raj (Slovak Paradise), another karst area about 40 km (25 miles) to the northwest (warm clothes are recommended for this cave). In 1995 all five were listed as UNESCO Sites.

Úhorná ④
Under the village of Úhorná, 14 km (9 miles) from Rožňava, is a reservoir, which was built in 1768 to prevent flooding. It supplied water to mines and iron mills.

Krásna Hôrka ③
One of Slovakia's finest castles, this is full of gorgeous furnishings. Nearby is the Art Nouveau mausoleum of the Andrássy family, who once owned the castle.

Betliar ②
The Andrássy family owned this whimsical hunting lodge, which houses a large collection of trophies and is decorated in a variety of styles. One of its most interesting rooms is the magnificent library.

■ Tour route
═ Other roads
❋ Viewpoint

0 kilometres   18
0 miles   9

Jaskyła Domica ①
Reputed to be the most beautiful cave in Slovakia, Jaskyňa Domica is also the longest. There is a boat ride along 140 m (460 ft) of the underground river.

Zádielska Valley ⑤
The valley is an impressive 3-km (2-mile) long canyon cut in white limestone rocks, with walls rising to 300 m (985 ft). Flowing along its floor is the small stream, Zádielski Potok.

TIPS FOR DRIVERS

Length: About 75 km (45 miles).
Stopping off points: Rožňava is a good base; other towns also have places for refreshments.
🛈 Brzotín, 2 km (1 mile) SW of Rožňava. *Tel* (058) 732 68 15.
www.slovenskyraj.sk
www.ssj.sk (cave information)

Jasov ⑥
Jasov features Slovakia's biggest monastery complex. Its interior contains fine examples of Baroque art.

Hačava

Lúčka

Bôrka

Moldava nad Bodvou

Jablonov nad Turňou

⑤   50 E571

Turňa nad Bodvou

50 E571

Košice

Turňa

Miskolc

Bodva

Bodva

550

Medzev ⑧
A landmark in this small town, which was founded in the 13th century by German settlers, is the tower of the Church of Mary the Queen of Angels.

Jasovska Jaskyňa ⑦
It is claimed that this cave was discovered by monks from the nearby monastery in Jasov. Its underground corridors feature numerous old writings and drawings, the oldest dating from 1452. Within the cave archaeologists have discovered traces of prehistoric habitation.

For hotels and restaurants in this region see pp364–5 and pp394–5

Spiš Castle ⓫

These forbidding castle ruins (Spišský hrad) are part of a historic complex, along with the small town of Spišské Podhradie (*podhradie* means "below the castle"), which lies between the castle and Spišská Kapitula *(see opposite)*, a settlement on a ridge 6 km (4 miles) to the northwest. Spiš Castle was the administrative capital of the Spiš region, a historic province populated by Saxon settlers. The oldest parts of the castle date from the 11th–12th centuries. After its 15th-century enlargement it contained five courtyards. In 1780 it burned down. It is gradually being restored. Most impressive from a distance, it is nonetheless worth a visit for its spectacular views.

Walls
The defensive walls were rebuilt, reinforced and equipped with new gun positions by the Zápolya family, who owned the castle in the 15th and 16th centuries.

Kruchová tower, dating from the first half of the 12th century, was used as a residence and an observation point.

Vast Fortress
Occupying an area of 4 ha (10 acres), Spiš Castle is the remains of the largest fortress complex in Central Europe. In the 17th century it had 2,000 inhabitants.

Gate
The entrance gate leads to a vast lower courtyard, nearly 300 m (985 ft) long and 115 m (380 ft) wide.

STAR FEATURES

★ Castle Chapel and Museum

★ Upper Castle

VISITORS' CHECKLIST

Road map E3. 🏠 *3,500
(Spišské Podhradie).* 🚆 🚌
*Spišské Podhradie, 3 km (2 miles)
NW.* **Tel** *(053) 454 13 36.*
Castle & Museum ⬭ *daily,
May–Sep: 8:30am–7pm; Oct:
9am–6pm; Nov: 9am–3pm daily.*
🖼 🎫 **www**.spisskyhrad.sk

★ Upper Castle
*Situated at the highest point,
the now-ruined upper castle,
with its tower and Roman-
esque palace, was built in the
14th century.*

Tournaments
*During the summer
season, colourful
historic pageants and
knights' tournaments
are held in the castle
courtyards.*

★ Museum
*Part of the chapel has been given
over to a small exhibition devoted to
the archaeology and history of Spiš
Castle, and to a collection of historic
arms and armour.*

★ Castle Chapel
*Six wooden statues of saints adorn the
interior of the 15th-century Gothic
chapel of the Zápolya family. In
2003 the chapel underwent a
complete renovation.*

Spišská Kapitula ⑫

Road map E3. 35 km (22 miles) W
of Prešov. 🚌

A small walled town on a
ridge west of Spišské
Podhradie, Spišská Kapitula
has been, since 1776, the seat
of the Spiš bishopric, the
ecclesiastical capital of the
Spiš region. Its dominant sight
is the Late-Romanesque,
twin-towered **St Martin's
Cathedral**, dating from 1245–
75 *(see also p251)*. It has two
Romanesque portals, an
unusual statue of a white lion
by the entrance, and unique
medieval frescoes in the
central nave. The interesting
burial chapel of the Zápolya
family, by the south wall, dates
from the 15th century. Also on
the town's one street is the
imposing Baroque **Bishop's
Palace** with a clock tower, and
a row of Gothic canons'
houses. Since 1993, Spišská
Kapitula has been on the
UNESCO World Cultural
Heritage listing, with Spišské
Podhradie and Spiš Castle.

🏛 **St Martin's Cathedral**
⬭ *Nov–Apr: 9am–2:30pm Mon–Fri;
May–Oct: 9am–4:30pm daily.* 🖼 🎫

Environs
Žehra, a village 6 km (4 miles)
southeast of Spišska Kapitula,
features a 13th-century Romanesque Church of the Holy Spirit
(sv. Duch), a white building
with a tower and a bell, topped
with onion-shaped wooden
cupolas. Inside the church are
magnificent 13th–15th-century
frescoes covering the presbytery and one wall of the nave,
and a 13th-century stone font.

**Church of the Holy Spirit in Žehra
from the south side**

TRAVELLERS'
NEEDS

WHERE TO STAY 342–365

WHERE TO EAT 366–395

SHOPPING 396–399

ENTERTAINMENT 400–403

SPORT AND LEISURE 404–409

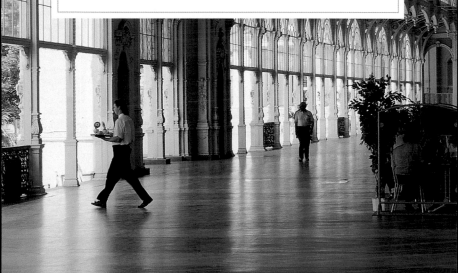

WHERE TO STAY

The Czech and Slovak Republics have a well-developed network of pleasant hotels, pensions and guesthouses, as well as rooms to let in private homes. Finding a bed for the night, even in a small town or a village, should never be a problem, although some places may be closed in the low season (usually October to April). In large cities, particularly Prague, it may be hard to find inexpensive

Doorman at Prague's Palace Hotel

accommodation, although there are a few budget hotels in the centre, and some small pensions on the outskirts. The chart of places to stay on the following pages lists the most attractive establishments in all price categories, including options such as youth hostels and mountain shelters. The listings for the Czech Republic are on pages 344–57; those for Slovakia are on 358–65.

CHOOSING A HOTEL

Both countries have relatively large numbers of hotels of various standards. Large towns, popular resorts and tourist regions offer a variety of accommodation from modern establishments belonging to large international chains and smart hotels set in historic buildings to humble hostels.

HOW TO BOOK

As in many other countries you can book a room by telephone, fax or the Internet. In both the Czech and Slovak Republics the local tourist offices can help with booking accommodation.

CHAIN HOTELS

Hotels belonging to a chain are usually situated in large towns and aim to attract business people. The Czech Republic has many luxury

hotels belonging to international chains, such as Ibis, Radisson SAS, Mercure, Inter-Continental and Holiday Inn. In Slovakia international hotel chains include Best Western and Radisson SAS. There are also local Slovak chains Sorea, Plus and Satel, as well as a range of small hunters' hotels belonging to the National Forestry Commission.

HOSTELS AND LODGES

The cheapest overnight accommodation in both the Czech and Slovak Republics is provided by hostels. In the Czech Republic these are known as *ubytovna*, and in Slovakia as *ubytovňa*. In the Czech Republic these are usually former (or current) workers' hostels, with shared bathroom facilities. Better standard rooms (with en-suite bathroom or even TV) are found in students' halls of residence (*kolej*), but they are open to visitors only from June

Grand Hotel Zvon in České Budějovice *(see p350)*

to August. Slovak hostels are usually located on the outskirts of towns; they often offer rooms with a bathroom.

Youth hostels (IYHF) are also available in the Czech Republic. Czech hostels are of a decent standard and provide overnight accommodation in multiple-occupancy rooms. Their network covers mainly the big towns and most popular tourist centres. There are some mountain hostels (*chata or bouda*) in the Krkonoše and Jeseníky ranges.

In Slovakia youth hostels are only found around Bratislava, but there are clusters of mountain hostels in the Tatras, Low Tatras, Malá and Veľká Fatra, Pieniny and Slovenský raj (Slovak Paradise). Slovak mountain hostels (*chaty*) usually provide basic facilities, with a shared bathroom, a modest buffet, and no access to cooking

Grand Hotel Pupp in Karlovy Vary *(see p352)*

◁ Mariánské Lázně railway station hall

Modest yet pleasant Hotel Ambassador in Košice, East Slovakia *(see p364)*

facilities. In both countries there are hotel-standard mountain hostels, but they tend to be pricey.

PENSIONS

There are large numbers of pensions, or guesthouses, in both countries, but particularly in the Czech Republic. Look out for their signs along the road: *pension* (in the Czech Republic) and *penzión* (in Slovakia).

In the Czech Republic these are usually cosy, inexpensive places offering rooms of a reasonable standard (with en suite bathroom), mostly with breakfast included. In Slovakia the term *penzión* covers provincial guesthouses, little different from private homes, but is also sometimes used by hotels with restaurants in large or historic town centres.

PRIVATE HOMES

Rooms in private homes for visitors to stay in are widely available in the Czech Republic. In Slovakia their numbers are growing fast. Some local tourist offices can help with advance bookings.

A room in the Carlton, Bratislava *(see p359)*

CAMP SITES

There are over 200 camp sites in the Czech Republic. In Slovakia, in the summer season there are about 100 (some also offering chalet and bungalow accommodation). Most have bathrooms, washrooms and kitchens available to all visitors; some also have a shop and a bar. They tend to be crowded in the high season.

AGRITOURISM

Slovakia is experiencing a growth in agritourism, which is where visitors have the chance to stay on a farm.

In the Czech Republic agritourism does not exist, as there is practically no private farming. Many Czech families, however, own summer houses, normally in attractive locations, which they rent out to visitors.

HIDDEN EXTRAS

Make allowances for extra expenses, such as tips for bringing in luggage to your room, or other services. While staying in a hotel it is worth checking whether parking and breakfast are included (particularly in Slovakia). Also check the cost of extras such as the minibar and telephone calls (particularly in the Czech Republic), as both can be much more expensive than elsewhere. Resorts in Slovakia tend to charge visitors a "climate tax", a small environmental tourist tax.

TRAVELLING WITH CHILDREN

In the Czech and Slovak Republics finding a place to stay with children does not present any major problems, and families are made welcome. In Slovakia many pensions, agritourism farms and private homes encourage families with children and try to provide entertainment and play areas for their youngest guests. Some hotels, particularly in the Czech Republic, will supply a cot and there may be a baby-sitting service.

DISABLED TRAVELLERS

Many Slovak hotels and better-class pensions can accommodate disabled guests; almost all new facilities are built with their requirements in mind. In the Czech Republic the needs of wheelchair users have been taken into account generally only by the top-class hotels, although this is slowly changing as new facilities are opened and are obliged to offer wheelchair access.

Hotels in the Czech Republic

These hotels have been chosen across a wide price range on the basis of their attractive location, high standards and range of facilities. Hotels are listed by region, starting with Prague and its environs, followed by the rest of the Czech Republic. Under each town or city, hotels are listed in alphabetical order within each price category.

PRICE CATEGORIES

Prices of accommodation in hotels and pensions are for a double room with bathroom and breakfast, and include tax.

Ⓚ under 3,000Kč
ⓀⓀ 3,000–4,500Kč
ⓀⓀⓀ 4,500–6,000Kč
ⓀⓀⓀⓀ 6,000–8,000Kč
ⓀⓀⓀⓀⓀ over 8,000Kč

PRAGUE – HRADČANY AND MALÁ STRANA

Pension Dientzenhofer
ⓀⓀ

Nosticova 2, Praha 1. **Tel** *257 311 319.* **Fax** *257 320 888.* **Rooms** *9*   **Map** *2 F4*

A pretty and well-kept pension, this was the birthplace of Baroque architect Kilian Ignaz Dietzenhofer. It is in a quiet street only three minutes' walk from Charles Bridge. Rooms are comfortable and all have en suite bathrooms, satellite TV and minibar. There is a small terrace for guests. Excellent wheelchair access. **www.dientzenhofer.cz**

Sax
ⓀⓀ

Jánský vršek 3, Praha 1. **Tel** *257 531 268.* **Fax** *257 534 101.* **Rooms** *22*   **Map** *2 D3.*

Situated close to Prague Castle, this Neo-Classical hotel is ideal for those who wish to be the first to arrive in the morning in Hradčany. The rooms are simply furnished, with windows facing the spectacular glass-roofed inner atrium. **www.sax.cz**

U Žluté boty
ⓀⓀ

Jánský vršek 11, Praha 1. **Tel** *257 532 269.* **Fax** *257 534 134.* **Rooms** *9*   **Map** *2 D3.*

Elegant rooms, plainly but tastefully furnished in a variety of styles; some have lots of wood, others are predominantly modern. All are large, with en suite bathrooms. A small garden square behind the hotel is particularly pleasant in the summer. **www.zlutabota.cz**

Best Western Kampa
ⓀⓀⓀ

Všehrdova 16, Praha 1. **Tel** *257 404 444.* **Fax** *257 404 333.* **Rooms** *84*   **Map** *2 E5.*

Housed in a 17th-century armoury, minutes away from the Charles Bridge, the hotel is tucked away in a quiet side street surrounded by beautiful gardens. The reception area leads into a bar and restaurant combined under lovely Baroque vaulted ceilings. Rooms are simply furnished, but clean. **www.euroagentur.cz**

Domus Henrici
ⓀⓀⓀ

Loretánská 11, Praha 1. **Tel** *220 511 369.* **Fax** *220 511 502.* **Rooms** *8*   **Map** *1 C3.*

This boutique hotel could hardly be nearer to the castle, the Loreto and Strahov Monastery. The rooms are huge and tastefully furnished. In summer the delicious breakfasts are served on the terrace with views over the Staré Město. **www.hidden-places.com**

U Brány
ⓀⓀⓀ

Nerudova 21, Praha 1. **Tel** *257 534 050.* **Fax** *257 532 767.* **Rooms** *17*   **Map** *2 D3.*

This is one of the best addresses in Prague. A popular place, U Brány is always full during high season, so book well in advance. The rooms, basically two-, three- and four-room suites, are elegantly furnished, and the bathrooms are just fantastic. **www.ubrany.cz**

Biskupský Dům (Bishop's House)
ⓀⓀⓀⓀ

Dražického náměstí 6, Praha 1. **Tel** *257 532 320.* **Fax** *257 531 840.* **Rooms** *45*   **Map** *2 F3.*

Fully restored in 1990, the hotel occupies a 16th-century building facing the Royal Route. The rooms are simply and comfortably furnished. Those on the upper floor feature exceptionally high ceilings with wooden beams, and all sorts of delightful nooks. **www.starshotelsprague.com**

Constans
ⓀⓀⓀⓀ

Břetislavova 309, Praha 1. **Tel** *234 091 818.* **Fax** *234 091 860.* **Rooms** *32*   **Map** *2 D3.*

Located in a quiet medieval street, below the castle. Newly refurbished, it combines old and modern styles in its airy interiors. The large rooms have huge beds and wooden floors. The charming hotel restaurant is a splendid place for dining. **www.hotelconstans.cz**

Dům U Červeného lva (Red Lion)
ⓀⓀⓀⓀ

Nerudova 41, Praha 1. **Tel** *257 533 832.* **Fax** *257 535 131.* **Rooms** *21*   **Map** *2 D3.*

With its lovely views over the Royal Route, the castle and peaceful Petřín hill, this former burgher's house is superbly located. Its rich interiors include painted Renaissance ceilings, the original period furniture and parquet floors. It also has a traditional beerhall. **www.hotelredlion.com**

Key to Symbols *see back cover flap*

U Zlaté Studně

U Zlaté Studně 166, Praha 1. **Tel** 257 011 213. **Fax** 257 533 320. **Rooms** 20   **Map** 2 E2.

A luxury hotel on four floors housed in a venerable old building. The view of the town, from the restaurant and the terrace, is simply stunning. The rooms are nicely furnished and bathrooms are very comfortable, which is a rarity in this part of town. **www.zlatastudna.cz**

Aria

Tržiště 9, Praha 1. **Tel** 225 334 111. **Fax** 225 334 666. **Rooms** 52   **Map** 2 E3.

In this charming, unusual hotel, the rooms are not very large and each of them is furnished in a style inspired by a different musical legend, such as "Dizzy" Gillespie, Puccini or Mozart. The hotel offers live music in its Winter Garden as well as a music library and a music salon with a real fire. **www.ariahotel.net**

Hoffmeister

Pod Bruskou 7, Praha 1. **Tel** 251 017 111. **Fax** 251 017 120. **Rooms** 37   **Map** 2 F2.

A high-class hotel, close to Prague Castle, the Hoffmeister has a spa and fitness club. Its large rooms are flamboyantly furnished and include colourful fabrics; they offer magnificent views over the Vltava. Located halfway up the hill leading to Chodkov. **www.hoffmeister.cz**

Savoy

Keplerova 6, Praha 1 **Tel** 224 302 430. **Fax** 224 302 128. **Rooms** 61   **Map** 1 B3.

A deluxe, modern hotel occupying a splendid, elegant building with an Art Nouveau façade. It prides itself on its service, and its amenities include a library and a fitness centre. The large, luxurious suites and rooms have perhaps the biggest bathrooms in Prague. Sometimes attracts celebrity guests. **www.hotel-savoy.cz**

Waldstein

Valdštejnské náměsti 6, Praha 1. **Tel** 257 533 938. **Fax** 257 531 143. **Rooms** 15   **Map** 2 E3.

Rooms of this elegant historic hotel in the centre of Malá Strana are furnished with antique pieces, but also provide Internet access, satellite TV and a kitchenette. Some have mosaics on the ceilings. Breakfasts, served in the original vaulted cellar, are delicious. **www.avehotels.cz**

PRAGUE – STARÉ MĚSTO AND JOSEFOV

Cloister Inn

Konviktská 14, Praha 1. **Tel** 224 211 020. **Fax** 224 210 800. **Rooms** 75   **Map** 3 B5.

This modern hotel, five minutes from the Charles Bridge, offers large, comfortably furnished rooms with pleasant bathrooms. Tasty breakfasts are served in a spacious dining room. Tea and coffee are freely available all day, and there is free Internet access for guests in the lobby. **www.cloister-inn.com**

U Klenotnika

Rytířská 3, Praha 1. **Tel** 224 211 699. **Fax** 224 221 025. **Rooms** 11   **Map** 3 B4.

A small but beautiful hotel and restaurant, halfway between Old Town Square and Wenceslas Square. The rooms are of a reasonable size and competitively priced. It also has a small bucket-lift for luggage. The hotel restaurant serves excellent breakfasts. **www.uklenotnika.cz**

Best Western Meteor Plaza

Hybernská 6, 110 00 Praha 1. **Tel** 224 192 559. **Fax** 224 220 681. **Rooms** 82   **Map** 4 D3.

This international chain hotel has a congenial, cosy old-world atmosphere. Despite having been modernized it still maintains its original character. Rooms are rather small. A pleasant restaurant is situated in the atmospheric wine cellar. **www.hotel-meteor.cz**

Betlem Club

Betlémské náměsti 9, Praha 1. **Tel** 222 221 574. **Fax** 222 220 580. **Rooms** 21   **Map** 3 B4.

Close to the Old Town Square, the hotel is housed in a beautiful medieval, pastel-green building standing in a quiet square. Rooms are small and plainly furnished, but all have bathrooms. Many times rebuilt, the house has a fascinating history and retains its original cellar. **www.betlemclub.cz**

U Zlatého Stromu

Karlova 6, Praha 1. **Tel/Fax** 222 220 441. **Rooms** 22   **Map** 3 B4.

The hotel is in a historic building. Rooms are small but have plenty of character. All the furnishings are tasteful and in keeping, including the wooden, beamed ceilings. Some windows face the courtyard, which is an oasis of peace; others overlook a very busy street. **www.zlatystrom.cz**

Bellagio

U Milosrdných 2, Praha 1. **Tel** 221 778 999. **Fax** 221 778 900. **Rooms** 46   **Map** 3 B2.

This lovely hotel, pastel-pink on the outside, stands in a peaceful street, close to the river. Tastefully furnished rooms, large and small, all have fair-sized bathrooms. The hotel bar is one of the most fashionable in Prague, and its Isabella restaurant is also becoming increasingly popular. **www.bellagiohotel.cz**

Grand Hotel Praha

Staroměstské náměsti 25, Praha 1. **Tel** *221 632 222.* **Fax** *221 632 204.* **Rooms** *31*   **Map** *3 C3.*

Due to its excellent location with a lovely view over the Old Town Square, the hotel fills up quickly, so book well in advance. Large rooms and suites have simple classic furnishings, but meet modern requirements. Breakfasts are served in the historic restaurant, U Orloje. **www.grandhotelpraha.cz**

Liberty

28 Řijna 11, Praha 1. **Tel** *224 239 598.* **Fax** *224 237 694.* **Rooms** *32*   **Map** *3 C4.*

Understated elegance and modern comfort are the hallmarks of this pleasant hotel, situated in the centre of Prague. There are spacious rooms and bathrooms, beautiful reception areas and exquisite service. The hotel health club, Relax, offers fitness facilities, massage and solarium. **www.hotelliberty.cz**

Metamorphis

Malá Štupartská 5, Praha 1. **Tel** *221 771 011.* **Fax** *221 771 099.* **Rooms** *24*   **Map** *3 C3.*

Located at the centre of the Staré Město, in the Týn courtyard, Metamorphis is in a venerable old house. It offers large rooms with pleasant bathrooms; some have antique furniture. The hotel restaurant makes its own delicious pizzas. **www.metamorphis.cz**

U Prince

Staroměstské náměsti 29, Praha 1. **Tel** *224 113 807.* **Fax** *224 213 807.* **Rooms** *24*   **Map** *3 C3.*

The hotel is popular with visitors thanks to the lovely view of the Staré Město from every room. The building itself is old, but the interior furnishings are super-modern. It boasts a magnificent terrace reached by a glass lift, and offers live jazz every evening. **www.hoteluprince.cz**

Grand Hotel Bohemia

Králodvorská 4, Praha 1. **Tel** *234 608 111.* **Fax** *222 329 545.* **Rooms** *78*   **Map** *4 D3.*

True to its name, this Art Nouveau hotel is opulent and dignified. Rooms are vast, the service is friendly, and the hotel café is a favourite meeting place for locals. The buffet breakfasts are very popular among regular visitors to Prague. **www.grandhotelbohemia.cz**

Ventana

Celetná 7, Praha 1. **Tel** *221 776 600.* **Fax** *221 776 603.* **Rooms** *29*   **Map** *3 C3.*

A classic Prague hotel, situated right at the centre of the Staré Město. Imaginatively furnished rooms, some split-level, all have four-poster beds. The reception area is boldly Art Deco in style. Extensive breakfasts are served in the library with a view over the Church of Our Lady before Týn. **www.ventana-hotel.net**

PRAGUE – NOVÉ MĚSTO

Pension Březina

Legerova 41, Praha 2. **Tel** *224 266 779.* **Fax** *224 266 777.* **Rooms** *35*   **Map** *6 D2.*

This somewhat run-down building houses a wonderful bed and breakfast establishment. Rooms are simple and modern, many facing a small garden at the back, and some with exposed wooden beams. It also has two suites, ideal for family accommodation. Breakfast is served in a small dining room. **www.brezina.cz**

Pension Museum

Mezibranská 15, Praha 1. **Tel** *296 325 186.* **Fax** *296 325 188.* **Rooms** *12*   **Map** *6 D1.*

The pension offers large rooms, most of them with a separate sleeping area and a small lounge. Excellent service, tasty breakfasts and a phenomenal location close to Wenceslas Square combine to make this the best bed and breakfast place in central Prague. Ideal for families. **www.pension-museum.cz**

Junior

Senovážné náměsti 21, Praha 1. **Tel** *224 231 754.* **Fax** *224 221 579.* **Rooms** *14*   **Map** *4 E4.*

An inexpensive hostel a few minutes' walk from Wenceslas Square. Rooms have two to six beds and are by no means luxurious, but are airy, comfortably furnished, and all have bathrooms. A popular pizzeria and a bowling alley are situated downstairs. **www.euroagentur.cz**

Na Zlatém Křiži

Jungmannovo náměsti 2, Praha 1. **Tel** *224 219 501.* **Fax** *222 245 418.* **Rooms** *8*   **Map** *3 C5.*

Probably the narrowest hotel in Prague, winner of many awards, this hotel offers large and luxurious double rooms and suites, all with bathrooms. Tasty breakfasts are served in the Gothic cellar. Can arrange transport to and from the airport. **www.goldencross.cz**

Opera

Těšnov 13, Praha 1. **Tel** *222 315 609.* **Fax** *222 311 477.* **Rooms** *67*   **Map** *4 F2.*

The hotel occupies an imposing late 19th-century Neo-Renaissance building close to the State Opera. Rooms with classic furniture and vast windows overlook the nearby park. The hotel bar has a good range of beers and is well worth visiting. **www.hotel-opera.cz**

Key to Price Guide *see p344* **Key to Symbols** *see back cover flap*

Tchaikovsky

Ke Karlovu 19, Praha 1. **Tel** *224 912 121.* **Fax** *224 912 123.* **Rooms** *19*   **Map** *5 C2.*

The hotel stands in a quiet street, five minutes' walk from Wenceslas Square. It offers charming traditional decor, understated elegance and refinement. Rooms are fairly large and beautifully furnished. A buffet breakfast is included in the price. **www.hoteltchaikovsky.com**

U Medvídků

Na Perštýne 7, Praha 1. **Tel** *224 211 916.* **Fax** *224 220 930.* **Rooms** *33*   **Map** *3 B5.*

Traditional Czech restaurant, pub and pension whose name translates as "The Little Bears". The most expensive rooms are larger and have wooden-beamed ceilings and a medieval flavour. It has a beerhall, which offers numerous Czech beers, and a beer museum in the cellar. **www.umedvidku.cz**

Elysee

Václavské námĕsti 43, Praha 1. **Tel** *221 444 111.* **Fax** *224 225 773.* **Rooms** *70*   **Map** *4 D5.*

If you are looking for a good but not luxurious hotel close to Wenceslas Square, this one will certainly provide the answer to your needs. The rooms are of a fair size and tastefully furnished, and the location is perfect. Effective sound-proofing eliminates street noises. Some apartments are available. **www.europehotels.cz**

Carlo IV

Senovážné námĕsti 13, Praha 1. **Tel** *224 593 111.* **Fax** *224 223 960.* **Rooms** *152*   **Map** *4 E4.*

This beautifully decorated hotel, with marble floors and wall paintings, occupies a Neo-Classical building at the heart of the city. It belongs to the Boscolo Group, and is magnificently luxurious, with the Box Block restaurant, a Cigar Bar, a spa and a wonderful swimming pool with mosaic floor. **www.boscolohotels.com**

Seven Days

Žitná 46, Praha 2. **Tel** *222 923 111.* **Fax** *222 923 222.* **Rooms** *50*   **Map** *6 D1/2.*

A marvellous Neo-Classical building at the centre of the Nové Mĕsto. The rooms are large, with excellent furnishings, and the communal areas are surprisingly opulent. A sauna and whirlpool are available for a small charge, and all rooms have Internet and TV. **www.hotelsevendays.cz**

Marriott

V Celnici 8, Praha 1. **Tel** *222 888 888.* **Fax** *222 888 889.* **Rooms** *293*   **Map** *4 E3.*

One of the most splendid of all Marriott hotels, this offers an excellent location right by the Old Town gate. All possible luxuries are available in each room. There is also a large health and fitness centre, with swimming pool. The hotel restaurant is one of the best in town. **www.marriott.com**

Radisson SAS Alcron

Štĕpánská 40, Praha 1. **Tel** *222 820 000.* **Fax** *222 820 100.* **Rooms** *211*   **Map** *6 D1.*

This large, luxurious hotel is in a superbly restored 1930s building near Wenceslas Square. The views from the upper floors of this hotel would provide a big enough attraction but there are others, including huge bathrooms and plush carpets. It is expensive, but worth the price. **www.radissonsas.com**

PRAGUE – ENVIRONS

Apollo

Kubišova 23, Praha 8. **Tel** *284 680 628.* **Fax** *284 684 570.* **Rooms** *42*

A modern, medium-size hotel offering plain rooms but with full facilities, including satellite TV, at reasonable prices. It is located in a quiet district 4 km (2 miles) north of the city centre. Tram and metro run regularly nearby. The price includes breakfast. **www.avehotels.cz**

Julián

Elišky Peškové 11, Praha 5. **Tel** *257 311 144.* **Fax** *257 311 149.* **Rooms** *32*

A good-quality hotel with small rooms but excellent service. The amenities include a sauna, solarium and a small fitness club. Children are welcome. There are also rooms available for wheelchair users, and one room has a specially adapted bathroom. Located near the river. **www.julian.cz**

Kafka

Cimburkova 24, Praha 3. **Tel** *224 225 769.* **Fax** *224 225 769.* **Rooms** *59*

Modest and clean but short on charm, this hotel is a brief walk from the Old Town. The large number of three- and four-bed rooms makes it particularly convenient and economic for families. Parking available at the hotel car park, but it has to be booked well in advance. **www.ckvesta.cz**

Kavalir

Plzeňska 177, Praha 5. **Tel** *257 216 565.* **Fax** *257 210 085.* **Rooms** *50*

The cheapest hotel of the H&Hotels group, the Kavalir is attractive, and lies south of Malá Strana. The rooms are exceptionally large, some with double beds. The hotel is well-kept, bright and clean; its friendly staff speak several languages. **www.europehotels.cz**

Abri
Jana Masaryka 36, Praha 2. **Tel** *222 511 568.* **Fax** *224 254 240.* **Rooms** *26*

This comfortable hotel stands in the quiet residential district of Vinohrady. Small rooms with bathrooms are all well equipped and furnished. The terrace in the small garden provides a pleasant place for a relaxing evening following a day of sightseeing. The amenities include a secure car park and a restaurant. **www.abri.cz**

Ariston
Seifertova 65, Praha 3. **Tel** *222 782 517.* **Fax** *222 780 347.* **Rooms** *61*

This good-quality three-star hotel is situated in a district close to the city centre. The rooms are a fair size, plain but clean, with high ceilings and solid wooden furniture. All have en suite bathrooms. There are also rooms for non-smokers, and some are adapted for disabled guests. **www.europehotels.cz**

Best Western Alta
Ortenovo náměstí 22, Praha 7. **Tel** *220 407 082.* **Fax** *222 822 833.* **Rooms** *87*

The hotel is located a fair distance from the city centre but close to an underground station. It belongs to the Best Western chain and therefore prides itself on unfailingly friendly and efficient service. A tasty breakfast is included in the price of the room. **www.hotelalta.com**

Duo
Teplická 492, Praha 9. **Tel** *266 131 111.* **Fax** *283 880 141.* **Rooms** *553*

A huge hotel situated in the northern part of the city with large rooms and excellent service. Some rooms have Internet access. It has the best sports centre in Prague, with swimming pool, fitness club, whirlpool, sauna and bowling alley. The beer garden is open in warm weather. **www.hotelduo.cz**

Green Garden
Fügnerovo náměstí 4, Praha 2. **Tel** *224 261 181.* **Fax** *224 262 182.* **Rooms** *55*   **Map** *6 D3.*

A comfortable, if not luxurious hotel, situated close to the main Prague-Brno motorway. The large, spacious, bright terrace under a huge glass roof, where you can pass a lazy afternoon over a cup of coffee overlooking the small green garden, is probably the greatest attraction of this place. **www.hotelgreengarden.cz**

U Blaženky
U Blaženky 1, Praha 5. **Tel** *251 564 532.* **Fax** *251 563 529.* **Rooms** *13*

Upon entering this grand villa in Prague's best residential district, you will feel your spirits soar. Everything in here is of good quality; the rooms are modern, spacious and tastefully furnished. The restaurant serves delicious local cuisine and offers a vast selection of wines. **www.ublazenky.cz**

U Tři Korunek
Cimburkova 28, Praha 3. **Tel** *222 781 112.* **Fax** *222 780 189.* **Rooms** *58*

The name of this hotel translates as "The Three Crowns"; the current price of the accommodation certainly exceeds this amount, but it is still not exorbitant. Rooms are modest, but well equipped. The hotel is situated in the district of Žižkov, about a 20-minute walk from Wenceslas Square. **www.3korunky.cz**

Arcotel Teatrino
Bořivojova 53, Praha 3. **Tel** *221 422 111.* **Fax** *221 422 222.* **Rooms** *73*

In the residential district of Žižkov, the hotel occupies a building that was once a theatre. It offers good-quality service, at affordable prices. Apart from the huge, well-furnished rooms it also has an excellent, quaintly furnished restaurant located in the former auditorium, surrounded by balconies and boxes. **www.arcotel.at**

Art Hotel Praha
Nad Královskou oborou 53, Praha 7. **Tel** *233 101 331.* **Fax** *233 101 311.* **Rooms** *24*

The hotel has a permanent exhibition of modern Czech art. Quiet and peaceful, it provides a good base for sightseeing in town. Each room has unique decor; all are furnished with taste and panache. The interesting lighting is subtle and romantic. Delicious breakfasts are included in the room price. **www.arthotel.cz**

Barceló
Na Strži 32, Praha 4. **Tel** *241 440 022.* **Fax** *241 441 023.* **Rooms** *213*

A fine hotel, located a fair distance from the city centre, it belongs to a Spanish chain. Barceló offers high-quality service, aiming mainly at large, organized groups of holidaymakers and business people. The rooms are spacious; those on upper floors have fine views over the city. **www.barcelopraha.com**

Carlton
Táboritská 18, Praha 3. **Tel** *222 711 177.* **Fax** *222 711 199.* **Rooms** *49*

An exquisite, high-class hotel in Žižkov. Large rooms at affordable prices. The most popular ones are those on the top floor, mainly due to their high ceilings and exposed wooden beams. One room is specially adapted for people with disabilities. Breakfast is served in a bright restaurant on the first floor. **www.europehotels.cz**

Mövenpick
Mozartova 1, Praha 5. **Tel** *257 151 111.* **Fax** *257 153 131.* **Rooms** *502*

Despite its location far from the city centre, this is an excellent hotel. It occupies two buildings, linked by a cable car. All rooms, some of them split-level, are large, comfortable and meet the highest standards. The hotel has two restaurants, and its lobby bar is famous for its delicious ice creams. **www.movenpick-prague.com**

Key to Price Guide *see p344* **Key to Symbols** *see back cover flap*

Praha Hotel

Sušická 20, Praha 6. **Tel** *224 341 111.* **Fax** *224 311 218.* **Rooms** *124*

When it first opened in 1981 this hotel was regarded by architects as the most modern in the republic, with unique interior furnishings. Originally used by state dignitaries, it is now open to everyone, but it still remains attractive to VIPs. **www.htlpraha.cz**

Ametyst

Jana Masaryka 11, Praha 2. **Tel** *222 921 921.* **Fax** *222 921 999.* **Rooms** *84*   **Map** *6 F3.*

Good, modern hotel with air-conditioned rooms, en suite bathrooms or showers and Internet access. The attic rooms with exposed beams are the most attractive. The hotel offers sauna facilities and massage and also has a small, pleasantly furnished restaurant. **www.hotelametyst.cz**

Mucha

Sokolovská 26, Praha 8. **Tel** *222 319 047.* **Fax** *224 816 641.* **Rooms** *39*   **Map** *4 F2.*

Despite being slightly overpriced, this is a very good hotel. It is named after the Czech artist Alfons Mucha. Reproductions of his works decorate the entire interior, which is a real Art Deco jewel. There is a restaurant, bar and sauna. **www.avehotels.cz**

Andel's

Stroupežnického 21, Praha 5. **Tel** *296 889 688.* **Fax** *296 889 999.* **Rooms** *239*

The hotel, representing the latest combination of elegance with functionality, was designed by an award-winning British team. The rooms are spacious, stylish and contemporary; the bathrooms have separate baths and showers, and the hotel restaurant is one of the best in Prague. **www.andelshotel.com**

Riverside

Janáčkovo nábřeží 15, Praha 5. **Tel** *234 705 155.* **Fax** *234 705 158.* **Rooms** *45*

The Riverside is a splendid hotel, offering unparalleled attention to comfort. Furnished with subtle elegance, it is virtually perfect – from the beautiful bathrooms to the original Czech art hung on the walls. As the name indicates, the hotel lies close to the river. **www.riversideprague.com**

CENTRAL BOHEMIA

BENEŠOV Atlas

Tyršova 2063, 256 01. **Tel** *317 724 771.* **Fax** *317 724 761.* **Rooms** *27*   **Road map** *B3.*

A modern hotel standing in the centre of Benešov, 2 km (1 mile) from Konopiště Castle. Two-, three- and four-bed rooms, with bathrooms and satellite TV; six rooms have a minibar. One room has wheelchair access. Restaurant with a summer terrace. **www.hotel-atlas.cz**

KOLÍN Chateau Kotěra

Ratboř u Kolina, Komenského 40, 281 41. **Tel** *321 613 111.* **Fax** *321 613 101.* **Rooms** *39*   **Road map** *B2.*

The hotel is situated 5 km (3 miles) southwest of Kolín, in a palace designed in Neo-Classical style by Czech Modernist architect Jan Kotěra. Luxuriously furnished rooms. The hotel restaurant specializes in Mediterranean cuisine and has wines from all over the world. Sauna, gymnasium, bicycle hire, tennis courts. **www.hotelkotera.cz**

KŘIVOKLÁT Roztoky

Roztoky u Křivoklátu 14, 270 23. **Tel** *313 558 931.* **Fax** *313 558 933.* **Rooms** *30*   **Road map** *B2.*

A quiet, inexpensive hotel about 1.5 km (1 mile) from Křivoklát Castle, adjacent to a protected nature area, Křivoklátsko. Stylish restaurant serving tasty food, and outdoor seating in the summer. A pub brews its own beer on the premises. **www.hotelroztoky.cz**

KUTNÁ HORA U Růže

Zámecka 52, 284 03. **Tel** *327 524 115.* **Fax** *327 563 202.* **Rooms** *14*   **Road map** *B2.*

The hotel is on the outskirts of Sedlec, close to the famous Ossuary. Its stylish interiors are furnished with original old furniture. It provides facilities for tennis, squash, bowling and paintball; it also has a swimming pool, sauna and fitness club. The restaurant offers a wide selection of Czech and European cuisine. **www.ruzehotel.cz**

KUTNÁ HORA Hotel U Zvonu

Zvonařská č.p. 286, 284 01. **Tel** *327 511 516.* **Fax** *327 516 571.* **Rooms** *7*   **Road map** *B2.*

A small congenial hotel located within the historic Old Town, in a peaceful street close to the town square and 200 m (220 yds) from the bus station. It occupies a Baroque 18th-century building. All rooms have en suite facilities, and the hotel has a pleasant restaurant *(see p378).* **www.uzvonu.cz**

KUTNÁ HORA U Vlašského dvora

28. října 511, 284 01. **Tel** *327 514 618.* **Fax** *327 514 627.* **Rooms** *10*   **Road map** *B2.*

A snug hotel in a historic 15th-century building in a quiet street in the medieval town centre. Park, swimming pool and tennis courts are all close by. Well-appointed rooms have views over the towers and steeples of the Old Town. Has a good restaurant *(see p378).* **www.vlasskydvur.cz**

MĚLNÍK Hotel Ludmila
`P` `11` ®

Pražská 2639, 276 01. **Tel** *315 622 419.* **Fax** *315 623 390.* **Rooms** *79* **Road map** *B2.*

A long-established hotel, located at the edge of the town, some 2 km (1 mile) from the centre. Ludmila offers comfortable rooms of standard and economy class. It has a restaurant *(see p379),* pub and sports bar attached, with a bowling alley; tennis courts nearby. **www.ludmila.cz**

MĚLNÍK U Rytířů
® `11` ®

Svatováclavská 17, 276 01. **Tel** *315 621 440.* **Fax** *315 621 439.* **Rooms** *8* **Road map** *B2.*

A charming little hotel, conveniently located in the historic town centre. A nearby viewpoint affords splendid views over the confluence of the Vltava and Labe rivers. The luxurious restaurant serves Czech and European specialities; vintage wines and a variety of beers are also on offer. **www.urytiru.cz**

MLADÁ BOLESLAV U Hradu
® `P` `11` ®

Staroměstské náměstí 108, 293 01. **Tel** *326 721 049.* **Fax** *326 721 039.* **Rooms** *30* **Road map** *B2.*

A smallish hotel in the town centre, at the foot of the castle. Pleasant rooms, with bathroom and TV, are clean and snug. There are two restaurants: one serving Czech cuisine, the other specializing in fish dishes and with a garden area for outdoor dining. **www.uhradu.cz**

MNICHOVO HRADIŠTĚ U Hroznu
® `11` ®

Masarykovo náměstí 27, 295 01. **Tel** *326 771 617.* **Fax** *326 771 246.* **Rooms** *20* **Road map** *B2.*

The hotel is very central. It offers pleasant, comfortable rooms with bathrooms, and two luxury suites. The stylish restaurant serves Czech and European cuisine, and Czech draught beer. Served in the stone-vaulted cellar are excellent Moravian wines and chef's specials.

PŘÍBRAM Modrý Hrozen
`P` `11` ®®

Náměstí T G Masaryka 143, 261 01. **Tel** *318 628 007.* **Tel/Fax** *318 628 901.* **Rooms** *21* **Road map** *B3.*

The hotel occupies a Baroque building right in the centre of the historic town, close to the steps leading to the Marian Sanctuary of Svatá Hora. Double rooms, two suites and a room for a family with children are all equipped to modern standards. There is a stylish restaurant *(see p379).* **www.modryhrozen.cz**

SÁZAVA Sázava
® `11` ®

Benešovská 44, 285 06. **Tel** *327 320 497.* **Fax** *327 321 117.* **Rooms** *8* **Road map** *B2.*

A bijou hotel set in a Baroque building. Rooms have a good range of facilities. Caters for families. Every couple checking in for the night receives a complimentary bottle of wine. The restaurant is famous throughout the Czech Republic for its excellent cuisine. **web.telecom.cz/hotel-sazava**

SOUTH BOHEMIA

ČESKÉ BUDĚJOVICE Hotel U Solné Brány
`P` `11` `大` ®

Radniční 11, 370 01. **Tel** *386 354 121.* **Fax** *386 354 120.* **Rooms** *12* **Road map** *B3.*

A small congenial hotel in the town centre, whose name translates as "The Salt Gate". Rooms with balconies or terraces. The hotel restaurant *(see p380)* offers a wide selection of dishes, including superb local fish and game, and a large choice of Moravian wines. **www.hotelusolnebrany.cz**

ČESKÉ BUDĚJOVICE Hotel U Tří Lvů
® `P` `11` `V` `&` ®

U Tří lvů 3a, 370 01. **Tel** *386 359 900.* **Fax** *386 359 780.* **Rooms** *36* **Road map** *B3.*

Modern, well-appointed hotel on the edge of the Old Town. Seven rooms and a terraced restaurant are adapted to the needs of disabled guests. All rooms have satellite TV, telephone, radio and minibar. The restaurant offers Czech, Slovak and international dishes. **www.hotelutrilvu.cz**

ČESKÉ BUDĚJOVICE Hotel Zátkův dům
® `P` `11` ®

Krajinská 41, 370 01. **Tel** *387 001 710.* **Fax** *387 001 711.* **Rooms** *10* **Road map** *B3.*

Occupying two Renaissance houses decorated with *sgraffito,* this is a small and friendly place. Comfortable rooms with modern furnishings including an office desk and Internet access. Considerable reductions are offered on Sunday nights. A buffet breakfast is included in the price. **www.zatkuvdum.cz**

ČESKÉ BUDĚJOVICE Grand Hotel Zvon
® `P` `11` `V` ®®®

Náměstí Přemysla Otakara II 28, 370 01. **Tel** *381 601 601.* **Fax** *381 601 605.* **Rooms** *70* **Road map** *B3.*

The hotel, occupying three historic buildings in the main town square, boasts traditions going back to the 16th century. The main reception area features some beautiful paintings and a 17th-century hand-carved ceiling. The rooms, of various sizes, are all of individual character. The hotel also has three restaurants.

ČESKÝ KRUMLOV Leonardo
`P` `11` ®

Soukenická 33, 381 01. **Tel** *380 725 911.* **Fax** *380 725 910.* **Rooms** *11* **Road map** *B3.*

A cosy, recently refurbished hotel situated in a historic building dating from 1582 and featuring lovely wooden ceilings and a Baroque staircase. It is centrally located near the main square. The price includes breakfast, which is served in the large dining room. **www.hotel-leonardo.cz**

Key to Price Guide *see p344* **Key to Symbols** *see back cover flap*

ČESKÝ KRUMLOV Pension Rosa

Linecká 54, 381 01. **Tel** *723 854 195.* **Rooms** *17* **Road map** *B3.*

This small, congenial pension in a pink Baroque building is located on the edge of the historic town centre but within easy reach of the main sights. It offers luxury rooms, adapted for people with disabilities, fitted with satellite TV and en suite bathrooms. **www.pension-rosa.cz**

ČESKÝ KRUMLOV Hotel U Města Vidně

Latrán 77, 381 01. **Tel** *380 720 111.* **Fax** *380 720 119.* **Rooms** *65* **Road map** *B3.*

The hotel, opened in June 2002, will satisfy even the most fastidious of guests, for a moderate price. Right in the heart of Latrán, it has luxurious rooms and suites, with satellite TV, Internet access and safes. The Vienna Garden restaurant offers up-to-the-minute cuisine. **www.hmv.cz**

ČESKÝ KRUMLOV Zlatý Anděl

Náměstí Svornosti 11, 381 01. **Tel** *380 712 310.* **Fax** *380 712 927.* **Rooms** *36* **Road map** *B3.*

In a Baroque building right at the town centre, opposite the town hall, this magnificent hotel perfectly combines tradition with modernity. All rooms, with en suite bathroom, satellite TV and minibar, are of a very high standard. The hotel has two restaurants, a cocktail bar, a café and a grill. **www.hotelzlatyandel.cz**

HLUBOKÁ NAD VLTAVOU Hotel Apartment Hluboká

Masarykova 972, 373 41. **Tel** *387 967 777.* **Fax** *387 967 787.* **Rooms** *10* **Road map** *B3.*

This luxury hotel is situated near the castle. It has ten suites, each consisting of two bedrooms, dining room, lounge, kitchen, separate bathroom and WC, offering comfort and good-value facilities for business travellers, individual tourists and families alike. **www.kamille.cz**

HLUBOKÁ NAD VLTAVOU Hotel Štekl

Bezručova 141, 373 41. **Tel** *387 967 491.* **Fax** *387 965 943.* **Rooms** *44* **Road map** *B3.*

A romantic hotel in a Neo-Gothic building in beautiful surroundings close to the castle. Room furnishings are reminiscent of castle interiors; no two are identical. Each room is decorated with copies of Old Dutch masters. The restaurant serves Czech and Thai cuisine.

JINDŘICHŮV HRADEC Vajgar

Náměstí Míru 162/I, 377 01. **Tel** *384 361 271.* **Fax** *607 853 976.* **Rooms** *18* **Road map** *B3.*

An inexpensive hotel of a decent standard. It is housed in one of the former merchants' dwellings in the central town square, surrounded by other historic houses. The restaurant serves traditional Czech cuisine, chef's specials and Moravian wines. **www.hotel-vajgar.cz**

PÍSEK Hotel Bílá růže

Šrámkova 169, 397 01. **Tel** *382 214 931.* **Fax** *382 219 002.* **Rooms** *35* **Road map** *B3.*

An elegant hotel in the town centre, with a name that translates as "White Rose". Rooms are equipped with bathroom, satellite TV and telephone. There is a restaurant and stylish cellar; the bar has live music and there is a beerhall with Czech cuisine and a dance floor. **www.hotelbilaruze.cz**

PRACHATICE Hotel Parkan

Věžní 51, 383 01. **Tel/Fax** *388 311 868.* **Rooms** *17* **Road map** *B3.*

The hotel is housed in a historic 14th-century building attached to the external city walls. In 1993 the building underwent reconstruction and its historic interiors have been supplemented with modern furnishings. The reception is in a Renaissance hall with a vaulted wooden ceiling. Pleasant restaurant *(see p381)*. **www.hotelparkan.cz**

PRACHATICE Koruna

Velké náměstí 48, 383 01. **Tel** *388 310 177.* **Rooms** *21* **Road map** *B3.*

In the predominantly Renaissance town centre of Prachatice, this hotel occupies a medieval building. Its rooms have en suite and satellite TV. The hotel restaurant will satisfy any gourmets, with its old Czech specialities and modern variations on local cuisine. The wine cellar is worthy of attention. **www.pthotel.cz**

ROŽMBERK NAD VLTAVOU Růže

382 18. **Tel** *380 749 715.* **Fax** *380 749 717.* **Rooms** *14* **Road map** *B3.*

A small congenial hotel occupying a 16th-century Renaissance house at the foot of the castle. It combines the romantic air of an old building with modern room furnishings. There are two suites – Komnata Petra Voka and Prechty z Rožmberka. Two restaurants serve Czech cuisine. **www.hotelruze.rozmberk.cz**

SLAVONICE Hotel Arkáda

Náměstí Míru 466, 378 81. **Tel** *384 408 408.* **Fax** *384 408 401.* **Rooms** *19* **Road map** *B3.*

The hotel occupies a beautiful pink and white Renaissance town house in the town square. Inside, the atmosphere is quiet and refined. The comfortable rooms have all modern facilities, and there is a restaurant. Bicycle hire is available for leisurely exploration of the area. **www.hotelarkada.cz**

TÁBOR Hotel Kapital

9. května 617, 390 01. **Tel** *381 256 096.* **Fax** *381 252 411.* **Rooms** *24* **Road map** *B3.*

Situated close to the medieval town centre, the Kapital offers clean rooms with all modern facilities. Restaurant with a terrace for summer dining *(see p382)*. Bicycle hire is available; the hotel can also arrange horse riding and jaunts in a horse and cart. **www.hotel-kapital.cz**

TŘEBOŇ Bohemia & Regent

U Světa 750, 379 01. **Tel** *384 721 394.* **Fax** *384 721 396.* **Rooms** *30*   **Road map** *C3.*

A complex of two hotels situated on the outskirts of town, close to the Svet pond, one of the largest of the area's many fish ponds. There are two restaurants in the complex, including one on the lakeside that specializes in fish dishes. **www.bohemia-regent.cz**

WEST BOHEMIA

CHEB Hvězda

Náměstí Krále Jiřího z Poděbrad 5, 350 02. **Tel** *354 422 549.* **Fax** *354 422 546.* **Rooms** *20*   **Road map** *A2.*

The hotel occupies an historic town house in the Old Town square and is near all the town's main sights. Rooms are well kept and pleasant, but not all have en suite bathrooms. The hotel has facilities for the disabled. Restaurant with a terrace. **www.hotel-hvezda.cz**

CHEB Penzion Hostel

Židovská 7, 350 02. **Tel** *354 423 401, 606 344 140.* **Fax** *354 423 401.* **Rooms** *8*   **Road map** *A2.*

A small pension of a higher than usual standard, situated in the Old Town, just off the the town square. High-ceilinged double rooms with bathrooms; the rooms can be combined into larger units. Breakfast is not included in the price. **www.penzionhostel-cheb.cz**

DOMAŽLICE Konšelský Šenk

Vodní 33, 334 01. **Tel** *379 720 200.* **Rooms** *10*   **Road map** *A3.*

In a medieval house, within Domažlice's Old Town centre, this hotel has views of the castle. Following its refurbishment the spacious rooms offer homely facilities and atmosphere. There is a beautifully kept garden for relaxation. In the hotel basement is a stylish restaurant-pizzeria. **www.konselskysenk.cz**

DOMAŽLICE Pension Family

Školní 107, 334 01. **Tel** *379 725 962.* **Fax** *386 356 843.* **Rooms** *10*   **Road map** *A3.*

Situated in Domažlice's historic town centre, 100 m (110 yds) from the main square, the pension offers plainly furnished but clean rooms with bathroom, at very attractive prices. There is also an apartment. The terrace is open in summer. Bicycle hire is available. **www.pensionfamily.cz**

FRANTIŠKOVY LÁZNĚ Spa Hotel Centrum

Anglická 392/5A, 351 01. **Tel** *354 543 156.* **Fax** *354 543 457.* **Rooms** *20*   **Road map** *A2.*

A comfortable, small, stylish hotel close to the main park. Elegant rooms and suites each have a bathroom and all the usual facilities. The hotel's spa centre offers baths, massage and an extensive range of treatments under medical supervision. **www.spahotelcentrum.cz**

HORŠOVSKÝ TÝN Šumava

Náměstí Republiky 11, 346 01. **Tel** *379 422 800.* **Rooms** *10*   **Road map** *A3.*

Excellent for business or tourist groups, this small, congenial hotel is in the town square. Offers a decent standard of rooms each with bathroom and a small TV set. Serves lunch and dinner, mainly Czech cuisine. Dogs and cats welcome. **www.hotel.htyn.cz**

KARLOVY VARY Hotel Kavalerie

T G Masaryka 43, 360 01. **Tel** *353 229 613.* **Fax** *353 236 171.* **Rooms** *5*   **Road map** *A2.*

A small hotel in the centre of the resort's pedestrianized zone, in a peaceful and quiet district within easy reach of bus and train stations. Large, bright rooms with pleasant decor and comfortable beds. Restaurant offers home cooking and some outdoor seating. **www.kavalerie.cz**

KARLOVY VARY Hotel Čajkovskij

Sadová 44, 360 01. **Tel** *353 237 520.* **Fax** *353 237 515.* **Rooms** *37*   **Road map** *A2.*

This newly refurbished, four-star hotel in a late 19th-century building close to the synagogue offers luxury conditions to its residents. The amenities include a spa, medical care and a restaurant serving international cuisine and Czech specialities. Special diets are catered for. **www.cajkovskij.com**

KARLOVY VARY Hotel Romance Puškin

Tržiště 37, 360 90. **Tel** *353 222 646.* **Fax** *353 224 134.* **Rooms** *37*   **Road map** *A2.*

Right at the centre of the resort, opposite the Royal Baths, this hotel offers comfortable, well-appointed rooms that are stylishly furnished. Modern spa centre complete with swimming pool. Restaurant with a summer terrace that offers running water.

KARLOVY VARY Grand Hotel Pupp

Mírové náměstí 2, 360 91. **Tel** *353 109 111.* **Fax** *353 224 032.* **Rooms** *112*   **Road map** *A2.*

One of the most famous Czech hotels, with traditions going back to the early 18th century. Luxuriously furnished rooms with minibar, safe, satellite TV and dazzling bathrooms. The amenities include restaurant *(see p382)*, casino, an impressive concert hall with Neo-Baroque interior, and of course a fabulous spa centre. **www.pupp.cz**

Key to Price Guide *see p344* **Key to Symbols** *see back cover flap*

LOKET Bílý kůň
T G Masaryka 109, 357 33. **Tel** *352 661 809.* **Fax** *352 661 877.* **Rooms** *31* **Road map** *A2.*

The name of this elegant, modernized hotel translates as "White Horse". It occupies a Neo-Renaissance house in the Old Town Square that J W Goethe visited many times. The amenities include restaurant, wine bar and summer terrace. **www.hotel-bilykun.cz**

MARIÁNSKÉ LÁZNĚ Hotel Maxim
Nehrova 141/1, 353 01. **Tel** *354 603 301.* **Fax** *354 603 303.* **Rooms** *28* **Road map** *A2.*

In a grand Neo-Classical building in the resort's centre, this hotel has retained its period interiors. Accommodation is in luxurious rooms. Offers medical treatment, therapy and rehabilitation; swimming pool (therapeutic baths). The restaurant menu is extensive. **www.hotelmaxim.cz**

MARIÁNSKÉ LÁZNĚ Hotel Excelsior
Hlavni 121, 353 01. **Tel** *354 622 705.* **Fax** *354 697 221.* **Rooms** *64* **Road map** *A2.*

Situated in a large, ornate building close to the "Singing Fountain", the hotel offers pleasantly furnished rooms, most with bathrooms. It is part of the Orea chain of hotels. The Restaurant 1900 serves international cuisine; there is also a summer terrace. **hotelexcelsior.cz**

PLZEŇ Hotel Continental
Zbrojnická 8, 301 00. **Tel** *377 235 292.* **Fax** *377 221 746.* **Rooms** *85* **Road map** *A3.*

Fully modernized in 1991, the Continental is in a building that dates from 1895. Its elegant rooms display individual character; a dozen or so have decor associated with certain themes, such as the sea, old Paris or London. Its former guests include celebrities, such as Marlene Dietrich and John Malkovich. Live music nightly. **www.hotelcontinental.cz**

PLZEŇ Hotel Irida
Na Poříčí 398/3, 301 00. **Tel** *373 729 612–15.* **Fax** *373 729 616.* **Rooms** *20* **Road map** *A3.*

This hotel, in a Neo-Classical building with a magnificent view over the river, is situated very close to the town centre. Clean, modern, well-equipped rooms with spotless bathrooms. Buffet breakfast. Sauna, hydro-massage, therapeutic gymnastics. Naturally, Pilsner Urquell is served in the bar. **www.irida.cz**

PLZEŇ Hotel Victoria
Borská 19, 301 00. **Tel** *377 221 010.* **Fax** *377 423 370.* **Rooms** *56* **Road map** *A3.*

The hotel occupies a grand, early 20th-century town house, a 10-minute walk from the town centre. Homely interiors create a relaxing, intimate atmosphere. The small walled terrace is a peaceful place to eat out in warm weather. Fitness club, massages, billiards. Bicycle hire is available. **www.hotel-victoria.cz**

PLZEŇ Parkhotel Plzeň
U Borského parku 31, 320 04. **Tel** *378 772 977.* **Fax** *378 772 978.* **Rooms** *72* **Road map** *A3.*

Opened in 2004, this hotel is in a beautiful area of Borský Park. Comfortable, luxuriously furnished rooms. Italian food is served in the romantic Emporio restaurant *(see p383)*, and there is an excellent wine bar. A golf driving range is attached to the hotel with facilities to hire equipment. **www.parkhotel-plzen.cz**

NORTH BOHEMIA

DĚČÍN Hotel Faust
U Plovárny 43, 405 01. **Tel** *412 518 859.* **Rooms** *50* **Road map** *B2.*

The hotel is located near a pond in the centre of Děčín, close to the town square. Well-appointed rooms with en suite bathrooms; one adapted for the disabled. Restaurant with a terrace and a specialist selection of South Moravian wines. **www.hotelfaust.cz**

HŘENSKO Hotel Mezni Louka
Mezná 71, 407 17. **Tel** *412 554 220.* **Tel/Fax** *412 554 027.* **Rooms** *25* **Road map** *B2.*

Enjoying a magnificent setting at the heart of České Švýcarsko National Park, the hotel occupies the building of a former gamekeeper's house, which in the late 19th century was turned into a hotel. It provides an excellent base for exploring the park. The facilities include mountain-bike hire, table tennis and billiards. **www.cztour.cz/meznilouka**

HŘENSKO Hotel Praha Hřensko
Hřensko 37, 407 17. **Tel** *412 554 006.* **Fax.** *412 554 162.* **Rooms** *30* **Road map** *B2.*

A beautifully located hotel in the town of Hřensko, on the edge of České Švýcarsko National Park. It occupies a stylish building representing the regional architecture, built in 1914 and modernized in 1995. It offers high standards and luxuriously appointed rooms. **www.hotel-hrensko.cz**

LIBEREC Hotel Praha
Železná 2/1, 460 01. **Tel** *485 102 655.* **Fax** *485 113 138.* **Rooms** *30* **Road map** *B2.*

In a lovely Art Nouveau building constructed as a hotel in 1905, the Hotel Praha is in a central location in the town square. It was modernized during the 1990s and now offers comfortable rooms, a good restaurant and stylish Art Nouveau interiors. **www.hotelpraha.net**

LIBEREC Hotel U jezírka   🅿   Ⓧ

Masarykova 44, 460 01. **Tel** *482 710 407.* **Fax** *482 710 254.* **Rooms** *38*   **Road map** *B2.*

The hotel is a 15-minute walk east of the town centre, in a leafy area close to the zoo and the botanical gardens. Nearby is an indoor swimming pool and aquapark. Bicycle trails lead from the hotel to the Jizerské hory mountains. **www.hotelujezirka.cz**

LIBEREC Impuls   🍴🅿⏱🍴   Ⓧ

Hodkovická 52, 463 13. **Tel** *277 25 10.* **Fax** *513 51 84.* **Rooms** *20*   **Road map** *B2.*

A stylish three-star hotel near the town centre, close to the Ješted sports complex and Babylon entertainment centre. Pleasant rooms with bathroom, satellite TV and telephone. The facilities include restaurant, bar, café and secure parking. **www.hotelimpuls.cz**

LIBEREC Košická   🅿   Ⓧ

Košická 471, 460 03. **Tel** *486 131 470, 608 001 168.*   **Road map** *B2.*

Hostel-type accommodation is offered in this inexpensive hotel. Rooms for two and four occupants, with one bathroom shared between two rooms; facilities are basic but clean. Apartments are available. Private car park. Close to railway and bus stations. **www.ubytovna-liberec.cz**

LITOMĚŘICE Dejmalik   🍴⛑🍴   Ⓧ

Sovová 3, 412 01. **Tel** *416 733 685.* **Fax** *416 733 686.* **Rooms** *9*   **Road map** *B2.*

A pleasant little hotel in the town centre, and a good base for visiting the Terezín fortress to the south. Baths have whirlpool massage. Horse riding can be arranged. Amenities nearby include an indoor swimming pool, thermal baths, sauna, solarium and bicycle trail.

TEPLICE Hotel Payer   🍴🅿⏱🍴🍴   ⓍⓍ

U Hadích lázní 1153, 415 00. **Tel** *417 531 446.* **Fax** *417 531 448.* **Rooms** *35*   **Road map** *B2.*

The elegant Neo-Classical building enjoys a magnificent view over the spa park. The hotel offers comfortable rooms with air conditioning, minibar and satellite TV. Facilities for the disabled. It has a new wing with slightly more expensive double rooms in a contemporary style. **www.hotelpayer.cz**

ŽATEC U Hada   🍴🅿⏱🍴🍴   Ⓧ

Náměstí Svobody 155, 438 01. **Tel & Fax** *415 711 000.* **Rooms** *21*   **Road map** *B2.*

The hotel is in the historic town centre, occupying a modernized burgher's house built in 1235, and featuring some original stonemasonry. Rooms are comfortable and it has two restaurants *(see p385)*. Solarium, swimming pool, fitness club, bowling and cinema are all close by. **www.uhada-zatec.cz**

EAST BOHEMIA

DVŮR KRÁLOVÉ Safari   🍴🅿⏱🍴   Ⓧ

544 01. **Tel** *499 628 255.* **Fax** *499 629 393.* **Rooms** *30*   **Road map** *C2.*

A luxurious, recently built hotel, close to the famous zoo. Well-equipped rooms all have French windows or balconies looking out over the central courtyard, which has an outdoor swimming pool. Bowling alley. Guests are entitled to a discount when visiting the zoo. **www.zoodk.cz**

HRADEC KRÁLOVÉ Hotelový Dům   🅿🍴   Ⓧ

Heyrovského 1177, 500 03. **Tel** *495 511 175.* **Rooms** *131*   **Road map** *C2.*

An inexpensive hotel standing on the southern outskirts of town, 1 km (half a mile) from the centre. Rooms are mainly doubles, and there is also a small dormitory. Bathrooms are shared between two rooms. A restaurant and a sauna are close by. **www.hotelovydum.cz**

HRADEC KRÁLOVÉ Nové Adalbertinum   🍴🅿   Ⓧ

Velké náměstí 32, 500 01. **Tel** *495 063 111.* **Fax** *495 063 405.* **Rooms** *35*   **Road map** *C2.*

A well-appointed pension with a restaurant housed in an historic Baroque building in the Old Town square. Rooms are simply furnished, but clean, all with bathroom, TV and telephone. Close by is a large car park, where hotel residents may leave their cars. **www.adalbertinum.diecezehk.cz**

HRADEC KRÁLOVÉ U Královny Elišky   🍴🅿🍴🍴🍴   ⓍⓍ

Malé náměstí 11, 500 03. **Tel** *495 518 052.* **Fax** *495 518 872.* **Rooms** *35*   **Road map** *C2.*

In the historic town centre, the hotel occupies two burghers' houses dating from the 14th century. The old cellars and vaulted ceilings have been left untouched during the modernization of the premises. The hotel offers a family atmosphere and traditionally furnished rooms. In the cellar a wine bar and a restaurant are available. **www.hotel-eliska.cz**

JIČÍN Jičín   🍴🅿⏱🍴   Ⓧ

Havlíčkova 21, 506 01. **Tel** *493 544 250.* **Fax** *493 544 251.* **Rooms** *16*   **Road map** *B2.*

The hotel is in the historic town centre, a short distance from the Valdice Gate. Its renowned restaurant serves game dishes and Czech cuisine. The shop in the cellar offers a wide selection of Bohemian, Moravian and foreign wines. **www.hoteljicin.cz**

Key to Price Guide *see p344* **Key to Symbols** *see back cover flap*

LITOMYŠL Petra

B. Němcové 166, 570 01. **Tel** *461 613 061.* **Fax** *461 613 061.* **Rooms** *4*   **Road map** *C2.*

A small congenial pension in a modernized Renaissance house, in the Old Town. The two rooms on the ground floor have vaulted ceilings in keeping with the building; all have bathrooms. Breakfast is included in the price. There is a pretty courtyard garden. **www.pension-petra.cz**

OPOČNO Opočno

U stadionu 670, 517 73. **Tel** *494 668 232.* **Fax** *494 667 480.* **Rooms** *50*   **Road map** *C2.*

Large, modern hotel close to the town square, aimed mainly at business travellers. It has good facilities for visitors with disabilities. It is situated within a sports complex that includes a stadium, playing fields, tennis courts, football pitch and swimming pool.

PARDUBICE Hotel 100

Kostelni 100, 530 02. **Tel** *466 511 179.* **Rooms** *10*   **Road map** *C2.*

Located in the historical centre of the city of Pardubice, Hotel 100 offers quiet, stylish accommodation. Double and single rooms are available as well as one apartment. Some rooms have views of the castle; all have ensuite bathrooms and satellite television. Free wirless internet access available. **www.hotel100.cz**

PARDUBICE Hotel Zlatá Štika

Štrossova 127, 530 02. **Tel** *466 052 100.* **Fax** *466 052 130.* **Rooms** *40*   **Road map** *C2.*

This luxurious, recently modernized hotel is at the edge of the town centre. It offers elegant, sunny rooms; in every one of them the guest will find a bottle of good wine. The amenities include a restaurant, wine bar, and alehouse refurbished in traditional style. **www.zlatastika.cz**

TRUTNOV Hotel Grand

Krakonošovo náměstí 120, 541 01. **Tel** *499 819 270.* **Rooms** *24*   **Road map** *C2.*

Making an excellent base for trips into Krkonoše, this three-star hotel is situated in the town square . Rooms have WC, shower, and satellite TV. Palmovka restaurant specializes in fish dishes, steaks and salads. A casino, solarium, hairdresser and beauty salon are all close by. **www.grandtu.cz**

VRCHLABÍ Hotel Gendorf

Krkonošská 153, 543 01. **Tel** *499 429 629.* **Fax** *499 429 632.* **Rooms** *39*   **Road map** *B2.*

A modern, central hotel, this forms part of a complex that includes a bank and shopping arcade. It is named after Christopher of Gendorf, a royal counsellor who made great contributions to the town's development. The hotel offers therapy and rehabilitation treatment – sauna, massage, cosmetic laser procedures, and others. **www.gendorf.cz**

NORTH MORAVIA AND SILESIA

BOUZOV Hotel u Cimbury

783 25. **Tel** *585 346 491.* **Fax** *585 346 282.* **Rooms** *13*   **Road map** *C3.*

Situated right in the town centre, at the foot of Bouzov Castle, the hotel offers rustic-style rooms with simple and comfortable furnishings, and a restaurant specializing in country cuisine *(see p387)*. An ideal place to stay when exploring the popular castle. **www.cimbura.hotel-cz.com**

JESENÍK Hotel Nodus

K vodě 430, 790 01. **Tel** *584 401 821.* **Fax** *584 403 001.* **Rooms** *23*   **Road map** *C2.*

This establishment enjoys a beautiful location on the outskirts of town, with views over the Jeseníki mountains. The adjacent field is equipped with tables for outdoor eating and has a barbecue area where residents can cook their own food. Well-appointed rooms. Services include sauna and massage. **www.nodus.hotel-cz.com**

NOVÝ JIČÍN Praha Hotel

Lidická 6, 741 01. **Tel/Fax** *556 701 229.* **Rooms** *24*   **Road map** *D3.*

An elegant hotel housed in an Art Nouveau building in the Old Town centre, close to the town square. Rooms have en suite bathroom, satellite TV and telephone; the suites also have a minibar. The large restaurant *(see p387)* is set in a grand period interior. **www.prahahotel.cz**

OLOMOUC Arigone

Univerzitní 20, 771 00. **Tel** *585 232 351.* **Fax** *585 232 350.* **Rooms** *14*   **Road map** *C3.*

A small, stylish hotel in the town centre. The building itself is a historic site and owes its name to the Italian painter, Francesco Arigone, who owned it in the 18th century. The restored interiors feature some remains of the original Romanesque stone masonry. Popular restaurant on two levels and bar. **www.arigone.cz**

OLOMOUC OLOMOUC Hotel Hesperia

Brněnská 55, 779 00. **Tel** *585 421 735.* **Fax** *585 412 367.* **Rooms** *58*   **Road map** *C3.*

This hotel is situated on the outskirts of town, a 10-minute stroll from the centre, along the main road to Brno. It offers luxurious rooms with all modern facilities. Internet room, Xerox and fax are all available to the residents. There is a large car park in front of the hotel. **www.hotel-hesperia.cz**

OLOMOUC Pension U Jakuba
Ulice 8. května 9, 772 00. **Tel/Fax** *585 209 995.* **Rooms** *5*   **Road map** *C3.*

Close to the Upper Market, this pension is in an historic Renaissance building, which dates back to the 15th century. In recent years the building has undergone a complete modernization. It offers four luxury studio-apartments, with fully equipped kitchens, and a three-bedroom attic apartment. **www.pensionujakuba.com**

OLOMOUC Hotel Gemo
Pavelčakova 22, 772 00. **Tel** *585 222 115.* **Fax** *585 231 730.* **Rooms** *34*   **Road map** *C3.*

The hotel is housed in a 13th-century building, whose interior decor, designed by Eugen Točik, uses only natural materials. Art Nouveau-style wooden furniture, handmade carpets and paintings by Moravian artists all add up to create an unforgettable atmosphere. Excellent restaurant *(see p387).* **www.hotel-gemo.cz**

OPAVA Iberia
Pekařská 11, 74 601. **Tel** *553 776 700.* **Fax** *553 776 702.* **Rooms** *16*   **Road map** *D2.*

A Spanish flavour distinguishes this recently modernized hotel in a 19th-century town house, close to the town square. Rooms are stylishly decorated and have bathroom, satellite TV, minibar and Internet access. The Castillo restaurant in the basement offers Spanish and Czech food and wine. **www.hoteliberia.cz**

OSTRAVA Hotel Nikolas
Nádražní 124, 702 00. **Tel** *596 134 164.* **Rooms** *20*   **Road map** *D2.*

Located along the main street that links the town centre with the railway station, this hotel is in a historic building with refurbished and modernized interiors. A pleasant wine bar is open in the evenings. A 20 per cent discount is offered at weekends.

OSTRAVA Polský Dům
Poděbradova 53, 723 00. **Tel** *596 122 001.* **Fax** *596 125 062.* **Rooms** *20*   **Road map** *D2.*

A well-appointed hotel with beautiful Art Nouveau interiors in Ostrava's town centre. The rooms are not very large, but they are clean and well equipped: all with en suite bathroom, satellite TV and telephone. There are two restaurants for residents; breakfast is from a self-service bar. **www.polskydum.cz**

ŠTERNBERK Hotel m
Čechova 11, 785 01. **Tel/Fax** *585 011 742.* **Rooms** *25*   **Road map** *C3.*

The hotel is situated in the town's historic centre close to Sternberg Castle. It is housed in a restored building, which succeeds in creating a pleasant family atmosphere and comfortable conditions in which to relax. An elegant restaurant. **www.hotelm.cz**

SOUTH MORAVIA

BRNO Amphone
Třída Kapitána Jaroše 29, 602 00. **Tel** *545 428 310.* **Fax** *545 428 311.* **Rooms** *54*   **Road map** *C3.*

A friendly family hotel set in a quiet street at the centre of Brno. It occupies a restored 19th-century town house. In addition to well-equipped double rooms, it has a small apartment. Excellent food, and in summer it is possible to eat outside on the terrace. Billiards, table tennis, sauna. **www.amphone.cz**

BRNO Hotel Bílá růže
Svatopetrská 26. **Tel** *545 233 500.* **Fax** *545 233 531.* **Rooms** *23*   **Road map** *C3.*

Business travellers as well as holidaymakers wishing to relax will enjoy this modern hotel a 10-minute walk from the town centre. Its elegant, well-equipped rooms are spacious and bright. Tennis courts for the use of residents. **www.hotel-bilaruze.cz**

BRNO Hotel Brno
Horní 19, 639 00. **Tel** *543 555 100.* **Fax** *543 215 308.* **Rooms** *90*   **Road map** *C3.*

The hotel stands in a peaceful area, not far from Brno's centre. Tastefully and simply furnished rooms and suites, including six rooms adapted for people with disabilities. Restaurant specializes in Moravian cuisine. **www.hotelbrno.cz**

BRNO Holiday Inn Brno
Křížkovského 20, 603 00. **Tel** *543 122 111.* **Fax** *543 246 990.* **Rooms** *202*   **Road map** *C3.*

Situated near the trade fair complex near the centre of Brno, this hotel has won numerous awards for its high-quality service. The rooms decorated in red and yellow are well-equipped and comfortable. The Prominent restaurant *(see p388)* serves dishes prepared in front of diners. There is also a hotel bar.

BRNO Hotel International Brno
Husova 16, 659 21. **Tel** *542 122 111.* **Fax** *542 210 843.* **Rooms** *262*   **Road map** *C3.*

Belonging to the Best Western Premier group, this modern hotel offers superbly equipped rooms and suites all with bathroom, satellite TV, minibar and safe. Its two restaurants, Lucullus and Pilsen, are among the most popular in Brno. **www.hotelinternational.cz**

Key to Price Guide *see p344* **Key to Symbols** *see back cover flap*

BRNO Hotel Voroněž 1

Křížkovského 47, 603 73. **Tel** *543 141 111.* **Fax** *543 212 002.* **Rooms** *75*   **Road map** *C3.*

This four-star hotel, modernized in 2002, has the region's largest business centre. Air-conditioned rooms, excellent service and hotel restaurants satisfy even the most fastidious of guests. There is a whisky bar with live music every evening, and a pub called the Moravian Cottage. **www.voronez.cz**

JIHLAVA Grand Hotel Jihlava

Husova 1, 587 52. **Tel** *567 303 541–2.* **Fax** *567 310 199.* **Rooms** *33*   **Road map** *C3.*

In a lovely Art Nouveau building dating from the early 20th century, this hotel is in the town centre, close to the town square. It offers rooms and three suites furnished with period furniture, in keeping with the hotel's character. Bureau de change and souvenir shop in the reception area. Restaurant and wine bar. **www.grandjihlava.cz**

KROMĚŘÍŽ Bouček

Velké náměstí 108, 767 01. **Tel** *721 223 844.* **Fax** *573 342 777.* **Rooms** *11*   **Road map** *D3.*

A small congenial hotel, occupying a Baroque house in the town square. Tastefully decorated rooms, some of which have views of the square and the castle. Restaurant *(see p389)* has an outdoor seated area open in the summer months in the arched entrance to the hotel. **www.hotelboucek.cz**

KROMĚŘÍŽ Pension Excellent

Riegrovo náměstí 7, 767 01. **Tel/Fax** *573 333 023.* **Rooms** *12*   **Road map** *D3.*

Located in the historical centre of Kroměříž, the Pension Excellent guesthouse is housed in a beautiful old building and offers comfortable accommodation. All rooms have satellite television and there is a lovely terrace and a restaurant serving traditional Czech cuisine. Sauna and free internet access. **www.excellent.tunker.com**

MIKULOV Réva

Česká 2, 692 01. **Tel/Fax** *519 512 076.* **Rooms** *20*   **Road map** *C3.*

Right in the centre of this small town, the Réva has rooms and a summer terrrace overlooking Mikulov Castle. The restaurant offers a wide selection of Czech dishes and local wines. There is also Italian cuisine on offer, with pizzas a speciality. **www.hotelreva.cz**

TELČ Hotel Na hrázi

Na hrázi 78, 588 56. **Tel** *567 213 150.* **Fax** *567 213 151.* **Rooms** *13*   **Road map** *B3.*

Beautifully located between the lakes that surround the Old Town centre. Comfortable, well-equipped rooms, all provided with easy access for wheelchair users. The hotel terrace and some balconies attached to the rooms offer magnificent views over the town. **www.nahrazi.cz**

TELČ Hotel Telč

Na Můstku 37, 588 56. **Tel** *567 243 109.* **Fax** *567 223 887.* **Rooms** *11*   **Road map** *B3.*

A small hotel in a street just off the main square in Telč, occupying a Renaissance town house. It offers a high standard, comfortable rooms and family atmosphere. Its associated restaurant, U Zachariáše, spills out on to the town square.

TELČ Penzion Steidler

Náměstí Zachariáše z Hradce 52, 588 56. **Tel** *567 243 424.* **Rooms** *3*   **Road map** *B3.*

Housed in one of the stunning, arcaded buildings that surround the historic town square, Penzion Steidler offers comfortable, simply furnished rooms, some with views towards the lake. A kitchenette is available for guests to use and there is a common room with a fireplace and television. **www.telc-accommodation.eu**

TŘEBÍČ Grand Hotel

Karlovo náměstí 5, 674 01. **Tel** *568 848 560.* **Fax** *568 848 563.* **Rooms** *67*   **Road map** *C3.*

Modern hotel in the town centre offering comfortable rooms of a high standard, simply furnished and with pale wooden floors. Amenities include a sauna, bowling alley and fitness club. The restaurant has local specialities and wines *(see p389)*. **www.hotel-trebic.cz**

VRANOV NAD DYJÍ Hotel Pod Zámkem

Náměstí 45, 671 03. **Tel** *515 296 216, 515 296 253.* **Rooms** *19*   **Road map** *C3.*

The hotel enjoys a prominent location on the main square directly below the castle, in a historic building known as "Peter's House", whose origins go back to 1524. The rooms are bright and comfortable; there is one apartment, and some four- and three-bed rooms as well as singles and doubles. **www.pod-zamkem.cz**

ŽĎÁR NAD SÁZAVOU Hotel

Strojírenská 372, 591 01. **Tel/Fax** *566 625 208.* **Rooms** *30*   **Road map** *C3.*

This modernized hotel in the style of a manor house is situated on the outskirts of town, and occupies a house dating back to 1908. Rooms are comfortably furnished. Spacious restaurant serving Czech cuisine, as well as a large hotel bar. **www.hotelh.cz**

ZNOJMO Hotel Morava

Horní náměstí 16, 669 01. **Tel** *515 224 147.* **Rooms** *10*   **Road map** *C3.*

The hotel is situated in the Old Town square, in a historic house. The rooms are comfortably and individually furnished. The restaurant offers an attractive choice of menu and local wines. There is a wine bar in the cellar with many local wines to choose from. **www.znojman.cz/morava**

Hotels in Slovakia

The hotels listed in this section have been selected for their attractive location, high standards and range of facilities. Hotels are listed by region, starting with Bratislava, followed by the rest of Slovakia. Under each town or city, hotels are listed in alphabetical order within each price category.

PRICE CATEGORIES
Prices of accommodation in hotels and pensions are for a double room with bathroom and breakfast, and include tax.
€ under 65 euros
€€ 65–130 euros
€€€ 130–200 euros
€€€€ 200–265 euros
€€€€€ over 265 euros

BRATISLAVA

Echo
€

Prešovská 39, 821 08 Bratislava 2. Tel (02) 55 56 91 70. Fax (02) 55 56 91 74. Rooms 34   Road map *C4.*

On the eastern edge of the city centre, the hotel is close to the sports hall, stadium, and swimming pools. All the rooms are spotlessly clean, comfortably furnished and have bathrooms. The hotel restaurant serves breakfast, lunch and dinner. **www.hotelecho.sk**

Hotel Incheba
€

Viedenská cesta 3–7, 851 01 Bratislava 5. Tel (02) 67 27 31 21. Fax (02) 67 27 25 42. Rooms 60   Road map C4.

The hotel is situated within the area of Incheba Expo Bratislava, a major exhibition centre on the right bank of the Danube. Rooms and suites all have an en suite bathroom and telephone. Fitness club, squash courts, sauna and solarium. Superb, generous breakfasts. During exhibitions the hotel is often fully booked. **www.incheba.sk**

Turist
€

Ondavská 5, 822 05 Bratislava 2. Tel (02) 55 57 27 89. Fax (02) 55 57 31 80. Rooms 99   Road map *C4.*

About 1.5 km (1 mile) from the historic town centre, the hotel offers plain yet comfortable conditions at reasonable prices. All rooms have balconies; some are provided with refrigerators. Breakfast included in the price. There are plenty of amenities nearby, including a park, swimming pool, ice rink and bowling alley. **www.turist.sk**

Barónka
€€

Murdochova 2, 835 27 Bratislava 37. Tel (02) 44 88 20 89. Fax (02) 44 88 54 00. Rooms 122   Road map *C4.*

Modern, three-star hotel situated in the Rača district, in an exceptionally picturesque wine-growing area 20 minutes by tram to the city centre. Smartly furnished rooms with satellite TV, radio and refrigerator; bathrooms with hairdryers. The facilities include restaurant, wine bar, summer terrace and a conference room. **www.baronka.sk**

Best Western Hotel West
€€

Cesta na Kamzík, 833 29 Bratislava 37. Tel (02) 54 78 86 92. Fax (02) 54 77 77 81. Rooms 49   Road map *C4.*

The hotel stands in a forested area northwest of the city, close to Kamzík mountain. Since 1999 it has been part of the international Best Western chain, which guarantees a high standard of service. The luxuriously furnished rooms include desks. The restaurant has an imposing interior and serves a wide variety of dishes. **www.hotel-west.sk**

Botel Marina
€€

Nábrežie arm. gen. L. Svobodu, 811 02 Bratislava 1. Tel (02) 54 64 18 04. Rooms 32   Road map *C4.*

This four-star hotel is located on a boat moored off the left bank of the Danube, at the foot of the castle. It offers comfortable cabins and suites with air-conditioning, Internet access and minibar. There is a nightclub on board. A unique atmosphere and in an ideal location. **www.botelmarina.sk**

City Hotel Bratislava
€€

Seberíního 9, 821 03 Bratislava 2. Tel (02) 20 60 61 50. Fax (02) 20 60 61 22. Rooms 240   Road map *C4.*

One of the city's biggest hotels, it is situated in the Ružinov district, between the city centre and the airport. The rooms are luxurious and stylish. There is a restaurant, lobby bar and grill bar. Large shopping and entertainment centres are close by. Well served by public transport. **www.cityhotelbratislava.sk**

Hotel Club
€€

Odbojárov 3, 831 04 Bratislava 4. Tel (02) 49 20 21 11. Fax (02) 44 63 57 39. Rooms 30   Road map *C4.*

Located near the National Tennis Centre, this hotel is about 10 minutes' drive from the centre. It offers comfortable accommodation, including an en suite bathroom in every room and satellite TV. A tennis court is available for guests. There is a pleasant restaurant. www.hotel-club.sk

Sorea
€€

Král'ovské údolie 6, 811 02 Bratislava 1. Tel (02) 54 41 44 42. Fax (02) 54 41 10 17. Rooms 39   Road map *C4.*

The hotel belongs to the Slovak Sorea hotel chain. It stands to the west of the castle, surrounded by greenery, about a 10-minute walk from the city centre. Modern, well-kept rooms of various categories. Breakfast bar. The Vitalcentre offers sauna, massage and a range of individual treatments. **www.sorea.sk**

Key to symbols *see back cover flap*

Tatra

Námestie 1. mája 5, 811 06 Bratislava 1. **Tel** *(02) 59 27 21 11.* **Fax** *(02) 59 27 21 35.* **Rooms** *86*   **Road map** *C4.*

On the outskirts of the Old Town, this luxurious hotel is aimed mainly at business people. Spacious rooms, with modern furnishings, some with air conditioning, afford magnificent views over the Presidential Palace gardens. The Old Bratislava restaurant is hung with paintings of the city. **www.hoteltatra.sk**

Antares

Šulekova 15/A, 811 03 Bratislava 1. **Tel** *(02) 54 64 89 71.* **Fax** *(02) 54 64 89 72.* **Rooms** *16*   **Road map** *C4.*

A small hotel with superb facilities, located in the quiet residential area at the foot of the castle. Rooms are decorated in a contemporary style, with air conditioning, satellite TV, wireless Internet connection, minibar and safe. In the summer breakfast is served in the peaceful garden. **www.hotelantares.sk**

Apartmánový hotel Residence Sulekova

Šulekova 20, 811 06 Bratislava 1. **Tel** *(02) 54 41 93 83.* **Fax** *(02) 54 41 93 88.* **Rooms** *32*   **Road map** *C4.*

The only apartment-type hotel in Bratislava. It offers beautifully fitted apartments with clean, modern decor, complete with kitchen and minibar. Convenient for a longer stay (reduced rates). Part of the Ma Maison chain, which operates hotels in the capitals of Central Europe. **www.residence-sulekova.com**

Devin

Riečna 4, 811 02 Bratislava 1. **Tel** *(02) 59 98 51 11.* **Fax** *(02) 54 43 08 58.* **Rooms** *94*   **Road map** *C4.*

Located in the historic centre of Bratislava, on the banks of the Danube. Comfortable rooms, with state-of-the-art facilities are furnished in natural materials and wood. All have views of the Danube or the city centre and castle. Plays host to heads of government during state visits. Superb restaurant *(see p391).* **www.hoteldevin.sk**

Holiday Inn Bratislava

Bajkalská 25/A, 825 03 Bratislava 2. **Tel** *(02) 48 24 51 11.* **Fax** *(02) 48 24 51 12.* **Rooms** *131*   **Road map** *C4.*

About 5 km (3 miles) from the city centre, this hotel is an ideal place for business travellers as well as holidaymakers. It offers comfortable, air-conditioned rooms and three restaurants with Slovak, Italian and international cuisine. There are also relaxation and business centres. **www.holiday-inn.com/bratislavasr**

Hradna Brana Devín

Slovanské nábrežie 15, Devín, 841 10 Bratislava 4. **Tel** *(02) 60 10 25 11.* **Rooms** *12*   **Road map** *C4.*

This small, congenial, luxurious hotel is situated close to the Devín Castle. Superbly equipped rooms, furnished according to Feng-shui principles. The hotel has facilities for the disabled; it also offers relaxation facilities. There is a restaurant, café and lobby bar. **www.hotelhb.sk**

Radisson SAS Carlton Hotel

Hviezdoslavovo nám. 3, 811 02 Bratislava 1. **Tel** *(02) 59 39 00 00.* **Fax** *(02) 59 39 00 10.* **Rooms** *168* **Road map** *C4.*

Situated at the heart of town, close to the Slovak National Theatre, the Carlton is housed in one of the capital's most imposing buildings, built in 1837. Each floor is dedicated to a different famous composer, and one suite is named after Maria Theresa. The Mirror Bar serves fantastic cocktails. **www.bratislava.radissonsas.com**

Danube

Rybné námestie 1, 813 38 Bratislava 1. **Tel** *(02) 59 34 00 00.* **Fax** *(02) 54 41 43 11.* **Rooms** *276*   **Road map** *C4.*

A top-class hotel set in the historic heart of Bratislava's Old Town with a splendid view over the Danube and the castle. Air-conditioned rooms with top-notch facilities, restaurant *(see p391)* and bar, excellent service and friendly atmosphere ensure a truly enjoyable stay. **www.hoteldanube.com**

Marrol's

Tobrucká 4, 811 02 Bratislava 1. **Tel** *(02) 57 78 46 00.* **Fax** *(02) 57 78 46 01.* **Rooms** *42*   **Road map** *C4.*

Modern, but in retro-style, this is one of the city's most exclusive hotels. Situated close to the exit from the Old Bridge. A range of beautiful rooms and three spectacular suites. Numerous events organized for the guests' entertainment. Private taxi service. **www.marrols.sk**

WEST SLOVAKIA

DUNAJSKÁ STREDA Bonbón

Alžbetínske námestie 1, 929 01. **Tel** *(031) 557 52 22.* **Fax** *(031) 557 57 77.* **Rooms** *70*   **Road map** *D4.*

A modern hotel in the town centre, Bonbón offers all kinds of recreation and relaxation and a high-quality service. There are family rooms and apartments as well as single and double rooms. In addition to a restaurant and café, there is a summer terrace leading to an outdoor pool. Geothermal baths nearby. **www.bonbon.sk**

KOMÁRNO Europa

M R Štefánika 1, 945 01. **Tel** *(035) 773 13 49.* **Fax** *(035) 773 13 51.* **Rooms** *37*   **Road map** *D4.*

Two-storey hotel in the central part of town. All rooms have an en suite bathroom, TV and refrigerator. There are two suites for business travellers and one for a family. The restaurant serves Slovak and international cuisine. There is also a coffee bar and a fast-food outlet. **www.hoteleuropa.sk**

LEVICE Lev ☑ P 🅿 ⬚ 🖥 €
Čsl. armady 2, 934 80. **Tel** *(036) 631 30 64.* **Fax** *(036) 622 97 39.* **Rooms** *29* **Road map** *D4.*

The hotel has been in business for over 100 years. It is housed in an imposing building in the centre of Levice and has a beautiful Art Nouveau conference hall. All rooms have en suite bathrooms and some have a balcony. Buffet breakfast included in the price.

MALACKY Atrium ☑ P 🅿 ⬚ 🖥 €
Zámocká 1, 901 01. **Tel** *(034) 772 31 61.* **Tel/Fax** *(034) 772 31 63.* **Rooms** *70* **Road map** *C4.*

Situated along the D2 motorway linking Bratislava with Brno and Prague, about 35 km (22 miles) from Bratislava. All rooms and 2-room suites have en suite bathrooms. The hotel restaurant and café offer a large choice of Slovak cuisine. There is a nightclub in the hotel. **www.hotelmalacky.sk**

MODRA Cottage Plus P 🅿 🎿 🖥 €
Piesok, 900 01. **Tel** *(02) 43 42 63 50.* **Fax** *(02) 43 29 33 78.* **Rooms** *10* **Road map** *C4.*

The pension enjoys a pleasant location within a wooded area of the Small Carpathian mountains, 37 km (23 miles) northeast of Bratislava. Well-appointed suites, friendly and helpful staff. Good opportunities for summer and winter sports. **www.hotely-plus.sk**

NITRA Best Western Hotel Koruna ☑ P 🅿 ⬚ 🖥 🖥 €€
Svätoplukova 2, 949 01. **Tel** *(037) 651 23 15.* **Fax** *(037) 651 23 18.* **Rooms** *16* **Road map** *D4.*

Located outside the town, on the slopes of Mount Zobor, on the site of a former vineyard and winery. The rooms are bright and spacious with air conditioning and en suite bathrooms. The restaurant has an excellent selection of wines. **www.hotelkoruna.sk**

NITRA Capital ☑ P 🅿 ⬚ €€
Farská 16, 949 01. **Tel** *(037) 692 52 01.* **Fax** *(037) 692 52 03.* **Rooms** *24* **Road map** *D4.*

This hotel is an oasis of beauty and tranquillity. All the facilities and service aim at ensuring the highest level of comfort and relaxation. The rooms have been furnished and equipped with great attention to detail. The lovely, stylish Symfónia restaurant *(see p392)* serves Slovak and international cuisine. **www.hotelcapital.sk**

NITRA Hotel Zlatý Kľúčik ☑ P 🅿 🎿 ⬚ 🖥 €€
Svätourbánska 27, 949 01. **Tel** *(037) 655 02 89.* **Fax** *(037) 655 02 93.* **Rooms** *27* **Road map** *D4.*

This modern hotel opened in 1994 on the slopes of Mount Zobor and offers a sweeping panorama of Nitra from many of its comfortably furnished rooms. It has an excellent restaurant *(see p392)* with a large selection of wines and an intimate lounge. Sauna, whirlpool and massages are available. **www.zlatyklucik.sk**

NITRA Park Hotel Tartuf ☑ P 🅿 🎿 ⬚ €€
Pustý Chotár 495, Beladice, 951 75. **Tel** *(037) 633 02 35.* **Fax** *(037) 633 06 82.* **Rooms** *11* **Road map** *D4.*

Housed in a beautiful Neo-Classical manor house built around 1820 and in an adjacent building, this hotel lies 18 km (11 miles) east of Nitra. Stylish interiors with luxurious furnishings, and a music room and billiard room. Superb restaurant and lovely coffee bar with summer terrace or an open fire in winter. **www.tartuf.sk**

NOVÉ ZAMKY Hubert ☑ P 🅿 ⬚ 🖥 €
Budovateľská 2, 940 60. **Tel** *(035) 642 64 80.* **Tel/Fax** *(035) 642 64 80.* **Rooms** *21* **Road map** *D4.*

Situated just outside the town on the road to Komarno. A pleasant, small and congenial hotel with traditionally and comfortably furnished rooms and professional service. The restaurant serves excellent seafood dishes and salads *(see p392)*. **www.hubertnz.sk**

NOVÉ ZAMKY Hotel Grand ☑ P 🅿 🎿 ⬚ 🖥 €€
Pribinova 19, 940 01. **Tel** *(035) 640 44 24.* **Tel/Fax** *(035) 640 44 25.* **Rooms** *22* **Road map** *D4.*

A luxury three-star hotel situated outside the town centre and surrounded by a park. The rooms are spacious and well furnished, with en suite bathroom. The hotel prides itself on its excellent restaurant with a wide selection of alcoholic drinks. In the summer you can enjoy a meal in the shady garden. **www.hotelgrandnz.sk**

PEZINOK Tilia ☑ P 🅿 €
Kollárova 20, 902 01. **Tel/Fax** *(033) 641 24 02.* **Rooms** *18* **Road map** *C4.*

Attractively located in the foothills of the Small Carpathians, at the centre of Pezinok, a small town famous for its wine-making traditions, 18 km (11 miles) northeast of Bratislava. It has a few apartments as well as rooms. The restaurant occupies a former wine cellar. **www.hoteltilia.sk**

PIEŠŤANY Hotel Balnea Esplanade ☑ P 🅿 ⬚ 🖥 💧 €
Winterova 29, 921 29. **Tel** *(033) 775 53 95.* **Fax** *(033) 762 37 43.* **Rooms** *258* **Road map** *D3.*

A luxurious spa hotel in Slovakia's largest health resort. It lies in a park, in the central part of the spa island. It offers a spa-rehabilitation centre and beauty salon. Guests have free use of Water World, which has indoor and outdoor

PIEŠŤANY Hotel Thermia Palace ☑ P 🅿 ⬚ 🖥 💧 €€
Winterova 29, 921 29. **Tel** *(033) 775 61 52.* **Fax** *(033) 762 25 04.* **Rooms** *122* **Road map** *D3.*

Architecturally the most beautiful hotel in Piešťany. The Art Nouveau building is in the southern section of the spa island, near the thermal springs and sources of mineral waters. It is linked with Irma spa house, allowing the residents to enjoy thermal baths regardless of the weather. Restaurant serves vegetarian dishes. **www.spapiestany.sk**

Key to Price Guide *see p358* **Key to symbols** *see back cover flap*

PIEŠŤANY Magnólia ⬛🅿️🍴🎛️♨️🛎️ €€

kpt. Nálepku 1, 921 01. **Tel** *(033) 762 62 51.* **Fax** *(033) 772 11 49.* **Rooms** *125* **Road map** *D3.*

The hotel stands on the banks of the Váh river, 1.5 km (1 mile) away from the bus and railway stations. Large, bright rooms are comfortable and provide a magnificent view over the river and Považský Inovec mountain. Free use of swimming pool and fitness club. **www.hotelmagnolia.sk**

SENEC Senec ⬛🅿️🍴♿♨️🛎️ €€

Slnečné jazerá–Sever, 903 01. **Tel** *(02) 45 92 72 55.* **Fax** *(02) 45 92 72 77.* **Rooms** *104* **Road map** *C4.*

Located amid the spectacular scenery of the Sunny Lakes, 18 km (11 miles) east of Bratislava, the hotel has a good restaurant *(see p392)* and excellent sports facilities. Indoor and outdoor pools, tennis and squash courts, table tennis, beach volleyball and more. Supervised activities for children. **www.hotelsenec.sk**

ŠTÚROVO Hotel Thermal ⬛🅿️🍴♿♨️🛎️♨️ €€

Pri Vadaši 2, 943 01. **Tel** *(036) 756 01 11.* **Fax** *(036) 756 01 01.* **Rooms** *47* **Road map** *D4.*

This imposing hotel stands close to the huge Vadaš thermal baths complex. In addition to hotel rooms, it offers luxury apartments (for 3 and 4 people) within the spa area, bungalows, a hostel and a restaurant. There is also a children's play area. **www.vadas.sk**

SVÄTÝ JUR Maxim ⬛🅿️🍴 €

Bratislavská 52/11, 900 21. **Tel** *(02) 44 64 73 37.* **Fax** *(02) 44 97 07 43.* **Rooms** *18* **Road map** *C4.*

The hotel is situated in this wine-producing town, at the foot of the Small Carpathians. Modern both inside and out, it has double rooms with a full range of facilities. It has a restaurant, café and wine cellar. Local and international specialities are served. **www.hotelmaxim.sk**

TRENČÍN Penzión Evergreen 🅿️🍴 €

Kubranská 8, 911 01. **Tel** *(032) 744 16 71.* **Fax** *(032) 743 37 87.* **Rooms** *12* **Road map** *D3.*

A small pleasant pension with modern furnishings, situated on the outskirts of town. Well-equipped rooms, and suites, as well as a restaurant, bar and summer terrace – all attractively priced. English breakfast is available but not included in the price.

TRENČÍN Hotel Tatra ⬛🅿️🍴♿♨️🛎️ €€€

M R Štefanika 2, 911 01. **Tel** *(032) 650 61 11.* **Fax** *(032) 650 62 13.* **Rooms** *70* **Road map** *D3.*

Established in 1901, the hotel enjoys an attractive location in a superb Art Nouveau building reconstructed in 1987–94. The rooms are comfortably furnished. Its renowned restaurants include the main restaurant *(see p392)*, the Slovak restaurant, which offers gypsy music, and the Art Nouveau café Sissi. **www.hotel-tatra.sk**

TRENČIANSKE TEPLICE Flóra ⬛🅿️🍴♨️🛎️ €

17 novembra 14, 914 51. **Tel** *(032) 655 29 81.* **Fax** *(032) 655 28 24.* **Rooms** *61* **Road map** *D3.*

The hotel is in the centre of this spa resort in extensive leafy grounds. All rooms have en suite bathrooms and many have been refurbished to a high standard. Most of the hotel balconies afford a breathtaking view. Facilities include rehabilitation treatment and thermal baths. **www.hotelflora.sk**

TRENČIANSKE TEPLICE Hotel Margit ⬛🅿️🍴🎛️♨️🛎️♨️ €

T G Masaryka 2, 914 51. **Tel** *(032) 655 10 28.* **Fax** *(032) 655 10 29.* **Rooms** *10* **Road map** *D3.*

An imposing building on the edge of the resort houses this well-equipped hotel. During the town's small international film festival in June the hotel is popular with visiting film stars. Previous guests include Sophia Loren and Alain Delon. Rehabilitation treatment, sauna and whirlpool baths. **www.hotel-margit.sk**

TRENČIANSKE TEPLICE Hotel Slovakia ⬛🅿️🍴♨️ €

T G Masaryka 3, 914 51. **Tel** *(032) 655 65 11.* **Fax** *(032) 655 35 04.* **Rooms** *92* **Road map** *D3.*

This is a large hotel on a promenade, offering comfortable, well-kept, plainly furnished rooms and suites; the suites have a minibar. It has a restaurant, café, summer terrace and nightclub. Massage, sauna and various therapies are available. **www.hotelslovakia.sk**

TRNAVA Penzión U MaMi ⬛🅿️🍴♿♨️🛎️ €

Jeruzalemská 3, 917 01. **Tel** *(033) 535 42 16.* **Fax** *(033) 535 42 17.* **Rooms** *14* **Road map** *D4.*

Situated in the town centre, in a peaceful street close to the Archbishop's Palace and St Nicholas' Cathedral, this hotel has 11 en suite rooms and three suites, all comfortably furnished. The restaurant is open only to residents. A fitness centre can be used free of charge by guests. **www.penzionumami.sk**

TRNAVA Apollo ⬛🅿️🍴♨️🛎️ €€

Štefánikova 23, 917 00. **Tel** *(033) 551 19 37.* **Fax** *(033) 551 19 38.* **Rooms** *21* **Road map** *D4.*

Conveniently located on one of the town's principal streets, the hotel offers spotless and comfortable double rooms all equipped with en suite bathroom, satellite TV and minibar. The facilities include a restaurant and café. High-speed Internet connection is available. **apollo.webpark.sk**

TRNAVA Dream ⬛🅿️🍴♨️🛎️ €€

Kapitulská 12, 917 01. **Tel** *(033) 592 41 11.* **Fax** *(033) 592 41 15.* **Rooms** *23* **Road map** *D4.*

The hotel enjoys an attractive location in a smartly painted historic building, close to the city walls. Stylishly furnished rooms and suites include air-conditioning and Internet access. The restaurant and bar offer a large selection of Slovak and international dishes, plus a good selection of wines. **www.hoteldream.sk**

CENTRAL SLOVAKIA

BANSKÁ BYSTRICA Dixon
Švermova 32, 974 01. **Tel** (048) 413 08 08. **Fax** (048) 423 11 91. **Rooms** 54   *Road map* E3.

A business-oriented hotel, the Dixon has good quality rooms with plain decor, plus one apartment. Guests can make use of the superb tennis courts (13 outdoor courts; 3 indoors for winter use) and squash courts. A swimming pool and sauna are also available, plus a games room with pool and table football. **www.dixon.sk**

BANSKÁ BYSTRICA Horský hotel Šachtička
Šachtička, 974 01. **Tel** (048) 414 19 11. **Fax** (048) 414 56 70. **Rooms** 47   *Road map* E3.

The hotel is set amid beautiful mountain scenery, in the Low Tatras, at the very heart of the skiing region. It is about 10 km (6 miles) from Banská Bystrica. There are both rooms and apartments. The hotel restaurant (see p393) offers Slovak and international cuisine. Modern sports hall; horse riding. **www.sachticka.sk**

BANSKÁ BYSTRICA Hotel Lux
Nám. Slobody 2, 974 00. **Tel** (048) 414 41 41. **Fax** (048) 414 38 53. **Rooms** 141   *Road map* E3.

Situated in the town centre, this modern, high-rise hotel has been in business for 35 years and provides excellent, professional service with pleasant rooms. A good restaurant (see p393) provides a wide selection of Slovak and international dishes, with an outdoor terrace in summer. **www.hotellux.sk**

BANSKÁ ŠTIAVNICA Salamander
Palárikova 1, 969 01. **Tel** (048) 691 39 92. **Fax** (048) 692 12 62. **Rooms** 16   *Road map* D4.

Conveniently located in the historic town centre in an imposing corner building is this welcoming hotel. It offers luxury rooms and suites, a restaurant, a wine bar with a wide and interesting selection of wines and a café. **www.hotelsalamander.sk**

BOJNICE Hotel Pod Zámkom
Hurbanovo námestie 2, 972 01. **Tel** 518 51 00. **Fax** 540 25 82. **Rooms** 67   *Road map* D3.

The hotel belongs to the European Wellness chain. It stands in the town centre, by the castle walls (its name means "under the castle"). A large variety of rooms are available, all pleasantly furnished. The hotel prides itself on individual service. **www.hotelpodzamkom.sk**

BOJNICE Kaskáda
Jánošíková 1301/24, 972 01. **Tel** (046) 518 30 10. **Fax** (046) 540 27 93. **Rooms** 70   *Road map* D3.

A modern hotel with its own Aquacentre (pool, hydro-massage, sauna, solarium). The comfortable rooms and apartments offer satellite TV, broadband Internet connection and minibar. The popular restaurant Kontesa de Jean Ville serves international and Slovak cuisine, accompanied by top-quality wines. **www.kaskada.sk**

DEMÄNOVSKÁ DOLINA Hotel Sorea SNP
032 51. **Tel** (044) 559 16 61. **Fax** (044) 559 16 64. **Rooms** 132   *Road map* E3.

The hotel is located in one of the most beautiful valleys in the Low Tatras (Nízke Tatry), to the south of Liptovský Mikuláš. Close by are stunning karst caves and Slovakia's largest skiing centre, Jasná. An excellent place for families who enjoy all types of sport and wish to relax in comfortable conditions. **www.sorea.sk**

GERLACHOV Hotel Hubert
Vila Horec, 059 42. **Tel** (052) 478 08 11. **Fax** (052) 478 08 05. **Rooms** 39   *Road map* E3.

The hotel enjoys an amazing location, 900 m (3,000 ft) above sea level, in the impressive setting of the High Tatras, overlooking their highest peak, Gerlachovský. Superb facilities include an indoor pool, fishing pond, horse riding, and a babysitting service. A good choice of food is available (see p393). **www.hotel-hubert.sk**

KREMNICA Centrál
Dolná 40, 967 01. **Tel** (045) 674 42 10. **Fax** (045) 674 42 14. **Rooms** 19   *Road map* D3.

Set in the romantic scenery of central Kremnica, the hotel offers a pleasant stay in well-appointed rooms and three suites. In the summer you can lounge on the sunny terrace; in the winter, relax in the sauna and enjoy a massage. The facilities include a conference centre. **www.hotel-central.sk**

KREMNICA Golfer
J Horvátha 910/50, 967 01. **Tel** (045) 674 37 67. **Fax** (045) 674 37 88. **Rooms** 35   *Road map* D3.

The only golf-orientated hotel in Slovakia. It offers bright and comfortable rooms. Golf course and golf lessons. Many other sports are available, winter and summer, including snowboarding, skiing, ice skating, mountain biking, tennis and basketball. **www.golfer.sk**

LIPTOVSKÝ JÁN Hotel Plus
Jánska dolina 163, 032 03. **Tel** (044) 526 34 07. **Tel/Fax** (044) 526 33 20. **Rooms** 42   *Road map* E3.

Located in the picturesque setting of the Jánska valley, one of the most beautiful spots in the Low Tatras and a well-known ski resort. Thermal baths are available year round. Two categories of rooms: one with en suite bathroom, and another, more modest, with a shared bathroom. **www.hotely-plus.sk**

Key to Price Guide see p358   **Key to symbols** see back cover flap

LIPTOVSKÝ JÁN Hotel Sorea Máj

032 03. **Tel** *(044) 520 81 00.* **Fax** *(044) 520 89 03.* **Rooms** *118*   **Road map** *E3.*

The hotel lies amid mountain scenery at the mouth of the Jánska valley. It belongs to the Slovak hotel chain Sorea. Restaurant, bar, bistro and espresso bar. Indoor pool, plus several outdoor thermal pools (about 28°C/82°F). Plenty of other sports facilities, including skiing, make it an ideal base year round. **www.sorea.sk**

LIPTOVSKÝ MIKULÁŠ Klar

1. mája 117, 031 01. **Tel** *(044) 552 29 11.* **Fax** *(044) 557 06 36.* **Rooms** *52*   **Road map** *E3.*

The hotel is in the western part of Liptovský Mikuláš, the best-known town in the foothills of the Low Tatras and the capital of the Liptov region. It offers basic, comfortable rooms in a small high-rise building. Thermal baths and skiing areas are nearby. **www.klar.sk**

LIPTOVSKÝ MIKULÁŠ Holiday Village Tatralandia

Ráztocká 21, 031 05. **Tel** *(044) 556 11 11.*   **Road map** *E3.*

A very child-friendly holiday village 2 km (1 mile) west of Liptovský Mikuláš, adjacent to the Aquapark Tatralandia. Bungalows and apartments are in different styles in different themed areas, such as the Fishing Cove, Liptov Village, Indian Settlement and Scouts' Camp. Comfortable accommodation and great facilities. **www.holidayvillage.sk**

MARTIN Hotel Grandis

Hrdinov SNP 350, 036 01. **Tel** *(043) 422 00 16.* **Tel/Fax** *(043) 422 00 15.* **Rooms** *24*   **Road map** *D3.*

Located on the outskirts of town, amid the Malá Fatra range, this is a welcoming hotel offering high-quality service. The rooms are cosily furnished. The restaurant serves gourmet food and has a summer terrace with mountain views. The café has an open fire. **www.grandis.sk**

ORAVSKÝ PODZÁMOK Oravan

Hviezdoslavovo nám, 027 41. **Tel/Fax** *(043) 589 31 15.* **Rooms** *8*   **Road map** *E3.*

Located at the foot of one of Slovakia's most imposing and best-preserved castles, the Oravan offers attractive rooms that are clean and comfortable, but not luxurious, decorated in pastel colours. The restaurant is pleasantly set out and there is a bar with a terrace. **www.hoteloravan.sk**

PRIBYLINA Grand Hotel Permon

Podbanské 18, 032 42. **Tel** *(052) 471 01 11.* **Fax** *(052) 449 01 33.* **Rooms** *286*   **Road map** *E3.*

In the Western Tatras, in a valley dominated by the peak of Kryváň, this is one of Slovakia's biggest and most exclusive hotels. Rooms are large and comfortable. It has a complex of steam and water baths, plus good sports facilities including tennis courts, bowling alley, and a gym. **www.hotelpermon.sk**

RUŽOMBEROK Kultúra

Antona Bernoláka 1, 034 01. **Tel** *(044) 431 31 11.* **Fax** *(044) 431 31 75.* **Rooms** *45*   **Road map** *E3.*

Conveniently located in the historic town centre, the hotel occupies the building of a former cultural centre that was founded in 1928. The building was thoroughly modernized in 2003, but its stylish interiors have been preserved with many rooms and facilities around a glass-roofed atrium. **www.hotelkultura.sk**

STARÉ HORY Altenberg

976 02. **Tel** *(048) 419 92 00.* **Fax** *(048) 419 92 03.* **Rooms** *21*   **Road map** *E3.*

This modern, high-standard chalet-style hotel is within fairly easy reach of Banská Bystrica (11 km/7 miles) and Donovale (10 km/6 miles). Many of the homely rooms have sloping roofs and great views. Three restaurants, including fish and pizza specialities. It provides sauna, massage and swimming pools. **www.altenberg.sk**

STARÝ SMOKOVEC Horský hotel Sorea Hrebienok

062 01. **Tel** *(052) 442 50 60.* **Fax** *(052) 442 50 63.* **Rooms** *137*   **Road map** *E3.*

Located in Hrebeinok, beside the terminus of the funicular railway that runs from Starý Smokovec, this hotel can only be accessed by funicular. Rooms are comfortable, with satellite TV and balconies. An excellent base for exploring the central region of the High Tatras on foot, by bike or on skis. **www.sorea.sk**

STARÝ SMOKOVEC Grand Hotel Starý Smokovec

062 01. **Tel** *(052) 478 00 00.* **Fax** *(052) 478 00 52.* **Rooms** *79*   **Road map** *E3.*

Situated at the centre of Starý Smokovec, at the foot of Slavkovský peak. A hotel with traditions (it has been in business since 1904), it occupies a romantic Bavarian-style building. Rooms and facilities are luxurious and there is great attention to detail. Excellent restaurant *(see p394).* **www.grandhotel.sk**

ŠTRBSKÉ PLESO Hotel Patria-Vysoké Tatry

059 85. **Tel** *(052) 449 25 91.* **Fax** *(052) 449 25 90.* **Rooms** *122*   **Road map** *E3.*

The most beautifully located hotel in the High Tatras, the Patria stands above Štrbské Lake at 1,355 m (4,445 ft) above sea level. Surrounded by wild scenery, it offers comfortable rooms, a good choice of food *(see p394),* recreation facilities and a full range of services. **www.hotelpatria.sk**

TATRANSKÁ LOMNICA Eurocamp FICC – bungalovy

059 60. **Tel** *(052) 446 77 41.* **Fax** *(052) 446 73 46.*   **Road map** *E3.*

One of the best camp sites in Slovakia, Eurocamp offers a perfect base for active holidays, including summer and winter sports. In a site surrounded by mountains, bungalows are available and there is a well-equipped campsite. Two restaurants *(see p394)* and many sports and relaxation facilities. **www.eurocamp-ficc.sk**

TATRANSKÁ LOMNICA Grand Hotel Praha

☐P⑪⚡⚒☷▥ €€

*059 60. **Tel** (052) 446 79 41. **Fax** (052) 446 78 91. **Rooms** 96* **Road map** E3.

A spectacular building in the form of a turreted castle, the hotel stands against the backdrop of the highest peaks of the High Tatras, crowned by Lomnický peak. Rich traditions, stylish interiors and sophisticated cuisine. The grand lounge and main restaurant *(see p394)* are particularly imposing in size and decor. **www.grandhotelpraha.sk**

ŽILINA Bránica

☐P⑪⚡⚒☷▥& €€

*Bránica, 013 05. **Tel** (041) 569 30 35. **Fax** (041) 569 30 39. **Rooms** 23* **Road map** D3.

This modern hotel stands 22 km (14 miles) east of Žilina at the foot of the Malá Fatra range. Tastefully furnished interiors; one room and one suite adapted for the disabled. Facilities for an active holiday, including tennis courts and a fitness club. **www.hotelbranica.sk**

ŽILINA Hotel Grand

☐P⑪⚡⚒☷▥▤ €€

*Sládkovičova 1, 010 01. **Tel** (041) 564 32 65. **Fax** (041) 564 32 66. **Rooms** 32* **Road map** D3.

A hotel that has been in business for 90 years, the Grand occupies a historic building refurbished in 2001, standing in a quiet part of Žilina's Old Town. Stylish interiors, some rooms with air conditioning and en suite bathrooms. It is just about possible to see the main square from some rooms. Private garage. **www.hotelgrand.sk**

EAST SLOVAKIA

BARDEJOV Hotel Satel Minerál

☐P⑪☷▥ €

*086 31 Bardejovské kúpele 26. **Tel** (054) 472 41 22. **Fax** (054) 472 41 24. **Rooms** 70* **Road map** F3.

The hotel is located in one of Slovakia's most popular resorts, amid the beautiful scenery of the Lower Beskydy mountains. An open-air museum of traditional buildings is close by. The facilities include restaurant, snack bar and pleasant wine bar. In winter ski lifts operate nearby. **www.satel-slovakia.sk**

BARDEJOV Bellevue

☐P⑪⚡☷▥▤ €€

*Mihálov 2503, 085 01. **Tel** (054) 472 84 04. **Fax** (054) 472 84 09. **Rooms** 25* **Road map** F3.

This small, congenial, comfortable hotel stands in a quiet suburban estate, 5 km (3 miles) south of Bardejov. It is particularly recommended for families. All rooms have a bathroom, satellite TV and air conditioning; suites with balconies have a magnificent view over the surrounding area. **www.bellevuehotel.sk**

KEŽMAROK Hotel Club

☐P⑪☷▥ €

*MUDr. Alexandra 24, 060 01. **Tel** (052) 452 40 51. **Fax** (052) 452 40 53. **Rooms** 19* **Road map** E3.

A small hotel situated in an old building in the historic town centre. The interiors are bright and modern and staff are welcoming. The well-regarded hotel restaurant specializes in game dishes and its walls are hung with a variety of hunting trophies.

KOŠICE Alessandria

☐P⑪☷ €€

*Jiskrova 3, 040 01. **Tel** (055) 622 59 03. **Fax** (055) 622 59 18. **Rooms** 12* **Road map** F3.

A small congenial hotel located east of the Old Town, offering traditionally furnished rooms with telephone, satellite TV, minibar and comfortable en suite bathrooms. The facilities include a pool table, bar and restaurant. **www.alessandria.sk**

KOŠICE Best Western Hotel Teledom

P⚡&▤ €€

*Timonova 27, 040 01. **Tel** (055) 55 23 74. **Fax** (055) 727 44 29. **Rooms** 20* **Road map** F3.

This three-star hotel and conference centre is located in the southwestern part of the Old Town. Well-equipped rooms are decorated in muted colours, each with bathroom; air-conditioned suites, some intended for non-smokers. The hotel is adapted for disabled guests. **hotel.teledom.sk**

KOŠICE Dália

☐P⑪☷▥ €€

*Löfflerova 1, 040 01. **Tel** (055) 632 59 49. **Fax** (055) 633 17 17. **Rooms** 11* **Road map** F3.

Aimed at visitors who favour peace and a family atmosphere, this small hotel is on the east of the Old Town. Attractive, tastefully furnished rooms create a feeling of utter comfort. The Dália restaurant, in addition to Slovak and international cuisine, offers a wide selection of vegetarian dishes. Sauna, hydro-massage. **www.hoteldalia.sk**

KOŠICE Hotel Ambassador

☐⑪▤ €€

*Hlavná 101, 040 01. **Tel** (055) 720 37 20. **Fax** (055) 720 37 27. **Rooms** 14* **Road map** F3.

At the centre of Košice, this is a newly modernized hotel offering simply and comfortably furnished rooms and suites. All have en suite bathrooms, with lift, TV, video. Its friendly restaurant. The Ambassador has a popular café with outdoor seating in summer on Košice s atmospheric main street *(see p343)*. **www.abba.sk**

LEVOČA Arkáda

☐P⑪ €

*Námestie Majstra Pavla 26, 054 01. **Tel** (053) 451 23 72. **Fax** (053) 451 22 55. **Rooms** 32* **Road map** E3.

An establishment in the historic setting of Levoča's town square, in a building that has a history going back to the Gothic era; it was modernized in the 1990s. The rooms are bright and airy, and all have en suite bathrooms. **www.arkada.sk**

Key to Price Guide *see p358* **Key to symbols** *see back cover flap*

LEVOČA Hotel Satel Levoča
⎙ P ⑪ ✚ ▒   €€

Námestie Majstra Pavla 55, 054 01. **Tel** *(053) 451 29 43.* **Fax** *(053) 451 44 86.* **Rooms** *23*   **Road map** *E3.*

The hotel is in a historic building, at the heart of Levoča's Old Town. The building's history goes back to the 14th century, and as early as the 16th century it was already an inn for travelling merchants. It was thoroughly refurbished in 1993. Besides restaurant and wine bar, the hotel boasts a terrace and an atrium with a fountain. **www.satel-slovakia.sk**

MEDZILABORCE Eurohotel Laborec
⎙ P ⑪   €

Andyho Warhola 195/28, 068 01. **Tel** *(057) 732 13 07.* **Fax** *(057) 732 29 94.* **Rooms** *54*   **Road map** *F3.*

This central hotel is close to the Warhol Family Museum of Modern Art. The original 1978 building was thoroughly modernized in 2002. Danova ski centre is nearby, and it provides an excellent base for exploring the nearby wooden Orthodox churches. **www.eurohotel.sk**

POPRAD Hotel Satel Poprad
⎙ P ⑪ ▢ ▒ ☰   €

Mnohel'ova 825, 058 01. **Tel** *(052) 716 11 11.* **Fax** *(052) 772 11 20.* **Rooms** *127*   **Road map** *E3.*

This central hotel was opened in 1991. Rooms are furnished in a modern style. The eating places and sports facilities are excellent, and there is a nightclub. It offers a wide choice of additional attractions, including scenic flights over the Tatras mountains. **www.satel-slovakia.sk**

POPRAD Aquacity Poprad
⎙ P ⑪ ☆ ▒ ☰   €€

Športová 1397/1, 058 01. **Tel** *(052) 785 12 22.* **Fax** *(052) 785 12 20.* **Rooms** *41*   **Road map** *E3.*

The hotel is part of a superb aquapark with thermal waters. Large, elegant rooms with stylish decor on a seasonal theme. The hotel guarantees relaxing conditions and welcomes families. Facilities include an Olympic-size swimming pool, fitness centre, horse riding and bicycle trails. **www.aquacity.sk**

PREŠOV Dukla
⎙ P ⑪ ☰   €€

Námestie Legionárov 2, 080 01. **Tel** *(051) 772 27 41.* **Fax** *(051) 773 21 34.* **Rooms** *61*   **Road map** *F3.*

Not particularly pretty, but conveniently located in the historic town centre, the hotel has been operating since 1951; the building was modernized in 2000. Well-equipped rooms with bathrooms offer comfort and a pleasant atmosphere. Enjoyable food at the restaurant and café. **www.hotelduklapresov.sk**

PREŠOV Senátor
⎙ P ⑪   €€

Hlavná 67, 080 01. **Tel** *(051) 773 11 86.* **Fax** *(051) 773 10 92.* **Rooms** *11*   **Road map** *F3.*

Small congenial hotel occupying a historic building, right at the centre of Prešov Old Town. Clean, bright and spacious rooms are tastefully furnished and well equipped. It has a restaurant and there is a wine bar in the cellar. **www.hotelsenator.szm.sk**

ROŽNAVA Hotel Čierny Orol
⎙ P ⑪   €

Námestie baníkov 17, 048 01. **Tel** *(058) 732 81 86.* **Rooms** *17*   **Road map** *E3.*

An elegant hotel with a famous restaurant. It occupies a historic, recently reconstructed burgher's house standing in the town square. The rooms and suites are furnished to a high standard and have shower and telephone. In the summer there is seating on the square for a drink or light lunch. **www.ciernyorol.sk**

ROŽNAVA Kras
⎙ P ⑪ ☰   €

Šafárikova 52, 048 01. **Tel** *058) 788 60 40.* **Rooms** *62*   **Road map** *E3.*

Conveniently located right at the centre of this mining town, the hotel offers rooms and suites with en suite bathroom, satellite TV and telephone. The amenities include restaurant, café and bar. The Mining Museum is close by. A good base for visiting the Slovenský kras. **www.hotel-kras.sk**

SPIŠSKÁ NOVÁ VES Hotel Metropol
⎙ P ⑪ ☰   €€

Štefánikovo nám. 2, 052 01. **Tel** *(053) 442 22 41.* **Fax** *(053) 442 22 43.* **Rooms** *39*   **Road map** *E3.*

This high-rise hotel at the centre of the historic capital of the Spiš region has been modernized to a high standard. Large, pleasant rooms decorated in a stylish, contemporary way are suitable for individual visitors, as well as for families with children. The restaurant *(see p395)* offers a huge choice. **www.hotel-metropol.sk**

SPIŠSKE PODHRADIE Kolpingov Dom
⎙ P ⑪ ☆ ☰   €€

Spišská Kapitula 15, 053 04. **Tel** *(053) 450 21 11.* **Rooms** *18*   **Road map** *E3.*

Situated in the former ecclesiastic capital of Spiš, the hotel occupies the restored building of the former canonry, part of the complex on the UNESCO World Heritage list. Close by are the ruins of Spiš Castle. The rooms are beautifully decorated and the restaurant superb. **www.hotelkolping.sk**

STARÁ LESNÁ Hotel Satel Horizont
⎙ P ⑪ ☆ ▒ ☰   €

059 60. **Tel** *(052) 446 78 81.* **Fax** *(052) 446 72 87.* **Rooms** *41*   **Road map** *E3.*

Located in between Poprad and the Western Tatras, the Horizont has a lovely panoramic view of the mountains. Rooms are well appointed. The facilities include a relaxation centre with sauna and hydro-massage, and a tennis court. **www.satel-slovakia.sk**

SVIDNÍK Dukla Senior
P ⑪ ☰   €

Sovietskych hrdinov 221, 089 01. **Tel** *(054) 752 33 88.* **Fax** *(054) 500 12 37.* **Rooms** *7*   **Road map** *F3.*

A small congenial hotel with a friendly atmosphere in leafy surroundings. Rooms and facilities are basic but clean and adequate. Provides a good base for exploring the surrounding area. The Museum of the Battle of Dukla and an open-air museum of traditional architecture are nearby.

WHERE TO EAT

The cuisines of both republics are perhaps not particularly famous in Europe but they are tasty and usually filling. In the Czech Republic the classic Czech dishes *(see pp368–9)* are served in most restaurants, often alongside local variations. The beer, of course, is world-famous *(see p370)*.

In Slovakia in recent years the quality of eating places has been rapidly improving. Many new restaurants are being

opened, often serving modern versions of traditional Slovak dishes, or very hearty soups.

While international cuisine is available in both countries, especially in large cities and in some hotel restaurants, Italian and Mexican places are very popular. Czechs and Slovaks enjoy eating out at any time, and you will find that traditional eateries and pubs are usually busy and also welcoming.

Statue of a chef outside a traditional restaurant

The Art Nouveau Hotel Evropa Café in Prague (see p376)

EATING PLACES

In the Czech Republic the word *restaurace* (restaurant) is a very broad term: it can apply to a luxurious establishment serving expensive and sophisticated dishes, or a popular local inn offering simple food, beer and vodka. Other types of eating place include *občerstvení*, a type of buffet bar with a limited selection of fast food, such as frankfurters, stews or soups. *Vinárna* (wine bars) usually serve food, as do some cafés (*kavárna*). Pubs known as *hospoda* or *hostinec* serve good-value, basic Czech food. In the Czech Republic, *pirnice* are pubs that do not serve food. There are many delicatessens where you can also order a stew, a salad, a pork chop or sandwiches to be consumed on the premises. Ice-cream kiosks, pizzerias and burger chains are all popular.

In Slovakia most restaurants (*reštaurácia*) are clustered within large towns and main regions. Away from the tourist trail there may not be a great choice of restaurants (it is best to look in hotels, pensions or hostels). When you succeed in finding one that is open, the choice of menu may prove to be limited.

A *vináreň* or wine cellar usually offers tasty food. A Slovak *pivnica* or *piváreň* (pub) also serves meals, but more cheaply. Slovak buffets, *občerstvenie*, serve simple hot dishes, plus a large selection of salads. *Jedáleň* (canteens) have a limited menu, but serve fresh, cheap dishes. Pizzerias and ice-cream parlours are widely found.

OPENING HOURS

Czech and Slovak restaurants usually open at 10am (in Slovakia sometimes at noon) and close at 10pm, or later. In small towns in the Czech Republic, where customers are scarce, eating places

U Kalicha, a famous Prague inn (see p377)

usually remain closed on a Monday, sometimes even from Monday to Wednesday. In Slovakia, quite a few establishments close from 3 to 6pm, though this traditional custom is slowly being abandoned. Some provincial restaurants open their doors only during the high season, and for the rest of the year they remain firmly shut. Buffet bars in both countries are usually open from about 6am all day.

PRICES AND TIPS

Prices of meals in Czech restaurants vary considerably. In small towns a meal with beer usually costs 120–150Kč, or less, per person. In smart restaurants in bigger towns, particularly in Prague, a similar meal is likely to cost up to several hundred crowns.

In Slovakia you can have a two-course meal with dessert, in a reasonable restaurant, for €7–€20 and in the best establishments in Bratislava for about €33.

In both republics service is included in the price, but it is customary, particularly in smart restaurants, to leave a tip of a dozen or so crowns, or 10 per cent of the bill. Credit cards are accepted only by a handful of restaurants in Prague, Bratislava and other large cities.

Diners outside Café Ister in Venturska, Bratislava

INTERNATIONAL MENU

Menus written in English (or German) are usual in most restaurants in Prague and Bratislava. In Czech provincial towns and villages you will occasionally be offered a German-language menu (in such cases the staff can manage at least a few sentences in German) but usually the menu is available only in Czech. Sometimes names of dishes are written in chalk, on a blackboard placed outside the restaurant. For assistance with decoding a Czech menu, *see p447;* for a Slovak menu *see p448.*

WHEN TO EAT

Breakfasts in the Czech and Slovak Republics do not differ much from those offered in other Central European countries, usually consisting of tea, coffee, rolls, cheese and cold meat. Upmarket hotels offer a wider breakfast choice. Lunch is often hearty but is served and eaten quickly. Restaurants fill up in the evening, mainly with beer drinkers. Snacks are popular at any time, with plenty of sweet and savoury options available *(see p369).*

RESERVATIONS

Tables can be reserved by telephone. Some restaurants can be booked on the Internet, via their website. There is no need to book for lunchtimes, but if you are planning a dinner on a Friday or Saturday evening, particularly in one of Prague or Bratislava's better-known eating places, it is advisable to contact them and make a reservation in advance.

DRESS CODE

Czechs and Slovaks tend to dress casually and are not too set on formality, so it is generally not necessary to dress up when going to a restaurant. Some of the more upmarket establishments in Prague and Bratislava are the exception; here you should put on smarter attire.

CHILDREN

Not many restaurants in the Czech Republic offer facilities for children or even children's menus, though some will provide half-portions.

In Slovakia there is usually no problem with ordering a half-portion for a child, and many restaurants offer a high-chair. Slovak menus also often include some children's favourites: pancakes *(palacéniki)* with a variety of fillings, usually accompanied by fruit and topped with cream; and chips *(hranolky).*

Pubs in both countries can be very smoky and so are not ideal for children.

VEGETARIANS

Meat is central to Czech and Slovak cuisine and it is hard to find a selection of vegetarian food outside the capitals. In the main cities, some upmarket places offer a greater choice of vegetarian dishes. Some menus have a section entitled "meatless dishes" (*bezmasna jídla* in Czech, *bezmäsite jedlá* in Slovak). In both countries it is best to ask what has gone into these dishes as many may include a meat stock or just less meat than usual.

DISABLED GUESTS

The sign of De Zwann café in Bratislava

Since restaurants providing good, level access are few and far between in the Czech Republic, disabled visitors must be prepared to encounter many difficulties. The situation is slightly better in Slovakia, but even here it is far from ideal.

SMOKING

In the Czech and Slovak Republics there are usually no restrictions concerning smoking in restaurants, although some places are starting to allocate non-smoking areas. Sometimes you can meet with a total ban on smoking during eating hours.

Grand interior of Kavárna Pošta, in Liberec, North Bohemia

The Flavours of the Czech and Slovak Republics

There is almost no discernable difference between the cuisines of the Czech and Slovak Republics. Both base their cooking around Central European staples such as potatoes, rice and cabbage, along with meat such as pork or beef, or fish such as carp or trout, which are almost always roasted or grilled, and accompanied by light sauces and vegetables. In the Czech Republic, especially around Prague, game is also popular. Other differences are mainly in the spelling of various dishes, for instance, the delicious sour soup known as *polévka* in the Czech Republic is *polievka* in Slovakia.

Blueberries

Atmospheric U Pinkasů cellar bar and restaurant, Prague *(see p376)*

lightly smoked meat usually eaten with bread at breakfast or with horseradish as a starter in the evening. Veal, usually served by Czechs as Wiener schnitzel *(smažený řízek)*, is popular and good. In Slovakia try the local goulash, *szegedinsky guláš*, a combination of stewed pork, sauerkraut, spices and cream.

Beef in the region is not up to international standards, and needs to be prepared well to be edible. Most beef in top restaurants is likely to be imported. The Czech favourite is *Pražská hovězí pečeně*, roast beef stuffed with bacon, ham, cheese, onion and eggs. When it is cooked long and slow, it can be tender and delicious. In Slovakia you'll find *viedenska rostenka*, a sirloin steak fried with onions. Czech or Slovak lamb *(jehněčí/jahnacie)* is not the best, either, though

MEAT

In both the Czech Republic and Slovakia, the favourite is pork *(vepřové/bravcové)*. It is served as steaks, chops or stuffed. It also appears in goulash, hams and sausages. Dumplings, frequently in slices, may be served on the plate with pork. Don't miss the celebrated Prague ham *(Pražska šunka)*, a succulent,

Apple strudel **Eclair**
Fruit buns **Chocolate cake** **Plum jam bun**
Apple crumble tart
Selection of typical Czech and Slovak cakes and pastries

REGIONAL DISHES AND SPECIALITIES

Knedlíky (dumplings) either savoury *(špekové)* in soups or sweet *(ovocné)* with fruits and berries, are perhaps the Czech Republic's best-known delicacy. Once a mere side dish, they have now become a central feature of the nation's cuisine as chefs rediscover their charms and experiment with new and different ways of cooking and serving them. In Slovakia, crêpes *(palačinky)* play a similar role, and are eaten savoury as an appetizer or sweet as a dessert. The Slovaks do have a famous dumpling dish, however: *bryndzove halusky* are stuffed with sheep's cheese and topped with bacon. Other specialities of the region include *drštková polévka/držková polievka*, a remarkably good tripe soup which, although an acquired taste, has seen a revival in recent years as better restaurants add it to their menus.

Halazsle
The Slovaks love this spicy fish soup, made with carp, trout and mackerel.

Wild chanterelle mushrooms from the forests across the region

VEGETABLES

Vegetables in both countries are excellent, if strictly seasonal. However, they can be overcooked. Although more imported, out-of-season vegetables are appearing in supermarkets, they command high prices. As a result, the cabbage is both countries' top vegetable, especially in winter, used raw as a salad or boiled and served with meats. Sauerkraut is ubiquitous.

from mid-March to mid-May good lamb is available in markets. Lambs are usually sold whole, with the head, which is used to make soup.

GAME AND POULTRY

A wide variety of game is found in the forests around Prague. In autumn you'll find duck, pheasant, goose, boar, rabbit, venison and hare on many menus. Duck is perhaps the most popular game dish, usually roasted with fruit or sometimes chestnuts, and served with red cabbage. Small pheasants, roasted whole with juniper and blueberries or cranberries, are also popular; venison is served grilled with mushrooms. Hare and rabbit are usually served in rich, peppery sauces.

Chicken is popular in Slovakia, where many restaurants roast them on a spit, known as *grilovane kurča*.

FISH

Fish is more popular in Slovakia than in the Czech Republic but, in both, fresh carp *(kapr/kapor)* is the traditional Christmas meal, usually baked and served with nuts. Trout is often stuffed with cheese and ham, and grilled.

Fresh vegetables on a Prague market stall

BEST LOCAL SNACKS

Sausages Street stalls and snack bars in cities and towns sell traditional sausages *(klobásy* and *utopenci)*, frankfurters *(párky)* or bratwurst, served in a soft roll with mustard.

Chlebíčky Open sandwiches on sliced baguettes are found in Czech city delicatessens or snack bars. Toppings are usually ham, salami or cheese, always accompanied by a gherkin *(okurkou)*.

Pivní sýr Beer cheese is soaked in ale until it becomes soft. It is served spread on bread and eaten with pickles or onions.

Syrečky These tasty cheese rounds from Olomouc have a pungent aroma and are served with beer and onions.

Palačinky Pancakes are filled with ice cream and/or fruits and jam, and are topped with lashings of sugar.

Plněná paprika
Peppers stuffed with mince and rice, in a spicy tomato sauce, are very popular.

Vepřové s křenem
Pork is served roasted, often on the bone, with red cabbage and sauerkraut or horseradish.

Ovocné knedlíky
Sweet dumplings are filled with fruit, usually blueberries or plums.

What to Drink

Slovak beer logo

Beer is the most celebrated drink in both the Czech and Slovak Republics. But perhaps nowhere else in Europe is alcohol so freely available and in so many forms. In both countries you can buy it not only in late-night shops and in almost all eating places, but even, for example, in railway station kiosks and buffets; these often serve wine and vodka alongside beer. Yet the best way to enjoy a drink is to join the locals for a glass or a tankard of beer in one of the many inns known as *hospoda* in Czech and *pivnica* in Slovak. You could also step into a beer hall or a wine bar where you can sample a wider range of drinks, and these are often accompanied by food.

Vinoteka sv. Urbana – a famous wine shop in Bratislava

Beer garden by the Vltava river in Prague

FAVOURITE BEERS

The best Czech beers are considered by many to be Pilsner Urquell (Plzeňský Prazroj) and Gambrinus, both made in Plzeň, Budvar from České Budějovice, Staropramen from Prague, Primator from Náchod, and Lev from Hradec Králové.

In Slovakia the most popular beers are Zlatý Bažant (Golden Pheasant), Topvar, Šariš, Steriger, Kelt and Urpin.

BEER (PIVO)

Both countries have many breweries. Normally served by the half-litre, beer is classed using the Balling scale, which measures the amount of sugar before fermentation. The most common types are *dvanáctka* (12 degrees) and *desítka* (10 degrees), *dvanáctka* being the stronger.

Beer classification

Percentage alcohol content

Czech Velkopopovický Kozel beer label
In the Czech Republic and Slovakia the word světlé *describes light beer. In both countries you can also get a dark lager* (tmavé).

Gambrinus (Czech)

Pilsner Urquell (Czech)

Kelt (Slovak)

Zlatý Bažant (Slovak)

Regent (Czech)

Budvar (Czech)

WINES

Neither the Czech Republic nor Slovakia could be termed major wine-producing countries; wines from here are intended mostly for home markets. In the Czech Republic wine is produced in South Moravia (in the Znojmo-Mikulov region) and in the Labe (Elbe) valley (the Mělník region).

The most famous wine district in Slovakia is the country's southeastern, low-lying region, bordering Hungary, which produces Tokaj wines. The Small Carpathians to the north of Bratislava, in the southwest of the country, are also a major wine-producing area.

Rulandské Biele, a white wine from Slovakia

White wine from Moravia (Czech Republic)

Czech wines in boxes decorated with Art Nouveau paintings by Alfons Mucha

SPIRITS AND LIQUEURS

Those who like to sample stronger spirits in the Czech Republic can chose from a number of vodkas, clear and flavoured. A flavoured vodka particularly worth recommending is *meruňkovice*, which has a delicate apricot flavour. Also popular is *slivovice*, a plum brandy. The best-known of the herb-flavoured spirits is Becherovka from the spa town of Karlovy Vary. Also worth trying is the slightly bitter *fernet*.

In Slovakia, there are several interesting spirits, including the juniper-flavoured *borovička*, produced from local berries and slightly resembling gin. There are two types of *demänovka* liqueur, the herbal (*bylinná*) and the dry (*horká*); the local rum is known as *tuzemak*.

Becherovka (Czech Republic)

Borovička Spiš (Slovakia)

Trenčianske Hradné (Slovakia)

SOFT DRINKS

Popular Slovak soft drinks *(nealko)* include Vinea and Kofola. Vinea is a drink produced from grape juice, and there are white (Vinea biela) and red (Vinea červena) varieties. Kofola is a cola-type drink. Slovaks drink a lot of mineral water. The country has 1,657 registered sources of mineral water, 106 of them commercially exploited. The most popular Slovak mineral waters include Budiš (a source regularly utilized since 1573), Fatra, Klaštorna, Baldovská and L'ubovnianka. Mineral water is also very popular in the Czech Republic. The best-known local brands include Mattoni, a fizzy water from Karlovy Vary, and Dobrá. In both countries mineral water is relatively inexpensive.

The most popular Slovak mineral waters

Becher, a Mineral Water Cup
Traditionally used in spas to take the waters, this cup is named after Dr Jan Becher, the first person to conduct scientific analysis of the mineral waters in Karlovy Vary.

Restaurants in the Czech Republic

The restaurants listed below have been selected for their excellent food, convenient location and value for money. They are divided into regions, as they appear in the guide. The entries appear alphabetically within each price category. Further information is provided in the form of symbols.

PRICE CATEGORIES
Price per person for a three-course meal with half a bottle of wine, including cover charge, service and tax.

Ⓚ under 250Kč
ⓀⓀ 250–450Kč
ⓀⓀⓀ 450–650Kč
ⓀⓀⓀⓀ over 650Kč

PRAGUE – HRADČANY AND MALÁ STRANA

Cantina   ⓀⓀⓀ
Újezd 38, Praha 1. **Tel** *257 317 173.*   **Map** *2 E5.*

Here everything is king-sized, from the large margaritas to the huge helpings of delicious Tex-Mex food. The menu includes all possible delicacies, including super burritos and genuine tacos. If you like your food really spicy, ask for additional seasonings.

Hungarian Grotto   ⓀⓀⓀ
Tomášská 12, Praha 1. **Tel** *257 220 370.*   **Map** *2 E3.*

This romantic, rustic-style restaurant, housed in a cellar, has been inspired by Hungary, the land of Tokay, goulash and paprika. Prices are modest. Some tables are set in a charming courtyard. The place is believed to be haunted by a 17th-century baker, who was betrayed by his wife.

Mount Steak   ⓀⓀⓀ
Josefská 1, Praha 1. **Tel** *257 532 652.*   **Map** *2 E3.*

A great place for meat-lovers. In addition to beef, it offers an enormous choice of over 60 types of steak such as wild boar, kangaroo, shark and ostrich meat. All are prepared to the guest's requirements, roasted, fried, or grilled, and are served with potatoes and vegetables. A large and tempting selection of salads is on offer.

Nebozízek   ⓀⓀⓀ
Petřínské sady 411, Praha 1. **Tel** *257 315 329.*   **Map** *2 D5.*

In spring and summer the particularly popular feature of this famous restaurant in Petřín Park is its patio with a magnificent view over Prague. The interior is snug and elegant. Menu includes seafood, steaks, Chinese food and Czech cuisine. Mouthwatering desserts, such as stuffed pear with ricotta cheese mousse.

Pálffy Palace Restaurant   ⓀⓀⓀ
Valdštejnská 14, Praha 1. **Tel** *257 530 522.*   **Map** *2 E2.*

On entering the house at Valdštejnská 14 climb the stone staircase to this most exquisite restaurant, where you will feel like you are dining in the private rooms of the aristocracy. Music carrying from the nearby Music Academy provides the perfect accompaniment to an international menu that changes daily.

Cowboys   ⓀⓀⓀⓀ
Nerudova 40, Praha 1. **Tel** *800 152 672.*   **Map** *2 D3.*

This flamboyant destination is a sprawling complex of bars and dining rooms, serving slightly overpriced but always enjoyable steaks and seafood against a backdrop of lavishly eccentric decor. The upper terrace affords one of the most spectacular views over central Prague. Book in advance.

David   ⓀⓀⓀⓀ
Tržiště 21, Praha 1. **Tel** *257 533 109.*   **Map** *2 E3.*

The restaurant is reached along a steep cobblestone lane, but it is easily worth the climb. The gourmet set lunch of traditional Czech specialities, including duck and rabbit, is a serious two- to three-hour affair. The food is accompanied by an interesting international selection of wines. Booking essential.

Kampa Park   ⓀⓀⓀⓀ
Na Kampě 8b, Praha 1. **Tel** *257 532 685.*   **Map** *2 F4.*

This upmarket restaurant nestling on the banks of the Vltava, with views of the Charles Bridge, was badly damaged in the floods of 2002. Now completely restored, its walls are once again covered with photos of its famous guests. ... Italian food and fish are among the specialities.

Peklo   ⓀⓀⓀⓀ
Strahovské nádvoří 1, Praha 1. **Tel** *220 516 652.*   **Map** *1 B4.*

Peklo is within the Strahov Monastery complex, which belongs to the order of Premonstratensians, who have been keeping wine in their cellars since the 14th century. The upmarket restaurant offers excellent Czech and international cuisine and a wide selection of wines. The name of this underground restaurant translates as "Hell".

Key to symbols *see back cover flap*

Square
Malostranské náměstí 5/28, Praha 1. **Tel** *257 532 109.*

Map 2 E3.

Established in 1874 as an inn, this building now houses a modern restaurant. It serves Italian and Mediterranean cuisine including tasty pasta and risotto. The board outside lists the day's specials, all of which are good value, so you can always find something to suit your taste. Good breakfasts.

U Malířů
Maltézské náměstí 11, Praha 1. **Tel** *257 530 318.*

Map 2 E4.

There has been a restaurant on this spot since 1543. Even back then U Malířů received high acclaim: Emperor Rudoph II's food tasters awarded it three royal stars. Expect the highest quality traditional and contemporary French cuisine, including a pricey Châteaubriand. The elegant decor is still worthy of royal guests.

U Tři Pštrosů
Dražického náměstí 12, Praha 1. **Tel** *257 532 410.*

Map 2 E3.

The dining room At the Three Ostriches is reminiscent of a Bavarian hunting lodge, but the food is cooked in genuine Czech style. Adventurous diners may wish to try the ostrich specialities of stew and roulade "Prague style" but you can also settle for something more traditional.

Valdštejnská Hospoda
Valdštejnské náměstí 7, Praha 1. **Tel** *257 531 759.*

Map 2 E3.

The Waldstein Inn was once a typical local pub, but renovations and redecorations have exposed the original features of this 15th-century building, such as the ceiling and stonework, making the setting very atmospheric. The menu consists of Czech favourites, with an emphasis on game.

PRAGUE – STARÉ MĚSTO AND JOSEFOV

Bohemia Bagel
Masná 2, Praha 1. **Tel** *224 812 603.*

Map 3 C3.

The best breakfast deal in Prague is available until late in the morning at this always-busy bagel shop and café. High-speed Internet connections are also provided at very reasonable rates. It has become so popular that a second Bohemia Bagel has opened across the Vltava, at Újezd 16.

Fish & Chips
Rytířská 19, Praha 1. **Tel** *224 226 105.*

Map 3 C4.

This almost genuine British restaurant was opened to meet the requirements of English solo travellers who were missing home cooking. It is also visited by the locals; sometimes, particularly at weekends, you might have to queue up for a while.

Beas
Týnská 19, Praha 1. **Tel** *608 035 727.*

Map 3 C3.

This inexpensive vegetarian North Indian curry restaurant with its Spartan furnishing enjoys enormous popularity. The food is mostly served on disposable plates, but it is delicious and imaginatively seasoned. It is served with water, to alleviate the effects of the hot spices.

Country Life
Melantrichova 15, Praha 1. **Tel** *224 213 366.*

Map 3 B4.

This belongs to an international group of vegetarian restaurants. Few Prague eateries can compete with its picturesque setting. It gets crowded at lunchtimes with vegetarians and non-vegetarians alike, hungry for the tasty pizzas, salads and soups.

Dahab
Dlouhá 33, Praha 1, **Tel** *224 873 375.*

Map 3 C3.

Right at the heart of the Old Town, Dahab is perhaps the only place in Prague where you can puff on a hookah pipe after your meal. This combination of a tea room, patisserie, café and restaurant has a nice selection of Middle Eastern dishes, including several vegetarian options.

Klub Architektů
Betlémské náměstí 5A, Praha 1, **Tel** *224 401 214.*

Map 3 B4.

This hidden gem is tucked away in a warren of tunnels and arches, reached through a courtyard near the Bethlehem Chapel. The servings are hearty and, unusually for an inexpensive Prague eatery, the menu includes a worthwhile vegetarian selection.

Orange Moon
Rámová 5, Praha 3. **Tel** *222 325 119.*

Map 3 C2.

Immensely popular since its opening, Orange Moon serves Thai, Indian and Burmese food. On the menu its dishes are marked with a one (spicy), two (very spicy) or three (burning) red pepper rating. There are also some unmarked dishes for those who prefer milder flavours.

Patriot X

V Celnici 3, Praha 1. **Tel** *224 235 158.* **Map** *4 D3.*

This is a Czech restaurant, café and bar, which, quite distinctively, takes a Scandinavian "less is more" approach to decor, yet it keeps the portions traditionally ample. The café is upstairs, while the restaurant and the bar with billiard tables are downstairs. The terrace has views of the Old Town.

Restaurace Století

Karolíny Světlé 21, Praha 1. **Tel** *222 220 008.* **Map** *3 A4.*

Arched ceilings, sepia prints and old Chinese porcelain all evoke a gentler era in this warm, friendly restaurant. The menu is inspired by the famous of yesteryear; for example, you can order a Marlene Dietrich (stuffed avocado with whipped Roquefort and marzipan) or an Al Capone (roast chicken leg with hot salsa and papaya).

U Provaznice

Provaznická 3, Praha 1 **Tel** *224 232 528.* **Map** *3 C4.*

An excellent pub with a long-standing tradition (and ghostly legend). Enchanting interiors with imaginatively painted walls. Matchless Czech cuisine in all its varieties; draught beer. Desserts and the selection of Czech liqueurs are well worth trying.

U Sádlů

Klimentská 2, Praha 1. **Tel** *224 813 874.* **Map** *4 D2.*

Who can decry the kitsch aspects of this medieval-themed restaurant when it is done with such aplomb? Every dish has a thematic name, in keeping with the general premise. Cheerful staff. Meat is of good quality and superbly cooked, with a choice of Czech-influenced sauces.

Barock

Pařížská 24, Praha 1. **Tel** *222 329 221.* **Map** *3 B2.*

An eclectic and excellent range of Thai and Japanese cuisine is served by efficient staff in this perennially fashionable restaurant. This is not a triumph of style over substance: the beautifully prepared and presented food is really up to international standards. Booking advisable.

Chez Marcel

Haštalská 12, Praha 1. **Tel** *222 315 676.* **Map** *3 C2.*

Chez Marcel is a touch of France in the centre of Prague. Its tables spill onto a quiet square, encouraging business people and students alike to come for reasonably priced regional *plats du jour*, and linger for steak *au poivre*, fresh mussels and the best fries (chips) in town.

Da Nico Wine Bar and Restaurant

Dlouhá 21, Praha 1. **Tel** *222 311 807.* **Map** *3 C3.*

Restaurant and bar serving mouth-watering Italian cuisine, including pizza, pasta dishes and risotto, and offering the best selection of Italian wines anywhere in the Czech Republic (over 300). Its cosy interior and efficient staff make it an ideal place for a romantic tryst, or for a business chat.

Dinitz

Na Poříčí 12, Praha 1. **Tel** *222 314 071.* **Map** *4 D4.*

Café, bar and bistro in the Jewish Quarter; it belongs to an Israeli who does not believe much in kosher food. It serves a variety of light meals, desserts and snacks, in exceptionally congenial surroundings. Very popular with the shoppers who throng the streets of nearby Náměstí Republicky.

Don Giovanni

Karolíny Světlé 34, Praha 1. **Tel** *222 222 060.* **Map** *3 A4.*

The first upmarket Italian restaurant to open in Prague (after 1989), this was named after the opera which Mozart premiered a short distance away in the State Opera. The seafood selection includes lobster and crab from the in-house fish tank.

James Joyce

Liliová 10, Praha 1. **Tel** *224 248 793.* **Map** *3 B4.*

The James Joyce was the first Irish pub in Prague. It serves hearty meals including Irish breakfasts, "door stopper" sandwiches and what most expatriates would still say is the best Irish stew in Prague. The atmosphere is lively and the staff are genuinely friendly.

La Provence

Štupartská 9, Praha 1. **Tel** *800 152 672.* **Map** *3 C3.*

A vibrant provincial French restaurant split over two levels, with the main restaurant downstairs, and a brasserie at street level. The menu of the main restaurant lists such country fare as rabbit or duck, and it could not be that "artistic disorder" is charming. Reasonable prices.

Les Moules

Pařížská 19, Praha 1. **Tel** *222 315 022.* **Map** *3 B2.*

A Belgian restaurant that serves the best Belgian beer, a true rarity in the capital. Its great attraction is the great pots of fresh mussels, flown directly from Belgium each day. The *pommes frites* are delicious, too. Other delicacies include rack of lamb cooked in beer.

Key to Price Guide *see p372* **Key to symbols** *see back cover flap*

Red, Hot and Blues
Jakubská 12, Praha 1. **Tel** *222 323 364.*   **Map** *3 C3.*

Located in what were the Czech king's stables some 500 years ago, this place is renowned for its good, home-style New Orleans and Creole cooking. Chilli, burgers with all the trimmings, soups and other American specialities are all on offer. There is live jazz or blues most nights.

Reykjavik
Karlova 20, Praha 1. **Tel** *222 221 218.*   **Map** *3 A4.*

This is an Icelandic restaurant that serves dependably good seafood favourites such as *frutti di mare*, shrimp cocktails and Icelandic salmon – in this case grilled *à la Norvégienne*. The service is unobtrusively efficient. It is a pleasantly cosy nook in which to sit on a cold winter's day. Outside dining is available in summer.

Kamenný Most
Smetanovo nábřeží 195, Praha 1. **Tel** *224 097 100.*   **Map** *3 A4.*

A visit to this restaurant may turn out to be an unforgettable experience due to its stunning views of the Charles Bridge. It serves modern and traditional Czech dishes and international cuisine and has a great wine list. There is also a live music bar, and an Irish pub.

King Solomon
Široká 8, Praha 1. **Tel** *224 818 782.*   **Map** *3 B3.*

The light, pleasant interior of the King Solomon extends to its conservatory. All the food is kosher, impeccably prepared and presented, complemented by kosher wines from the Czech Republic and beyond. They also deliver special Sabbath meals to hotels throughout Prague.

La Bodeguita del Medio
Kaprova 5, Praha 1. **Tel** *224 813 922.*   **Map** *3 B3.*

In this eclectic and uniquely decorated Cuban restaurant the diners relish their seafood dishes and spiced delicacies. After dinner it is worth moving upstairs, where you can enjoy imaginative drinks, cocktails and large selection of Havana cigars late into the night.

Le Saint-Jacques
Jakubská 4, Praha 1. **Tel** *222 322 685.*   **Map** *3 C3.*

Le Saint-Jacques is managed by a French proprietor who is as attentive as his immaculate cuisine is sumptuous. Try any dish from the constantly evolving menu, though the fish is always good. French classics of frogs' legs and snails are also cooked to perfection. A pianist and violinist serenade patrons every night.

Mlýnec
Novotného lávka 9, Praha 1. **Tel** *221 082 208.*   **Map** *3 A4.*

The chef, Marek Purkart, is the first in the Czech Republic to be awarded the Michelin Bibendum three times, so here you can expect the best food and the highest prices. Crisp roasted duck served with white and red cabbage and Karlovy Vary dumplings are certainly worth recommending. Traditional Czech cuisine perfected.

Opera Grill
Karolíny Světlé 35, Praha 1. **Tel** *222 220 518.*   **Map** *3 A4.*

There are only seven tables in the Opera Grill, one of Prague's best-known restaurants, which gives it the feel of a private dining room – but this also makes it a good idea to book ahead. The menu features international dishes, superbly prepared, such as lamb, pasta and steak.

Pravda
Pařížská 17, Praha 1. **Tel** *222 326 203.*   **Map** *3 B2.*

A stylishly decorated, restaurant offering superb service and a buzzy atmosphere. Pravda will tempt the adventurous with its beautifully presented Asian and Scandinavian-inspired fare. This includes relatively expensive seafood dishes like Cajun crayfish and poached cod. Excellent puddings.

7 Angels
Jilská 20, Praha 1. **Tel** *224 234 381.*   **Map** *3 B4.*

There has been a restaurant on this spot since the 13th century, but whatever the changes of management have been since then, 7 Angels remains one of the most charming small dining rooms in Central Europe. The house speciality is traditional Bohemian cuisine with the focus on game.

Staroměstská
Staroměstské náměstí 19, Praha 1. **Tel** *224 232 534.*   **Map** *3 C3.*

Housed in a medieval building on Staroměstské náměstí square, this long-standing popular inn is famous for its classic Czech cuisine and Pilsner beer. The menu includes steaks, salads and home-made desserts. Dine inside or, during the summer months, choose a table overlooking the square.

U Modré Růže (The Blue Rose)
Rytířská 16, Praha 1. **Tel** *224 225 873.*   **Map** *3 B4.*

There is something for everyone on the Czech and international menu that includes beef, lamb, game, seafood and vegetarian dishes. Dishes are beautifully presented and the setting is certainly unique, in beautifully restored 15th-century catacombs.

PRAGUE – NOVÉ MĚSTO

ABA Restaurant, Bar and Night Club
Žitná 4, Praha 2. **Tel** *222 232 315.* **Map** *5 C1.*

The ABA has a welcoming interior of brick walls, graceful arches and original candelabra. The feeling of comfort is further boosted by the food – steaks, sirloin, fish, salads and a delicious apple pie for dessert – and a good selection of beers and wines. Large parties often make for a lively atmosphere.

U Holanů
Londýnská 10, Praha 1. **Tel** *222 511 001.* **Map** *6 E3.*

Tuck into a plate of pickled sausages or herring at Vinohrady's favourite no-nonsense pub. The decor here is simple and clean with dark wood panelling and the service is efficient but perfunctory. There is live music in the evenings.

Buffalo Bill's
Vodičkova 9, Praha 1. **Tel** *224 948 624.* **Map** *5 C1.*

Quite a sensation when it opened 10 years ago on this busy thoroughfare, Buffalo Bill's still draws locals, expatriates and tourists alike with its mixture of Tex Mex dishes and its range of ribs and wings from the American grill. Definitely child-friendly. **www.buffalobill.cz**

Café Imperial
Na Poříčí 15, Praha 1. **Tel** *246 011 440.* **Map** *4 D3.*

This high-ceilinged café is covered in beautiful, original Art Deco tilework. Its atmosphere is that of a stylish old European coffee-house, yet the prices are affordable. It serves light breakfasts, lunches, suppers and snacks. The wide-ranging menu includes Chinese dishes and choices for kids.

Hotel Evropa Café
Václavské náměstí 25, Praha 1. **Tel** *224 228 117.* **Map** *4 D5.*

This is a classic Art Nouveau restaurant, though slightly shabby around the edges. It has been extremely popular for years, particularly among Prague's writers. Its small terrace is one of the nicest in town. The food is average, but people come for the ambience and company.

Jáma
V jámě 7, Praha 1. **Tel** *224 222 383.* **Map** *5 C1.*

A popular place, particularly during the lunch hours, when it serves mainly burgers and burritos and is frequented by office workers and tourists. In the evenings it transforms itself into one of Prague's most congenial bars, where it is difficult to get a table without advance booking.

Radost FX Café
Bělehradská 120, Praha 1. **Tel** *224 254 776.* **Map** *6 E2.*

Good vegetarian food is a rarity in Prague, but the dishes are so good that vegetarians and non-vegetarians alike make a beeline here for lunch. Beyond the restaurant is a bar serving lethal absinthe cocktails, and an art gallery. Downstairs is a disco.

U Fleků
Křemencova 11, Praha 1. **Tel** *224 934 019.* **Map** *5 B1.*

This is a combination of restaurant, pub and brewery set in a maze of rooms resembling caves and caverns. It is said that some of them date from 1499; the brewery was founded in the early 20th century. Book in advance for the restaurant, which serves robust Czech pub fare *(see also p96).*

U Pinkasů
Jungmannovo náměstí 16, Praha 1. **Tel** *221 111 150.* **Map** *3 C5.*

This inexpensive, good-quality beer hall has been here since 1843. The food is simple yet tasty, and therefore the place is popular, particularly during lunch hours. It is arranged on three levels: the basement houses a traditional beer hall, the ground floor is a bar serving light meals and snacks, and above it is a traditional beer hall.

Beograd
Vodičkova 5, Praha 1. **Tel** *724 903 734.* **Map** *5 C1.*

Once a Serbian restaurant, and retaining its old name, Beograd has changed into a Czech establishment. The beer is highly recommended, served directly from large copper tanks. The food is carefully prepared and tasty, though a little overpriced, and the menu includes game.

Café Louvre
Národní třída 20, Praha 1. **Tel** *224 930 912.* **Map** *3 B5.*

An excellent place for breakfast, Café Louvre has been in business since the early 1900s. As well as a full restaurant menu of Czech and European fare, they have an excellent selection of cakes and pastries. There's also a smart billiard room on the premises.

Key to Price Guide *see p372* **Key to symbols** *see back cover flap*

Cicala

Žitná 43, Praha 1. **Tel** *222 210 375.* **Map** *6 D1.*

The owner is an Italian who does not speak English and has only a rudimentary knowledge of Czech. This is the most genuine Italian restaurant, the walls hung with photos of the best dishes, which taste like "mamma's food". Its *zuppa di cozze* (mussel soup) is the tastiest in Prague.

Marie Teresie

Na Příkopě 23, Praha 1. **Tel** *224 229 869.* **Map** *3 C4.*

A fluorescent-lit shopping arcade is left behind on entering this spacious cellar restaurant, named after the Habsburg empress. The fare is traditional Czech, served with a silver service flourish. "Maria Theresa's Platter" is pork, duck, smoked meat, white and red cabbage, and three kinds of dumpling.

U Kalicha

Na bojišti 12–14, Praha 1. **Tel** *296 189 600.* **Map** *6 D2.*

The look of this restaurant, including its cartooned walls, is based on the famous Czech novel *The Good Soldier Švejk*. Its author, Jaroslav Hašek, was a frequent visitor. Traditional, heavy Czech cuisine such as roast goose or pork with cabbage is available. Lively musicians play on a tuba and accordion as you eat.

U Korbele

V celnici 7, Praha 1. **Tel** *221 822 433.* **Map** *4 E3.*

Set in the Renaissance Prague Hotel, beautifully decorated in wood, with decorative Moravian plates, this restaurant surprises visitors with its superb Bohemian cuisine and relatively low prices. This truly attractive place specializes in seasonal dishes, so the menu changes every few months. Added to this is an enormous array of Czech beers.

Zahrada v Opeře

Legerova 75, Praha 1. **Tel** *224 239 685.* **Map** *6 E1.*

The "Garden at the Opera" lies between the National Museum and the State Opera. It has a sophisticated menu, which includes some imaginative salads, and the decor is sleek and modern. Outstanding value for money, it makes a perfect gourmet dinner choice before or after a night at the opera.

Aromi

Mánesova 78, Praha 1. **Tel** *22 27 13 222.* **Map** *6 E1.*

One of Prague's finest Italian restaurants, Aromi offers an authentic taste of Italy in simple surroundings. The cream and brown decor is restrained and the atmosphere relaxed. Specialities here are seafood and pasta and there are also excellent wines from around the world. Good value.

El Gaucho

Václavské náměstí 11 – Kenvelo Centre, Praha 1. **Tel** *221 629 410.* **Map** *3 C5.*

Step downstairs from a mini mall and into a surprisingly genuine Argentine restaurant. Steaks are cooked on an authentic "Asado" grill, food is hearty and plentiful, waiters are dressed as gauchos, and there is a good selection of South American wines.

PRAGUE – ENVIRONS

Ambiente

Mánesova 59, Praha 3. **Tel** *222 727 851.* **Map** *6 E1.*

This eclectic and good-value restaurant, which features everything from American Southwestern to Italian cuisine, is renowned for its salads – they serve probably the best Caesar salad in Prague. Desserts are also wonderful, so leave some room.

Koliba Prague

Gregorova 8, Praha 11. **Tel** *272 941 340.*

This large, relaxed, open-plan restaurant, set on a hill above Prague, fills up with diners every evening during the summer months. Gypsy musicians encourage locals and visitors alike to join in with the singing. Simple but toothsome steaks and fish dishes.

Krásná Řeka

Anglická 6, Praha 3. **Tel** *224 218 154.* **Map** *6 E2.*

This is still the best Chinese restaurant in Prague, although the portions are small and so you may decide to order an additional main course. The dishes range from tofu to duck, and, unusually for many Chinese restaurants, there is a good variety of vegetarian options.

U Marčanů

Veleslavínská 14, Praha 6. **Tel** *235 360 623.*

Folk music, dancing and singing every night make this restaurant very popular with visitors to Prague. It is situated in a lovely villa, a fair distance from the city centre, so you have to take a taxi. Czech food is served on long communal tables. The portions are enormous, and the beer glasses are even bigger. Reservation essential.

CENTRAL BOHEMIA

BEROUN Harmonie Restaurant
Na Ostrove 816, 266 01. **Tel** *311 713 100.* ⊗ **Road map** B2.

Modern interior with light-coloured walls contrasting with the dark woodwork and furniture, making an excellent setting for the meals served in here. Among many interesting dishes, the ones particularly worth recommending are asparagus cocktail, onion soup, beef in wine sauce with croquettes and salad, and pancakes with ice cream.

DOBŘÍŠ Zámecka Restaurace
Zámek Dobříš, 263 01. **Tel** *318 520 525.* ⊗⊗ **Road map** B3,

Situated in Dobříš Castle, this restaurant serves Czech and European cuisine, including an enormous mixed grill (beef sirloin, pork loin, turkey, potatoes roasted with cheese, rice and thin pancakes). On tap is Staropramen beer, light and dark. There is also a café.

KARLŠTEJN Koruna Restaurant
Karlštejn 13, 267 18. **Tel** *311 681 465.* ⊗ **Road map** B2.

This hotel restaurant is furnished in traditional style. Koruna offers Bohemian dishes that are not particularly sophisticated, but really tasty. Especially good are scrambled eggs with caviar, onion soup, mixed grill with chips or rice, and blueberry tart.

KARLŠTEJN Restaurant U Karla IV
Karlštejn 173, 267 18. **Tel** *311 681 226.* ⊗ **Road map** B2.

The restaurant stands only a few paces from the castle walls. It has three rooms and three terraces, plus a beer-garden with a grill. Traditional Bohemian cuisine including fish, poultry and grilled food. It also puts on knights' tournaments, traditional dance shows and fireworks.

KOLÍN U ostrova
Sokolská 10, 280 02. **Tel** *321 720 293.* ⊗ **Road map** B2.

The restaurant is scenically located on an island in the Labe river. Meat dishes, grilled and spit-roasted, are cooked to order. Delicious fish and seafood. Prazdroj and Gambrinus beer from Plzeň. The summer garden offers a lovely view of the river.

KOLÍN U Rabina
Karoliny Světlé 151, 280 02. **Tel** *321 724 463.* ⊗ **Road map** B2.

A restaurant in a welcoming pension. It has an interesting though ascetic interior and serves Bohemian, Moravian and Italian cuisine; fish and steaks are particularly tasty. Highly professional service and congenial atmosphere. There is also a wine bar.

KUTNÁ HORA Čínský restaurant
Náměstí Narodniho odboje 48, 284 01. **Tel** *327 514 151.* ⊗ **Road map** B2.

The restaurant specializes in Bohemian and Chinese cuisine; it serves mainly snacks, fish, vegetarian food and salads. An excellent place for family celebrations and large social gatherings, it also has a child-friendly section of the menu with smaller portions.

KUTNÁ HORA U kamenné kašny
Husova 140, 284 01. **Tel** *327 512 855.* ⊗ **Road map** B2.

The restaurant is set in a 15th-century Gothic house and serves traditional Bohemian cuisine. Prazdroj and Gambrinus beer from Plzeň. The chef's specials include *Vepřový řizek pana Boháčka* (Mr Boháček's pork chops) and *Malínský biftek* (minute steak).

KUTNÁ HORA U Vlašského dvora
28 Řijna 511, 284 01. **Tel** *327 514 618.* ⊗⊗ **Road map** B2.

A pleasant restaurant located on the ground floor of the hotel of the same name. Excellent Czech and French cuisine and professional service. Large selection of Moravian wines. A garden with grill opens at the back of the hotel in the summer, and there is also sunny outdoor seating at the front.

KUTNÁ HORA U Zvonu
Zvonařská 286, 284 01. **Tel** *327 511 516.* ⊗⊗ **Road map** B2.

Restaurant belonging to a small hotel situated in the town centre. It ... Bohemian cuisine, but the menu also includes a choice of international dishes. A ... local and foreign wines is on offer. The decor is plain and slightly rustic.

KUTNÁ HORA Pivnice Dačický
Rakova 8, 284 01. **Tel** *327 512 248.* ⊗⊗⊗ **Road map** B2.

This large, traditional beer hall/restaurant situated in the town centre offers flamboyant Bohemian cuisine (such as baked ostrich steak in coconut cream sauce with garlic-parmesan potatoes), a large selection of desserts, plus vodkas, wines and seven brands of draught beer. Guests are often treated to live music.

Key to Price Guide *see p372* **Key to symbols** *see back cover flap*

MĚLNÍK Bravo

Náměstí Míru 30, 276 01. **Tel** *315 625 548.* **Road map** B2.

The restaurant is conveniently situated in the town square. On offer is a good range of Bohemian and European cuisine; the pizzas and the seafood dishes in particular are well worth a try. Draught beer and many other kinds of alcohol and spirits.

MĚLNÍK Restaurant Local

Hotel Ludmila, 276 01. **Tel** *315 622 419.* **Road map** B2.

Simple, modern interior tastefully decorated in pastel shades, wood and rustic brickwork. Dishes worth recommending include prawn cocktail, garlic soup, chicken with apricot and cheese, and chocolate fondue with fruit. Plenty of drinks and snacks to choose from, too.

MLADÁ BOLESLAV La Romantica

Vinična 1343, 293 01. **Tel** *326 734 054.* **Road map** B2.

A restaurant serving an appetizing variety of Mediterranean dishes. The setting is interesting – partly within the rock under the church. Excellent seafood and salads. Very tasty Parma ham with melon, and a refreshing tzatziki. Good selection of wines.

MLADÁ BOLESLAV Stardust

Staroměstské náměstí 6, 293 01. **Tel** *326 326 222.* **Road map** B2.

This friendly restaurant serving hearty food is conveniently situated in the town square. The menu is straightforward and consists mainly of meat dishes, with a large selection of steaks and sauces. Budvar beer is on tap. A selection of wines and spirits.

MLADÁ BOLESLAV Hotel Galatea

Pod koupalištěm 881, 293 06. **Tel** *326 721 920.* **Road map** B2.

This hotel restaurant, with its modern decor and wooden furniture, favours European cuisine. Large and varied menu includes black caviar on toast with lemon, home-made goulash, grilled breast of chicken with herbs, apple pie with ice cream and whipped cream. **www.galatea.cz**

MNICHOVO HRADIŠTĚ Podzámecká restaurace

Arnoldova 91, 295 01. **Tel** *326 773 091.* **Road map** B2.

This good-value and serviceable restaurant is centrally situated in Mnichovo Hradiště, close to the castle. Inside, the walls are hung with old views of castles. It distinguishes itself by its friendly service, tasty Czech cuisine (over 150 different dishes are on offer) and attractive prices.

NELAHOZEVES Zámek Nelahozeves

Zámek Nelahozeves. **Tel** *315 709 111.* **Road map** B2.

Set in an impressive Renaissance castle, this restaurant has a good choice for a quick lunch stop, but is equally pleasant for passing a summer afternoon over cold snacks and hot dishes. A large selection of drinks includes Roudnice wine and Lobkowicz beer.

PODĚBRADY Bašta U krále Jiřího

Jiřího náměstí 7/2, 290 01. **Tel** *325 612 532.* **Road map** B2.

Furnished in traditional Bohemian style, this restaurant serves a menu dominated by European and local cuisine. Unusually for outside Prague, there is a good choice of vegetarian dishes and they are particularly popular. A large selection of beers.

PŘÍBRAM Restaurace Zlatý Soudek

Náměstí T G Masaryka 98, 261 01. **Tel** *318 623 245.* **Road map** B3.

A lively restaurant with 150 seats, that mainly caters for families with children. It has a decent menu, specializing in fish, poultry and pork dishes. The fruit goblet is worth ordering. In summer some tables are set out on the pleasant new terrace.

PŘÍBRAM Modrý Hrozen

Náměstí T G Masaryka 143, 261 01. **Tel** *318 628 007.* **Road map** B3.

The interior of this hotel restaurant, with its rich stucco wall decoration, resembles a palace banqueting hall, but the food served in here is simple, unsophisticated and extremely tasty. The dishes worth recommending include small vegetarian pancakes, broth with noodles, fried fish fillets, and fruits of the forest goblet.

ROUDNICE NAD LABEM U Petráčků

Nerudova 35, 413 01. **Tel** *416 837 346.* **Road map** B3.

A traditional restaurant with a long history located right in the town centre. Good basic Bohemian food is on offer: set menus and dishes à la carte. Beer is well kept in the cellar, and there is a choice of Staropramen beers as well as several others; Czech wines. Popular with locals.

SLANÝ Hotel Hejtmanský Dvůr, Atrium Restaurant

Masarykovo náměstí 114, 274 01. **Tel** *312 527 110.* **Road map** B2.

Restaurant in a beautiful atrium, with a glass roof providing additional illumination; lots of natural greenery. Bohemian and international cuisine. Typical, tasty dishes include salade Niçoise, potato soup with wild mushrooms and croutons, or Wiener schnitzel with potatoes and lemon.

SOUTH BOHEMIA

ČERVENÁ LHOTA Červená Lhota Restaurant

Červená Lhota 6, 378 21 Kardašova Řečice. **Tel** *384 384 305.*   **Road map** *B3.*

This restaurant, situated directly opposite the Červena Lhota Castle, offers light meals of international cuisine, all served with an imaginative variety of sauces. Here you can order vegetarian dishes, as well as delicious fish and meat dishes.

ČESKÉ BUDĚJOVICE Pizzeria Regina

Krajinska 11, 370 01. **Tel** *386 350 999.*   **Road map** *B3.*

A new, stylish restaurant and pizzeria right in the town centre in the Hotel Zátků v Dům. Sensational salads, excellent pizzas and pastas, but also steaks. A separate area has been set aside for non-smokers, and there are tables outside in warm weather.

ČESKÉ BUDĚJOVICE Potrefená husa IX

Česká 66, 370 01. **Tel** *387 420 560.*   **Road map** *B3.*

Restaurant/beer-hall serving Staropramen, Velvet and Kelt beers, as well as several Belgian brands. Divided into two parts, the main bar and the pub. The chef's specials include grilled chicken legs and neck of pork. A large terrace overlooks the river.

ČESKÉ BUDĚJOVICE Hotel Klika

Hroznová 25, 370 01. **Tel** *387 318 171.*   **Road map** *B3.*

A hotel restaurant whose interior resembles an old inn. The food is good, straightforward and traditional, in keeping with the decor: cheese with olives, beef stew with fried dumplings, pork fillet with pepper and fried potatoes, and cinnamon cake with cream.

ČESKÉ BUDĚJOVICE Hotel U Solné Brány

Radniční 11, 370 01. **Tel** *386 354 121.*   **Road map** *B3.*

The interior of this modern hotel restaurant is hung with tapestries and paintings. It serves international cuisine with strong French accents: onion soup with cheese, roast halibut with rosemary, hot raspberries with raspberry ice cream.

ČESKÉ BUDĚJOVICE U Rytíře

Náměstí Premysla Otakara II č. 33, 370 01. **Tel** *386 358 151.*   **Road map** *B3.*

This restaurant is located in the Old Town square and has medieval-themed decor and menu. It offers a large selection of traditional Bohemian cuisine. Delicious fish and sumptuous home-made desserts. A good selection of Bohemian and Moravian wines.

ČESKÉ BUDĚJOVICE Restaurant Gourmet Symphony

Náměstí Premysla Otakara II 28, 370 01. **Tel** *387 311 384.*   **Road map** *B3.*

Hotel restaurant situated on the ground floor, with a charming view of the town square. Stylish interior with a historic ceiling. The menu is dominated by Bohemian dishes, such as potato soup and roast neck of pork with sauerkraut and dumplings but the international cuisine on offer is also excellent.

ČESKÝ KRUMLOV Bílá Paní

Soukenická 42, 381 01. **Tel** *380 711 977.*   **Road map** *B3.*

The restaurant is in the historic city centre, close to the town square. It is set in one of the oldest buildings in town, dating from 1460. The dining room features an old wooden ceiling. A stylish wine bar is located in the cellar. Particularly worth recommending is the garlic soup with cheese served in a hollowed-out loaf.

ČESKÝ KRUMLOV Hacienda Mexicana

Linecká 42, 381 01. **Tel** *380 712 852.*   **Road map** *B3.*

One of several Mexican chain restaurants in the Czech Republic, it occupies a 15th-century building with Mexican interior decor and South American cuisine. The food is tasty and hearty and the atmosphere lively and very child friendly. Salsa sounds in the background.

ČESKÝ KRUMLOV Katakomby

Náměstí Svornosti, 381 01. **Tel** *380 772 500.*   **Road map** *B3.*

The restaurant of the Old Inn Hotel offers excellent Bohemian food grilled on a wood fire. It is set in the medieval 13th-century catacombs. Draught beers, light and dark, includi̇̇ng͏ from a local brewery. Large selection ͏of ̇beerṡ ҉

ČESKÝ KRUMLOV Restaurant Don Julius

Náměstí Svornosti 11, 381 01. **Tel** *380 712 310.*   **Road map** *B3.*

A witty, unconventional interior with an open hearth and walls decorated with a relief of the town square. From its large selection of Bohemian and international dishes it is worth trying tomatoes stuffed with cheese salad, potato soup, Wiener schnitzel, and tart with berries and whipped cream.

Key to Price Guide *see p372* **Key to symbols** *see back cover flap*

ČESKÝ KRUMLOV Gourmet Restaurant

*Latran 77, 381 01. **Tel** 380 720 111.* **Road map** *B3.*

The solemn atmosphere of the interior, with monastery vaults filled with warm light, creates an unforgettable impression. Added to this is an international cuisine with French accents, such as asparagus in milk with rosemary dumplings, wild Norwegian salmon fillet in Béarnaise sauce, hot marzipan, and strawberries in vanilla sauce.

JINDŘICHŮV HRADEC Grand Hotel Restaurant

*Náměstí Miru 165, 377 01. **Tel** 384 361 252.* **Road map** *B3.*

The restaurant's interior seems to have been transported from an Italian palazzo. The cuisine is obviously Mediterranean, but with the addition of Bohemian dishes. Delicious broccoli soup with croutons, pasta with ham and cheese sauce, fruit salad.

JINDŘICHŮV HRADEC Francův Dvůr

*Jemčinska 125/4, 377 01. **Tel** 777 303 030.* **Road map** *B3.*

The interior, although modern, is decorated in the style of an old inn, with exposed rafters. The cuisine is mainly Bohemian and Hungarian, including sheep cheese soup, carp with onion and mushrooms, and cake with fruit and whipped cream.

JINDŘICHŮV HRADEC Golden Goose Restaurant

*Náměstí Miru 141, 377 01. **Tel** 384 362 320.* **Road map** *B3.*

The Golden Goose offers top-class Bohemian cuisine and fish dishes. Particularly worth recommending are chicken cocktail with pineapple, Viennese soup with sesame oil and bacon, rump steak with mushroom sauce and grilled aubergines, and pancake with fruit.

JINDŘICHŮV HRADEC U Papoušků

*Na Příkopech 188/II, 377 01. **Tel** 384 362 235.* **Road map** *B3.*

Restaurant with a terrace, in a pension of the same name, set in the town centre. It serves Bohemian, Italian, Chinese and Mexican dishes with a non-standard selection of vegetables. Here, you can spend a delightful evening by candlelight, drinking excellent wines from the house cellar.

PÍSEK U Zlatého býka

*Kocínova 1, 397 01. **Tel** 382 221 286.* **Road map** *B3.*

A pleasant restaurant with pastel decor, situated opposite the city walls, with a view of the Putimska Gate. A large selection of Bohemian and European dishes is on offer. Grilled food is served in the summer. Friendly service and a romantic atmosphere.

PRACHATICE Restaurace Bocelli

*Velké náměstí 39, 383 01. **Tel** 721 719 692.* **Road map** *B3.*

A cosy and well-situated restaurant in the town centre offering superbly prepared Italian cuisine and a large selection of Italian wines. Here, you can enjoy a choice of excellent pizza, spaghetti or risotto, served in a congenial atmosphere.

PRACHATICE Restaurace a pivnice hotelu Park

*Věžní 51, 383 01. **Tel** 388 311 424.* **Road map** *B3.*

The restaurant is situated in the basement of the Hotel Park. In its pleasant dining room you can enjoy excellent Bohemian, Moravian, traditional old-Czech or international cuisine. The chef's speciality is fish dishes. Smoking is prohibited during lunch hours.

PRACHATICE Národní dům

*Velké náměstí 10, 383 01. **Tel** 608 111 481, 608 111 482.* **Road map** *B3.*

This restaurant is located in the town square, in the historic city centre. It offers a large selection of dishes, and is particularly good value at lunchtime (between 10am and 2pm), when it serves an inexpensive menu of the day. Live music and dancing on Saturday evenings.

STACHY Restaurace Hotel Churáňov

*Zadov 13, 384 73. **Tel** 388 428 107.* **Road map** *B3.*

The restaurant is located in the newly refurbished Churáňov Hotel in the Šumava mountain range. Gourmets will appreciate this Bohemian and international cuisine. The wine list offers a large selection of wines from all over the world. In summer you can sit on the terrace and enjoy the magnificent views.

STRAKONICE U Madly

*Velké náměstí 53, 386 01. **Tel** 383 323 158.* **Road map** *B3.*

This simple and elegant restaurant, situated in the town square, is decorated with a British feel. A large selection of Bohemian and international dishes are on offer. The atmospheric wine bar in the cellar serves good wines and 19 brands of beer.

TÁBOR Hospůdka u Plísňáka

*Křížová 94, 390 05. **Tel** 602 476 974.* **Road map** *B3.*

A pleasant pub in the Old Town, which opens from 3pm, concentrating mainly on serving beer and wine (with an excellent choice of Moravian wines). This is not the place for a main meal, but there is a selection of cheese dishes to complement your drinks.

TÁBOR Hotel Relax U Drsu

Varšavská 2708, 390 05. **Tel** *381 263 905.*   **Road map** *B3.*

A hotel restaurant, with cosy (albeit traditional) decor, serving Czech and international cuisine. The menu includes cheese dumplings, garlic soup, fried carp with fried potatoes, and honey gateau with nuts and cream. Outdoor seating is available in summer.

TÁBOR Hotel Kapitál

tr. 9. května 617, 390 01. **Tel** *381 256 096.*   **Road map** *B3.*

Hotel Kapitál restaurant generates a tranquil homely atmosphere, and the food served here adds to the enjoyment. Among the choices are tomatoes stuffed with cheese salad, soup with meat and dumplings, turkey steak stuffed with ham and cheese, and banana in chocolate.

TŘEBOŇ Rychta

Masarykovo náměstí 107, 379 01. **Tel** *384 757 111.*   **Road map** *B3.*

A restaurant situated in the Zlatá Hvězda Hotel in the town centre. Food is cooked to traditional Bohemian recipes and includes delicious fish and game. Draught beer is straight from the Formakna brewery. Large selection of alcoholic and non-alcoholic drinks.

TŘEBOŇ Supina

Valy, 379 01. **Tel** *384 21 149.*   **Road map** *B3.*

The traditional fishing region of Southern Bohemia is reflected in the decor of this fish restaurant; nets hang from the ceiling and down between the tables. The restaurant serves fresh, locally-caught fish; recommendations include the carp with dill and mushroom sauce.

WEST BOHEMIA

CHEB U Čechů

Kamenná 28/203, 350 02. **Tel** *377 062 755.*   **Road map** *A2.*

A reliable restaurant set in the historic city centre, close to the town square. It offers well-prepared traditional Bohemian cuisine and a selection of draught beers. Its very friendly staff help to create an excellent atmosphere.

DOMAŽLICE Konšelský šenk

Vodní 33, 334 01. **Tel** *379 720 222.*   **Road map** *A3.*

This small congenial restaurant in a Baroque building known as Konšelský Šenk is close to the town square. It specializes in Italian cuisine, serving numerous types of pizza and other Italian dishes, as well as vegetarian variations. Dogs are also welcome.

FRANTIŠKOVY LÁZNĚ Tři Lilie

Národní 3/10, 351 01. **Tel** *353 825 756.*   **Road map** *A2.*

Luxurious restaurant belonging to the resort hotel of the same name. It offers beautifully prepared Bohemian food, on a set or à la carte menu. Excellent game dishes are available, and there is a large selection of both alcoholic and non-alcoholic drinks.

HORŠOVSKÝ TÝN Zámecká Restaurace

Náměstí Republiky 1, 346 01. **Tel** *379 423 483.*   **Road map** *A3.*

Located in the main square of this small town, the restaurant has a very pleasant, quiet and intimate atmosphere. It serves traditional Bohemian dishes and a good choice of beers. The food is unsophisticated, but it is tasty and reasonably priced.

KARLOVY VARY Poštovní dvůr

Slovenská 2, 360 01. **Tel** *353 224 119.*   **Road map** *A2.*

This luxurious restaurant is located near the spa centre, in a restored building of a former 18th-century post inn. It features a stylish interior with a wooden ceiling. Bohemian and European cuisines are prepared with taste and imagination. Wine bar and garden pavilion.

KARLOVY VARY Restaurant Dvořák

Nová Louka 11, 360 01. **Tel** *353 102 119.*   **Road map** *A2.*

Modern, cosy interior decorated in warm colours. Bohemian and international cuisine. The most interesting items on the menu include tuna and soy salad, roast rabbit with spring vegetables, and orange and banana ice cream.

KARLOVY VARY Grand Restaurant Pupp

Mírové náměstí 2, 360 91. **Tel** *353 109 111.*   **Road map** *A2.*

A very elegant restaurant in the world-famous Grand Hotel Pupp *(see p352),* with stylish decor based on stucco wall decoration and light-coloured soft furnishings. Menu highlights include smoked fish served with balsamic sauce, salmon cream soup, and roasted sea fish with jasmine rice, pepper and saffron.

Key to Price Guide *see p372* **Key to symbols** *see back cover flap*

KLATOVY Harmonie 🍴P◫♫ ⊗

Nádražní 185/III, 339 01. Tel 376 358 312. **Road map** A3.

A small, stylish wine bar near the town centre, close to the bus station. It offers a wide selection of wines, both local and international, and an excellent range of Bohemian cuisine. Although fully air-conditioned, it also offers a separate room for non-smokers.

KLATOVY Restaurace Střelnice 🖫🖦 ⊗

Pražská 22, 339 01. Tel 376 322 366. **Road map** A3.

Located in the town centre, the restaurant is decorated with photographs and historic artifacts associated with beer-making. It serves delicious Bohemian cuisine, complemented with Plzeň beer. A programme of music is presented every night; you can also take to the dance floor. A pleasant garden is open in the summer.

KLATOVY Restaurace Tep P ⊗

Náměstí Míru 151, 339 01. Tel 376 311 958. **Road map** A3.

Located in the historic town square, this comfortable restaurant offers a wide selection of Bohemian cuisine, as well as two unique dishes prepared from sea fish and game. There is a choice of grilled food. All dishes are beautifully prepared and presented.

LOKET Bílý kůň 🍴P🖦 ⊗⊗

T.G. Masaryka 10, 357 33. Tel 352 685 002. **Road map** A2.

This elegant restaurant in the Bílý kůň hotel serves Bohemian and European cuisine. Its spacious, leafy terrace has a magnificent view over the Ohře valley and offers a relaxed evening's dining. It also has a lively tavern (open Thu–Sun 7pm–3am).

MARIÁNSKE LÁZNĚ U Zlaté koule 🍴P♫ ⊗⊗⊗⊗

Nehrova 26, 353 01. Tel 354 624 455. **Road map** A2.

An elegant restaurant, open since 1993. Its style is that of a romantic, cosy inn; it offers good quality food and drink. In 2003 it was voted the best restaurant in the Czech Republic. Traditional Bohemian cuisine, set and à la carte menus, all top-notch. It has a wide choice of fish and game dishes such as venison with dumplings.

PLZEŇ Gurmánská orlice 🍴 ⊗

Sady 5. května 32, 301 00. Tel 377 222 025. **Road map** A3.

An elegant restaurant in the historic town centre, close to the main square. Besides classic Bohemian cuisine it also offers French specialities. A large selection of Czech, French and Italian wines. Some dishes on the menu are partially cooked at the guest's table.

PLZEŇ Parkhotel Plzeň, Emporio Restaurant 🍴P🏃 ⊗

U Borského parku 31, 320 04. Tel 378 772 977. **Road map** A3.

A warm, homely atmosphere has been achieved through carefully selected furniture and decor, which emphasize the food's flavour: simple, yet delicious. The best includes chicken salad in mustard mayonnaise, bread filled with traditional home-made Bohemian potato soup, chicken breast with courgettes, and gingerbread.

PLZEŇ Pivovarská rychta 🍴P ⊗

Riegrova 12, 320 04. Tel 377 328 822. **Road map** A3.

Three restaurants are housed in one building. Fast food and pizzas are served in the basement and on the ground floor. Above are two restaurants serving a large selection of Bohemian and European cuisine. Five brands of beer, including Staropramen, Prazdroj and Krušovice.

PLZEŇ Hotel Central 🍴P🖦 ⊗⊗

Náměstí Republiky 33, 301 00. Tel 377 226 757. **Road map** A3.

This modern, spacious restaurant decorated in pastel shades is one of the most popular in town. Among its many dishes, highlights include home-made pâté, hunter's soup with beans and sausage, venison roulade cooked in wine, fried potato dumpling, and baked ice cream with chocolate and cream.

PLZEŇ Hotel Panorama 🍴P🏃◫🖦 ⊗⊗⊗⊗

V Lomech 11, 323 00. Tel 377 534 323. **Road map** A3.

A highly congenial interior decorated in warm colours, but with modern accents. The restaurant offers a very simple menu with Bohemian and international cuisine, including ham with melon, hunter's soup, meat fondue accompanied by a large platter of vegetable salads, and tiramisu.

NORTH BOHEMIA

DEČÍN U přístavu P🖦 ⊗

Labské nábřeží 669/2, 405 02. Tel 412 532 557. **Road map** B2.

Scenically located on the shores of the Labe, the restaurant's decor is on a marine theme and includes ropes, nets, anchors and ship's wheels. It specializes in grilled dishes, particularly fish, of course, but also game. Ingredients are all fresh and carefully prepared.

DEČÍN Hongkong   🎞️📦📋♿   ⓧⓧ

Masná 5, 405 02. **Tel** *412 516 925.*   **Road map** *B2.*

A cosy family restaurant with air conditioning. Unusually, it specializes in both Chinese and Argentinean cuisine, and serves the best steak in town. The tasty food is complemented by a large selection of beers. The staff speak English and German.

FRÝDLANT Restaurace u vévody fridlanstkého   🖼️   ⓧⓧ

Míru 34, 434 01. **Tel** *482 311 296.*   **Road map** *B2.*

The restaurant is located in the centre of this small town, in a Renaissance town house with an atmospheric mainly wood interior. Bohemian and old-Czech cuisine; fish dishes are popular but also Chinese and other Oriental foods. Highlights include spit-roasted pork knuckle.

LIBEREC Ananda   📦📋♿   ⓧ

Frýdlantská 210, 460 01. **Tel** *606 601 122.*   **Road map** *D2.*

Situated between the town hall and Varsava cinema, this is a light and airy space, one of a handful of Czech vegetarian restaurants. The chef does not even use eggs. Besides soups and main courses it also serves excellent breakfasts. It also has facilities for the disabled.

LIBEREC U Severů   📦🖼️   ⓧ

5. května 350/52, 460 01. **Tel** *485 105 321.*   **Road map** *B2.*

A small, family restaurant with friendly service, and relaxing ambience, offering tasty Bohemian cuisine and Moravian wines. In the summer tables are set outside; there is also an outdoor grill. The chef's special is the *Český talíř* (Czech plate).

LIBEREC Bílý mlýn   🎞️📦📋🖼️   ⓧⓧ

tř. Svobody 295/30, 460 01. **Tel** *482 750 863.*   **Road map** *B2.*

Restaurant with a café, situated on the outskirts of the town centre, in the Stary Harcov district, on the shores of an artificial lake. Modern interior includes a huge tank with piranha. It specializes in game, lamb and fish. Also on offer are Italian dishes and grilled food. A large selection of Czech and foreign wines.

LIBEREC Rybářská bašta   🖼️   ⓧⓧ

Masarykova 29, 460 01. **Tel** *482 710 177.*   **Road map** *B2.*

This restaurant, near the zoo, on the shores of Labuthio Lake, offers the best fish dishes in town, including fresh-water and sea varieties. Carp, trout, catfish and salmon are all cooked in a variety of ways and styles. Particularly worth recommending are Atlantic salmon medallions on herbs, in cream sauce.

LIBEREC Grand Restaurant   🎞️📦🅿️🚹   ⓧⓧⓧ

Grand Hotel Zlatý Lev, Gutebergova 126/3, 460 01. **Tel** *485 256 700.*   **Road map** *B2.*

Stylish, intimate interior, lavishly decorated with fabrics, their textures and vibrant colours accentuated by candelabra lighting. The menu at this hotel restaurant includes salmon caviar; Russian borsch; "Golden Lion" beef steak, and chocolate cake.

LITOMĚŘICE U zlatého bažanta   🚹🖼️   ⓧⓧ

Mírové náměstí 13/21, 412 01. **Tel/Fax** *416 732 454.*   **Road map** *B2.*

The restaurant is in a small historic house, right in the town centre, with an atmospheric, vaulted interior. Traditional Bohemian cuisine, including game. The delicious cakes and bread are baked on the premises. The only non-smoking restaurant on the town square.

LOUNY Pod kostelem   🎞️   ⓧ

Pivovarská 17, 440 01. **Tel** *395 653 470.*   **Road map** *B2.*

Situated close to St Nicholas' church, the restaurant offers Bohemian and traditional Czech cuisine, specializing in grilled meats. Service is friendly and this makes a good spot for lunch or an evening meal. The draught beers include Velkopopovický kozel and Radegast.

LOUNY U Svatého Huberta   🎞️🖼️   ⓧⓧ

Pražska 105, 440 01. **Tel** *415 652 072.*   **Road map** *B2.*

Situated in the centre of town, the dining room of this small, friendly restaurant is simply furnished with wooden furniture and white tablecloths. The menu includes delicacies such as deer carpaccio with grilled vegetables and creamed goat's cheese starters, followed by buck medallions filled with camembert and cranberries.

OSEK Restaurace Černý Orel   🖼️   ⓧ

Vilová 18, 417 05. **Tel** *417 837 082.*   **Road map** *B2.*

A slightly unusual restaurant with stone-and-wood interior decor that is reminiscent of Alpine mountain inns. The menu is dominated by Bohemian cuisine, but you may also wish to try its excellent seafood and fish. Large selection of alcoholic drinks.

TEPLICE U královny Judity   🛏️   🍴

Zámecké náměstí 347/7, 415 01. **Tel** *417 579 316.*   **Road map** *B2.*

Conveniently located in the centre of the Teplice spa zone, this wine bar is on two floors – at street level and in a pleasant cellar. It offers tasty food at attractive prices (including a selection of grilled steaks) and, of course, a large selection of wines. Open 24 hours.

Key to Price Guide *see p372* **Key to symbols** *see back cover flap*

TEPLICE Restaurant U Petra

*Rooseveltova 1, 415 01. **Tel** 417 538 337.*

Road map B2.

Stylish, historic castle interior, where both international and French cuisines achieve a new dimension. Particularly worth recommending are the cheese plate, onion soup, Chateaubriand with herb butter, and pancakes with stewed fruit and whipped cream.

ÚSTÍ NAD LABEM Fírova Bašta

*Stará 1094/76, 401 34. **Tel** 475 221 336.*

Road map B2.

Situated in the town centre, this restaurant offers a wide choice of tasty Bohemian specialities. Vegetarians will also find various dishes to their liking. There is a room reserved for non-smokers. The summer garden has an open-air grill, and there is a children's play area outside.

ÚSTÍ NAD LABEM Restaurace ve Střední Evropě

*Lidické náměstí 7, 401 34. **Tel** 475 200 928.*

Road map B2.

An elegant restaurant with a pleasant interior, right in the centre of town. It offers set menus as well as à la carte dishes, with a choice of Bohemian and international cuisine. A truly hospitable venue, it stays open until the last guest leaves.

ŽATEC U Hada

*Náměstí Svobody 155, 438 24. **Tel** 417 552 025.*

Road map A2.

A small hotel restaurant specializing in Bohemian and European cuisine, situated right in the town centre. The decor is stylish, with great attention to detail and wonderful fresh flowers. Menu includes a vast selection of salads, steaks and fish dishes.

EAST BOHEMIA

ČERNÝ DŮL Aurum

*Hotel Aurum, 543 44. **Tel** 499 435 169.*

Road map C2.

A snug restaurant in the Aurum Hotel; in the morning it serves breakfast to hotel residents. In the summer you can have a meal on the terrace, and enjoy a lovely view. A great variety of food, mainly Bohemian cuisine, and drinks. There is an alehouse in the same hotel.

DVŮR KRÁLOVE Hospoda u Svobodných pánů

*Náměstí T G Masaryka 84, 544 01. **Tel** 603 104 011.*

Road map C2.

A tiny restaurant set in a small historic town house, in the main square, serving an interesting choice of Bohemian and European cuisine. Particularly recommended is the soup served in hollowed-out bread. Highly efficient service and a quiet, intimate atmosphere.

HAVLÍČKŮV BROD Rusticana

*Na Výsluní 1814, 580 01. **Tel** 569 425 932.*

Road map C3.

The restaurant offers Balkan cuisine, including fish, grilled steaks, pasta, meats and salads, as well as the more usual, but nonetheless high quality, traditional Bohemian cuisine. The chef's special is the roast duck. In summer you can eat in the garden.

HAVLÍČKŮV BROD Švejk Restaurant

*Jihlavská 1985, 580 01. **Tel** 569 496 200.*

Road map C3.

A smart restaurant in the Slunce hotel. The interiors are furnished in Empire style, with period furniture and attention to the smallest details. The walls are hung with stained glass and paintings depicting Good Soldier Švejk and the Emperor Franz Josef. Bohemian cuisine, and Pilsner beer. There's a room for non-smokers.

HRADEC KRÁLOVÉ Danup restaurant

*Tř. ČSA 353, 500 02. **Tel** 495 511 026.*

Road map B2.

An inexpensive restaurant on the edge of the Old Town, situated in a modernized Art Nouveau building. Traditional Bohemian cuisine, fish, poultry, game and grilled food. A good selection of vegetable salads. The chef's special is stuffed beef sirloin.

HRADEC KRÁLOVÉ Na Hradě

*Velké náměstí, Špitálská 175, 500 02. **Tel** 495 581 941.*

Road map B2.

A classic Czech pub with long wooden tables and benches and rustic artifacts adorning the walls. It serves Bohemian and Moravian cuisine, also old Czech dishes. You can pop in for a quick lunch, or for an excellent leisurely dinner. The place is popular with students.

HRADEC KRÁLOVÉ Satchmo

*Dlouhá 96, 500 02. **Tel** 495 514 590.*

Road map B2.

An elegant restaurant situated in the Old Town, between the two town squares. The wine bar in the cellar has a large selection of Moravian wines. Bohemian and European cuisine with a great variety of fish dishes. The best coffee in town. There is live jazz from time to time. Closed on Sundays.

HRADEC KRÁLOVÉ U Královny Elišky

Malé náměstí 117, 500 02. **Tel** *495 518 052.*   **Road map** *B2.*

This hotel restaurant has an idiosyncratic interior, with brick-arched ceilings, simple yet cosy. The menu has something on offer for everybody; there is carpaccio of salmon with herbs, soup with meat and dumplings, trout fried in butter and fruits of the forest in dry sparkling wine.

JIČÍN Restaurace U Anděla

Valdštejnovo náměstí 34, 506 01. **Tel** *493 533 023.*   **Road map** *B2.*

The restaurant set in a Baroque house in Jičín town square has a simple, unadorned interior. The menu is extensive, and one of the chef's specials is delicious roast duck served with *knedlíky* (dumplings) and salad. Several varieties of Budvar beer.

KUKS U Zlatého slunce

544 43. **Tel** *774 692 158.*   **Road map** *C2.*

Established in 1699 by the founder of the Kuks spa, Count Sporck, this restaurant has been in business non-stop for over 300 years. It offers an array of dishes, salads and desserts on set menus. In summer it also serves food à la carte. Closed Mon–Wed. Out of season it opens only during weekends.

LIPNICE NAD SÁZAVOU U České Koruny

Lipnice nad Sázavou 55, 582 32. **Tel** *569 486 126.*   **Road map** *C2.*

It was to this pub that Jaroslav Hašek, the author of *The Good Soldier Švejk* adventures, used to come, to sit, drink and write. But this is not the only attraction of this place; it also offers delicious Bohemian cuisine cooked to old recipes; added to this is the fine Plzeň beer.

LITOMYŠL Zlatá Hvězda

Smetanovo náměstí 84, 570 01. **Tel** *461 615 338.*   **Road map** *C2.*

This elegant hotel restaurant in the town centre has been visited by many political celebrities, including Václav Havel. Bohemian and European cuisine are served. Specialities include stew with wild mushrooms, omelette with bacon and artichokes, and roast duck with dumplings.

NÁCHOD Restaurace U Beránka

Masarykovo náměstí 74, 547 01. **Tel** *491 422 248.*   **Road map** *C2.*

The restaurant is situated in the U Beránka hotel. The menu includes Bohemian and European cuisine. After a good dinner it is worth moving to the café for a cup of coffee, or to the wine bar for a glass of local wine. There is a ban on smoking between 11am and 2pm. Dogs are always welcome.

PARDUBICE Restaurace Rybárna

Bulharská 1784, 532 10. **Tel** *466 614 056.*   **Road map** *C2.*

The restaurant is scenically located in a park on the lakeshore just to the east of the Old Town. Smart and imaginative interior includes a fish tank, leaving no doubt about which food is the speciality here. Organizes grills and country music evenings.

PARDUBICE Restaurace Bazalka

Pernštýnská 15, 532 10. **Tel** *466 513 100.*   **Road map** *C2.*

This restaurant is listed among the 100 best in the Czech Republic. Besides Bohemian specialities it serves dishes from all over the world (mainly Balkan, Mediterranean and South American food); excellent grills and fish. A separate room is provided for non-smokers.

RYCHNOV NAD KNĚŽNOU Hotel Panorama

Masarykova 941, 516 01. **Tel** *494 534 619.*   **Road map** *C2.*

Boldly designed, cosy yet classic interior with a view of the mountains. Serves European cuisine. Particularly worth trying are tomatoes stuffed with chicken salad served with toast, mushroom soup, pork loin stuffed with hot red chilli peppers and apple pie with whipped cream.

ŠPINDLERŮV MLÝN Harmony

Bedřichov 106, 543 51. **Tel** *499 469 111.*   **Road map** *C2.*

In the congenial surroundings and pleasant atmosphere of this hotel restaurant, with its excellent service, you can enjoy delicious Bohemian and international cuisine, as well as top-class wines. Leave some room for the mouthwatering home-made desserts and ice creams.

SRCH Na Výsluní

Na Výsluní 236, 532 10. **Tel** *466 414 459.*   **Road map** *C2.*

A new restaurant near Pardubice. It has pleasant modern decor and serves excellent food; grilled meat and steaks are particularly recommended. The menu also includes seafood and vegetarian dishes and there is a choice of dishes for children.

TRUTNOV Restaurace U Kostela

Kostelní, 541 01. **Tel** *777 605 150.*   **Road map** *B2.*

Restaurant and café with modern interior furnishings, located close to the Baroque church. The restaurant (upstairs) is reached by wooden stairs. Dishes worth recommending include onion soup with toast and chicken breast on crisp vegetables. In summer, meals are also served in the small garden.

Key to Price Guide *see p372* **Key to symbols** *see back cover flap*

NORTH MORAVIA AND SILESIA

BOUZOV Hotel U Cimbury restaurant

783 25. **Tel** *585 346 491.* **Road map** *C3.*

A small congenial hotel restaurant decorated with hunting trophies. U Cimbury serves excellent Bohemian and international cuisine, and offers both set and à la carte menus. The restaurant specializes in simple country fare, using fresh, local ingredients.

JESENÍK Křížový vrch

Za Pilou 6, 790 01. **Tel** *584 402 063.* **Road map** *C2.*

This huntsman-style restaurant is housed in the oldest building in the district, reconstructed after a fire of 1994. It serves mouthwatering local cuisine; the chef's specialities include roast duck, and saddle of wild boar in cream, with cowberries. Self-service bar with a large selection of salads.

JESENÍK Akropolis

Masarykovo náměstí, 790 01. **Tel** *584 413 883.* **Road map** *C2.*

The restaurant offers a wide selection of Bohemian dishes (fish, poultry, pork) but many guests come here to enjoy the Greek food. Particularly recommended is the large platter of grilled meats (sirloin, pork, chicken breast) served with tzatziki (cucumber and yogurt salad).

NOVÝ JIČÍN Praha Hotel-restaurant

Lidická 6, 741 01. **Tel/Fax** *556 701 229.* **Road map** *D3.*

An elegant restaurant with stylish Art Nouveau interiors. Bohemian and European cuisine. Well prepared food, beautifully presented. Friendly, smiling staff. There is an outdoor terrace open in the summer months, and a well-stocked cocktail bar.

OLOMOUC Caesar

Horní náměstí-radnice, 771 00. **Tel** *585 229 287.* **Road map** *C3.*

Restaurant-café, situated in Gothic rooms of the historic town hall alongside an interesting commercial gallery. Top-notch Italian cuisine and a large selection of alcoholic drinks, coffee and other beverages. The café garden overlooks the Olomouc town square.

OLOMOUC Hospoda U Dášenky

Masarykova 3, 771 00. **Tel** *585 224 171.* **Road map** *C3.*

The restaurant is set in a somewhat gloomy cellar with a fireplace. Serves Bohemian specialities, including steak and chicken dishes. The choice of beers is good, with Velkopopovicky Kozel and Pilsner Urquell among others. There is a TV in the bar area.

OLOMOUC Hotel Gemo

Pavelčákova 22, 772 00. **Tel** *585 222 115.* **Road map** *C3.*

Modern yet cosy interior; its quiet decor includes some Art Nouveau elements. Excellent food, varied and superbly flavoured; includes vegetables with mozzarella, basil and olive oil, cream of mushroom soup, salmon fillet in cream sauce with pasta, and baked vanilla ice cream.

OPAVA U Krbu

Masařská 3, 746 01. **Tel** *553 613 488.* **Road map** *D2.*

Located in the historic town centre, this restaurant offers a large selection of Bohemian and European dishes from cabbage soup to frogs' legs. It also has a Mexican kitchen with specialities such as burritos and Tex-Mex chilli con carne. Salads and desserts are both substantial.

OSTRAVA U Dvořáčků

Hladnovská 19, 710 00. **Tel** *596 245 454.* **Road map** *D2.*

A huntsman-style restaurant serving classic Bohemian and Moravian cuisine, and old-Czech fare. Game is on the menu, including rabbit and pheasant, and the chef's special is roast duck. There is a large selection of grilled dishes, particularly poultry and fish.

OSTRAVA Hotel Atom Ostrava

Zkrácená 2703, 710 00. **Tel** *596 702 111.* **Road map** *D2.*

The cosy interiors of this modern hotel restaurant open onto the surrounding greenery. International dishes with French and Italian accents include beef medallions with blue cheese and salad, cream of asparagus with ham dumplings and whipped cream, spaghetti with *frutti di mare*, and omelette with fruit, cinnamon and sugar.

OSTRAVA Jarmark

Novinářská 6a/3178, 710 00. **Tel** *596 616 516.* **Road map** *D2.*

Located in a shopping mall, Jarmark is an award-winning self-service restaurant which offers fresh food cooked to order in front of the diners. It offers some local dishes as well as fresh salads, a variety of seasonal vegetables and home-made pasta of all sorts.

PŘEROV Hotel Jana

Koliby 2, 750 02. **Tel** *581 204 466.*   **Road map** *D3.*

Located in a modern hotel with an interesting central spiral atrium. The chef is dedicated to indulging all customers' gastronomic tastes, so the menu is large and varied, with choices such as ham with melon, sauerkraut soup with sausages, turkey fillet with almond stuffing, and fruit salad.

PŘIBOR Mexico

Frenštátská 166, 742 58. **Tel** *556 725 831.*   **Road map** *D3.*

This Mexican restaurant lies along the main road that runs through Příbor. Meals are served at the fast food bar, or brought to the table. The decor is rustic with Mexican touches, and there are booths, which give it a cosy feel. Some Bohemian specialities also make it on to the menu.

SOUTH MORAVIA

BRNO Havana Restaurant

Masarova 9, 628 00 Brno-Líšen. **Tel** *544 238 380.*   **Road map** *C3.*

Cuban restaurant, where you can enjoy Caribbean food, such as *pollo frito a la Criola* (fried Creole chicken), as well as local and international cuisine. The decor is spectacular, with the building made to look like a crumbling Havana mansion complete with pillars and tropical plants.

BRNO Restaurant Bugatti

Lidická 23, 659 89. **Tel** *541 321 207.*   **Road map** *C3.*

The modern decor of this hotel restaurant has a striking gold and blue colour scheme. Particularly recommended is peach filled with chicken salad, Peking soup, breast of duck in saffron sauce with wild mushrooms, and hot apple pie with vanilla cream and blueberries.

BRNO La Rossa

Sportovní 2a. **Tel** *541 638 344.*   **Road map** *C3.*

Located in the Bobycentrum Hotel, this pizzeria serves 18 varieties of pizza, plus pasta, gnocchi, fish, steaks and salads. There is a wide choice of Moravian, Italian and world wines and beer enthusiasts will be delighted with the famous Pilsner Urquell beer on draft. Excellent home-made desserts.

BRNO Gourmand

Josefská 14. **Tel** *542 211 030.*   **Road map** *C3.*

Located in the city centre, the restaurant's decor evokes the end of the 19th century. Bohemian and Moravian cuisine, with lovingly prepared dishes such as eel with garlic, rosemary, sage, thyme, wine and cream. Extensive menu of steaks, chicken, fish, and seasonal salads, with some vegetarian dishes. A large selection of wines. **www.gourmand.cz**

BRNO Moravská Chalupa

Křížkovského 47, 603 73. **Tel** *543 143 101.*   **Road map** *C3.*

An unusual restaurant occupying a rustic building– the name means "Moravian Cottage" – within the Voroněž hotel complex. It serves Bohemian and Moravian cuisines, and the best-known brands of beer. There is a beer tavern and a wine bar in the cellar plus an adjoining bowling alley.

BRNO Cěrný Medvěd

Jakubské náměstí 1. **Tel** *542 210 054.*   **Road map** *C3.*

An elegant restaurant in the historic town centre, close to the main square. Vast selection of Bohemian specialities; also French cuisine. The wine list offers mainly Moravian varieties, but there are also some French, Italian and South African wines.

BRNO Restaurant Prominent

Křížkovského 20. **Tel** *543 122 111.*   **Road map** *C3.*

This modern hotel restaurant has a warm Scandinavian-style interior. Menu includes breast of duck slices served cold with apricots and roasted pistachio, chicken broth with home-made dumplings and minced duck liver, roast goose with red and white cabbage and dumplings, and baked apple en croute, with marzipan filling.

BRNO U Minoritů

Orlí 17, 602 00. **Tel** *542 215 614.*   **Road map** *C3.*

A stylish restaurant in the Old Town, housed in a building of the old Minorite monastery established in 1230. The rooms are decorated with Baroque sculptures. The themed menu uses various ecclesiastical names for dishes, and the food includes Bohemian delicacies and some vegetarian choices. Moravian wines are on offer.

JIHLAVA Amazonia Club Café

Husova 26/1643, 602 00. **Tel** *567 300 280.*   **Road map** *C3.*

The interior decor of this unusual restaurant has been inspired by ancient Latin American culture. Serves international cuisine and vegetarian dishes as part of an extensive menu, which also has a section for children. A large selection of beers and wines adds to the convivial atmosphere.

Key to Price Guide *see p372* **Key to symbols** *see back cover flap*

KROMĚŘÍŽ Bouček Hotel Restaurant

Velké náměstí 108, 767 01. **Tel** *573 338 100.*
Road map *D3.*

This hotel restaurant is situated in the historic town centre. It serves Bohemian and international specialities. In summer there are tables outside in the arcaded hotel entrance with a wonderful view of the town square and the castle. Live music and dancing on Fridays and Saturdays. Large selection of wines.

NEDVĚDICE Pod Pernštejnem

Nedvědice 76, 592 62. **Tel** *603 423 977.*
Road map *C3.*

Situated close to Pernštejn Castle, this restaurant of long-standing traditions was established in the early 1920s. The well-prepared food is mainly Bohemian, with dishes such as spicy pork wrapped in a potato pancake, and grilled trout. Gambrinus, Pilsner Urquell and Pernštejn beers. Closed on Monday.

SLAVKOV U BRNA Sokolský dům

Palackého náměstí 75, 684 01. **Tel** *544 221 103.*
Road map *C3.*

The restaurant belongs to a hotel of the same name, situated in the centre of Slavkov. Bohemian and international dishes with grilled food a speciality. An open-air terrace has seating in the summer. In the adjoining pub there is a good choice of draught beer.

TELČ Restaurace U Zachariáše

Náměstí Zachariáše z Hradce 33. **Tel** *567 243 672.*
Road map *B3.*

A large, elegant restaurant in a hotel in the town square. The high-ceilinged, airy indoor restaurant spreads over two rooms, while there is outdoor seating overlooking the square in the summer. Bohemian and European dishes are on the menu. The wine list offers a large selection of Moravian wines.

TIŠNOV Loria

Brněnská 6, 666 01. **Tel** *549 410 335.*
Road map *C3.*

The extensive premises include a beer hall and a restaurant on the ground floor, and a wine bar with restaurant in the basement. On the menu is a variety of grilled dishes. The tasty food is accompanied by a large selection of Moravian wines.

TŘEBÍČ Restaurace Fantazie

Modřínova 599, Třebíč-Hajek. **Tel** *568 827 261.*
Road map *C3.*

A large restaurant set in an amusement centre. Here you can play billiards and mini-golf indoors. Steaks and pizzas feature heavily on the menu, and the chef's specials include pork ribs and tuna steak cooked with garlic. Ideal for families or groups.

TŘEBÍČ Grand Hotel

Karlovo náměstí 5, 674 01. **Tel** *568 848 560.*
Road map *B3.*

The Grand Hotel restaurant is situated in the town centre. Its attractions include Moravian evenings with wine tasting and sampling of traditional local dishes. The regular menu is mainly Bohemian cuisine. The decor is modern and slightly cold.

ŽĎÁR NAD SÁZAVOU Radniční Restaurace

Náměstí Republiky, 591 01. **Tel** *566 623 188.*
Road map *C3.*

A pleasant restaurant in the middle of the town. Located in the basement of the old town hall, it has an interesting history and was at one time the local prison. It serves Bohemian and European dishes. Outdoor tables are available in the summer. Friendly service.

ZLÍN Hacienda Mexicana

Náměstí Práce 1335, 762 70. **Tel** *577 560 200.*
Road map *C3.*

A popular Mexican restaurant with a congenial atmosphere. The internal decor is typical of a Mexican themed venue. All food is prepared in accordance with traditional recipes; some ingredients are imported from Mexico. The menu also includes Mediterranean and American dishes, and there is a great choice for kids.

ZLÍN Záložna

Náměstí Míru 174, 760 01. **Tel** *577 019 343.*
Road map *C3.*

Situated in the town centre, Zalozna has pleasant interiors that make a feature of a large, colourful fish tank. An eclectic menu includes Bohemian, Asian and Mexican food, with plenty of steaks and grilled meat. A large selection of Moravian and French wines is on offer.

ZNOJMO Na Věčnosti

Velká Mikulášska 11, 669 02 . **Tel** *606 838 524.*

The restaurant is housed in a Renaissance building, with a pub in the basement and an art gallery and restaurant on the ground floor. The menu is dominated by vegetarian cuisine. A large selection of wines. It is worth a visit for its interesting interiors and congenial atmosphere alone.

ZNOJMO Hradní restaurace

Hradní, 669 02. **Tel** *515 228 164.*
Road map *C3.*

A stylish restaurant in the Gothic rooms of Znojmo Castle. The menu is dominated by Bohemian cuisine, specializing in grilled and spit-roasted fare. In spring and summer you can sit outside and enjoy historic vignettes played out on the castle's front courtyard.

Restaurants in Slovakia

The restaurants listed below have been selected for their excellent food, convenient or attractive location and value for money. They are divided into regions, as they appear in the guide. The entries are ordered alphabetically within each price category. Further information is provided in the form of symbols.

PRICE CATEGORIES
Price per person for a three-course meal with half a bottle of wine, including table charge, service and tax.

€ under 12 euros
€€ 12–20 euros
€€€ 20–35 euros
€€€€ over 35 euros

BRATISLAVA

Bagel & Coffee Story   🗐 ♿   €

Štúrova 13, 811 02. **Tel** *(02) 52 63 16 56.*   **Road map** *C4.*

An original American-style restaurant. Bagel-type sandwiches in a variety of options (such as French, Italian, New York, vegetarian) and salads. Fantastic selection of drinks from cappuccinos, lattes and flavoured coffees to milkshakes and fresh juices.

Gremium   🗐 🅿 🚹 ♿ 🎵 🎏   €

Gorkého 11, 811 01. **Tel** *(02) 54 13 10 26.*   **Road map** *C4.*

Restaurant and modern, relaxed bar, which is in a friendly pension located near the National Theatre and Opera House. A fairly informal atmosphere makes customers feel at ease. Coffee, drinks, cocktails, beer, salads, ribs, chicken wings and pasta.

Trafená hus   🗐 🅿 🚹 ♿ 🎵 🎏   €

Šafárikovo námestie 7, 811 02. **Tel/Fax** *(02) 52 92 54 73.*   **Road map** *C4.*

Owned by the same group as the Gremium (above), this modern place has an easy-going atmosphere. The restaurant and the bar serve excellent Czech and Belgian beers. For diners there are grill specials, stews and other Slovak, European and American dishes.

Caribic's   🗐 🅿 🎏   €€

Žižková 1/A, 811 02. **Tel** *(02) 54 41 83 34.*   **Road map** *C4.*

An original restaurant offering Caribbean cuisine, located at the foot of Bratislava Castle. Menu dominated by fish and seafood. The restaurant's highlights include sea fish baked in a banana leaf, salmon steak tartare with sesame oil, and steamed fresh crayfish.

Chez David   🗐 🅿 🎵 🎏   €€

Zámocká 13, 811 01. **Tel** *(02) 54 41 38 24.*   **Road map** *C4.*

Located near the castle, this kosher restaurant has been in business for over 10 years. Chez David specializes in dishes from Europe and Israel, and there are also international dishes on offer. Kosher wines and Jewish music.

Paparazzi   🗐 🎵   €€

Laurinská 1, 811 01. **Tel** *(02) 54 64 79 71.*   **Road map** *C4.*

This Italian restaurant is located in the historic town centre, in a 19th-century Neo-Classicial building. Particularly worth recommending are *fettucine con gamberoni* pasta, and roast veal in an almond crust, with Williams pears. The cocktail bar serves Italian-style cocktails and other drinks.

Preégo   🗐   €€

Žilinská 4, 811 08. **Tel** *(02) 52 62 57 02.*   **Road map** *C4.*

This award-winning restaurant and café is rapidly gaining in popularity. Modern interior decor; international uisine. The chef's specials include beef steak with spinach and salmon steak in cream sauce with prawns, dill and white wine.

Slovenská reštaurácia   🗐 🚹   €€

Hviezdoslavovo námestie 20, 813 36. **Tel/Fax** *(02) 54 43 48 83.*   **Road map** *C4.*

This award-winning restaurant is situated near the National Theatre. Slovenská reštaurácia serves contemporary and traditional Slovak cuisine, including a variety of meats in cream sauces, and potato dishes. The wine list is tempting.

Traja Musketieri   🗐 🅿 🚹 ♿   €€€

Sládkovičova 7, 811 04. **Tel/Fax** *(02) 54 43 00 19.*   **Road map** *C4.*

Named after the novel by Alexander Dumas, the Three Musketeers restaurant is decorated in Louis XIV style. The menu gives names of dishes straight from the era of the Sun King, such as valet Mousqueton's poultry pâté with prunes and pistachios; or Koketa – roast chicken breasts in sesame.

Key to symbols *see back cover flap*

Mezzo-Mezzo €€€

Rybárska brána 9, 811 01. **Tel** *(02) 54 43 43 93.* **Road map** *C4.*

This restaurant has a modern interior decor and is located near the National Theatre. Mezzo-Mezzo's specialities are meat dishes, fish and spaghetti; try the grilled octopus served with a toasted baguette and salsa sauce. Serves breakfast.

Poľovnícka reštaurácia sv. Huberta €€€

Dulovo námestie 1, 821 08. **Tel** *(02) 55 96 85 50.* **Road map** *C4.*

Huntsman-style restaurant in the Apollo Hotel, decorated with numerous hunting trophies. One of the best of its kind in Slovakia. Menu dominated by game (venison, pheasant and wild boar). Full list of the best Slovak and Moravian wines.

Tempus Fugit €€€

Sedlárska 5, 811 01. **Tel** *(02) 54 41 43 57.* **Road map** *C4.*

Attractively located in a 14th-century Gothic building in Bratislava's Old Town. The restaurant's name (Time Flies) does not seem to affect its leisurely charm. The menu is contemporary and includes roast suckling pig and smoked salmon with avocado and crayfish. Cigars available – for those who like them.

Francúzska reštaurácia €€€€

Riečna 4, 811 02. **Tel** *(02) 59 98 58 52.* **Road map** *C4.*

This French restaurant in the Devin Hotel has been enjoying well-deserved fame for the past 20 years. The chef's specialities include breast of duck in orange served with home-made pasta. French-style service and wine selection. Added to this are Slovak dishes and wines, and international cuisine.

Le Monde €€€€

Rybárská Brána 8, 811 01. **Tel** *(02) 54 41 54 11.* **Road map** *C4.*

The restaurant and the bar are situated in historic rooms of the Kernov House. It favours French cuisine, although, as its name implies, you can also order all sorts of other dishes from around the world (Asia, Central Europe, Scandinavia, Mediterranean), including meat and fish.

Romeo e Giulietta €€€€

Rybné námestie 1, 813 38 . **Tel** *(02) 59 34 08 12.* **Road map** *C4.*

This newly opened Italian restaurant in the Danube Hotel is run by native Italians. It (naturally) specializes in all types of pasta and risotto, as well as grilled lamb and tiramisu dessert. Its wine cellar is well stocked with Italian and the best Slovak wines.

Savoyka €€€€

Mostová 4, 814 02. **Tel/Fax** *(02) 54 43 20 02.* **Road map** *C4.*

A small restaurant close to the National Theatre. Its warmly coloured interior is decorated with Picasso-style paintings and panoramas of old Pressburg and contemporary Bratislava. Its main dishes include neck of rabbit in honey and Tokaj sauce. For dessert try the white chocolate mousse with fruit.

WEST SLOVAKIA

KOMÁRNO Banderium €€

Námestie Mr Štefánika II, 945 01. **Tel** *(035) 773 01 56.* **Road map** *D4.*

An elegant restaurant situated in the town centre in a pension that occupies an 18th-century building. The culinary traditions of this place go back to the 19th century, yet the stylish interior looks completely up to date. International cuisine.

MALACKY Klub milovníkov vín D €

Hollého, 901 01. **Tel** *(034) 772 33 05.* **Road map** *C4.*

Wine bar (wine-lovers' club) located on the outskirts of the town centre, behind a cinema. The wines on offer are mainly from the Small Carpathians region. But you can also get something to eat in here, such as grilled steak or Milan-style trout in cream.

MODRA Vinohradnícky dom €

Štúrova 108, 900 01. **Tel** *(02) 647 41 00.* **Road map** *C4.*

A stylish restaurant offering a wide array of dishes and vintage wines. It is one of the attractions of the Small Carpathians' Wine Trail. It houses the first European private gallery of postage stamps. An attractive courtyard with climbing vines.

NITRA Mexiko €

Štefánikova 5, 949 01. **Tel** *(037) 652 53 81.* **Road map** *D4.*

An original Mexican-themed restaurant housed in the basement of the Zobor Hotel. Menu dominated by Mexican food but it also includes Slovak and Bohemian dishes (served in the Gastro Grill, Mon–Fri 7am–8pm, Sun 2–11pm). Occasionally it organizes all-night discos.

NITRA Symfónia

*Farská 16, 949 01. **Tel** (037) 692 52 01.*

€€

Road map D4.

A stylish restaurant in the Capital Hotel building. The restaurant, decorated in pinks and greens, offers a large choice of tasty Slovak and international cuisine, and has a menu for children. In the same hotel are a wine bar, café and pub.

NITRA Zlatý Klúčik

*Svätourbanská 27, 949 01. **Tel/Fax** (037) 655 02 05.*

€€

Road map D4.

Beautifully located above the town on the slopes of Mount Zobor. Serves mainly regional food but it also offers a choice of international cuisine. Delicious desserts, including chocolate mousse with pear and cinnamon. Slovak and foreign wines.

NOVÉ ZÁMKY Koliba dolina

*Športová 4, 941 01. **Tel** (035) 642 60 55.*

€

Road map D4.

The restaurant is run by the association of catering colleges and staffed by trainee catering students. Located above the Kaufland shop, it offers a large and regularly changing selection of good quality and freshly prepared dishes at very affordable prices.

NOVÉ ZÁMKY Hubert

*Budovateľská 2, 940 60. **Tel/Fax** (035) 642 64 80.*

€€

Road map D4.

A modern restaurant and café with summer terrace, Japanese garden and air-conditioned interiors. Specializes in sea and freshwater fish and game. Offers a large selection of salads and dishes for people who want to eat healthy yet tasty food.

PEZINOK Surini

*Bernolákova 82, 902 01. **Tel** (033) 342 66 17.*

€

Road map C4.

A small congenial restaurant with pleasant decor, situated along the Small Carpathian Wine Trail. Serves a good selection of game, fish and poultry dishes. It is an ideal place to come with friends for a leisurely lunch or an evening get-together.

PEZINOK Zámocká vináreň

*Mladoboleslavská 5, 902 01. **Tel** (033) 641 23 60.*

€€

Road map C4.

A combination of restaurant and wine bar with 50 years of tradition behind it, attractively located in a 13th-century castle. The menu includes classic Slovak cuisine, with a particular emphasis on game and fish. Good selection of local wines and beers.

SENEC Senec

*Slnečné jazerá – sever, 903 01. **Tel** (02) 45 92 72 55.*

€

Road map D4.

A modern hotel restaurant with a summer terrace overlooking the Sunny Lakes beach and sports area. The menu lists a variety of meats, poultry, and even ostrich, as well as vegetarian dishes. The fish selection is good, with trout, carp and catfish, as well as Goulash à la Danube, with four kinds of fish.

TRENČÍN Tatra

*Gen M R Štefánika, 911 01. **Tel** (032) 650 61 02.*

€€

Road map D3.

A hotel restaurant attractively located in a 19th-century building at the foot of Trenčín Castle. Serves international dishes, including grilled breast of duck with roasted apples filled with almonds or goats' cheese, served on a bed of lettuce with blueberries and pine nuts. French wines.

TRENČIANSKE TEPLICE Dedinka

*Kúpeľná 13, 914 51. **Tel** (032) 655 14 76.*

€€

Road map D3.

Located in a quiet part of the resort, in a lovingly restored burgher's house, it offers typically Slovak cuisine with traditional names, such as *Pachove gule* (stuffed potato balls with smoked meat and stewed cabbage) or *Zbojnícke dukáty* (Highland robber's ducats), which is pork roasted with bacon and sheep's cheese.

ŽELIEZOVCE Reštaurácia Csiko Csarda

*Rozmárinová 1, 937 01. **Tel/Fax** (036) 771 19 75.*

€€

Road map D3.

Hungarian-style restaurant, the interior decor redolent of the 1920–30s. Wide selection of game, poultry and fish dishes. The chef's showpiece is Piramida (Pyramid) – a dish of turkey, pork loin, and roast goose slices with layers of blue cheese. Pear with salmon mousse is also worth trying.

CENTRAL SLOVAKIA

BANSKÁ BYSTRICA Hotel Šachtička

*Šachtičky 34, 974 01. **Tel** (048) 414 19 11.*

€

Road map E3.

Šachtička is a hotel restaurant enjoying an attractive location in the winter sports centre. The restaurant's huge windows offer superb views over the wooded mountain slopes. Slovak and international cuisine served to the music of a Gypsy band.

Key to Price Guide *see p390* **Key to symbols** *see back cover flap*

BANSKÁ BYSTRICA Hotel Dixon

Švermová 32, 974 04. **Tel** *(048) 413 08 08.* **Road map** *C4.*

A hotel restaurant situated close to the sports complex. Excellent for business meetings and banquets. It offers Slovak and international cuisine at reasonable prices. Although the restaurant is large, its warm colours and softly lit interior give it an intimate atmosphere.

BANSKÁ BYSTRICA Lux

Námestie Slobody 2, 974 00. **Tel** *(048) 414 41 41-45.* **Road map** *E3.*

Located in the Lux Hotel, in the town centre, with an attractive view over the Old Town. Menu includes a wide choice of vegetarian dishes, as well as poultry (such as Côte d'Azur duck breast in orange sauce), beef, veal and pork. Home-made sweets.

BREZNO U Draka

B Nemcovej 6, 977 01. **Tel** *(048) 611 53 02.* **Road map** *C4.*

A small congenial restaurant situated in the foothills of the Low Tatras. Its name translates as "At the Dragon". Diners are seated on long wooden benches. Menu consists mainly of Slovak dishes, specializing in grilled meats. In summer tables are placed outdoors.

ČERVENÝ KLÁŠTOR Goralská reštaurácia U Petríka

Červený Kláštor 61, 059 06. **Tel** *(055) 482 27 84.* **Road map** *E3.*

This country-style restaurant, celebrating the folklore of the Pieniny highlanders, is situated at the centre of town. It has simple decor with plenty of natural wood, and offers dishes from highland and Slovak cuisines. It also organizes picnics with highland music.

GERLACHOV Reštaurácia Hotel Hubert

Vila Horek, 059 42. **Tel** *(052) 478 08 11.* **Road map** *E3.*

A catering complex (two restaurants, café, wine bar, hunter's lounge and shepherd's hut) set amid the romantic scenery of the High Tatras, overlooking the Gerlach summit. Menu includes fish, poultry and game. Trout fillet with prawns and salmon sauce is particularly recommended. A very large selection of wines.

JASNÁ Tri Studničky

Demänovská dolina 5. **Tel** *(044) 547 80 00.* **Road map** *E3.*

The name of this restaurant translates as "Three Wells". The signature dish of the chef, Vojtech Arts, is the grilled venison with cherry sauce, in a potato shell, decorated with baked apple and fresh vegetables. An outstanding dessert is toffee apples in a pancake batter.

MARTIN Grandis, Hotel Grandis

Hrdinov SNP 90. **Tel/Fax** *(043) 422 00 15.* **Road map** *D3.*

Set in a picturesque location on the outskirts of town amid the mountain scenery of Malá Fatra, the restaurant serves dishes such as turkey with asparagus and basil, and pancakes with chestnut purée, plus the best Slovak and Moravian wines. An adjacent café permits smoking.

NOVÝ SMOKOVEC Atrium

Nový Smokovec 42, 062 01. **Tel** *(052) 442 23 42.* **Road map** *E3.*

A very smart, modern hotel restaurant with a light and airy interior and amazing mountain views from the windows of the restaurant. Menu includes Slovak and international dishes. Outdoor dining in summer. Within the same hotel are a wine bar and pub.

PARTIZÁNSKE Afrodita

Prievidzská 30, 972 46 Čevenany. **Tel/Fax** *(905) 354 538.* **Road map** *D3.*

One of the best restaurants in the country. Extensive and imaginative menu including original seafood dishes. Also cream of snail soup with roasted almonds, or marinated salmon with prawns in a prawn sauce. Save some room for one of the delicious desserts. Large no-smoking room.

PÚCHOV Wili

1 mája 899, 020 01. **Tel** *(042) 463 14 51.* **Road map** *D3.*

The restaurant belongs to the modern Hotel Wili. The interior is crisply decorated, and the food very well presented. Salmon with spinach garnished with Orava bacon comes well recommended. A delicious dessert is pear baked in red wine filled with vanilla cream and nuts.

RUŽOMBEROK Panský dom

Námestie A Hlinku 43, 034 01. **Tel** *432 82 06.* **Road map** *C4.*

With its excellent location in the town's central square, in a historic craftsman's house, the restaurant is reputed to be the best in this part of Liptov. It offers regional delicacies consisting of fish and game. Wild boar medallions with thyme and blueberry sauce, served with grilled potatoes, is definitely a dish worth trying.

STARÝ SMOKOVEC Reštaurácia Grand Hotel Starý Smokovec

Starý Smokovec 25, 062 01. **Tel** *442 51 91.* **Road map** *E3.*

A modern gastronomic complex within a hotel, with the main restaurant in an imposing, high-ceilinged room, and a nearby bistro and café. From time to time it organizes Slovak Food Days. In summer wooden tables are placed outside for alfresco dining.

ŠTRBSKE PLESO Koliba na Sanovej Polianke   🖪P🏃♿🎵   €

059 85. Tel 449 22 21.   **Road map** *E3.*

Stylish restaurant, café, wine bar and pub situated at the foothills of Tatras Mountains within the National Park. A variety of traditional Slovak dishes, live music and an excellent atmosphere. In the summer some tables are put outside for diners. Welcomes children and has a kids' menu.

ŠTRBSKE PLESO Slnečná reštaurácia   P🏃♿🎵   €€

059 85. Tel 449 25 91.   **Road map** *E3.*

The restaurant belongs to Patria – one of the most beautifully located hotels in the Tatras Mountains. Dine in an elegant and spacious interior and choose from a large selection of dishes that represent the world's cuisine. A popular spot for walkers.

TATRANSKÁ LOMNICA Koliba   🖪P♿🎵🏠   €

059 60. Tel 446 77 41.   **Road map** *E3.*

The restaurant, which has an open hearth, is the smallest and cosiest of the three eating places situated on the FICC camping site. The menu includes Slovak cuisine. There is live music played by a Gypsy band. The Koliba also serves breakfast.

TATRANSKÁ LOMNICA Restaurant Grand Hotel Praha   🖪P🏃♿🎵🏠   €€

059 60. Tel 446 79 41.   **Road map** *E3.*

A luxurious hotel gastronomic complex including restaurant, café and bar. Varied menu and a full array of services; you can even order a photographer to record your visit for posterity. The main restaurant is imposing with chandeliers and voluminous curtains.

ŽDIAR Goralska Krčma   P   €

059 55. Tel/Fax 449 81 38.   **Road map** *C4.*

The restaurant is in the Ždiar pension building standing along the main road to the border with Poland. Offers highland specialities. The decor is rustic with wooden floors and walls, and the walls are bedecked with hunting trophies. Superb mountain views.

ŽILINA Gastro Nóvum   🖪P🏃🍽♿🎵🏠   €

Závodská cesta 2961, 010 01. Tel/Fax 723 31 10.   **Road map** *D3.*

The restaurant, run by the association of catering colleges, has plenty of Slovak dishes, some cooked in front of guests. Famous for its desserts, including the home-baked Swiss roll with nuts. The interior is fairly plain and brightly lit.

ŽILINA Gold Wing   🖪P🏃🍽♿🎵🏠   €€

Mariánske námestie 30/5, 010 01. Tel 564 06 85.   **Road map** *D3.*

Located in the town centre, this is one of the most elegant restaurants in Žilina. It also includes a snack-bar. The chefs, with international experience, prepare all kinds of dishes from around the world. Particularly worth recommending is turkey roulade filled with carrot and asparagus purée; also beef steak with prawns.

ZVOLEN Poľana   🖪P🏃🍽♿🎵🏠   €€

Námestie SNP 64/2, 960 01. Tel/Fax 532 01 24.   **Road map** *D3.*

The town's most famous restaurant. It leans towards Slovak cuisine and potatoes in any form: boiled, roasted or made into pancakes *(haruľa)*. Slovak dishes are served with Slovak wines. Also international cuisine. The delicious desserts include pear with caramel and ice cream.

EAST SLOVAKIA

KEŽMAROK Reštaurácia Hotel Club   🖪P🏃♿🎵🏠   €

MUDr. Alexandra 24, 060 01. Tel (052) 452 40 51.   **Road map** *E3.*

The town's most elegant restaurant. Its interior is decorated with hunting trophies. A wide selection of Slovak and international dishes, and its specialities include venison, and whole roast pig (which needs to be ordered in advance). In spring and summer you can dine outdoors.

KOŠICE 12 Apoštolov   🖪   €€

Kováčska 51, 040 01. Tel 729 51 05.   **Road map** *F3.*

The restaurant has been in business since 1910. It is located in Košice Old Town, in a 14th-century burgher's house. Snug interior; extensive menu and wine list – Slovak and foreign. The chef's specials include breast of duck with almonds and orange salsa; also turkey roulade.

KOŠICE Krčma Letna   🖪   €€

Letná 1, 040 01. Tel 633 34 05.   **Road map** *F3.*

One of the best restaurants in Košice, it specializes in traditional Slovak cuisine, supplemented by international dishes. It offers as many as 180 Slovak and French wines. House specials include breast of duck with pineapple sauce, beans and potatoes; and *foie gras* with Cumberland sauce.

Key to Price Guide *see p390* **Key to symbols** *see back cover flap*

KOŠICE Monte Bianco

🅿 €€

Kováčska 11, 040 01. **Tel** 025 21 15. **Road map** F3.

An Italian restaurant situated in the town centre. Pleasant atmosphere and efficient service. A large selection of Italian dishes and wines. Panna cotta and other Italian desserts are well worth recommending. On warm days you can sit at the outdoor tables on the attractive terrace.

KOŠICE Uhorsky Dvor

🎜🅿 €€€

Bočná 10, 040 01. **Tel** 055 728 84 93. **Road map** F3.

Košice has a strong Hungarian community and this restaurant offers the best of their cuisine. The smart restaurant is decorated in a traditional folk Hungarian style and there is also a beer-hall serving grilled meats. Chicken legs cooked in dark beer with dry plums and bacon is recommended. Vegetarian dishes are also available.

LEVOČA Reštaurácia u 3 apoštolov

🎛 €€

Námestie Majstra Pavla 11, 054 01. **Tel** 451 23 02. **Road map** E3.

An elegant restaurant (Restaurant At the Three Apostles) situated at the centre of this historic town. It offers excellently prepared dishes representing traditional Slovak cuisine. Menu includes a large selection of fish, at reasonable prices, and vegetarian dishes.

POPRAD Forum Sabbathae

🎜🅿🎎🖹♿🎵🎛 €€

Sobotské námestie 43, 058 01. **Tel/Fax** (052) 776 96 02. **Road map** E3.

Restaurant, café and wine bar belonging to a congenial pension in Spišská Sobota, the historic district of Poprad. Housed in a Renaissance building, it serves a lovely venison steak. A well-stocked wine cellar offers a choice of over 200 Slovak and foreign wines.

POPRAD Sabato

🎜🅿🎎🖹♿🎵🎛 €€

Sobotské námestie 1730/6, 058 01. **Tel/Fax** (052) 776 95 80. **Road map** E3.

The restaurant belongs to a small pension in a 17th-century building in Spišská Sobota. It serves Slovak and international cuisine, including lamb steak with spinach and baked *pierogi* (dumplings). An attractive summer garden in historic surroundings. Open fires in winter.

PREŠOV Carpe Diem

🎜 €€

Hlavná 95, 080 01. **Tel** 758 11 17. **Road map** F3.

Situated in an old house in the historic centre of Prešov, Carpe Diem also has a café, a wine bar and a cosy sheltered terrace, all with a congenial atmosphere. On the menu are Slovak and international dishes; particularly worth recommending is the salmon in orange sauce.

PREŠOV La Cucaracha

🎜 €€

Hlavná 72, 080 01. **Tel** 772 06 00. **Road map** F3.

The restaurant is located near Prešov's historic centre. La Cucaracha specializes in Mexican cuisine – the chilli con carne and tacos are excellent – but the menu also features sea fish and grilled meat. The delicious, home-made desserts are highly recommended.

SLOVENSKÝ KRAS Restaurant U Železného Grófa

🅿🎎♿🎵🎛 €

Rožňavská 635, 049 41. **Tel/Fax** 732 99 80. **Road map** E3.

A cosy restaurant located in a building scenically set at the foot of one of Slovakia's most famous castles. It offers generous portions of traditional Slovak cuisine. Service is friendly and the atmosphere is pleasant. In summer there is an outdoor terrace for diners, and a children's play area.

SPIŠSKÁ NOVÁ VES Nostalgie

🎜🎛 €€

Letná 49, 052 01. **Tel/Fax** 441 41 44. **Road map** E3.

Located in the town centre in a historic building, the restaurant favours fusion cuisine, combining American, Mexican and Italian elements. Particularly recommended are the König (king) salmon, grilled breast of duck with peas, fried potatoes and rosemary sauce, and the Italian desserts.

SPIŠSKÁ NOVÁ VES Reštaurácia Hotel Metropol

🎜🅿♿🎛 €€

Stefanikovo námestie 2, 052 01. **Tel** 442 22 41–3. **Road map** E3.

The elegant restaurant of the Metropol Hotel offers a large selection of international dishes. The restaurant specializes in meat and fish dishes as well as delicious desserts. There is a patio open during the summer months where you can enjoy an aperitif before dinner.

SPIŠSKÁ STARÁ VES Diana

🅿 €

SNP 134, 061 01. **Tel/Fax** 482 29 69. **Road map** E3.

Located in the Diana pension, in the centre of the small town of Spišská Stará, this restaurant has been decorated in the style of a hunting lodge. The specialities here are game dishes such as duck. Punters can also have a drink and play on the billiard table.

SPIŠSKÉ PODHRADIE Spišský salaš

🅿🎎🎵🎛 €€

Levočská cesta 11, 053 04. **Tel** 454 12 02. **Road map** E3.

This long-standing restaurant has been in business since 1964. The menu features regional cuisine, consisting mainly of traditional Spiš dishes such as sheep's-cheese dumplings. A playground and pony rides are provided for younger guests.

SHOPPING IN THE CZECH REPUBLIC

In many ways shopping is undergoing great changes in the Czech Republic, with shopping malls springing up in large and medium-sized towns, and international chains opening branches. This means that many standard essentials can be easily bought here. For a choice of goods with more of a Czech flavour, Prague cannot be beaten, particularly around Wenceslas Square and in the Staré Město. Elsewhere you can still

Beautifully decorated Czech tankard

pick up good quality and sometimes quirky regional items in individual specialized shops – and browsing is an essential part of the pleasure. Typical Czech products include crystal glassware, craft items, wooden toys and antiques. Lovely Czech gems are also worth investigating, particularly garnets. There are some excellent book and music shops in Prague and around the country.

One of Prague's numerous antique shops

OPENING HOURS

Most shops open from 9am to 5pm, Monday to Friday; shopping centres and supermarkets usually stay open for longer, both earlier and later. Small shops may close for an hour at lunchtime. On Saturdays shops close at 1 or 2pm, with large shopping centres remaining open until 8pm. On Sundays only large shopping centres and selected food stores open for business, and in small towns and villages all shops may remain closed, or some may open for just a few hours in the morning.

SALES

From time to time some Czech shops offer seasonal price reductions, especially at the end of a season and after Christmas.

HOW TO PAY

Larger shops accept major credit and debit cards, but smaller outlets prefer cash. Visitors from non-EU countries can claim a VAT refund of up to 14 per cent of the purchase price of some goods on leaving the country.

MARKETS

Prague has several famous markets. During its Christmas and Easter markets, the Old Town Square and Wenceslas Square fill with festive and traditional goods. There are two permanent markets. The central, open-air **Havel Market** sells fruit and vegetables as well as some toys and ceramics; it is open from April to

September. The huge, mainly indoor **Prague Market** sells all sorts of consumer goods.

Outside Prague local markets in most towns and cities sell produce and other everday items, and sometimes crafts. In large cities you can find markets where Vietnamese vendors sell Asian clothes. Along the border with the former East Germany Vietnamese sellers also trade in cigarettes, alcohol, and even Czech glass and crystal. The biggest concentration of such trade is the Hrensko border crossing, along the road from Děčín to Dresden. A large market selling mainly alcohol has developed near the border with Poland, at the Kudowa-Náchod crossing.

GLASS AND CERAMICS

Bohemia is famous for its high-quality lead crystal and ornamental glass. The main glass-producing regions are Krušné hory and the Šumava. In every town it is possible to find a shop specializing in glass and crystal artifacts, and in the Staré Město in Prague there are literally scores of them; some of the best known are **Český Křišťál, Dana Bohemia, Moser** and **Sklo**. One large crystal wine glass, gilded and hand-painted with

A decorative lamp from Harrachov

decorations, can cost in excess of 1,000Kč, but truly beautiful products are worth their price.

Another interesting souvenir from the Czech Republic is a traditional earthenware beer tankard decorated with a Czech brewery logo.

HANDICRAFTS AND FOLK CRAFTS

Traditional crafts are alive and well in the Czech Republic. The range of original souvenirs includes ceramics, wooden vessels and wooden toys. The largest selection of such goods can be found at local markets, but gift and souvenir shops may also have some interesting items on offer.

ANTIQUES

The Czech Republic is a country rich in antiques. During the 1990s many shops opened specializing in antiques and now you can find them (called *Starožitnosti*) in almost every town. They are, of course, most numerous in Prague's Old Town. Well-known examples in the Old Town

Fruit and vegetable market in Brno

The famous Czech "spa wafers"

include **Bazar Nábytku, Dorotheum** and **Starožitnosti Uhlíř**. Their range of goods includes mostly antique furniture, paintings, porcelain and a variety of old bric-a-brac. Prices are often more reasonable than in western Europe.

FOOD

Czech chocolates are particularly good. The great variety of types includes boxed chocolates, bars *(tyčniky)* and wafers. Spa wafers are traditionally taken with spa water; spa hotels and speciality shops often sell these. The Czech Republic is also a country producing excellent cheeses. In some delicatessens you can buy long strings of smoked cheese. *Olomoucke*

rožki, oval cheeses with a distinct flavour, are also excellent. Department stores, found in almost every large town, are a good bet for food shopping. Their food sections are usually on the ground floor.

ALCOHOLIC DRINKS

Famous Czech beers Pilsner Urquell (Prazdroj) and Budvar, which make excellent presents, can be bought in practically every food store. It is also worth boosting your own stock with a supply of local, lesser-known brands. When it comes to vodkas, virtually all Czech brands, including the famous Becherovka, are available throughout the country. Absinthe and *slivovice* (plum brandy) are other popular Czech spirits.

Wines from South Moravia and the Mělník area are the finest and well worth taking back home. In Prague a good selection of alcoholic drinks can be found in **Jan Paukert** delicatessen (*lahůdky*). If you are in the wine-producing areas, you can usually visit the vineyards to taste and buy.

DIRECTORY

MARKETS

Havel Market
Havelská, Prague 1.
Map 3 B4.

Prague Market
Holešovice, Prague 7.

GLASS AND CERAMICS

Český křišťál
Železná 14, Prague.
Map 3 C4. **Tel** 224 227 118.

Dana-Bohemia
Národní 43, Prague.
Map 3 A5.
Tel 224 214 655.

Glass Studio Liberec
Vlčí Vrch 85, Liberec.

Helena Bonevová – Repliky vitráží
Újezd 21, Prague.
Map 2 E4.
Tel 257 311 496.

Hracky
Loretánské náměstí 3.
Prague.
Map 1 B3.
Tel 603 515 745.

Moser
Na Příkopě 12, Prague.
Map 3 C4.
Tel 224 211 293.

Sklárny Bohemia
Náměstí T G Masaryka 1130, Poděbrady.

Sklo
Malé náměstí 6, Prague.
Map 3 B4.

Zdeněk Kleprlík – Veste Glass
Dědinova 2011, Prague 4.
Tel 272 934 117.

ANTIQUES

Art Gallery
Maiselova 9, Josefov,
Prague. **Map** 3 B3.
Tel 222 319 816.

Bazar nábytku
Libenský ostrov, Prague 8.
Tel 266 310 726.

Dorotheum
Ovocný trh 2, Prague.
Map 3 C3.
Tel 224 222 001.

Elart
Mostecká 7, Malá Strana,
Prague. **Map** 3 B4.
Tel 257 530 722.

Na Staré Poště
Starožitnosti Náměstí
Kinskyeh 7, Prague.
Map 3 B4.
Tel 257 311 245.

Starožitnosti Uhlíř
Mikulandská 8,
Prague.
Map 3 B5.
Tel 224 930 572.

FOOD AND ALCOHOLIC DRINKS

Jan Paukert Delicatessen and Wine Bar
Národní 17,
Prague.**Map** 3 A5.
Tel 224 214 968.

SHOPPING IN SLOVAKIA

The souvenirs and presents most often brought back from Slovakia are handcrafted goods, such as traditional clothing, tablecloths, lace, wooden or china figurines, sculptures, ceramics and paintings – on glass, wood or ceramic. An original, although somewhat bulky, souvenir would be a vast mountain horn up to 4 m (13 ft) in length! Visitors to the Tatras mountains can bring back a *valaška* – a highlander's walking stick.

Slovak ceramic plaque

The local cheeses are varied and delicious, and Slovak wines, beers and spirits are good value.

Shops in Slovakia range from small local outlets and bazaars and markets to department stores and supermarkets belonging to large international chains. The best places to buy Slovak handcrafted goods are at the numerous folk festivals, but you can also get them in specialist shops, which you will generally find in any of the larger towns.

A souvenir stall

OPENING HOURS

Shops in Slovakia are generally open from 9am to 6pm, although some food stores open as early as 6am and do not close until 8 or even 9pm. Some shops open on Saturdays and Sundays, usually until 1pm. Many close for lunch, which lasts from noon until 1pm, or longer.

Shops belonging to large chains, like Carrefour, Billa or Hypernova, are usually open every day of the week until late at night (Saturdays and Sundays until 5pm). Out-of-town hypermarkets such as Tesco are open 24 hrs. These are not to be confused with Tesco town centre department stores, which are open the same hours as smaller shops.

Until recently many village shops opened only between 7 and 9am and again between 5 and 7pm; outside these hours people worked in the fields,

so there were no customers. Today this practice is being slowly abandoned.

HOW TO PAY

As in the Czech Republic, larger shops will accept major credit and debit cards, but smaller outlets will accept only cash.

SALES TAX

In the Slovak Republic sales tax is known as DPH *(daň z pridanej hodnoty)*. It is charged on most goods at a flat rate of 16 per cent.

When they leave the country, visitors from non-EU countries can claim a refund of sales tax of up to 14 per cent of the purchase price of goods over €165.

DEPARTMENT STORES

Most large department stores in town centres date from the Communist era, but their interiors have been adapted to modern trade requirements. Some have been taken over by the Tesco group. The range of goods on offer is practically the same as that found on the shelves of all large stores in Europe.

MARKETS

In many Slovak towns and villages the traditional market day is Saturday. This is when locals come out to buy the best local fruit, vegetables and meat. The most famous weekly produce market takes place in the twin central market squares in Bratislava (Hlavné námestie and Františkánské námestie).

At Slovak markets, besides buying all sorts of goods, you

Goods on sale inside an ULʼUV shop, Bratislava

Europe Place square and shopping mall in Komárno, West Slovakia

can also taste local delicacies, such as potato pancake *(lokša)* and fried garlic cakes *(langoš)*, as well as local wines.

CERAMICS

Slovakia has some interesting ceramics. Majolica from Modra is particularly popular; the factory shop in Modra, **Slovenská ľudová majolika**, has a superb selection, but its china is sold all over Slovakia.

ANTIQUES

Antique shops *(starožitnosti)* are not as prevalent as in the Czech Republic, but are still found in most towns, and there are many interesting items and sometimes bargains to be snapped up.

HANDICRAFTS AND TRADITIONAL ART

The agricultural character of most of Slovakia's regions has helped to preserve a great many traditions and customs throughout the country.

An excellent present from Slovakia might be a doll dressed in traditional costume. Other interesting traditional Slovak items include embroidery, table-cloths, wood-carvings, painted Easter eggs, dolls made of dried corn leaves or wire, and secular or religious paintings on glass, wood or ceramics. Slovak traditional artists are also renowned for their wood-carvings, mostly depicting saints and Nativity

figures. Complete Nativity scenes are quite pricey but make superb and unique presents or mementos that last for decades. Models of traditional Slovak wooden buildings are also beautiful items to bring home.

Traditional crafts and art products can be bought relatively easily in larger towns and tourist resorts. Try **U Žofky** in Bratislava, **Krausk a syn** in Bojnice, or **U Kráľa Mateja** in Spišská Sobota. **UĽUV** (Centre for Folk Art Production) is a chain of stores specializing in selling Slovak handicrafts.

FOOD AND DRINK

Slovak shops sell a variety of traditional local food products, such as sheep cheeses, including *brynza*, smoked *oštiepky* and steamed *parenice*. The culinary speciality of the Malá Fatra region are *korbáčiki* – strings of plaited smoked and steamed cheeses.

Those who enjoy a tipple might like to bring home from Slovakia a few bottles of a local wine, liqueurs, the famous plum brandy *slivovice*, or cognac. They are all relatively inexpensive. Slovak Zlatý bažant bottled beer is excellent.

DIRECTORY

CZECH ENTERTAINMENT

The Czech Republic offers a wide variety of entertainment for its visitors, with something for every taste and interest. Those who enjoy nightlife will get the most from Prague, with its scores of nightclubs, theatres, cinemas and music venues. Outside Prague the options are more limited, but most other large towns and cities have a lively cultural scene, though it may be mostly for Czech speakers. During the main holiday period, numerous Czech castles stage knights' tournaments with brilliant displays of fencing or swordsmanship. In the evenings dramatic episodes associated with the site's history are performed. Concerts of early and Baroque music and organ recitals take place in castles and churches. Many towns and tourist resorts organize club nights and rock concerts featuring local and international artists.

Detail from the Puppet Theatre in Ostrava

An outdoor performance of a play in Český Krumlov, South Bohemia

INFORMATION

Information on what is on and where in Prague can be found in the listings of the weekly English-language *Prague Post*, sold in the city and available on the Internet *(www.praguepost.com)*. Here and elsewhere, tourist offices are also a good source of information, and look out for free leaflets and posters in the local area.

BOOKING AND PRICES

Tickets for cultural events in the Czech Republic are not excessively expensive: they range from around 100Kč (for one of the smaller theatres in Prague) up to 3,000Kč (for a concert by a major orchestra).

Concert and theatre tickets can be booked by telephone or by letter. Tickets to Prague's National Opera or National Theatre can also be purchased on the Internet. Group tickets to the most popular performances can be booked well in advance. If you are visiting in the summer, it makes sense to book ahead for performances you particularly want to see and they will deliver the tickets to your hotel.

CINEMA

There are cinemas throughout the country, even in small towns. They show the latest foreign releases (often Hollywood blockbusters), as well as Czech productions. Most foreign films are shown in their original language with Czech subtitles. One of the biggest multi-screen cinemas in Prague is the **Cinema City Flora** complex. The largest Czech cinema event is the annual **International Film Festival** held in late June and early July in Karlovy Vary.

THEATRE

Most large towns have a theatre, often a historic building with a beautiful interior. Czech theatre has a long tradition. Prague's **National Theatre** *(see pp94–5)* is the city's main theatre, but there are many mainstream and fringe theatres, such as the **Laterna Magika** and the **Komedie**, both of which stage more avant-garde productions.

As a rule, theatres display the plays that are currently in repertoire on the front of the building, but posters advertising current productions can also be seen locally. Few productions outside Prague are in English.

CLASSICAL MUSIC AND OPERA

Classical music has a long tradition in the Czech Republic. The country has produced some great composers, including Bedřich Smetana, Antonín Dvořák, Leoš Janáček, and Bohuslav Martinů. Works by Czech composers figure in the repertoires of local orchestras

Classical music concert in Prague's State Opera

all year round. Although most orchestras and concert halls close for the holiday season, that is when numerous classical music concerts are staged in churches, castles and palaces. Many churches, in Prague and several other large cities, organize concerts of Baroque music.

The **Rudolfinum** *(see p82)* is the home of the Czech Philharmonic Orchestra. The Prague Symphony Orchestra is based at the **Municipal House** *(see pp84–5)*. The **State Opera** and the **Estates Theatre** in Prague stage first-class operas and ballets.

Brno has a very active classical music scene; the **National Theatre** is a superb concert venue.

MUSIC FESTIVALS

Another great attraction for music lovers are the Czech music festivals (for specific festivals, *see pp28–31)*. The most famous is **Prague Spring International Music Festival**. Prague also stages an **International Jazz Festival** in October.

One of the best ways to sample Czech folk music is at one of its many folk festivals; enquire at tourist offices for details of events, which can be very crowded.

Imposing façade of the Mahenovo Theatre in Brno

NIGHTLIFE

There are large numbers of music and dance clubs that specialize in different kinds of music, so that most music fans will be able to find something to their liking. Every large Czech town has a music club, although their greatest numbers are in Prague.

The best-known cultural centre in Prague is **Palace Akropolis**. This complex includes a theatre, concert hall, exhibition space, café and restaurant. It hosts many world music artists. **Agharta Jazz Centrum** is perhaps Prague's best jazz club; it is very popular so if you want to see a particular performer it is vital to book. **Malostranská Beseda** puts on rock, jazz, blues, country and folk music.

Outside Prague, check the flyposters for the current information on gigs and clubs. Most cities and larger towns have venues with live music nightly, mainly from Czech bands and musicians. Techno and dance is very popular throughout the country. Top Czech and some foreign DJs can be seen; again, check flyposters for details.

For gay and lesbian visitors, Prague has the most nightlife to offer. The magazine *Amigo* has listings. **Valentino** is one of the most popular gay bars. Outside Prague and Brno, gay venues are much scarcer.

DIRECTORY

TICKETS

www.ticketpro.cz

CINEMA

Cinema City Flora
Vinohradská, Prague 3.
Tel 255 742 021.
www.cinemacity.cz

THEATRES

Komedie Theatre
Jungmannova 1, Prague 1.
Map 3 C5.
Tel 224 222 734.
www.divadlokomedie.cz

Laterna Magika
Národní 4, Prague 1.
Map 3 A5.
Tel 224 931 482.

National Theatre
Národní 2, Prague 1.

Map 3 A5.
Tel 224 901 448.
www.nationaltheatre.cz

CLASSICAL MUSIC AND OPERA

Estates Theatre
Ovocný trh 1, Prague 1.
Map 3 C4.
Tel 224 215 001.
www.narodni-divdlo.cz

Municipal House
Náměstí Republiky 5,
Prague 1. **Map** 4 D3.
Tel 222 002 101.
www.obecnidum.cz

National Theatre, Brno
Dvořakova 11, Brno.
Tel 542 158 111.
www.ndbrno.cz

Rudolfinum
Alšovo Nábřeži 12, Prague .
Map 3 A3. *Tel 227 059 352.* www.rudolfinum.cz

State Opera
Wilsonova 4, Prague 1.
Map 4 E5. *Tel 224 227 266.* www.opera.cz

MUSIC FESTIVALS

International Jazz Festival
www.jazzfestivalpraha.cz

Prague Spring
www.praguespring.cz

NIGHTLIFE

Agharta Jazz Centrum
Železná 16, Prague 1.
Map 3 C4.

Tel 222 211 275.
www.agharta.cz

Malostranská Beseda
Malostranské nám. 21,
Prague 1. **Map** 3 C4.
Tel 257 532 092.

Palace Akropolis
Kubelíkova 27, Prague 1.
Tel 296 330 913.
www.palacakropolis.cz

Rock Café
Národní 20, Prague 1.
Map 3 B5.
Tel 608 702 008.
www.rockcafe.cz

Valentino
Vinohradskaho, Prague 2.
Map 6 F1.
Tel 222 513 491
www.club-valentino.cz.

SLOVAK ENTERTAINMENT

In Slovakia, the wide-ranging cultural entertainment on offer should satisfy most visitors. There are scores of theatres, cinemas, discotheques, dance clubs, concert halls, art galleries and museums. Visitors can see performances given by world-class artistes (mainly in large towns), as well as attend numerous folk festivals (more likely in the provinces). The best-known Slovak cultural event is the Bratislava Cultural

Slovak fiddle player

Summer, which runs from June to September and includes classical, jazz and folk music performances as well as theatre and cinema shows. Similar festivals take place in other larger towns in the summer, as well as in some smaller tourist centres and spa resorts. Summer and autumn are the liveliest times to visit in terms of cultural events, but there is a great deal of interest all year round, particularly in Bratislava and the other major cities.

Performers at a pop concert in Bratislava

INFORMATION

The free English-language weekly *The Slovak Spectator* is a good source of information about what's on in the capital and around the country. The monthly magazine *What's on – Bratislava & Slovakia* is also very informative and has some good reviews. Try tourist offices for up-to-date local information.

TICKET PRICES

It is hard to generalize about prices but a ticket to a Slovak Philharmonic concert will cost about €10–€20, and to the Slovak National Theatre €10–€50; a cinema ticket may cost as much as €5.

CINEMA

Slovakia has a relatively large number of cinemas particularly in Bratislava but also in small towns and villages. The country has film clubs and alternative cinemas,

which show non-commercial films. Most films are subtitled.

Modern multiplex cinemas can be found only in Bratislava. Slovakia's only 3-D cinema is the **Orange IMAX**, also in Bratislava.

THEATRE

The beginnings of Slovak theatre go back to the Middle Ages. Out of the 24 national theatres that exist in Slovakia, a few give performances in

foreign languages. These include Hungarian theatres in Košice and Komárno; Romany in Košice; and Ukrainian-Ruthenian in Prešov. Few performances are in English. Particularly outstanding is the contemporary theatre in Bratislava, **Astorka**. Other theatres that enjoy spectacular successes include **Radošin Naive Theatre** (Radošinské naivné divadlo), the avant-garde **GUnaGU** and **S.T.O.K.A.**, and the Jewish folklore theatre **Pressburger Klezmer Band**. All are based in Bratislava, but productions may go on tour.

Slovakia also plays host to several international theatre festivals, including the biennial Bábkarska Bystrica (festival of puppet theatres) in Banská Bystrica, and Kaulkiar held in the **Aréna** mime theatre in Bratislava. Such mime and puppet events enable non Slovak speakers to enjoy Slovakia's rich traditions.

CLASSICAL MUSIC, OPERA AND BALLET

The main establishments associated with classical music, opera and ballet have their home in the capital. The **Slovak Philharmonic Orchestra** has been housed in the Neo-Baroque **Reduta** building (*see p282*)

Foyer with bar in a Bratislava cinema

since 1949. In 1960 it gave birth to the Slovak Chamber Orchestra. The country's best opera and ballet theatre is the **Slovak National Theatre** *(see p282)*.

MUSIC FESTIVALS

Each year numerous music events and festivals take place throughout Slovakia *(see also pp256–9)*. The most prominent are the **Bratislava Music Festival** and **Bratislava Jazz Days**, both in the autumn.

The best-known Slovak festival of popular music is Bratislava Lyre, which used to be one of the flagship national entertainment events under Communist rule, and now is a nationwide song festival. The most important and the biggest folk festivals take place in Výhodná, Myjava, Detva, Zuberec, and Červený Kláštor.

NIGHTLIFE

Bratislava pulsates with life round the clock. From April until early October countless outdoor areas for beer, wine and music spring up around the town. In the evenings the focus of social life is in bars

Performance by the Slovak Philharmonic Orchestra

and pubs on the outskirts of the Old Town, in Korzo. Late at night you may choose to venture into a fashionable discotheque or visit one of the capital's music clubs housed, for example, in the post-Communist nuclear shelters. The flourishing nightlife is encouraged by the relatively low prices of drinks.

The best-known and most popular clubs and discos in Bratislava include: **17's Bar** (rock), **Café Kút** (reggae), **Jazz Café** (jazz), **Cirkus Barok** (on a boat), **Flamenco** (Latino disco), **Harley Davidson** (rock), and **Laverna Klub** (disco).

Club life is not limited to the country's capital city – those who enjoy spending their time this way can also find something to their liking in Košice, Trnava, Martin, Lučenec and in the foothills of the Tatras, although the entertainment on offer will be rather modest compared with that of Bratislava.

Inevitably, Bratislava is the place with the most nightlife to offer gay men and lesbians. Two established gay clubs are **D4** and **Apollon**.

DIRECTORY

CINEMA

Orange IMAX
Ivánska cesta 12, Bratislava.
Tel (02) 43 42 30 33.

THEATRES

Aréna Theatre
Viedenská cesta 10,
Bratislava.
Tel (02) 67 20 25 57.

Astorka Theatre
Suché mýto 17, Bratislava.
Tel (02) 54 43 20 93.

GUnaGU
Na Františkánskom
námestie 7, Bratislava.
Tel (02) 54 43 33 35.

**Pressburger
Klezmer Band**
www.klezmer.sk

**Radošin Naive
Theatre**
Škultétyho 5, Bratislava.
Tel (02) 55 56 35 08.

S.T.O.K.A.
Pribinova 1, P.O.Box 235,
810-00 Bratislava.
Tel (09) 05 21 10 31.

CLASSICAL MUSIC, OPERA AND BALLET

**Slovak National
Theatre**
Gorkého 4, Bratislava.
Tel (02) 54 43 30 83.
www.snd.sk

**Slovak
Philharmonic
Orchestra**
Palackého 2, Bratislava.
Tel (02) 59 20 82 33.
www.filharm.sk

MUSIC FESTIVALS

**Bratislava Jazz
Days**
www.bjd.sk

**Bratislava Music
Festival**
Michalská 10, Bratislava.
Tel (02) 54 43 03 78.

NIGHTLIFE

17's Bar
Hviezdoslavovo námestie
17, Bratislava.
Tel (09) 03 63 70 38.

Apollon Gay Club
Panenská 24, Bratislava.
Tel (02) 91 54 80 31.
www.apollon-gay-club.sk

Café Kút
Zámočnícka 11, Bratislava.
Tel (02) 54 43 49 57.

Cirkus Barok
Rázusovo nábrežie 2,
Bratislava.
Tel (02) 54 64 20 91.

D4
Jedlíkova 9,
Bratislava.

Flamenco
Štefánikova 14,
Bratislava.
Tel (02) 90 56 12 90.

Harley Davidson
Rebarborová 1, Bratislava.
www.harley-davidson.sk

Jazz Café
Ventúrska 5,
Bratislava.
Tel (02) 54 43 46 61.
www.jazz-cafe.sk

Laverna Klub
Laurinská 19, Bratislava.
Tel (02) 54 43 31 65.

SPORT AND LEISURE IN THE CZECH REPUBLIC

Visitors to the Czech Republic can find plenty of opportunities for all kinds of leisure pursuits, and it is possible to plan a whole trip here around a particular activity. The mountains provide ideal areas for hiking and rock-climbing in summer, as well as being a paradise for snow enthusiasts in winter. An interesting way to explore the country is by bicycle; although the climbs can be steep, the surroundings are spectacular. Natural mineral spas have attracted visitors for centuries, and many resorts, especially in the west, are based around these spas. Canoeing along Czech rivers is becoming increasingly popular, while numerous reservoirs are suitable for sailing. There are also many opportunities for running, horse riding, golf and tennis. Tourist information offices have information on what is available.

Hiking, a popular form of recreation in the Czech Republic

HIKING

The mountains and foothills offer many opportunities for hiking. Almost every region has a dense network of marked trails, which makes it easy to reach destinations by following the most interesting routes. The many excellent hiking areas include the Šumava (see pp148–9), Krkonoše (see pp208–9) and the Český ráj (see pp206–7). A great help to hikers are the **Czech Hiking Club** (Klub Českých turistů) hiking maps, at a scale of 1:50,000, which include the marked trails and are available from most Czech bookshops.

The most convenient and cheapest form of overnight accommodation, particularly in the mountains, are hostels and shelters (see p342). Some bus and train routes link with points along the trails, making it easy to do a linear hike.

CYCLING

Bicycles are plentiful in the Czech Republic. Numerous hotels and tourist resorts offer bicycles for hire, and many regions provide special marked trails for cyclists. These are in addition to international routes that run through the country. Special

Cyclists on a quiet rural road in the Czech Republic

maps for cyclists can be obtained from bookshops. There are no problems with transporting a bicycle (kolo) on a train.

SKIING AND SNOWBOARDING

The most popular skiing region is the Krkonoše mountains, with its famous ski jump in Harrachov. There are also well-maintained ski runs and lifts in the Jeseníky mountains in North Moravia, the Šumava (see pp148–9) in South Bohemia and other areas. Cross-country skiing is also widely enjoyed in the Czech Republic, with many regions providing marked routes for its enthusiasts. Snowboarding is growing in popularity and there are facilities in major winter sports resorts.

ROCK CLIMBING

The country abounds in areas suitable for rock climbing. The best known among them is the Český ráj (see pp206–7), north of Prague, where keen climbers will find numerous weathered sandstone rocks, with marked climbing trails representing various degrees of difficulty. Another region popular with climbers is the Adršpach and Teplice Rocks (see p210) in East Bohemia, close to the Polish border. The tourist offices in these regions can provide excellent information, including details of mountaineering clubs.

Canoeists on the Vltava, near Nova Pec, South Bohemia

some of the medicinal treatments on offer, which differ from spa to spa. The Czech Republic's most famous spas are in West Bohemia and include Karlovy Vary *(see pp174–5)*, Mariánské Lázně *(p169)*, and Františkovy Lázně *(p172)*. There is also Luhačovice in South Moravia *(p239)*, Teplice in North Bohemia *(p191)*, and Jeseník in North Moravia *(p221)*.

GOLF AND TENNIS

Golf is gaining in popularity here. Currently there are over 100 golf clubs affiliated to the **Czech Golf Federation** (Česká Golfová Federace) and their total membership is over 20,000. Tennis courts can be used, for a fee, in any town that has a sports centre. Many hotels have tennis facilities, some open to non-residents.

WATER ACTIVITIES

Many Czechs are water sports enthusiasts, enjoying windsurfing, sailing, canoeing, swimming and angling. This landlocked country has numerous lakes and reservoirs offering excellent conditions for these sports, as well as many rivers. Canoeing along turbulent mountain rivers is a relatively new sport here, with a particularly good stretch on the Labe (Elbe) in Krkonoše. Equipment can be hired from the many sport centres beside every lake.

Fishing is highly regulated so needs some planning. Contact the **Czech Fishing Union** (Český Rybářský Svaz) for detailed information, including times of seasons.

SPAS

Spas have been popular for several hundred years *(see p174)* and still have thousands of visitors annually. Visitors drink the often foul-tasting spa water, traditionally using a special vessel called a *becher (see p371)*. They also bathe in the warm waters, and undergo

Anglers on the shore of Lake Lipno in the Šumava, South Bohemia

DIRECTORY

HIKING

Czech Hiking Club
Archeologická 2256/1,
155 00 Prague 5.
Tel 251 610 181.
www.kct.cz

SKIING

Czech Skiing Association
Zátopkova 2,
160 17 Prague 6.
Tel 296 118 368.

Jeseníky Tourist Information Centre
Masarykovo nám. 1/167,
790 01 Jeseník.
Tel 584 498 155.

Železná Ruda Information Centre
Javorská 124, 340 04
Železná Ruda, Šumava.
Tel 376 397 033.
Fax 376 397 033.

ROCK CLIMBING

Český ráj Information Centre
Náměstí Českého
ráje 26, 511 01 Turnov.
Tel 481 366 255.
Fax 481 366 256.
www.cesky-raj.info

Czech Climbing Organization
www.czechclimbing.com

FISHING

Czech Fishing Union
Nad Olšinami 31,
100 00 Prague 10.
Tel 274 811 751.
www.rybsvaz.cz

SPAS

Czech Spa Information
Masarykovo náměstí 20,
379 01 Třeboň.
Tel 384 721 459.
www.spas.cz

Františkovy Lázně
www.frantiskovylazne.cz

Karlovy Vary
www.karlovyvary.cz

Luhačovice
www.luhacovice.cz

Mariánské Lázně
www.marianskelazne.cz

Teplice
www.lazneteplice.cz

GOLF AND TENNIS

Czech Golf Federation
Strakonická 2860,
150 00 Prague 5.
www.cgf.cz

Czech Tennis Association
Ostrov Štvanice 38,
170 00 Prague 7.
Tel 222 333 444.

Spectator Sports in the Czech Republic

The most popular spectator sport in the Czech Republic is undoubtedly football. Matches played by the national team as well as club matches are followed with great interest. Since some individual Czech players have been reasonably successful internationally, the Czechs also like following foreign games. Attending a match or watching live in a Czech pub is a memorable event. Czechs are truly world class in ice hockey, and matches often generate an emotional reaction from spectators. Another sport with an enthusiastic following is motorcycle racing; the Grand Prix competitions held in Brno are major international events.

Motocross, a sport with many keen spectators

Czech tennis player Jiří Novák

TENNIS

Although some of the major international Czech stars of tennis, such as Martina Navrátilová, Ivan Lendl and Jana Novotná perhaps now have their greatest successes behind them, the sport still enjoys considerable popularity in the Czech Republic. As well as watching matches, many people like to play tennis, as can be seen by the large numbers of tennis courts in towns and cities around the country.

FOOTBALL

The Czechs have always been great fans of soccer, and in recent years, following the successes of their national team in European Championships in Holland and Portugal, their interest has grown even further. The local clubs, such as AC Sparta Praha, and FC Brno, are well known in Europe. Some Czech players, such as Pavel Nedvěd or Milan Baroš, who play for European clubs, are also famous. The season is from September to December and March to June.

ICE HOCKEY

Czech ice hockey players can be seen on the winners' rostrum of virtually every world championship held in this sport. The national team won gold in the 1998 Winter Olympics. The leading Czech ice hockey clubs include HC Slavia Praha and HC Sparta Praha. The ice hockey season is from September to April.

MOTORCYCLE SPORTS

The Czech Republic has been a manufacturer of quality motorcyles for many decades, and motorcycle sports such as motocross and cinder-track racing are both avidly followed here. The Czechs have some high-class competitors and enjoy watching them battling. Brno Grand Prix cinder-track races attract thousands of spectators from all over Europe.

DIRECTORY

FOOTBALL

Football Association of the Czech Republic
Diskařská 100,
160 17 Praha 6.
Tel 233 029 111.
Fax 233 353 107.
www.fotbal.cz

ICE HOCKEY

Czech Ice Hockey Association
1. pluku 8-10,
186 00 Praha 8.
Tel 233 379 248.
Fax 233 336 096.

MOTORCYCLE SPORTS

Czech Autoclub
Opletalova 29,
110 00 Praha 1.
Tel & Fax 224 223 363.

The Ice Hockey World Championships in Prague, 2004

SPORT AND LEISURE IN SLOVAKIA

Slovaks love all types of outdoor activities and fresh-air pursuits and their country is full of areas and facilities devoted to amateur sports. The favourite game year round is football, and athletics is also popular. In winter, ice hockey is enthusiastically pursued. In mountain sports skiing and ice climbing are the Slovaks' speciality. The country has a well-developed infrastructure for

Young skier

hiking and bicycle touring, both excellent ways to explore the landscape. It is also possible to take to the water on one of the many lakes and rivers, which offer an exciting variety of conditions. People wishing to pamper themselves could visit one of the Slovak health resorts and spas. Tourist offices are the best places for information about local leisure facilities.

Cross-country skiing, as popular as downhill

SKIING AND SNOWBOARDING

Slovakia has ideal conditions and facilities for many winter sports. The Slovak Carpathians feature numerous downhill runs and ski lifts. The best-known ski resorts are Jasná, which is south of Liptovský Mikuláš, and Ružomberok, both in the Tatras mountains. In East Slovakia there is Kojšovská Hoľa near Košice. The lower mountain ranges offer ideal conditions for cross-country skiing. Snowboarding can be practised at all ski resorts.

HORSE RIDING

The popularity of equestrian sports in Slovakia is on the rise. New studs and riding centres are springing up all over the country, mainly near large towns and in tourist regions. The area that is the most ideally suited for horse riding is the sparsely

populated border region of Lower Beskydy (Bukovské vrchy). One of the best-known riding events in Slovakia is the annual Mengusovské Rodeo, held in the village of Mengusovské, in the foothills of the Tatras mountains.

HIKING

A dense network of clearly signposted walking trails makes hiking relatively straightforward, particularly in the mountain regions. The trails are marked with their degree of difficulty, which is helpful when organizing an excursion. Maps at various scales with the trails marked are widely available, as are English (and German) walking guides to the country. The most rewarding areas include the High Tatras *(see pp316–7)* and the gentler Vihorlat range *(see p332)*. Wear several layers of warm clothing at all times in the High Tatras.

ROCK AND ICE CLIMBING

The best mountaineering area in Slovakia is the High Tatras *(see pp316–7)*. The local hostels make excellent bases for expeditions into the upper regions of the mountains. You can also practise rock climbing in the Malá Fatra, Slovenský raj and Pieniny National Park *(see p307)*. For ice climbing a popular destination is the frozen waterfalls of the Slovenský raj.

CAVE EXPLORATION

Around 3,900 caves have been found in Slovakia, mainly in the regions of the Slovenský raj, Slovenský kras *(see pp336–7)*, Low Tatras, and Tatras. Twelve are open to visitors. The biggest known cave system in Slovakia, which is over 30 km (18 miles) long, is in the Demänovská valley, near Liptovský Mikuláš.

Pony trekking in the region of Spiš Castle, East Slovakia

CYCLING

Cycling holidays are rapidly gaining popularity with the Slovaks. As part of the European cycle network, Slovakia has marked cycling routes that cover about 3,500 km (2,175 miles) and this network is being constantly extended. Mountainous areas offer strenuous but rewarding cycling, while the going is easier along the Danube, or following the Váh river valley, and in the East Slovakian Lowlands.

WATER ACTIVITIES

Although Slovakia is a landlocked country with no large lakes, watersports enthusiasts can enjoy themselves on dammed reservoirs, many of which have jetties and equipment hire facilities. The most popular Slovak artificial lakes include Liptovska Mara and Slňava on the Váh, near Piešt'any.

White-water rafting can be experienced on the Belá river, and also on stretches of the Váh. The longest artificial rafting run in Central Europe is situated in Čuňo, near

Bratislava. Mountain canoeing enthusiasts can certainly enjoy trips down the Danube, Hornad and Váh rivers, as well as on the artificial canoe course in Liptovský Mikuláš. The Dunajec Gorge in Pieniny National Park is a beautiful and popular spot for both rafting and canoeing (see p317).

Cycling in Slovakia

SPAS

Slovakia is famed for its mineral and medicinal springs, boasting numerous modern resorts with a range of effective treatments and therapies on offer to a local and international clientele.

The best-known Slovak resorts include Piešt'any (see

p300), Trenčianske Teplice (see p301) and Bardejovske Kúpele in East Slovakia. Some of them have relatively small bathing facilities in the form of single pools (often in historic buildings); others have large complexes or even vast aquaparks.

GOLF AND TENNIS

Golf courses are still a novelty in Slovakia. The best-known are around Bratislava and the Tatras mountains. A few are attached to large hotels. Ask for information at the local tourist office on the closest course.

Tennis is a fairly popular sport in Slovakia. You can find tennis courts at sports centres in larger towns, also at hotels and recreation centres in tourist resorts and spas. Many are open to visitors and non-residents.

Messing about in a boat on a lagoon near Košice, East Slovakia

DIRECTORY

SKIING AND SNOWBOARDING

Skipark Kojšovská Hol'a
Letná 42, 040 01 Košice.
Tel (055) 489 83 91.

Skipark Ružomberok
Hrabovská cesta 1679/31, Ružomberok.
Tel /Fax (044) 432 26 06.
www.skipark.sk

Ski Park Vyšné Ružbachy
[illegible]
Tel 0903 999 912.
Fax (052) 418 01 50.
www.skiparkvruzbachy.sk

Snowboarding Association of Slovakia
Jnácka 6, 832 80 Bratislava.

HIKING

High Tatras
www.tatry.sk

ROCK CLIMBING

International Mountaineering & Climbing Federation
www.theuiaa.org

CAVE EXPLORATION

Cave Locations
www.slovakia.org/tourism/nature.htm

CYCLING

Slovak Cycling Club
Hotel Piešt'any, A.Trajana 2, 921 01 Piešt'any.
Tel (033) 774 31 33.

SPAS

Bardejovské Kúpele
086-31 Bardejovské Kúpele.
Tel (054) 477 44 70.
Fax (054) 472 35 49.
www.kupele-bj.sk

Kúpele Rajecké Teplice
Tel (041) 549 42 56.
Fax (041) 549 36 74.
www.spa.sk

Slovak Health Spa Piešt'any, Inc.
Winterova 29,

921 29 Piešt'any.
Tel (033) 775 77 33.
Fax (033) 775 77 39.
www.piestany-spa.sk

Slovak Spas
www.slovakia-spa.sk

Slovenské Liečebné Kúpele Trenčianske Teplice
914 51 Trenčianske-Teplice.
Tel (032) 655 22 88.
Fax (032) 655 29 60.
www.slktn.sk

GOLF

Slovak Golf Union
[illegible]
82 109 Bratislava.
Tel (02) 523 18 90.
Fax (02) 521 88 34.

Spectator Sports in Slovakia

Sport is a very important part of life for the Slovaks. This can be clearly seen in the impressive numbers of sports centres and facilities. The expansion of the sports infrastructure has resulted in a substantial increase in the successes achieved by Slovaks in the highest ranking international events, including world championships and Olympic Games. The disciplines in which they excel, and which are most closely followed by spectators, are ice hockey, soccer and tennis. Canoeing and kayaking also draw the crowds.

Michal Martikán in the Olympic slalom canoeing race, Athens, 2004

Miroslav Šatan, captain of the Slovak national ice hockey team

ICE HOCKEY

The national sport of the Slovaks is ice hockey. In fact, the professional players who won the ice hockey world championship in 2002 for their country are regarded as real heroes. The legends of Slovak ice hockey are: Stan Mikita, Peter Šťastny, Václav Nedomansky, Vladimir Dzurila and Josef Golonka. Many Slovak players play regularly in the North American National Hockey League (NHL).

FOOTBALL

This is the second most popular sport in Slovakia. Up to now, however, the greatest achievement of Slovak players in the international arena has been when FC Artmedia Petržalka (from near Bratislava) reached the UEFA Champions' League in 2005.

SKIING AND SNOWBOARDING

Slovaks are very proud of their prowess in snow sports. Slovak skiers are starting to score international successes in Alpine and Classic skiing. The most recent star is the young Alpine skier Veronika Zuzulova, hailed as the future of Slovak skiing. The top Slovak cross-country skier is Ivan Batory. Snowboarders are also doing well, with Radoslav Zidek winning a silver medal in the snowboard cross event (downhill snowboard racing) at the 2006 Winter Olympics.

OTHER SPORTS

Slovak competitors are also successful in sports such as swimming, shooting and mountain canoeing. Michal Martikán is one of the stars of slalom canoeing, having won three Olympic medals.

Tennis is another popular game. The most successful current players are Dominik Hrbaty, Karol Kučera and Karol Beck. Major tournaments are held at the National Tennis Centre in Bratislava.

DIRECTORY

ICE HOCKEY

Slovenský zväz ľadového hokeja
Junácka 6,
832 80 Bratislava.
Tel (02) 492 49 179.
Fax (02) 442 58 344.
www.szlh.sk

FOOTBALL

Slovak Football Association
Junácka 6,
832 80 Bratislava.
Tel (02) 492 49 161.
Fax (02) 492 49 595.
www.futbalsfz.sk

SKIING

Slovak Ski Association
Junácka 6,
832 80 Bratislava.
Tel (02) 492 49 208.
Fax (02) 492 49 565.
www.slz.sk

Veronika Zuzulova, successful Slovak skier

SURVIVAL
GUIDE

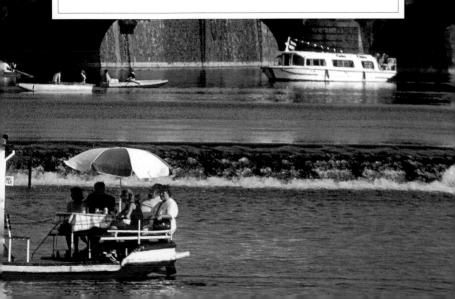

PRACTICAL INFORMATION

The Czech and Slovak Republics are both very friendly destinations for visitors. Numerous historic sights and attractions, good roads (particularly in the Czech Republic), efficient internal transport, tasty local food and a wide choice of accommodation result in the steadily growing numbers of visitors to these countries. Once

Tourist bus belonging to the Czech company Martin Tours

you have arrived, a well-developed network of tourist information offices, which in both countries can be found in even quite small places, provides invaluable help to travellers. The practical information below and opposite concerns the Czech Republic; pages 414–15 give practical information on visiting Slovakia.

WHEN TO VISIT THE CZECH REPUBLIC

The best time of year for visiting the country is between May and September. During these months the warm weather makes for pleasant camping, mountain trekking or relaxing by or swimming in lakes and rivers. Some castles, museums and other historic sights, particularly in small towns and villages, open their doors to visitors only during this high season.

During school holidays (July and August) campsites and some resorts tend to fill up, so it is better to visit in May, June or September if you want to avoid the crowds. Prague in particular is inundated with visitors in July and August and can be unbearably crowded.

Late September is an interesting time to visit Moravia for its grape harvest season. In winter many regions of the Czech Republic offer good snow conditions.

VISA AND CUSTOMS REGULATIONS

Citizens of EU countries do not need a visa when entering the Czech Republic; it is enough to carry a passport (valid for at least 6 months beyond your return date) or an ID card. UK citizens are entitled to stay for up to 180 days without a visa. EU, New Zealand, Australian, US and Canadian citizens can stay for up to 90 days. For up-to-date information, consult your nearest Czech Embassy (or visit *www.mfa.cz*).

Customs regulations do not apply to visitors from within the EU as long as they stay within the EU guidelines for personal use. When entering the Czech Republic you must carry 1,000Kč for every day of your planned visit, though for EU residents this is checked only in exceptional cases.

A tourist information office, Tábor

EMBASSIES

For selected embassies in the Czech Republic, see the directory opposite. The consulates for Australia and New Zealand and the Canadian Embassy in Prague also cover Slovakia.

TOURIST INFORMATION

The Czech Republic has a very efficient network of tourist information offices, which can be found in almost every town, village and resort. In large cities they are usually in railway stations; otherwise they are often in the town square. They are open from 9am to 5pm (7pm in Prague) and provide information on accommodation, eating places, museums, art galleries and historic sights; they also offer free booklets and sell maps, guidebooks and postcards. Staff can usually speak fluent German and good English. It is worthwhile contacting a Czech tourist office where you live before leaving to help plan your trip.

Charles Bridge in Prague – a popular destination all year round

◁   **View from the Vltava to Prague's National Theatre**

Horse-drawn transport in Karlovy Vary, West Bohemia

BUSINESS HOURS

Most banks and offices are open from 9am to 5pm; some have a lunch break. (For shop opening hours, *see p396*.)

MUSEUMS AND HISTORIC SIGHTS

Between May and September museums in most large Czech towns are open Tuesday to Sunday from 9am to 6pm. From October to April many open from 9am to 5pm, sometimes changing to Monday to Friday. In smaller towns many museums are open only from May to October, 9am–4pm, or 5pm; some open only at weekends.

Other sights, such as castles, churches, convents and monasteries, are open to visitors from May to September, Tuesday to Sunday 9am–4pm, or 5pm. Many close for lunch between noon and 1pm. In April and October some provincial sights are open only at weekends; from November to April many are closed, though a few can be visited by appointment. Many historic sights can be visited only by guided tours (at least five

Tickets to some of the main tourist sights in Prague

people). In smaller places the keys to buildings may be with a custodian (often a private individual); a notice on the door says who to contact.

ADMISSION PRICES

Admission to museums and historic sights outside the capital is not expensive, costing around 40–60Kč. Children over six and students are generally given a discount of 30–50 per cent, while under sixes are often free. Expect higher ticket prices in Prague.

TRAVELLING WITH CHILDREN

Children are welcomed, although there are few facilities (such as play areas) specifically for them. There are, however, plenty of open spaces in which children can let off steam. (For eating with children, *see p367*).

DISABLED TRAVELLERS

Despite some improvements, the Czech Republic is still not that easy to negotiate for disabled travellers. In some places, particularly in Prague, there are hotels, restaurants, bars, museums and historic sights that have been adapted to the needs of the disabled. However, in many towns and cities, the prevalence of cobbles means that wheelchair users will find getting about uncomfortable, but possible.

Accessible public transport is patchy. A number of railway stations and trains, and some of the capital's metro stations and newer buses, do have wheelchair access. The Prague

Public Transport Offices have a list of wheelchair accessible transport *(www.dpp.cz)*.

LANGUAGE

While many people in Prague speak English, knowledge of English in the provinces is minimal, and so it is useful to know some Czech basics. The most popular greeting is *dobrý den* (good day), or in the morning *dobre rano* (good morning). When parting you can say *aboj* (cheers), or *na shledanou* (goodbye) or *nashle.* (*see also* Phrasebook, *pp447–8.*)

MEASURES AND ELECTRICAL APPLIANCES

The Czech Republic uses the metric system. The mains voltage is 220–230 volts. Standard Continental European two-pin plugs are used.

DIRECTORY

EMBASSIES AND CONSULATES IN THE CZECH REPUBLIC

Australian Consulate
Klimentská 10, 110 00 Prague 1.
Tel 296 578 350, 296 578 351.

British Embassy
Thunovská 14, 118 00 Prague 1.
Tel 257 402 111.

Canadian Embassy
Muchova 6, 160 00 Prague 6.
Tel 272 101 800.

New Zealand Consulate
Dykova 19, 101 00 Prague 10.
Tel 222 514 672
or 0049 30 20 62.

US Embassy
Tržiště 15, 118 01 Prague 1.
Tel 257 530 663.

EMBASSIES IN THE SLOVAK REPUBLIC

British Embassy
Panská 16, 814 99 Bratislava.
Tel (02) 59 98 20 00.

US Embassy
Hviezdoslavovo námestie 4,
811 02 Bratislava.
Tel (02) 54 43 08 61.

WHEN TO VISIT SLOVAKIA

Slovakia is an attractive destination for visitors throughout the year. Spring and autumn are good times for mountain hikes, bike tours and cave exploration. Summertime is excellent for swimming in the numerous pools and bathing centres (ordinary and thermal) and for enjoying water sports on its artificial lakes. In winter, Slovakia tempts visitors with its excellent ski slopes, and more unusual attractions such as swimming in outdoor thermal pools.

Those interested in visiting museums, open-air museums (skansens) and castles should bear in mind that from October to May many of them are closed, particularly those situated in the provinces. However, sights in Bratislava and other large towns generally remain open throughout the year.

VISA AND CUSTOMS REGULATIONS

Nationals of EU countries are admitted to Slovakia on presenting a valid passport or an ID Card, but if they intend to remain in the country for more than 90 days, they are required to report to the police and apply for a resident's permit.

Foreigners entering the Slovak Republic have to carry €108, or the equivalent in any convertible currency, in the form of travellers' cheques, cash or credit cards, for each

day of their intended stay (children up to the age of 16 need half this amount). This rule is, however, applied to EU citizens only in exceptional circumstances. The sum may be reduced on the presentation of documents confirming advance payment for some services, such as hotel bookings or car hire.

At customs, as in the Czech Republic, EU nationals can bring into Slovakia the maximum allowed within the EU guidelines for personal use.

Information brochures from Slovak tourist information offices

EMBASSIES

For selected embassies in the Slovak Republic, see the directory (p413). The consulates for Australia and New Zealand and the Canadian embassy in Prague cover their nationals when travelling in Slovakia.

TOURIST INFORMATION

Local tourist information centres provide details on accommodation, the region's

natural attractions, also its cultural and sporting events. The most reliable information can be obtained from any of the 49 AICES affiliated offices (Asociácia informačných centier Slovenska), with their head office in Liptovský Mikuláš (www.infoslovak.sk). In addition, many places have their own information centres providing the same type of services. These may sell parking permits and local discount cards for tourists; they may also exchange foreign currencies. In some of these centres (although still very few) it is possible to book hotel accommodation.

Unfortunately, almost none of the maps, guidebooks and information brochures that can be obtained from tourist information offices are free; the best you can hope to be given for free are a few pamphlets.

Tourist information offices are usually open 9am to 5pm, occasionally until 4pm or 6pm. Some of them close for an hour at lunchtime. On Saturdays many such offices close at 1pm, and on Sundays many remain closed all day. Their staff usually speak English and German.

Slovak tourist offices abroad are few and far between, but it is worth consulting websites such as www.slovakije.com or www.slovakiatourism.sk for information when planning your trip.

MUSEUMS AND HISTORIC SIGHTS

Slovakia has numerous interesting historic sites from various eras: from the Neolithic and Bronze Ages to relatively recent times. In most towns you can find regional, historic or local museums. These often open all year from 9am to 5pm, though they may open Tuesday to Sunday in summer and Monday to Friday in winter.

The most interesting open-air museums (skansens), exhibiting traditional rural buildings, can be found in the country's northern regions, in Martin-Jahodniki (from all

Tourist bus in Bratislava's Old Town

Waiting to get started at a ski school

over Slovakia), Zuberec (Orava), Stará L'ubovňa (Spiš), Svidník (Ukrainian-Ruthenian); and Humenn (Zemplinský). The historic villages of Čičmany and Vlkolínec enjoy the status of "living skansens". Opening hours vary, with some staying open all year and others just during the summer months.

Many Slovak castles and historic buildings are open from May to September, Tuesday to Sunday between 9am and 5pm, closing for an hour for lunch. They open at weekends in April and October, and then some close completely from November to March. Opening hours of major sights are listed in this guide. Many can be seen only on a guided tour; ask if there is an English guide as otherwise tours are usually in Slovak.

Some large churches and cathedrals open on the same basis as museums. Others are open only when a service is in progress. At other times, seek admission from the local caretaker or priest, whose address is often given on the door.

ADMISSION PRICES

Museum entrance fees are not very high in Slovakia– they vary from €1 to €2, with concession tickets for children and students at around 50 cents to €1. A few major castles charge more. At Bojnice, for instance, a standard ticket costs €4, and concessions are €2. At Orava a standard ticket is €3, while a concession ticket is €1.

TRAVELLING WITH CHILDREN

Slovakia is a child-friendly country. Public parks feature many playgrounds; there are also children's play areas in some supermarkets. The most attractive places are the numerous swimming pools, with ordinary and thermal pools. The country's best-known aquapark is Tatralandia, near Liptovský Mikuláš. Its competitor is the ever-expanding Aquacity park in Poprad. Children are also sure to enjoy the zoos in Bratislava, Bojnice, Košice and Spišská Nová Ves

The youngest travellers can expect generous discounts in hotels, as well as on public transport; for example, a child up to the age of six travels free on Slovak railways.

DISABLED TRAVELLERS

Facilities for disabled visitors are limited in Slovakia. Many of the trains have wheelchair access to at least one carriage, but it is often difficult to negotiate the station itself in order to reach the train. Many older

buildings are gradually being adapted to the needs of disabled users. (For access in hotels, *see p343*; for restaurants, *see p367*).

LANGUAGE

Slovakia's official language is Slovak, commonly spoken by about 86 per cent of the population. In the country's southern region, with its Hungarian minority (about 10 per cent of the population), the signs and names of places are given in both Slovak and Hungarian. Bilingual signs can also be seen in northeastern regions inhabited by, amongst others, the Ruthenian (Ukrainian) minority. You can also communicate in Czech anywhere in Slovakia without any problem. In towns and tourist resorts a knowledge of English and German is reasonably widespread.

MEASURES AND ELECTRICAL APPLIANCES

Slovakia uses the metric system. The mains voltage is 220–230 volts. Standard Continental European two-pin plugs are used.

LOCAL TIME

Slovakia's clocks are set to Central-European time (GMT + 1), that is, the same as most of the countries of Continental Europe. As in neighbouring countries, the clocks are put forward by one hour on the last Sunday in March (summer time) and back again by one hour on the last Sunday in October (winter time).

Children playing in front of Grassalkovich Palace, Bratislava

Personal Security and Health in the Czech Republic

The Czech Republic is a relatively safe country. Outside the capital, thefts and muggings are rare, and therefore it is safe to walk the streets even late at night. However, in Prague it is wise to be more safety conscious as pickpockets often target visitors, but even here the situation is better than in many other large European urban areas.

A historic pharmacy in the town of Klatovy, West Bohemia

A "black sheriff"   A police officer

POLICE

The Czech police (policie) wear black uniforms with the silver police emblem displayed on the chest. Like everywhere, they attend to safety on the streets and roads and pursue criminals. They drive white cars with a green stripe and the word "Policie" along the side.

Large towns also have municipal police (městská policie), who deal with illegal parking. A special police branch is responsible for border control. "Black sheriffs" are private security guards.

If you have a crime to report, the municipal police should be your first point of contact. Ask for a translator if no English is spoken.

GUARDING AGAINST THEFT

In large towns, and particularly in Prague, in crowded places (such as Prague Castle or the metro) you should be on the alert for pickpockets. Always keep your money and documents in a safe place and out of view, and be extra vigilant if anyone seems to be crowding you. At night it is best not to carry large amounts of money on you. If a hotel safe is available, keep valuables locked away. Make a photocopy of your passport and write down credit card numbers. Cars parked in the street are generally safe, but you should not leave luggage or valuable objects in view.

HEALTH CARE

There is a fair standard of health care in the Czech Republic, and medical help can be obtained anywhere in the country without any problems. In emergencies and in life-threatening situations, EU nationals with an EHIC card are entitled to receive free medical treatment, but in all other cases hospitalization or medical help has to be paid for. It is advisable to take out travel insurance to cover any medical costs incurred abroad. The water is safe to drink, but mineral water is more palatable.

Czech police car

PHARMACIES

For minor ailments and accidents you can turn for advice to the nearest pharmacy (lekárna). Pharmacies may be found in large towns. They are generally open on weekdays from 8am until 6pm, and on Saturdays until 2pm. You will find 24-hour pharmacies only in major cities.

DIRECTORY

EMERGENCY NUMBERS

Ambulance *Tel* 155.

Police *Tel* 158.

Municipal Police *Tel* 156.

Fire Brigade *Tel* 150.

Roadside Assistance *Tel* 154.

Emergency Operator (English) *Tel* 112.

MEDICAL HELP

Army Hospital
U Vojenské Nemocnice 1200, Prague.
Tel 973 203 203.

Dental Emergencies
Palackého 5, Prague. **Map** 3 C5.
Tel 224 946 981.

Fakultní poliklinika (hospital)
Karlovo náměstí 32, Prague.
Map 5 B2.
Tel 224 964 111.

24-Hour Pharmacy
Štefanikova 6, Prague.
Tel 224 946 982.

Personal Security and Health in Slovakia

In Slovakia, crime that is directed at tourists remains relatively rare, and Slovaks are peaceful people, who try to solve any disagreements by way of negotiation rather than open confrontation. Nevertheless, as in other countries it is always advisable to follow a few basic rules of safety, particularly if you are in a large city.

Slovak policeman   **Slovak municipal police officer**

POLICE

The police patrol the streets on foot (in large town centres) or travel in marked radio-cars. Some towns also have a municipal police (*mestská polícia*).

In a threatening situation, contact the police (Policajný zbor Slovenskej republiky, PZ SR) by calling the emergency numbers, or by going immediately to a local police station (Obvodné oddelenie PZ SR), to the district command (Okresné riaditeľstvo PZ SR) or to the regional command (Krajské riaditeľstvo PZ SR).

GUARDING AGAINST THEFT

The best way to protect yourself against losing documents, cash or other valuables is to take a few basic precautions, particularly in crowded places. Keep your money in a safe place, out of view. On public transport you should pay attention to any unexpected and unforced contacts or collisions with other passengers. It is also unwise to sleep on the train if you are travelling alone. In a parked car do not leave money, cameras, or any other valuables in view.

Make a photocopy of your passport and write down credit card numbers, and keep valuables that you don't need on a daily basis locked away in the safe if you are staying in a hotel.

HEALTH CARE

In emergencies and in life-threatening situations EU nationals with an EHIC card are entitled to receive free medical treatment, but in all other cases hospitalization or medical help has to be paid for. The cost of a visit to a doctor is about €13. A one-day stay in hospital costs about €40, to which you have to add the cost of examinations, tests, medicines and transport.

Slovak pharmacy sign

It is best to take out travel insurance providing good cover, and if you do need to claim, keep all documentation. Foreigners travelling to Slovakia do not require any immunizations or vaccinations. The water is safe to drink, but mineral water, which is more pleasant to drink, is widely available.

PHARMACIES

Pharmacies (*lekareň*) can be found in all towns and larger villages. In minor emergencies their staff will recommend suitable medication. They are generally open 8am–6pm. In larger towns there is usually a pharmacy open 24 hours.

DIRECTORY

EMERGENCY NUMBERS

Ambulance *Tel* 155, 112.

Police *Tel* 158, 112.

Fire Brigade *Tel* 150, 112.

Municipal Police *Tel* 156.

Emergency Breakdown Assistance *Tel* 1230, 1240.

Mountain Rescue *Tel* 18 300.

MEDICAL HELP

Dental Emergencies
Bezručova 5, Bratislava.
Tel (02) 62 92 36 30.

Nemocnica Staré Mesto (Old Town Hospital)
Mickiewiczova 13, Bratislava.
Tel (02) 57 29 01 11.

Pharmacy
Ružinovská 12, Bratislava.
Tel (02) 43 33 11 43.

Poliklinika Tehelná (A&E)
Tehelná 26, Bratislava.
Tel (02) 44 37 26 68.

Slovak ambulance

Banks and Currency in the Czech Republic

Bureau de change sign

The Czech currency is the Czech crown. Although the republic is part of the EU, the euro is not generally accepted, particularly outside Prague. The best way to take money with you is in the form of a debit card, and to draw out the money you need as you go along. In this way you can avoid carrying large sums with you, and, by using ATMs you can withdraw money outside banking hours. Banks and bureaus de change also change money.

ATMS

There is a wide network of ATMs, which can be found even in small towns. Most of them accept foreign cards, such as MasterCard, VisaPlus, Visa Electron or Cirrus/Maestro. You can use these to withdraw cash as you need it.

BANKS AND BUREAUS DE CHANGE

Every town has a branch of the major banks such as **Komerční Banka** or **Česká Spořitelna** (at the post office), where you can exchange money. The rate used is the exchange rate labelled *valuty nákup* ("we buy"). Banks are generally open Monday to Friday, from 9am until 5pm. The commission on exchanging money is usually 2 per cent. Money can also be changed

ATM in Louna

at Čedok travel agents, who also charge 2 per cent commission. Private bureaus de change sometimes add higher commission charges, and the rate of exchange is often much less favourable than that offered by banks. It is not worth changing money in hotels, which offer the worst rate of exchange. You should also not change money with street touts. They generally do not offer better rates than the banks, and often try to cheat visitors by handing them forged banknotes.

CREDIT CARDS

Credit cards can be used to pay in upmarket hotels and restaurants, and in large shops. In the provinces many small shops do not accept credit cards, so it is always advisable to carry some cash.

Modern building of the Czech National Bank, in Ústí nad Labem

TRAVELLERS' CHEQUES

If you wish to avoid carrying large sums of money with you, you can buy travellers' cheques before leaving home, and then cash them on arrival or as you travel. The most popular cheques in the Czech Republic are American Express and Citicorp, but larger banks will accept any type. Some major hotels in large towns will also accept payment by travellers' cheque.

CURRENCY

The country's monetary unit is the Czech crown (Kč), which is divided into 100 hellers. When you are touring small towns and villages, it is always preferable to carry lower denominations of Czech banknotes because many smaller establishments may find it difficult to give change for a 1,000, 2,000 or 5,000Kč note.

Banknotes
Czech banknotes are in denominations of 20, 50, 100, 200, 500, 1,000, 2,000 and 5,000Kč.

20Kč note

50Kč note

100Kč note

200Kč note

500Kč note

1,000Kč note

2,000Kč note

5,000Kč note

50 crowns (50Kč) 20 crowns (20Kč) 10 crowns (10Kč) 5 crowns (5Kč) 2 crowns (2Kč)

1 crown (1Kč)   50 hellers

Coins
Czech coins come in the following denominations: 50 hellers and 1, 2, 5, 10, 20 and 50 crowns (Kč). All coins have the Czech emblem (a lion rampant) on the reverse.

Banks and Currency in Slovakia

The national currency of Slovakia is the euro. The largest of the Slovak banks accept travellers' cheques, which can also be cashed in the bureaus de change found in tourist areas and cities. ATMs can be found everywhere. Also, increasing numbers of services and retail outlets now accept credit card payments. Prices will be quoted in both Slovak korunas and euros on a mandatory basis until 31 December 2009, although the koruna is no longer legal tender. This may be continued on a voluntary basis until June 2010.

ATMS

Credit- or debit-card holders will find ATMs installed outside virtually every bank and operating 24 hours; they accept Maestro, MasterCard, Visa, Diners Club, American Express, and other cards. Before withdrawing money from an ATM, find out the rate of commission charged by the bank for the service.

ATM in Skalica

BANKS

In towns and large tourist resorts there are no problems with finding a bank for changing or withdrawing money. The most frequently encountered are branches of large banks: **Slovenská sporiteľňa**, **VÚB**, **Tatra Banka** and **OTP**. Slovak banks are generally open from 8am to 5pm (the smaller the town, the earlier the closing time). Sometimes they close for an hour for lunch.

TRAVELLERS' CHEQUES

Travellers' cheques issued by Thomas Cook, American Express and Visa area accepted at branches of VÚB, Tatra Banka, Slovenská sporiteľňa, and in selected bureaus de change. Their commission is usually about 1 per cent of the cheque's face value; the lowest commissions are charged on US dollar and pound sterling cheques.

CREDIT CARDS

Credit cards are accepted at petrol stations, larger shops and some hotels. The number of places in Slovakia that accept "plastic money" is growing all the time, however, as with the Czech Republic, in the provinces many small shops do not accept credit cards, so it is always advisable to carry some cash.

Bank façade in Banská Bystrica

DIRECTORY

MAIN BRANCHES OF SELECTED BANKS

Slovenská sporiteľňa
Central Office
Suché Mýto 6,
Bratislava.
Tel (02) 68 50 41 64.
Fax (02) 59 57 40 22.
www.slsp.sk

Branches
Námestie SNP 18,
Bratislava.
Tel (02) 59 77 11 11.
Fax (02) 59 77 25 14.

Krížna 23,
Bratislava.
Tel (02) 50 10 97 11.
Fax (02) 55 42 11 40.

Pribinova 4,
Košice.
Tel (055) 682 35 50.
Fax (055) 682 35 83.

Tatra Banka
Central Office
Hodžovo námestie 3, Bratislava.
Tel (02) 68 66 10 00.
www.tatrabanka.sk

Branches
Zohorská 1, Bratislava.
Námestie SNP 21, Bratislava.
Vajanského nábr. 5, Bratislava.
Rooseveltova 1, Košice.

SELECTED BRANCHES OF BUREAUS DE CHANGE

Prvá devízová spol. s r.o.
Mostová 16,
Ružomberok.
Tel (044) 430 44 34.
Fax (044) 430 44 36.

Scars
Hviezdoslavova 21,
Zvolen.
Tel & *Fax* (045) 533 33 30.
www.scars.sk

Zmenáreň Aurika
Námestie sv. Egídia 22,
Poprad.
Tel (052) 772 34 83.

THE EURO

Sixteen member states of the EU have now replaced their traditional currencies with a single European currency, the euro. Austria, Belgium, Cyprus, Finland, France, Germany, Greece, Ireland, Italy, Luxembourg, Malta, the Netherlands, Portugal, Slovakia, Slovenia and Spain have all chosen to join the new currency; the UK, Denmark and Sweden have stayed out. The euro was introduced in Slovakia on 1 January 2009, with notes and coins coming into circulation. A very short transition period of only two weeks allowed euros and the Slovak koruna to be used simultaneously. All euro notes and coins can be used anywhere inside the participating member states.

Bank Notes

Euro bank notes have seven denominations. The €5 note (grey in colour) is the smallest, followed by the €10 note (pink), €20 note (blue), €50 note (orange), €100 note (green), €200 note (yellow) and €500 note (purple). All notes show the stars of the European Union.

5 euros

10 euros

20 euros

50 euros

100 euros

200 euros

500 euros

2 euros

1 euro

50 cents

20 cents

10 cents

Coins

The euro has eight coin denominations: €1 and €2; 50 cents, 20 cents, 10 cents, 5 cents, 2 cents and 1 cent. The €2 and €1 coins are both silver and gold in colour. The 50-, 20- and 10-cent coins are gold. The 5-, 2- and 1-cent coins are bronze.

5 cents

2 cents

1 cent

Telephone and Mail Services in the Czech Republic

Telephone and mail services in the Czech Republic are very efficient. Every town and large village has a post office and public telephones can be found even in small villages and are usually in good order. Post offices are similarly widespread and efficient, delivering international mail reliably. Internet access is springing up in many locations so should not be a problem.

Public telephone kiosk

USING PUBLIC TELEPHONES

The landline telephone network in the Czech Republic is run by Český Telecom. Yellow kiosks marked with the company's logo contain card-operated telephones; the cards can be bought at post offices and newsstands. If you are travelling to remote villages, take a phonecard with you as they may be hard to find. Their price varies from 150 to 300Kč. Most public telephones are kept in good

working order, but it is better to avoid the few remaining coin-operated telephones, as they do not work very well. The call tariffs from public telephones vary depending on the distance (local or long-distance calls) and the time of day. One minute of an international call costs between 10 and 20Kč. Calls can also be made from hotel rooms but charges are often much higher.

MOBILE PHONES

If you wish to use your own mobile phone, you need to arrange for a roaming service with your operator before leaving home. Mobile phone operators in the Czech Republic include Eurotel, Oskar and T-mobile.

CZECH NUMBERS

All numbers consist of nine digits and the area code is an integral part of the telephone number. Even when making a call from within a town, it is necessary to dial the area code. If you experience problems with getting through, it is likely that the number has changed.

MAIL SERVICES

At a post office you can send a letter or parcel, make a telephone call and buy postage stamps *(známky)*. The latter are also sold at news kiosks. A postage stamp for a postcard to any EU country costs 17Kč. It is best to send international parcels from main offices. Czech letter boxes are painted orange. At the main post office in every large town (marked Pošta 1), you can use the poste restante service for receiving mail; you need to present your passport to collect any letters. Post offices also offer a money exchange service. Their opening hours are 7am to 7pm on weekdays, and 7am to noon on Saturdays.

Logo of the Czech Post Office, a post horn

INTERNET AND E-MAIL

All towns have at least one Internet café, where you can access the Internet and send e-mails. Ask at the local tourist office for the nearest if you cannot find one. Many hotels also offer Internet access, sometimes free and, in larger business hotels, wireless. Prices for access are generally reasonable; the connections are fast, so that fans of web surfing can indulge in their favourite pastime without any problems.

USEFUL NUMBERS

- Dial these prefixes before the Czech number when calling from abroad: from the UK and Ireland 00420; from USA and Canada 011420; from Australia and New Zealand 0011420.
- Directory enquiries: 1180
- International info: 1181.

USING A PHONECARD TELEPHONE IN THE CZECH REPUBLIC

1 Lift the receiver and wait for the dialling tone.

2 The message *Vložte telefonní kartu* tells you to insert the card into the slot. The display shows you the credit left on your card.

3 When the words dial and wait to be connected.

4 The card is ejected automatically when it runs out.

By pressing this red button you can hear instructions in English.

Emergency numbers

Telephone and Mail Services in Slovakia

Slovak telephone and mail services are widely available and efficient. Public phones are mostly in good working order, and there are generally no problems with making a call, local or international. Post offices can be found in all towns and larger villages. The number of Internet cafés is steadily increasing; they are mostly situated in the centres of large towns.

Slovak news kiosk, one of many selling telephone cards

USING TELEPHONES

The payphones in Slovakia are both coin and card-operated. The service is quick and efficient, but not all public telephones allow for international calls. Those that do not allow outgoing calls to international and mobile numbers are marked with an orange sticker. If you are in doubt, seek advice at a post office. Phone cards can be purchased at post offices and news kiosks and are easier to use for international calls. They are sold in 75 and 150 units.

Some major towns have telephone exchanges in which you can make a phone call and pay the total cost at the end. Calls from hotel telephones tend to be expensive; it is advisable to check the rates before making an outward call. There are currently two mobile phone operators in Slovakia: Orange and EuroTel.

Slovak post box

SLOVAK NUMBERS

The Slovak telephone network is currently undergoing modernization, which can make life harder when you are trying to get a connection. Three-digit area codes have been introduced (the first digit is always 0), and when making a long-distance call you should dial the area code of the town or the region, followed by the subscriber's number. Local calls do not need the area code. The new area codes for Slovak telephone numbers are included in this guide.

MAIL SERVICES

Post offices can be found in all towns and larger villages. They generally open from 8am until 6pm, Monday to Friday, and 8am until 1pm on Saturday. In large towns you can find some post offices that open on Sundays. A postage stamp (*známky*) for an ordinary letter costs €1; a parcel up to 2 kg (4.4 lb) costs €4; an international package up to 1 kg (2.2 lb) in weight costs €25.

As in the Czech Republic, a poste restante service is available in the main post office (Pošta 1) in each major town. You will need your passport in order to collect your mail.

INTERNET AND E-MAIL

Internet cafés are not quite as prevalent as in the Czech Republic, but can nevertheless be found in many towns. They are opening up on a regular basis, so finding them should not present too many difficulties. Sometimes a sign may be hung along the main street, but the actual entrance may lead through gates, corridors and back yards. These kinds of establishments are often located in cellars. They charge about €1.50–€2 per hour, with the total charges being calculated by the minute. Many hotels offer Internet access to guests.

USING A PHONECARD TELEPHONE IN SLOVAKIA

1 Lift receiver and wait for dialling tone.

2 Insert card with arrow pointing upwards.

3 Display will show number of units left, and instruct you to dial number.

4 Dial number and wait to be connected.

5 Press this button if you wish to make another call, without replacing the receiver. The card slides out when you replace the receiver.

USEFUL NUMBERS

- Dial these prefixes before the Slovak number (including area code) when calling from abroad: from the UK and Ireland 00421; from USA and Canada 011421; from Australia and New Zealand 0011421.
- International directory enquiries: 0149.
- Directory enquiries within Slovakia: 120.

GETTING TO THE CZECH AND SLOVAK REPUBLICS

The easiest way to reach both the Czech and Slovak Republics is by air. Prague airport is served by many airlines, including several low-cost carriers. Bratislava has fewer flights, and one option is to fly to Vienna, just 50 km (31 miles) from Bratislava, which is better connected. Travelling by train or coach is also possible; it is often cheaper than air travel and enables you to see more of the country, though may take longer. Road and rail links are excellent from most of Europe.

ČSA (Czech Airlines) aircraft

TRAVELLING BY AIR TO THE CZECH REPUBLIC

The country's biggest air transport hub is Prague's Ruzyně Airport, for both international and domestic flights. You can fly there from almost any large European city in less than two-and-half hours. The main Czech carrier is **ČSA** (Czech Airlines), although Prague is also served by most major European airlines, and an increasing number of low-cost carriers, including **easyJet**, **Ryanair** and **SkyEurope** from the UK and Ireland.

Those travelling from Australia, New Zealand, the US and Canada usually have to fly to another European capital and take a connecting flight to Prague.

FROM RUZYNĚ AIRPORT TO PRAGUE

Prague's Ruzyně airport is located about 20 km (12 miles) from the city centre. Connecting buses are the 119 (to Dejvicka metro station, line A, green) or 100 (to Zličín metro station, line B, yellow). The buses run from around 4:30am to 11:30pm. A ticket costs 12Kč, and the journey takes about 30 minutes. Another option is to catch the six-seater minibuses from the airport, which charge 90Kč.

Alternatively you can take a taxi. Their fares are negotiable, but you should not agree to pay more than 500Kč for the journey between the airport and the capital. To avoid any dispute, ask about the maximum fare before starting the journey.

OTHER CZECH AIRPORTS

The other main airports in the Czech Republic are in Ostrava, Brno and Karlovy Vary. Domestic routes are served by ČSA and Air Ostrava. Specialist airlines operate small-aircraft fleets which can be chartered for private clients and offer pleasure flights for tourists.

Porters at Ruzyně Airport in Prague

AIRLINES SERVING THE CZECH AND SLOVAK REPUBLICS

Air Slovakia
Pestovateľská 2, Bratislava.
Tel (02) 43 42 27 42.
www.airslovakia.sk

Austrian Airlines
www.aua.com

British Airways
Tel 239 000 299.
www.ba.com

ČSA
V Celnici 5, Prague.
Tel 239 007 007.
www.csa.cz

easyJet
www.easyjet.com

Lufthansa
www.lufthansa.co.uk

Ryanair
www.ryanair.com

SkyEurope
www.skyeurope.sk

Prague's Ruzyně Airport's modern interior

TRAVELLING BY AIR TO SLOVAKIA

Bratislava's M R Štefánika Airport is served by airlines from all over Europe, including an increasing number of low-cost carriers. A further option for visitors to southern Slovakia is to fly to Vienna's Schwechat International Airport, less than 50 km (30 miles) from the border (see below). Vienna may also be the most convenient gateway for travellers from North America and Australasia.

Visitors heading for the mountain region of northern Slovakia might consider taking a flight to Krakow in Poland, which is nearer than Bratislava, and heading south from there.

TRANSPORT FROM THE AIRPORT TO BRATISLAVA

Bratislava's airport is 12 km (7 miles) from the city centre; the bus journey (on bus no. 61) takes 30 minutes and a taxi takes 15 minutes. Vienna's airport, 50 km (31 miles) from Bratislava, operates a regular bus service to the Slovak capital.

OTHER SLOVAK AIRPORTS

Slovakia's internal airports are in Košice, Piešťany, Sliač and Tatra-Poprad (5 km/ 3 miles from Poprad). Both Czech Airlines and Air Slovakia serve these airports.

Glazed interior at Bratislava Airport

TICKET PRICES

Prices of air tickets vary tremendously: they depend on the airline, the time of year, the type of ticket ("open" or with a fixed return date), the validity period, and many other factors, as well as where you purchase the ticket. Most airlines offer special concessions for children; some also offer reductions to families and group travellers. It is also worth looking for special promotions that are, from time to time, offered by various airlines, for selected routes. Usually, it is worth booking the ticket well in advance. The Internet is a good starting point for shopping around for a good deal.

A welcome to visitors at Štefánika Airport

LOW-COST AIRLINES

Low-cost airlines offer a good range of deals on flights to Prague, Brno, Bratislava and Krakow in Poland, and the number of routes is increasing all the time. For the lowest fares you should book via the Internet as far in advance as possible. Flights generally do not include in-flight meals, although refreshments are usually sold on board. A useful website for checking the latest low-cost routes is *www.flycheapo.com*.

BY COACH

You can get to both the Czech and Slovak Republics by coach operated by one of the international carriers who run scheduled services between main European cities. Travelling by coach is generally less expensive than by air, but it may sometimes be less comfortable, and – above all – takes much longer. The coaches on international routes are generally well equipped with air conditioning and have reclining seats. Further details are available from the operator before you book. It is worth taking a blanket or a sleeping bag with you and, for a cold night, a flask filled with a hot drink.

BY TRAIN

Train travel offers more comfortable conditions than travel by coach (particularly if you pay for a couchette), but it should be stressed that standard fares on international train routes are usually very high – the cost of such a journey may not be much lower than travelling by air, for example. It could, however, be considerably reduced if you buy discounted international tickets in advance, or passes for travellers under 26 or over 60. Details and application forms can be obtained from ticket offices at international railway stations.

Bratislava Airport

Travelling in the Czech Republic

Travelling by train is a great way to see the Czech Republic. They are inexpensive; run frequently and usually arrive on time, and they enable you to reach virtually any town. Taking a bus is somewhat more expensive but can be faster. The ČSAD buses (Czech Bus Transport Company) run services to every town and village in the country. Bus and train timetables can be found at the website address *www.jizdnirady.cz*. The republic has a network of well-maintained roads so using a car (whether hired or your own) is an ideal way to visit remote places.

Train conductor

TRAIN TICKETS

Tickets for train travel must be booked in person, at railway station ticket desks, or in ČS kancelář ČD offices. These offices are those of Czech Railways' own travel agency and can be found in most large towns throughout the country. Unfortunately, there are no facilities for reserving tickets by telephone or on the Internet. Tickets bought at railway stations have to be paid for in cash, but the ČS kancelar ČD offices do also accept credit cards.

TRAVELLING BY TRAIN

The rail network is run by Czech Railways (České dráhy/**ČD**); it is most developed in the northern and western regions of the country; in the south and east there are fewer train services. Detailed information on train and bus services is available at the website address *www.cd.cz.*

There are several kinds of train in the Czech Republic. The slowest and the cheapest is the stopping train *(osobní vlak),* which runs on local routes. This kind of train, often with only one or two carriages, resembles a tram and uses similar-sounding warning signals. It stops at every station and travels at a speed of only 30 km/h (19 mph) or so. The fast trains *(rychlík)* operate on long-distance routes and do not stop at every station. They include first- and second-class carriages. On this type of train you may reserve a seat *(místenka),* although it is not compulsory.

Fast trains have several levels and prices. On express trains it is best to reserve a seat if you want to guarantee one. On more upmarket express trains, such as InterCity and EuroCity, it is compulsory to make a seat reservation. The highest standard is offered by SC trains (SuperCity), which have only first class carriages; you need to reserve a seat in advance. These trains run on the Prague to Ostrava route. For overnight travel you can opt to pay extra for a couchette *(lehátkový vůz).*

The main railway station in Prague

Children up to the age of six travel free on Czech railways, and young travellers, up to the age of 12, are entitled to a 50 per cent reduction. Note that a return ticket will cost you less than two singles.

The international InterRail tickets, which entitle holders to unlimited travel for one month throughout Europe, are honoured in the Czech Republic. Also honoured are the Euro Domino tickets, entitling the holder to a certain number of travel days within one month.

RAILWAY STATIONS

Czech railway stations, even those found in small towns, offer a full range of facilities necessary for travellers. All stations, from the largest to the smallest, are clean and well-kept; almost all of them have restaurants or a bar selling beer and other alcoholic drinks, and a ticket office. Many stations

Inside Masarykovo Railway Station in Prague

in small or middle-sized towns do not have traditional, raised platforms; instead they have a system of open tracks, and the station-master sets up boards giving details of the trains that are just about to arrive and depart.

LUGGAGE

At all larger railway stations you can deposit your luggage at the left-luggage office, or leave it in a self-service locker. On large stations there are also porters who help with the luggage.

TRAVELLING BY BUS

Czech bus transport functions very efficiently. The ČSAD, Čcská Autobusová Doprava (the country's largest bus company), runs a nationwide network of services that includes virtually all towns and villages, even the most remote ones. Travelling by bus is generally more expensive than by train, but it is also quicker. Bus stations are usually a short walk from the centre of a town, and often near the train station.

Tickets are available from ticket desks at bus stations in large towns, and it is worth buying in advance for weekends when services are less regular. On minor routes tickets are usually bought from the driver. The country's largest bus transport hub is the Prague Florenc station. Prague and Brno also have regular bus links with many European cities.

A ČSAD bus – run by the Czech Bus Transport Company

TRAVELLING BY CAR

Well-maintained roads and long sections of motorway make driving one of the best methods of exploring the country. A foreigner driving on Czech roads must carry a valid international driver's licence, an ID card (visitors from outside the EU must also carry passports), the vehicle registration document and a third-party insurance policy ("Green card").

The car should be marked with letters identifying its country of origin (if not, you may incur an on-the-spot fine). The driver must carry inside the vehicle a warning sign in the form of a red triangle and a first-aid kit. Babies and children must always be strapped in appropriate seats.

Motorcyclists and their passengers must wear crash helmets in the Czech Republic. The maximum speed per-

An information sign about speed limits

mitted for cars and buses is 50 km/h (30 mph) in built-up areas, 90 km/h (55 mph) on open roads and 130 km/h (80 mph) on motorways.

From 15 October to 15 March, drivers must use dipped headlights at all times.

Driving after consuming any alcohol at all is strictly prohibited and if discovered the driver may have to pay a stiff fine, or risk being detained by the police.

ROADS AND ROAD SIGNS

Czech motorways are marked with the letter D followed by a number; the major roads are indicated by the letter E and a number. The Czech motorway network is not very extensive compared to that in many other European countries but it is growing steadily. In order to be allowed to use it, you have to buy a disc, available at border crossings and larger petrol stations. The disc should be displayed on the windscreen. Not doing so could incur a very heavy fine.

City roads tend to be busy, while outside these conurbations traffic is minimal.

CAR HIRE

It is possible to hire a car in advance via a major car hire firm. Local representatives, found at airports and in upmarket hotels, may offer cheaper deals. In order to hire a car you must be at least 18 years of age, have a valid driver's licence and an identity document recognized in the Czech Republic, with a photo.

Czech country road

DIRECTORY

TRAIN TRAVEL

ČD (České dráhy)
28 Jianguo Men Wai Jie.
Tel 00420 412 503 113.
www.cd.cz

Travelling in Slovakia

Slovak trains are clean and fast, and railway stations are often located in interesting historic buildings. There are fewer railway lines than in the Czech Republic, however, mainly due to the country's mountainous terrain. Travelling on inter-city buses is relatively cheap, fast and reliable but the service can be patchy in some areas. The most convenient way to travel around the country is by car, particularly the further east you go, as the public transport network becomes sparser.

Railway station building in Piešťany

TRAVELLING BY TRAIN

Trains in Slovakia are run by **ŽSR** (Železnice Slovenskej republiky). They run frequently, are usually clean and punctual, and the quality of the track makes for a fast and smooth journey. Travelling on some of the routes that run through scenic mountain ranges (particularly the Banská Bystrica to Divaky and Brezno to Margecany sections) is in itself a tourist attraction. Some of the local routes are served by railbuses, called *motorki*, that stop at every station.

Slow trains (*osobný vlak*) are indicated on timetables (*cestovný poriadok*) with the letters "Os", and, if the route is also served by a railbus, with "MOs". A slightly higher level of service is provided by limited-stop trains (*zrýchlený vlak*), marked with the "Zr" symbol; tickets cost virtually the same as for the slow trains. These stop only at some stations, although more frequently than fast trains.

Fast trains (*rýchlik*), marked with the symbol "R", operate on longer routes between towns and cities. A ticket for a fast train, including a reserved seat, costs about €1–€1.50 more than for a slow train. Even faster, but no more expensive, are express trains

(*explesný vlak*), marked with the symbol "Ex". These link all major towns in Slovakia, and some of them go also to the Czech Republic. The top category of trains are the fast EuroCity (marked "EC") and InterCity (marked "IC"). They link Bratislava with Košice and Banská Bystrica; also Košice with Prague and Budapest. Tickets for these trains are not all that expensive – about €2.50 more (including a reserved seat) than for a slow train.

TRAIN TICKETS

Slovak railways are relatively inexpensive. The cost of a journey by slow train per kilometre works out at about 40 cents. A return ticket (*spiatočny lístok*) is 20

per cent cheaper than two single tickets. Fare reductions of 20 to 60 per cent (depending on the age of the passengers) are offered to groups (with a minimum of six people). Children up to the age of six travel free. A family ticket for three to six people, including up to four children up to the age of 15, offers a 20 per cent fare reduction. Holders of the International Student Identity Card (ISIC) receive a 50 per cent reduction.

RESERVATIONS

Seat reservation may be compulsory (*povinne*) or optional (*nepovinne*) on fast, express, EuroCity and InterCity trains. This information is given in the timetables against each train. For some overnight trains it is also possible to buy a couchette (*ležadolový lístok*) or a bed in a sleeping compartment (*lôžkový listok*). Places can be reserved at railway station ticket offices and at selected travel agents.

RAILWAY STATIONS

Slovak railway stations (*železničná stanica*) in large towns are generally clean and well-maintained. They often occupy historic buildings dating from the days of the Austro-Hungarian empire. In smaller towns and villages their standard is also fair, although often they do not have ticket offices (*pokladňa*). If this is the case, you have to buy the ticket from a conductor on the train.

Train travelling through a beautiful tract of Slovak countryside

Slovak bus serving local routes

LUGGAGE

At all larger railway stations you can leave your luggage at the left-luggage office (*úschovňa batožín*), or deposit it in a self-service locker (*úložné skrinky*).

TRAVELLING BY BUS

Bus stations (*autobusová stanica*) are not the world's cleanest but buses run quite frequently, and tickets are fairly cheap. Bus stations are often located near a town's railway station. You need, however, to be careful when consulting timetables, as they are often speckled with countless additional symbols, which indicate, for instance, that the bus in question runs only spasmodically (*premáva*), and at weekends does not run at all (*nepremáva*). Older buses tend to operate on local routes, but the situation is somewhat better on inter-city routes. Private bus companies run some routes. You can buy tickets at the bus station, or on local trips, directly from the driver.

TRAVELLING BY CAR

Roads are reasonable and do not present any special problems to drivers, particularly since traffic is not very heavy. Visitors from the EU arriving in Slovakia by car are not required to have a "Green Card" or an international driving licence. It is necessary, however, to carry the vehicle registration document with you.

Slovak regulations require every car to be equipped with a first-aid kit, a warning triangle, a tow rope and a set of spare bulbs. Children up to the age of 12, or up to 150 cm (5 ft) tall, must travel strapped in appropriate seats in the back of the vehicle.

Sign showing speed limits in Slovakia

Seat belts should be kept fastened throughout your journey. From 15 October until 15 March dipped headlights must be permanently switched on. Motorcyclists are obliged to wear crash helmets. It is not permitted to drive at all with any alcohol in your bloodstream.

The maximum permitted speed on Slovak motorways is 130 km/h (80 mph) for cars and 110 km/h (70 mph) for buses; elsewhere it is 90 km/h (55 mph) on open roads and 60 km/h (37 mph) within built-up areas. People under 18 are not permitted to drive vehicles on Slovak roads, even if they hold a valid driving licence from another country.

ROADS AND ROAD SIGNS

Signposting on trunk roads in Slovakia is clear; the problems start only when entering large towns. The highest category of Slovak roads are the motorways (*dial'nica*), marked with a D followed by a number, set on a blue background. All motorways are toll roads. The toll is paid by buying a disc. This can be annual (€20); or valid for 15 days (€3.50). The disc should be placed in the upper corner of the windscreen. Discs can be purchased at border crossings, in petrol stations and at larger post offices. Dual carriageways are also toll roads.

CAR HIRE

The number of car hire companies (*autopožičovňa*) in Slovakia is on the increase. Most are found in Bratislava and Košice. The international companies, such as Hertz, Avis, Europcar and Budget, offer mainly Western makes of car. There are also local firms, such as **Auto Danubius**, which hire Škodas.

DIRECTORY

TRAIN TRAVEL

ŽSR

www.zsr.sk

CAR HIRE

Auto Danubius

Trnavska 39, Bratislava.

Tel (02) 443 72 502.

www.autotudanubius.sk

The New Bridge across the Danube in Bratislava

Getting Around Prague

Prague metro sign

The historic centre of Prague is a relatively small area that is best explored on foot. There is also an efficient network of buses, trams and metro trains. This public transport system (*dopravní podnik* or DP) has offices in metro stations and at some major route junctions which have transport maps and timetables, and sell tickets and passes. Three- or seven-day passes can be used on trams, trains and buses.

THE METRO

The Czech capital is served by three metro lines: A (green), B (yellow) and C (red). They crisscross, making it easy to change trains and, as a result, travel around virtually the entire city quickly. The metro service operates from 5am until midnight. During morning and evening rush hours the trains run every 3–5 minutes; early in the morning and late at night, and during weekends and on public holidays their frequency is every 8–12 minutes.

DRIVING AND PARKING

Due to the volume of traffic and narrow streets, driving around Prague is difficult. There are also many pedestrianized areas and restrictions on cars. During the rush hour the streets frequently get jammed. It is therefore not a good idea to try to see Prague by car. If you have a car and wish to make a one-day trip into the city, you can leave the car on the outskirts and use the Park and Ride car parks, intended for people who wish to travel

The direction in which a tram is heading

Name of the stop

Numbers indicating which trams stop here

Prague tram stop

in by metro. Central Prague has allocated areas for paid parking, so if you are lucky enough to find a space (which is not easy), you will have to pay at the meter. Illegally parked cars get clamped or towed away to a special police compound.

BUSES AND TRAMS

The MHD (Městská Hromadná Doprava, Municipal Transport System) buses run according to the timetables displayed at every bus stop. Buses on some of the routes are modern, low vehicles that are suitable for wheelchairs and pushchairs.

Prague and other large towns (Ostrava, Brno, Plzeň, Liberec, Olomouc and České Budějovice) also have trams. As they move along, the driver calls the stops through the microphone. Prague's tram network has 26 lines. During weekends from the end of March until November there is also a historic tram line, no. 91 (*nostalgická linka*), from the Střešovice depot to the city centre. Tickets can be bought from attendants on board.

NIGHT TRANSPORT

Night buses (no. 601 upwards) and trams (51 upwards) run in Prague after midnight. The main junction for night transport is Lazarská in Nové Město.

TAXIS

Taxis are the most comfortable, but also the most expensive method of getting around town. You can find them at taxi ranks, hail them on the street, or call them by telephone or via the Internet. Prague taxis do not come in any one colour, and their only distinctive mark is the illuminated TAXI sign on the roof. Prices vary: 20–30Kč for "slamming the door" and 17–30Kč for every kilometre, depending on the company.

BICYCLES

Prague has many bicycle lanes, to which new ones are always being added. However, they run outside the historic centre. The traffic and cobbles mean that cycling in Prague is not particularly comfortable. Bicycles can be hired in special shops, as well as in many hotels and hostels.

WALKING

If you wish to explore Prague on foot, you should equip yourself with a street map. Small maps can be obtained free of charge at tourist information offices.

The interior of Můstek metro station in Prague

Getting Around Bratislava

The best way to see the mostly pedestrianized historic centre of Slovakia's capital city is on foot. For longer journeys, or outside the centre, Bratislava has a well-developed network of bus, tram and trolleybus services, although some of the fleet have seen better days. Those who enjoy night-time entertainment can return home via the night services. Car drivers may find it difficult to get a parking space, and leaving a car illegally parked could incur a very heavy fine. Cycling is a good alternative.

Bratislava trolleybus

BUSES, TRAMS AND TROLLEYBUSES

Bratislava has an excellent network of bus services. Some of the older vehicles are being replaced with modern ones. There are also trams *(električka)* running within Bratislava (and in Košice). The stops *(zastávka)* are marked with appropriate signs. Bratislava also has a trolleybus service, as do Košice, Prešov, Zlín and Banská Bystrica. In Bratislava, a standard ticket is valid on buses, trams and trolleybuses. You need to buy your ticket in advance and validate it on board the vehicle, or obtain a one- or two-day pass if you are making several journeys.

Between the hours of 11pm and 5am the capital city is served by 18 night-time lines, including trams, trolleybuses and buses (nos. 501–518).

DRIVING AND PARKING

Driving is far from the best way to see Bratislava. Traffic packs the streets and there are many one-way and pedestrianized streets. Finding a place to park in Bratislava and other large towns (outside weekends and evenings) is virtually impossible. If you do find a

space you need to pay for parking at the meters (ensure you have enough loose change), or use a ticket *(parkovacia karta)*, on which you have to mark the time of leaving the vehicle. These tickets can be purchased at shops and kiosks. Parking charges vary from 30 cents to €2 per hour. A one-off payment for leaving a car (€1.50–€2 on average) is charged by car parks situated close to tourist attractions.

Non-payment or illegal parking is penalized by wheel-clamping or towing the vehicle to a police

Pedestrian-only zone

compound. Having your vehicle released in Bratislava will cost you €165.

TAXIS

Taxis are available in Bratislava and other Slovak towns, and also in major tourist resorts. The average charge is €1 per kilometre. Before starting on a journey you should ask the driver how much he will charge you for the trip, and, just to be sure, check the initial reading of the meter.

BICYCLES

Bratislava and its environs have eight marked bicycle routes; their total length is 75 km (45 miles). One of their advantages is the logical, clear layout: six routes spread radially; the remaining two link them to form wide rings. Bicycle lanes have also been provided in Košice, Banská Bystrica and Zilina, and their environs.

WALKING

Exploring Bratislava and other major cities on foot is an excellent idea. Most of the historic town centres and their attractions are clustered within a small area, and, besides, almost every town has a pedestrianized zone *(pešia zóna)*. Tourist information offices provide a free street map of the centre of Bratislava.

One of Bratislava's old trams, which offer tours of the city

General Index

Acknowledgments

Hachette Livre Polska wishes to thank the following people at Dorling Kindersley:

Publisher
Douglas Amrine

Publishing Manager
Anna Streiffert

Managing Art Editor
Kate Poole

Project Manager
Jacky Jackson/Wordwise Associates Ltd

Consultant Editor
Ferdie McDonald

Cartography
Uma Bhattacharya, Mohammad Hassan, Stuart James, Jasneet Kaur, Casper Morris

DTP Designers
Vinod Harish, Vincent Kurien, Natasha Lu, Alistair Richardson, Azeem Siddiqui

Factchecker
Dr Tomas Kleisner

Proofreader
Stewart Wild

Indexer
Helen Peters

Jacket Designer
Sonual Bhatt

Hachette Livre Polska also wishes to thank the following people and institutions who assisted in the preparation of this book:

Additional Text
Lucy Mallows, Beth Potter, Jakub Sito Barbara Studnik Wócikowowska

Additional Illustrations
Dorota Jarymowicz

Additional Photography
Nigel Hudson, Oldřich Karasek, Ian O'Leary, Robert Pasieczny, Clive Streeter, Barbara Sudnik-Wójcikowska

Additional Picture Research
Rhiannon Furbear, Ellen Root

Additional Editorial and Design
Lydia Baillie, Maite Lantaron, Marianne Petrou

Maps
Jarosław Talacha, Michał Zielkiewicz

The Publishers also thank the following individuals and institutions for permission to reproduce photographs or photograph their establishments; to take photographs inside their premises; and to use photographs from their archives:

Artothek (Susanne Vierthaler).

Chram sv. Barbory, Kutna Hora, for permission to photograph inside the church.
Corbis (Bartłomiej Sych).
Kunsthistorisches Museum, Wien (Ilse Jung)
Muzeum Kroměříž (Jiři Stránský)
Muzeum Města Brna (Pavel Ciprian) for permission to photograph Špilberk.
Muzeum Jindřichohradecka (Jaroslav Pikal)
Národni památkový ústav (Jaromir Kubů) for permission to photograph inside Karlštejn Castle.
Národni památkový ústav, Brno (Zdeňka Dokoupilova) for permission to photograph inside Kroměříž Castle.
Národni Knihovna Česke Republiky v Praze (Renáta Sádlova).
Oblastní Galerie, Liberec (Zdenka Huškova).
Barbora Ondrejčakova of the International Film Festival in Karlovy Vary.
Országos Széchényi Könyvtar (Orsolya Karsay)
Obecni dům, Prague (Augustina Vaňková) for permission to photograph the interiors and for her kind help.
Náměstí na Hane Palace for permission to photograph their coach.
Jaroslav Pecha for permission to photograph inside Panna Mária church in Banská Bystrica.
Slovak National Tourism Centre (Ján Bošnovič) for materials, photographs and information, and for his extraordinary help and kindness.
Slovenska Narodna Galeria, Bratislava (Maria Corejova). Uměleckoprůmyslové museum v Praze (Alena Zapletalová) Židovske Muzeum v Praze (Michael Dunayevsky).

Picture Credits
t = top; tr = top right; tl= top left; ta = top above; tb = top below; c = centre; cla = centre left above; ca = centre above; cra = centre right above; cl = centre left; cr = centre right; clb = centre left below; cb = centre below; crb = centre right below; b = bottom; bl = bottom left; br = bottom right; bra = bottom right above; brb = bottom right below; bla = bottom left above; blb = bottom left below.

Works of art on the pages detailed have been reproduced with the permission of the following copyright holders:
Aristide Maillol *Pomona* 1910 © ADAGP, Paris and DACS, London 2006 102cr; Alphonse Marie Mucha *The Arts: Dance* 1898 ©ADAGP, Paris 2006 24cr, *The Arts: Music* 1898 ©ADAGP, Paris 2006 25cl, *Poster for Sokol Movement* 1912 ©ADAGP, Paris 2006 97bl; Marie Cernisova Toyen *The Dangerous Hour* 1942 © ADAGP, Paris and DACS, London 2006 25br.

4CORNERS IMAGES: Borchi Massimo 245br; SIME/Gräfenhain Günter 10br.
AKG-IMAGES: 33c, 33bc, 34bc, 38cbl, 78cla, 79bc; ALAMAY IMAGES: Alan Copson City Pictures 31b; Danita Delimont 272, 325b; eye35.com 70; f1 online 290; Chris Fredriksson 369c, 52; Eddie Gerald 114–5; isifa Image Service s.r.o. 205b, 212, 213b, 245clb; 428; Jon Arnold Images/ Walter Bibikow 306; JTB Photo Communications, Inc. 244bl; Pegaz cr; © Profimedia CZ s.r.o 14, 118, 128–9, 150–151, 242–3; Profimedia International

s.r.o 11 bl; Michaela Dusíková 11tc, Ivcta Mudrochová 47tl; Jan Wlodarczyk 245tc; zdspics 244ca; ARCHÍV HLAVNIHO MESTA, PRAHY (CLAM-GALLASUV PALÁC): 39bl, 74tr, ARCHIWUM ZDJEÇ KARELA KRYLA: 23c; ART ARCHIV: Janaček Museum Brno/Dagli Orti 23t; ARTOTHEK: 24cr, 25cl, 25br; AV STUDIO: 262t, 263t, 263bra.

BRIDGEMAN ART LIBRARY: Jean-Loup Charmet Collection 43tl, 72cl; *The Meeting of Napoleon and Francis I*, by Jean Antoine Gros. 40crb; Rosegarten Museum, Constance 36cla; B&W: 99cb (Wojciech Wójcik).

CORBIS: 22b, 34c, 41ba, 42cl, 42tr, 101t; © Alinari Archives 174b; © Paul Almasy 46bra, © Archivo Iconografico, S.A. 40cr; © Austrian Archives; Haus-, Hof- und Staatsarchiv, Vienna 34brb, 266bra; © Yannis Behrakis/Reuters 409t; © Bettmann 26c, 41bb, 46t, 46brb, 131t; © Stefano Bianchetti 265tr; © Mike Blake/Reuters 409b; © David W. Černy/Reuters 267bra; © John Dakers; Eye Ubiquitous 426c; © Franz-Marc Frei 20tlb, 22tl; © Marc Garanger 267t; © Hulton-Deutsch Collection 22tr, (Lancaster) 47t; © Petr Josek/Reuters 406b; © George D. Lepp 17tla; © Buddy Mays 30tr; © Gail Mooney 369tl; © Ali Meyer 40t, 264c; © Reuters 47brb, 256c, 406c; © Galen Rowell 189t; © Rykoff Collection 44brb; © Scheufler Collection 43cla, 43b, 44bra, 44bla, 266t; © Liba Taylor 248b; © Peter Turnley 14b, 47bc, 47bla; © Miroslav Zajic 46c; Zefa 43cra; JOE CORNISH: 48–9; 97cr.

ROMAN DELIKÁT: 264b.

SAMANTHA VON GERBIG: 39t; GETTY IMAGES: Imagno/Contributor 269c; Adam Jones 10cla.

HEMISPHERE IMAGES: Monde/Pawel Wysocki 410–11.

INTERNATIONAL FILM FESTIVAL, KARLOVY VARY: 29cr.

JON ARNOLD IMAGES: Walter Bibikow 2–3, 302–3.

KANCELÁR PREZIDENTA REPUBLIKY: 33br; OLDŘICH KARASEK: 18cr, 20cl, 28c, 31t, 58tr, 65t, 208bl, 209cb, 209ca, 209t, 337t, 340–341, 370cl; JAROSLAV KLENOVSKY: 237cr; DALIBOR KUSÁK: 104bl; ARCHIVE OF MARLENE KRYL: 23cr; KUNSTHISTORISCHES MUSEUM, WIEN: portrait of *Emperor Sigismund*, by Pisanello 36clb.

LEBRECHT MUSIC AND ARTS PHOTO LIBRARY: RA 27b.

MARY EVANS PICTURE LIBRARY: 9, 36t, 37t, 41t, 44t, 45t, 45bla, 45blb, 49t, 115t, 411c; MESTSKE MUZEUM,

BRATISLAVA: 261 265c; MUSEUM OF THE HISTORY OF SCIENCE, OXFORD: Samantha von Gerbig, 39tl; MUZEUM KROMĚŘÍŽ: *Pink Portrait* by Max Švabinsky 25tr.

NÁRODNÍ GALERIE V PRAZE: Graficka sbirka 37br, 39cbr, 95br; Klaster sv Anezky 77cl; Klaster sv. Jiri **32**; Milan Posselt 55cb; Šternberský Palac 60–61 all; Veletrzni Palac 102–3 all; NÁRODNÍ KNIHOVNA ČESKÉ REPUBLIKY: 38tl; NARODNI MUSEUM V PRAZE: Vlasta Dvorakova 35cr, 36bl, 36–7c, 37c, 37cl, 38bc, 39bc, 74bl; Muzeum Bedricha Smetany 42bl; Tyrsovo Muzeum 97bl; NÁRODNI PAMÁTKOVÝ ÚSTAV: *St Elizabeth*, by Master Teodoryk 24cl.

OBLASTNÍ GALERIE, Liberec: *Manor House in Benatky*, by August Pettenkofen 183c; OBRAZÁRNA PRAŽSKEHO HRADU: 56tl; ORSZÁGOS SZÉCHÉNYI KÖNYVTAR: *Tartar's Raid* miniature 262crb.

PHOTOLIBRARY.COM: Jon Arnold Images: 8–9.

REGIONAL MUSEUM IN VYSOKÉ MÝTO: Jíří Junek 26br.

SLOVAK NATIONAL TOURISM CENTRE: 257t, 258t, 259b, 312b, 312c, 312tra, 313t, 313ca, 313cb, 317br, 322c, 339b, 339cb, 339ca, 343b, 371bl, 398b, 402t, 402c, 402b, 403t, 409c, 425b, 425c, 425t, 428b; SLOVENSKA NARODNA GALERIA, BRATISLAVA: *Jan Francisci, Captain of Slovak Insurgents*, painting by Peter Michal Buhúň: 260; STÁTNÍ ÚSTREDNI ARCHIV: 34tc; STÁTNÍ ŽIDOVSKÉ MUZEUM: 51tr, 79br; LUBOMÍR STIBUREK: 89ca; BARBARA SUDNIK-WÓJCIKOWSKA: 17bla, 252tl, 252cl, 252b, 253cl, 253cr; SVATOVÍTSKÝ POKLAND, PRAŽHÝ HRAD: 35cl, 35bc.

MIKOŁAJ TAŁANDZIEWICZ: 318–319.

U PINKASÚ RESTAURANT: 368cl; UMĚLECKOPRŮMYSLOVÉ MUZEUM V PRAZE: 40bc, 97br; GABRIEL URBÁNEK/UMP: 25bl.

ZEFA: 170–171.

Jacket

Front – ALAMY IMAGES: Gavin Hellier main photograph; CORBIS: Werner Forman Archive crb; DK IMAGES: Dorota i Mariusz Jarymowiczowie clb; GETTY IMAGES: Stone/Rex Ziak cb. Back – ALAMY IMAGES: Robert Harding tl; DK IMAGES: Dorota i Mariusz Jarymowiczowie br. Spine – ALAMY IMAGES: Gavin Hellier.

All other images © Dorling Kindersley For further information see: www.dkimages.com

English–Czech Phrase Book

In an Emergency

Where is the telephone?	Kde je telefón?
the nearest hospital?	nejbližší nemocnice?
Help!	Pomoc!
Please call a doctor!	Zavolejte doktora!
Please call an ambulance!	Zavolejte ratunkowe! sanitku!
Please call the police!	Zavolejte policii!

Communication Essentials

Yes/No	Ano/Ne
Please	Prosím
Thank you	Děkuji vám
Excuse me/forgive me	Promiňte
Hello/Good morning	Dobrý den
Goodbye	Na shledanou
Good evening	Dobrý večer
Goodnight	Dobrou noc
What is it?	Co to je?
Why?	Proč
Where?	Kde?
When?	Kdy?
today	dnes
tomorrow	zítra
yesterday	včera
morning	ráno
afternoon	odpolední
evening	večer
there	tam
here	tady, zde
How are you?	Jak se máte?
Very well thank you	Velmi dobře, děkuji
Where is/are...?	Kde je/jsou ...?
How far is it to ...?	Jak je to daleko?
Do you speak English?	Mluvíte anglicky?
I don't understand	Nerozumím
Pardon?	Prosím?
big/large	velký
small	malý
hot	horký
cold	studený
open	otevřeno
closed	zavřeno
entrance	vchod
exit	východ
toilets	toalety, záchod
men/gentlemen	muži, páni
women/ladies	ženy, damy
vacant	volno
engaged	obsazeno

Sightseeing

art gallery	galerie
castle	hrad, zámek
church	kostel
garden	zahrada
old town/city	staré město
palace	palác
railway station	nádraží
square	náměstí
street	ulice
stop (bus, tram)	zastávka
theatre	divadlo
ticket	lístek
tourist information	turistické informace

Shopping

I would like...	Chtěl(a) bych ...
Do you have... ?	Máte ...?
How much does it cost?	Kolik to stojí?
What time do you open/close?	V kolik otevíráte/zavíráte?
expensive	drahý
cheap	levný
size	velikost
number (size)	číslo
colour	barva

Shops

antiques	starožitnictví
bakery	pekárna
bank	banka
bazaar/market	trh
bookshop	knihkupectví
camera shop	obchod s fotoaparáty
clothes shop	oděvy
department store	obchodní dům
glass, china	sklo, porcelán
news kiosk	novinový stánek
pharmacy	lékárna
post office	pošta
shoe shop	obuv

In a Hotel

Do you have a vacant room?	Máte volný pokoj?
with a bathroom	pokoj s koupelnou
with a shower	se sprechou
I have a reservation	Mám reservaci
key	klíč
porter	vrátný

Eating Out

Do you have a table free for .?	Máte volný stůl pro ...?
I'd like to reserve a table	Chtěl(a) bych rezervovat stůl
I am a vegetarian	Jsem vegetarián(ka)
Waiter!	Pane vrchní!
The bill, please	Prosím, účet
breakfast	snídaně
lunch	oběd
dinner	večeře
fixed-price menu	standardní menu
starter/snack	předkrm
dish of the day	nabídka dne
main course	hlavní jídlo
dessert	dezert
wine list	nápojový lístek
tip	spropitné
bill	účet

Menu

bramborove hranolky	chips
brambory	potatoes
chléb	bread
citrón	lemon
cukr	sugar
čaj	tea
džus	juice
houby	mushrooms
houska	roll
hovězí	beef
husa	goose
jablko	apple
jahody	strawberries
jehněčí	lamb
kachna	duck
kapr	carp
káva	coffee
knedlíky	dumplings
krúta	turkey
kuře	chicken
máslo	butter
maso	meat
minerálka	mineral water
šumivá	fizzy
nešumivá	still
mléko	milk
ovoce	fruit
palačinky	pancakes
pečené	baked/roasted
pepř	pepper
polévka	soup
pivo	beer
ryba	fish
rýže	rice
salát	lettuce, salad
smažené	fried
sůl	salt
sýr	cheese
šunka	ham
uzeniny	cold meats
vejce	egg
vepřové	pork
víno	wine
voda	water
zákusky	cakes
zelenina	vegetables
zmrzlina	ice cream

English-Slovak Phrase Book

In an Emergency

Where is the telephone?	Kde je telefon?
the nearest hospital?	najbližšia nemocnica?
Help!	Pomoc!
Please call a doctor!	Prosím, zavolajte lekára!
Please call an ambulance!	Prosím, zavolajte sanitku!
Please call the police!	Prosím, zavolajte políciu!

Communication Essentials

Yes/No	Áno/nie
Please	Prosím
Thank you	Dakujem
Excuse me/forgive me	Prepáčte
Hello/Good morning	Dobrý deň
Goodbye	Dovidenia
Good evening	Dobrý večer
Goodnight	Dobrú noc
What is it?	Čo to je?
Why?	Prečo?
Where?	Kde?
When?	Kedy?
today	dnes
tomorrow	zajtra
yesterday	včera
morning	ráno
afternoon	odpoludnia
evening	večer
there	tam
here	tu, sem
How are you?	Ako sa máš?
Very well thank you	Dakujem, dobre!
Where is/are...?	Kde je/sú...?
How far is it to ...?	Ako ďaleko je do...?
Do you speak English?	Hovoríte po anglicky?
I don't understand	Nerozumiem
Pardon?	Počúvam, prosím?
big/large	veľký
small	malý
hot	horúci
cold	studený
open	otvorené
closed	zatvorené
entrance	vhod
exit	východ
toilets	toalety, WC
men/gentlemen	muži, páni
women/ladies	ženy, damy
vacant	voľné
engaged	obsadené

Sightseeing

art gallery	galéria
castle	hrad, zámok
church	kostol
garden	záhrada
old town/city	staré mesto
palace	palác, kaštieľ
railway station	vlaková stanica
square	námestie
street	ulica
stop (bus, tram)	zastávka
theatre	divadlo
ticket	lístok
tourist information	turistické informačné centrum

Shopping

I would like...	Chcel/a/ by som...
Do you have... ?	Máte...?
How much does it cost?	Koľko to stojí?
What time do you open/ close?	O ktorej otvárate? zatvárate?
expensive	drahý
cheap	lacný
size	veľkosť
number (size)	číslo
colour	parba

Shops

antique	antikvariát
bakery	pekáreň
bank	banka
bazaar/market	tržnica
bookshop	kníhkupectvo
camera shop	potoslužba
clothes shop	odevy
department store	obchodný dom
glass, china	sklo, porcelán
news kiosk	novinový stánok
pharmacy	lekáreň
post office	pošta
shoe shop	obuv

In a Hotel

Do you have a vacant room?	Máte voľnú izbu?
with a bathroom	Izba s kúpeľňou
with a shower	Izba so sprchou
I have a reservation	Mám zarezervované
key	Kľúč
porter	vrátnik

Eating Out

Do you have a table free for.?	Máte voľný stôl pre...?
I'd like to reserve a table	Chcel/a/ by som zarezervovaň stôl
I am a vegetarian	Som vegetarián /nka/
Waiter!	Vrchný, čašník
The bill, please	Prosím si účet
breakfast	raňajky
lunch	obed
dinner	večera
fixed-price menu	pevná /stála/ cena
dish of the day	ponuka dňa
starter/snack	predjedlo
main course	hlavné jedlo
dessert	dezert, můčnik
wine list	vinná karta
tip	prepitné
bill	účet

Menu

bravčové	pork
čaj	tea
chlieb	bread
čierne korenie mleté	pepper
citrón	lemon
cukor	sugar
džús	juice
hovädzie	beef
huby	mushrooms
hus	goose
koláč	roll
jablko	apple
jahňacie	lamb
jahody	strawberries
kačka	duck
kapor	carp
káva	coffee
knedlíky	dumplings
kuracina	chicken
maslo	butter
mäso	meat
minerálna voda	mineral water
sýtená	fizzy
nesýtená	still
mlieko	milk
morčacie	turkey
ovocie	fruit
palacinky	pancakes
pečené	baked/roasted
polievka	soup
pivo	beer
ryba	fish
ryža	rice
šalát	lettuce, salad
soľ	salt
syr	cheese
šunka	ham
údeniny	cold meats
vajíčka	egg
víno	wine
voda	water
vyprážané	fried
zákusky	cakes
zelenina	vegetables
zemiakové hranolky	chips
zemiaky	potatoes
zmrzlina	ice cream

Road map of the Czech & Slovak Republics